Countries and Concepts
Politics, Geography, Culture

Michael G. Roskin
Lycoming College

Prentice Hall

UPPER SADDLE RIVER, NEW JERSEY 07458

Library of Congress Cataloging-in-Publication Data

Roskin, Michael
   Countries and concepts: politics, geography, culture/Michael G. Roskin.—7th ed.
    p. cm.
   Includes bibliographical references and index.
   ISBN 0-13-086758-6
    1. Comparative government.   I. Title

JF51.R54 2000
320.3—dc21
                                     00-034662

VP, Editorial director: Laura Pearson
Director of marketing: Beth Gillett Mejia
Assistant editor: Brian Prybella
Editorial assistant: Beth Murtha
Editorial/production supervision: Kari Callaghan Mazzola
Prepress and manufacturing buyer: Ben Smith
Electronic page makeup: Kari Callaghan Mazzola and John P. Mazzola
Interior design: John P. Mazzola
Cover director: Jayne Conte
Cover design: Bruce Kenselaar
Cover art: © Ralph Mercer/DS8 #7

This book was set in 10/11.5 Goudy by Big Sky Composition
and was printed and bound by RR Donnelley & Sons Company.
The cover was printed by Phoenix Color Corp.

 © 2001, 1998, 1995, 1992, 1989, 1986, 1982 by Prentice-Hall, Inc.
A Division of Pearson Education
Upper Saddle River, New Jersey 07458

Printed in the United States of America
10 9 8 7 6 5 4 3 2 1

ISBN 0-13-086758-6

PRENTICE-HALL INTERNATIONAL (UK) LIMITED, *London*
PRENTICE-HALL OF AUSTRALIA PTY. LIMITED, *Sydney*
PRENTICE-HALL CANADA INC., *Toronto*
PRENTICE-HALL HISPANOAMERICANA, S.A., *Mexico*
PRENTICE-HALL OF INDIA PRIVATE LIMITED, *New Delhi*
PRENTICE-HALL OF JAPAN, INC., *Tokyo*
PEARSON EDUCATION ASIA PTE. LTD., *Singapore*
EDITORA PRENTICE-HALL DO BRASIL, LTDA., *Rio de Janeiro*

Contents

PART II FRANCE 86

Feature Boxes

A Note to Instructors

My feelings about the seventh edition of *Countries and Concepts* are contained in a possibly apocryphal early edition of *Pravda*, printed at the height of the Bolshevik Revolution, that advised its readers: "No news today. Events moving too fast." This edition of *Countries and Concepts* is full of changes. Britain, France, and Germany have replaced their conservative governments with ones of the center-left. Russia may be lurching toward authoritarianism. Only Japan does not change in any dramatic way. A tour of Japan convinced me that Japan does change, but slowly and reluctantly, always trying to preserve its core of Japaneseness.

New to This Edition

The major innovation in the seventh edition is the building into the text of the booklet *Political Geography of Countries and Concepts*, which was earlier offered as a supplement. Beth Gillett Mejia, former Executive Editor for this book and now Director of Marketing, feels that geography is so important that it should not be left as a side issue. Students are often weak in geography these days; the subject seems to have been dropped from most school curricula. I have been offering Political Geography at Lycoming for some years, at the behest of Lycoming's education department, because students were doing poorly on the geography section of state teacher exams. I hear concerns about students' lack of geographical knowledge from other instructors, so *Countries and Concepts* tries to remedy this.

Other changes in the text are the addition of several instructional features to help emphasize concepts and definitions:

- Key Websites: Each part opens with an annotated list of key website addresses to help students with further research.
- Questions to Consider: Each chapter opens with a list of "Questions to Consider" to prime students for the main points.
- Key Terms: Chapters now have running marginal glossaries, labeled "Key Terms," to make sure students are building their vocabularies as they read. The definitions listed are those of a political scientist; in other contexts one might find different definitions. For further review, a list of key terms has been added to the end of each chapter. The page number that follows each

listed key term indicates the page upon which the corresponding marginal definition box appears. (These terms and their definitions also appear in the end-of-book Glossary.)

- Feature Boxes: Most of the feature boxes now have category heads—Geography, Democracy, Political Culture, Comparison, or Key Concepts—to give them greater focus and continuity.

Structure and Purpose

The structure and purpose of *Countries and Concepts* continue as before. The book analyzes four European nations and Japan at some length and four Third World nations more briefly. It does not attempt to create young scholars out of college sophomores. Rather, it sees comparative politics as an important but usually neglected grounding in citizenship that we should be making available to our young people. I agree with the late Morris Janowitz (in his 1983 *The Reconstruction of Patriotism: Education for Civic Consciousness*) that civic education has declined in the United States and that this poses dangers for democracy. Our students are often ill-prepared in the historical, political, economic, geographical, and moral aspects of democracy, and to expose such students to professional-level abstractions in political science ignores their civic education and offers material that is largely meaningless to them. An undergraduate is not a miniature graduate student.

Accordingly, the seventh edition of *Countries and Concepts* is designed to include a good deal of fundamental vocabulary and concepts, buttressed by many examples. It is readable. Many students don't do assigned readings; with *Countries and Concepts*, they have no excuse that the reading is long or boring.

Some reviewers have noted that *Countries and Concepts* contains values and criticisms. This is part of my purpose. The two go together; if you have no values, you have no basis from which to criticize. Value-free instruction is probably impossible. If successful, it would produce value-free students, and that, I think, should not be the aim of the educational enterprise. If one knows something with the head but not with the heart, one really doesn't know it at all.

Is *Countries and Concepts* too critical? It treats politics as a series of ongoing quarrels for which no very good solutions can be found. It casts a skeptical eye on all political systems and all solutions proposed for political problems. As such, the book is not out to "get" any one country; it merely treats all with equal candor. *Countries and Concepts* tries to act as a corrective to analyses that depict political systems as well-oiled machines or gigantic computers that never break down or make mistakes. Put it this way: If we are critical of the workings of our own country's politics—and many, perhaps most, of us are—why should we abandon the critical spirit in looking at other lands?

The seventh edition continues the loose theoretical approach of the previous editions with the simple observation that politics, on the surface at least, is composed of a number of human conflicts or quarrels. These quarrels, if observed over time, usually form patterns of some durability beyond the specific issues involved. What I call patterns of interaction are the relationships among politically relevant groups and individuals—what they call in Russian *kto-kovo*: Who does what to whom? There are two general types of such patterns: (1) between elites and masses, and (2) among and within elites.

Before we can appreciate these patterns, however, we must first study the political culture of a particular country, which leads us to its political institutions and ultimately to its political history. Thus we have a five-fold division in the study of each country. We could start with a country's contemporary political quarrels and work backward, but it is probably better to begin with the underlying factors as a foundation from which to understand their impact on modern social conflict. This book goes from history to institutions to political culture to patterns of interaction to quarrels. This arrangement need not supplant other approaches. Instructors have had no trouble utilizing this book in connection with their preferred theoretical insights.

Inclusion of the Third World in a first comparative course is problematic. The Third World is so complex and differentiated that many (myself included) suspect the concept should be discarded. The semester is only so long. But if students are going to take only one comparative course—all too often the case nowadays—they should get some exposure to three-quarters of humankind. We continue, therefore, with briefer treatment of four non-European systems: China, Brazil, South Africa, and Iran. They are not "representative" systems—what Third-World countries are?—but are interesting in their four different relationships to democracy: (1) democracy in China blocked by a Communist elite; (2) democracy returned to Brazil after a military interlude; (3) the difficult founding of a nonracial democracy in South Africa; and (4) democracy blanketed by an Islamic revolution in Iran. These four systems provide a refreshing counterpoise to the more settled systems of Europe and Japan. Instructors can and do omit some or all of these Third-World systems—for lack of time or in order to focus more closely on Europe—but this does not destroy the continuity of the text.

Supplements

Companion Website

www.prenhall.com/roskin   This new website brings an online study guide to students, absolutely free. When students log on, they will find a wealth of study and research resources. Chapter outline and summary information, true/false tests, fill-in-the-blank tests, and multiple-choice tests, all with immediate feedback and chapter page numbers, give students ample opportunity to review the information. The site also includes an archive of the maps that are found in the text, as well as links to sites pertaining to the countries that are covered in the text.

Instructor's Manual and Test Item Files

An instructor's manual with test item files on diskette are available to instructors from their Prentice Hall representative.

Acknowledgments

I welcome your suggestions on any area of the book and its supplementary materials. Many have generously offered their comments, corrections, and criticism. Especially valuable were the comments of Christian Soe, California State University at Long Beach; Cheryl L. Brown, University of North Carolina at Charlotte; Karl W. Ryavec, University of Massachusetts at Amherst; Frank Myers, State University of New York at Stony Brook; Ronald F. Bunn, University of Missouri-Columbia; Said A. Arjomand, State University of New York at Stony Brook; Larry Elowitz, Georgia College; Arend Lijphart, University of California at San Diego; Cheryl Brown, University of North Carolina at Charlotte; Thomas P. Wolf, Indiana University, Southeast; Susan Matarese, University of Louisville; Marianne C. Stewart, Rutgers University (on Brazil); Hanns-D. Jacobsen, Free University of Berlin (on Germany); Ruth Grubel of Kwansei Gakuin, Nishinomiya; Ko Shioya of *Bungei Shunju* (on Japan); Carol Nechemias, Penn State at Harrisburg; Yury Polsky, West Chester University, and Marcia Weigle, Bowdoin College (on Russia); Dan O'Connell of Palm Beach Community College (on China); and Lycoming colleagues Mehrdad Madresehee and Bahram Golshan (on Iran), Carla Damiano (on Germany), and Garett Heysel (on France). All errors, of course, are my own. Instructors may send professional comments and corrections to me personally at Lycoming College, Williamsport, PA 17701, or e-mail roskin@lycoming.edu. I am grateful for any suggestions for subsequent editions.

Michael G. Roskin

The Concept of Country

Questions to Consider

1. What is the difference between nation and state?
2. Why are standard definitions of nation-state sometimes inadequate?
3. What key factors produced the modern state?
4. Where did nationalism originate?
5. What does the author mean by "quarrels"?
6. How do we define Europe's regions?
7. At what level of economic development does democracy become stable?
8. What is a political institution?
9. What is political culture?
10. How are generalizations and theories related?
11. At what point should we replace the study of individual European nations with a study of the European Union?
12. What is "redistribution" and why is it never settled?

What are we chiefly studying? **Nations**? The Latin root of nation means "birth," so nation suggests people with some blood linkage, now rarely the case. Trying to define the nation in terms of blood ties is unreal and racist. Now, nationality generally means a group of people with a sense of identity and often their own language, culture, or religion. Modern France is a collection of peoples of many origins, united by language and culture. The United States is a bizarre collection of peoples, processed over time into a shared political culture.

Should we call them **states**? Obviously we are not using "state" in the sense of the fifty U.S. states, which lack **sovereignty**, because ultimately Washington's laws prevail. State means governmental

Key Terms

nation   The cultural element of a country; people psychologically bound to one another.

state   The institutional or governmental element of a country.

sovereignty   The last word on law in a given territory; boss on your own turf.

1

structure. Historically, states preceded and often formed nations. Over the centuries, the French government, by decreeing the use of a certain dialect and spelling and enforcing nationwide educational standards, molded a French consciousness. The French state invented the French nation.

We might settle on "countries." Country originally meant countryside or rural area where people shared the same dialect and traditions. It has broadened in meaning until most people use it as synonymous with nation or state.

The Classic Nation-State

Some use "nation-state" to combine the psychological and structural elements, but the term did not catch on. Nation-states were often defined as having territory, population, independence, government, and sometimes other attributes. By each of these features, however, we might place some question marks.

Territory would seem to be basic, but what about peoples who have a strong sense of peoplehood but lack real estate? For example, the Jews who turned their sense of people-hood into Israel and the Palestinians who now define themselves as a nation and are poised to declare statehood. This immediately brings up the next problem: What happens when territorial claims overlap? How do you tell which claim is just? History is a poor guide, as typically many tribes and ethnic groups have washed over the land through the centuries. France's Alsatians, on the west bank of the Rhine River, speak German and have Germanic family names. But they also speak French and think of themselves as French. Should Alsace belong to France or Germany? Wars are fought over such questions.

Population is obviously essential. But many countries are **multinational**, with popu-lations divided by language or **ethnicity**. Sometimes the nationalities are angry and wish to break away. Like the ex-Soviet Union, ex-Yugoslavia was composed of several quar-relsome nationalities, most of whom (Slovenes, Croats, Macedonians, Bosnian Muslims) left the Yugoslav state, which, they believed, was unfairly dominated by the largest nationality, the Serbs. Yugoslavia is an example of a recent (1918) and artificial creation that did not jell as a nation-state. All countries, to be sure, are more or less artificial, but over time some, such as France, have psychologically inculcated a sense of common nationness that overrides earlier regional or ethnic loyalties. Germany has done this more recently.

Key Terms

multinational A country composed of several peoples with distinct national feelings.

ethnicity Cultural characteristics differentiating one group from another.

diplomatic recognition One state announces it is ready to do business with another.

Independence means that the state governs itself as a sovereign entity. Colonies, such as Algeria under the French, become nation-states when the imperial power departs, as the French did in 1962. **Diplomatic recog-nition** by other countries, especially by the major powers, confirms and deepens a country's independence. Without such recognition, South Africa's four nominally independent black homelands were fake little countries that were dissolved in 1994. Some countries are more sovereign and independent than others. East European lands during the Cold War were Soviet satellites, less than sovereign since the last word ultimately came from Moscow. Are Central American "banana republics" under U.S. supervision truly sovereign and independent? Only in a rather artificial and legal sense. All countries place great value on their sovereign inde-pendence, but not all of them achieve it fully.

Government is probably the crux of being a state. Without government there is anarchy, with the high probability that the country will fall apart or be conquered. Sometimes government can precede states. The Continental Congress preceded and founded the United States. A government can be in exile, as was de Gaulle's Free French government during World War II. The mere existence of a government does not automatically mean that it effectively governs the whole country. In much of the Third World, the government's writ falls off as one travels from the capital. In Brazil's vast Amazon region, cattle ranchers, gold prospectors, and rubber tappers fight Wild West style while the Brazilian government tries to bring the chaos under legal control.

In sum, nation-states are not as clear-cut as supposed; their realities are messy but interesting. This is one reason for using the admittedly vague term "country": It avoids **reification**, a constant temptation in the social sciences, but one we must guard against.

The Modern State

Whatever we call it—country, state, or nation-state—we must recognize that its current form is relatively recent. To be sure, we can find states at the dawn of written history. (Ancient kingdoms, in fact, developed writing for communication and record-keeping.) But the modern state is only about half a millennium old and traces back to the replacement of old European feudal monarchies by what were called "new monarchies" and subsequently the "strong state." There are many factors in this shift; it is impossible to pinpoint which were the causes and which the consequences. **Causality** is always difficult to demonstrate in the social sciences, but the box discusses some of the changes that ushered in the modern State.

By the end of the Thirty Years' War in 1648, the feudal system had been displaced by the modern state. **Feudalism** balanced power between monarch and nobles; it was loose and sloppy and did not tolerate strong national government. It was not oriented to change or expansion. The new monarchies were **absolutist**, concentrating all power in themselves, disdaining the old medieval constitution in which their powers balanced with nobles, and using new economic, administrative, and military tools to increase their power. Royalist philosophers extolled the strong monarch, and coined the term *sovereignty*. In consolidating their powers, monarchs had the nation celebrated, giving rise to the concept of nationality, of belonging to a nation rather than merely being the subject of an hereditary ruler.

Key Terms

reification Taking a theory as reality.

causality Proving that one thing causes another.

feudalism Political system of power dispersed and balanced between king and nobles.

absolutism A royal dictatorship in which the king amasses all power.

The Rise of Nationalism

The French Revolution unleashed modern nationalism. As German armies closed in on the Revolution in 1792, the French people rallied *en masse* to repel the foe, believing they were defending both the Revolution and the *patrie* (fatherland), and the two concepts merged. France, in the eyes of its revolutionaries, was destined to liberate and reform the

GEOGRAPHY

WHAT MADE THE MODERN STATE?

1. The Turks used gunpowder and cannon to crack the walls of Constantinople in 1453. Within a few years, all of Europe knew of these new weapons, and monarchs quickly acquired cannons and with them subdued the nobles and consolidated their kingdoms.

2. The economy greatly expanded with commerce, banking, and accounting. The English learned to make steel with coal (coke) instead of charcoal, thus founding the industrial revolution. Major trade routes developed, all of them taxed by monarchs who needed the revenue to govern and expand their realms.

3. The New World opened, starting in 1492. Those monarchs with access to the sea promoted overseas exploration and colonies for the sake of national wealth and power.

4. The invention of printing increased the rate of diffusion of information, speeding up all other process and displacing Latin by local tongues. Printing also increased the ability of the national capital to govern the outlying provinces.

5. The Catholic church lost **temporal** power. Monarchs chose to crown themselves (the **investiture crisis**). Then Protestant kings split from Rome and set up national churches, as in England and Sweden.

6. This led to the wars of religion, first the Schmalkaldic War of 1545–55 and then the devastating Thirty Years' War of 1618–48. The net impact of these conflicts was increased state power in the hands of monarchs and secularization, getting religion out of the daily affairs of state, which promoted modernization.

7. State administration greatly improved, as warring monarchs were always desperate for money and needed reliable tax bases and tax collectors. The state got its own budget, separate from the royal household budget. Before, the treasury had been the king's piggy bank; now it belonged to the state. During the Thirty Years' War, France's Richelieu and Sweden's Oxenstierna invented modern, rational administration, designed to control and tax an entire country.

rest of Europe. The concept of a nation embodying everything good was thus born and spread throughout Europe by Napoleon's enthusiastic legions.

By its very nature, nationalism couldn't stay confined to the French soldiers, who soon turned into brutal and arrogant occupiers. All over Europe, local patriots rose up against them with the same kind of nationalistic feelings the French had brought with them. The spillover of French nationalism thus gave rise to Spanish, German, and Russian nationalism. By the late nineteenth century, with German and Italian unification, most Europeans had either formed nationalistic states or desired to do so (for example, Poland). Thinkers such as Germany's Hegel and Italy's Mazzini extolled the nation as the highest level of human (or possibly divine) development.

Key Terms

temporal Of this world; opposite of spiritual.

investiture crisis Fight between popes and monarchs over who had the right to crown the latter.

The modern state and its nationalism did not stay in West Europe. Driven to expand, the Europeans conquered Latin America, Asia, and Africa. Only Japan and Turkey kept the Europeans out; Meiji Japan carried out a brilliant "defensive modernization."

The European imperialists introduced nationalism to their subject peoples. By their very integration and administration of previously fragmented territories, the British in India, the French in Indochina, and the Dutch in Indonesia taught "the natives" to think of themselves as a nation that of right deserved to be independent. Now virtually the entire globe is populated by national states, each jealous of their sovereign independence and many of them fired by nationalism.

Looking for Quarrels

One way to begin the study of a political system is to ask what its people fight about. There is no country without political **quarrels**. They range from calm discussions over whether to include dental care in nationalized health insurance to angry conflicts to murderous civil wars over who should rule the country.

Key Term

quarrels   As used here, important, long-term political issues.

You can get a fair idea of a country's quarrels by talking with its people, interviewing officials, following the local media, and attending election rallies. This is the way journalists work. Political scientists, however, go further. They want to know the whys and wherefores of these controversies, whether they are long-standing issues or short-term problems. Our next step, then, is to observe the quarrels over time. If

Comparing Some Basic Figures

	Population		Per Capita GDP		Workforce	Infant Mortality
	In Millions 1999	Average Annual Growth 1990–97	ppp* 1998	Growth 1998	in Agriculture	per 1,000 Live Births
Britain	59	0.3%	$21,200	2.6%	2%	7
France	59	0.5	22,600	3.0	4	7
Germany	82	0.5	22,100	2.7	3	7
Russia	146	−0.1	4,000	−5.0	18	20
Japan	126	0.3	23,100	−2.6	3	5
China	1,267	1.1	3,600	7.8	50	34
Brazil	168	1.4	6,100	0.5	35	44
South Africa	43	1.7	6,800	0.3	30	50
Iran	65	2.4	5,000	−2.1	30	33
United States	276	1.0	31,500	3.9	3	7

*Purchasing Power Parity, explained on page 366.

Source: *CIA World Factbook*, World Bank, UNDP, and OECD. Regard all such tables with skepticism. Figures from non-OECD countries are often rough estimates. Population growth includes immigration. Changing currency rates throw off GDP growth comparisons. Averages deceive: South African figures, for instance, do not show the major gaps between black's and white's in income, population growth, and infant mortality. Even something as standard as the U.S. labor force in agriculture can vary greatly, depending on whether illegal or temporary foreign workers are counted.

the basic quarrel lasts a long time, we are on to an important topic. To explain the quarrel, we must dig into the country's past, its institutions, and its culture.

In this book, we look at nine countries, considering each in five sections, each focusing on a subject area. We start with the underlying causes of current quarrels:

- The Impact of the Past
- The Key Institutions
- The Political Culture

We study the past, including the country's geography, in order to understand the present. We are not looking for the fascinating details of history but for the major patterns that have set up present institutions and culture. We study institutions to see how power is structured, for that is what institutions are: structures of power. We study culture to get a feel for the way people look at their social and political system, how deeply they support it, and how political views differ among groups.

Moving from underlying factors to current politics brings us to the next two areas:

- Patterns of Interaction
- What People Quarrel About

Here, we get more specific and more current. The previous sections, we might say, are about the traditions, rules, and spirit of the game; the patterns of interaction are how the game is actually played. We look here for recurring behavior. The last section, the specific quarrels, represents the stuff of politics, the kind of things you see in a country's newspaper.

The Impact of the Past

We look first at a country's geography. *Physical geography* concerns the natural features of the earth, whereas **political geography** studies what is largely human-made. There is, of course, a connection between the two, as physical limits set by nature influence the formation, consolidation, and governing mentality of political systems.

Next, moving on to history, was the country unified early or late? For the most part, countries are artificial—not natural—entities, created when one group or tribe conquers its neighbors and unifies them by the sword. The founding of nations is usually a bloody business, and the longer ago it took place, the better. We look at Sweden and say, "What a nice, peaceful country." We look at Somalia and say, "What a ghastly bloodbath of warring clans." We forget that long ago Sweden resembled Somalia.

The unification and consolidation of a country usually leaves behind regional resentments of incredible staying power. People whose ancestors were conquered centuries ago may still act out their resentments in political ways, in the voting booth, or in civil violence. This is one way history has an impact on the present.

Becoming "modern" is a wrenching experience. Industrialization, urbanization, and the growth of education and communications uproot

Key Term

political geography   The ways territory and politics influence each other.

GEOGRAPHY

There are no binding definitions of Europe's regions, but the end of the Cold War made the old division into eastern and western obsolete. There is still, to be sure, a West Europe, which may be defined as those states that touch the Atlantic, plus Italy and Switzerland. The ex-Communist countries in what used to be called East Europe, though, need to be separated into Central Europe (a pre-World War II term now revived) and the Balkans, for these two areas are very different.

Central Europe is the region between West Europe and Russia from Hungary north. It used to be, in whole or in part, the Habsburgs' Austro-Hungarian Empire. It includes Austria, Hungary, the Czech Republic, Slovakia, and Poland (southern Poland was Austrian-ruled before World War I, as was part of northern Italy). These countries are predominantly Catholic and (with the exception of Austria, which was never Communist) poorer than West Europe. Freed from Communist rule, they turned quickly to democracy and market economies.

The Balkans (Turkish for mountain), for centuries part of the Ottoman Turkish Empire, are largely Eastern Orthodox and a more backward area that includes Romania, Bulgaria, Albania, Greece (which was never Communist), and half of Yugoslavia. These countries lag behind Central Europe in setting up democracies and market economies. Yugoslavia presents a special problem, because half of it (Slovenia and Croatia) was under the Habsburgs while the other half (Serbia, Bosnia, and Macedonia) was under the Turks. And it is precisely on this fault line that Yugoslavia violently split apart in the early 1990s, with half Central European in character and the other half Balkan. Russia, because it reaches clear to the Pacific is, along with other ex-Soviet republics, sometimes called "Eurasia."

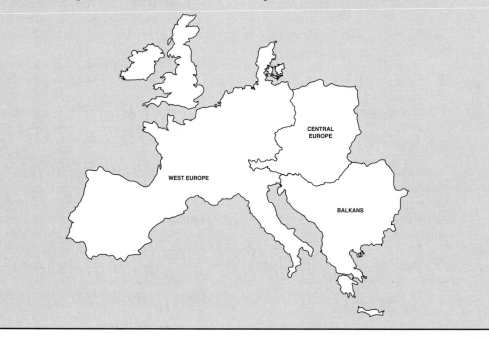

Key Terms

elite   A member of the top or most influential people.

mass   Most of the citizenry; everyone who is not an *elite*.

democracy   Political system of mass participation and competitive elections, with an emphasis on human and civil rights.

GDP   Gross Domestic Product: the sum total of goods and services produced in a country in one year.

per capita   GDP divided by population, giving an approximate level of well-being.

electoral franchise   The right to vote.

symbol   The use of a political artifact to stir mass emotions.

people from their traditional villages and lifestyles and send them to work in factories, usually in cities. In the process, previously passive people become aware of their condition and willing to do something to change it. They become ready to participate in politics, demanding economic improvements, and are often mobilized by new parties. It's a delicate time in the life of nations. If the traditional **elites** do not devise some way to take account of newly awakened **mass** demands, the system may be heading toward revolution.

No country has industrialized in a nice way; it is always a process marked by low wages, bad working conditions, and, usually, political repression. The longer in the past this stage has happened, the more peaceful and stable a country is likely to be. We must look for the stage of development a country is in. A country just undergoing industrialization can expect domestic tensions of the sort that existed earlier in Europe.

Religion is a crucial historical question. Does the country have its church-state relationship settled? If not, it's a lingering political sore. Protestant countries had an easier time of it; their churches cut their ties to Rome, the state became stronger than the church early on, and the church stayed out of politics. In Roman Catholic countries, where the church had power in its own right, there was a long church-state struggle called the "clerical-anticlerical split," which is still alive today in France: Conservatives are more religious and liberals and leftists are indifferent or hostile to religion. Iran is now struggling with this question.

At a certain point in their development, countries become ready for **democracy**. Very few poor countries can sustain democracy, which seems to require a good-sized middle class to work right. Attempts to implant democracy in countries with **per capita GDPs** below $5,000 generally fail, but democracy seems to come naturally to countries that have per capita GDPs above $6,000. Notice in the table on page 5 that several of our countries are in this borderline area. This is one way economics influences political culture.

Americans often think elections are cures for all political ills, but elections in developing countries are seldom free and fair. Democracy can also come too late. If the traditional elite waits too long, the masses may mobilize, turn radical, and fall into the hands of revolutionary demagogues. What happened in Russia in 1917 happened again in Iran in 1979. The gradual expansion of the **electoral franchise**, as in Britain, is probably best.

The widening of the franchise means the rise of political parties. On what was a party first based? When was it founded? What were its initial aims, and how has it changed over the years? Was the party strongly ideological? Left-wing parties argued that government should provide jobs, housing, medical care, and education. Other parties, on the political center or right, either reject the welfarist ideas, compromise with them, or steal them. Gradually, the country becomes a welfare state with a heavy tax burden.

Finally, history establishes political **symbols** that can awaken powerful emotions. Flags, monarchs, religion, national holidays, and national anthems often serve as the cement that holds a country together, giving citizens the feeling they are part of a common enterprise. To fully know a country, one must know its symbols, their historical origins, and their current connotation.

DEMOCRACY

WAVES OF DEMOCRACY

Harvard political scientist Samuel P. Huntington saw democracy as spreading in three waves. The first wave, a long one, lasted from the American and French Revolutions through World War I. It gradually and unevenly spread democracy through most of West Europe. But between the two world wars, a "reverse wave" of communist and fascist **authoritarian** regimes pushed back democracy in Russia, Italy, Germany, Spain, Portugal, and Japan.

The second wave, a short one, lasted from World War II until the mid-1960s. It brought democracy to most of West Europe plus the many Asian and African colonies that got their independence. Most of Asia, Africa, and Latin America, however, quickly turned authoritarian.

Huntington's third wave began in the mid-1970s with the return of democracy to Portugal, Spain, and Greece, and thence to Latin America and East Asia. In 1989, as Communist regimes collapsed, it took over much of East Europe and even, with the Soviet collapse of 1991, Russia. At least on paper, roughly half of the world's 193 countries are democratic. But, warns Huntington, get ready for another reverse wave as some shaky democratic regimes revert to authoritarianism.

The Key Institutions

A political **institution** is a web of relationships lasting over time, an established structure of power. An institution may or may not be housed in an impressive building. With institutions we look for durable sets of human relationships, not architecture.

One way to begin our search is to ask, "Who's got the power?" A nation's **constitution**—itself an institution—may give us some clues, but it does not necessarily pinpoint real power centers. Britain's monarch and Germany's president are more for decoration than governing. The French constitution changed, giving more power to prime ministers and less to presidents.

Is the system presidential or parliamentary (see box on page 42)? Both systems have **parliaments**, but a presidential system has a president who is elected and serves separately from the legislature; the legislature cannot vote out the president. The United States and Brazil are presidential systems. In parliamentary systems, action focuses on the prime minister, who is usually a member of parliament and who is delegated by it to form a government (another word for cabinet). The prime minister and his or her cabinet can be ousted by a vote of no-confidence in parliament. Americans used to assume presidential systems were better and

Key Terms

authoritarian Non-democratic or dictatorial politics.

institution Established rules and relationships of power.

constitution The written organization of a country's institutions.

parliament A national assembly that considers and passes laws.

more stable than parliamentary systems. Recent problems might make Americans aware of the advantages of a parliamentary system, which can easily oust a chief executive. Besides, parliamentary systems, with the proper refinements such as Germany's, can be quite stable.

How powerful is the legislature? In most cases it is less powerful than the executive, and its power is generally declining. Parliaments still pass laws, but most of them originate with the civil servants and cabinet and are passed according to party wishes. In most legislatures (but not in the U.S. Congress), party discipline is so strong that a member of parliament simply votes the way party whips instruct. Parliaments can be important in nonlegislative ways: They represent citizens, educate the public, structure interests, and, most important, oversee and criticize executive-branch activities.

Does the parliament have two chambers (bicameral) or one (unicameral)? Two chambers are necessary in federal systems to represent the territorial divisions, but they are often extra baggage in unitary systems. Most of the countries studied in this book have bicameral legislatures.

How many parties are there? Are we looking at a one-party system, such as China; two-party systems, such as Britain and the United States; or multiparty systems, such as France, Germany, and Russia? Party system is partly determined by a country's electoral system, of which there are basically two types, majoritarian and proportional. A majoritarian system, as in the United States and Britain, enables one party to have a majority in parliament. This encourages two-party systems. Proportional systems, where parliamentarians are elected according to the percentage of the vote their party won, as in Germany and Israel, produce parliaments where no one party dominates. Proportional representation encourages multiparty systems, which in turn may contribute to cabinet instability as coalition members quarrel.

How powerful is the country's permanent civil service—its bureaucracy? The bureaucracy today has eclipsed both cabinet and parliament in expertise, information, outside contacts, and sheer numbers. Some lobbyists no longer bother with the legislature; they go where the action is, to the important decision makers in the bureaucracy.

Political Culture

Key Terms

political culture The values and attitudes of citizens in regard to politics and society.

cynical Untrusting; believing that a political system is wrong and corrupt.

legitimacy Mass perception that a regime's rule is rightful.

After World War II, political scientists shifted their emphasis from institutions to attitudes. The institutional approach had become suspect. On paper, Germany's Weimar constitution was a magnificent achievement after World War I, but it didn't work in practice because too few Germans really supported democracy. By the late 1950s a new **political culture** approach to comparative politics that sought to explain systems in terms of peoples' attitudes became prominent. This is a two-way street, however, because attitudes determine government, and government determines attitudes. Americans became much more **cynical** in the wake of Vietnam and Watergate, while Germans became more committed democrats as their country achieved economic success and political stability.

Legitimacy is a basic political attitude, originally meaning that the rightful king was on the throne, not a usurper. Now it means a mass attitude

POLITICAL CULTURE

THE CIVIC CULTURE STUDY

In a massive 1959 study, political scientists Gabriel Almond and Sidney Verba led teams that asked approximately one thousand people in each of five countries—the United States, Britain, West Germany, Italy, and Mexico—identical questions on their political attitudes. The Civic Culture study, which was a benchmark in cross-national research, discerned three types of political culture:

1. *Participant,* in which people know a lot about politics and feel they should and do participate in politics.
2. *Subject,* in which people are aware of politics but cautious about participating; they are more conditioned to obeying.
3. *Parochial,* meaning narrow or focused only on their immediate concerns, is one in which people are not even much aware of politics and do not participate.

Almond and Verba emphasized that each country is a mixture of these types, with perhaps one type dominating: participant in America, subject in West Germany and Italy, parochial in Mexico. A good mixture, which they found in America and Britain, produces what they called "the civic culture." Question: If Americans are so participant, why do they vote so little?

that people think the government's rule is valid and that it should generally be obeyed. Governments are not automatically legitimate; they have to earn the respect of their citizens. Legitimacy can be created over a long time as a government endures and governs well. Legitimacy can also erode as unstable and corrupt regimes come and go, never winning the people's respect. One quick test of legitimacy is how many police officers a country has. With high legitimacy, it doesn't need many police because people obey the law voluntarily. With low legitimacy, a country needs many police. Regimes attempt to shore up their legitimacy by manipulating symbols.

One symbol frequently manipulated is **ideology**. An ideology is a grand plan to save or improve the country (see box on page 12). Typically, leaders at the top of a system take their ideology with a grain of salt. But for mass consumption, the Soviets and Chinese cranked out reams of ideological propaganda (which, in fact, most of their people ignored.)

Most of the other political systems explored in this book are not so ideologically explicit, but all are committed to various ideologies to greater or lesser degrees: German Social Democrats are committed to the welfare state, British Conservatives to free-market economics, and Chinese Communists to "socialism with Chinese characteristics." Does every system have some sort of ideology? Probably. A system run on purely **pragmatic**

Key Terms

ideology A belief system contending that society can be improved.

pragmatic Without ideological considerations; based on practicality.

grounds—if it works, use it—would be unideological, but such systems are rare. Even Americans, who pride themselves on being pragmatic, are usually convinced of the effectiveness of the free market (Republicans) or moderate government intervention (Democrats). Thus, one of our questions: How ideological or pragmatic is a particular system and its political parties?

KEY CONCEPTS

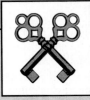

WHAT IS "IDEOLOGY"?

Political ideologies can be an important part of political culture. They are belief systems—usually ending in -ism—that claim to aim at improving society. Believers in an ideology say: "If we move in this direction, things will be much better. People will be happier, catastrophe will be avoided, society will become perfected." An ideology usually contains four elements:

1. The *perception* that things are going wrong, that society is headed down the wrong path. Fanatic ideologies insist that catastrophe is just around the corner.
2. An *evaluation* or analysis of why things are going wrong. This means a criticism of all or part of the existing system.
3. A *prescription* or cure for the problem. Moderate ideologies advocate reforms; extremist ideologies urge revolution and overthrow of the present system.
4. An effort to form a *movement* to carry out the cure. Without a party or movement, the above points are just talk without serious intent.

Marxism-Leninism is a perfect example of ideology. First, we have Marx's perception that capitalism is unjust and doomed. Second, we have his analysis, that capitalism contains its own internal contradictions, which bring economic depressions. Third, we have a Marxist prescription: Abolish capitalism in favor of collective ownership of the means of production—socialism. And fourth, especially with Lenin, we have the determined movement to form a strong Communist party—the "organizational weapon"—to put the cure into effect by overthrowing the capitalist system.

There are some other interesting points about ideologies. They are usually based on a serious thinker, often an important philosopher. Communism traces back to Hegel, classic liberalism to John Locke. But the philosopher's original ideas become popularized, vulgarized, and often distorted at the hands of ideologists who are trying to mass-market them. Deep thoughts are turned into cheap slogans. It often ends up that the original philosopher would reject what's being done in his name. Toward the end of his life, Marx worried about the distortions of his ideas by younger thinkers and sadly commented, "One thing is for sure: I am not a Marxist."

An important point about ideologies is that they are always defective; that is, they never deliver what they promise: perfect societies and happy humans. Classic liberalism produced an underclass, while Marxism-Leninism produced brutal dictatorships. Even Islamic fundamentalism did not make Iranians happy.

KEY CONCEPTS

THE POLITICS OF SOCIAL CLEAVAGES

Most societies are split along one or more lines. Often these splits, or "cleavages," become the society's fault lines along which political views form. Here are some of the more politically relevant social cleavages.

Social Class Karl Marx thought social class determined everything and was the only important social cleavage, that whether one was bourgeois or proletarian determined one's political orientation. Marx held that middle- and upper-class people were conservative and working-class people were progressive or radical. But experience makes it hard to accept this narrow view. Some poor people are extremely conservative while some middle-class intellectuals are radical.

Still, social class does help structure attitudes. The working class does tend toward the left, but never 100 percent. Further, the left they tend toward is apt to be the moderate left of social democracy rather than the radical left of communism. Such is the case of the German Social Democratic party.

The student of comparative politics has to put class into perspective. By itself, social class is seldom a sufficient explanation for political orientation. Other ingredients are usually present. The question, as Joseph LaPalombara put it, is, "Class plus what?"

Geographic Region Most countries have regional differences, and often they are politically important. Once a region gets set in its politics it can stay that way for generations. Often the attitude is a remembrance of past conquests and injustices. Scotland still resents England, and likewise the south of France resents the north. The student should learn to inquire about the regions of a nation, what their politics are, and how they got to be that way.

Religion We considered how religious struggles were one of the more politically relevant items in a nation's history. In some countries they are still quite important. You can predict with fair accuracy how a French person will vote by knowing how often he or she attends Mass. You can partly predict how a German will vote by knowing if the citizen in question is Protestant or Catholic (and which region he or she lives in). In Iran, religion dominates politics. It has been shown that religion accounts for the formation of more political parties than does social class.

Urban-Rural Urban dwellers tend to be more aware of politics, more participatory, and more liberal or leftist. This is especially true in the Third World, where the countryside remains backward while the cities modernize (e.g., China has a major urban-rural split in terms of living conditions, education, and political orientation).

There are other possible politically relevant social cleavages. In some situations gender matters, as in the United States, where women vote more Democrat than men. Occupation, as distinct from social class, can also influence political attitudes. A miner and a farmer may make the same amount of money, but chances are the miner will be leftist and the farmer conservative. Age can sometimes be an important political factor. Young people are usually more open to new ideas and more likely to embrace radical and even violent causes than older citizens. Germany's terrorists, China's Red Guards, and Iran's *hezbollahi* were all young.

Almost any social cleavage or category can become politically relevant. Students of comparative politics can become sensitive to these categories by asking themselves from where they got the political views they hold. Is it their age? Did they get them from family? And why do their families hold these views? Is it their religion? Their ethnic group? Their regional tradition?

DEMOCRACY

CRISIS OF DEMOCRACY?

Worldwide, social scientists worry that the attitudes in firmly established democracies are becoming more cynical about government. If the trend deepens, it could undermine the basis of democracy. Observers focus on two trends: (1) A falloff of roughly 10 percent in voting turnout from the 1950s to the 1990s. (2) Public-opinion polls that show Americans, Europeans, and Japanese all trust government and politicians less. Is democracy doomed?

Be careful of doomsters; their predictions are usually wrong. The voting falloff may be due in part to the lowering of the voting age in the early 1970s nearly everywhere from 21 to 18. Young people vote less. The cynical opinions may be due to increased expectations that government must provide jobs, health, and happiness—often hyped by politicians—that government cannot possibly deliver. Viewed in this light, democracy may have been too successful.

Democracy is not necessarily doomed. It may be entering a new phase in which better-educated citizens know more and criticize more. Citizen efforts to fight corruption, curb the influence of powerful interest groups, and reform defective institutions are widespread. What, for example, will be the effects on democracy of the Internet?

Another contributor to political culture is a country's educational system. Almost universally, education is the main path to elite status. Who gets educated and in what way helps structure who gets political power and what they do with it. No country has totally equal educational opportunity. Even where schooling is legally open to all, social-, economic-, and even political-screening devices work against some sectors of the population. Most countries have elite universities that produce a big share of their political leadership, at times a near monopoly. Elite views are a major determinant of a country's politics.

Patterns of Interaction

Here we come to what is conventionally called "politics." We look for who does what to whom. We look for the interactions of parties, interest groups, individuals, and bureaucracies. Elites play a major role in these interactions. Even democratic politics is usually the work of a few. Most people, most of the time, do not participate in politics. But there are various kinds of elites, some more democratic and dedicated to the common good than others. How much of these interactions are an elite game with little or no mass participation?

Do groups come together to compete or to strike deals? How do political parties persuade the public to support them? We look not for one-time events but for things that occur with some regularity. Finding such patterns is the beginning of making **generalizations**, and making generalizations is the beginning of **theory**. Once we have found a pattern, we ask why. The answer will be found partly from what we have learned about each country in preceding chapters and partly from the nature of political life in which struggle and competition are normal and universal.

Some interactions are open and public; others are closed and secretive. The interactions of parties and citizenry are mostly open. Every party tries to convince the public that their party is the one fit to govern. This holds equally true for democratic and authoritarian systems. Do they succeed? Whom do the parties aim for, and how do they win them over? By ideology? Promises? Common interests? Or by convincing people the other party is worse?

The parties interact with each other, sometimes cooperatively but more often competitively. How do they denounce and discredit each other? Under what circumstances do they make deals? Is their competition murderous or moderate?

Key Terms

generalization The finding of repeated examples and patterns.

theory Firm generalizations supported by evidence.

euro (symbol: €) Currency introduced in 1999 for most of West Europe; approximate value $1.

European Union (EU) Federation of most West European states; began in 1957 as Common Market.

GEOGRAPHY

HOW IMPORTANT IS THE EUROPEAN UNION?

With the debut of the **euro** currency in 1999, pretty important. Some observers of the European scene argue that it makes less and less sense to consider the nations of West Europe separately, because increasingly it is the **European Union** that determines the politics, laws, and economy of West Europe. They have a point. In standardizing currency, taxes, and policies it is increasingly the EU that calls the tune.

But the EU is not yet a union in the way the United States is. Some EU nations ignore provisions they dislike. Of the EU's fifteen members, only eleven adopted the euro in 1999. Sovereignty still resides in London, Paris, Berlin, and other national capitals rather than at EU headquarters in Brussels. Institutionally, the EU structure is still rather corrupt and undemocratic. The EU's inability to do anything about Bosnia illustrates the EU's lack of concerted foreign and security policies. European unity is building, but it will be some time before it blots out the distinctive politics of its member countries.

COMPARISON

THE IMPORTANCE OF BEING COMPARATIVE

UCLA's late, great James Coleman used to tell his students, "You can't be scientific if you're not comparing." Countries are not unique; they are comparable with other countries. When we say, for example, the parliament of country X has become a rubber stamp for the executive, this is not a very meaningful statement until we note it is also the tendency in countries Y and Z.

The "uniqueness trap" often catches commentators of the American scene off-guard. We hear statements such as: "The U.S. political system is breaking down." Compared to what? To France in 1958? To Russia today? Or to the United States itself in 1861? Compared to these other cases, the United States today is in great shape. We hear statements like: "Taxes in this country are outrageous." But what percentage of GDP do Americans pay in taxes compared to Britons, French, and Germans? Our thinking on politics will be greatly clarified if we put ourselves into a comparative mood by frequently asking, "Compared to what?"

Parties also interact with the government. In China, the Party nearly is the government. In more politically open countries, parties try to capture and retain governmental power. How do parties form coalitions? Who gets the top cabinet jobs? Once in power, is the party able to act, or is it immobilized by contrary political forces? These are some questions to ask.

Politics within the parties is an important point. We ask if a party has factions. In Japan, the factions of the leading party are more important than most of the other separate parties. Does the party have a left wing and a right wing? How do its leaders hold it together? Do they pay off factions with key jobs or merely with lip service? Do factional quarrels paralyze the party? Could it split? Do its more extreme factions frighten away voters?

Parties also interact with **interest groups**. Some groups enjoy "structured access" to like-minded parties. In Europe, labor unions are often linked formally to political parties. Here we need to know: Does the party co-opt the interest group, or vice versa? How powerful are interest-group views in determining party policy?

As mentioned earlier, interest groups often decide it's not worth working on the electoral-legislative side and instead focus their attention on bureaucracies. One of the key areas of politics is where bureaucracies and businesses interface. Are interest groups controlled by government, or vice versa? What kind of relationships do businessmen and bureaucrats establish? Which groups are the most influential? These important interactions are generally out of the public sight and often corrupt. Does money change hands?

Key Term

interest group
Association aimed at getting favorable policies.

What People Quarrel About

Here we move to current issues, the political struggles of the day. We start with economics, the universal and permanent quarrel over who gets what. Politics and economics are closely connected; one can make or break the other. (Political scientists should have a grounding in economics; take an economics course.)

First, we inquire if the economy of the country is growing. Rapidly or slowly? Why? Are workers lazy or energetic? Are managers inept or clever? How much of the economy is supervised and planned by government? Is government interference a hindrance on the economy? If the economy is declining, will it lead to political upheaval (as in the Soviet Union)? Why are some countries economic success stories and others not? How big a role does politics play in economic growth?

Other issues: Are unions restrained or militant? What political payoffs do unions seek? Are wage settlements in line with productivity, or are they inflationary? Does government try to influence wage increases? Do workers and management cooperate or battle each other? Do workers have any say in running their companies? How much imported labor is there? How much unemployment?

Once we have a realistic picture of the economic pie, we inquire who gets what slice. How equal—or unequal—is the distribution of income and wealth? Does the government redistribute incomes to make people more equal or does it let inequality grow? Does unequal distribution lead to social and political resentment? **Redistribution** is another name for a

Key Term

redistribution   Taxing the better off to help the worse off.

welfare system, and all advanced democracies are to some extent welfare states. How high and how progressive are taxes? How many welfare benefits exist and how generous are they? Do people want more welfare and higher taxes or less welfare and lower taxes? Which people want what? If stuck with an overgenerous welfare system, can the government cut it?

There are, to be sure, noneconomic quarrels as well. Regionalism is persistent and even growing. Even Britain and France have breakaway regional movements. In Germany, the east and the west resent each other. What are a country's regions? Which of them are discontent? Over what? How does the discontent manifest itself? Does it include violence? Are there ideas to decentralize or devolve power to the regions? One nasty quarrel throughout West Europe is what to do with the millions of immigrants, usually from Third World lands: Let in more or keep them out? Integrate them or send them home?

Key Terms

absolutism (p. 3)	investiture crisis (p. 4)
authoritarian (p. 9)	legitimacy (p. 10)
causality (p. 3)	mass (p. 8)
constitution (p. 9)	multinational (p. 2)
cynical (p. 10)	nation (p. 1)
democracy (p. 8)	parliament (p. 9)
diplomatic recognition (p. 2)	per capita (p. 8)
electoral franchise (p. 8)	political culture (p. 10)
elites (p. 8)	political geography (p. 6)
ethnicity (p. 2)	pragmatic (p. 11)
euro (p. 15)	quarrels (p. 5)
European Union (EU) (p. 15)	redistribution (p. 17)
feudalism (p. 3)	reification (p. 3)
GDP (p. 8)	sovereignty (p. 1)
generalization (p. 15)	state (p. 1)
ideology (p. 11)	symbol (p. 8)
institution (p. 9)	temporal (p. 4)
interest group (p. 16)	theory (p. 15)

Further Reference

Almond, Gabriel, and Sidney Verba. *The Civic Culture: Political Attitudes and Democracy in Five Nations*. Princeton, NJ: Princeton University Press, 1963.

Ashford, Douglas E. *The Emergence of the Welfare States*. New York: Basil Blackwell, 1986.

Colomer, Josep M., ed. *Political Institutions in Europe*. New York: Routledge, 1996.

Huntington, Samuel P. *The Third Wave: Democratization in the Late Twentieth Century*. Norman, OK: University of Oklahoma Press, 1991.

Keating, Michael. *The Politics of Modern Europe: The State and Political Authority in the Major Democracies*. Brookfield, VT: Edward Elgar, 1994.

Klingemann, Hans-Dieter, and Dieter Fuchs, eds. *Citizens and States*. New York: Oxford University Press, 1995.

Lane, Ruth. *The Art of Comparative Politics*. Needham Heights, MA: Allyn & Bacon, 1997.

Lijphart, Arend. *Electoral Systems and Party Systems: A Study of Twenty-Seven Democracies, 1945–1990*. New York: Oxford University Press, 1994.

Lipset, Seymour Martin. *Political Man: The Social Bases of Politics*, expanded and updated ed. Baltimore, MD: Johns Hopkins University Press, 1981.

Mair, Peter, ed. *The West European Party System.* New York: Oxford University Press, 1990.

Peters, B. Guy. *Comparative Politics: Theory and Method.* New York: New York University Press, 1998.

Rokkan, Stein. *State Formation, Nation-Building, and Mass Politics in Europe.* New York: Oxford University Press, 1995.

Sullivan, Michael J. *Comparing State Polities: A Framework for Analyzing 100 Governments.* Westport, CT: Greenwood, 1996.

Tilly, Charles, ed. *The Formation of National States in Western Europe.* Princeton, NJ: Princeton University Press, 1975.

PART I

Key Websites

Magna Carta   From the National Archives and Record Administration, this site offers a translation of the Magna Carta as confirmed by Edward I with his seal in 1297.
http://www.nara.gov/exhall/charters/magnacarta/magtrans.html

English Bill of Rights 1689   This site discusses an act declaring the rights and liberties of the subject and settling the succession of the crown.
http://www.yale.edu/lawweb/avalon/england.htm

The House of Commons and Members of Parliament   This site has information on the House of Commons and Parliament, including the following: a list of members, ministers and committees; a brief guide to the UK Parliamentary System; and over 60 Factsheets describing various facets of the House of Commons (available for downloading in pdf format).
http://www.parliament.uk/commons/cminfo.htm

The House of Lords   The home page of the House of Lords covers various topics of interest, including the following: an agenda of future business; a list of publications on the Internet; general information on specific subject-oriented investigative Select Committees; and judicial work and judgments.
http://www.parliament.the-stationery-office.co.uk/pa/ld/ldhome.htm

The Labour Party   This site covers the basic principles and history of the Labour Party. The site also tracks current events and features the full text of the Labour manifesto—see also The Labour Party's home page <http://www.labour.org.uk/>.
http://www.bbc.co.uk/politics97/parties/palab.shtml

The Conservative Party   This site discusses the Conservative Party's history, current events, and poll results. The site also features the Conservative manifesto of 1997—see also The Conservative Party's home page <http://www.conservative-party.org.uk/>.
http://www.bbc.co.uk/politics97/parties/pacon.shtml

10 Downing Street   This site offers a News Center, Interact, Live Broadcasts, and an Information Center. The News Centre features daily news direct from 10 Downing Street regarding government activities. Interact receives regular updates on government activities via email. Live Broadcasts covers events involving the Prime Minister and other senior government officials. The Information Centre provides lists of subcommittees and members for each of the committees listed, and also features recent speeches and statements.
http://www.number-10.gov.uk/index.html

The British Monarchy   This is the official website of the Monarch, and includes topics on the following: the Queen and her role within Parliament, with the Prime Minister, and with the Privy Council; information about accession, coronation, and succession; and a brief history of the monarchy through the ages.
http://www.royal.gov.uk/index.htm

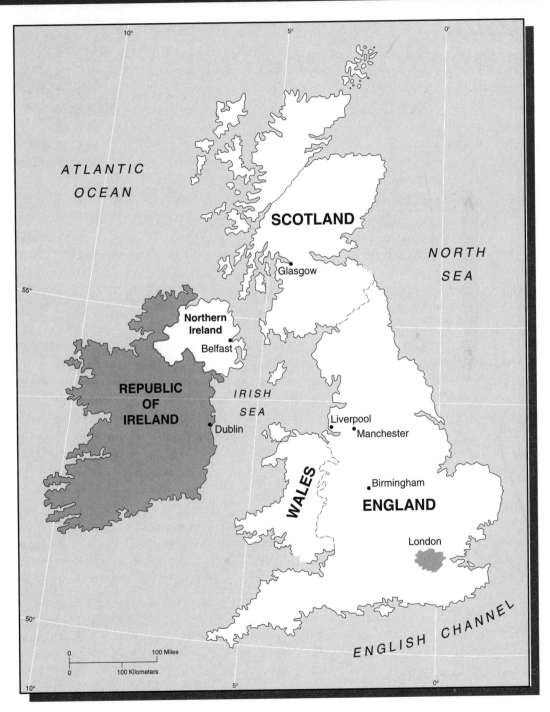

Britain:
The Impact of the Past

2

Questions to Consider

1. How has geography influenced British development?
2. What does the Union Jack stand for?
3. What did the Magna Carta preserve?
4. What is the Common Law?
5. When did Parliament eclipse the monarch?
6. How did Puritanism influence democracy?
7. How did democracy come to Britain?
8. What was the difference between Hobbes and Locke?
9. How are Britain and Sweden so comparable?

A Polish student I once knew at UCLA had to write a paper for her English class on what she most wished for her native land. She took the question as a geographical one and wrote: "I wish Poland be island like England." She would like to fix Poland's problem, its location on a plain between large, hostile neighbors (Germany and Russia) that has given it a sad history of invasion and partition.

England long ago had been invaded many times. For a millennium and a half, waves of **Celts**, Romans, Angles and Saxons, Danes, and finally **Normans** washed upon Britain. One tribe of Celts, the Britons, gave their name to the entire island. Britishers, like most peoples, are not of one stock but of many.

The fierce Germanic tribesmen who rowed across the North Sea during the third to fifth centuries A.D. brought over Anglisch, what we call Old English, the language of the Angles, close to the Frisian of the Netherlands and German coast. "England" was simply the land of the Angles. The Angles and Saxons slowly moved across England, destroying towns and massacring inhabitants. The Celts were pushed back to present-day Wales and Scotland, which became a "Celtic fringe" to England. Some Celts fled over to France and gave their name to Brittany. Preserving their distinct identity and languages (Cymric in Wales, Gaelic in Scotland), Britain's Celts never quite forgot what the newer arrivals did to them.

Key Terms

Celts Pre-Roman inhabitants of Europe.

Normans Vikings who settled in and gave their name to Normandy, France.

GEOGRAPHY

INVADABILITY

Britain is hard to invade. The last successful invasion of England (which was by the Normans) was in 1066. The barrier posed by the English Channel has kept French, Spaniards, and Germans from conquering Britain. Politically, this has meant that England could develop its own institutions without foreign interference, a luxury not enjoyed by most Continental lands.

Militarily, it has meant that England rarely needed or had a large army, a point of great importance in the seventeenth century when British kings were unable to tame Parliament precisely because the monarch had few soldiers.

Other invaders followed. In the ninth century, Danish Vikings held much of eastern England (the Danelaw), but they were eventually absorbed. Another group of Vikings had meanwhile settled in France; these Norsemen (Normans) gave their name to Normandy. In 1066, with the English throne in dispute, William of Normandy put forward his own dubious claim to it and invaded with a force gathered from all over France. He defeated the English King Harold at the famous battle of Hastings, and England changed dramatically.

William the Conqueror replaced the entire Saxon ruling class with Norman nobles, who earned their **fiefdoms** by military service. At first the Norman conquerors spoke only French, so vast numbers of French words soon enriched the English language. Backed by military power, administration was better and tighter. William ordered a complete inventory of all lands and population in his new domain; the resulting Domesday Book provided a detailed tool for governance. The **Exchequer**—the name derived from the French word for a checkered counting table—became the king's powerful treasury minister, a title and office that still exists. Furthermore, since William and his descendants ruled both England and parts of France, England was tied for centuries to the affairs of **the Continent**.

Magna Carta

The Normans brought to England a political system that had first emerged on the Continent—*feudalism*. The feudal system was a contractual agreement between lords and vassals in which the lords would grant the vassals land (or the use of it) and protection while the vassal would support the lord with military service. Feudalism tends to appear naturally when central authority has broken down and a money economy disappears, for then land and fighting ability take on tremendous importance. In Europe, the collapse of the Roman Empire meant kings could survive and thrive only if they had enough lords and knights to fight for them. The lords and knights in turn got land. Power here was a two-way street: The king needed the nobles and vice versa.

Key Terms

fiefdom Land granted by a king to a noble in exchange for support.

Exchequer Britain's treasury ministry.

the Continent British term for the continent of Europe, implying they are not part of it.

GEOGRAPHY

THE UNITED KINGDOM

The full and official name of Britain is the United Kingdom of Great Britain and Northern Ireland. "Great Britain" refers to the whole island that includes Wales and Scotland as well as England.

The British flag, the "Union Jack," stands for three saints representing different parts of the United Kingdom. The larger red cross is the Cross of St. George of England, the diagonal white cross is that of St. Andrew of Scotland, and the thinner, diagonal red cross is that of St. Patrick of Ireland. (Note this cross is off center.) Now some English nationalists wave just the English flag (red cross on a white field) and some Scottish nationalists their flag (diagonal white cross on a blue field), an indication that the United Kingdom has grown less united. Symbols matter.

The **mixed monarchy** of the Middle Ages was a balance between king and nobles. Its essence can be summed up in the oath the nobles of Aragon (in the northeast of Spain) swore to a new ruler: "We who are as good as you swear to you, who are no better than we, to accept you as our king and sovereign lord provided you observe all our statutes and laws; and if not, no."

Centuries of English history were dominated by the struggle to make sure the king did not exceed his feudal bounds and become an absolute monarch (which is what happened in most of Europe). This English struggle laid the foundation for limited, representative government, democracy, and civil rights, even though the participants at the time had no such intent.

The Great Charter the barons forced upon King John at Runnymede in 1215 is nothing so far-reaching or idealistic; it never mentions liberty or democracy. What the barons and top churchmen wanted from John was to stop his encroachment on feudal customs, rights, and laws by which they held sway in their localities. In this sense the **Magna Carta**, one of the great documents of democracy, was feudal and reactionary. Far more important than its actual content, however, was the principle of limiting the monarch's powers and making sure he stayed within the law.

Key Terms

mixed monarchy King balanced by nobles.

Magna Carta The 1215 agreement to preserve the rights of English nobles.

The Magna Carta meant the king stayed in balance with the nobles, thus preventing either despotism or anarchy, the twin ills of the Continent. In Europe, countries either went to *absolutism*, as in France, or broke up into small principalities, as in Germany. British, and by extension, American democracy owes a lot to the stubborn English barons who stood up for their traditional rights.

The Rise of Parliament

During the same century as the Magna Carta, English kings started calling to London, by now the capital, two to four knights from each shire (roughly a county) and a similar number of **burghers** from the towns to consult with the king on matters of the realm. Kings did this not out of the goodness of their hearts but because they needed to raise taxes and to firm up the support of those who had local power. The fact that English kings also had French holdings meant that England fought wars in France. These were expensive, and the only way to raise revenues to pay for them was by inviting local notables to participate, at least symbolically, in the affairs of state. Little did the kings know they were founding an institution in the thirteenth century that would overshadow the monarchy by the seventeenth century.

Parliament began as an extension of the king's court, but over the centuries took on a life of its own. Knights and burghers formed what we call a lower house, the House of Commons. Those of noble rank, along with the top churchmen, formed what we call an upper house, the House of Lords. In time, a leading member of the Commons became its representative to the king; he was called the Speaker. In order that business could be conducted unhampered, parliamentary privileges developed to prevent the arrest of members.

The House of Commons at this stage was not a "representative" institution, at least not in our sense. It represented only people who were locally wealthy or powerful, not a cross-section of the English people. That came much later, in the nineteenth century. But Parliament played a role even more important than accurate representation of the nation. It continued the blocking mechanism of the Magna Carta: It diffused power and prevented the king from getting too much. Parliament thus laid one of the foundations of democracy without knowing it.

Henry VIII

Parliament got a major boost during the reign of Henry VIII (1509–47), when Henry declared a partnership with Parliament in his struggle against Rome. On top of underlying tensions between the **Vatican** and London—the universal Church on the one hand and growing nationalism on the other—Henry wanted the pope to grant him a divorce. His marriage to Catherine of Aragon had failed to produce the male heir Henry felt he needed to ensure stability after him. (Ironically, it was his daughter Elizabeth who went down in history as one of the greatest English monarchs.)

The pope refused—Catherine's Spanish relatives at that time controlled the papacy—so Henry summoned a parliament in 1529 and kept it busy for seven years, passing law after law to get England out of the Catholic church and the Catholic church out of England. The

COMPARISON

COMMON LAW

One of England's contributions to civilization is the **Common Law**, the legal system now also practiced in the United States, Canada, Australia, and other countries once administered by Britain (but not South Africa). Common Law grew out of the customary usage of the Germanic tribal laws of the Angles and Saxons, which stressed the rights of free men. It developed on the basis of **precedent** set by earlier decisions and thus has been called "judge-made law."

When the Normans conquered England, they decided the purely local nature of this law was unsuitable to governing the country as a whole, so they set up central courts to systematize the local laws and produce a "common" law for all parts of England—hence the name.

Common Law differs from the Roman Law that is practiced throughout Continental Europe (and in Scotland). Common Law emphasizes precedent while Roman Law stresses fixed legal codes. This gave the Common Law flexibility to adapt and change gradually over time.

Key Terms

Common Law System of judge-made law developed in England.

precedent Legal reasoning based on previous cases.

Anglican Church of England, Episcopalian in America.

anticlerical Favoring getting the Roman Catholic church out of politics.

secularization Diminishing the role of religion in society and government.

new **Anglican** church was at first identical to the Roman Catholic church (it turned Protestant later), but it was led by an Englishman, not the pontiff of Rome. The new church granted Henry his divorce in 1533. He married a total of six wives (and had two of them beheaded). Henry was not simply eager for young brides; he was desperate for a male heir for dynastic reasons.

The impact of Henry's break with Rome was major. England was cut free from Catholic guidance and direction. Countries that stayed Catholic, such as France, Spain, and Italy, experienced wrenching splits for centuries between prochurch and **anticlerical** forces. England (and Sweden) avoided this nasty division because the state early on was stronger than the church and controlled it. This meant that in England it was far easier to **secularize** society and politics than in Roman Catholic countries, where the church was still an independent power.

Parliament became more important than ever; Henry needed its support for his momentous break with Rome. In 1543 Henry praised Parliament as an indispensable part of his government: "We be informed by our judges that we at no time stand so highly in our estate royal as in the time of parliament, wherein we as head and you as members are conjoined and knit together into one body politic." A century later Parliament chopped the royal head off one of his successors.

Parliament versus King

In the late fifteenth century several European monarchs were able to expand their powers and undermine the old feudal mixed monarchy. The weakened power of Rome in sixteenth-century England gave kings more independence and introduced the notion that kings ruled by divine right, that is, that they received their authority directly from God without the pope as intermediary. Political theorists searched for the seat of *sovereignty* and concluded it must lie in one person—the monarch. This gave rise to absolutism. By 1660 absolute monarchs governed most lands of Europe—but not England.

The seventeenth century brought uninterrupted turmoil to England: religious splits, civil war, a royal beheading, and a military dictatorship. The net winner, when the dust had settled, was Parliament.

Trouble started when James I came down from Scotland to take over the English throne after the death of Elizabeth I in 1603. James united the crowns of Scotland and England, but they remained separate countries until the 1707 Act of Union. James I was intelligent and well-educated but imbued with absolutist notions then common throughout Europe. He didn't like to share power and thought that existing institutions should simply support the king. This brought him into conflict with Puritanism, an extreme Protestant movement that aimed to reform the "popish" elements out of the Anglican church. James preferred the Anglican church to stay just the way it was, for it was one of the pillars of his regime. James's harassment of Puritans caused some of them to run away to Massachusetts.

By now Parliament had grown to feel equal with the king and, in the area of raising revenues, superior to him. Hard up for cash, James tried to impose taxes without the consent of Parliament, which grew angry over the move. James's son, Charles I, who took over in 1625, fared even worse. He took England into wars with Spain and France; both were unsuccessful and increased the king's desperation for money. Charles tried to play the role of a Continental absolute monarch, but the English people and Parliament wouldn't let him.

When the **Royalists** fought the **Parliamentarians** in the English Civil War (1642–48), the latter proved stronger, for the Parliamentarian cause was aided by Puritans and the growing merchant class. The Parliamentarians created a "New Model Army," which trounced the Royalists. (The king, as was mentioned, had no standing army at his disposal.) Charles was captured, tried by Parliament, and beheaded in 1649.

Key Terms

Royalists   Supporters of the king in the English Civil War.

Parliamentarians Supporters of Parliament.

landlocked   A country with no seacoast.

GEOGRAPHY

SEACOAST

A country with outlet to the sea has a major economic advantage over **landlocked** countries. Sea transport is cheap and does not require crossing neighboring countries. Usable natural harbors also help. Peter the Great battled for years to obtain Russian outlets on the Baltic and Black Seas, something England and France had from the start. England's Atlantic orientation contributed to its empire, early industrialization, and prosperity.

DEMOCRACY

"ONE MAN, ONE VOTE"

Among the antiroyalists were a group of out-and-out **republicans**, called **Levellers**, who wanted to make men politically equal. Sergeants and enlisted men in the New Model Army argued that people like themselves—tradesmen, artisans, and farmers—should have the vote. They were influenced in their thinking by Puritanism, which among other things taught that all men were equal before God and needed no spiritual or temporal superiors to guide them. (This Puritan influence also had a powerful impact on American democracy.)

One group of Levellers, meeting in Putney in 1647, even went so far as to advocate "one man, one vote." This radical idea was a good two centuries ahead of its time, and the more conservative forces of England, including Cromwell himself, rejected it out of hand. Still, the Putney meeting had introduced the idea of the universal franchise—that is, giving everybody the right to vote.

Cromwell's Commonwealth

Key Terms

republican In its original sense, favoring getting rid of monarchy.

Levellers Radicals during the English Civil War who argued for equality and "one man, one vote."

republic A country not headed by a monarch.

commonwealth A republic.

From 1649 to 1660 England had no king. Who then was to rule? The only organized force left was the army, and it was led by Oliver Cromwell. Briefly, England became a **republic** called the **Commonwealth**, and Cromwell was the leading figure. Discord, however, grew worse. To restore order, Cromwell in 1653 was designated Lord Protector, a sort of uncrowned king, and soon imposed a military dictatorship on England. When Cromwell died in 1658, most Englishmen had had enough of turbulent republicanism and longed for stability and order. In 1660, Parliament invited Charles II, son of the beheaded king, to return from Dutch exile and reclaim the throne. The English monarchy was restored, but it was a different kind of monarchy, one in which Parliament was much stronger and had to be treated with respect.

The "Glorious Revolution"

Charles II knew he could not be an absolute monarch; instead, he tried to manipulate Parliament discreetly. A showdown arose over religion. Charles was pro-Catholic and secretly ready to return his allegiance to Rome. In 1673 he issued the Declaration of Indulgence, lifting laws against Catholics and non-Anglican Protestants. What we might see as an act of tolerance toward minority religions, Parliament saw as an illegal return to Catholicism, and it blocked the royal move. Anti-Catholic hysteria swept England with fabricated stories of popish plots to take over the country.

When Charles II died in 1685, his openly and proudly Catholic brother, James, took the throne as James II. Again, a Declaration of Indulgence was issued, and again Parliament took it as a return to both Catholicism and absolutism. Parliament dumped James II (but let him escape) and invited his Protestant daughter, Mary, and her Dutch husband, William, to be England's queen and king. This was the "Glorious Revolution" of 1688: A major shift of regime took place with scarcely a shot fired. (In 1690, William beat James in Ireland, but that was after the Revolution.) In 1689 a "Bill of Rights"—unlike its U.S. namesake—spelled out Parliament's relationship to the Crown: no laws or taxes without Parliament's assent.

The majority of Englishmen approved. If it wasn't clear before, it was now: Parliament was supreme and had the ability to invite and dismiss monarchs. In 1714, for example, Parliament invited George I from Hanover in Germany to become king; the present royal family is descended from him. Since that time, the English monarch has been increasingly a figurehead, one who reigns but does not rule.

The Rise of the Prime Minister

One of the consequences of bringing George I to England was that he couldn't really govern even if he had wanted to. He spoke no English and preferred Hanover to London. So he turned to an institutional device that had been slowly developing and allowed it to assume top executive power—the cabinet, composed of ministers and presided over by a first, or prime, minister. Headed by Sir Robert Walpole from 1721 to 1742, the cabinet developed nearly into its present form, but lacked two important present-day features: The **prime minister** could not pick his **ministers** (that was reserved for the king), and the cabinet was not responsible—meaning, in its original sense, "answerable"—to Parliament.

Royal power had one last gasp. George III managed to pack the Commons with his supporters and to govern with the obedient Lord North. One unforeseen result of this temporary absolutist resurgence was the U.S. Declaration of Independence, which sought to regain the traditional rights of Englishmen against a too-powerful king. Following this British defeat, William Pitt the Younger restored the cabinet and prime ministership to

---

Key Terms

prime minister The chief of government in parliamentary systems.

minister Head of a major department (ministry) of government.

DEMOCRACY

"POWER CORRUPTS"

The nineteenth-century British historian and philosopher Lord Acton distilled the lessons of centuries of English political development in his famous remark: "Power tends to corrupt; absolute power corrupts absolutely." Acton feared the tyrannical tendencies of the modern state. Lord Acton's dictum underlays much democratic thinking power and made them responsible only to the Commons, not to the King. This began the tradition—it has never been written into law—that the "government" consists of the leader of the largest party in the House of Commons plus other people he or she picks. As party chief, top person in Parliament, and head of government combined, the prime minister became the focus of political power in Britain.

The Democratization of Parliament

Parliament may have been supreme by the late eighteenth century, but it was hardly democratic or even representative. In the country, the right to vote was limited to those who owned land that yielded an income of at least forty shillings a year. In towns, there were often not more than a dozen or so men eligible to vote, although in the cities the franchise was much wider.

In the eighteenth century, parties began to form. At first they were simply parliamentary caucuses, meetings of people from the same area. Only in the next century did they begin to strike roots in the electorate outside of Parliament. The labels **Whig** and **Tory** first appeared under Charles II, connoting his opposition and his supporters, respectively. Both were derisive names: The original Whigs were Scottish bandits, and the original Tories were Irish bandits.

During the nineteenth century, a two-party system emerged. The Whigs grew into the Liberal party and the Tories into the Conservative party. British Conservatives to this day are nicknamed Tories. Whatever their party label, parliamentarians were not ordinary people. The House of Lords, of course, was limited to hereditary peers. The House of Commons, despite its name, was the home of gentry, landowners, and better-off people. Elections were often won by bribing the small number of voters.

By the time of the American and French revolutions in the late eighteenth century, however, Parliament noticed the winds were stirring in favor of expanding the electorate. People began talking about political democracy and the right to vote. Under the impact of the industrial revolution and economic growth, two powerful new social classes arose— the middle class and the working class. Whigs and Tories, both heavily aristocratic in their makeup, at first viewed demands for the mass vote with disdain and even horror; it reminded them of how democracy ran amok during the French Revolution.

Gradually, though, it dawned on the Whigs that the way to head off revolution was to incorporate some of the new social elements into politics and give them a stake in the system. Furthermore, they realized that the party that supported broadening the franchise would most likely win the votes of those who were newly enfranchised. After much resistance by Tories in the Commons and by the entire House of Lords, Parliament succeeded in passing the **Reform Act** of 1832.

At the time, the Reform Act hardly looked like a momentous breakthrough. It allowed more of the middle class to vote but still only expanded the electorate by about half: Only about 7 percent of adults could then vote. The Reform Act established the principle, though, that the Commons ought to be representative of, and responsive to, the broad mass of citizens, not just the notables. In 1867, it was the Conservatives' turn. Under Prime Minister Benjamin Disraeli, the Second Reform Act doubled the size of the electorate, giving about 16 percent of adult Britons the vote. In 1884, the Third Reform Act added farm workers to the electorate and thus achieved nearly complete male suffrage. Women finally got the vote in 1918.

Key Terms

Whigs   A faction of Parliament that became the Liberal party.

Tories   A faction of Parliament that became the Conservative party.

Reform Acts   Series of laws expanding the British electoral franchise.

THREE BRITISH GENIUSES: HOBBES, LOCKE, BURKE

Thomas Hobbes lived through the upheavals of the English Civil War in the seventeenth century and opposed them for making life insecure and frightening. Hobbes imagined that life in "the **state of nature**," before "**civil society**" was founded, must have been terrible. Every man would have been the enemy of every other man, a "war of each against all." Humans would live in savage squalor with "no arts; no letters; no society; and which is worst of all, continual fear, and danger of violent death; and the life of man, solitary, poor, nasty, brutish, and short." To get out of this horror, people would—out of their profound self-interest—rationally join together to form civil society. Society thus arises naturally out of fear. People would also gladly submit to a king, even a bad one, for a monarch prevents anarchy.

John Locke, saw the same upheavals but came to less-harsh conclusions. Locke theorized that the original state of nature was not so bad; people lived in equality and tolerance with one another. But they could not secure their property: There was no money, title deeds, or courts of law, so their property was uncertain. To remedy this, they contractually formed civil society and

thus secured "life, liberty, and property." Locke is to property rights as Hobbes is to fear of violent death. Some philosophers argue that Americans are the children of Locke. Notice the American emphasis on "the natural right to property."

Edmund Burke was a Whig member of Parliament who was horrified at the French Revolution, warning well in advance it would end up a military dictatorship (it did). The French revolutionists had broken the historical continuity, institutions, and symbols that restrain people from bestial behavior, argued Burke. Old institutions, such as the monarchy and church, must be pretty good because they have evolved over centuries. If you scrap them, society breaks down only to end under a tyranny. Burke understood that **conservatism** means constant, but never radical, change. Wrote Burke: "A state without the means of some change is without the means of its conservation." Progress comes not from chucking out the old but from gradually modifying the parts that need changing while preserving the overall structure, keeping the form but reforming the contents.

The interesting point about the growth of the British electorate is that the process was slow. New elements were added to the voting rolls only gradually, giving Parliament time to assimilate the forces of mass politics without going through an upheaval. The gradual tempo also meant citizens got the vote when they were ready for it. In some countries where the universal franchise—one person, one vote— was instituted early, the result was fake democracy, as crafty officials rigged the voting of people who didn't understand electoral politics. Spain, for example, got universal suffrage in the 1870s, but election results were set in advance. By the time the British working class got the vote, they were ready to use it intelligently.

With the expansion of the voting franchise, political parties turned from parliamentary clubs into modern parties. They had to win elections involving thousands of voters. This meant

Key Terms

state of nature   Humans before civilization.

civil society   Humans after becoming civilized. Modern usage: associations between family and government.

conservatism   Ideology aimed at preserving existing institutions and usages.

COMPARISON

THE ORIGINS OF TWO WELFARE STATES

Both Britain and Sweden are welfare states. How did this come to be? In comparing their histories, we get some clues.

- Swedish King Gustav Vasa broke with Rome in the 1520s, a few years earlier than Henry VIII. In setting up churches that were dependent on their respective states—Lutheran in Sweden, Anglican in England—the two countries eliminated religion as a source of government opposition.

- Politics in both lands did not get stuck in a clerical-anticlerical dispute over the Church's role, as was the case in France, Italy, and Spain. In Britain and Sweden, the main political split was along class lines, working class versus middle class.

- Britain and Sweden both developed efficient and uncorrupt civil services, an absolute essential for the effective functioning of welfare programs.

- Both countries formed strong—but not Marxist—labor movements, the TUC in Britain and LO in Sweden.

- These two labor movements gave rise to moderate, worker-oriented parties, Labour in Britain and the Social Democrats in Sweden, which demanded, and over time got, numerous welfare measures passed. One big difference is the Social Democrats have been in power in Sweden for all but a few years since 1932 and have implemented a more thorough—and more expensive—welfare state.

organization, programs, promises, and continuity. The growth of the electorate forced parties to become vehicles for democracy.

The Rise of the Welfare State

By the beginning of the twentieth century, with working men having the right to vote, British parties had to pay attention to demands for welfare measures—public education, housing, jobs, and medical care—that the upper-crust gentlemen of the Liberal and Conservative parties had earlier been able to minimize. Expansion of the electoral franchise led to the growth of the **welfare state**.

One force goading Liberals and Conservatives into supporting welfare measures was the new Labour party, founded in 1900. At first, Labour worked with the Liberals—the "Lib-Lab" coalition—but by the end of World War I, Labour pushed the Liberals into the weak third-party status they have languished in to this day. Unlike most Continental socialists, few British Labourites were Marxists. Instead, they combined militant trade unionism with intellectual social democracy to produce a pragmatic, gradualist ideology that sought to level class differences in Britain. As one observer put it, the British Labour party "owed more to Methodism than to Marx."

Key Term

welfare state Political system that redistributes wealth from rich to poor; standard in West Europe.

The British labor movement of the late nineteenth century was tough. Resentful of being treated like dirt, many working men went into politics with a militancy that still characterizes some of their heirs. In the 1926 General Strike, the trade unions attempted to bring the entire British economy to a halt to gain their wage demands. They failed.

Briefly and weakly in power under Ramsay MacDonald in the 1920s, Labour won resoundingly in 1945 and implemented an ambitious program of welfare measures. Since then, the chief quarrel in British politics has been between people who like the welfare state and people who don't.

Key Terms

Anglican (p. 26)

anticlerical (p. 26)

burghers (p. 25)

Celts (p. 22)

civil society (p. 31)

Common Law (p. 26)

Commonwealth (p. 28)

conservatism (p. 31)

Continent, the (p. 23)

Exchequer (p. 23)

fiefdom (p. 23)

landlocked (p. 27)

Levellers (p. 28)

Magna Carta (p. 24)

minister (p. 29)

mixed monarchy (p. 24)

Normans (p. 22)

Parliament (p. 25)

Parliamentarians (p. 27)

precedent (p. 26)

prime minister (p. 29)

Reform Acts (p. 30)

Republic (p. 28)

republican (p. 28)

Royalists (p. 27)

secularization (p. 26)

state of nature (p. 31)

Tories (p. 30)

Vatican (p. 25)

welfare state (p. 32)

Whigs (p. 30)

Further Reference

Beloff, Max. *Wars and Welfare: Britain 1914–1945.* London: Edward Arnold, 1984.

Callaghan, John. *Socialism in Britain since 1884.* Cambridge, MA: Basil Blackwell, 1990.

Chrimes, S. B. *English Constitutional History.* London: Oxford University Press, 1967.

Clarke, Peter. *Hope and Glory: Britain 1900–1990.* New York: Penguin, 1996.

Colley, Linda. *Britons: Forging the Nation, 1707–1837.* New Haven, CT: Yale University Press, 1992.

Davies, Norman. *The Isles: A History.* New York: Oxford University Press, 1999.

Greenleaf, W. H. *The British Political Tradition,* 3 vols. London: Methuen, 1987.

Hibbert, Christopher. *Cavaliers & Roundheads: The English Civil War, 1642–1649.* New York: Scribner's, 1993.

Kishlansky, Mark. *A Monarchy Transformed: Britain, 1603–1714.* New York: Allen Lane/Penguin Press, 1997.

McKibben, Ross. *Classes and Cultures: England 1918–1951.* New York: Oxford University Press, 1998.

Thorpe, Andrew. *A History of the British Labour Party.* New York: St. Martin's, 1997.

Williams, Glyn, and John Ramsden. *Ruling Britannia: A Political History of Britain, 1688–1988,* 2nd ed. New York: Longman, 1990.

Britain:
The Key Institutions

3

Questions to Consider

1. What did Bagehot mean by "dignified" as opposed to "efficient" office? Examples?
2. How may Britain be described as "prime ministerial government"?
3. Does Britain have checks and balances?
4. Describe Blair's political positions.
5. When does Britain hold general elections?
6. What are the differences between presidential and parliamentary systems?
7. What did Blair do with the House of Lords?
8. Describe the British electoral system.
9. What are Britain's main parties?

It is commonly said that Britain has no written constitution. This is not completely true, for parts of the British constitution are written. It is more correct to say the British constitution does not consist of a single document but is rather a centuries-old collection of Common Law, historic charters, acts passed by Parliament, and, most important, established custom.

This **eclectic** quality gives the British constitution flexibility. With no single, written document to refer to, nothing can be declared "unconstitutional." Parliament—specifically the House of Commons—can pass any law it likes. The British political system can therefore grow and change over time without suffering a systemic crisis. Franklin D. Roosevelt's problems with the Supreme Court, which ruled some of his measures unconstitutional, could not have come up in Britain.

The negative side to this, however, was that Britain had nothing to guarantee human rights. In 1991, six men convicted as IRA bombers in 1975 were freed with the shameful admission that confessions had been beaten out of them and the police had rigged evidence. The European Court of Human Rights, located in Strasbourg, France, ruled against British

Key Term

eclectic Drawn from a variety of sources.

justice in several such cases, a considerable embarrassment for Britain. In 2000, Britain adopted the European Convention on Human Rights as domestic law, finally giving Britons the equivalent of a U.S. Bill of Rights.

The British often speak of "the **Crown**" but have trouble defining it; often they don't even try. The Crown is an all-encompassing term meaning the powers of government in general. Originally, the Crown meant the king, but over the centuries it has broadened to include everyone helping the king or queen: This includes Parliament, the cabinet, and civil servants. Let us consider some of these.

The Monarch

In Britain there is a clear distinction between "head of state" and "chief of government." In America this distinction is ignored because the two are merged into one in the presidency. In most of the rest of the world, however, there is a top figure without much power who symbolizes the nation, receives foreign ambassadors, and gives speeches on patriotic occasions. This person—often a figurehead—can be either a hereditary monarch or an elected president, although not a U.S.-style president. Britain, Sweden, Norway, Denmark, the Netherlands, Belgium, and Spain are monarchies. This doesn't mean they aren't democratic; it just means the head of state is a carry-over from the old days.

A hereditary head of state can be quite useful. Above politics, a monarch can serve as psychological cement to hold a country together without taking an important role in government. Because, theoretically, the top position in the land—what royalist philosophers used to call the sovereign—is already occupied, there are no political battles over it. The nastiest struggles in the world are precisely over who is to be sovereign; in Britain, the issue has long been settled.

The great commentator on the British constitution, Sir Walter Bagehot, divided it into **dignified** and **efficient** parts. The monarch, as head of state, is a dignified office with lots of symbolic but no real political power. He or she "reigns but does not rule." The king or queen nominally appoints a cabinet of His or Her Majesty's servants (see box on page 38), but otherwise a monarch is more like an official greeter.

The "efficient" office in Britain is the chief of government, the prime minister, a working politician who fights elections, leads his or her party, and makes political deals. Despite the prestige attached to being prime minister, it does not carry the degree of "dignity" that being the monarch does. There is an advantage in the way Britain and other countries split the two positions: If the chief of government does something foolish or illegal, he or she will raise the public's ire, but the blame will fall on the individual prime minister, and respect will not diminish for the head of state, the "dignified" office. The system retains its legitimacy. Where the two offices are combined, as in the United States, and the president is involved in something like Watergate, the public gets disgusted with both the working politician and the nation's symbolic leader. "The British don't need to love their prime minister," said one diplomat. "They love their queen."

The 1997 death of Princess Di, ex-wife of Prince Charles, jolted Britain, including the royal family. Di was the only royal with the common touch; her charity work and love life upstaged the cold and remote House of Windsor. Amidst the outpouring of grief for Di came mutterings that the royal family really didn't much care.

Key Terms

Crown   The powers of the British government.

dignified   In Bagehot's terms, the symbolic or decorative offices.

efficient   In Bagehot's terms, the working, political offices.

Prince Charles, Britain's future king and head of the state, in happier days with his then-wife, the late Princess Diana, and their children, Prince William, also a future king, and Prince Henry. The divorce of Charles and Diana in 1996 did not affect Charles's succession to the throne. (Central Office of Information, London)

Some even thought it might be time to dump the monarchy. But old dynasties know how to survive, and quickly the Queen and Prince Charles became more public and outgoing.

Although few would exchange the monarchy for a republic, some (including Queen Elizabeth herself) suggest reforms that would cut government funds for the royal house and make female heirs to the throne the equal of males. Look for a major decision point when Queen Elizabeth dies. Will Charles automatically accede to the throne? Even if he is remarried? To a commoner (herself divorced)? The last time this happened, in 1936, King Edward VIII abdicated, but we need not expect a replay. Britain will likely retain a monarchy, but it may be a monarchy with reduced financial support and political roles.

The Cabinet

The British cabinet also differs from the U.S. cabinet. The former consists of members of Parliament (most in Commons, a few in Lords) who are high up in their parties and important political figures. Most have lots of experience, first as ordinary **MPs** (members of Parliament), then as **junior ministers**, and finally as cabinet ministers. The American cabinet, which seldom now meets and counts for little, usually consists of experts from universities, law offices, and businesses, mostly without political experience, who serve as administrators, not policy innovators. Some observers claim British cabinet government has been declining since World War I, which required speedy, centralized decisions. Now Prime Minister Blair develops policy with a small personal staff and then informs the cabinet of it. Some British commentators fear the rise of a "command premiership" in this development.

Key Terms

MP   Member of Parliament.

junior minister   An MP with executive responsibilities below that of cabinet rank.

DEMOCRACY

THE LAST POLITICAL MONARCH

Unlike other European monarchs, King Juan Carlos of Spain retains some crucial political functions. Juan Carlos took over as head of state after Franco's death in 1975 and initiated and backstopped a process that turned Spain from dictatorship to democracy. He named a prime minister who dismantled the Franco structure, carried out Spain's first free elections in forty-one years, and drafted a new constitution—all with the open approval of the king.

Juan Carlos's real test as a defender of democracy came in 1981 when some disgruntled officers tried to carry out a coup; they actually held the entire **Cortes** at gunpoint. In full military uniform, the king addressed the nation on television and ordered the troops back to their barracks. They complied, and democratic Spaniards of all parties thanked God for the king. Democracy and monarchy are not **antithetical**; one can support the other. *¡Viva el rey!*

Originally, the British cabinet consisted of ministers to the king. Starting in the seventeenth century, however, the cabinet became more and more responsible to Parliament and less and less to the king. A British minister does not necessarily know much about his or her **portfolio** but is carefully picked by the prime minister for political qualifications. Both major British parties contain several viewpoints and power centers, and prime ministers usually take care to see they are represented in the cabinet. When Prime Minister Thatcher ignored this principle by picking as ministers only Tories loyal to her and her philosophy, she was criticized as dictatorial and ultimately lost her job. Balancing party factions in the cabinet helps keep the party together in Parliament and in power.

The British cabinet bridges a gap between "executive" and "legislative." British ministers are both; the elaborate American separation of powers (adopted by the Founding Fathers from an earlier misperception of British government by Montesquieu) doesn't hold in Britain or in most of the world. The United Kingdom has a combining or **fusion of powers**.

The British cabinet practices "collective responsibility," meaning they all stick together and, in public at least, support the prime minister. Occasionally, a minister resigns in protest over a major controversy.

In recent years, the cabinet has consisted of more than twenty ministers, although this number and portfolio titles change. The Commons routinely approves the prime minister's requests to add, drop, or combine ministries. In the late 1990s, Prime Minister Blair's cabinet consisted of the following "secretaries," or ministers:

Lord Chancellor (member of Lords, heads judiciary)
Foreign secretary
Home secretary (internal governance, including police)
Chancellor of the Exchequer (treasury)
Environment secretary

Key Terms

Cortes   Spain's parliament.
antithetical   Ideas opposed to one another.
portfolio   Minister's assigned ministry.
fusion of powers   The combination of executive and legislative, as in parliamentary systems; opposite of the U.S. separation of powers.

Defense secretary
Education secretary
Transport secretary
Social Security secretary
Agriculture secretary
Employment secretary
Northern Ireland secretary
Welsh secretary
Scottish secretary
National Heritage secretary (preservation of buildings and monuments)

In addition, the leaders of both the House of Commons and the House of Lords are in the cabinet, along with a chief secretary for the cabinet as a whole.

Below cabinet rank are more than thirty noncabinet "departmental ministers" and a similar number of "junior ministers" assigned to help cabinet and departmental ministers. All totaled, at any given time about a hundred MPs are also serving in the executive branch. The hope of being named to one of these positions ensures the loyalty and obedience of most younger MPs.

For all intents and purposes, in Britain (and in most parliamentary systems) cabinet equals **government**; the two terms are used interchangeably. One speaks of the "Blair government." (Only the United States uses the word "administration.") When the "government falls" it simply means the cabinet has resigned. Britain is often referred to as "cabinet government," although some call it "prime ministerial government."

Key Term

government   A particular cabinet; what Americans call "the administration."

DEMOCRACY

THE QUEEN CHOOSES A NEW PRIME MINISTER

In May 1997 an old ritual was repeated. Ostensibly Queen Elizabeth II chose a new prime minister, but of course she really had no choice at all. Events unrolled according to the fiction that the prime minister is still chief advisor to the monarch.

Britain's governing Conservative party saw their voter support erode due to some unpopular policies of Prime Minister Margaret Thatcher and the weak leadership of her successor, John Major, who had narrowly won the 1992 elections. The House of Commons can go up to five years between elections, so in 1997 Major had to call them. His Conservatives lost massively to a resurgent Labour party.

No longer leader of the party with a majority of the Commons seats, Major could not remain prime minister, so the day following the elections he called on the Queen to formally resign as first minister to Her Majesty. (He continued as a member of parliament but was dumped as Tory leader.) That same day the Queen called Tony Blair, as leader of what was now the largest party in the Commons, to Buckingham Palace and "asked" him to form a new government. He accepted.

Who Was When: Britain's Postwar Prime Ministers

Clement Attlee	Labour	1945–51
Winston Churchill	Conservative	1951–55
Anthony Eden	Conservative	1955–57
Harold Macmillan	Conservative	1957–63
Alec Douglas-Home	Conservative	1963–64
Harold Wilson	Labour	1964–70
Edward Heath	Conservative	1970–74
Harold Wilson	Labour	1974–76
James Callaghan	Labour	1976–79
Margaret Thatcher	Conservative	1979–90
John Major	Conservative	1990–97
Tony Blair	Labour	1997–

The Prime Minister

The prime minister, PM for short (don't get it confused with MP, which he or she also is), is the linchpin of the British system. In theory, the PM's powers could be nearly dictatorial. Because the prime minister picks and controls the cabinet and heads the largest party in Parliament, theoretically he or she should be able to get nearly any measure passed. British parliamentarians are well-disciplined; party **whips** make sure their MPs turn out for **divisions** and vote the straight party line. Yet even with the reins of power so tightly held by one person, prime ministers still do not turn into dictators.

The chief reason is that general elections are never more than five years away. Prime ministers are usually cautious about introducing measures that might provoke public ire. When John Major saw his popularity slipping, he knew he would lose if he "went to the country" with new elections, so he tried to stall, hoping his party's fortunes would rise before the five years were up. Typically, prime ministers introduce moderate, piecemeal measures to avoid offending key blocks of voters. The fear of losing the next election keeps most prime ministers (but not Thatcher) cautious.

Furthermore, a prime minister has to be careful of the major currents of opinion within party ranks. As in the United States, the two large British parties contain left, right, and center wings, as well as regional and idiosyncratic viewpoints. As was mentioned earlier, a prime minister usually constructs the cabinet with top MPs representing several views within the majority party. In cabinet meetings the PM tries to fashion a consensus from the several stands.

Then the cabinet has to sell the policy to their MPs back in Commons. Party discipline is good but rarely total. The prime minister, through the chief whip, has a hold on the MPs. One who does not "take the whip" (follow the party line on a vote) risks losing his or her nomination for reelection—in effect, getting fired from Parliament. But this is a two-way street. If a party policy really bothers an MP, the member can threaten to quit and make a stink. Every few years an MP "crosses the aisle" and joins the other party in protest (as did the young Winston Churchill). In 1995 one

Key Terms

whip A parliamentary party leader who makes sure members obey the party in voting.

division A vote in the House of Commons.

moderate Conservative MP was so upset by what he saw as right-wing domination of his party that he quit the Tories and ran (successfully) as a Labourite, the ultimate slap at party leadership. If a PM fails badly, he or she can even be dumped by MPs. Several times in the past two decades, both Labour and Conservative cabinets have had to withdraw or water down their legislative proposals for fear of backbenchers' revolt within the ranks of their own party. A backbenchers' revolt helped oust Thatcher in 1990.

THE IMPORTANCE OF BEING BLAIR

At age 43 in 1997, Tony Blair became Britain's youngest prime minister since 1812. To win, he had recast the Labour party—which he called "New Labour"—into a reformist but not radical centrist party. Blair jettisoned uncritical support for unions, higher taxes, and the welfare state in favor of Clinton-type ideas on economic growth and getting people off welfare. With an upbeat personality, he trounced the Conservatives and John Major, who had trouble leading a divided party, in the 1997 general elections to form the first Labour government since 1979.

Some called Blair's ideology—a "Third Way" between capitalism and socialism—vague. Like Clinton, Blair had stolen much of the right's economic agenda but put a smiling face on it. Within two years, leaders across Europe wanted to be like Tony Blair, the man with a vision of a humane but flexible market-based system who refused to get stuck in yesterday's thinking.

And the rest of Europe needed a model. Eleven of the EU's fifteen countries had elected socialist governments by the late 1990s (those that did not: Spain, Belgium, Luxembourg, Ireland) but most of them were not quite sure what they stood for. For many, the traditional socialist dream of welfare for all has been shattered by high costs and high unemployment. What then to offer the electorate? Anyone around here have a vision? Ah, that Englishman Blair has one! Not only did socialists such as France's Lionel Jospin and Germany's Gerhard Schröder proclaim themselves to be like Blair, so did conservatives like Spain's José María Aznar and many German Christian Democrats.

Blair supported market economics but concentrated on modernizing Britain's sometimes creaky institutions. His measures devolved considerable powers to Northern Ireland, Scotland, and Wales. He drastically reformed the House of Lords and launched important initiatives in education. He gave Britain the equivalent of a U.S. Bill of Rights. He even considered changing Britain's hallowed electoral system in favor of proportional representation. By tackling problems that his predecessors ignored, Blair showed himself to be a great modernizer.

Tony Blair. (British Information Services)

The PM does, however, have a potent political weapon: the power to call new elections whenever he or she wishes. By law, the Commons can go up to five years without a general election. **By-elections** when an MP dies or retires can come any time; they are closely watched as political barometers. A crafty prime minister calls for new general elections when he or she thinks the party will do best. A good economy and sunny weather tend to produce a happy electorate, one that will increase the seats of the incumbent party. In 1974 Britain held two general elections because Prime Minister Harold Wilson thought he could boost Labour's strength in the Commons. (He did.) In 1987 Margaret Thatcher called elections a year early to take advantage of good economic news and disarray in the Labour party; she won handily. Public-opinion polls and by-elections help the prime minister decide when to ask the queen to dissolve Parliament and hold new elections.

Since 1735 British prime ministers have resided in an ordinary brick row house, No. 10 Downing Street. Except for a couple of London bobbies on guard outside, a passer-by might take it for a private home. But this is deceptive, for behind the walls, Downing Street is actually the nerve center of **Whitehall**. Upstairs at No. 10, the prime minister has his or her apartment. On the ground floor, in the back, the cabinet meets in a long white room. No. 10 connects to No. 12 Downing Street, the residence of the chief whip, the prime minister's parliamentary enforcer. They can visit without being seen from the street. Also connecting out of sight is No. 11 Downing Street, residence of the important Chancellor of the Exchequer, head of the powerful Treasury Ministry. Next door is the Foreign Office. At the corner of Downing Street, also with a connecting door to No. 10, is the cabinet secretariat, responsible for communication and coordination among the departments.

The Commons

One can look at the cabinet as a committee of the House of Commons sent from **Westminster** to nearby Whitehall to keep administration under parliamentary control. Another way is to view the Commons as an electoral college that stays in operation even after it has chosen the executive (the cabinet).

The two main parties in Commons—Conservative and Labour—face each other on long, parallel benches. The largest party is automatically Her Majesty's Government and the other Her Majesty's **Opposition**. The physical structure of the House of Commons explains a lot. It is very small, measuring only 45 by 68 feet (14 by 21 meters) and was originally designed for only about 400 members. How then can it possibly hold the current membership of 659? (A number that increases over the years as Britain's population grows in some areas more than in others. Parliament may add constituencies but is reluctant to drop old ones.) It doesn't, at least not comfortably. Members have no individual desks, unlike most modern legislators. When there's an important vote, MPs pack in like sardines and sit in the aisles.

By keeping the House of Commons building small, the British ensure that members can face each other in debate a few yards apart. The parallel benches go well with the two-party system; the half-circle floor plan of most Continental legislatures facilitates pielike division into multiparty systems. But the main reason for

Key Terms

by-election A midterm election for a vacant seat in Parliament.

Whitehall The main British government offices.

Westminster The Parliament building.

Opposition In parliamentary systems, the parties in parliament that are not in the cabinet.

COMPARISON

PARLIAMENTARY VERSUS PRESIDENTIAL SYSTEMS

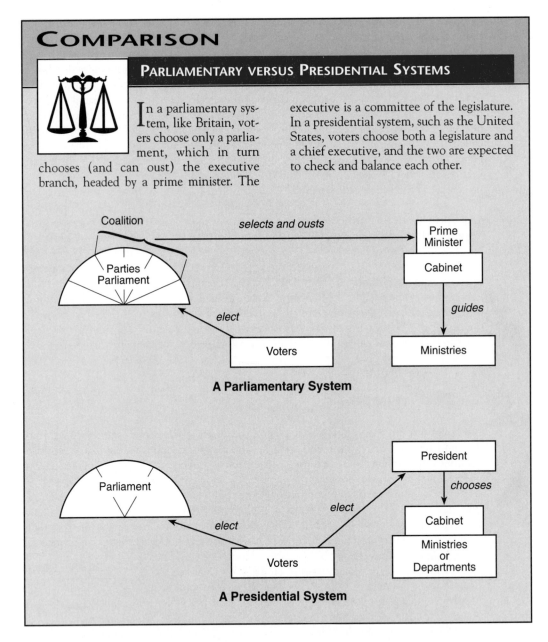

In a parliamentary system, like Britain, voters choose only a parliament, which in turn chooses (and can oust) the executive branch, headed by a prime minister. The executive is a committee of the legislature. In a presidential system, such as the United States, voters choose both a legislature and a chief executive, and the two are expected to check and balance each other.

A Parliamentary System

A Presidential System

the chamber's small size is that it was always small, ever since 1547 when Henry VIII first gave Commons the use of the St. Stephen's royal chapel. During World War II when Commons was damaged by German bombs, Prime Minister Winston Churchill ordered it rebuilt exactly the way it had been.

On each side of the oblong chamber there are five rows of benches. The front row on both sides is reserved for the leading team of each major party, the cabinet of the government party, and the "shadow cabinet" of the opposition. Behind them sit the "backbenchers," the MP rank and file. A neutral Speaker, elected for life from the MPs, sits in a thronelike chair at one end. The Speaker, who never votes or takes sides, manages the floor debate and preserves order. In 1992, Commons elected its first woman Speaker, Labourite Betty Boothroyd.

A table in the center, between the party benches, is where legislation is placed (the origin of the phrase "to table" a proposal). The Speaker calls the house to order at 2:30 P.M., and sessions can go on until late in the evening. Unless "the whip is on"—meaning an MP had better be there because an important vote is expected—many MPs are busy elsewhere.

How the Commons Works

Each year Parliament opens in November with a Speech from the Throne by the queen, another tradition. The MPs are ritually summoned by Black Rod, the queen's messenger, from Commons and file into the nearby House of Lords. (Neither monarchs nor lords are allowed to enter the House of Commons.) From a gold-paneled dais in Lords, Her Majesty reads a statement outlining what policies "my government" will pursue. The speech has been written by the prime minister with the queen serving merely as an announcer. A conservative king, George VI, had to read a Labour speech in 1945 promising extensive nationalization of industry. This he did without batting an eye.

Just as the queen takes her cues from the cabinet, so does Commons. Practically all legislation is introduced by the "government" (that is, the cabinet), and it stands a high chance of passing nearly intact because of the party discipline discussed previously. What

---

COMPARISON

HOW MUCH ARE PARLIAMENTARIANS PAID?

Compared to other advanced democracies, British MPs are paid little and do not enjoy substantial allowances. And this is after a substantial pay raise for MPs in 1996.

Many MPs work at other jobs, some as "consultants" for interest groups. This has given them a reputation for "sleaze" that they detest. Many MPs would like to stop or limit outside pay, but the cost of living in London is high, and MPs' salaries are totally inadequate. The huge allowances for U.S. Representatives (Senators can get almost $2 million) illustrate the strong constituency orientation of U.S. legislators: They need large, specialized staffs both to help the folks back home and to study current issues, functions that are not as highly developed in other parliaments.

Member of	Salary	Allowances
British House of Commons	$67,000	$72,000
French National Assembly	94,400	14,600
German Bundestag	89,000	110,700
Russian Duma	7,000	—
Japanese Diet	146,200	108,900
U.S. House of Representatives	133,600	887,000

House of Commons in session. Notice how small it is. (British Information Service)

the cabinet wants, the cabinet usually gets. When a Labour cabinet introduces bills into Commons, Labour MPs—unlike their American counterparts in Congress—rarely question them. Their job is to support the party, and individual conscience seldom gets in the way.

The task of challenging proposals falls to the opposition, seated on the Speaker's left. From the opposition benches come questions, denunciations, warnings of dire consequences, anything that might make the government look bad. A spirit of bipartisanship seldom gets in the way. Government MPs, particularly the cabinet and subcabinet ministers on the front bench, are duty-bound to defend the bills. In situations like these, the rhetorical skill of MPs produces debates in the House of Commons unmatched in any other legislature.

Although the rhetoric is brilliant and witty, the homework is weak. Because they are expected simply to obey their party, few MPs bother specializing. Traditionally, British parliamentary committees were also unspecialized; they went over the precise wording of bills but called no witnesses and gathered no data. The structure of legislative committees is an important key to their power, and gradually some MPs saw the need for a more American type of committee system. In 1979, fourteen **select committees** were set up to scrutinize the workings of each ministry; they have the power to take written and oral evidence. The select committees, with permanent, stable membership, resemble to some extent U.S. Congressional committees.

Key Term

select committee A specialized committee of the Commons focusing on a ministry.

Neither Tory nor Labour governments have been enthusiastic about specialized committees that monitor and criticize executive functions. That may be part of the U.S. system of separation of powers, some have argued, but it has no place in the U.K. system of fusion of powers. In general, the British cabinet would like to use the Commons to rubber-stamp its decisions. Fortunately, such rubber-stamping is not always the case, as we shall see later.

The New House of Lords

In 1999, Parliament drastically reformed the House of Lords by kicking out most of its hereditary peers. The British Parliament is nominally bicameral, but Lords has seen Commons limit its powers over the centuries, so that now when one says "Parliament" it really means the House of Commons. Early on, Commons established supremacy in the key area of money: raising revenues, and spending them. (The U.S. Constitution provides that money bills originate in the lower chamber, the House of Representatives, an echo of the English tradition.) Britain's seventeenth century battles centered around the power of Commons, and it emerged the winner; Lords gradually took a back seat. By 1867 Bagehot considered Lords a "dignified" part of the constitution.

Since Britain's unwritten constitution does not specify or make permanent the powers of the two chambers, it was legally possible for Commons to change Lords. Its powers now are severely limited. The 1911 Parliament Act allows Lords to delay legislation not more than thirty days on financial bills and two years (since 1949, one year) on other bills.

Lords can amend legislation and send it back to Commons, which in turn can (and usually does) delete the changes by a simple majority. Every few years, however, Lords jolts the government by forcing Commons to take another look at bills passed without sufficient scrutiny. Lords, then, is somewhat more important than a debating club. It is the only British institution in a position to check the potentially dictatorial powers of a prime minister who has a large and disciplined majority in Commons. It can thus be seen as a weak analog to the U.S. Supreme Court, a sort of "conscience of the nation." They are also able to debate questions too hot for elected officials to handle—for example, laws concerning abortion and homosexuality.

There are over thirteen hundred Lords and Ladies of the Realm; about 650 of the titles are hereditary, but since 1958 an increasing number (now close to 600) have been named as nonhereditary **life peers** for distinguished contributions in science, literature, politics, business, and the arts. Usually, fewer than three hundred lords turn up in the House of Lords; a quorum is three. A few lords are named to the cabinet or to other high political or diplomatic positions. The chamber is also home to the five **Law Lords**, life peers who are the top judges in the British court system to whom cases may be appealed. (Unlike the U.S. Supreme Court, however, they lack the power to declare anything unconstitutional.)

Most Britons agreed that Lords was an **anachronism** ripe for reform but couldn't agree on how to do it. Blair solved the problem in 1999 by legislation that deprived most hereditary peers of their seats in Lords, chopping its membership in half. Only ninety-two hereditaries were allowed to remain among 567 life peers. Some hereditary dukes, earls, and viscounts protested bitterly, but many did not care. Although Lords is now more democratic, the move did nothing to enhance its weak powers to debate and delay.

Key Terms

life peers Distinguished Britons named to the House of Lords for their lifetimes only (does not pass on to children).

Law Lords Britain's top judges; members of Lords.

anachronism Something from the past that doesn't fit present times.

The Parties

The House of Commons works as it does because of the British party system. This is a fairly recent development; only since the time of the French Revolution (1789) has it been possible to speak of coherent parties in Britain. Parties are now the cornerstone of British government. If a party elects a majority of the MPs, that party controls Commons and forms the government.

British parties are more cohesive, centralized, and ideological than American parties. It's fair to say there are more differences within the two big U.S. parties than between them. Now, however, like their U.S. counterparts, the two large British parties tend to converge to the center. Earlier, British Labourites, who were sometimes called Socialists— a term most of them didn't object to—favored nationalization of industry, more welfare measures, and higher taxes. Conservatives urged less government involvement in society and the economy and lower taxes. Internal party differences arose from the degree to

---

KEY CONCEPTS

BRITAIN'S TWO-PARTY SYSTEM

Britain is usually described as a two-party system. This is not completely accurate, for there are small parties that are sometimes politically relevant. In 1979, for example, the withdrawal of support by the eleven Scottish Nationalists in the Commons brought down the Callaghan government in a rare vote of no-confidence. The Liberal Democrats may get one vote in five, forcing the Labour and Conservative parties to move to more centrist positions.

Britain's electoral system keeps two parties big and penalizes smaller parties. Britain, like the United States and Canada, uses **single-member districts** as the basis for elections. This means that each electoral district or constituency sends one person to the legislature, the candidate that gets the most votes even if less than a majority, sometimes called **FPTP** (first past the post). In 1992, for example, a Lib Dem in Scotland won with just 26 percent of the vote. This system of single-member districts with **plurality** victors tends to produce two large political parties. The reason? There is a big premium in such districts to combine

small parties into big ones in order to edge out competitors. If one of the two large parties splits, which sometimes happens, the election is thrown to the other party, the one that hangs together. In proportional-representation electoral systems there is not such a great premium on forming two large parties, and that contributes to multiparty systems.

The countries that inherited the British **majoritarian** system tend toward two large parties at the national level, one a bit left, the other a bit right (e.g., the U.S. Democrats and Republicans). Canada used to be one until the Progressive Conservatives collapsed and the socialistic New Democrats, the separatist Bloc Québécois, and the Reform party in the West rose.

Until recently, New Zealand used the Anglo-American system, and it too yielded two large parties. It also upset many New Zealanders, because other viewpoints got ignored, so in 1993 a new electoral law went into effect, modeled on Germany's hybrid system of half single-member districts and half proportional representation (see Chapter 13). New Zealand soon developed a more complex party system.

which party members supported these general points of view. Now, as we shall explore subsequently, differences between the two parties are muted.

In 1981, the more moderate wing of the Labour party split off to form a centrist Social Democratic party. They argued that Labour had fallen under the control of radicals who turned the party sharply leftward. The Social Democrats faced the problem that had long beset Britain's third party, the middle-of-the-road Liberals, namely, that single-member plurality districts severely penalize smaller parties.

The Liberal party illustrates how smaller parties suffer under the British system of electing MPs. In the last century the Liberals were one of the two big parties, but by the 1920s they had been pushed into a weak third place by Labour. Now, although the Liberals are often able to win nearly 20 percent of the vote, they rarely get more than a few dozen seats in the Commons because their vote is territorially dispersed, so in few constituencies does it top Tories or Labourites.

In 1983 and 1987, the Liberals and the Social Democrats ran jointly as the "Alliance," and in 1988 they merged into the Liberal Democratic party. Because they are spread rather evenly, the "Lib Dems" still get shortchanged on seats in the Commons (see box on p. 65). The Liberal Democrats would like to move away from the majoritarian system and bring in a bit of **proportional representation** (PR), something Blair pledged to hold a referendum on. The leading proposal is to keep FPTP but "top off" seats to more accurately reflect nationwide party strengths. (The German system, by contrast, starts with PR but adds FPTP.)

Scottish and Welsh nationalist parties have had spurts of growth and decline. Their territorial concentration enables them to obtain a few seats in Westminster and a good portion of the seats in the Scottish and Welsh assemblies instituted in 1999. We will explore patterns of interaction among the parties and the voters in Chapter 5.

Key Terms (sidebar)

single-member district A district that sends one representative to parliament.

FPTP "First past the post": a short way of saying "single-member districts with plurality win."

plurality The largest quantity, even if less than a majority.

majoritarian An electoral system that encourages dominance of one party in parliament, as in Britain and the United States.

proportional representation Electoral system of multimember districts where seats are awarded by percentage a party wins.

Key Terms

anachronism (p. 45)	FPTP (p. 47)	portfolio (p. 37)
antithetical (p. 37)	fusion of powers (p. 37)	proportional representation (p. 47)
by-election (p. 41)	government (p. 38)	select committee (p. 44)
Cortes (p. 37)	junior minister (p. 36)	single-member district (p. 47)
Crown (p. 35)	Law Lords (p. 45)	Westminister (p. 41)
dignified (p. 35)	life peers (p. 45)	whip (p. 39)
division (p. 35)	MP (p. 36)	Whitehall (p. 41)
eclectic (p. 34)	opposition (p. 41)	
efficient (p. 35)	plurality (p. 47)	

Further Reference

Birch, Anthony H. *The British System of Government*, 9th ed. New York: Routledge, 1993.

Blackburn, Robert. *The Electoral System in Britain*. New York: St. Martin's, 1995.

Bogdanor, Vernon. *Power and the People*. London: Victor Gollancz, 1997.

Brazier, Rodney. *Ministers of the Crown*. New York: Oxford University Press, 1997.

Carmichael, Paul, and Brice Dickson, eds. *The House of Lords: Its Parliamentary and Judicial Roles*. Portland, OR: Hart, 1999.

Giddens, Anthony. *The Third Way: The Renewal of Social Democracy*. London: Polity Press, 1998.

Hennessey, Peter. *Whitehall*. New York: Free Press, 1989.

James, Simon. *British Cabinet Government*. New York: Routledge, 1992.

Jogerst, Michael. *Reform in the House of Commons: The Select Committee System*. Lexington, KY: University Press of Kentucky, 1993.

Mount, Ferdinand. *The British Constitution Now*. London: Heinemann, 1992.

Norton, Philip. *The British Polity*, 4th ed. White Plains, NY: Longman, 1998.

Rhodes, R. A. W., and Patrick Dunleavy, eds. *Prime Minister, Cabinet and Core Executive*. New York: St. Martin's, 1995.

Riddell, Peter. *Parliament Under Pressure*. London: Victor Gollancz, 1998.

Thomas, Graham P. *Prime Minister and Cabinet Today*. New York: St. Martin's, 1998.

British Political Culture

4

> ## Questions to Consider
>
> 1. What's the difference between a wage and a salary? In class terms?
> 2. What's the difference between objective and subjective?
> 3. What is a British "public" school?
> 4. How does an "Oxbridge" education form an elite?
> 5. What is "class voting," and has it declined?
> 6. What story does a map of the 1997 elections tell?
> 7. What sort of center-periphery tension does Britain have?
> 8. Have British parties always been pragmatic?
> 9. What does poll data tell politicians about the shape of the electorate?
> 10. How did Northern Ireland become such a problem?

"England is a snob country," one longtime American resident in London told me. She added: "And I'm a snob, so I like it here." Her candor touched one of the facets of British political life, one that explains a great deal about modern England: the large and often invidious distinctions made between and by social classes.

Social class can be analyzed in two ways, objectively and subjectively. The objective approach uses data such as income and neighborhood to put people into categories. The subjective approach asks people to put themselves into categories. There are often discrepancies between the two, as when a self-made businessman, thinking of his humble origins, describes himself as **working class**, or when a poorly paid schoolteacher, thinking of her university degrees, describes herself as **middle class**. In Britain and in most industrialized democracies, the main politically relevant distinction is between working class and middle class.

Objectively, class differences in Britain are not so great; they

Key Terms

social class   A layer or section of a population of similar income and status.

working class   Related to those paid an hourly wage; typically less affluent and educated.

middle class   Related to professionals or those paid salaries; typically educated beyond secondary school.

objective   Judged by observable criteria.

Key Terms

subjective   Judged by feeling or intuition.

solidarity   Feeling of cohesion within a social class.

public school   In Britain, a private boarding school, equivalent to a U.S. prep school.

old boy   Someone you knew at public school.

grammar school   A private nonboarding school, equivalent to a U.S. day school.

comprehensive school   A publicly funded secondary school, equivalent to a U.S. high school.

are basically no greater than in the rest of West Europe. The time has long passed when Disraeli could write that Britain was not one nation but two, the rich and the poor. Since that time, the British working class has grown richer, the middle class bigger, and the small upper class poorer.

But **subjectively** or psychologically, class differences remain. Working-class people live, dress, speak, and enjoy themselves in markedly different ways from the middle class. Britons seem to like these differences and try to preserve them.

According to German sociologist Ralf Dahrendorf, the key word in Britain is not class but **solidarity**. While there has been a leveling of objective class differences, Dahrendorf holds, the idea of individual competition and improvement has not caught on in Britain as in other industrial countries. Rather than struggling to improve themselves individually, many Britons relish the feeling of solidarity they get by sticking with their old jobs, neighborhoods, and pubs. "Britain is a society in which the values of solidarity are held in higher esteem than those of individual success at the expense of others," Dahrendorf wrote.

Whether one calls it class or solidarity, these divisions influence British politics in many ways. They contribute to the way Britons vote. They color the attitudes of labor unions and of the Labour party. And—very importantly—they give birth to Britain's elites through the education system.

"Public" Schools

One pillar of the British class system is the **"public" school**. These schools got their name from their original purpose of training boys for public life in the military, civil service, or politics. Their costs put them beyond the reach of working-class families. Eton, Harrow, Rugby, St. Paul's, Winchester, and other famous academies have for generations molded the sons of the upper and upper-middle classes into a ruling elite.

What a small minority of young Britons learn from ages thirteen to eighteen is more than their demanding curriculum. At least as important is the personal style they develop: self-confident to the point of arrogance, self-disciplined, bred to rule. Spy novelist John Le Carré recalled with loathing his years in a public school during World War II: "We doubled up with mirth at the sound of lower-class accents." His schoolmates called such people "oiks" and felt nothing but contempt for them. In 1945 Attlee was simply "a Leftie who had seduced the oiks into getting rid of Churchill." In terms of class relations, added Le Carré decades later, "nothing, but absolutely nothing, has changed" since the 1940s.

The British private-school system generates an **old boy** network that assists graduates later in life. The years of floggings, vile food, and bullying by upper-classmen forge bonds among old schoolmates, and they often arrange for each other to get positions in industry and government. A large portion of Britain's elite have gone to private boarding schools, including some two-thirds of Conservative MPs (but few Labour MPs).

While the upper and upper-middle classes send their children to boarding schools, the middle class send theirs to private **grammar schools**, where pupils wear uniforms but do not live in. Until after World War II, there was no free high-school system in Britain. Now some 80 percent of English schoolchildren go to state-funded **comprehensive** and technical schools

DEMOCRACY

WHAT TO DO WITH "PUBLIC" SCHOOLS?

The British Labour party long sought to do away with the country's private boarding schools. Labourites regarded them as undemocratic, part of a class system where boys of better-off families learn about privilege. Most Conservative politicians have attended "public" schools, but few Labour politicians have. Conservatives want to maintain the schools, arguing that they train the best people and imbue them with a sense of public service.

In actual practice, Labour governments essentially let the private boarding schools alone while they try to upgrade the quality of publicly supported "comprehensive" schools. Blair's emphasis on education, for example, leaves the public schools untouched. The problem may be solving itself: Boarding-school enrollment has slumped while day-school popularity has climbed. Changing lifestyles have convinced many British parents that sending their children away is cruel and unloving.

that lead most of them to the workplace. Only 65 percent of British seventeen-year-olds are still in school (including technical training), the lowest level of any industrial land. (Comparative figures: Germany, 97 percent; United States, 88 percent; Japan, 83 percent.) In spite of the efforts of the Labour party since World War II, British education is still strongly divided along class lines.

"Oxbridge"

The real path to position and power in Britain is through the elite universities of Oxford or Cambridge. Nearly half of Conservative MPs are Oxford or Cambridge graduates (usually after attending a public school, such as Eton), while a quarter of Labour MPs are **Oxbridge** products. In the cabinet, these percentages are higher. And prime ministers are almost always graduates of either Oxford or Cambridge. Blair, for example, is an Oxford man. The only exceptions in recent years have been Labour Prime Minister James Callaghan (1976–79) and John Major (1990–97). Of the ministers in Major's first cabinet, 76 percent had attended "public" schools and 71 percent were Oxbridge graduates. Perhaps in no other industrialized country are the political elite drawn so heavily from just two universities.

As with secondary (high-school) education, British university education is also elitist. A greater proportion of Americans go to a university than do Britishers. British university admission until recent decades was slanted in favor of better-off families, especially those whose children go to private schools. Since World War II, education opened to the working and lower-middle classes by direct-grant secondary schools and scholarships for deserving youths. Oxford and Cambridge became less class-biased in their admissions, and many **redbrick** universities were founded or expanded.

Key Terms

Oxbridge Slang for Oxford and Cambridge universities.
redbrick British universities other than Oxbridge.

Key Terms

Rhodes scholarship
Founded by South African
millionaire; enables top
English-speaking students to
attend Oxford.

class voting   Tendency of
a given class to vote for a
party that claims to
represent its interests.

Only a small percentage of Oxbridge students go into politics, but those who do receive a major boost. In the first place, an Oxford or Cambridge degree—which takes three years to earn—commands respect. Furthermore, the Oxbridge experience hones political skills. One popular major for aspiring politicians is "PPE"—philosophy, politics, and economics—in effect, how to run a country. Debating in either the Oxford or Cambridge Unions trains students to think on their feet and confound their opponents with rhetorical cleverness, a style that carries over into the House of Commons. Perhaps the main advantage of an Oxbridge education, however, is the "sense of effortless superiority" the graduate carries all his or her life.

In 1993, an Oxford man became the U.S. president, and he named three other Oxonians to his cabinet. Two U.S. Supreme Court justices are also Oxford men. All these Americans had received **Rhodes scholarships**.

Class and Voting

Britain used to be offered as a good example of **class voting**—a situation where most of the working class votes for the left party (in this case, Labour) while most of the middle class votes for the right (in this case, Conservative). Actually, class voting in Sweden is higher than in Britain, but nowhere is it 100 percent. Two shifts dilute class voting in Britain and elsewhere: (1) Some working-class people vote Conservative, and (2) some middle-class people vote Labour. Class differences may be part of Britain's political culture, but they do not translate into class voting on a one-to-one basis.

What dilutes class voting? Some working-class people are simply convinced that Conservatives do a better job governing than Labourites. Some workers have a sentimental attachment to the country's oldest party. Some issues have little to do with class. The Tories win a large part of the working class on the issues of economic growth, keeping taxes down, and keeping out immigrants.

Going the other way, many middle-class and educated people are intellectually convinced that the Labour party is the answer to what they see as an establishment-ruled, snobbish class system. Such intellectuals provide important leadership in the Labour party. The leader of the Labour left for a long time was an aristocrat, Anthony Wedgewood Benn, or, as he liked to be known, Tony Benn. Furthermore, some middle-class people grew up in working-class families and have sentimental ties to the way their parents voted.

Class voting changes over time. The British generation that came to political maturity during and after World War II, especially the working class, has been quite loyal to the Labour party, which it swept into power in 1945. Since then, class voting has fallen off in Britain and other advanced, industrialized democracies, including the United States. Class is not what it used to be in any country's voting patterns.

It is, however, still a noteworthy factor. Typically, political scientists find voting behavior is influenced by social class plus one or more other factors, such as region, ethnic group, religion, and urban-rural differences. The 1997 British general election partially bears this out (see box on page 54). Tories were strongest in England, especially the south of England, and in small towns and rural areas. They were weaker in Scotland and Wales and in the big industrial cities, places with a long-term Labour identification and concern over unemployment. Class by itself explains only a part of British voting patterns. Class plus region explains a good deal more.

The Deferential British?

One old image of the British is that they are **deferential**, that is, the average Briton defers to the political judgment of elites. According to the deferential model, working- and middle-class Britons recognize the superior leadership qualities of the Oxbridge-educated **Establishment** and let it take the lead.

The deferential model of British political culture was oversold and is now obsolete. Perhaps in earlier decades, when class differences were enormous, the working class deferred to its social betters. But while they were tipping their hats, they were also building a store of resentment. As noted in Chapter 2, the labor movement came into British politics in the last century with a snarl. In some sectors of the British working class, resentment is still strong and comes out in the militant socialism on the left wing of the Labour party and in indifferent work attitudes and a readiness to go out on strike. The deferential model cannot explain such behavior.

The "working-class Tory" has been explained as a working-class person who defers to the Conservatives and votes for them. But the working-class Tory voter can be explained without the notion of deference. Many such voters think the Conservatives have the right policies, the Labour party had swung too far left, and there are too many nonwhite immigrants. Furthermore, the 1997 elections saw a return of the "middle-class Labour voter," a shift that has nothing to do with social deference.

British Civility

In Britain, **civility** is based on a sense of limits: Don't let anything go too far; don't let the system come unstuck. Thus, while Labourites and Conservatives have serious arguments, neither party, when in power, moves in for the kill. The game is not one of total annihilation, as it has sometimes been in France, Germany, and Russia. Accordingly, British politicians are fairly decent toward each other.

But civility in Britain does not preclude **heckling**. In Parliament a cabinet minister presenting a difficult case might face cries of "Shame!" or "Treason!" from the opposition. Margaret Thatcher faced Labourites chanting "Ditch the bitch." Insults and heckling are part of British debates and are not viewed as inappropriate; some see them as tests of a debater's cool.

Civility is usually the case in public also—but not always. Amateur orators at the famous Speakers' Corner of Hyde Park in London can have their say on any subject they like, although they too must face heckling. British politics turned very uncivil on the question of race, which we'll discuss later, and there have been riots and demonstrations that have resulted in deaths. Murder rather than civility became the norm for Northern Ireland. British civility has been overstated; Swedes are considered by many to be far more civil.

Pragmatism

As noted in Chapter 1, *pragmatic* has the same root as *practical* and means using what works without paying much attention to theory or ideology. British attitudes, like American or Swedish ones, are generally pragmatic. The Conservatives used to pride themselves on being the most pragmatic of all British parties. They were willing to adopt the policies of another party if they were vote catchers. In the nineteenth century, Disraeli crowed he had "dished the Whigs" by stealing their drive to expand the voting franchise. In the 1950s, the returning Conservative government did not throw out Labour's welfare state; instead they boasted that Tories ran it more efficiently. This changed with the laissez-faire economic program of Prime Minister Thatcher. The fixity of her goals contributed to ideological debates within and between the two large and usually pragmatic parties. Pragmatism returned to the Tories after Thatcher.

The British Labour party had historically been mostly uninterested in Marxism or any other theory. With the Callaghan government in the 1970s, ideological controversy engulfed Labour. Callaghan was a very moderate, pragmatic Labourite, hard to distinguish from some Conservatives. Many Labour personalities, including some union heads, resented

THE 1997 ELECTIONS: CLASS PLUS REGION

Labour won a thumping victory in 1997, but the areas where they scored above average tell a repetitive story: Scotland, Wales, and the industrial areas of London, Liverpool, Yorkshire, and the Northeast, areas the Thatcher revolution passed by. Labour scores especially well among people who feel disadvantaged: the Scots, the Welsh, and the poor. The areas where the Conservatives fared above average (the shaded portion) are mostly in England, especially in rural and suburban parts. In a nearly universal political pattern, large cities tend to vote left.

Where Tories Won above Average in 1997

GEOGRAPHY

CENTERS AND PERIPHERIES

A country's capital is often called its "center," even though it may not be in the precise geographical center of the land. Closer to the boundaries of the state are the **peripheral** areas. Often these are more recent additions to the territory of the state. Some of them still speak a different language and resent rule by the capital. This is called **center-periphery tension** and is nearly universal.

Over the centuries, England added Wales, Scotland, and Ireland. Resentment was so high in Ireland, however, that Britain had to grant it independence earlier in the twentieth century. Now Britain retains only Northern Ireland, long a source of resentment and violence. Scotland and Wales also harbor grudges against rule by London, and these grudges fed the devolution movement. As we shall consider in Chapter 6, Tony Blair's Labour government attempted to calm these feelings by granting Scotland and Wales their own legislatures.

The U.S. Civil War was an effort by the southern periphery to cast off rule by Washington. In terms of attitudes and economics, the North and South really were two different countries, a gap that has been largely closed since then. The center of U.S. population, politics, economics, communications, education, and culture long remained in the northeast. This still fosters slight center-periphery tension; some western politicians express irritation at rule by Washington.

Callaghan's centrism and rammed through a clearly socialist party platform despite him. The moderate wing of the Labour party split off in 1981 to form a centrist party, the Social Democrats. As we shall consider in Chapter 5, a series of Labour party leaders pushed the party back to the center, leading to its 1997 electoral victory.

There is and always has been a certain amount of ideology in British politics, but it has usually been balanced with a shrewd practical appreciation that ideology neither wins elections nor effectively governs a country. The ideological flare-up of the 1980s in Britain made it perhaps the most polarized land of West Europe. Ironically, at this same time, French parties, long reputed to be far more ideological than British parties, moved to the center, where British parties used to cluster.

One aspect of British pragmatism is their "muddling-through" style of problem solving. The British tend not to thoroughly analyze a problem and come up with detailed options or "game plans." They try to "muddle through somehow," improvising as they go. This often works with small problems, but with a big problem, such as the situation in Northern Ireland, it amounts to a nonsolution.

Traditions and Symbols

British politics has a good deal of tradition. Things are often done in the old ways, even by left-wing Labourites, who, whether they recognize it or not, subscribe to Burke's idea of keeping the forms but

Key Terms

periphery   The nation's outlying regions.

center-periphery tension   Resentment of outlying areas at rule by the nation's capital.

Key Terms

authority   The power of a political figure to be obeyed.

hooliganism   Violent and destructive behaviour.

center-peaked Distribution with most people in the middle; a bell-shaped curve.

center-seeking   Tendency of political parties toward moderate politics calculated to win the center.

changing the contents. As Burke saw it, traditions and symbols contribute to society's stability and continuity; people feel disoriented without them.

The British man or woman in the street usually likes traditions and symbols. Although some Britons dislike the tabloid lifestyle of the younger generation of "royals," only a minority would abolish the monarchy in favor of a republic with a president. Parades with golden coaches and horsemen in red tunics are not just for tourists—although they help Britain's economy—they also serve to deepen British feelings about the rightness of the system.

Traditions can also tame political radicals. Once they win seats in the Commons, radicals find themselves having to play according to time-hallowed parliamentary usages. "Well, it simply isn't done, old boy," is the standard lesson taught to newcomers in Parliament. In a few years, the would-be radicals are usually more moderate. In terms of parliamentary behavior, it's hard to distinguish Labour from Tory MPs.

Legitimacy and Authority

One definition of legitimacy is a feeling of rightness about the political system. As was pointed out in Chapter 1, the word originally meant the right king was on the throne, not a usurper. As used by political scientists, it refers to public attitudes that the government's rule is rightful. Legitimacy is a feeling among the people; it does not mean "legal." When a political system enjoys high legitimacy, people generally obey it. They will even do things they don't want to, such as paying their income taxes.

Legitimacy is closely related to **authority**, obeying duly constituted officials. British legitimacy and authority were long cited as models, but they were exaggerated and oversold. British policemen used to be famous for not carrying guns and for their good relations with the people on their beat. Political scientists used to cite such points to illustrate Britain's nonviolent qualities. During the 1970s, however, Britain turned more violent. The

POLITICAL CULTURE

FOOTBALL HOOLIGANISM

Underscoring the decline in British civility was the rise of football **hooliganism**, the gleeful rioting of some British soccer fans. Often drunk at games, some team groupies charge onto the field in the middle of a game. In 1985, Liverpool fans killed thirty-eight Italian spectators by causing their bleachers to collapse. All over Europe, the English fanatics were feared and sometimes barred from games.

What causes the violence? Some blame unemployment; the games offer the jobless one of their few diversions. But most hooligans are employed and some earn good livings. Others see hooliganism as the erosion of civilization itself. "The truth is," said one self-confessed Manchester hooligan, "we just like scrappin'."

Irish Republican Army (IRA) spread their murderous tactics from Ulster, planting bombs that killed dozens. In 1984, one bomb blew up near Thatcher. Criminals started using handguns. In Britain's inner cities, relations between police and youths, especially black youths, grew hateful and contributed to urban riots (which, nonetheless, cost very few lives). A minority of British policemen now carry guns and riot gear, a symbol of the erosion of legitimacy and authority in Britain.

Key Term

Irish Republican Army
Anti-British terrorists who seek unification of all Ireland.

POLITICAL CULTURE

THE SHAPE OF THE BRITISH ELECTORATE

Virtually all modern democracies show a strong clustering in the ideological center, with a tapering off toward the extremes: bell-shaped curves. Such a **center-peaked** distribution is probably necessary to sustain democracy, for it encourages **center-seeking** politics. A U-shaped distribution would indicate extreme division, possibly getting ready for civil war (example: Spain, 1936). Pollsters and political consultants constantly remind their clients of the distribution of ideological opinion and warn them not to position themselves too far to the left or right. It took the Labour party several electoral defeats to get the message. Tony Blair finally pushed Labour into about the 5 position (exact center) with vague but upbeat party positions.

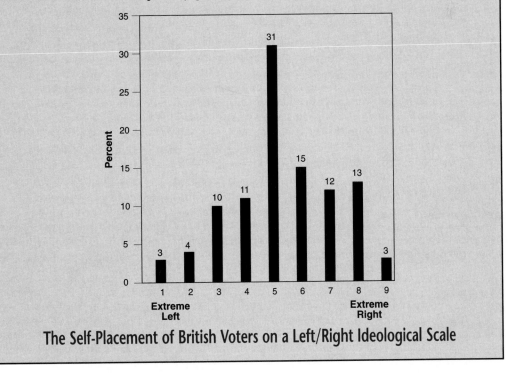

The Self-Placement of British Voters on a Left/Right Ideological Scale

POLITICAL CULTURE

THE IRA: BALLOTS AND BULLETS

The Irish Republican Army is illegal in both Eire and Northern Ireland, but its political arm, Sinn Fein (pronounced *shin fain*) is not. Many Northern Irish Catholics vote for Sinn Fein candidates and in 1983 and 1987 elected IRA apologist Gerry Adams to Parliament from West Belfast. Adams, who as an act of protest never took his seat in Westminster, denies belonging to the IRA but did not condemn its violence: "I honestly see no other way by which the British can be forced to withdraw from this country, except by a mixture of struggle which involves properly controlled, interactive armed struggle." He has since mellowed but still calls Queen Elizabeth "Mrs. Windsor."

Electing IRA people is not new for Ulster's Catholics. In 1981 they elected Bobby Sands, an imprisoned IRA gunman, who starved himself to death in a hunger strike. The fact that so many men and women of Ulster are willing to vote for an extremist party indicates the depth of hatred and the difficulty of compromise.

The Ulster Ulcer

While we can say Britons on the whole still have attitudes of civility, pragmatism, legitimacy, respect for authority, and nonviolence, we must also note Northern Ireland (sometimes called Ulster) as a massive exception. Northern Ireland illustrates how a system that works when there is widespread legitimacy fails when it is lacking. Unlike the rest of Britain, Ulster is a split society, more like those of Latin Europe—France, Spain, Italy—where part of the population does not see the government as legitimate.

The Ulster problem has its roots in history. For eight centuries England ruled Ireland, at times treating the Irish as subhuman, seizing their land, deporting them, even outlawing the Catholic faith. A low point came with the 1846–54 Potato Famine in which a million Irish starved to death while the English, with plentiful food stocks, watched. (An example of what happens when you make too many babies, admonished English **Malthusians**.) At that time about a million and a half Irish emigrated, mostly to the United States. The Irish problem was the great issue of nineteenth-century British politics, "the damnable question" of whether to keep it firmly under British control or grant it **home rule**.

Key Terms

Malthusian   The view that population growth outstrips food.

home rule   Giving a region some autonomy to govern itself.

Eire   The Republic of Ireland.

In the spring of 1916, while the English were hard-pressed in World War I, the "Irish Volunteers," in what is known as the Easter Rising, rose up with guerrilla-warfare tactics in an attempt to win freedom for Ireland. (In 1919, they renamed themselves the IRA.) By 1922, after brutally crushing the rising, the British had enough; Ireland became a "free state" of the British Commonwealth. In 1949, the bulk of Ireland ended this status and became independent **Eire**.

But this did not solve the Ulster problem; 57 percent of the 1.5 million people in these six northern counties are Protestant (descended from seventeenth-century Scottish immigrants) and are determined to remain part of Britain.

Fiercely Protestant, for years these **Orangemen** treated Northern Irish Catholics as a different race and feared "popish" plots to bring Northern Ireland into the Catholic-dominated Irish Republic to the south. The Protestant majority systematically shortchanged the Catholic minority in jobs, housing, and political power. For many years, most Catholics didn't even have the right to vote for the local legislature.

In 1968 Catholic protests started, modeled on U.S. civil-rights marches. But peaceful demonstrations turned violent. A "provisional" wing of the IRA emerged to enroll Catholic fanatics in a program of murder. Protestant counterparts, such as the Ulster Defense Association, reciprocated in kind. Assassination became nearly random. Over 3,600 people have been killed—including MPs, Earl Mountbatten, British soldiers, but mostly innocent civilians—making the United Kingdom the most violent nation in West Europe.

> ### Key Terms
>
> **Orangemen** After King William of Orange (symbol of the Netherlands royal house); Northern Irish Protestants.
>
> **anglophile** Someone who loves England and the English.
>
> **francophobe** Someone who dislikes France and the French.

A Changing Political Culture

We are trying to put British political attitudes into some kind of perspective. Britons are neither angels nor devils. Political scientists used to present Britain as a model of stability, moderation, calm, justice, and just plain niceness. In contrast, France was often presented as a model of instability and immoderate political attitudes. The contrast was overdrawn; neither the British nor the French are as good or as bad as sometimes portrayed.

Observations of a country's political culture can err in two ways. First, if you are favorably disposed toward a country—and many Americans are great **anglophiles** (while many are **francophobes**)—you may tend to overlook some of the nasty things lurking under the surface or dismiss them outright as aberrations. For years American textbooks on British politics managed to ignore or play down the violence in Northern Ireland. Such "incivility" seemed so un-British that no one wanted to mention it. Riots in impoverished parts of British inner cities caught many observers by surprise.

Second, we may forget that studies of political culture are carried out during particular times, and things change. The data for Almond and Verba's 1963 *Civic Culture* (see box on p. 11), were collected four decades ago. The authors' composite portrait of Britain as a "deferential civic culture" is no longer valid. Since the late 1950s, Britain has undergone some trying times, especially in the area of economics. This did not erase British attitudes wholesale; they simply made manifest what had been latent. Political attitudes change; they can get nastier or better.

Key Terms

deferential (p. 53)
Eire (p. 58)
Establishment (p. 53)
francophobe (p. 59)
grammar school (p. 50)
heckling (p. 53)
home rule (p. 58)
hooliganism (p. 56)
Irish Republican Army (p. 57)
Malthusian (p. 58)
middle class (p. 49)
objective (p. 49)

old boy (p. 50)
Orangemen (p. 59)
Oxbridge (p. 51)
periphery (p. 55)
public school (p. 50)
redbrick (p. 51)
Rhodes scholarship (p. 52)
social class (p. 49)
solidarity (p. 50)
subjective (p. 50)
working class (p. 49)

Further Reference

Adams, Ian. *Ideology and Politics in Britain Today*. New York: St. Martin's, 1998.

Adonis, Andrew, and Stephen Pollard. *A Class Act: The Myth of Britain's Classless Society*. London: Hamish Hamilton, 1997.

Dahrendorf, Ralf. *On Britain*. Chicago, IL: University of Chicago Press, 1982.

Field, William H. *Regional Dynamics: The Basis of Electoral Support in Britain*. Portland, OR: F. Cass, 1997.

Jowell, Roger, John Curtice, Lindsay Brook, and Daphne Ahrendt, eds. *British Social Attitudes: The 11th Report*. Brookfield, VT: Dartmouth, 1994.

Madgwick, Peter, and Richard Rose, eds. *The Territorial Dimension in United Kingdom Politics*. Atlantic Highlands, NJ: Humanities Press, 1982.

Miller, William L., Annis May Timpson, and Michael Lessnoff. *Political Culture in Contemporary Britain: People and Politicians, Principles and Practice*. New York: Oxford University Press, 1996.

Mitchell, Paul, and Rick Wilford, eds. *Politics in Northern Ireland*. Boulder, CO: Westview, 1999.

Parry, Geraint, George Moyser, and Neil Day. *Political Participation and Democracy in Britain*. New York: Cambridge University Press, 1991.

Rose, Richard, and Ian McAllister. *The Loyalties of Voters: A Lifetime Learning Model*. Newbury Park, CA: Sage, 1990.

Ruane, Joseph, and Jennifer Todd. *The Dynamics of Conflict in Northern Ireland*. New York: Cambridge University Press, 1996.

Townshend, Charles. *Making the Peace: Public Order and Public Security*. New York: Oxford University Press, 1993.

Wald, Kenneth D. *Crosses on the Ballot: Patterns of British Voter Alignment since 1885*. Princeton, NJ: Princeton University Press, 1983.

Britain: Patterns of Interaction

5

Questions to Consider

1. What's the difference between party image and party ID?
2. What is a "safe seat" and how do you get one?
3. Who names British candidates?
4. What did Tony Blair call his party? What did it mean?
5. Why do the Liberal Democrats have such an uphill struggle?
6. How did Thatcher differ from a traditional Tory?
7. What is the big British labor confederation? How big is it?
8. Where and what is the Question Hour?
9. How democratic is Britain? As much as the United States?

In Britain, as in most democratic countries, the relationship between people and political parties is complex, a two-way street in which each influences the other. The parties project something called **party image**, what people think of the party's policies, leaders, and ideology. Most voters, on the other hand, carry in their heads a **party identification**, a long-term tendency to think of themselves as "Tory" or "Democrat" or whatever. The strategy of intelligent party leadership is to project a party image that will win the loyalty of large numbers of voters and get them to identify permanently with that party. If they can do this, the party prospers and enjoys many electoral successes.

Both party image and party identification are reasonably clear in Britain: Most Britons recognize what the main parties stand for in general terms, and a large portion of British voters identify with a party. The situation is never static, however, for the parties constantly change the images they project, while some voters lose their party identification and shift their votes.

In every country, parents contribute heavily—but never totally—to the party identification of their children. In Britain, if both parents are of the same party, most of their children first identify with that party, although this may later erode as young people develop their own perspectives. By the same token, party images are rather

Key Terms

party image The way the electorate perceives a given party.

party identification The psychological attachment of a voter to a particular political party.

Key Terms

swing vote   Those voters who switch parties from one election to the next.

seat   Membership in a legislature.

safe seat   Constituency where voting has long favored a given party.

constituency   The district or population that elects a legislator.

carpetbagger   In U.S. usage, an outsider attempting to run in a different constituency.

central office   London headquarters of British political party.

clear, and most Britons are able to see differences between their two largest parties: Labour aiming at helping people through social and educational reforms, and Conservatives aiming at economic growth through hard work with little state intervention.

For deeply confirmed Labour or Conservative voters—those whose party identification closely matches the image of their preferred party—there is little doubt about whom to vote for. Until recently, most British voters were reliably Labour or Conservative. The **swing vote** are those who move their votes among parties, either because their party identification is not strong, or their perceptions of the parties' images shifts, or both. A swing of a few percentage points can determine who will form the next government, for if each constituency shifts a little one way, say, toward Labour, the Labour candidate will be the winner in many constituencies. Single-member districts often exaggerate percentage trends and turn them into large majorities of **seats**.

The game of British electoral politics consists of the parties trying to mobilize all of their party identifiers—that is, making sure their people bother to vote—plus winning over the uncommitted swing vote. In 1970 the Labour government of Harold Wilson suffered a surprise defeat by the Conservatives under Edward Heath. It wasn't that Labour identifiers suddenly switched sides—they didn't—but rather that some were unhappy with Wilson's policies and simply stayed away from the voting booth.

National and Local Party

Political scientists used to describe the British national party—Conservative or Labour—as nearly all-powerful, able to dictate to local party organizations whom to nominate for Parliament. As usual, though, when you look more closely you find that things are more complicated.

The name of the game for parliamentary candidates is the **safe seat** and getting adopted by the local **constituency** organization to run for it. Party leaders are normally assigned very safe seats, for it is highly embarrassing if one of them loses his or her seat in the Commons. About 450 (of 659) seats are usually considered safe. There is a bargaining relationship between the parties' London headquarters and the local constituency party. The local party often requests lists of possible candidates from headquarters, settles on one, and then gets it approved by the central headquarters. Unlike the U.S. system, there is both national and local input into British candidate selection with a veto on both sides.

Some constituency organizations insist that a candidate actually live in the district. Americans expect all candidates to reside in the district they represent; those who don't are called **carpetbaggers** and have an uphill battle. Most countries, however, including Britain, impose no such requirements, although being a local person can help. Some British constituencies like their people to establish a residence there once they've won. But many constituencies couldn't care less if their MP actually lives there; after all, the MP's job is mainly in London, and periodic visits are sufficient for him or her to hear complaints and maintain ties with electors. Besides, in Britain, party is more important than personality. In any given House of Commons, probably a minority of MPs are natives of the constituency they represent.

What about the unsafe seats, those where the other party usually wins? These are the testing grounds for energetic newcomers to politics. The Conservative or Labour **central offices**

DEMOCRACY

1997: FINALLY, LABOUR

In April 1997, after eighteen years in opposition, Britain's Labour party won and won big. Their overall national percentage jumped almost eight points from the 1992 elections for a gain of 148 seats in Parliament, giving them a comfortable majority out of the 659 total seats. Remember, with Britain's electoral system a swing of only a few percent means dozens of seats change from one party to another. As usual for Britain, this election gave Labour only a plurality of the votes cast; since 1935 no British party has scored an actual majority. Unusual for Britain, in 1997 seven Tory cabinet members lost their normally safe seats.

As polls predicted, the Conservatives suffered a major (pun intended) loss, dropping over 12 percentage points from their narrow victory in 1992. The Liberal Democrats ac-

tually slumped a little, to under 17 percent of the vote, but they more than doubled their number of seats because their voters were more territorially concentrated. The rest of the vote, almost 10 percent, was scattered among small, mostly regional parties.

For many British voters, John Major was a poor leader, and the Tories had been in office too long and were out of ideas. The Tories were rocked by several scandals, both financial and sexual, and were angrily split over joining Europe's common currency. Labour's Tony Blair was not only a nice man but had turned Labour decisively away from its left and into a centrist party. Now it was the Tories' turn to redefine themselves. To do this, they dumped Major and elected William Hague, age 36, as party chief, the youngest Tory leader since 24-year-old William Pitt in 1783.

	% Votes		Seats	
	1997	1992	1997	1992
Labour	43.1	35.2	419 (63%)	271 (42%)
Conservative	30.6	42.8	165 (25%)	336 (52%)
Liberal Democrat	16.7	18.3	46 (7%)	20 (3%)

in London may send a promising beginner to a constituency organization that knows it doesn't have much hope of winning. Again, the local unit must approve the candidate. Even if the candidate loses, his or her energy and ability are carefully watched—by measuring how much better the candidate did than the previous one—and promising comers are marked. For the next election, the London headquarters may offer the candidate a safer constituency, one where he or she stands a better chance. Finally, the candidate either wins an election in a contested constituency, is adopted by a safe constituency, or bows out of politics. Many of Britain's top politicians, including several prime ministers (Blair among them), lost their first races and were transferred to other constituencies. There's no stigma attached; it's normal, part of the training and testing of a British politician.

Politics within the Parties

British political parties, like British cabinets, are balancing acts. A party leader must neither pay too much attention to his or her party's factions nor totally ignore them. In constructing their policies, leaders usually try to give various factions a say but keep the whole thing under moderate control with an eye to winning the next election.

Party leaders must balance between sometimes extremist party militants and a generally moderate voting public. If a party takes too firm an ideological stand—too left in the case of Labour or too right in the Conservative case—it can cost the party votes. Thus party leaders tend to hedge and moderate their positions, trying to please both the true believers within their party and the general electorate. If they slip in this balancing act, they can lose either party members or voters or both. When Labour veered left in the 1980s and the Conservatives followed their hard-right Thatcher course, the centrist Liberal Democratic Alliance (later turned into a party) won a quarter of the 1983 vote, a warning to both major parties.

Although long described as ideologically moderate, both the British Labour and Conservative parties have important ideological viewpoints within their ranks. The Labour party is divided into "left" and "right" wings. The Labour left, springing from a tradition of militant trade unionism and intellectual radicalism, wants more nationalization of industry, the dismantling of "public" schools, higher taxes on the rich, leaving the European Union, and no nuclear weapons—British or U.S. Some **Marxists** and **Trotskyists** have won Labour offices. The Labour right, on the other hand, is moderate and centrist. It favors some of the welfarist approach of Continental social-democratic parties, such as the German SPD, but now wants no government takeovers of industry or higher taxes. It is pro-NATO, pro-Europe, and pro-American in foreign policy. The rightists in Labour argue that the left wing's ideas are extremist and cost the party votes. With Tony Blair, the Labour right won and told the left to shut up. Blair called his party **New Labour**, friendly to business, personal freedom, political reform, and the Liberal Democrats. Some wondered if a resurrection of the old Lib-Lab coalition was in the making.

As an amorphous party proud of its pragmatism, Conservatives were long thought immune to ideological controversy or factional viewpoints. This is not completely true, for the Tories comprise two broad streams of thought, which we might label as traditional and Thatcherite tendencies. The former is not a U.S.-style conservative, advocating a totally free economy with no government intervention. Instead, the **traditional Tory** wants a party that takes everybody's interests into account, plus traditional ways of doing things, and under the guidance of people born and bred to lead. This has been called a "one-nation" Tory.

The **Thatcherite** wing (which traces back to nineteenth-century liberalism and is called **neoliberalism** in Europe) is like American conservativism: They want to roll back government and free the economy. After World War II this view crept into the Conservative party and, with the 1975 election of Margaret Thatcher as party chief, moved to the forefront. Under Thatcher, the traditional Tories were dubbed **wets**, the militant Thatcherites **dries**. (The terms were taken from boarding-school slang. "Wets" are frightened little boys who wet their pants; "dries" are strong and brave lads who do not.)

Key Terms

Marxist   Follower of the socialist theories of Karl Marx.

Trotskyist   Follower of the Marxist but anti-Stalin theories of Leon Trotsky.

New Labour   Tony Blair's name for his very moderate Labour party.

traditional Tory   Moderate or centrist Conservative; not a follower of Thatcher.

Thatcherite   Free-market, anti-welfarist ideology of former British Prime Minister Margaret Thatcher.

neoliberalism   The revival of free-market economics, exemplified by Margaret Thatcher.

wets   In Thatcher's usage, Tories too timid to apply her militant neoliberalism.

dries   In Thatcher's usage, Tories who shared her neoliberal vision.

DEMOCRACY

THE STRUGGLE OF THE LIBERAL DEMOCRATS

Public-opinion polls sometimes suggest the new Liberal Democratic party could become Britain's second-largest party. But what Britons tell pollsters and how they vote are two different things; they speak more radically than they vote. Still, widespread disillusionment with the two large parties could give the Liberal Democrats a chance for major-party status.

The Liberal Democrats were born of the 1988 merger of the old Liberal party and the small, new Social Democratic party that in 1981 had broken away from Labour. The two strands did not see eye-to-eye. On many questions—especially on the economy and defense matters—the Social Democrats were more conservative than the Liberals. The Liberals tended to be ultra-liberal on questions of gay rights and open immigration. They wanted Britain out of NATO and nuclear weapons—both U.S. and British—out of Britain. True to their origins in the right wing of the Labour party, the Social Democrats were not unilateral disarmers and felt that lifestyle questions cost the party votes. The new party is a parallel to the many and incoherent viewpoints of the two big U.S. parties.

The British electoral system—single-member districts with plurality win—is brutal on third parties (just as it is in the United States), especially those like the Liberal Democrats that are territorially dispersed. This discourages potential voters, who don't want to waste their votes on a party they fear will never win many seats. The Liberal Democrats' only hope is adoption of some elements of a proportional-representation election system.

The trouble here is that some old-style British Conservatives find total capitalism almost as threatening as socialism. As industries went bankrupt in record number, Thatcher faced a revolt of Tory "wets" against her "dry" policies. After Major took over, Thatcherite MPs sought to dump him. Attitudes toward European unity also split the Tories. Thatcher and her followers favored the Common Market but opposed turning it into a European Union; they wanted free trade but not a surrender of British sovereignty to Brussels. (They were dubbed **Eurosceptics**.) Major and his followers were enthusiastically pro-Europe (**Europhiles**), including the 1993 Maastricht Treaty, which took European unity a big step forward. In short, the Conservatives have as many and as deep rifts as Labour.

Parties and Interest Groups

What politicians say and what they deliver are two different things. Politicians speak to different audiences. To party rank and file they affirm party gospel (championing either the welfare state or free enterprise, as the case may be). To the electorate as a whole they usually tone down their ideological statements and offer vague slogans, such as "You've never had it so good" or "Time for a change." But

Key Terms

Eurosceptic Does not wish to strengthen the EU at the expense of national sovereignty.
Europhile Likes the EU and wishes to strengthen it.

DEMOCRACY

SAVING LABOUR FROM THE UNIONS

From its 1983 electoral disaster, the Labour party struggled to recover. Part of its problem was a too-left party image. Another part was its doddering and ineffective leader, Michael Foot. At its annual conference that fall, the Labour party tried to repair both areas by overwhelmingly choosing as its new leader Neil Kinnock, a silver-tongued Welshman as charming as Margaret Thatcher was aloof. At 41, Kinnock, son of a coal miner, was the youngest Labour leader ever. Kinnock first had to curb Labour extremists; he got the Trotskyist Militant Tendency faction expelled (it formed a miniparty). Kinnock did well, lifting Labour from 27.6 percent of the popular vote in 1983 to 35.2 percent in 1992. But Kinnock came across as too slick and was hurt by the Tory charge that Labour was dominated by the unions. Labour indeed was founded by and heavily based on trade unions, some led by militant socialists who would rather lose elections than lose their principles.

Following Labour's fourth defeat in a row in 1992, Kinnock resigned, making way for John Smith, a 53-year-old Scottish lawyer even more pragmatic than Kinnock. Smith, a wooden speaker with little **charisma**, set out to reorient Labour more to the middle than the working class. Higher taxes and public ownership were out; discipline in education was in. But Smith had to break the union hold on the Labour party. Many union leaders resisted; they liked being able to control—through the proxy votes of millions of union members—90 percent of the vote at Labour's annual conferences. This union domination, often with a strong leftist slant, rendered Labour unacceptable to most British voters. In 1993, Smith got a change in Labour's rules to return the candidate selection process back to local party organizations; unions now control only 50 percent of conference votes. In 1994 Smith died of a heart attack.

Tony Blair then took on the unions and got the party to drop its Clause Four, part of its constitution since 1918, that called for the "common ownership of the means of production," in other words, socialism. With Blair's very moderate 1996 manifesto, Labour—which Blair called "New Labour"—started looking a lot like the U.S. Democrats. Labour's membership and electoral support climbed. It was not just Blair's doing, though; the process of pushing Labour back to the center had been underway since Kinnock began it in 1983.

quietly, usually behind the scenes, politicians are also striking important deals with influential interest groups representing industry, commerce, professions, and labor. About half of the British electorate belong to at least one interest group.

Some 25 percent of the British work force, for example, is unionized, down from 40 percent but still a higher percentage than in the United States or France (but only half that of Sweden). Labor unions are constituent members of the Labour party, and until recently controlled a majority of votes at Labour's annual conference, contributed the most to the party's budgets and campaign funds, and provided grass-roots manpower and organization. Especially important are the views of the head of the **Trades Union Congress** (TUC). No Labour party leader can totally ignore the wishes of Britain's union leaders.

Key Terms

charisma   Pronounced "kar-isma"; Greek for gift; political drawing power.

Trades Union Congress (TUC)   British labor federation equivalent to the U.S. AFL-CIO.

This opened up Labour to charges that it is run by and for the unions, which earned a reputation as too far left, too powerful, and strike-happy. To counteract this, both Labour party and union leaders deny union dominance. Indeed, one Labour party campaign tactic is to claim that only the Labour party can control the unions, rather than the other way around. Tony Blair forcefully pointed out to union chiefs the folly of losing one election after another. The close association of labor federation to social-democratic party is the norm for the industrialized countries of Northern Europe, as we shall see when we study Germany.

Dozens of union members sit as Labour MPs in Parliament; dozens more MPs are beholden to local unions for their election. This union bloc inside the Labour party can force a Labour government to moderate measures that might harm unions. At times, however, Labour party chiefs have made union leaders back down, explaining to them that if the unions get too much, the Labour party will lose elections. To reiterate, to be a party leader means performing a balancing act among several forces.

MPs known to directly represent special interests—an **interested member**—are not limited to the Labour side. Numerous Tory MPs are interested members for various industries and do not try to hide it. When the connection is concealed or when money changes hands, an MP pushing for favors to a group becomes known as sleazy. The **sleaze factor** hurt the Tories under Major, but several Labourites under Blair got caught accepting money from questionable sources; some resigned. Politicians taking money on the side is found everywhere, in all parties.

The Conservative counterpart of the TUC is the **Confederation of British Industry** (CBI), formed by an amalgamation of three smaller groups in 1965. The CBI speaks for most British employers but has no formal links to the Conservative party, even though their views are often parallel. The CBI was delighted at Thatcher's antinationalization policies, although British industrialists gulped when they found this meant withdrawal of **subsidies** to their industries. Thatcher could not totally ignore them, for CBI members and money find their way into Tory circles, and dozens of CBI-affiliated company directors occupy Conservative seats in Commons.

Key Terms

interested member   An MP known to represent an interest group.

sleaze factor   Public perception of politicians on the take.

Confederation of British Industry   Leading British business association; equivalent to U.S. National Association of Manufacturers.

subsidy   Government financial help to private individual or business.

Question Hour   Time reserved in the Commons for MPs to question members of the cabinet.

The Parties Face Each Other

There are two ways of looking at British elections. The first is to see them as three-week campaigns coming once every few years, each a model of brevity and efficiency, especially compared to the long, expensive U.S. campaigns. Another way, however, is to see them as nearly permanent campaigns that begin the day a new Parliament reconvenes after the latest balloting. The formal campaign may be only a few weeks, but long before then the opposition party is thinking of little but ousting the current government.

The chief arena for this is the House of Commons. Unlike the U.S. Congress, British parliamentarians are seldom animated by a spirit of bipartisanship. The duty of the opposition is to oppose, and this they do by accusing the government of everything from incompetence and corruption to sexual scandal. The great weapon here is embarrassment, making a cabinet minister look like a fool. The time for this is the **Question Hour**, held Monday through

POLITICAL CULTURE

THE PROFUMO SCANDAL

In the game of embarrassment played in the House of Commons, the classic play came with the 1963 Profumo affair. The Labour opposition got wind that Tory War Minister (at the departmental, not the cabinet, level) John Profumo was dating a party girl who at the same time was also dating the Soviet naval attaché, a known spy. Questioned by Labour in the Commons, Profumo swore there had been no impropriety in his relationship with Christine Keeler and threatened to sue anyone who said otherwise. Being a gentleman of impeccable credentials—Harrow, Oxford, army brigadier—Profumo was believed by the Macmillan government. But the scandal refused to die down; it began to appear that se-

curity had been breached and that Profumo was being set up for blackmail.

Sensational news stories charged the Conservative government with laxity on national security, covering up for one of its "old boys," and debauchery at the highest levels of the Establishment. There was some truth to the charges, and Profumo resigned in shame. It was not, however, the shame of a married man, 48, caught with a 21-year-old call girl. That was forgivable. What was unforgivable was that a gentleman had lied to Parliament. The Tory government mishandled the incident; Conservative MPs lost confidence in Prime Minister Macmillan, and voters lost confidence in the Conservative party, which was voted out the following year.

Key Terms

permanent secretary   The highest civil servant who runs a ministry, nominally under a minister.

knighthood   The lowest rank of nobility; carries the title of "Sir."

Thursday from 2:30 P.M. (when the Commons opens) to 3:30 P.M. By tradition, this hour is reserved for MPs to aim written questions at cabinet ministers, who are on the front bench on a rotating basis (e.g., most Thursdays might be the turn of the education secretary). The PM is usually there once a week, along with most of the cabinet. Each written question can be followed by supplementary oral questions. The opposition tries to push a minister into a position where he or she has to tell a lie, fluff an answer, or burst into anger. Then the opposition, in effect, smirks, "You see, they're not fit to govern."

The Cabinet and the Civil Servants

As we discussed earlier, British cabinet ministers are generalists, not specialists, and are chosen more for political reasons than for any special ability to run their departments. Who then does run them? The nominal head of each British department is the minister; he or she represents that ministry in cabinet discussions and defends it in the Commons. But the minister doesn't run the department; civil servants do.

Ministers come and go every few years; the highest civil servants, known as **permanent secretaries** are there much longer. The permanent secretary often has an edge on his or her minister in social and economic terms as well. Most permanent secretaries are knighted while few ministers are. Although **knighthood** is now purely honorific in Britain, it still conveys a certain social superiority. Permanent secretaries earn more than ministers, in some cases nearly twice as much. A minister finds it nearly impossible to fire or transfer a permanent secretary. Furthermore, permanent secretaries have a say in determining who will replace them when they retire or leave for lush positions in private industry; they tend to be a self-selecting elite. Permanent secretaries always play the role of humble, obedient servants, but some ministers come to wonder just who the boss really is.

The permanent secretary is assisted by several deputy secretaries who in turn are supported by undersecretaries and assistant secretaries. These names look like those of an American department, but there's a major catch: In most U.S. departments, all or most of these people are political appointees, serving at the pleasure of the president and resigning when a new president takes office. In Britain, only the ministers assisted by some junior ministers—about a hundred persons in all—change with the political winds. What in America are temporary political appointees are permanent officials in Britain.

Key Term

rule of anticipated reactions Friedrich's theory that politicians plan moves in anticipation of how the public will react.

DEMOCRACY

HOW DEMOCRATIC IS BRITAIN?

The power of bureaucrats brings us to a fine irony. In centuries of British political evolution, we have seen how Britons marched toward democracy by first limiting the power of the monarch and then expanding participation. If we look closely, though, we notice that much important decision making is only partly democratically controlled. Civil servants make much policy without any democratic input.

Does this mean there is no real democracy in Britain? No, it means we must understand that no country exercises perfect control over its bureaucracy and that parties and elections are only attempts to do so.

Indeed, most of the interactions we have talked about are not under any form of popular control. Ideological infighting, the influence of interest groups on parties and the bureaucracy, the relationship of top civil servants with ministers, the granting of titles—these and other interactions are removed from democratic control. The people do not even choose whom they get to vote for; that is a matter for party influentials. All the people get to do is vote every few years, and the choice is limited.

Again, does this mean there is no democracy in Britain? No, not at all. Some people have an exaggerated vision of democracy as a system in which everyone gets to decide on everything. Such a system never existed at the national level, nor could it. The most we can ask of a democracy is that the leading team—in Britain, the prime minister and cabinet—are held accountable periodically in elections. This keeps them on their toes and anxious to pay attention to the public good, holds down special favors and corruption, and makes sure the bureaucracy functions. It is in the fear of electoral punishment that Britain, or any other country, qualifies as a democracy. What the great Carl J. Friedrich called the **rule of anticipated reactions** keeps the governors attentive. We will learn not to expect much more of political systems.

Key Term

Treasury British ministry that supervises economic policy and funding of other ministries.

This gives them power. They are not amateurs but know their ministry—its personnel, problems, interests, and desires. Knowledge is power, and over time, top civil servants come to quietly exercise a lot of it. While a permanent secretary or his or her assistants never—well, hardly ever—go public with their viewpoints, they reveal them through the kinds of ideas, programs, bills, and budgets they submit to the minister, their nominal boss. The minister theoretically can command them, but in practice he or she simply doesn't know enough about the workings of the ministry. Instead, the minister relies on them. Accordingly, while most bills and budget proposals pass through the cabinet, they do not originate there. The permanent civil servants do the jobs that are the stuff of governance.

The real power among the many British ministries is the **Treasury**. Sometimes called the "department of departments," Treasury not only supervises the main lines of economic policy but has the last word on who gets what among the ministries. Anyone with a bright idea in British government—a new minister or an innovative civil servant—soon comes up against the stone wall of Treasury, the ministry that says "no."

Britain's treasury minister goes by the old name of Chancellor of the Exchequer—originally the king's checker of taxes—and is now the second most powerful figure in the cabinet, the first being the prime minister. Many Chancellors of the Exchequer later become prime ministers, so the person in that office is watched closely.

Under the Chancellor are the usual secretaries and civil servants, but they are a breed unto themselves, smarter and more powerful than other bureaucrats. Operating on a team-spirit basis, Treasury chaps trust only other Treasury chaps, for only Treasury can see the whole picture of the British government and economy and how the many parts interrelate. The other departments see only their corner, hence they should not be heeded. This attitude gives Treasury and its people an image of cold, callous remoteness, "government by mandarins"—but no one has tried to replace them.

The Civil Service and Interest Groups

We mentioned earlier the relationship between interest groups and political parties. But this is only one way interest groups make their voices heard; it is often not the most important way. Much of the impact of interest groups is in their quiet, behind-the-scenes contact with the bureaucracy. Indeed, with Parliament's role curtailed as a result of powerful prime ministers and cabinets, and the cabinet ministers themselves dependent on the permanent civil servants, many interest groups ask themselves, "Why bother with Parliament? Why not go straight to where the action is, the bureaucracy?"

This approach is especially true of business and industry; the major effort of the unions is still focused on the Labour party. The reason for this is partly in the nature of what trade unions want as opposed to what business groups want. Unions want general policies on employment, wages, welfare, and so on, that apply to tens of millions of people. Industry usually wants specific, narrow rulings on taxes, subsidies, regulations, and the like that apply to a few firms. Thus unions tend to battle in the more open environment of party policy while business groups often prefer to quietly take a government official to lunch.

In working closely with a branch of Britain's economic life, a given ministry comes to see itself not as an impartial administrator but as a concerned and attentive helper. After all, if that industry falters, it reflects on the government agency assigned to supervise it. In this

POLITICAL CULTURE

THE UTILITY OF DIGNITY

A seemingly quaint British holdover from the past is the monarch's bestowal of an honor such as knighthood. But more than just a quaint practice, it's a clever payoff system that serves a number of purposes. The granting of titles is a reward and an encouragement to retire, solving the problem of senility and dead wood at the top. A person looking forward to a knighthood (Sir) or a **peerage** (Lord) is more likely to go quietly. Getting one of these honors also has a civilizing effect on the recipients; even the most militant union leaders and rapacious businessmen start talking philosophically about the common good once they have a title in front of their name.

Although the queen awards these and other distinctions, she does so only on the advice of the prime minister. A small staff keeps track of meritorious civil servants, business people, unionists, soldiers, politicians, scholars, artists, and writers and recommends who should get what. In addition to becoming knights and peers, distinguished Britons may be named to the Order of the British Empire, Order of the Garter, Order of Merit, Order of the Bath, the Royal Victorian Order, and many others. The granting of honors is a part of British political culture, a way of bolstering loyalty to and cooperation with the system.

---

manner civil servants come to see leaders of economic interest groups as their "clients" and to reflect their clients' views. When this happens—and it happens in every country—the industry can be said to have "captured" or "colonized" the executive department.

Reinforcing this pattern is the interchange between civil service and private industry. A permanent secretary can make much more money in a corporation than in Whitehall; every now and then one of them leaves government service for greener pastures. (We will also see this pattern in France and Japan.) By the same token, business executives are sometimes brought into high administrative positions on the dubious theory that if they can run a company well, they can do the same for government. The point is that fairly cozy relationships develop between civil servants and private business.

Key Term

peerage   A Lord or Lady; higher than knighthood.

Key Terms

carpetbagger (p. 62)

central office (p. 62)

charisma (p. 66)

Confederation of British Industry (p. 67)

constituency (p. 62)

dries (p. 64)

Europhile (p. 65)

Eurosceptic (p. 65)

interested member (p. 67)

knighthood (p. 68)

Marxist (p. 64)

neoliberalism (p. 64)

New Labour (p. 64)

party identification (p. 61)

party image (p. 61)

peerage (p. 71)

permanent secretary (p. 68)

Question Hour (p. 67)

rule of anticipated reactions (p. 69)

safe seat (p. 62)

seat (p. 62)

sleaze factor (p. 67)

subsidy (p. 67)

swing vote (p. 62)

Thatcherite (p. 64)

Trades Union Congress (TUC) (p. 66)

traditional Tory (p. 64)

Treasury (p. 70)

Trotskyists (p. 64)

wets (p. 64)

Further Reference

Barberis, Peter. *The Elite of the Elite: Permanent Secretaries in the British Higher Civil Service.* Brookfield, VT: Ashgate, 1996.

Butler, David, and Dennis Kavanagh. *The British General Election of 1997.* New York: St. Martin's, 1998.

Crewe, Ivor, Brian Gosschalk, and John Bartle, eds. *Political Communications: Why Labour Won the General Election of 1997.* Portland, OR: F. Cass, 1998.

Evans, Brendan, and Andrew Taylor. *From Salisbury to Major: Continuity and Change in Conservative Politics.* New York: St. Martin's, 1996.

Garner, Robert, and Richard Kelly. *British Political Parties Today,* 2nd ed. New York: St. Martin's, 1998.

Kelly, Richard, ed. *Changing Party Policy in Britain: An Introduction.* Malden, MA: Blackwell, 1999.

King, Anthony, ed. *New Labour Triumphs: Britain at the Polls.* Chatham, NJ: Chatham House, 1998.

McKinstry, Leo. *Fit to Govern.* London: Bantam Press, 1996.

Norris, Pippa, and Joni Lovenduski. *Political Recruitment: Gender, Race and Class in the British Parliament.* New York: Cambridge University Press, 1995.

Norton, Philip, ed. *The Conservative Party.* Upper Saddle River, NJ: Prentice Hall, 1996.

Panitch, Leo, and Colin Leys. *The End of Parliamentary Socialism: From New Left to New Labour.* New York: Norton, 1997.

Reitan, Earl A. *Tory Radicalism: Margaret Thatcher, John Major, and the Transformation of Modern Britain, 1979–1997.* Lanham, MD: Rowman & Littlefield, 1997.

Seldon, Anthony, and Stuart Ball, eds. *Conservative Century: The Conservative Party Since 1900.* New York: Oxford University Press, 1994.

Weir, Stuart, and David Beetham. *Political Power and Democratic Control in Britain: The Democratic Audit of the United Kingdom.* New York: Routledge, 1999.

Whiteley, Paul, Patrick Seyd, and Jeremy Richardson. *True Blues: The Politics of Conservative Party Membership.* New York: Oxford University Press, 1995.

What Britons Quarrel About

6

Questions to Consider

1. What's the difference between relative and absolute decline?
2. How did Thatcher aim to cure Britain's economy? Did it work?
3. What is the Beer thesis on Britain's decline?
4. What is productivity and why is it so important?
5. In what areas could Britain undergo constitutional reform?
6. Did Britain's National Health Service work? Compared to the United States?
7. What is devolution? Does it indicate quasi-federalism?
8. Did Northern Ireland return to peace? Why or why not?
9. What is Britain's stance on the European Union? On the *euro*?

Britain was in economic decline for decades. At first it was only **relative decline** as the economies of West Europe and Japan grew more rapidly than the British economy. By the 1970s, however, Britain was suffering **absolute decline** that left people with lower living standards as inflation outstripped their wage increases. The first industrial nation was embarrassed to see Italy overtake it in per capita GDP in the 1980s. Likewise, Britain's former colonies of Hong Kong and Singapore have higher per caps than does Britain. In Britain, **deindustrialization** seemed to be taking place; in some years the British GDP shrank. They called it the "British disease," and some Americans feared it was contagious.

Key Terms

relative decline   Failing to keep up economically with other nations.

absolute decline   Growing weaker economically compared to one's own past.

deindustrialization
Decline of heavy industry.

The "British Disease"

Why did Britain decline? There are two basic approaches to such a complex problem. One begins with what happens in people's attitudes—a psycho-cultural approach. The other begins with what happens in the physical world—a politico-economic approach. The two are

Key Terms

consumption Buying things.

production Making things.

productivity The efficiency with which things are produced.

inflation An increase in almost all prices.

monetarism Friedman's theory that the rate of growth of the money supply governs much economic development.

not mutually exclusive but have a chicken-egg relationship to each other: One feeds into the other.

Some writers put their emphasis on British nonwork attitudes as the root of the problem. The old feudal aristocracy, which disdained hard work as tawdry moneymaking, was never thoroughly displaced in Britain. Rather, the rising entrepreneurs tried to ape the old elite and become gentlemen of leisure and culture. In public schools and Oxbridge, young Britons learn to despise commercial and technical skills in favor of the humanities. The emphasis was on having wealth rather than creating it. Accordingly, Britain tended to lack daring and innovative capitalists. Many Britons prefer more leisure time to more money.

The British class system makes matters worse. British managers—mostly middle class—are snobbish toward workers; they do not mix with them or roll up their sleeves and get their hands dirty. British workers react by showing solidarity with their "mates" and more loyalty to their union than to their company. If the psycho-cultural approach is correct, the only way to save Britain is to change British attitudes. But deep-seated attitudes resist change.

The other approach, the politico-economic, argues that the bad attitudes are a reflection of faulty government policy. Change the policy so as to make a new context, and attitudes will change. The Thatcherites were among the chief proponents of this view. The problem, they argued, is the growth of government, especially since Labour won with its socialistic program in 1945. The welfare state let many **consume** without **producing** and subsidized inefficient industries. Unions, given free rein by previous governments, raised wages and lowered **productivity**. The growing costs of the welfare state drained away funds that should have gone for investment. Insufficient investment meant insufficient production, which meant stagnating living standards. Cut both welfare benefits and industry subsidies and you will force—with some pain—a change in attitudes, they argued.

The Thatcher Cure

The Thatcher cure for Britain's economic problems is still debated in Britain. Thatcherites argue that her policies were not implemented thoroughly and long enough. Anti-Thatcherites in all the parties argue the policies had been brutal and ineffective. The way Thatcherites see it, the permissive policies of both Labour and previous Conservative governments had expanded welfare programs beyond the country's ability to pay for them. Unions won wage increases out of line with productivity. Nationalized and subsidized industries lost money. The result: **inflation** and falling productivity that were making Britain the sick man of Europe. The cure, in part, came from the **monetarist** theory of American economist (and Nobel Prize winner) Milton Friedman, which posits too-rapid growth of the money supply as the cause of inflation. Thatcher cut bureaucracy, the growth of welfare, and subsidies to industry in an effort to control Britain's money supply and restore economic health.

Some Britons wondered if the cure wasn't worse than the disease. Unemployment at one point reached 14 percent of the work force, thousands of firms went bankrupt, and Britain's GDP growth was still anemic. Even moderate Conservatives pleaded for her to relent, but Thatcher wasn't called the Iron Lady for nothing. "The lady's not for turning," she intoned. She saw the economic difficulties as a purge Britain had to experience to get well. One of her

KEY CONCEPTS

"PLURALISTIC STAGNATION"

Harvard political scientist Samuel Beer advanced a provocative thesis on the cause of Britain's decline: too many interest groups making too many demands on parties who are too willing to promise everyone everything. The result was **pluralistic stagnation** as British groups scrambled for welfare benefits, pay hikes, and subsidies for industry. The two main parties bid against each other with promises of more benefits to more groups. In the late 1960s, a strong **counterculture** emerged in Britain, which wrecked traditional attitudes of civility and deference and made groups' demands more strident. With every group demanding and getting more, no one saw any reason for self-restraint that would leave them behind. Government benefits fed union wage demands, which fed inflation, which fed government benefits....

The interesting point about the Beer thesis is that it blamed precisely what political scientists long celebrated as the foundation of freedom and democracy: **pluralism**. Beer demonstrated, though, that it can run amok; groups block each other and government, leading to what Beer called the "paralysis of public choice." Any comparison with your system?

economists said: "I don't shed tears when I see inefficient factories shut down. I rejoice." Thatcher and her supporters repeated endlessly, "You can't consume until you produce."

Gradually the argument began to take hold. Many Britons had to admit they had been consuming more than they were producing, that subsidized factories and mines were a drain on the economy, and that bitter medicine was necessary to correct matters. It was almost as if Britons had become guilty about their free rides and knew they now had to pay up. In the 1980s, more working-class Britons voted Tory than voted Labour.

But did Thatchernomics work? By the time the Tories left office in 1997 the picture was mixed but generally positive. Inflation was down and economic growth among the fastest in Europe. State-owned British Steel, British Leyland (motor vehicles), and other industries that had been nationalized since the war to prevent unemployment trimmed their bloated work forces and raised productivity. Many state-owned plants were sold off, a process called **privatization**. Competition was increased through **deregulation**. Renters of public housing got the chance to buy their homes at low cost, a move that made some of them Conservatives. Unions eased their wage and other demands, and union membership dropped sharply. Many weak firms went under, but thousands of new small and middle-sized firms sprang up. Capital and labor were channeled away from losing industries and into winners, exactly what a good economic system should do. A California-like computer industry produced a "silicon glen" in Scotland and a "software valley" around Cambridge University.

Key Terms

pluralistic stagnation Beer's thesis that out-of-control interest groups produce policy log jams.

counterculture Rejection of conventional values, as in the 1960s.

pluralism The autonomous interaction of social groups on themselves and on government.

privatization Selling a state-owned industry to private interests.

deregulation Cutting governmental rules regulating industry.

COMPARISON

THE COST OF THE WELFARE STATE

The other side of the welfare state is how expensive it is. In the late 1990s, all types of taxes at all levels of government took the following percentages of GDP:

Sweden	53
France	46
Italy	44
Germany	42
Canada	38
Britain	38
Spain	34
United States	30
Australia	30
Japan	29

Source: OECD.

Part of the impact of Thatchernomics came from jolting workers out of their trade-union complacency ("I'm all right, Jack"). In 1984, when the government's National Coal Board decided to close hundreds of unprofitable pits and eliminate twenty thousand jobs, miners staged a long and violent strike, which was supported by some other unionists. Thatcher would not back down; after a year, the miners did. (At about the same time, President Reagan faced down striking air-traffic controllers.) New legislation limited union chiefs' abilities to call strikes, and the number and length of strikes in Britain dropped drastically.

As in the United States under Reagan, income inequality grew in Britain. The number of Britons in families with less than half the average income increased under Thatcher and Major from 5 million in 1979 to 14 million in 1993. High youth unemployment led to urban riots. Major regional disparities appeared between a rich, resurgent South of England, with new high-tech industries, and a decaying, abandoned North, where unemployment hit hardest. Thatcher never did get a handle on government spending, much of which, like U.S. **entitlements**, must by law be paid. British welfare benefits actually climbed sharply during the Thatcher and Major years despite their best efforts to trim them. Cutting the welfare state is tempting but rarely successful; too many people have come to depend on its benefits. In the late 1980s, a credit and spending boom kicked inflation back up to over 10 percent, and the economy slumped into **recession**. Competitively, British productivity was low and its wages high, so Britain continued to lose manufacturing jobs to other countries.

Key Terms

entitlement   Spending programs citizens are automatically entitled to, such as Social Security.

recession   An economy that is shrinking, indicated by a falling GDP.

Thatcher's main legacy is the changed terms of Britain's political debate. In 1945, Labour had shifted the debate to the welfare state, and Tories had to compete with them on their own terms, never seriously challenging the underlying premise that redistribution is good. Thatcher changed this all around and made the debate one about productivity and economic growth; now Labour had to compete on *her* terms. It was a historic shift, and one that influenced the political debate in other lands, including the United States. Labour Prime Minister Blair did not repudiate the broad outlines of Thatcher's free-market economics.

COMPARISON

THE PRODUCTIVITY RACE

No production, no goodies. Production is what gets turned out. Productivity is how efficiently it gets turned out. You can have a lot of production with low productivity, the Soviet problem that brought down the Communist regime. Among the major economies, Britain's productivity was weak. In 1995, French manufacturing value added per hour was 85 percent that of the United States, West German 81 percent, Japan 73 percent, and Britain 70 percent.

The growth of productivity—the additional amount a worker cranks out per hour from one year to the next—is the measure of future prosperity. Rapid growth in productivity means quickly rising standards of living; low growth means stagnation or even decline. The table at the top of the righthand column shows the percent of average annual growth in manufacturing from 1979 to 1994.

The U.S. figure indicates the relatively

Japan	4.2
France	3.1
Italy	3.9
Germany	2.3
Belgium	3.8
Britain	3.9
United States	2.5

Source: OECD

low cost of U.S. labor, which makes it cheaper to hire more workers than to install automation. (Side effect: U.S. unemployment rates are half those of West Europe.) It also reflects the large size of the U.S. services sector, where productivity gains are harder to come by than in manufacturing.

Low U.S. productivity growth meant a stagnating average U.S. standard of living from 1973 until the late 1990s. At the close of the century, U.S. productivity seemed to be climbing, ascribed by some to a "New Economy" based on computers and the Internet.

The Trouble with National Health

The centerpiece of Britain's extensive welfare state is the National Health Service (NHS), which went into operation in 1948 as part of Labour's longstanding commitment to improving the lot of working Britons. Before World War II, British medical care was spotty. When millions were examined for military service during the war, many were scrawny and unhealthy. Conservatives and the British Medical Association fought the NHS, but the tide was against them.

Did the NHS work? The answer is both yes and no. The British population is much healthier than it used to be. Infant mortality, one key measure of overall health standards, dropped from 64 out of 1,000 live births in 1931 to 7 now. The British working class has especially benefited. Britons spend only 6.7 percent of their GDP on health care but are as healthy as the Americans, who spend 14 percent.

But NHS has some negative aspects. Costs skyrocketed. The British population has become more elderly, and old people consume many times as much medical care as younger people. Technical advances in medicine work wonders, but they are terribly expensive. The

DEMOCRACY

WHICH BLAIR PROJECT?

Blair's chief project was not Britain's economy but its institutions. His bold constitutional reforms modernized Britain's political institutions, many of which had been little changed in centuries. Note that some of his projects have already been passed into law while others are still debated. Blair will go down as Britain's great modernizer.

1. A written constitution: With no fixed limits, power can be abused in Britain. Written rules could make Britons freer, especially with the addition of …
2. A bill of rights, U.S.-style: Blair accomplished this by having Parliament adopt the European Convention on Human Rights as domestic law, bringing Britain into line with the rest of the EU starting in 2000. For the first time Britons got legal guarantees of media freedom and protection from heavy-handed police methods.
3. Judicial review: Any bill Parliament passes is automatically constitutional in Britain. As in most of the world, British courts cannot check executive excesses. Many Britons admired the role of the

U.S. Supreme Court, which, among other things, guarantees …
4. Freedom of information: Britain has an Official Secrets Act that comes close to censorship. All manner of government wrongdoing is concealed. Many Britons admired the U.S. Freedom of Information Act.
5. A meaningful upper house: As we discussed in Chapter 3, in 1999 Blair modernized Lords by kicking out most hereditary peers and leaving it largely in the hands of life peers. This still left it with little power. A next step would be to give it some powers to check Commons and the cabinet.
6. Devolution: Blair carried this out smartly in granting extensive home rule and elected assemblies to Northern Ireland, Scotland, and Wales. (See the subsequent discussions.)
7. A new electoral system: As we considered in Chapter 3, the traditional FPTP system overrewards some parties and penalizes third parties. Adding some PR ("topping off"), as was done in the 1999 elections for the new Scottish and Welsh parliaments, would be much fairer, especially to the Lib Dems.

system requires many bureaucrats. With a staff of 1 million, the NHS is the largest employer in West Europe, but personnel and facilities have not kept pace with demand. The money simply isn't there. If surgery isn't for an emergency, patients may wait a year or more. Over 1 million Britons are on waiting lists for medical treatment.

The upshot is that private medical care quietly returned to Britain. About 13 percent of Britons pay for speedy and personal care through private medical insurance. Labour's great effort to provide medical treatment for all succeeded but class differences remain. Most Britons like the NHS but want it reformed.

Is Northern Ireland Settled?

Good Friday agreement
1998 pact to share power in
Northern Ireland.

consociation   Sharing of
political power at the
executive level, giving all
major parties cabinet
positions.

subject   Originally, a
subject of the Crown; now
another term for British
citizen.

After thirty years of violence, peace glimmered in Northern Ireland. In 1998, on Good Friday, the two sides reached a power-sharing agreement, but extemists tried to undermine it. A breakaway group, the Real IRA, set off a bomb on a crowded street in Omagh, killing twenty-eight (most of them Catholic). This horrified everyone and solidified the agreement. Even Gerry Adams, the Sinn Fein chief who once advocated violence, said violence "must be for all of us now a thing of the past, over, done with and gone." Most agreed.

Prime Minister Tony Blair took some of the credit for the **Good Friday agreement**; his Conservative predecessors would not negotiate with Sinn Fein. Militants on both sides had exhausted themselves. Britons and Irish alike were disgusted by the bloodshed and wanted the horror over with.

The key elements of the agreement were to reopen the Northern Ireland parliament at Stormont, which had been closed since 1974. Previously dominated by Protestants, it was one of the reasons for Catholic protest. Now it is freely elected, using the type of proportional representation that is also used in the Republic of Ireland. Ministries are awarded on a balanced basis; most of the nine parties in Stormont got at least one. First minister, for example, is David Trimble, leader of the (Protestant) Ulster Unionist party, but his deputy is Seamus Mallon, leader of the (Catholic) Social Democratic and Labour party. Political scientists call such an arrangement **consociation** and find it useful to hold together badly fractured societies.

Stormont's powers and budget are not trivial. It runs Northern Ireland's education, medical, social, housing, and agricultural services. In addition, a "north-south council" of officials from Northern Ireland and the Republic of Ireland supervises cross-border policies. The whole process stalled in 2000 when the IRA refused to turn in its weapons.

British Racism

British intellectuals, especially those on the left, used to criticize the United States for racism. Then the British left took to denouncing South Africa. That sort of thing, Britishers used to say, could never happen in tolerant, civilized Britain. At least since the 1958 Notting Hill race riot in London, the English have had to face the fact that they, too, have a race problem and that there are no easy solutions to it.

The race problem in Britain is a legacy of empire. Britain in 1948 legally made the natives of its many colonies British **subjects**, entitled to live and work in the United Kingdom. Although the colonies were granted independence in the 1950s and 1960s, as members of the British Commonwealth—a loose organization of countries that were at one time British colonies—their people were still entitled to immigrate to Britain. In the 1950s, West Indians arrived from the Caribbean, then Indians and Pakistanis. Immigrants were willing to take the lowliest jobs that many Englishmen didn't want. Then they would send for their wives, children, fiancées, and cousins. Immigrants and their offspring now form about 5 percent of Britain's population.

White resentment soon grew, especially among the working class, who believed the recent immigrants wanted their housing, jobs, wallets, and daughters. Britons began to discover they were racists, sometimes violent racists. In 1967 an openly racist National Front party formed,

GEOGRAPHY

DEVOLUTION FOR SCOTLAND AND WALES

Along with Northern Ireland, Scotland and Wales represent center-periphery tensions, something that afflicts many countries. In general, the farther you go from the nation's capital, the more regional resentment you hear. Aggravating this problem in Britain are the long Celtic memories of Scots and Welsh. Wales has been a part of England since the Middle Ages; the thrones of England and Scotland were united in 1603, and in 1707 both countries agreed to a single Parliament in London. But old resentments never quite died. Wales and Scotland were always poorer than England, provoking the feeling among Welsh and Scots that they were economically exploited.

In the twentieth century the political beneficiary of these feelings has been the Labour party, which holds sway in Wales and Scotland. Voting Labour in Scotland and Wales became a form of regional nationalism, a way of repudiating rule by England, which goes Conservative. Center-periphery tensions almost always reveal themselves in voting patterns. In the 1960s the small Plaid Cymru (pronounced plyde kum-REE, meaning "Party of Wales") and the Scottish Nationalist party began to grow. In the 1997 elections, the Welsh Nationalists won four Commons seats and the Scottish Nationalists six.

Local nationalism grew in many countries during the 1970s besides Wales and Scotland: Corsican and Breton in France, Quebecker in Canada, Basque and Catalan in Spain. In the 1990s, the Soviet Union and Yugoslavia fell apart. It was hard to pinpoint the cause for this upsurge in local separatism. Economics plays a role; local nationalists usually claim their regions are shortchanged by their central governments. Nationalists often emphasize their regions' distinct languages and cultures and demand that they be taught in schools. Some of the impulse behind local nationalism is the bigness and remoteness of the modern state, the feeling that important decisions are out of local control, made by far-away bureaucrats. And often smoldering under the surface are historical resentments of a region that once was conquered, occupied, and deprived of its own identity. Whatever the mixture, local nationalism sometimes turns its adherents into fanatics willing to wreck the entire country to get their way. Happily, this did not happen in Britain. The Scots and Welsh never became as extreme as Basques in Spain or Corsicans in France.

In Scotland, the economic factor played a large part in its rising nationalism. When oil was discovered in the North Sea off Scotland in the 1960s, some Scots didn't want to share the petroleum revenues with the United Kingdom as a whole. "It's Scotland's oil!" cried the Scottish Nationalists whose electoral fortunes rose with the offshore discoveries. Oil offered Scotland the possibility of economic independence and self-government, of becoming something more than a poor, northerly part of Britain.

The leading issue for Welsh nationalists has been language, the ancient Celtic tongue of Cymric (pronounced *kim-rick*). Fewer than one Welsh person in five speaks Cymric, and most are elderly. In recent years, however, there has been an upsurge of people learning Welsh, and the language is now officially co-equal with English within Wales. There is even a Welsh TV channel.

The strategy of the Labour party has been to offer home rule or autonomy to Scotland and Wales. This was called **devolution**, the granting of certain governing powers by the center to the periphery. A 1977 devolution bill to set up Scottish and Welsh assemblies failed in **referendums**.

After the parliamentary elections of 1997, in which Scotland and Wales stayed overwhelmingly Labour, Tony Blair again offered Scotland and Wales their own parliaments, and this time the referendums passed. In 1999, at about the same time Ulster got home rule, Scots and Welsh elected regional parliaments with a new voting system that could be what Blair has in mind for Britain as a whole. The German-style system (see page 190) gave each voter two votes, the first for FPTP single-member districts and the second for parties in multimember districts. The results of the second vote were used to "top off" the number of seats for each party until they were roughly proportional to its share of the votes. Labour took the most seats in both Scotland and Wales but not a majority, forcing them to form coalitions. This too could be a harbinger for things to come in Britain. The new assemblies have some powers in education, economic planning, and taxation. Britons don't use the word, but these moves amount to **quasi-federalism**. Will it solve Britain's problem or just whet appetites for more? The Scot Nats and about half the people of Scotland still say they want full independence.

In addition, the Blair government set up eight Regional Development Agencies for England, whose task was economic growth.

Some took these agencies as the beginnings of federalism within England. As we will see in France, regional planning councils can turn into political units. The shifts are examples of unitary systems loosening up into quasi-federalism or "regionalism."

advocating the expulsion of all "coloureds" back to their native lands. Some National Front leaders had earlier been members of Britain's tiny Fascist party. Skinheads, some supporting the Front or the rival National party, went in for murderous "Paki bashing." With slogans such as "Rights for Whites," votes for the two small parties grew, although neither won a seat in Parliament. Meanwhile, the minute Trotskyist Socialist Workers party attacked racist rallies, and hundreds of police had to hold the two sides apart.

The British race question is not confined to the fringes of politics. Many ordinary Britons view nonwhites as a social problem and would like them to return to their native lands, although by now many are born in Britain. Some of the swing to the Conservatives was attributed to Margaret Thatcher's call for a "clear end to immigration" before it "swamped" British culture.

In point of fact, immigration to Britain has been successively tightened by both parties since 1962 and has now become quite restrictive. Demographers say there is no chance that the immigrants will swamp anything. But the question poses serious ethical dilemmas. The British gloried in their empire for more than a century; now they have responsibility for what they created. Particularly poignant was the situation of "Asians" (Indians and Pakistanis) in East Africa. Brought to Kenya and Uganda by the British decades ago as laborers, Asians soon became small-business people and monopolized commercial life. Native Africans bitterly resented the Asians and applauded government policies to "Africanize" commerce—meaning kicking out the Indians and Pakistanis. The Asians pleaded to be let into Britain. As Hong Kong reverted to Communist China in 1997, many residents of that British crown colony likewise pleaded to be let into Britain.

Key Terms

devolution   A central government turning some powers over to regions.

referendum   A vote on an issue rather than for an office.

quasi-federal   Halfway federal.

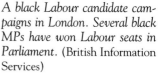

A black Labour candidate campaigns in London. Several black MPs have won Labour seats in Parliament. (British Information Services)

Britain and Europe

Until recently, the British never thought of themselves as Europeans. Indeed, most English people look down upon anyone from across the English Channel, even if their income is higher. Rather than working toward a united Europe after World War II, as the main Continental countries did, Britain emphasized its Commonwealth ties and its "special relationship" to the United States. London faced westward, across the Atlantic, rather than eastward, across the Channel.

Rather than signing the 1957 Treaty of Rome, which set up the European Community (EC, since 1993 the EU, for European Union), Britain in 1960 built a much looser grouping known as the European Free Trade Association (EFTA). While the EC Six (France, West Germany, Italy, Belgium, the Netherlands, Luxembourg) surged ahead economically, the EFTA Outer Seven (Britain, Austria, Denmark, Finland, Iceland, Norway, Portugal, Sweden, and Switzerland) found themselves slowly cut off from the main European market. In 1963, Britain applied to get into the Common Market. French President Charles de Gaulle vetoed British entry, charging that Britain was still too tied to the Commonwealth and the United States to be a good European. He was right.

By the time de Gaulle resigned in 1969, Britain was again ready to join the EU, but there were domestic political complications. Not all Britons like the idea. For traditional Tories, it meant giving up some British sovereignty to the EU headquarters in Brussels and even treating Europeans as equals. For everyone it meant higher food prices. For manufacturers it meant British products have to compete with often better and cheaper Continental imports that now come in tariff-free. For fishermen it meant British fishing areas are open to all EU fishermen. For workers it meant the loss of some jobs. In short, many Britons want to stay firmly British.

The arguments in favor of the EU stress that Britain needs change and competition, the very forces that had invigorated European industries. Furthermore, geographically, strategically, economically, even spiritually, Britain really is part of Europe and should start

GEOGRAPHY

THE EU MEMBERS

Although likely to grow, perhaps until it encompasses all of Europe, the European Union (formerly the Common Market) has at present fifteen members: Britain, France, Germany, Belgium, Netherlands, Luxembourg, Italy, Spain, Portugal, Sweden, Denmark, Finland, Greece, Ireland, and Austria.

Grouping the members into five groups of three each may help you remember them: The Big Three of West Europe—Britain, France, and Germany; the small "Benelux" countries; the Latin countries of South Europe; three Nordic lands; and three lands at the periphery. Eleven EU members went to the *euro* currency; Britain, Sweden, Denmark, and Greece do not yet participate.

acting like it. Britain is no longer a great empire and cannot stand on its own; the "special relationship" with the United States is unreliable and makes Britain into a U.S. dependency.

The Euro-debate cuts across party lines, sometimes producing a strange coalition of right-wing Tories and left-wing Labourites, each opposing Europe for their own reasons. In 1971, under a Tory government, the Commons voted 356 to 244 to join; 69 Labour MPs defied their party whip to vote in favor while 39 Conservatives, freed from party discipline, voted "no" along with Labour. The vote graphically demonstrated that British party discipline is not perfect. On January 1, 1973, Britain, along with Denmark and Ireland, made the Common Market Six, the Nine.

When Labour returned to power, Prime Minister Harold Wilson offered the British public a first—a referendum, something quite common in France. But Britain, with its tradition of parliamentary supremacy, had never held one before. The 1975 British referendum found that most Britons wanted to stay in Europe, but one-third voted no.

Thatcher, a British nationalist and "Eurosceptic," took a tough line on the EU. A common market was fine, she argued, but not turning it into a supranational entity that would infringe on Britain's sovereignty. Many Britons emphatically reject joining the European Monetary Union (EMU) or its new *euro* currency. The EMU indeed takes away an important part of sovereignty, the ability of each country to control its currency, and gives it to the European Central Bank in Frankfurt. Many Britons (and some other Europeans) feared that Europe's strongest economy—Germany—would dominate the EMU and that policy on money supply and interest rates would be set by the Bundesbank. Briton and three other EU members stood aside as the euro was introduced in 1999; Blair preferred to wait and see how it works out. As before, Britain hung back in building Europe.

Great Britain or Little England?

The question "Great Britain or Little England?" sums up the dilemma of modern Britain: the problem of scaling down its vision of itself. Britain, in the course of a century, has clearly declined, both internationally and domestically. When Britain was a mighty empire and the most

Key Terms

unilinear Progressing evenly and always upward.
human capital The education, skills, and enthusiasm of a nation's work force.
underclass Permanently disadvantaged people.

industrialized country in the world, it had power, wealth, and a sense of mission. This in turn fostered order, discipline, and deference among the British people. Losing its empire and slipping out of the front rank of the economies of West Europe, decay, violence, and resentment appeared.

Britain offers a refutation of the idea that progress is **unilinear**. In the case of Britain we see that what goes up can eventually come down. But this process is never static. Now that Britain is adjusting to its new reality—as one European country among many—regeneration may have begun. To see how another country has turned around, how a society and economy can change from static to dynamic, let us now consider France.

COMPARISON

BRITAIN'S EDUCATION DILEMMA

One limit to sustained British economic growth is poor educational levels, something Tony Blair vowed to correct. Britain's **human capital** does not compare favorably with Europe or America. The percent of 18-year-olds entering some form of higher education in 1991 was as follows:

United States	65
Japan	53
France	43
Germany	42
Britain	20

Source: OECD

In a comparative math and science test of thirteen-year-olds, Britain (and the United States) came in way down the list (the winner: Singapore). Like many Americans, millions of adult Britons have trouble reading and doing basic math. The Nissan car factory in Britain found that seven out of ten job applicants could not pass its verbal-reasoning test.

The problem stems from Britain's over-concentration on its top students and neglect of everyone else. Britain's brainiest test their way into fine universities, where they get very good and nearly free educations. The others in secondary school, who fear they will not pass the demanding college-prep exams (the A-levels) might as well drop out. And they do: Close to two out of three young Britons (including young John Major) leave school as soon as they can. There are few German-style apprentice programs or U.S.-type community colleges to impart job skills to British students not of the university level. The result is a serious shortage of skilled technicians and foremen. This takes its toll on productivity. Using the exact same automated equipment, British workers produce 40 percent less than Japanese workers.

Thatcher, with her emphasis on excellence, largely neglected the problem of "school-leavers." A variety of public-private and school-business partnerships have been tried to teach them job skills; none have been very successful (except in Scotland). The result has been the growth of a U.S.-style **underclass**. One solution being implemented: City Technology Colleges in inner cities. The real problem with British education traces back to a snobbish, class-ridden society, and it will be hard for Tony Blair to change that.

Key Terms

absolute decline (p. 73)

consociation (p. 79)

consumption (p. 74)

counterculture (p. 75)

deindustrialization (p. 73)

deregulation (p. 75)

devolution (p. 81)

entitlement (p. 76)

Good Friday agreement (p. 79)

human capital (p. 84)

inflation (p. 74)

monetarism (p. 74)

pluralism (p. 75)

pluralistic stagnation (p. 75)

privatization (p. 75)

production (p. 74)

productivity (p. 74)

quasi-federal (p. 81)

recession (p. 76)

referendum (p. 81)

relative decline (p. 73)

subject (p. 79)

underclass (p. 84)

unilinear (p. 84)

Further Reference

Boyle, Kevin, and Tom Hadden. *Northern Ireland: The Choice.* New York: Penguin, 1995.

Brown, Alice, David McCrone, and Lindsay Paterson. *Politics and Society in Scotland.* New York: St. Martin's, 1996.

Burgess, Michael. *The British Tradition of Federalism.* Rutherford, NJ: Farleigh Dickinson, 1995.

Edwards, Brian. *The National Health Service: A Manager's Tale.* London: Nuffield Provincial Hospitals Trust, 1993.

Freedman, Leonard. *Politics and Policy in Britain.* New York: Longman, 1996.

Jenkins, Simon. *Accountable to None: The Tory Nationalisation of Britain.* London: Hamish Hamilton, 1995.

Owen, Geoffrey. *From Empire to Europe.* New York: HarperCollins, 1999.

Paul, Kathleen. *Whitewashing Britain: Race and Citizenship in the Postwar Era.* Ithaca, NY: Cornell University Press, 1997.

Pierson, Paul. *Dismantling the Welfare State?: Reagan, Thatcher, and the Politics of Retrenchment.* New York: Cambridge University Press, 1994.

Pilkington, Colin. *Issues in British Politics.* New York: St. Martin's, 1998.

Rubinstein, W. D. *Capitalism, Culture and Decline in Britain: 1750–1990.* New York: Routledge, 1993.

Samuel, Raphael. *Island Stories: Unravelling Britain.* New York: Verso, 1998.

Stevenson, Jonathan. *We Wrecked the Place: Contemplating an End to the Northern Irish Troubles.* New York: Simon & Schuster, 1997.

Studlar, Donley T. *Great Britain: Decline or Renewal?* Boulder, CO: Westview, 1996.

PART II

Key Websites

The Government of France   This site contains a plethora of information about France, including data about administrative divisions; executive, legislative, and judicial branches; and political parties.
http://www.emulateme.com/france.htm

The European Union   This site offers a chronology of the European Union beginning in 1950 and is differentiated by institutional category.
http://europa.eu.int/abc/obj/chrono/en/them1.htm

Elections in France   This site contains election results for candidates, National Assembly seats, and Senate seats. It also investigates political parties recently in Parliament and those not in Parliament.
http://www.agora.stm.it/elections/election/country/fr.htm

Office of the French President   From Elysée Palace, this site has documents and descriptions of the president, including the following: Institutions—the founding texts, the presidents of the Fifth Republic; The President—a portrait of Jacques Chirac, his staff, and the presidential role; France and Europe—the European Union, the Council of Europe; and Official foreign policy statements.
http://www.elysee.fr/ang/index.shtm

Henri Petain   This site contains a biography of the military hero Henri Petain, who was head of the collaborationist Vichy regime.
http://gi.grolier.com/wwii/wwii_petain.html

Le Monde   This site, updated daily, features France's leading newspaper—*Le Monde*—in French. *Le Monde* has a somewhat leftist slant.
http://www.lemonde.fr

UNITED

KINGDOM

NETHERLANDS

BELGIUM

GERMANY

ENGLISH CHANNEL

NORD

LUXEMBOURG

HAUTE-
NORMANDIE

PICARDIE

BASSE-
NORMANDIE

CHAMPAGNE

LORRAINE

BRETAGNE

Paris

REGION DE
PARIS

ALSACE

PAYS DE LA LOIRE

CENTRE

BOURGOGNE

FRANCHE-COMTE

BAY

FRANCE

SWITZERLAND

OF

POITOU-
CHARENTES

BISCAY

LIMOUSIN

AUVERGNE

RHONE-ALPES

ITALY

AQUITAINE

MIDI-PYRENEES

LANGUEDOC

PROVINCE
COTE D'AZUR

ANDORRA

CORSICA

SPAIN

MEDITERRANEAN

SEA

0   100   200 Miles

0   100   200 Kilometers

5°   50°   45°   5°

France:
The Impact of the Past

7

Questions to Consider

1. Compare the Roman influence in France and Britain.
2. How does France have a perfect example of a core area?
3. Who epitomized French absolutism?
4. What was the theory of mercantilism?
5. What were the main causes of the French Revolution?
6. How did great French thinkers differ from the British?
7. What is Brinton's theory of revolution?
8. With what regime did France become a stable democracy?
9. What did the Dreyfus Affair show?
10. Who ran France during World War II?
11. How did de Gaulle come to power?

"France has everything," the French like to boast. They are nearly right. Roughly the shape of a hexagon, with three sides on seas and three on land, France is simultaneously an Atlantic country, a Mediterranean country, and an Alpine country. It has lush farmland, navigable rivers, many minerals, and a moderate climate. It does not, however, have the safety of England's moat. France is vulnerable to land attack from the north and the east. While England historically did well without standing armies, France needed large armies, a point that helps explain the rise of French absolutism. French kings had their troops to rely on.

Internally, France is divided into a North and a South. Culturally and temperamentally, the two regions are rather different and, until the late Middle Ages, even spoke different languages. The Germanic northerners spoke *langue d'oïl*, "the tongue of *oïl*," their word for yes, which grew into the modern French *oui*. The Mediterranean southerners spoke *langue d'oc*, after their word for yes, *oc*. It declined after the Paris kings conquered the South in the thirteenth century. To this day, southerners may speak with a different accent and resent the region's subjugation to Paris. The region is still called Languedoc.

GEOGRAPHY

RIVERS

Navigable rivers serve as economic lifelines, tying a country together and sometimes boosting international trade. England's Thames also gives it an inland outlet to the sea. France's Seine, Rhine, Rhone, and Loire roughly cover the four points of the compass, giving trade routes and outlets to the sea in all directions. French kings supplemented the rivers with an ambitious system of canals, some of which are still in use. The Rhine has for centuries served as a sort of West European highway; it touches Switzerland, France, Germany, and the Netherlands. The Danube helped stitch together the Austro-Hungarian Empire, but for centuries its outlet in the Black Sea was controlled by the hostile Turks. Russia's rivers, it has been said, flow the wrong way, either to the Arctic Ocean or to the Black Sea, where the Ottomans held the vital Turkish Straits. China's economic and political life grew up around the Yangtze River.

The Roman Influence

Like most peoples, the French are a mixture of ethnic stocks. In the centuries before Christ, tribes of Celts pushed into France and merged with the native Ligurians. The Romans conquered the area and called it *Gallia* (Gaul). The Roman influence in France was longer and deeper than in England. The Anglo-Saxons obliterated England's Roman influence, but the Germanic tribes that moved into Gaul became Romanized themselves. Thus, English is a Germanic language and French is a Romance language.

By the time the Roman Empire collapsed, one Germanic tribe, the Franks, had managed to take over most of present-day France. Their chief, Clovis—from whom came the name Louis—was baptized in 496, and France has been mostly Catholic ever since, the "eldest daughter of the Church." The Franks under Charles Martel turned back the invading Moors in 732, possibly saving Christianity in Europe. Charles Martel's grandson, Charlemagne, carved out a gigantic kingdom—the Holy Roman Empire—that encompassed what someday would amount to most of the six original EU countries. Although the empire soon disintegrated, Charlemagne had planted the idea of European unity.

The Rise of French Absolutism

In the confusion that followed the death of Charlemagne, France was reduced to several petty kingdoms and dukedoms, as was Germany. While Germany stayed divided until the nineteenth century, French kings pursued unification and centralization of their power with single-minded determination. Pushing outward from the Paris area, the *Ile de France* (Island of France), French kings added territory while retaining control in Paris.

Feudalism in France began to give way to absolutism with Louis (pronounced Lwie) XI,

GEOGRAPHY

CORE AREAS

Most countries have an identifiable **core** area, a region where it might be said that the state originated. Some countries, to be sure, contain more than one core area, and this may indicate regional tension. Typically, the country's capital is in its core area. Farther out are the peripheral areas, often more recent additions where people may speak a different language and resent rule by the core area. At times, the resentment can turn deadly, as when breakaway provinces, such as Serbia's Kosovo, Turkey's Kurdish area, and China's Taiwan refused to be ruled by the center. Part of the tragedy of Kosovo is that it was the medieval Serbian core, but after Turkish conquest in 1389, Serbs were displaced northward, and Kosovo slowly became a majority Albanian. Looking to their history, Serbs refused to give up their ancient heartland.

France is an almost perfect example of a core area, centered on Paris, spreading its rule, language, and culture with an eye toward perfecting national integration. This has been a slow process and one still not complete. In the nineteenth century, there were regions of France that spoke strange dialects. By deliberate educational policy, corps of schoolteachers directed by Paris spread across France to turn "peasants into Frenchmen," in the words of historian Eugen Weber. Some peripheral areas still harbor resentments against Paris. Brittany, Corsica, and Languedoc try to keep alive local dialects and regional culture. Extremists in Corsica practice occasional violence.

England is the core area of the United Kingdom, but a German core area is much less clear. The many German ministates of the Middle Ages kept their sovereignty and dialects unusually long. Prussia led German unification in the nineteenth century, and Berlin indeed became the nation's capital. But many regions accorded Prussia little respect; Catholic lands such as Bavaria and the Rhineland disliked Prussia's authoritarianism and Protestantism. Germany remained riven by **particularism**, a factor that contributed to present-day federalism. Some thinkers see in Nazism a contrived effort to bring all German regions and dialects under central control by means of lunatic nationalism. The addition of East Germany to the Federal Republic has set up a new tension, with old West Germany as the capitalist and democratic core and old East Germany as the disgruntled periphery that feels it's not getting its share of economic prosperity. This will likely fade with time.

The Soviet Union represented a huge gap between its Slavic core area and its non-Slavic peripheral areas. Russia's numerous nationalities are still distinct and discontent. Lacking the kind of cohesion of other nation-states, the Soviet Union was better seen as the last old-fashioned colonial empire. The Slavic core of Russia, Belarus, and Ukraine gradually beat back Tatars, Turks, and Swedes until it straddled the vast belt where Europe meets Asia. Then the tsars sent expeditions eastward to claim Siberia to the Pacific. In the mid-nineteenth century Russia acquired most of the Muslim-Turkic peoples of Central Asia. **Russification** proved impossible and fostered nationalist hatred against Moscow. The breakaway of republics from the Soviet Union may be seen as decolonization. The remaining Russian Federation still contains lands like Chechnya that would like to break away.

China's core area was the Yangtze Valley, but by the time of Christ, China had consolidated a major kingdom. So numerous and united—despite occasional civil wars—were the **Han** Chinese that the addition to the kingdom of a few outer barbarians (Mongols, Tibetans, Turkic Muslims, and others) bothered the Han little. Recently, however, Central Asian dissidents have set off bombs to protest rule by Beijing.

The original area of settlement in Brazil was the Northeast, but economic interest and immigration soon shifted southward, to the present core area of the states of Rio de Janeiro, São Paulo, and Minas Gerais, the areas of heaviest settlement and the seats of political and economic power. The drought-stricken and impoverished Northeast is now the periphery. By deliberate government design, Brazilians were encouraged to populate the vast Amazonian periphery. To this end, Brasilia, deep in the interior, was made the capital in 1960.

Under white rule, South Africa had two core areas, the English on the coast from Cape Town to Natal and the Afrikaners inland, in the Transvaal and Orange Free State. In an effort to resolve this tension, South Africa's parliament was located in Cape Town and its executive departments in Pretoria. This arrangement did nothing for South Africa's black majority, which was kept partially confined to peripheral farming and tribal areas.

One interpretation of current South African politics, now in the hands of an elected black government, is an attempt to close the gap between the "have" core areas, dominated by whites, and the "have not" peripheral regions to which most Africans had been consigned.

Japan, with Tokyo-Yokohama as its core area, has only a little center-periphery tension between East and West Japan and from the claims of agricultural and fishing prefectures. Iran has non-Persian-speaking peripheral areas that resent rule by Tehran.

The U.S. core area began with the thirteen colonies along the Atlantic seaboard, especially the northern ones. The Civil War can be seen as an effort by the southern periphery to cast off rule by the northern core. In terms of attitudes and economics, the North and South really were two different countries, a gap that has been largely closed since then. Still, the center of population, politics, economics, communications, education, and culture long remained in the northeast. This still fosters slight center-periphery tension; some western politicians express irritation at rule by Washington.

---

who ruled from 1461 to 1483. The crafty Louis XI doubled the size of France until it was nearly its present shape, weakened the power of the feudal nobles, ignored the **Estates-General**, and developed a royal bureaucracy to increase taxation. It was a pattern that was to be strengthened for at least three centuries, leaving the France of today still highly centralized. Louis XI also cultivated relations with Rome. There was never an English-style break with the Vatican; instead, the Catholic church became a pillar of the French monarchy. The **Huguenots**, were controlled, massacred, and driven into exile. In 1589, however, the royal line of succession fell to a Huguenot, Henry of Navarre. The Catholic church offered the throne to Henry only if he would convert to Catholicism. In what has become a model of opportunism, Henry accepted with the words, "Paris is worth a Mass."

Under Louis XIII, Cardinal Richelieu became chief minister and virtual ruler from 1624 to 1642. Obsessed with French power and glory, Richelieu further weakened the nobles, recruited only middle-class bureaucrats, and sent out **intendants** to control the provinces for Paris. Richelieu was an organizational genius who put his bureaucratic stamp on France for all time.

Key Terms

core The region where a state originated.

particularism A region's sense of its difference.

Russification Making non-Russian nationalities learn Russian.

Han Original and main people of China.

Estates-General Old, unused French parliament.

Huguenots French Protestants.

intendants French provincial administrators, answerable only to Paris; early version of *prefects*.

The French nobles did try to fight back, but they lost. In 1648 and again in 1650 some French **aristocrats** staged an uncoordinated revolt called the *Fronde*. Recall that at this time English nobles and their commoner allies beheaded a king who tried to act like an absolute monarch. In France, the nobles were quickly broken and lost the **autonomy** enjoyed by English lords.

Louis XIV: The High Point of Absolutism

Key Terms

aristocrat   Person of inherited noble rank.

autonomy   Partial independence.

Versailles   Palace and estate on outskirts of Paris, built by Louis XIV.

courtier   Person who hangs around a royal court.

mercantilism   Theory that nation's wealth is its gold and silver, to be amassed by government controls on the economy.

ancien régime   French for old regime; the monarchy that preceded the Revolution.

"*L'état, c'est moi* [The state—that's me]," Louis XIV is often quoted as saying. By the time Louis XIV became king in 1661, French absolutism was already well developed; he brought it to a high point. Louis's emblem was the sun, around which all things revolved. The "Sun King" further increased centralization and bureaucratization, all aimed at augmenting his own and France's power. Louis used his large army in almost continual warfare. He acted as his own prime minister and handled much administration personally. He never bothered convening the Estates-General. He constructed **Versailles** and made thousands of nobles live there, diverting them from power seeking to game playing—games of intrigue, love, and flattery. While English lords ruled as small kings on their estates, French nobles were reduced to **courtiers**.

Louis's policies of "war and magnificence" were huge financial drains. To harness the French economy to serve the state, Louis's minister Colbert practiced **mercantilism**—the theory that a nation is as wealthy as the amount of gold it possesses, and the way to amass gold is for the government to supervise the economy with plans, subsidies, monopolies, and tariffs. This helped set a pattern found in most European countries and in Japan: Instead of purely free-market economics, the government is expected to play a supervisory role.

Louis XIV was an able monarch who impressed all of Europe; other kings tried to imitate him. French cuisine, architecture, dress, and language dominated the Continent. From the outside, the France of Louis XIV looked more impressive than England. Without "checks and balances" to get in the way, the centralized monarchy of France accomplished great things. But the English, by developing political participation, devised a more stable system.

Why the French Revolution?

For all its external splendor, France in the eighteenth century was in difficulty. Its treasury was often near bankruptcy. Especially costly was French support for the American colonists against Britain; the French did it more for revenge than for love of liberty. The bureaucracy was corrupt and inefficient. Recognizing too late that mercantilism was bad economics, the regime tried to move to a free market, but by then French industry and agriculture had become used to state protection and objected. Also important was the spread of new ideas on "liberty," "consent of the governed," and "the general will." Ideas can be dynamite, and great thinkers expounded ideas that undermined the **ancien régime**.

As Alexis de Tocqueville pointed out, revolutions seldom start when things are bad but, rather, when they are getting better. The French people enjoyed improving economic

GEOGRAPHY

BOUND FRANCE

An old technique in the teaching of geography has been largely forgotten; we are going to revive it. It requires the student to cite, from forced recall, the boundaries of a given country in the following form:

Bound France

France is bounded on the north by Belgium and Luxembourg;

on the east by Germany, Switzerland, and Italy;

on the south by the Mediterranean Sea and Spain;

and on the west by the Atlantic Ocean.

The four directions need be only approximate. Germany is also on France's northern border, but Germany is mainly to the east of France. This bounding exercise is a more effective learning tool than labeling a blank map, as a map gives several clues. Bounding forces students to reconstruct the map in their minds without clues. To reinforce your knowledge, from the map on p. 87 sketch out and label France and its neighbors. Next do it again from memory. Once you can bound each of our nine countries, you will be able to label much of all the continents except Africa, which is extremely fragmented and complex. To fill in the blank spots, we will also include other countries in our bounding exercises. Bounding has only limited utility for Britain, as the United Kingdom has only one land boundary. What is it?

---

conditions for most of the eighteenth century, which increased expectations and spurred jealousy of people who were getting richer faster. As we shall see in Iran under the Shah, economic growth can be highly destabilizing. Furthermore, Louis XVI had decided to reform the political system and provide for some kind of representation. But as we shall see in Russia and South Africa, the reforming of an unjust and unpopular system is extraordinarily difficult, often leading to revolution.

In the spring of 1789, Louis XVI convened the Estates-General for the first time since 1614. Its three estates—the clergy, the nobility, and the commoners—were elected by nearly universal male suffrage. The **Third Estate**, the commoners, demanded that all three houses meet together, so that the more numerous Third Estate could override the conservative First and Second Estates. The Third Estate argued that it represented the popular will, but Louis resisted. By the time he gave in, many parliamentarians were angry and radicalized and voted themselves into a **National Assembly**, its name today.

Shortly afterward, the common people of Paris, furious over rising bread prices, stormed the **Bastille** on July 14, 1789. Bastille Day became the French national day. Upon hearing of the Bastille incident the king exclaimed, *"C'est une révolte,"* meaning something that could be put down. A duke corrected him: *"Non, Sire, c'est une révolution."* It was the first modern usage of the word **revolution**.

Key Terms

bound   To name bordering countries.

Third Estate   Largest chamber of the Estates-General, representing commoners.

National Assembly   France's parliament.

Bastille   Old and nearly unused Paris jail, the storming of which signaled the start of the French Revolution in 1789.

revolution   The sudden and complete overthrow of a regime.

One of the reasons Louis XVI was unpopular was his frivolous, extravagant Austrian-born queen, Marie Antoinette. She was said to have once inquired why there had been riots and was told it was because the people had no bread. "No bread?" she tittered. "Then let them eat cake." The masses hated her. She was guillotined in 1793 a few months after Louis XVI.

From Freedom to Tyranny

In 1791 the National Assembly constructed a **constitutional monarchy**, and if things had stopped there, the **French Revolution** might have resembled the English Revolution of a century earlier. But the French constitutional monarchy was undermined from two sides: from

---

THREE FRENCH GENIUSES: VOLTAIRE, MONTESQUIEU, ROUSSEAU

Three eighteenth-century thinkers—Voltaire, Montesquieu, and Rosseau—helped persuade many French, especially middle-class intellectuals, that the *ancien régime* was rotten and that a better system could be constructed. Their common weapon was reason (abstract, **Cartesian**, logical), in contrast to English thinkers, who relied on empirical reality. The French dislike reality for failing to live up to their logical constructs, an approach that lends itself to radicalism.

Voltaire (1694–1778) was the epitome of the **Enlightenment**, ridiculing everything stupid he saw, of which there was plenty. His main target was the Catholic church, which he saw as intolerant, irrational, and hypocritical. Voltaire's phrase *"Ecrasez l'infáme"* ("crush the infamous thing," meaning the Catholic church) became the founding cry of anticlericalism and spread through most Catholic countries. (But not Ireland or Poland. Any idea why?)

The Baron de Montesquieu (1689–1755) traveled all over Europe to gather material for one of the first books of comparative politics, *The Spirit of the Laws*. Montesquieu, like Voltaire, was especially impressed with English liberties, which he thought resulted from the "checks and balances" of the different parts of their government. Montesquieu was actually describing an idealized model of an English system that had already passed into history, but the American Founding Fathers read him literally. Montesquieu's book suggested that countries could more or less rationally choose their governmental institutions. The French have been choosing and discarding them ever since.

Jean-Jacques Rousseau (1712–78), who was born in Geneva but lived mostly in France, was the most complex and some say the most dangerous of these thinkers. Rousseau hypothesized man in the state of nature as free, happy, and morally good. Society corrupted man with private property, which leads to inequality and jealousy. In a famous phrase at the beginning of his book *The Social Contract*, Rousseau said: "Man is born free but everywhere he is in chains." Rousseau further hypothesized that beneath all the individual, petty viewpoints in society there is a **general will** for the common good. This could be discovered and implemented even though some people might object; they would be "forced to be free." Critics of Rousseau charge that he laid the intellectual basis for both nazism and communism because his theory provided dictators with the rationale that they "really know" what the people want and need.

The French political thinkers tended to call for major, sweeping change; English thinkers, for slow, cautious change. The French thinkers fundamentally hated their government; the English didn't.

the king and some aristocrats who wanted to restore absolute power, and from a militant faction known as the Jacobins, who wanted a radical revolution. Their cry: "*Liberté, Egalité, Fraternité!*" The king was found to be conspiring with foreign princes to invade France and restore him to full power. And the attempted invasion of 1792 helped the Jacobins take over. With a makeshift but enthusiastic citizen army—"the nation in arms"—they repelled the invaders at Valmy.

Power fell into the hands of the misnamed Committee of Public Safety under Maximilien Robespierre, a provincial lawyer and fanatic follower of Rousseau who was determined to "force men to be free." Instituting the **Reign of Terror**, Robespierre and his followers guillotined more than twenty thousand people, starting with the king, queen, and nobles but soon spreading to anyone who doubted Robespierre. Finally, in 1794, during the revolutionary calendar's month of Thermidor, Robespierre's comrades, afraid they might be next, guillotined him, and the Terror ended.

During all this turmoil, the army became the only coherent institution, especially one young artillery officer, the Corsican Napoleon Bonaparte, who had won fame leading French armies in Italy and Egypt. In 1799 a **coup d'état** overthrew the weak civilian Directory and set up a Consulate with Bonaparte as First Consul. Brilliant in both battle and civil reform, Napoleon crowned himself emperor in 1804.

Above all, Napoleon loved war. As Henry Kissinger pointed out, a revolutionary power, like France, in the midst of hostile conservative monarchies can feel secure only by conquering its neighbors. Napoleon made France master of all Europe, using dashing tactics and an enthusiastic army to crush one foe after another until at last they went too far. Facing a British-led coalition,

Key Terms

constitutional monarchy A monarchy whose powers are limited.

French Revolution 1789 popular ouster of the monarch.

Cartesian After French philosopher René Descartes; philosophical analysis based on pure reason without empirical reference.

Enlightenment Eighteenth-century philosophical movement advocating reason and tolerance.

general will Rousseau's theory of what the whole community wants.

Reign of Terror Robespierre's 1793–94 rule by guillotine.

coup d'état Military takeover of a government.

DEMOCRACY

LEFT, RIGHT, AND CENTER

The way delegates were seated in the National Assembly during and after the French Revolution gives us our terms for radical, conservative, and moderate. In a half-circle chamber, the most radical delegates, those representing the common people, were seated to the left of the speaker's rostrum, the most conservative, those representing the aristocracy, to the right. This allowed like-minded legislators to caucus and separated delegates who might start fist fights.

The precise meanings of left, right, and center have varied through the ages and from country to country. In general, however, the left favors greater equality of incomes, welfare measures, and government intervention in the economy. The right, now that it has shed its aristocratic origins, favors individual achievement and private industry. The center tries to synthesize the moderate elements in both viewpoints. Those just a little to one side or the other are called center-left or center-right.

KEY CONCEPTS

BRINTON'S THEORY OF REVOLUTION

The great Harvard historian Crane Brinton in 1938 published *The Anatomy of Revolution*, which argued that all revolutions pass through similar stages. He compared several revolutions, but his main model was the French. Brinton's stages are as follows:

- The old regime loses its governing effectiveness and legitimacy. It becomes inept and indecisive. Intellectuals especially become **alienated** from it. An improving economy provokes discontent and jealousy.
- The first stage of revolution comes with the growth of antiregime groups. Triggering the revolution is a political problem—such as whether the three estates should meet separately or together—that the old regime can't solve. Rioting breaks out, but troops sent to crush it desert to the rioters. The antiregime people easily take over power amidst popular rejoicing.
- Moderates initially seize power. They opposed the old regime, but as critics rather than as revolutionaries. They want major reform rather than total revolution. Extremists

accuse them of being weak and cowardly, and true enough, they are not ruthless enough to crush the extremists.

- Extremists take over because they are more ruthless, purposeful, and organized than moderates. In what Brinton likened to a high fever during an illness, the extremists whip revolution into a frenzy, throwing out the old, forcing people to be good, and punishing real or imagined enemies in a reign of terror. In France, this stage came with Robespierre; in Iran, with Khomeini.
- A **Thermidor**, or calming-down period, ends the reign of terror. Every revolution has a Thermidor, which Brinton likened to a convalescence after a fever, because human nature can't take the extremists and their revolutionary purity for too long. Power may then fall into the hands of a dictator who restores order but not liberty—a Napoleon.

Brinton's theory has largely stood the test of time. Revolutions do seem to pass through stages, although their timing cannot be predicted with accuracy. Iran, as we shall see, has followed the Brinton pattern.

Key Terms

tyrannical   Coercive rule, usually by one person.

plebiscite   Referendum; a mass vote for an issue rather than for a candidate.

chauvinism   After a Napoleonic soldier named Chauvin; fervent, prideful nationalism.

harassed by guerrilla warfare in Spain, and frozen in the Russian winter, Napoleon was defeated and exiled to the Mediterranean island of Elba in 1814. The next year he tried a comeback and thousands of his old soldiers rallied around him to fight at Waterloo and lose.

Napoleon left an ambiguous legacy. While he claimed to be consolidating the Revolution, he actually set up a **tyrannical** police state. Trying to embody Rousseau's elusive general will, Napoleon held several **plebiscites**, which he always won. He unleashed **chauvinism** by proclaiming France to be Europe's liberator. Napoleon was not just a historic accident, though, for we shall see similar figures emerging in French politics. When a society is badly split, as France was over the Revolution, power tends to gravitate into the hands of a savior, and democracy doesn't have a chance.

The Bourbon Restoration

Europe breathed a sigh of relief once Napoleon was packed off to a remote island in the South Atlantic and the brother of Louis XVI was restored to the French throne as Louis XVIII. In the **Bourbon** Restoration, exiles from all over Europe returned to France to claim their old rights. Many French disliked the returning Bourbons and sighed, "They learned nothing and they forgot nothing."

France was badly split. Most aristocrats hated the Revolution, while most commoners supported at least a version of it. The Catholic church was reactionary, for the Revolution had confiscated church lands and ended its tax privileges. French Catholics for generations hated the anticlericalist republicans and democrats, who in turn mistrusted the Church. Residuals of the clerical-anticlerical split persist to this day. But France had also changed quite a lot in the quarter-century since the Revolution. Parliaments now counted for something; kings could no longer rule without them. The civil reforms of Napoleon were preserved. People insisted on equality before the law.

At first the French, tired from upheaval and warfare, accepted the Bourbons. But by 1830 they proved to be as pig-headed as ever, and rioting broke out. In a semilegal switch, the liberal Duc d'Orleans, Louis-Phillipe, replaced the last Bourbon, Charles X. He too proved inept,

Key Terms

alienated Psychologically distant and hostile.

Thermidor Month when Robespierre fell; a calming down after a revolutionary high.

Bourbon French dynasty before the Revolution.

A Tale of Two Flags

The Bourbon flag had been blue and white with *fleur-de-lis* (iris). The Revolution introduced the tricolor of red, white, and blue.

The post-Napoleon restoration brought back the old flag, for the tricolor symbolized everything the Bourbons hated. In 1830, the Orleanist monarchy, to mollify revolutionary sentiment, brought back the tricolor, France's flag ever since.

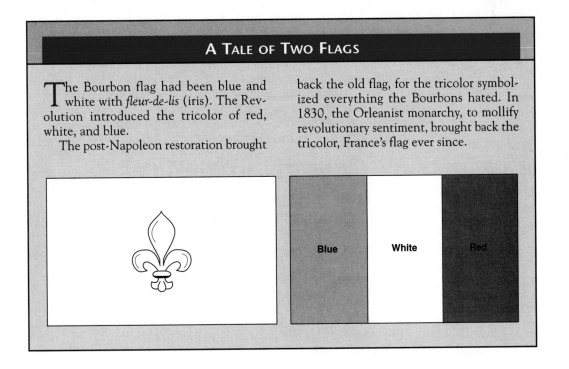

and a small uprising in that revolutionary year of 1848 brought the Second Republic. This didn't last long either.

The French have historically tended to turn from tumultuous democracy to authoritarian rule. In 1848 they overwhelmingly elected Napoleon's self-proclaimed nephew, Louis Napoleon, as president. Using plebiscites, in 1852 he turned the Second Republic into the Second Empire with himself as Emperor Napoleon III. This brought two decades of peace and progress until Louis Napoleon, in 1870, allowed himself to be goaded into war with Prussia. Bursting with overconfidence, the French were quickly trounced. The Germans surrounded Paris and shelled it daily, but there was no French government that could surrender. In Paris itself, a revolutionary takeover by common citizens brought the short-lived **Paris Commune**, which conservative French troops crushed, killing some twenty thousand Parisians. Karl Marx mistakenly saw the Commune as the first proletarian uprising, and among leftists the Commune grew into a legend of worker power.

The Third Republic

Amidst near anarchy, the **Third Republic**, France's first stable democracy, was born. Its first task was a humiliating peace with Germany that cost France the province of Alsace (which has many German-speaking people) plus a billion dollars in gold. The enraged French ached for revenge and transferred their traditional hatred of Britain to Germany.

Curiously, the accidental Third Republic turned out to be the longest-lasting French regime since the ancien régime. The Third Republic was basically fairly conservative and **bourgeois**. France was not healed during its long tenure; indeed, social tensions mounted. A **reactionary** Catholic right dreamed of an authoritarian system, while the left organized Socialist and later Communist parties. Economic and population growth was slow, and France slipped further behind the rapidly growing Germany.

Still, the Third Republic staggered through the ordeal of World War I. At first the French were delighted with a chance for revenge against Germany, but soon the appalling losses—a million and a half French lives—turned France bitter and defeatist even though it was on the winning side. France regained Alsace but had no stomach to fight again.

The defeatism played right into the hands of Nazi Germany, which swept easily through France in May–June 1940. Only one French unit fought well, a tank column commanded by an obscure colonel named de Gaulle, who had been warning for years of the need to develop a better French armored force. The French thought they could prevent a repetition of the World War I bloodshed by hiding behind the **Maginot Line**, but fixed defenses can't move; the Germans simply went around them on the north.

Key Terms

Paris Commune Takeover of Paris government by citizens during the German siege of 1870–71.

Third Republic France's democratic regime from 1871 to 1940.

bourgeois Middle-class.

reactionary Seeking to go back to old ways; extremely conservative.

Maginot Line Supposedly unbreachable French defenses facing Germany before World War II.

Vichy Nazi puppet regime that ran France during World War II.

Vichy: France Splits Again

The Germans largely let the French run occupied France. Named after the town of Vichy in central France where it was set up, the **Vichy** government was staffed by the same sort of reactionaries who earlier had reviled Dreyfus, people who hated democracy and admired

POLITICAL CULTURE

THE DREYFUS AFFAIR

Nothing better illustrates the deep division of French society in the late nineteenth century than the trial of Captain Alfred Dreyfus, a Jewish officer on the French general staff. In 1894, Dreyfus was accused of selling secrets to the Germans; he was given a rigged military trial with fake evidence and sent to Devil's Island for life. It soon became clear that Dreyfus was not the culprit and had been convicted by bigoted officers simply because he was a Jew, a handy scapegoat.

France split in two. Those defending Dreyfus—the *Dreyfusards*—felt they were defending the republican traditions of equality. These tended to be people on the left. Novelist Emile Zola published his famous letter *J'accuse!* (I accuse!), charging the government

with covering up for the military. The *Anti-Dreyfusards*—reactionary aristocrats, army officers, fanatic Catholics, and anti-Semites—grew equally passionate in defense of their prerevolutionary values. Most French people took one side or the other; there was even street fighting.

Finally, in 1906, Dreyfus was exonerated, but his trial had left deep scars. It showed how underneath the beautiful, civilized veneer of **belle époque** France lurked the primitive passions of reaction and anti-Semitism. The lesson was not lost on one Viennese journalist covering the trial. Theodore Herzl was so shocked by the anti-Semitism he had seen in France that he immediately organized a world **Zionist** movement to save Jews from what he feared would be other, similar outbursts.

---

the authoritarian Germans. The aged Marshal Pétain, hero of World War I, became chief of state, and an opportunistic politician, Pierre Laval, became premier without benefit of elections. Some French thought Vichy was an improvement over the Third Republic, which had voted the **Popular Front** into power in 1936. "Better the Nazis than the Communists," muttered Vichy supporters. French SS units fought in Russia. French police rounded up Jews for deportation to death camps. French workers volunteered to work in Germany. Although most French people today hate to admit it, many collaborated with the Germans and even liked them.

Other French, however, hated the Germans and Vichy. Some joined the **Résistance**, a loosely knit underground network that sabotaged and spied on the Germans, rescued British and American airmen, and occasionally killed collaborators. Again, France split. The Vichy period was, in the words of political scientist Stanley Hoffmann, "a Franco-French war." The Resistance attracted French people of many political persuasions, but the left predominated. The Communists, who refused to attack Germans until the 1941 invasion of Russia, became the most effective underground fighters and emerged from the war with prestige and a good organization.

The rallying point of the Resistance was Charles de Gaulle (promoted to general in the last days of the Third Republic), who broadcast from London: "France has lost a battle, but France has not lost the war!" Organizing French-speaking people around the world—

Key Terms

belle époque The "beautiful epoch"; France around 1900.

Zionism Jewish nationalist movement; founded Israel.

Popular Front Coalition government of all leftist and liberal parties in France and Spain in the 1930s.

Résistance Underground French anti-German movement of World War II.

POLITICAL CULTURE

FRANCE'S POLITICAL ERAS

The political history of France is rich and complex. Notice how conservative and radical eras approximately alternate. It is more difficult to construct such a table for British political development because it has had no drastic regime changes since the Commonwealth in the seventeenth century.

Name	Years	Remembered for
Old Regime	–1789	Absolutist monarchy; centralized administration; supervised economy.
Revolution	1789–1799	Tumultuous; repel invaders; Reign of Terror; Thermidor.
Napoleon	1799–1814	Redoes civil code; conquers most of Europe; crowns self emperor.
Bourbon Restoration	1815–1830	Try to restore monarchy in badly split France.
Orleanist	1830–1848	Liberal monarchy.
Second Republic	1848–1852	Attempted liberal republic.
Second Empire	1852–1870	Louis Napoleon's conservative stability.
Third Republic	1871–1940	Bourgeois liberal democracy.
Vichy	1940–1944	German puppet government.
Provisional Government	1944–1946	De Gaulle-led coalition.
Fourth Republic	1946–1958	Unstable, fractious, immobilized; Indochina and Algeria.
Fifth Republic	1958–	De Gaulle strong president; state-led modernization.

France had sizable colonies and thousands of able-bodied men who fled from France—de Gaulle declared a provisional government comprised of **Free French** expatriates. Participating in military action in North Africa, the Normandy landings, and the liberation of Paris in 1944, the Free French Army was of considerable help to the **Allies**. During the war de Gaulle came to think of himself as the savior of France, a modern Joan of Arc.

The Fourth Republic

From 1944 to early 1946, de Gaulle headed a provisional government. A newly elected constituent assembly, dominated by parties of the left, drafted a constitution for the **Fourth Republic** that gave great power to the legislative branch. De Gaulle opposed the new constitution and resigned with the warning that the Fourth Republic would have the same institutional weaknesses as the Third. He retired to the small town of Colombey-les-Deux-Eglises, not to return to power until the people called him back to save France again late in the next decade.

He was right about the Fourth Republic resembling the Third: From its inception the Fourth was plagued by a weak executive, a National Assembly paralyzed by small, squabbling parties, and frequent changes of cabinet. The result was, as before, **immobilisme**. Politicians played games with each other; they were good at wrecking but not at building.

Still, like the Third Republic, the Fourth might have endured had it not been for the terrible problems of **decolonization**, problems the fractious parliamentarians could not solve. The first problem was Indochina, a French colony for nearly a century, occupied by the Japanese in World War II and then reclaimed by France. War with the Communist-led Viet Minh broke out in 1946 and dragged on until the fall of the French fortress of Dienbienphu in 1954. (The United States came close to jumping into the Vietnam conflict that year but backed off.)

The **Indochina War** was bad for France, but Algeria was worse. The French had been there since 1830, at first to vanquish pirates but later to settle. Close to a million Europeans dominated Algerian economic, social, and political life; Algeria was even declared a part of France. The revolt of Algerian nationalists started in 1956 with urban terrorism. This time the French army was determined to win. They hunted down nationalists and tortured them. When the civilian politicians in Paris started opposing the Algerian War, the French army in Algeria began a coup d'état in 1958. Paratroopers were ready to drop on their own country; France tottered on the brink of civil war. At the last minute both sides agreed to call back General de Gaulle. The army assumed he would keep Algeria French. (He didn't.) De Gaulle, acting as if he had known all along that history would recall him to lead France, demanded as his price a totally new constitution, one that would cure the ills of the Fourth Republic. He got it. In the next chapter, we explore the institutions of the Fifth Republic.

Key Terms

Free French   De Gaulle's World War II government in exile.

Allies   World War II anti-German military coalition.

Fourth Republic   1946–58 French regime.

immobilisme   Inability of a government to solve big problems.

decolonization   The granting of independence to colonies.

Indochina War   The first Vietnam war, 1946–54, between French and Communist Viet Minh.

Key Terms

intendants (p. 91)   Résistance (p. 99)
Maginot Line (p. 98)   revolution (p. 93)
mercantilism (p. 92)   Russification (p. 91)
National Assembly (p. 93)   Thermidor (p. 97)
Paris Commune (p. 98)   Third Estate (p. 93)
particularism (p. 91)   Third Republic (p. 98)
plebiscite (p. 96)   tyrannical (p. 96)
Popular Front (p. 99)   Versailles (p. 92)
reactionary (p. 98)   Vichy (p. 98)
Reign of Terror (p. 95)   Zionism (p. 99)

Further Reference

Arendt, Hannah. *On Revolution*. New York: Viking, 1963.

Beevor, Antony, and Artemis Cooper. *Paris after the Liberation, 1944–49*. New York: Doubleday, 1994.

Bernier, Olivier. *Louis XIV: A Royal Life*. New York: Doubleday, 1987.

Brinton, Crane. *The Anatomy of Revolution*. New York: Vintage Books, 1965.

Burns, Michael. *Dreyfus: A Family Affair, 1789–1945*. New York: HarperCollins, 1992.

Hazareesingh, Sudhir. *Political Traditions in France*. New York: Oxford University Press, 1994.

McMillan, James F. *Dreyfus to De Gaulle: Politics and Society in France, 1898–1969*. New York: Edward Arnold, 1985.

Rousso, Henry. *The Vichy Syndrome: History and Memory in France since 1944*. Cambridge, MA: Harvard University Press, 1991.

Schama, Simon. *Citizens: A Chronicle of the French Revolution*. New York: Knopf, 1989.

Tilly, Charles. *The Contentious French*. Cambridge, MA: Harvard University Press, 1986.

Tocqueville, Alexis de. *The Old Regime and the French Revolution*. New York: Doubleday, 1955.

Weber, Eugen. *The Hollow Years: France in the 1930s*. New York: W. W. Norton, 1994.

Williams, Charles. *The Last Great Frenchman: A Life of General De Gaulle*. New York: Wiley, 1995.

Zuccotti, Susan. *The Holocaust, the French, and the Jews*. New York: Basic Books, 1993.

France:
The Key Institutions

8

Questions to Consider

1. What are the weaknesses of multiparty parliamentary systems?
2. How is the French system "semipresidential"?
3. What problem did "cohabitation" solve?
4. How does the French electoral system work?
5. What is a "technocrat"? Does the United States have any?
6. How has the French parliament been weakened?
7. What good is the French Senate? How does it compare with the U.S. Senate?
8. Compare the French and British party systems: Why are they different?
9. Is France still a highly centralized unitary system?

The British constitution grew piecemeal and has not yet been formalized into one document. French constitutions—and there have been fifteen of them since the Revolution—are all written, although often altered in practice. Americans regard their Constitution with an almost religious awe, not to be touched in its basic provisions, but the French and most other Europeans have seen constitutions come and go and are not averse to rewriting the basic rules of their political game every few decades.

By 1958, many French agreed that the Fourth Republic was inherently flawed and unable to settle the ghastly Algerian War. The chief problem, as defined by de Gaulle, lay in the weakness of the executive, the **premier**. The **president** was simply a figurehead, typical of European republics. The premier depended on unstable **coalitions**. Faced with controversial issues, one or more coalition parties would often drop out, vote against the government in a **vote of no-confidence**, and thereby bring it down. In all, there were twenty cabinets ("governments") in less than twelve years. Personal jealousies sometimes played a role; if a premier was too effective, other politicians

Key Terms

premier French for prime minister.

president An elected head of state, not necessarily powerful.

coalition Multiparty alliance to form a government.

vote of no-confidence Parliamentary vote to oust a cabinet.

sometimes voted against him out of resentment. Pierre Mendès-France, for example, settled the Indochina War in 1954, but that made him too popular and effective, so the National Assembly voted him out a few months later.

The Fourth Republic embodied all the weaknesses of a multiparty parliamentary system that still plague Italy. Such a system can work well and with stability, as in Sweden, but it depends on the party system and the national political style. Given French parties and political style, however, it is doubtful that a pure parliamentary system could ever work well.

A Semipresidential System

De Gaulle hated the executive weakness of the Fourth Republic, but neither did he like the American-style presidential system with its checks and balances that might hamper his style. So he devised what has been called a **semipresidential system**, a hybrid with both an executive president and a premier (see box on pages 106 and 107). For over a quarter-century, however, instead of some kind of balance between the powers of the president and those of the premier, the president held sway by virtue of commanding the largest bloc of votes in the National Assembly. Thus, for most of the history of the **Fifth Republic**, the system functioned as a presidential or even "superpresidential" system. Only with the parliamentary elections of 1986—which produced a conservative National Assembly while a Socialist president was still in office—did we finally see semipresidentialism in action.

Let us first examine the "old" system of the Fifth Republic, the one de Gaulle devised and commanded from 1958 to 1969. The general structure of it, of course, continues to this day, but the powers of its components have changed. The French president is elected for seven years and may be reelected without limit. Originally, the president was selected by an electoral college of parliamentarians and local office holders. De Gaulle soon discovered he wanted nothing—certainly no politicians—to stand between him and the people, so in 1962, by means of a **referendum**, he changed the constitution to provide for direct election of the president. It has been that way ever since.

The constitution specifies some powers as belonging to the president and some to the premier, but the practice was unclear. On paper, the president appoints a premier (but cannot fire him) who then selects his own cabinet. No parliamentary approval is required for this. Until 1986 the president was so assured of an obedient National Assembly that he handpicked both premier and cabinet ministers as mere helpers to carry out the president's program. The president presides at cabinet meetings. Virtually all foreign and defense affairs were in his hands (still mostly the case). The **Élysée** originated most legislation, often with the advice of ministers, and could even force the National Assembly to vote on executive proposals in a simple yes-or-no manner. The president, however, does not have the power to veto legislation. De Gaulle saw the role of president in almost mystical terms, as a "guide" and "arbiter" of the nation.

One important—and perhaps overused—power de Gaulle liked is the calling of referendums. You'll recall that such mass votes on issues are alien to British tradition but very much a part of French usage, especially by figures who believe they embody the general will and communicate directly with the people, bypassing the politicians. De Gaulle called five such plebiscites (see Chapter 10) and won each except the last. Feeling repudiated, he resigned, perhaps establishing another constitutional tradition.

Key Terms

semipresidential system System with features of both presidential and parliamentary systems.

Fifth Republic Regime devised by de Gaulle, 1958 to present.

referendum A mass vote on an issue rather than on candidates; same as *plebiscite*.

Élysée Presidential palace in Paris, equivalent to the U.S. White House.

Who Was When: The Fifth Republic's Presidents

Charles de Gaulle		1959–69, reelected in 1965, resigned in 1969
Georges Pompidou	Gaullist	1969–74, died in office
Valéry Giscard d'Estaing	UDF	1974–81, served one term
François Mitterrand	Socialist	1981–95, reelected in 1988
Jacques Chirac	Gaullist	1995–

Another potentially major power at the disposal of the French president is the ability to invoke "emergency powers" in time of danger to the nation. While many democracies have such an emergency provision, there is always the fear that it can be abused, as Hitler used Article 48 of the Weimar constitution to snuff out freedom. Article 16 of the French constitution seems to place no limits on what a president can do during an emergency, a situation that is up to the president to define. During such an emergency the National Assembly must meet, but it has no power to block presidential decisions. The emergency clause has been invoked only once—in 1961, when the same generals who put de Gaulle into power tried to overthrow him for pulling out of Algeria—and many agreed it was a genuine emergency.

The presidential paradise ended when the National Assembly elections of 1986 produced a legislature dominated by conservative parties. The problem was that President François Mitterrand, a Socialist, had two years remaining in his seven-year term. For the first time in the history of the Fifth Republic, a president did not control the National Assembly. No one could predict what was going to happen; the constitution was unclear. Some feared a hostile deadlock and paralysis of government. Others thought Mitterrand would have to resign to make way for the election of a conservative president. Instead, Mitterrand played a waiting game that preserved him as president but reduced the powers of the presidency. Mitterrand thus clarified the French constitution and set a precedent when the same situation occurred in 1993 and 1997.

In 1986 Mitterrand called on the leader of the largest conservative party (sometimes called **neo-Gaullist**), Jacques Chirac, to become premier, and went along with most of Chirac's cabinet choices. Mitterrand also did not block most of Chirac's legislative program, which rolled back many of Mitterrand's socialist experiments in the economy. The two struck an informal bargain—called **cohabitation**, living together but not married—in which Chirac concentrated on domestic affairs and Mitterrand on foreign policy. Mitterrand took a back seat and contented himself with foreign and defense affairs and the symbolic functions of the presidency. In 1993, faced with another conservative victory in parliamentary elections, Mitterrand named another neo-Gaullist, Eduard Balladur, as his premier. In 1997, faced with a Socialist victory in the early parliamentary elections he had called (see box on page 114), Chirac named Socialist chief Lionel Jospin as premier. Cohabitation had become routine; institutions evolve.

If the French want to avoid cohabitation and its uncertainties, they could cut the last link between legislative and executive branches (the "can-censure" arrow) and become a straight presidential system, U.S.-style. Some also talk about shortening the seven-year presidential term so that it matches the five-year term of the National Assembly to avoid the two lame-duck years that came at the end of each Mitterrand term. True, the U.S. system often deadlocks between the White House and Capitol Hill, but the president still has plenty of power to govern without permission from Congress.

Key Terms

neo-Gaullist Chirac's revival of the Gaullist party; the Rally for the Republic (RPR).

cohabitation Arrangement in which the French president was forced to name as premier the leader of the opposing party.

COMPARISON

PARLIAMENTARY VERSUS PRESIDENTIAL SYSTEMS

Most European governments are parliamentary; that is, they depend on votes in parliament to put a cabinet into executive power and keep it there. The cabinet is usually composed of members of parliament and can be seen as a sort of parliamentary steering committee that also guides the ministries or departments. If no party in parliament has a majority, a coalition of parties is necessary, and this may be unstable. In policy splits, a *vote of no-confidence* may oust the cabinet. Where a single party dominates the parliament—which is mostly the case in Britain—the system can be very stable.

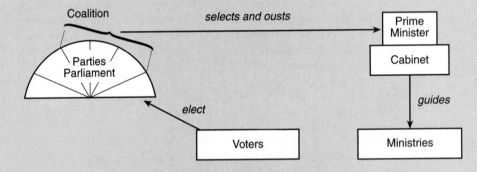

A Parliamentary System

In a presidential system, such as the United States and Brazil, the executive does not depend on parliamentary support, for here the chief executive is elected more or less directly for a fixed term. The parliament can do what it wants, but it cannot oust the president in a vote of no-confidence. (It may try to impeach the president.) The advantages of a presidential system is its stability and certainty: There will always be a president to lead. The disadvantage is that the president and the legislature may **deadlock**, producing something similar to the *immobilisme* that plagues parliamentary systems.

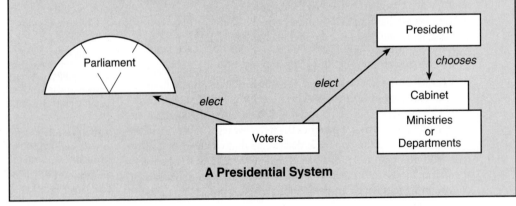

A Presidential System

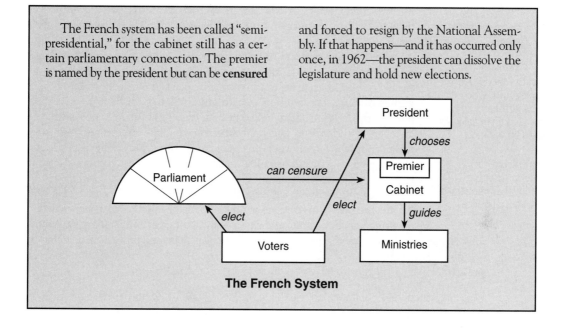

The French system has been called "semi-presidential," for the cabinet still has a certain parliamentary connection. The premier is named by the president but can be **censured** and forced to resign by the National Assembly. If that happens—and it has occurred only once, in 1962—the president can dissolve the legislature and hold new elections.

The French System

Premier and Cabinet

Until cohabitation, French ministers, including the prime minister, served as little more than messenger boys for the president. The premier's main function was to push presidential measures through parliament. Under cohabitation, however, Premiers Chirac, Balladur, and Jospin restored much of the power of that office by pursuing their own legislative agendas.

The French president chooses a premier, who in turn picks a cabinet. Chirac named fellow neo-Gaullist Alain Juppé, who had been foreign minister in the outgoing Mitterrand government, as his new premier. Ministers do not have to be approved by the National Assembly but usually are. A cabinet not to the liking of parliament could be censured and ousted. Accordingly, Socialist Mitterrand felt he had to name neo-Gaullists Chirac and Balladur, because they had majority support in parliament. This is the general basis for selecting prime ministers throughout Europe (compare with Britain, page 38, and Germany, page 182).

The president cannot directly fire a premier, but, if they are of the same party, the president may persuade the premier to resign. In 1988 Mitterrand named the bright Michel Rocard, but had him resign in 1991 when he became too obvious a rival for the leadership of the Socialist party. Then Mitterrand named the fiery Edith Cresson, France's first woman premier, a person of strong opinions but shaky leadership qualities; she served ten months until Mitterrand got her to resign. In 1992, Mitterrand named Pierre Bérégovoy, a seasoned politician but one who could not stem the Socialist slide to electoral defeat in early 1993; he lasted eleven months in office. (Under suspicion of corruption, Bérégovoy committed suicide a few weeks later.) With this setup, cohabitation actually improves a premier's tenure in office, because the president cannot use party pressure to get a resignation. During the

Key Terms

deadlock U.S. tendency of the executive and the legislature, especially when of opposing parties, to block each other.

censure Condemnation of executive by legislative vote.

Key Terms

deputy   A member of French parliament (and many other parliaments).

technocrat   An official, usually unelected, who governs by virtue of economic and financial skills rather than by winning election.

interior ministry   In Europe, department in charge of local administration and national police.

first two cohabitation periods, Mitterrand had no internal party leverage over his neo-Gaullist premiers, Chirac and Balladur, who lasted two years until new elections.

A French twist found in few other parliamentary democracies is that a **deputy** chosen to be a minister must resign his or her seat. (A replacement is elected along with each deputy, so there is no need for by-elections.) De Gaulle wanted to make sure ministers wouldn't run back to parliament to protest his policies. By the same token, unlike Britain, French ministers do not have to be members of parliament; many are experienced administrators and non-party **technocrats** who have never been elected to anything. De Gaulle picked as one of his premiers Georges Pompidou, a man who had no elected political experience (but who went on to become an effective president in his own right).

Like most European cabinets, the French cabinet can be easily remade to suit the premier. Ministries are not quite the same as U.S. departments, which are firmly fixed by statute and change only after great deliberation. Paris ministries are almost ad hoc combinations of existing French agencies and bureaus, which change according to the policy goals of the executive. The cabinet named by Premier Jospin in 1997 consisted of twenty-six persons (five of them women) for the following:

Employment and Solidarity	Youth and Sport
Justice	European Affairs
Education	Research and Technology
Interior	Overseas Departments
Foreign Affairs	Health
Economy	Cooperation (foreign aid)
Defense	Housing
Infrastructure and Transportation	Foreign Trade
Culture and Communications	Budget
Agriculture	Commerce and Trades
Environment and Land Use	Industry
Parliamentary Relations	Veterans
Government Reform and Decentralization	Tourism

In general, left-wing governments seek large and specialized cabinets since they propose major changes under government supervision. Conservative governments, on the other hand, usually like smaller cabinets, as they do not plan to remake society. Repeated changes in ministries sounds chaotic to Americans, but bear in mind that the career civil servants in the various bureaus change very little; the changes are at the very top as to who is their ultimate boss. As the French have said for decades: "*Plus ça change, plus c'est la même chose.*" (The more it changes, the more it stays the same.)

The National Assembly

During the Third and Fourth Republics the National Assembly was dominant. Making and unmaking cabinets, the parliament controlled the executive. Some say this sort of parliamentary system has a weak executive and strong legislature. That's not quite accurate. In this case the

DEMOCRACY

FRANCE'S PRESIDENTIAL ELECTION OF 1995

In the spring of 1995, after fourteen long years of Socialist President Mitterrand, France elected the neo-Gaullist mayor of Paris and leader of opposition in parliament Jacques Chirac, then 62. It was Chirac's third try; he had been beaten by Mitterrand in 1981 and 1988. French elections are held in two rounds. The first round showed the following results:

Lionel Jospin	(Socialist)	23.3%
Jacques Chirac	(Neo-Gaullist)	20.8
Eduard Balladur	(Neo-Gaullist)	18.6
Jean-Marie Le Pen	(National Front)	15.0
André Lajoinie	(Communist)	6.8

What was curious about this election is that two neo-Gaullists (who disliked each other) ran in the first round. For the second round two weeks later, all but the top two are eliminated. During this period deals are made. In this case, Balladur (who had served as premier under President Mitterrand) patched things up with party chief Jacques Chirac and urged his first-round voters to support Chirac on the second round. Its results:

Chirac	52.6%
Jospin	47.4

Newly installed President Chirac already had a big conservative majority of the National Assembly, which had held elections in 1993, so he did not need to call for new elections, as Mitterrand had done after each of his presidential victories.

legislature wasn't strong either. Divided into several quarrelsome parties that were unable to form stable coalitions, the French National Assembly was no more able to govern than were the cabinets. The government "fell" every few months on the average.

This is not quite so chaotic as it sounds. When a government in a parliamentary system "falls," it does not mean the entire structure of government collapses; indeed, little changes. It just means there has been a policy quarrel among the parties so that the cabinet coalition no longer commands a majority of the parliament. The cabinet then either resigns, is ousted in a vote of no-confidence, or limps along as a minority government. After several days or even weeks of negotiations, another cabinet is put together that wins majority approval. Often this cabinet is composed of the same ministers in the same jobs as the previous cabinet. Instead of too much change, parliamentary systems often suffer from too little. Premiers have their hands so full just keeping the coalition together that they are often unwilling to risk doing anything that might make it come apart. The result is *immobilisme*.

Meeting in the windowless **Palais Bourbon**, deputies prior to 1958 tended to play politics with each other and ignore what was happening outside. In a massive avoidance of responsibility, deputies concentrated on either getting into the cabinet or bringing it down. Things changed with the Fifth Republic; the legislators' paradise came to an abrupt end.

The National Assembly no longer makes cabinets; today that power belongs to the premier, in consultation with the president.

Key Term

Palais Bourbon Paris building of the French National Assembly.

Indeed, the relationship between the cabinet and the legislature has been deliberately weakened; as noted earlier, a deputy named to the cabinet must resign his or her seat. One link does remain: The National Assembly can censure a cabinet, indicating its extreme displeasure. The president on the other hand, can dissolve the National Assembly for new elections before the end of its normal five-year term, which is what Chirac did in 1997. The president is limited to one dissolution per year.

CHIRAC: A BRAINY GAULLIST AS PRESIDENT

In many ways, French President Jacques Chirac was the opposite of his immediate predecessor, François Mitterrand. The two, although they governed together during the 1986–88 cohabitation period, hated each other. Mitterrand, who died of cancer shortly after completing two full terms, was a left-leaning mystic. Chirac was right-leaning and governed by means of administrative and economic expertise. Mitterrand was a quiet and abstract intellectual and poet, a graduate of the Sorbonne. Chirac was an energized problem-solver, a graduate of the elite Ecole Nationale d'Administration. Mitterrand hated de Gaulle for his haughty ways during World War II; Chirac made his political career by worshipping Charles de Gaulle. Mitterrand carried on the traditional French presidential style of aloofness and distance from the public; Chirac was more of a crowd-stirring populist.

But in some ways the two antagonists resembled each other. Both were extremely brainy, the norm for French leaders. Both created their respective political parties. Mitterrand, for years a leader of small centrist parties, took over the Socialists in 1971 when they were at a low ebb and remade them into a vote-getting center-left party, with which he rode into the presidency a decade later. Chirac took over and reorganized the moribund Gaullists in 1976, turning them into the biggest right-wing party, the Rally for the Republic, often known as "neo-Gaullist." (De Gaulle left office in 1969 never having bothered to build a strong Gaullist party.)

For years, even as a leading member of the National Assembly, Chirac was also the elected mayor of Paris, something perfectly legal and normal in France. (More than half the National Assembly's deputies and most ministers are also mayors; it firms up their power base. While premier under Chirac, Juppé was elected mayor of Bordeaux.)

Chirac served as premier under center-rightist Valéry Giscard d'Estaing from 1974 to 1976, but the two parted in jealous anger over who was to be the leading figure on the French right. Chirac then served as premier under Mitterrand from 1986 to 1988, time enough for Mitterrand to get Chirac to catch the blame for economic problems and enable Mitterrand to win reelection in 1988. Another point Mitterrand and Chirac have in common: Both know how to wait, and both won the presidency on their third try.

Jacques Chirac. (French Embassy Press and Information Division)

The premier and the president, not the legislature, now hold key powers of legislation. Most bills originate with the government. The government sets the agenda. If the government specifies, its proposals must be considered without amendments on a take-it-or-leave-it basis called a "blocked vote." That is to prevent parliamentary dilution of legislation. The National Assembly no longer has the time or structure to consider legislation closely: Its sessions are limited to five and a half months a year; it has only six committees; and a bill cannot be bottled up in committee but must be reported out.

The government is able to pass many laws by simple decree, provided the premier and the president agree (and sometimes they don't). The 1958 constitution specifies the types of laws that must go through parliament; all others presumably don't need to. While most decrees concern details, the power of government decree also extends to the budget. Here, the legislature has lost its original, most fundamental, power—the power of the purse. Any parliamentary motion to either decrease revenues (a tax cut) or increase spending (a new program) are automatically out of order. And if the parliament can't settle on the budget within seventy days, the government may make it law by simple decree.

A Senate That Fights Back

Most parliaments are composed of two chambers, and most don't know what to do with the upper chamber. Sweden simply abolished its upper house. The greatest value of an upper house is in representing territorial subunits, as the U.S. Senate represents the states. Where the system is unitary (Britain, France, Sweden) rather than federal (the United States, Germany, Russia, Brazil) an upper chamber doesn't have much use.

COMPARISON

THE ISRAELI PARLIAMENTARY SYSTEM

Israel to some extent followed in France's footsteps. Both had a weak executive dependent on a shaky coalition of parties elected by proportional representation. Both modified their systems. De Gaulle ended the Fourth Republic's parliamentary system and founded the Fifth's semipresidential one. Israel stayed purely parliamentary until recently.

Israel's single house, the 120-member Knesset, is elected by proportional representation, a system that permits any party that wins at least 1.5 percent of the national vote to have at least a few seats in parliament. (It used to be only 1 percent.) Israel has a dozen or more parties—some based on a single personality—none of them having a majority in parliament. Thus every Israeli government has been a coalition and prone to breakup when the parties in it quarreled. Israel too suffered immobilism in the face of major problems.

Taking a turn to semipresidentialism, Israel for the first time directly elected its prime minister in 1996 by popular vote. This was designed to bring greater stability to Israel's chief executive, but that is not necessarily the case, because the new, directly elected prime minister is still responsible to parliament and can still be ousted on a vote of no-confidence.

France's main legislative body, comparable to the British House of Commons, is also the lower house, the 577-member National Assembly elected every five years (or sooner if the president wishes it). The upper house, the *Sénat*, has 316 members elected for nine years each—with elections for about a third every three years—by a gigantic electoral college made up of National Assembly deputies plus more than 100,000 regional and municipal councilors. De Gaulle thought that these councilors, because they would disproportionately represent rural and small-town France, would produce a conservative Senate amenable to Gaullist direction.

Rural and small-town France is not necessarily conservative; it looks out for farming. Above all, the *Sénat* represents farmers' viewpoints; it has been called the agricultural chamber. The French Senate has criticized and amended numerous government bills. *Sénateurs* aren't under pressure like lower-house assembly members to pass what the government wants. The French Senate is listened to by the government on farm matters, for when French farmers get mad they can create havoc. Still, when the government wants a measure passed, it can override Senate objections by a simple majority in the National Assembly.

The French Senate, although not equal in power to the National Assembly, cannot be dissolved by the government. Apparently, de Gaulle came to regret that he had allowed the Senate an autonomous existence, for in 1969 he tried to dilute its power by means of another plebiscite. The French people, annoyed by de Gaulle, supported their Senate, the last area of French parliamentary freedom, and rejected the referendum.

The French Multiparty System

Parties can make or break a political system. Britain's stability and efficiency would diminish if instead of one party with a solid majority in Commons there were half a dozen parties of about equal size. Much of what was wrong with the Third and Fourth Republics was not government institutions but the parties that tried to operate them.

We must avoid evaluating all two-party systems as good and all multiparty systems as bad. Americans especially are disdainful of multiparty systems and often cite Italy and the Fourth Republic as examples of the ills they create. But several multiparty parliamentary democracies with institutions not too different from Italy's and the Fourth Republic's are stable and effective, for example, Sweden, Switzerland, Holland, and Belgium. At least as much depends on the way the parties behave as on how many parties there are.

By the same token, the Fifth French Republic wouldn't have worked the way it did had not the Gaullist party ballooned into the largest of all French parties. Indeed, if the Fourth Republic had been preserved but with Gaullists occupying the largest slice of the National Assembly, the most troublesome problem of that system—*immobilisme*—would have disappeared, for de Gaulle would have had a stable majority at his disposal.

France has at present three large parties and three small ones, plus a sprinkling of minor parties. The Socialists (PS) occupy the center-left and for most of the 1980s were the largest party. But two parties allied in 1986, 1993, and 1995—the center-right Union for French Democracy (UDF) and the farther-right neo-Gaullists (RPR)—to win a majority of parliament and then the presidency. Flanking the large parties are the Communists on the left and the racist National Front on the right. Fitting in somewhere on the left, the Greens finally got into the National Assembly in 1997. (For more on French parties, see Chapter 10).

France's Electoral System

French legislative elections come every five years (or sooner in case the president wishes it), presidential elections every seven years (or sooner if the president resigns or dies). Legislative and presidential elections were intended to be deliberately out of kilter. President Mitterrand solved this problem following his elections in both 1981 and 1988 by immediately dissolving the National Assembly so that his Socialists could increase their number of seats.

The traditional electoral system of the Fifth Republic—single-member districts with runoff—is actually taken from the Third Republic. Like the British and American systems, the French use single-member districts. But unlike the Anglo-American systems, where a simple plurality is all that's required to win (FPTP), the French victor needs a majority (more than 50 percent). If the candidate doesn't get it on the first ballot—and that is usually the case—the contest goes to a runoff a week later, this time with candidates that got under 12.5 percent of the district's registered voters eliminated and only a simple plurality needed to win. The second round, then, is the decisive one; the first round is the functional equivalent of the U.S. primaries.

For the 1986 parliamentary elections, however, the Mitterrand government, as they had long promised, reverted to **proportional representation** (PR), which had also been used by the Fourth Republic. Instead of single-member districts with runoffs, the PR system used multimember districts and only one round. Voters cast a ballot for a party, not an individual, and seats were awarded according to the percentage won by each party. In Europe generally, parties of the left favor PR, arguing that it is inherently fairer and gives adequate representation to the parties of the poor and working class. Critics charged Mitterrand with changing the rules to favor his Socialist party, which did somewhat better under PR than with single-member districts. They pointed out that PR enabled the extremist **National Front** to obtain seats in the National Assembly; under single-member districts it wins few or none. Inadvertently, Socialists aided racists. The 1986 experiment in PR was short-lived, and France returned to single-member districts with runoffs. Presidential elections are played out under similar rules. All but the top two candidates for president are eliminated in the first round; a second round two weeks later decides between the top two (see box on page 109).

The French system permits or encourages several parties to exist; the Anglo-American systems frankly discourage third parties. Unlike proportional representation, the French (like the British) system penalizes small parties. In Germany, for example, a Green vote of over 5 percent wins them dozens of seats. Some have suggested that adoption of the one-round English-style FPTP would help the French reduce the number of their parties by forcing smaller parties to amalgamate with larger ones. But the French party system is rooted in French society, and this is a more complex and fragmented society than the British or American. The French have several parties because they need them, and any attempt to reduce them to two might lead to two big extremist parties rather than two big moderate parties. In any case, the French party system seems to be coalescing into two large blocs, one left and one right. Over the decades, there have been fewer and fewer relevant parties in France.

The Constitutional Council

In the 1980s, a little-noticed branch of the French government started taking on a life of its own: the Constitutional Council. Although it was part of the 1958 constitution, it came into its own as a buffer

Key Terms

proportional representation   Electoral system that assigns parliamentary seats in proportion to party vote.

National Front   French anti-immigrant party.

DEMOCRACY

FRANCE'S PARLIAMENTARY ELECTIONS OF 1997

In France, as in Britain, parliament can go up to five years between elections, but the chief executive (as in most of Europe and in Canada) can call elections early. This President Chirac did, with great damage to himself. The parliamentary elections of 1993 had given Chirac's supporters (his own RPR and the allied UDF) 80 percent of the National Assembly. And Chirac had ten months before elections were scheduled.

Chirac called **snap elections** because he was in trouble. Although Chirac had won the presidential election in 1995 (see earlier box on page 109), he quickly became unpopular. His promises to lower unemployment (at a postwar high of 12.8 percent), cut taxes (which ate 45 percent of France's GDP), and bring down France's budgetary deficit (in order to join the planned euro currency) were contradictory and impossible. In trying to implement them, his premier, Alain Juppé, grew even more unpopular. Chirac's big parliamentary majority splintered, and Chirac figured he'd lose big if elections were held in 1998 but might squeak through if elections were held earlier. He erred.

Many RPR and UDF candidates ran against Chirac's policies, as did the Socialists, who promised to create 700,000 new jobs (half of them in the public sector) by reducing the work week from 39 to 35 hours for the same pay (a dubious notion advanced earlier by the German Social Democrats). All promised no new taxes.

The ruling RPR and UDF, compared to the first round of the 1993 elections, lost in the first round of the 1997 National Assembly elections held May 25, 1997.

	1993	1997
Rally for the Republic (RPR, neo-Gaullist)	20.4%	15.7%
Union for French Democracy (UDF)	19.1	14.2
Socialists (and allies)	20.3	25.0
National Front	12.4	14.9
Communists	9.2	9.9
Greens and Ecology	7.6	3.2

A few candidates won actual majorities in their districts, and they were declared winners immediately. In almost all districts, however, voters had to go to a runoff a week later. Candidates who had polled less than 12.5 percent of their district's registered voters in the first round were dropped. In most districts weaker candidates also withdrew and endorsed the candidate who most matched their preferences. For example, by prearrangement among the two large conservative parties, an RPR candidate who scored lower would withdraw and urge his supporters in the first round to vote for the better-scoring UDF candidate in the second round.

Hoping to save the center-right coalition, Premier Juppé resigned between the two rounds, but the Socialists still won nearly a majority of seats in the runoff a week later. Still a few seats short, the Socialists formed a coalition with the Communists and Greens in a cabinet headed by Lionel Jospin, and that gave the left a majority in parliament. Compared to the 1993 results, here are the second-round percentages of vote from June 1, 1997, and number of seats:

	1993		1997	
RPR (neo-Gaullists)	28.3%	257	23.7%	140
Union for French Democracy (UDF)	25.8	215	21.0	108
Socialists (and allies)	28.3	57	38.9	246
National Front	5.7	0	5.6	1
Communists	4.6	23	3.8	37
Greens	—	0	1.6	8
Others	4.0	25	5.5	37

The racist National Front won a seat for the first time since 1988 (when it also won one seat). The real loser of the 1997 elections was Chirac's policy of budgetary austerity aimed at joining the euro. Although Jospin pledged to go with the euro, he dropped the austerity policy.

between Mitterrand and the conservative-dominated parliament during his two cohabitation periods. Some started comparing it to the U.S. Supreme Court. The comparison is shaky.

- Both have nine members, but the French serve for nine years, not for life. Three members of the French court are appointed each by the president, the speaker of the National Assembly, and the speaker of the Senate.
- The French Council members are rarely lawyers and see their role as political rather than legal. The U.S. Supreme Court sees its role the other way around.
- The scope of the French Council is much more limited. It can review the constitutionality of laws only after they've been passed by parliament but before they've been signed by the president. It considers cases not from lower courts but on demand by the executive or any sixty members of either chamber of parliament.
- Rather than establishing legal precedents as the U.S. Supreme Court does, the French Constitutional Council has acted as a brake against hasty and ill-considered legislation. As such, the ruling parties in France tend to dislike its decisions while the opposition parties often like them.
- In 1999 the head of the Constitutional Court had to step down over allegations that he had siphoned off vast sums from a giant state-owned oil company he had earlier headed. This did the Court's reputation no good.

The role and powers of the U.S. Supreme Court are unique. Some French thinkers would like to see their council become more like the U.S. Supreme Court. The German Federal Constitutional Court is one of the few that approach the Supreme Court in importance.

Key Terms

snap election   An election called on short notice, ahead of schedule.

unitary system   System in which power is centralized in capital, and component areas have little or no autonomy.

first-order civil division The main units countries are divided into, such as departments in France.

prefect   French *préfet*; administrator of a department.

Midi   French for "noon"; the South of France.

département   Department; French first-order civil division, equivalent to British county.

GEOGRAPHY

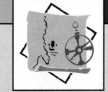

DECENTRALIZING UNITARY SYSTEMS

The way a state is organized territorially, its "civil divisions" and their relationship to the capital, can heighten center-periphery tensions. There is no sure-fire formula for calming such tensions. Basically, there are two approaches, **unitary** and federal. More than Britain, France is an example of the unitary system, a carry-over from monarchical times, whereby the **first-order civil divisions**—counties in Britain, departments in France, prefectures in Japan—have little autonomy and serve mostly as administrative conveniences for the national capital.

These units can be changed and their boundaries redrawn with little ado. The leading executives in these civil divisions are appointed and supervised by the national government. France's **prefects** are perhaps the best examples of how the unitary state rules. There are elected county, departmental, and municipal councils, but their powers to tax and spend are limited. Any major project must be cleared with and usually funded by the national authorities. Most countries in the world are unitary systems. (U.S. states, although they look like federal systems, are actually unitary.)

A unitary system gives greater control to the center for rational administration and modernization. Standards can be enforced nationally. Central administration can knead disparate groups into a single nationality, as France has done over the centuries. The unitary system is generally best suited to a country like Japan that is not too large or does not contain different cultures and languages.

One difficulty with unitary systems is that they may ride roughshod over the wishes and feelings of local people, especially those at the periphery. Crushing the **Midi** left behind centuries of resentment. Many of today's *méridionaux* (southerners) deliberately cultivate their distinct accent and regard themselves as

a race separate from the haughty northerners. Thus instead of dampening center-periphery tensions, a unitary system may preserve them. Corsican and Breton violence testifies to the failure of complete integration of France's regional subcultures into a French whole.

Further, a unitary system, by virtue of its uniformity, can be overly rigid and make big, nationwide mistakes that in a federal system would be implemented and corrected piecemeal, as the components tried various policies. Often there is too much national control over purely local, even trivial issues. Even small matters such as a new traffic light might have to be approved by Paris or Tokyo.

Britain, France, and Spain in recent years have moved to correct some of the inflexibility of their unitary systems by instituting regional autonomy. Britain has devolved some home rule to Scotland, Wales, and Northern Ireland. France's twenty-two regions and Spain's seventeen *autonomías* now have elected councils with considerable decision-making powers on economic growth, education, housing, and other regional concerns. Although not nearly federalism, it would be fair to say that these unitary systems have moved in a somewhat federal direction.

The change in France under Mitterrand is particularly striking, for it rolled back a tradition that started with Louis XI. French monarchs tried to erase regional differences but sometimes only worsened local resentments. Napoleon perfected this centralizing and homogenizing pattern. He abolished the historic provinces and replaced them with smaller, artificial units called **départements** named after rivers. The departments were administrative conveniences to facilitate control by Paris.

Each department—there are now ninety-six (plus five for overseas territories)—is administered by a prefect, a lineal descendant of Richelieu's old intendant, now an official of the Interior Ministry. Prefects, very bright and highly trained, monitored laws, funds, and mayors with Olympian detachment.

In 1982, Mitterrand got a law that reduced the domain of prefects and increased local autonomy. Elected councils in the departments and regions won policy-setting and taxation powers in education, urban and regional planning and development, job training, and housing. French local and regional government became more important, and elections to their councils were hotly contested. Competition set in as cities, departments, and regions sought to attract new industries. Local taxes increased, but the ways of assessing them became widely divergent and innovative.

The subnational units of French government started acting somewhat like U.S. states, developing their own strategies for prosperity. France in no sense became a federal system, but its decentralization was Mitterrand's most important and lasting contribution to the French political system.

Key Terms

censure (p. 107)

coalition (p. 103)

cohabitation (p. 105)

deadlock (p. 107)

département (p. 115)

deputy (p. 108)

Élysée (p. 104)

Fifth Republic (p. 104)

first-order civil division (p. 115)

interior ministry (p. 108)

Midi (p. 115)

National Front (p. 113)

neo-Gaullist (p. 105)

Palais Bourbon (p. 109)

prefect (p. 115)

premier (p. 103)

president (p. 103)

proportional representation (p. 113)

referendum (p. 104)

semipresidential system (p. 104)

snap election (p. 115)

technocrat (p. 108)

unitary system (p. 115)

vote of no-confidence (p. 103)

Further Reference

Cole, Alistair, and Peter Campbell. *French Electoral Systems*, 3rd ed. Brookfield, VT: Gower, 1989.

Gaffney, John, and Lorna Milne, eds. *French Presidentialism and the Election of 1995*. Brookfield, VT: Ashgate, 1997.

Lewis-Beck, Michael, ed. *How France Votes*. New York: Chatham House, 2000.

Loughlin, John, and Sonia Mazeyln, eds. *The End of the French Unitary State? Ten Years of Regionalization in France 1982–1992*. Portland, OR: Frank Cass, 1995.

Poulard, Jean V. "The French Double Executive and the Experience of Cohabitation." *Political Science Quarterly* 105 (summer 1990): 2.

Safran, William. *The French Polity*, 5th ed. New York: Longman, 1998.

Schmidt, Vivien A. *Democratizing France: The Political and Administrative History of Decentralization*. New York: Cambridge University Press, 1991.

Stevens, Anne. *The Government and Politics of France*, 2nd ed. New York: St. Martin's, 1996.

Stone, Alec. *The Birth of Judicial Review in France: The Constitutional Council in Comparative Perspective*. New York: Oxford University Press, 1992.

Thody, Philip. *The Fifth French Republic: Presidents, Politics and Personalities*. New York: Routledge, 1998.

French Political Culture

9

Questions to Consider

1. Describe the split nature of French political culture.
2. What is statism? Is it still found in Europe?
3. What was the slogan of the French Revolution?
4. What is anticlericalism? Where else is it found?
5. What would be the typical education path into the French elite?
6. What is the ENA and why is it important?
7. How do presidential press conferences show differences of political culture?
8. What happened to Marxism in France?

wo Parisian families I knew during the Bicentennial of the French Revolution in 1989 illustrate the deeply divided nature of French society. One couple, although not university-educated, were bright and hard-working and had turned their small suburban house into a tidy and pleasant home. They read the conservative daily *Le Figaro* and the Catholic weekly *La Voix*. They did not like the current Socialist government. When they entered a church, they crossed themselves. They showed little interest in celebrating the Bicentennial July 14 and cautioned me about the crowds in Paris. They suggested a picnic in the countryside instead.

The other family were typical Parisian intellectuals, both university-educated, inhabiting a charming, book-strewn older apartment not far from one of Paris's great boulevards. They read the leftish *Le Monde* and were indifferent to religion. They liked the current Socialist government. They urged me to join the street festivities the night before July 14 and then try to catch the spectacular parade. They thought the French Revolution was really something worth celebrating.

There, in miniature, was conservative France and radical France, the former indifferent or even a little hostile to the French Revolution, the latter enthusiastically in favor of it. The split created by the French Revolution continues to this day, although in subdued form. Conservative France no longer battles radical France; rather, the two preserve a chilly distance.

Both families deeply love France, but they love different facets of France. France has a

mystique, a kind of drawing power that can equally attract conservatives such as de Gaulle and Socialists such as Mitterrand. The conservatives are drawn to French civilization, its Catholic roots, and its
grandeur (greatness). Liberals and leftists, on the other hand, are drawn
to the ideals of the French Revolution—liberty, equality, fraternity—
and see France as the repository of these ideals. Some French envision
their land as a person, a princess, or even a Madonna. They have a rev-
erence for their country that few Americans or Britons can match.
The dramatic and stirring "**La Marseillaise**" (see box on page 120),
gives one a sense of the depth of French patriotism.

Key Terms

"**La Marseillaise**"   French national anthem.
omnipotent   All-powerful.
statism   The idea that a strong government should run things, especially major industries.

French patriotism in the abstract, however, does not carry over into the real, grubby, daily
life of French politics. The French are usually far more cynical about politics than Britons or
Americans. Some describe the French as the world's greatest complainers: Nothing works right;
all governments are crooked. France in the abstract is glorious; France in the here and now is
shabby. This is why de Gaulle said France needs national greatness, for only with a vision of
something great can French people rise above the sordid reality and pursue the mythical ideal.

Mitterrand was elected in part because of his ability to project an idealistic vision of France
with a leftist twist. "It is natural for a great nation to have great ambitions," he proclaimed. "In
today's world, can there be a loftier duty for our country than to achieve a new alliance between
socialism and liberty?" The French liked the sentiment, but once Mitterrand was in power
they grew quickly disillusioned with the reality.

Historical Roots of French Attitudes

Where did this French political schizophrenia come from? Part of the problem is historical,
traceable to the centralization of French kings, who implanted an **omnipotent** state, a state that
tried to supervise everything. In theory, a centralized system should be capable of planning and
building rationally. In practice, it often falls short of the goal. The French, trained to expect a
powerful government to help them (the ideal), are always disappointed when it doesn't (the real).

French **statism** also stunted the development of a voluntary, do-it-ourselves attitude,
something taken for granted in the United States. France simply has no tradition of voluntary

---

GEOGRAPHY

SAILING THE MEDITERRANEAN

On your luxury yacht, you are sailing in a great, clockwise circle around the Mediterranean Sea, always keeping the shore a few kilometers to port (left, for you landlubbers).
You enter through the Strait of Gibraltar.

Which countries do you pass one after another on your left?

Spain, France, Italy, Slovenia, Croatia, Bosnia (minute shoreline), Croatia again,
Montenegro (part of rump Yugoslavia), Al-
bania, Greece, Turkey, Syria, Lebanon, Israel,
Egypt, Libya, Tunisia, Algeria, and Morocco.

POLITICAL CULTURE

"LA MARSEILLAISE"

Possibly the world's greatest national anthem is the French "Marseillaise." Dashed off in a single night in 1792 by a 32-year-old army officer, Rouget de Lisle, to accompany volunteers from Marseille headed north to defend the Revolution, the "Marseillaise" soon became the Revolution's, and then France's, anthem.

Extremely stirring and bloodthirsty, it is the perfect song for fighting for a nation. The refrain:

*Aux armes, citoyens, formez vos
    bataillons!
Marchons! Marchons!*

Qu'un sang impur abreuve nos sillons!
(To arms, citizens, form your
    battalions!
We march! We march!
Until [the enemy's] impure blood
    overflows our furrows!)

If you've never heard it sung, catch the movie *Casablanca* on late-night television. Like the French flag, the "Marseillaise" became a controversial political symbol. Part of the Revolution, it was banned by Napoleon and the Bourbons, accepted by the liberal Orleans monarch in 1830, banned again by Napoleon III, and made the national anthem in 1879. In a split society, nothing is simple.

groups of neighbors undertaking local governance. When local groups take responsibility and something goes wrong, you can only blame yourselves. In France, with all responsibility, until recently, in the hands of the central government, people blame Paris.

Centuries of **bureaucratized** administration also left the French used to living by uniform, impersonal rules—and lots of them. This creates hatred, the hatred of the little citizen on one side of the counter facing the cold, indifferent bureaucrat on the other.

Centralization and bureaucratization are the products of the "order and reason" approach to governance that has been practiced in France for centuries. Order and reason, unfortunately, are mere ideals. Since they are always deficient in practice, the French become unhappy with a reality that always falls short of ideals.

A Climate of Mistrust

In personal relations, French people are sometimes distant and mistrustful to people outside their family. Indeed, attitudes of mistrust are widespread throughout Latin Europe—they are extremely pronounced in Italy—while trustful attitudes are more common in North Europe. American scholar Laurence Wylie found villagers in the Vaucluse, in the south of France, constantly suspicious of *les autres*, "the others," those outsiders who talk behind your back, blacken your name, and meddle in your affairs. The best way to live, people there agreed, was not to get involved with other people and to maintain only correct but distant relations with neighbors. With modernization, such extreme mistrust has receded.

Key Term

bureaucratized Heavily controlled by civil servants.

French philosopher and playwright Jean-Paul Sartre voiced a very French feeling about interpersonal relationships when he wrote, "*L'enfer, c'est les autres*" (Hell is other people). He meant, in his play *No Exit*, that having to get along with other people was his idea of hell.

Foreigners notice how shut off the French family is. Typical French houses are surrounded by high walls often topped by broken glass set in concrete. Shutters aren't just for decoration; they bang shut as if to tell the world to mind its own business. Traditionally, French people rarely entertained at home—they'd go to a restaurant instead; inviting outsiders to your table was an invasion of family privacy. This has changed, however; I have been invited into several French homes for superb meals.

Special mistrust is reserved for the government. In Wylie's village it was taken for granted that all government is bad, a necessary evil at best. The duties of a good citizen, which schoolchildren memorize in their civics course, are mere ideals, but in the real world, government is corrupt, intrusive, and ineffective. French children learn to love **la patrie** in the abstract but to disdain politics in the here and now. Politics are also best kept private and personal; discussing politics with others only leads to arguments. Besides, it's none of their business.

Key Terms

patrie French for fatherland.

culmination Logical outcome or end.

POLITICAL CULTURE

HOW TO CELEBRATE A 200-YEAR-OLD REVOLUTION

The French Revolution was still a divisive political issue in 1989. Even choosing the official historian for the Bicentennial was a political problem. Conservative historians called the Revolution a giant mistake, the root of France's subsequent troubles. Such viewpoints anger the left and were hardly a way to celebrate the Bicentennial. Radical or leftist historians, on the other hand, read into the Revolution the harbinger of all things good and of the Bolshevik Revolution in Russia. This was hardly acceptable to conservative France.

In François Furet the Mitterrand government found their historian: a former Marxist who had turned away from radicalism to produce a moderate and sober synthesis with something for everyone. Furet finds nothing wrong with the revolutionary ideals of *liberté, egalité, fraternité*, but he argued that with the collapse of the monarchy and takeover of the revolution by extremists, the revolution had to "skid out of control" (*dérapage*). It was not just evil or foolish people that caused the revolution to skid out of control, Furet argues, but the logic of revolutions themselves. Furet's thinking parallels that of Crane Brinton, discussed in Chapter 7.

A change in the current political context enabled Furet and other French intellectuals to accept this troubling analysis of the French Revolution. For decades, many French intellectuals naively celebrated the 1917 Russian Revolution as a continuation of the French Revolution. With the erosion of French leftism and decay of Soviet communism, French intellectuals saw that the Bolshevik Revolution had been a mistake. But if 1917 was the **culmination** of 1789, then logically the French Revolution itself must have been badly flawed. The new attitude about communism forced the French to reevaluate their own revolution.

The Nasty Split

Catholic countries have a serious problem that Protestant (and Eastern Orthodox) countries don't have to worry about: the role of the Church. When Britain and Sweden broke with Rome and established national churches, they also subordinated churchmen to the state. The Anglican church in Britain and the Lutheran church in Sweden depended strictly on London and Stockholm, respectively, for support; they could not turn to Rome. As a result, in these societies the Church no longer played an independent political role.

In Latin European countries—France, Italy, Spain—the Roman Catholic faith retained its political power, supporting conservative regimes and getting special privileges, such as control of education, tax exemption for church lands, and a considerable say in government policy. Because of this temporal power, many people in Latin Europe developed anticlerical attitudes. Their most brilliant spokesman was Voltaire (see Chapter 7). Anticlericalism was not necessarily antireligion; it rather sought to get the church out of government, what Americans call the separation of church and state.

Anticlericalism spread in Latin Europe, especially among intellectuals. After the French Revolution and Italian unification (in mid-nineteenth century), many people wanted a purely secular state, that is, one with no church influence in government. That was easy to do in America, where there was no single established church, but it was hard in France, Italy, and Spain, where church and state were intertwined. To separate them required drastic surgery: sale of church lands, banning of some Catholic orders (such as the Jesuits), and state rather than church control of schools. The reaction to this was predictable. Just as the Republic was anticlerical, the church turned anti-Republic. Church sentiment went from conservative to reactionary, and the Roman Catholic faith became a pillar of monarchical restoration because that meant a return of church privileges.

KEY CONCEPTS

THE PERSISTENCE OF RELIGION

The first ballot of the 1981 French presidential election provides a graphic illustration of how religion is still part of politics in France.

The two leading candidates were Socialist François Mitterrand on the left and Republican Valéry Giscard d'Estaing on the right. A poll showed the more religious were also the more conservative.

Attend Mass	Mitterrand	Giscard d'Estaing
Weekly	8%	48%
2 or 3 times a month	17	34
Less often	20	27
Never	24	16

Source: IFOP survey reproduced in Howard R. Penniman, ed., *France at the Polls, 1981 and 1986: Three National Elections* (Durham, NC: AEI/Duke University Press, 1988), p. 161.

COMPARISON

FRENCH AND AMERICAN PARTY IDENTIFICATION

Philip E. Converse and Georges Dupeux, in a famous if somewhat old study, compared French and American party identification. What they found was startling. Most Americans were able to quickly identify which party they preferred; most French people could not. Where did this difference come from? Converse and Dupeux also found that 76 percent of Americans could name their father's party while only 25 percent of the French could even specify their father's general political tendency (left or right). Many French respondents reported that their fathers had never talked about politics.

The Converse-Dupeux study illustrated that in French families, politics was not a fit topic for conversation. This lack of political guidance from the old generation to the young contributed to political confusion in France; for example, the rapid shift in votes between parties and the quick rise and fall of protest parties. People who have not been socialized by their family toward one party or another are like ships without anchors, easily moved from one party to another.

In this way conservative France retained its Catholic viewpoint, while revolutionary France became strongly anticlerical. The battle raged for more than a century. At one point the Vatican instructed faithful Catholics to steer clear of any political involvement with the "Jacobin" Republic. During the Dreyfus affair, French clericalists and anticlericalists lined up on opposing sides. Finally, in 1905, the National Assembly completed the separation of church and state; France no longer had an established church. Until this century, to be in favor of the Republic meant to be anticlerical. The great premier during World War I, Georges Clemenceau—*le tigre*—was a passionate republican and supporter of Dreyfus. He recalled how his father used to tell him, "There's only one thing worse than a bad priest—and that's a good one."

The parties of the French left (Socialist and Communist) still draw mostly anticlerical supporters. The parties of the right (Gaullist and UDF) attract mostly pro-church supporters. In all of Latin Europe—Italy, Spain, and Portugal, as well as France—how often a person goes to Mass usually predicts his or her vote; strongly Catholic usually means politically conservative.

Some 90 percent of French babies are baptized into the Catholic faith, but less than 10 percent of French people regularly attend Mass. The great battles between clericalists and anticlericalists have subsided, but some issues can reawaken the old quarrel. The abortion controversy and question of state control of Church schools can still stir protest in the streets of Paris. Once established, social and political cleavages have tremendous staying power.

School for Grinds

Another contributor to French political culture is schooling. The curriculum was set generations ago and is changed only slowly and reluctantly. Heavy on rote memorization, French education tends to produce diligent grinds rather than lively intellects. Even small children lug home briefcases bulging with books. A "good" child is one who puts in long homework hours.

POLITICAL CULTURE

THE INSTABILITY OF SPLIT SOCIETIES

Unlike the stable and settled countries of North Europe, such as Britain and Sweden, the countries of Latin Europe continued to experience political upheavals well into the twentieth century. In France, Italy, and Spain, regimes have tended to be personal creations (for example, those of de Gaulle, Mussolini, and Franco) that end or change with the demise of their creator.

The underlying factor in this instability seems to be the split quality of French, Italian, and Spanish political culture that is rooted in their histories. Roughly half the population of each country is Catholic and conservative and favors strong executive leadership; the other half is anticlerical and liberal or radical and favors a strong parliament. The center is small; people in Latin Europe historically tended to identify with either the left or right camp, each severely mistrusting the other.

When the right was in power—historically, most of the time—the left denounced the government with shrill Marxist rhetoric as the tool of capitalists. When the left was in power, the right denounced them as dangerous incompetents, possibly serving Moscow's interests. At any given time, roughly half the country regarded the government as illegitimate, and this stunted feelings of legitimacy about government in general. In Latin Europe, few take pride in their nation's governmental institutions.

In the absence of shared values and underlying consensus, political difficulties can lead to violence, coups, and even civil war, which in turn leads to authoritarian rule. In the 1930s, Spain split into left and right camps and exploded into a vicious civil war won by the Catholic and conservative forces of General Franco. Disgruntled rightists in the Spanish military attempted a coup as recently as 1981. Portugal had a coup in 1974. In 1958 France very nearly had a military coup. In opposition, François Mitterrand referred to the Gaullist constitution as a "permanent coup." (In office, he found that the powers it gave him as president really weren't so bad.)

Until recently, everywhere in the country French children learned the same thing, as established by the Ministry of Education in Paris, with no local input. One legendary story has it that some decades ago an education minister looked at his watch and told an interviewer what Latin verb was being conjugated all over France. Since then, the French school curriculum has become less centralized and less classical.

The curious thing about the standardized, memorized French education, however, is its deeply humanistic and individualistic content. Outwardly, French schoolchildren appear to be mechanically digesting the inflexible, unimaginative curriculum; inwardly, they are exposed to ideas that would be banned in many American schools. This tension between outward conformity and inward freedom gives rise to **privatistic** attitudes and occasional eruptions of rebellion. It encourages young French people to keep their thoughts to themselves. In this way, a set, rigid educational pattern may actually contribute to French individualism.

The French pride themselves on the equality of educational opportunity that their system offers. "No English-style private schools for the rich here," they seem to say, "With us, everybody has the same chance." This picture is not

Key Term

privatistic   Tending to purely private and family concerns.

quite accurate. While the French school system on paper is open to all, the lofty content of French education is tilted toward the children of middle- and upper-class homes. Working-class and peasant children, not exposed at home to correct speech—and the French are maniacs about their language—or abstract, intellectual thoughts, begin school at a disadvantage and are often discouraged from staying in school beyond age sixteen.

The great gateway to social, economic, and political power in France is the **lycée**. Napoleon developed lycées to train army officers. Most lycées are state-run. Admission is competitive, and the curriculum is demanding. Not all communities have lycées, which are concentrated in cities. A successful student completes the lycée with an examination at age 18 and gets a **baccalauréat**, which entitles the student to university admission. Now, as the result of government policy to upgrade French educational levels, more than half of French young people earn the "*bac*," but they still tend to be from middle-class families.

Key Terms

lycée   French academic high school.

baccalauréat   Exam by which French finish high school.

grande école   French for "great school"; an elite, specialized institution of higher education.

The "Great Schools"

Just as Oxford and Cambridge tower over other English universities, the **grandes écoles** dominate French higher education. French universities, which stress the "impractical" liberal arts, have long been regarded as unimportant. To get into a French university is not hard; indeed, so many have flooded the lecture halls that standards have dropped and graduates have trouble getting jobs. Altogether, some 45 percent of French twenty- to twenty-four-year-olds are in full-time education, the highest percentage in Europe and comparable to the United States.

But few make it to one of the "Great Schools." Skimming off the brightest and most motivated few by means of rigorous entrance exams, the schools train (rather than "educate") French youths in the practical matters of running a country and then place them in top civil-service and managerial positions. The Great Schools form the people who run France. No other country has anything quite like them. It would be as if West Point produced not army

---

HOW WOULD YOU DO ON THE "BAC"?

In about twelve hours of nationwide essay exams spread over a week, France's seventeen- or eighteen-year old lycéens face questions like the following, taken from the philosophy section of a recent baccalauréat exam. How would you do? Choose one. Spend no more than two hours.

Why defend the weak?
Comment on Rousseau's declaration that "one must have societies where inequality is not too great, where the tyranny of opinion is moderated and where voluptuousness reigns more than vanity."
What is it to judge?
Is it reasonable to love?

French students now get their choice of bac exams. Some are scientific or technical; the most prestigious is math. The French government is trying to move students from the humanities to technology.

THE UNITED STATES AND FRANCE: A LOVE-HATE RELATIONSHIP

The French have contradictory attitudes toward America. At times, anti-Americanism seems to be a part of French political culture. Many French, especially intellectual and political elites, dislike the United States, its compassionless capitalism, its lack of culture, and its global **hegemony**. The United States has become a *"hyperpuissance"* (hyperpower) that tries to remake the world in its own image. But France, they say, will go its own way, based on its own traditions and culture. Millions of ordinary French people, however, like America and happily flock to U.S.-made movies and cheer American bicycling champions.

What's eating the French elites? First, they look back to the time when French power, language, and culture dominated Europe and much of the world. They resent being replaced by U.S. power and English. De Gaulle, angered at not being treated as an equal by Roosevelt and Churchill during the war, led France on nationalistic and anti-U.S. paths.

France, not the United States, was to lead Europe. Many French, especially in the Foreign Ministry, still follow this design.

French elites do all they can to hold back the tide of Americanization. They outlaw English words (*"franglais"*). They limit the number of U.S. movies and TV shows. They reject a totally free market and cling to state ownership and supervision.

The French try to retain their Frenchness, much as the Japanese try to retain their Japaneseness. Neither are completely successful. Little by little, French ways resemble American ways, *"le business à l'américaine"* (an example of franglais). The international economy requires it; much business is now global and conducted in English. French firms buy American firms and vice-versa. Some French Great Schools now offer English-language MBAs. Some French think they are fighting American cultural domination, but they are really fighting modernization.

officers but leading administrators. Some denounce the *grandes écoles* as elitist and undemocratic, but few suggest abolishing them. Indeed, their stranglehold on French leadership seems to grow stronger.

Although there are several Great Schools, three are politically the most important. The *Ecole Polytechnique* was used by Napoleon to train military engineers. Called X for short, *xiens* have their pick of technology and management jobs when they graduate. The *Ecole Normale Supérieure*, founded by Napoleon to create loyal lycée instructors, still produces many of France's leading intellectuals—among its graduates have been Jean-Paul Sartre, Raymond Aron, and President Georges Pompidou. The newest Great School, founded by de Gaulle in 1945, is the *Ecole Nationale d'Administration* (ENA), which quickly became the most important. Many of the country's top civil servants are "enarchs," as they call themselves.

Like all Great Schools, the ENA is extremely selective. Entrance is slanted in favor of the best graduates of the *Institut d'Etudes Politiques* in Paris, a university-level school, which itself is hard to get into. This in effect screens out persons of working-class origin who haven't gone to a top lycée. For the ENA, typically, fewer than one in ten passes the legendary written and oral exams to join the entering class of about a hundred. Once in, ENA students get monthly stipends to cover their living. About half of their twenty-seven months is spent interning in government ministries. Upon graduation, rewards are great. At age twenty-five, the average ENA

Key Term

hegemony Being the top or commanding power.

graduate obtains a high position in government, diplomatic service, or private business and banking. About one-third of France's prefects and ambassadors are ENA graduates. All cabinets are dominated by enarchs. President Chirac ('59) and Premier Jospin ('65) graduated ENA, which has a near-lock on France's political elite.

Training in a Great School epitomizes the best and worst of French education. You have to be very smart and hard-working, but you also have to be cold, logical, and removed from ordinary people. Products of the *grandes écoles* may be brilliant, but they often lack common sense and humanity. Some critics call them, pejoratively, "technocrats," people who rule by technical criteria. The perfect (negative) example is Alain Juppé, a brilliant ENA graduate ('72) and Chirac's first premier, whose cold, technocratic leadership made him the most unpopular premier of the Fifth Republic and the biggest single cause of his party's setback in the 1997 parliamentary elections.

The Fear of "Face to Face"

Whatever the educational institution—lycée, university, or Great School—the teaching style is similar: cold, distant, uninvolved. Class discussion is discouraged. Questions are from the instructor, not the students. When I taught at the University of Toulouse, I was determined to

GEOGRAPHY

THE PERSISTENCE OF REGION

In 1936 the leftist Popular Front won in the shaded départements (map left). In 1981, Socialist François Mitterrand won the presidency with a very similar pattern (map right). Region, as well as social class and religion, often produces distinct and durable voting patterns.

1936: Popular Front Vote

1981: Mitterand Vote

Key Term

compartmentalization
Mentally separating and
isolating problems.

break this pattern; I urged and demanded that my students ask questions and participate in discussion. The result was stony silence; what I requested was totally outside the experience of French students.

By the time they are teenagers, French adolescents have picked up one of the basic characteristics of French culture, what sociologist Michel Crozier called "*l'horreur du face-à-face*." Aside from family and intimate friends, French people feel uncomfortable with warm, cozy, face-to-face relationships. Sometimes tourists say the French are unfriendly to foreigners. They really aren't; they are simply reserved and formal to everyone, including other French people. The French style is opposite that of the American, which places a premium on informality and friendliness. In the United States everyone is supposed to be outgoing, call others by their first names, smile, and say, "Have a nice day." Such behavior—much of it shallow—boggles the French mind.

To avoid face-to-face relationships, the French prefer a highly structured system with clear but very limited areas of competence and set, impersonal rules. That way people know exactly where they stand and nobody butts into another's private domain. British-style pragmatism and "muddling through" are definitely not the French style either.

Freedom or Authority?

The points discussed so far—lack of trust, fear of face-to-face relationships, rigid and rote education—all contribute to a French political personality that can't make up its mind whether it wants freedom or authority. Actually, it wants both, the abstract *liberté* extolled by philosophers and the controlled hierarchies built for centuries by French bureaucrats. What happens is **compartmentalization**: The private French person loves freedom, while the public French person—in school, on the job, facing the bureaucracy—knows he or she needs reason, order, and formal, impersonal rules. A typical French person has been described as an anarchist who secretly admires the police but could equally be a policeman who secretly admires the anarchists.

The result of this mental split is a continual longing for freedom and a perfect society but an equal tendency to surrender to authority and a highly imperfect society. The balance is unstable; from time to time the quest for liberty bursts out, as in 1789, 1830, 1848, the Paris Commune of 1871, and the Events of May of 1968. We will explore this pattern more fully in the next chapter, but it is interesting to note that each of these outbursts ended with a surrender to authority. French political culture has been described as limited authoritarianism accompanied by potential insurrection. When they vote, some French say half in jest, "The heart is on the left, but the billfold is on the right."

Legitimacy in France is weaker than in Britain. Rather than a strong feeling of the rightness of institutions and authority, some French accord their system only half-hearted support. A few, on the extreme left and right, hate it.

Social Class

As is Britain, France is a class society. The gap between French working and middle class is one of the biggest in Europe and—with the educational system slanted in favor of middle-class children—social mobility is not what it could be. In France, as in Britain, if you're born into the working class you'll probably stay there. Distribution of income in France is more unequal than in Britain or even Spain. The rich live superbly in France; the poor scrape by.

Comparison

French and American Press Conferences

A French presidential press conference offers a quick insight into French political style. A rare event—maybe once or twice a year—the press conference takes place in an imposing salon of the Elysée Palace, the French White House. The president is seated. On the wall behind him is either a brocade or tapestry. In keeping with the elegant setting, the president is attired in a conservative suit and plain tie.

The journalists sit quietly taking notes. The president expounds abstractly on progress, national greatness, reason, and order, like a professor giving a lecture. He speaks beautiful French, slowly and clearly, with utter confidence and literate, witty phrases, for he is the product of an elite education. Then, if there's time, the president takes a few questions from the reporters. The questions are polite, even timid, for no one dares try to trip up or embarrass the president. The president in return treats the journalists like small children who do not understand the logic and clarity of his policies. The president is, in keeping with French political style, magisterial, rational, and very much in command.

The American presidential press conference, held more frequently, takes place against a White House corridor. The president stands at a lectern. He is wearing an indifferent suit and striped tie. The president is nervous and ill-at-ease, for he knows that the newspeople are out to get him, just as they have been out to get every president. As they see it, that's their job. He offers a few opening remarks in an almost defensive tone to explain his recent actions. Then, with a forced smile, he throws the conference open to questions from the floor. The journalists descend like a wolf pack, clawing at the air with their upraised hands, each one demanding attention.

The newsperson called upon—often by name, as the president wants to show he cares about them personally—gives a little lecture setting the background for his or her question. The question itself—on how the president's policies contradict themselves or on a sexual scandal—is hostile in tone, trying to catch the president in an uncomfortable situation. The president replies in stammering, ungrammatical English, for he is the product of an American college. The president, in keeping with the democratic American style, tries to treat the journalists as friends and equals, but his smile and handshakes as he leaves can scarcely conceal his adversarial relationship with the media.

Class differences tend to reinforce other cleavages in French society—clerical-anticlerical, urban-rural, radical-conservative, even to a certain extent North-South. That is, these factors tend to line up on one side—never perfectly, of course—but enough to produce a left-right split in French voting. Very broadly, here are the typical characteristics of French voters for the left and the right:

Left Voter	*Right Voter*
Working class	Middle class
Anticlerical	Pro-church
Urban	Rural or small town

GEOGRAPHY

"EVERY COUNTRY HAS A SOUTH"

Much truth is contained in this old saw. Except for very small countries, the south of most lands in the northern hemisphere is poor and less developed than the north. Industry has tended to cluster in the north of England, France, Germany, Italy, Spain, and the United States. People in the south of these countries are often described as fun-loving but slow and lazy. The northern people are often described as efficient and hard-working. The south usually votes differently from the north. People of the *Midi* describe themselves as a different, Mediterranean race that doesn't like the cold and germanic northern French.

The picture breaks down when you go too far north; development in the Scandinavian countries and Russia generally centers on the temperate areas and avoids the frozen north. And in the southern hemisphere, nearly the reverse is true, for there the more southerly areas are more temperate. Why should political and economic growth be more closely associated with temperate or even slightly chilly zones? Is it climate or culture? Does the former give rise to the latter?

The Great Calming Down

French intellectuals, some of them from the same *grandes écoles* as the governing elite, were for a long generation attracted to Marxism. Observing the huge gap between the ideal of equality and the reality of gross inequality, many educated and middle-class French turned to Marxist explanations and sometimes to membership in the Communist party. Philosopher Jean-Paul Sartre backed every leftist cause he could find and urged other intellectuals to become likewise *engagé*. Another *normalien*, his adversary Raymond Aron, disparaged Marxism as "the opium of the intellectuals," a play on Marx's famous statement that "religion is the opium of the masses."

Under Mitterrand, if not before, this changed. French intellectuals became disillusioned with Marxism, communism, and traditional leftist positions. There seem to be several reasons for this major shift, which has long-term implications for French political life. A new generation of French intellectuals scathingly criticized the Soviet Union and communism. In the early 1980s, many West German intellectuals turned anti-American over how to deal with the Soviets and especially over the stationing of new U.S. missiles on German soil. There is no love lost between French and German intellectuals, and the French were happy to repudiate what they regarded as naive German pacifism. The Soviet-approved coup in Poland by a Polish general in late 1981 chillingly reminded many French of the takeover of France by Marshal Pétain in the service of Germany during World War II.

But most important, with the election of a Socialist government in 1981, the left was in power. It was one thing to criticize a conservative government but quite another to run a government yourself. French intellectuals and leftists saw how difficult it was to improve the economy, assume a role in world affairs, and transform French society. Clever slogans do not translate into effective policy, and many French intellectuals became middle-of-the-roaders. Some celebrated free-market capitalism, a strange position for French intellectuals. The Mitterrand presidency contributed a lot by freeing French society from the allure of leftist ideology and guiding it to a middle-of-the-road pragmatism. French politics became centrist, a bit like American politics. With the onset of the Bicentennial, much of the passion that earlier surrounded the French Revolution seemed to go out of it. French politics entered into what might be termed "the great calming down" of de-ideologized pragmatism. As François Furet put it, "The Revolution is over." Most French people seemed to agree.

DEMOCRACY

THE FRENCH TURN CENTRIST

The real winner of recent French elections has been neither the left nor the right but the center. Observers referred to the "normalization" of French political life and a healing of the great split in French society. Politicians of the left and right tended to move to the center. Gone are the old ideological visions; moderation and pragmatism are now fashionable.

Underscoring this was a 1992 poll that asked Frenchmen to place themselves on a nine-point ideological scale, ranging from extreme left to extreme right. The results are not too different from Britain (page 57) and Germany (page 209): Most people are centrist. French politicians are thus on notice: Any party or candidate perceived as too far left or right will lose. This helps explain the miserable showing of the Communists. Once this lesson sinks in, France may turn into a "two-plus"-party system, like many other industrialized democracies.

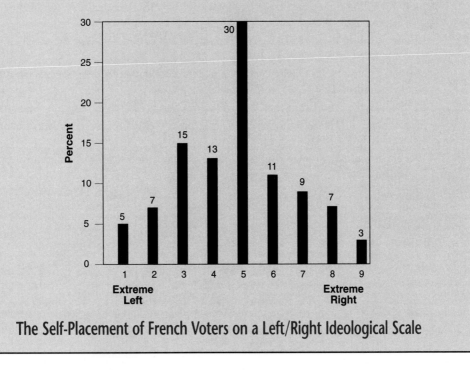

The Self-Placement of French Voters on a Left/Right Ideological Scale

Key Terms

baccalauréat (p. 125)   "La Marseillaise" (p. 119)
bureaucratized (p. 120)   lycée (p. 125)
compartmentalization (p. 128)   omnipotent (p. 119)
culmination (p. 121)   patrie (p. 121)
grande école (p. 125)   privatistic (p. 124)
hegemony (p. 126)   statism (p. 119)

Further Reference

Bernstein, Richard. *Fragile Glory: A Portrait of France and the French.* New York: Alfred A. Knopf, 1990.

Converse, Philip E., and George Dupeux. "Politicization of the Electorate in France and the United States," *Public Opinion Quarterly* 1 (spring 1962).

Crozier, Michel. *The Bureaucratic Phenomenon.* Chicago, IL: University of Chicago Press, 1964.

Ehrmann, Henry W., and Martin Schain. *Politics in France,* 5th ed. New York: Harper-Collins, 1992.

Judt, Tony. *Past Imperfect: French Intellectuals, 1944–56.* Berkeley, CA: University of California Press, 1993.

Khilnani, Sunil. *Arguing Revolution: The Intellectual Left in Post-War France.* New Haven, CT: Yale University Press, 1994.

Mahoney, Daniel J. *De Gaulle: Statesmanship, Grandeur, and Modern Democracy.* Westport, CT: Praeger, 1996.

Reader, Keith A. *Intellectuals and the Left in France since 1968.* New York: St. Martin's, 1986.

Singer, Daniel. *Is Socialism Doomed? The Meaning of Mitterrand.* New York: Oxford University Press, 1988.

Weber, Eugen. *My France: Politics, Culture, Myth.* Cambridge, MA: Harvard University Press, 1991.

Wylie, Laurence. *Village in the Vaucluse.* Cambridge, MA: Harvard University Press, 1957.

France: Patterns of Interaction

10

Party image and voter identification with parties are less developed in France than in Britain. Many French voters do not have long-term party preferences, and French parties tend to come and go and change their names, blurring their images. The result is a large number of voters not firmly attached to one party, who shift parties from one election to another. In most of West Europe, elections show only small swings of a few points from the previous contest. In France, new parties sometimes rise and fall within a few years. French parties may gain ten to twenty percentage points from their previous showing. French voting can be **volatile**.

Few French parties haven't changed their names at one time or another. Founded in 1905, the Socialists originally called themselves the French Section of the Workers International, or SFIO. In 1969, merging with some smaller left groups, they changed the name to the *Parti Socialiste* (PS). In 1981, the PS under Mitterrand won both the presidency and the National Assembly. It again became the largest party in parliament in 1997, but still less than majority.

The Gaullists seemed to have a new name for each election. From 1947 to 1952 they called themselves the Rally of the French People (RPF). With de Gaulle's coming to power in 1958, it became the Union for the New Republic (UNR), then in 1967 the Democratic Union for the Fifth Republic (UDV^e), in 1968 the Union for the

Key Term

volatile   Rises and falls quickly.

Defense of the Republic (UDR), in 1971 the Union of Democrats for the Republic (with the same initials, UDR), and in 1976 the Rally for the Republic (RPR). Jacques Chirac, who founded and headed the RPR, was elected president in 1995.

The French center is unusually messy, possibly because many figures strive for prominence and do not like to merge into one party. The Union for French Democracy (*Union pour la Démocratie Française*, UDF), now one of the three largest parties, began as a parliamentary grouping in 1962 and first ran in elections in 1966 as the Republicans. In 1974 its leader, Valéry Giscard D'Estaing, was elected president and later merged several small centrist parties with the Republicans to form the UDF, a loose federation of five center-right parties. In 1998, the Republicans, now renamed Liberal Democracy, split from the UDF.

One French party does not play around with name changes, the Communists (PCF), although they too have trouble with their party's image. The Communists plunged from 25 percent of the French vote in 1972 to only 10 percent in 1997. On the other side of the spectrum, the National Front emerged in 1986 as the party of racial hatred. To make things even more confusing, left parties often run jointly as the Union of the Left or Common Program (Socialist and Communist), and right parties as the Majority or Alliance (Gaullists and UDF).

The Emerging Party System

The French party system is not as complex as it used to be; it is down from ten parties in 1958 to four or five relevant ones today. Smaller parties have been dropping out, and larger ones are consolidating and forming into two **blocs**—one left and one right. Schematically it looks like this:

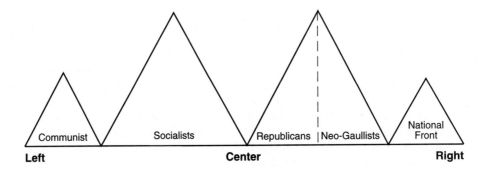

The two blocks are by no means internally harmonious. As we shall see, the Communists are always feuding with the Socialists and the Republicans constantly striving for the predominance with the Gaullists. If they can help it, none of the other parties wants anything to do with the racist National Front. In terms of voter appeal, however, the two blocs fit into two great French tendencies of which we spoke earlier. The left favors ways to make people more equal, by taxing the rich, controlling or nationalizing some industries, and continuing extensive welfare benefits. The right also claims to be for change, but much more cautiously, based on capitalistic economic growth and modest reforms. The National Front wants expulsion of North African immigrants.

The Socialists and the Communists

In most countries, Socialist and Communist parties have been natural enemies ever since the Communists followed Lenin's command and broke away from the Socialists shortly after World War I. Typically, when one is strong the other is weak. Britain, Sweden, Germany, and Spain all have large socialist-type parties and small Communist parties. In Italy, on the other hand, a large Communist party—now renamed the Democratic Party of the Left—overshadows the Socialists. In France it used to be that way, but during the 1970s and 1980s the Socialists grew and the Communists shrank, so that now the PS is the largest left party in France.

The two parties have common roots. In fact, the PCF is a 1920 offshoot of the Socialists. In a battle that has raged throughout the twentieth century, the Communists claim that the Socialists aren't militant enough, that they have abandoned revolutionary Marxism to settle for gradual, pragmatic reformism. Since its founding, the PCF had been faithful to Moscow. As was the case worldwide, the Communists didn't join in the Resistance until Germany attacked the Soviet Union in 1941. Since Stalin's time, however, the PCF had been gradually becoming more moderate. It denounced the 1968 Soviet invasion of Czechoslovakia and claimed to favor the moderate path of **Eurocommunism**. French voters can't trust the Communists, though, for old **Stalinist** tendencies reappear—as when the party expels a dissenting intellectual, lays down a dogmatic line, or stabs fellow leftists in the back.

The result is an unstable alliance of Socialists and Communists. The two parties hate each other but know they need each other. The second round, or runoff, of a French election places a great premium on combining parties, for in the French runoff a simple plurality wins. If the Communists and Socialists ran separately on the second ballot they would always lose to the combined Gaullists and Republicans. Accordingly, the left parties—the PS, PCF, and sometimes leftist splinter groups—generally support the strongest left candidate, regardless of party, on the second ballot. It is the French electoral system that drives two rivals on the French left together.

Their alliance, or misalliance, seldom lasts, however. The Communists are disciplined and doctrinaire, always citing the "correct" Marxist interpretation of events. The Socialists are loose and sloppy, home to a wide variety of people ranging from Marxists to moderate Social Democrats who do not oppose a market economy. The PS even permits the organization of factions within its ranks, something no Communist party ever allows.

The two parties speak to different electorates. The Communists concentrate on the urban proletariat; some of their greatest strength is in the industrial "Red belt" around Paris. The Socialists typically try to reach the more middle-class civil servants and skilled workers; they have been called "the party of schoolteachers." The leadership of the PS is composed almost completely of intellectuals; that of the PCF is heavily working class.

The Fractured Right

Most countries have one large party on the right; France has at least three. Some trace the division of the French right back to the Revolution, which led to (1) an ultraconservative monarchist right, (2) a moderate Orleanist right, and (3) a populist Napoleonic right. Today, these three strands are represented by the (1) National Front (FN), (2) UDF, and (3) Gaullists (RPR).

Key Terms

Eurocommunism Move in the 1970s by Italian Communists away from Stalinism and toward democracy.

Stalinist Brutal central control over a Communist party.

THE FRENCH LEFT: SMOTHER THY BROTHER

When François Mitterrand took over the shrunken and demoralized Socialist party in 1971, it was overshadowed on the French left by the Communists, who regularly won a fifth of the vote. Given France's peculiar electoral system—single-member districts with runoff—Mitterrand knew the PS couldn't grow on its own. He also knew that a good third of the Communist vote was not from committed Communists; it was a **protest vote** that could be won over by an attractive Socialist party. His plan was to embrace the Communists, use them, win away their lukewarm supporters, and then discard them. He did that, and it worked.

In 1972 the PS and PCF worked out their Common Program, spelling out what they would do in power: some nationalization of banks and industry, wage increases, and more welfare funding. They agreed to support each other in the second round of parliamentary and presidential balloting. The Socialist vote grew, in part at the expense of the Communists. Many French on the left and center didn't trust the Communists but found Mitterrand and the reinvigorated PS attractive. By 1977 the PCF was getting worried and sabotaged the Common Program by making it more radical—something the Socialists refused to go along with. This effectively lost the 1978 National Assembly elections for the left, even though public-opinion polls foresaw them beating the Gaullist and Republican "majority."

But it was too late for the PCF to dominate the left; the PS was bigger, and the Communists were discredited for wrecking Common Program and for applauding the Soviet invasion of Afghanistan. In 1981 they went into the first round of the presidential elections denouncing the Socialists, but fared so poorly—they lost a quarter of their vote—that they meekly supported Mitterrand on the second round. Mitterrand had them where he wanted them: junior partners on whom he depended not at all, for the Socialists held an absolute majority of the National Assembly. Why then did Mitterrand bring the PCF into his cabinet with four rather minor ministries?

The United States was upset with this move that brought Communists into a West European government; Vice President Bush went to Paris to protest. He needn't have worried; Mitterrand knew what he was doing. The Communists in the cabinet (1) kept them from criticizing the government, (2) held down strikes by the largest, Communist-led union, and (3) humiliated the PCF by making it follow Mitterrand's policies, which included a pro-American tilt to build Western defenses against the Soviets. In 1984 a shrunken, demoralized PCF left the cabinet and has done poorly in elections ever since. The crafty Mitterrand had destroyed them.

The current Alliance consists of the Gaullists, UDF, and newly independent Liberal Democracy, which peeled away from the UDF in 1997 in a Thatcherite direction. The UDF itself is a loose coalition of five smaller parties. Further right, outside of the Alliance, the National Front and some small groups spit venom at immigrants and the European Union.

For the right, ideology and doctrine are less important than personality. Gaullists traditionally have been skeptical of European unity and the free market, while most UDF parties have been for them. But in speaking to the same middle-class electorate, the UDF and Gaullists often cooperate so closely they agree on a single parliamentary candidate on the first ballot.

Key Term

protest vote   Ballot cast against the existing regime.

For a while, it looked like the two parties would merge, and a big majority of their voters think they should. But merger never happened and likely won't because on the right—and this is true of many countries—personality becomes the dominant issue.

Here, the shadow of de Gaulle still looms. The French right is torn between those who want to keep his image alive and those who favor more traditional center-right politics. De Gaulle, a Napoleonic figure above parties, never aimed at founding a political party. Like Franco, Mussolini, and Latin American military dictators, de Gaulle hated parties, blaming their incessant squabbles for all the troubles of the Third and Fourth Republics. De Gaulle didn't even much care for the Gaullist party; he never formally headed or endorsed it. His attitude seemed to be: "All right, if you must, go ahead and worship me." During his long reign (1958–69), the Gaullist party was simply a tool for his control of the National Assembly. In the legislative elections of 1968, the Gaullists won 46 percent of the popular vote and an outright majority of National Assembly seats.

A single charismatic figure leading a national movement is a tough act to follow. A charismatic leader doesn't tolerate other important personalities around him; he prefers obedient servants and yes-men. As a result, when de Gaulle departed in 1969, he left a vacuum that no one in the Gaullist party could really fill. His former premier, Georges Pompidou, won the presidency that year, but by the time Pompidou died in 1974, the Republican candidate, Valéry Giscard d'Estaing (who later formed the UDF), was more attractive than the Gaullist candidate. Because de Gaulle disdained parties, he never bothered institutionalizing his movement into a durable party. The real genius in politics is the one who builds lastingly; de Gaulle didn't.

Trying to fill the vacuum, Jacques Chirac in 1976 reorganized the moribund Gaullists into the Rally for the Republic, commonly called the "neo-Gaullists." A slick performer who alienated many French people by his high-handedness, Chirac alternately quarreled and made up with the UDF. Pushed into a less-active role when he was forced to cohabit with a Socialist cabinet after his 1997 snap-election debacle, Chirac gave up party leadership. In 1999, Michèle Alliot-Marie, was elected head of the RPR, the first woman to lead a major party in France. A law professor and former minister for sport, Alliot-Marie had her hands full to hold together the splintering neo-Gaullists, some of whom deserted it to form rival parties. Her big task: find new, vote-getting policies for Gaullism, a label most French consider **passé**, a vaguely conservative mood rather than a party.

Key Term

passé Outmoded; receded into the past.

The relationship of the French right parties is similar to that of the French left parties: The electoral system makes sure they compete with each other on the first round but need each other on the second round. The difference on the right is that the hatred is largely personal, a struggle between bright, ambitious party leaders who want to be president. Current UDF chief François Léotard and Liberal Democracy leader Alain Madelin are examples. Just plain jealousy plays a role. If parties merge, it means the leaders of one party become second fiddle, something most politicians do not like. Before you condemn French politicians as unusually petty and jealous, ask yourself if American politicians are much different.

Some observers fear that if the RPR and UDF do not merge and come up with an attractive, modern program, the National Front will grow into the largest party on the right. The good news here is that the FN itself split over personal rivalry. The Front's leader Jean-Marie Le Pen in 1998 expelled brainy Bruno Mégret (who has a master's degree from Berkeley), who took some of the FN with him. In France, everything fragments.

MITTERRAND SKUNKS CHIRAC

President Mitterrand, losing his Socialist majority in parliament in 1986, amazingly turned the loss to his advantage. He had to name his political archenemy, Neo-Gaullist leader Jacques Chirac, as premier. Now all the dirty work fell to Chirac, especially difficult problems of economic growth and unemployment. Mitterrand, by giving up day-to-day political tasks to Chirac, re-

gained popularity while Chirac's popularity plummeted. Mitterrand's old image of the "tranquil force" served him well as the Olympian president above the fray, and after a year he was the most popular political figure in France. All agreed that Mitterrand, simply by staying quiet and dignified, had skunked the energetic but effusive Chirac.

The Stalemate Cycle

French politics seems to run in a roughly cyclical pattern. "Normal" politics in France usually means a stalemate in which political groups, constantly feuding among themselves, block major change. This is punctuated every generation or two by an explosion, a crisis the stalemated system can't handle. To get out of the fix, the French people have repeatedly turned to a hero, a charismatic figure who hasn't been sullied by "status quo" politics. French politics seems to require a Napoleon from time to time.

After a dozen years of revolutionary turmoil, France welcomed the first Napoleon as a hero who would end chaos. Half a century later, they turned to Louis Napoleon for the same reason. In 1940 the French parliament actually voted dictatorial powers for the aged Marshal Pétain. Pierre Mendès-France was the thinking-person's hero in 1954 when he got France out of Indochina, but he lacked the charisma of the outsider who is above ordinary politics. That figure arrived in 1958 in the person of de Gaulle, who saved France from civil war over Algeria.

De Gaulle believed he had put an end to France's recurrent stalemates and crises by constructing a Fifth Republic with a strong president. But did the Fifth Republic really transcend French history? At first it appeared to. France withdrew from the Algerian tragedy, streamlined its party system, and surged ahead economically. In 1968, however, all hell broke loose (see box on page 139), and people began to wonder if the Fifth Republic wasn't suffering from some of the same ills that had plagued predecessors.

Mitterrand also found that the transformation of French politics was not as complete as de Gaulle believed. De Gaulle's personal popularity ensured not only his election as president but a large Gaullist party in the National Assembly. This made it easy to govern; any law or budget de Gaulle wanted was rubberstamped in the Palais Bourbon. The Fifth Republic did not depend on the unstable coalitions of the Third and Fourth in order to govern. But how much did it depend on the same party maintaining control of both the executive and legislative branches?

France found out in 1986. With the election of a National Assembly dominated by the Republicans and Gaullists, Mitterrand named a conservative as premier but stayed on as president. Cohabitation (see Chapter 8) kept the government functioning, but only because Mitterrand consented to letting Premier

Key Terms

Events of May Euphemism for the riots and upheaval of May 1968.

CRS Republican Security Companies; French riot police.

Chirac pretty much have his way in naming ministers and pursuing conservative policies. Mitterrand played a waiting game, letting Chirac take the blame for unpopular policies. After some time, when Mitterrand's popularity eclipsed Chirac's, Mitterrand began to oppose some of Chirac's policies. A U.S.-style deadlock emerged as neither the president nor the premier could get his way. Chirac controlled parliament, but Mitterrand could denounce his legislative program and criticize him personally. The second cohabitation period was somewhat more relaxed as Mitterrand, probably aware he was dying, attempted to do little. The third

POLITICAL CULTURE

THE EVENTS OF MAY 1968

Just ten years after the near civil war over Algeria that brought de Gaulle into office, his regime suffered another explosion almost as powerful, the **Events of May**. A month of student and worker strikes and battles with police revealed that under the law-and-order surface of Gaullist France throbbed the old revolutionary tradition. The great split that had plagued France for generations had not completely healed; the cleavage still ran through French society like an earthquake fault line in California, ready to crack open without warning.

Trouble began at the University of Nanterre in a suburb of Paris. Students—fed up with overcrowded facilities, a rigid curriculum, and complete lack of student input—staged a strike. The students' immediate grievances were real and specific. But the strike spread like wildfire because it also appealed to the revolutionary dreams of left-wing students. Soon, most universities in France were occupied by students playing at revolution. Slogans went up on campus walls: "Be realistic, demand the impossible." "I am a Marxist—of the Groucho tendency." For the students, the Events of May was a cross between the Paris Commune and Woodstock.

It wasn't quite so funny when the student protests spread to workers. With some seven million workers on strike, France virtually shut down. Workers' complaints were more

concrete: low wages and long hours. In several occupied factories, workers put up the red flag. Lycéens and professional employees joined in the strike. The Communist reaction to all this illustrates how far the party had come from its revolutionary origins. The PCF and its CGT trade union opposed the strikes! Fearing a loss of their dominant position on the French left, the Communists denounced the strikers as adventurers who thought they could change society overnight. In some respects the Communists had become a conservative force in French politics, antileft leftists.

The police waded into protesters with tear gas and truncheons. The paramilitary **CRS** (*Compagnies Républicains de Sécurité*) seemed to enjoy cracking student skulls. De Gaulle quietly conferred with the French army stationed in Germany, and troops and tanks could be seen around Paris.

But then the revolution—if that's what it was—burned out, like many previous uprisings in French history. De Gaulle went on television with soothing words; he had heard the demand for more participation and would submit himself to the voters' approval in a referendum. De Gaulle changed his mind about a plebiscite and held parliamentary elections instead. The 1968 elections showed, once again, that only part of France was revolutionary, for a majority of the voters supported conservative candidates; Gaullists won an actual majority of seats in the National Assembly.

cohabitation period, which opened in 1997 with Chirac naming Jospin premier, worked smoothly. The economy improved, and the public gave Chirac high approval ratings. But they gave even higher ratings to Premier Jospin, who hoped to win the next presidential election.

Referendum Madness

One technique French leaders revert to is the plebiscite or referendum. This poses major questions directly to the people without going through elected representatives in parliament. The referendum, almost unknown in Britain, has been used eighteen times since 1793 in France. It fits neatly into a very French tradition: Rousseau's idea of the general will. On the surface, nothing could be more democratic than consulting the people directly on their wishes.

In reality, plebiscites can be very tricky, an authoritarian tool that manipulates the citizenry. The key power in a referendum belongs to the one who writes the question. The question can be posed in such a simplified way that one almost has to vote yes. Furthermore, a referendum often comes after the decision has already been made and the leader just wants popular endorsement.

De Gaulle played the plebiscite game to the hilt. For de Gaulle, the purpose of a referendum was not merely to gain mass approval for a given policy, but to reinforce his personal rule. After every plebiscite he could turn to his old enemies, the traditional politicians, and say, "You see, the people understand and support me. Who needs you?" In French political theory, again derived from Rousseau, a nation run by a leader who stands in direct communication with the people—without parties, parliaments, politicians, or interest groups getting in the way—is the ideal democracy. Some, however, see in this model the seeds of dictatorship.

De Gaulle attached his personal prestige to each referendum. "If the nation rejects the measure," he in effect told France, "it also rejects me, and I shall resign." This blunt approach worked every time until the last. In 1958 people were glad to see a new constitution. In 1961 and 1962 they were delighted to see Algeria become independent and French troops come home. But de Gaulle's second referendum of 1962 raised some questions. De Gaulle had made a mistake in the 1958 constitution in having the president chosen by a gigantic electoral college composed of local office holders, whom he assumed would be conservative and pro-de Gaulle; they weren't. So in October 1962, bypassing the National Assembly, he asked the voters to amend the constitution to allow direct election of the president. The referendum passed with a 62 percent yes vote, but this represented only 46 percent of the total electorate, far less than de Gaulle expected.

The hint was clear—the French people were happy to get out of Algeria but not so happy about tinkering with the constitution—but de Gaulle ignored it. In 1969, after riding out the

The Five Plebiscites of de Gaulle

Year	Question	"Yes"
1958	New constitution for Fifth Republic	79%
1961	Self-determination for Algeria	75
1962	Approve Algerian independence	91
1962	Direct election of president	62
1969	Reform of Senate and regions	47

1968 Events of May with resounding electoral success, de Gaulle once again sought to demonstrate that the people were behind him. He picked a rather technical issue that didn't require a plebiscite: the reform (that is, weakening) of the Senate and the setting up of regional subunits. The French people said no, and true to his word, de Gaulle resigned. He went back to Colombey-les-Deux-Eglises, where he died the following year.

Since then, there have been only three referendums. In 1972 Pompidou proposed enlarging the Common Market to include Britain, Ireland, and Denmark. Mitterrand held a referendum in 1988 on granting the Pacific territory of New Caledonia greater independence. It passed, as expected, but only 37 percent of the voters bothered turning out. In 1992, Mitterrand brought the Europe-unifying Maastricht Treaty before the French electorate, who narrowly endorsed it. In none of these cases were referendums really needed to solve a political impasse, and only the last aroused any popular interest. Rather, both presidents tried to use a referendum to bolster mass support and deflect attention away from more serious matters. Voter apathy suggests that the French have tired of referendums. (Have Californians?)

Fragmented Labor Unions

In Britain we saw how interest groups were well-organized and powerful, especially big labor and big business. This pattern is true of North Europe in general, as we shall consider when we come to Germany. In France, and in Latin Europe in general, there are also plenty of interest groups, but they are usually splintered along party lines.

In Britain (and Germany and Sweden), for example, there is one big labor federation. In France (and Italy and Spain) there are several labor unions—Communist, Socialist, Catholic, and independent unions—competing against each other. The Communist-led CGT (*Confédération Generale du Travail*) is considered powerful in France, but on a comparative basis it isn't powerful at all. It speaks for perhaps 10 percent of the French work force. Indeed, fewer than 10 percent of French labor is organized into unions; even U.S. unions are proportionally bigger (about 14 percent of the workforce).

French unions also quarrel among themselves. The CGT has collided angrily with the the smaller, Socialist-oriented CFDT (*Confédération Française Démocratique du Travail*) and nonparty *Force Ouvrière*. Labor's voice in France is weak and divided. Accordingly, French unions are strong neither in bargaining with management nor in making an impact on government. There are many strikes in France, but they tend to be short because unions lack strike funds.

Part of the problem with French unions is their political slant. Since the largest union, the CGT, is led by Communists, the other parties, especially those who control the government, ignore their demands. French unions engage in political strikes, actions aimed at government policy rather than bread-and-butter demands. In the 1980s and 1990s French unions often

Latin Europe's Divided Unions

	France	*Italy*	*Spain*
Communist	CGT	CGIL	CO
Socialist	CFDT	—	UGT
Catholic	—	CISL	—
Other	FO (centrist)	UIL (soc. dem.)	CNT (anarchist)

protested closures or layoffs at state-owned industries, much as in Thatcher's Britain. Few French unions take the American view that a union is a device for negotiating better terms with management, not a political tool.

The relative weakness of French unions has an important side effect: It makes them more, rather than less, militant and ideological. Feeling that the government has turned its back on them, French workers are more bitter than the workers of Germany and Sweden, where strong unions have an important voice in government. In those two countries, large and well-organized unions have become moderate and pragmatic.

Business and the Bureaucracy

French business is perhaps less fragmented than labor, for businesspeople rarely dabble in ideology if the present system suits them. The French Enterprise Movement (*Mouvement des Enterprises de France*, Medef) speaks mostly for large firms and generally enjoys good relations with the government, for both are committed to economic growth. Indeed, the state sees its role as guiding and helping industry, a pattern of statism going back centuries (and highly developed in Japan).

At first, Mitterrand thought he could ignore business interests and pursue a leftist economic program. This worried businesses, and they cut investment in France; some French firms invested in the United States. Mitterrand backed off and tried to make peace with French business. Premier and later President Chirac, borrowing a leaf from Reagan and Thatcher, announced himself to be totally probusiness and proceeded to "privatize" large sections of France's nationalized industries, including a state-owned television network.

The **Medef** is probably not as influential as the CBI in Britain because of the French tendency toward individualism. A French firm may belong to the Medef, for example, but rely only on its own resources for discreet contacts with the bureaucracy.

The big advantage business has over labor in dealing with government contacts is that the French business executive and civil servant are the same kind of people, often graduates of the same *grande école*, who move back and forth between top jobs in government and industry. Such connections give France's major firms **structured access** to the machinery of administration, something small-business people, farmers, and labor unionists don't have. Frustration builds in the latter groups and explodes from time to time in flash parties such as the National Front, in produce dumping by farmers, and in wildcat strikes. The political-bureaucratic systems of North Europe, by providing access for all major groups, generally avoid such outbursts.

But neither do French businesspeople dominate government decision making. French political tradition is stacked against it. In the Anglo-American tradition, pluralism—the open interplay of interest groups with government—is respected, sometimes even celebrated. When farmers, businesspeople, trade unionists, and ethnic groups lobby in Washington, it is considered perfectly normal. In Britain's Commons, "interested members" make no secret of the fact that they represent certain industries. French political theory, however, still devoted to Rousseau's notion that interest groups are immoral—because they represent partial wills rather than the general will—tends to view such groups as illegitimate. The French tradition is **dirigiste**, from the top down, ignoring interest-group demands, and doing what civil servants deem best for French power and prestige. This gives great power to bureaucrats.

Key Terms

Medef   French business association.

structured access   Permanent openness of bureaucracy to interest-group demands.

dirigiste   Bureaucrats directing industry; closely connected to French statism.

DEMOCRACY

BORING! BORING! NO NEW FACES

Few of France's major political figures has changed in two or even three decades. The major contenders of the 1970s are still the major contenders at the turn of the century, and most are in their sixties or even seventies. Current President Chirac had been running for the presidency since 1981; he won on his third try at age 62. Even Michel Rocard, the bright young kid of the Socialist party, first stood for the presidency in 1969. There is something about the French party system and political culture that does not replace leaders even when they have been unsuccessful. U.S., British, and German parties usually abandon losers.

The thought of a 46-year-old like Bill Clinton becoming president is mind-boggling to the French. Said one French politician, "The French like to have a father figure for their president." Both de Gaulle and Mitterrand served until 78; age was never held against them. A young premier is possible: Brainy Laurent Fabius was all of 37 when Mitterrand appointed him in 1984. But, said Mitterrand, "he needs time to suffer and mature."

The trouble with a political system that offers no new faces in several decades is that it gets boring. French voters, especially young ones, get turned off and turn away from all the major parties. They think no one speaks to their needs. Their discontent then builds until it becomes explosive. Unlike the American system, where state governorship may open the way for the presidency (Carter, Reagan, Clinton), in France, as in most of Europe, people must slowly work their way up through party ranks. You can't "come from out of nowhere" as in America. As we will consider again in Germany, the boredom problem is not a trivial one in European politics.

The Eternal Bureaucracy

France has been developing its bureaucracy for five centuries. Almost every change of regime has led to growth in the number and functions of French bureaucrats. During the revolving-door cabinets of the Fourth Republic, people used to say that the fall of governments didn't really matter that much because the bureaucracy ran the country anyway.

In France, civil servants oversee a great deal more than do their U.S. counterparts. The closest parallel to the power of French bureaucrats are Japanese bureaucrats, who have a similar frame of mind. France has several nationalized industries—aircraft, automobiles, coal mines, banks, steel, gas, and electricity—in addition to the areas that are state-run throughout Europe, such as the "PTT" (post, telephone, and telegraph) and the railroads. Workers in these industries are not considered civil servants, but top management people are. Every French teacher, for that matter, from kindergarten to university, is a civil servant.

The civil servants we are concerned with, however, are the several thousand who staff the Paris ministries, the **Grands Corps**, most of whom are graduates of one of the Great Schools. Even more powerful than their British counterparts, French civil servants of the administrative class (about the top 20 percent) run France. If anything,

Key Term

Grands Corps Top bureaucrats of France.

Key Term

tutelle   French for tutelage; bureaucratic guidance.

the bureaucrats' power was enhanced with the coming of the Fifth Republic, for de Gaulle so hamstrung the National Assembly that it could no longer provide a policy counterweight to, or check on, the actions of the top civil servants. Furthermore, by long French tradition, many top politicians were themselves civil servants, now often graduates of the ENA or of another *grande école*. Three-fourths of Jospin's ministers and half the National Assembly's deputies are former civil servants: government of the bureaucrats, by the bureaucrats, and for the bureaucrats.

This is not to say that French bureaucrats run things badly; often they do their jobs very well. It's the bureaucratic attitude that alienates their countrymen: aloof, arrogant, cold, logical, and rigid. It's not that they don't meet and interact with other Frenchmen; civil servants sit on some fifteen thousand committees and councils all over the country with representatives of business, labor, and farming. The highest of these is the national Social and Economic Council, but even it has a purely advisory capacity, and often advice is ignored as "unobjective." The composition of many of these consultative bodies is increasingly bureaucratic; some 30 percent of the Social and Economic Council is named by the government, for example. The French bureaucratic approach is expressed in their term **tutelle**, for they act more as tutors than as servants of the public.

Government by Bureaucracy

More than in Britain, the civil service in France constitutes a powerful governing body uncontrolled by elected officials, who sometimes denounce the bureaucracy as an "administrative labyrinth" or even as "administrative totalitarianism." But they can't seem to do much about it.

We should not think France is unique in this regard, for no country has devised a way to keep its bureaucracy under control. France, with a longer history of bureaucratization and the Great Schools' monopoly over the top civil service, merely reveals the pattern more fully. In Japan, it reaches a kind of high point. In trying to reform, trim, or democratize a bureaucracy we run into a problem: Almost any solution we can think of requires adding more bureaucrats. In France, for example, Mitterrand once tried a ministry for the reform of administration—still more bureaucracy.

"PUTTING ON THE SLIPPERS"

The movement of top civil servants to the executive suites of industries is so well-known in France that they even have a word for it, *pantouflage*, or "putting on the slippers." This means that a graduate of the *Ecole Polytechnique* or the ENA, after a few years in a Paris ministry, can slip into a cushy, high-paying management job, often in a firm he or she used to deal with as an official. Over half the chief executives of France's largest firms are former high civil servants, and two-thirds are graduates of the ENA or X. *Pantouflage* is an important connecting link between French business and bureaucracy. It also invites corruption, which seems endemic in France. In 1999, France's brilliant finance minister resigned over charges he collected big private fees for which he did no work, a standard French method of payoffs.

THE REAL POWER: THE INSPECTION

Some say the real elite running France is the *Inspection Générale de Finance*. Selected from among the top ten ENA graduates (see pages 125–27) each year, the superbright *inspecteurs de finances* snoop all around France to see how public funds are spent. Virtually all levels of French government are afraid of them. Few countries have the precise equivalent of the **Inspection**. It would be as if the U.S. General Accounting Office (a branch of Congress) had the enforcement powers of the FBI. *Inspecteurs* (among them: Giscard d'Estaing and Juppé) of all ranks and ages agree to always see each other. Inspectors who chose to "put on the slippers" (see box on page 144) still have clout, as they offer each other the best public and private jobs. And if they tire of these, they can return to the IGF at a top salary.

We can see here why the French people, faced with an unresponsive, undemocratic bureaucratic maze, turn frustrated and bitter. Where bureaucracy thrives, democracy shrivels. In trying to fix this, Mitterrand stepped into a contradiction. Socialism needs lots of bureaucracy—to run welfare programs, supervise industry, and plan the economy. But decentralization means loosening bureaucratic controls and returning power to local decision-making bodies. It took Mitterrand about three years to realize he had been working at cross purposes; he turned away from socialism and continued with decentralization.

Key Term

Inspection   Short for General Finance Inspection; the very top of French bureaucracy, with powers to investigate all branches.

Key Terms

bloc (p. 134)

CRS (p. 138)

dirigiste (p. 142)

Eurocommunism (p. 135)

Events of May (p. 138)

Grand Corps (p. 143)

Inspection (p. 145)

Medef (p. 142)

passé (p. 137)

protest vote (p. 136)

Stalinist (p. 135)

structured access (p. 142)

tutelle (p. 144)

volatile (p. 133)

Further Reference

Bell, David Scott, and Bryon Criddle. *The French Communist Party in the Fifth Republic.* New York: Oxford University Press, 1994.

Charlot, Jean. *The Gaullist Phenomenon: The Gaullist Movement in the Fifth Republic.* New York: Praeger, 1971.

Converse, Philip E., and Roy Pierce. *Political Representation in France*. Cambridge, MA: Harvard University Press, 1986.

Frears, John. *Parties and Voters in France*. New York: St. Martin's, 1991.

Friend, Julius W. *The Long Presidency: France in the Mitterrand Years*. Boulder, CO: Westview Press, 1998.

Hewlett, Nick. *Modern French Politics: Analysing Conflict and Consensus since 1945*. Malden, MA: Blackwell, 1998.

Levy, Jonah D. *Tocqueville's Revenge: State, Society, and Economy in Contemporary France*. Cambridge, MA: Harvard University Press, 1999.

Marcus, Jonathan. *The National Front and French Politics: The Resistible Rise of Jean-Marie Le Pen*. New York: New York University Press, 1996.

Morris, Peter. *French Politics Today*. New York: St. Martin's, 1994.

Penniman, Howard R., ed. *France at the Polls, 1981 and 1986: Three National Elections*. Durham, NC: Duke University Press, 1988.

Pierce, Roy, *Choosing the Chief: Presidential Elections in France and the United States*. Ann Arbor, MI: University of Michigan Press, 1995.

Suleiman, Ezra N. *Elites in French Society: The Politics of Survival*. Princeton, NJ: Princeton University Press, 1978.

Tiersky, Ronald. *France in the New Europe: Changing Yet Steadfast*. Belmont, CA: Wadsworth, 1995.

Wilson, Frank L. *Interest-Group Politics in France*. New York: Cambridge University Press, 1988.

What the French Quarrel About

11

Questions to Consider

1. Why did the French economy improve after World War II?
2. Why are too many small shopkeepers and farmers a problem?
3. Why is the state sector of the French economy still large?
4. How does French conservatism differ from the U.S. variety?
5. Why is European unemployment so high?
6. Compare U.S. and European views on welfare.
7. So far, has cutting the work week lowered unemployment?
8. How does France's racial problem resemble America's?
9. How do France's education problems differ from America's?

The French economy has been almost the opposite of the British. Britain's economy after World War II declined, dropping Britain further and further back among the industrialized countries. The French economy, which had grown only slowly in the nineteenth and early twentieth centuries, awoke as if from a slumber after World War II and zoomed ahead. With growth rates reaching 6 percent a year, France became the world's fourth-largest industrial power (after the United States, Japan, and Germany).

What did the trick in France after World War II? The typical French business firm prior to the war was a small family affair. Growth was not emphasized; keeping it in the family and earning just enough for a good living was all that mattered. This meant lots of little companies and stores rather than a few big ones. Rather than compete by cutting prices or offering better goods and services, the French, with a **petit bourgeois** mentality, sought to hide behind a protective government that would set prices and keep out foreign competition by high tariffs. It was a cozy arrangement for French business families, but it kept France economically backward.

World War II produced quite a jolt. The French elite, smarting from the German conquest and eager to restore France to world leadership, realized the economy had to change. A Planning Commission was set up to make "indicative plans" to encourage—but not force—French businesspeople to expand in certain sectors and

Key Term

petit bourgeois Small shopkeeper.

Key Terms

indicative planning
Government suggestions to
industry to expand in certain
areas.

protective tariff   Tax on
imported goods to prevent
them from undercutting
domestic products.

regions. Quite distinct from Communist-style centralized planning, **indicative planning** in effect said, "Look, everything is favorable for a new widget factory in the southwest. If you build one you'll probably make a lot of money." As we saw in the last chapter, there are warm connections between French bureaucracy and business, and it didn't take businesspeople long to get the hint. The French Planning Commission provided the business community with economic research and gentle nudges to push it along what were deemed desirable paths.

Foreign competition was another jolt. First, the European Coal and Steel Community in 1952, then the Common Market in 1957, dismantled France's **protective tariffs**. At first French businesspeople were terrified, sure that more aggressive German industry would swamp them. But gradually they learned that French firms could be quite competitive and enjoy the enlarged sales opportunities afforded by the Common Market. French business firms changed, becoming bigger, more modern, and expansion-oriented. But success brought its own problems.

COMPARISON

NUCLEAR POWER À LA FRANÇAISE

The French complain and quarrel about many things, but, curiously, nuclear energy isn't one of them. The French mostly accept nuclear energy, and none of the major parties is against it. The anti-atom Greens won a few seats in the 1997 legislative elections as part of a Socialist-Communist-Green alignment.

The French, short of other energy sources, have gone all-out for nuclear-generated electricity and have made a success of it. France has sixty nuclear power stations that produce 77 percent of its electricity (compared to 36 percent in Japan, 28 in Germany, 27 in Britain, 19 in the United States, 13 in Russia, 1.2 in China, and 1.1 in Brazil). In the United States, astronomical cost overruns have meant no more nuclear-plant construction. Some U.S. plants have been scrapped before they were finished. Overall, French nuclear-generated electricity costs less than half of America's, and New Hampshire's problem-plagued Seabrook reactor could have been built by the French for one-sixth its actual cost.

How do the French do what Americans can't? Here, we see some of the occasional advantages of centralized, technocratic rule. The state-owned utility, Electricité de France, developed a single type of reactor and stuck with it. Competing U.S. manufacturers proffer a variety of designs, some not well-tested. When Paris gives the word to build a reactor, the political, financial, regulatory, and managerial sectors mesh under central direction, and the project gets done on time. In the United States, those sectors quarrel with no central guidance, and the project takes years longer than it should. Environmentalist groups in France—not very big anyway—have no legal power to block or delay projects. The centralized French system is also better able to train personnel; there have been no Three Mile Islands in France. Nuclear power plants are an important and growing part of France's export trade. The very strengths of the American system—decentralization, competition, light regulation, and pluralist interplay—tripped up the U.S. nuclear industry.

Big Guys versus Little Guys

On a street where I lived in Toulouse, in the space of a few blocks, there were not only pharmacies, bakeries, butchers, cafés, and houseware, furniture, vegetable, and tobacco shops, but at least three of each type of store. Perhaps two miles distant, in a suburb, was a one-stop **hypermarché** fittingly named Mammouth. There, under one roof, were a combined supermarket (offering perhaps a hundred different cheeses), discount house (everything from clothes to auto parts), and cafeteria. Not only was the selection bigger at Mammouth than among the myriad neighborhood stores, but prices were lower, too.

Such developments have been going on throughout France for years. Some call it the Americanization of France, but it's really just the modernization of an old-fashioned economy. The impact on the small shopkeepers is predictable: They are being squeezed out, screaming all the way. What they regarded as their birthright—the small, family-owned, uncompetitive shop—is being destroyed. As Marx put it: "One capitalist kills many."

A parallel problem hits French farmers; there are also too many small farms; half are run part-time. France remained a nation of peasants for an unusually long time. A third of the French workforce was still on the land at the end of World War II. With postwar industrialization, this changed; now only 4 percent of the labor force works on the land, but this may still be too many. Since 1950, three-fourths of France's farms, mostly small, have disappeared. Still, French agriculture, like its U.S. counterpart, frequently overproduces, and French farmers often dump produce on highways to protest what they regard as inadequate prices. France is the world's second largest food exporter (first place: the United States) and the EU's largest food producer. The EU's expensive **Common Agricultural Program (CAP)** subsidies go disproportionately to French farmers. German taxpayers are awfully tired of paying for this, and the CAP became a nasty quarrel within Europe that begged to be reformed. One French idea: Instead of paying farmers to produce more than is needed, pay them to look after the environment.

The small shopkeepers and farmers who are being squeezed out contribute to France's electoral volatility. They shift allegiances rapidly, to whoever promises their survival. The Gaullists have been a major beneficiary, but the frightened little shopkeepers have also contributed to extremist parties. There is no nice solution to the problem of too many small shops and farms; they've got to go, and it hurts. Attempts to retain them are hopeless and even reactionary, the stuff demagoguery is made of.

In 1953, for example, Pierre Poujade founded the Union for the Defense of Shopkeepers and Artisans (UDCA) to protect small-business people from the bigger, more efficient department stores and supermarkets that were driving many of them out of business. Tinged with reaction and anti-Semitism, Poujadism caught fire, and in the parliamentary elections of 1956 won 12 percent of the popular vote; some thought it was the coming party. It turned out to be a **flash party**, however; Poujadism disappeared in 1958 when de Gaulle took over the French right. Le Pen was a Poujadist and, some say, continued its views in his National Front.

The Privatization Question

For much of the postwar period, one-fourth of French business and industry was state-owned, more than any other West European country. Now, after major privatization programs, less than one-tenth is still state-owned. Some nationalization of French industry took place

Key Terms

hypermarché   French for "hypermarket"; a store that sells everything.

Common Agricultural Program (CAP)   An EU program to subsidize farmers; the biggest single part of the EU budget.

flash party   A party that quickly rises and falls.

GEOGRAPHY

BEYOND THE NATION-STATE?

Many thinkers suggest that the nation-state has outlived its usefulness. By jealously guarding its sovereignty, the modern state whips up destructive nationalism, spends too much on arms, engages in unnecessary wars, impedes the free flow of trade and travel, and is unable to tackle global problems such as hunger, overpopulation, and environmental degradation. The fact that the modern state is only about five centuries old suggests that it is not the last or highest form of human organization. Humanity may be headed toward **supranational** forms of organization.

The European Union—known as such since 1993—is our best example of a supranational political entity. The EU uses economic means to a political end: European unification. It started with the six-nation European Coal and Steel Community in 1952 but expanded the concept of trade without tariffs in the 1957 Treaty of Rome. By cutting 10 percent of their tariffs with each other every year, after a decade goods, capital, and labor flowed freely from one member country to another. At the beginning of 1993, the EU became one economy, which means that it is also becoming one political entity.

The Common Market was a resounding economic success story, and it led to the gradual and cautious transfer of certain economic aspects of sovereignty from national capitals to Brussels, home of the EU Commission. With this developed some supranational political power. As the EU introduced a common currency, the euro, at the beginning of 1999 and forges a combined foreign policy, it will become more than a trade bloc and start taking on the characteristics of a nation, except that it will be composed of many states who will never fully surrender their sovereignty. It will be a new entity, one that we do not yet have a good name for.

And it will surely grow. For a European country, there is little or no choice: enjoy the advantages of a gigantic market or go it alone in a world of intense economic competition. Sweden, Finland, and Austria joined in late 1994. (Norwegians voted to stay out for the second time; they think they can go it alone with their oil.) The eastern part of Germany automatically became a member with unification in 1990. The newly non-Communist states of Central Europe immediately applied for associate membership. West Europe is their natural market, source of investment capital, and outlet for surplus labor. To stand outside the EU is to risk economic stagnation.

In the EU do we glimpse the future? Its parallel is the North American Free Trade Area that links Canada, the United States, and Mexico in a common market that may expand southwards, eventually combining with Mercosur (see Chapter 29). There are some good and some bad things going on with supranationalism. The economic growth is good, but if the blocs erect trade barriers to keep out the goods of other blocs, international tension will climb. One of the great international questions today is whether to build regional trade blocs or skip the blocs and work on opening the entire world to unrestricted trade.

right after World War II. Louis Renault, founder and owner of the auto firm, had collaborated with the Germans, so the Free French seized his empire in 1944. Other industries, such as steel, were taken over by the state because without government subsidies they'd go under, creating unemployment. Still other areas, such as aviation, are prestige industries aimed at boosting France's world standing.

The left in France traditionally demanded more nationalization, including all big banks and industries. They argued that under state control big industries would pay workers more, hire more workers, and produce what French people really need rather than capitalist luxuries only a few can afford. Traditionally, much of the French right also liked state-owned industries, believing that they contributed to national power and greatness and could be best run by brilliant *xiens* and *énarques* (see pages 125–27). De Gaulle, for example, supported a major state sector in heavy and high-tech industry, what the French call *étatisme* (statism). Remember, **conservatism** in Europe is not the same as conservatism in America.

France has been treated to waves of privatization and deregulation by Socialists and Gaullists alike. The French have been forced to admit that statism tends to retard growth. But France had so much state ownership, controls, and rules that there is always more to be done. Most French leaders flinch at thorough privatization because they fear making unemployment, already high, any worse. Like welfare, statist economies are terribly difficult to cut back; too many people have too much at stake.

The center-right UDF under Giscard had perhaps the strongest commitment to privatization, but the pain of change led to the Socialist victory of 1981. Good economics is sometimes bad politics. Unfortunately, as Mitterrand discovered, good politics is sometimes bad economics. Generous policies on welfare, wages, and the work week brought inflation, stagnation, and higher unemployment. The Socialists nationalized several large firms and banks only to find that they were money-losers. In 1983, Mitterrand reversed course in favor of private business and a market economy. "You don't want more state?" asked Mitterrand. "Me neither." (Compare with Clinton: "The era of big government is over.") Believers in socialism had received a real slap in the face and abandoned their leftism for neoliberalism. Chirac, first as premier and later as president, reoriented the Gaullists toward privatization of state-owned industry. Much was sold, but unemployment was so huge it led to the Socialists' 1997 parliamentary election victory. Jospin promised to slow or reverse privatization, but in practice he sold more French state-owned enterprises than all five of his immediate predecessors put together. He never, however, used the word "privatization," for that would be giving in to the Anglo-Saxons.

What to Do about Unemployment

In the late-1990s, U.S. unemployment was under 5 percent of the work force; in West Europe as a whole it was more than 10 percent (the worst: Spain, with over 20 percent unemployment). For a time, one out of eight French workers was jobless, and it has not improved much. And this high unemployment was occurring when, for the most part, Europe's economies were growing. France's GDP, for example, grew a healthy 3.2 percent in 1998. But this only slightly improved the unemployment problem.

THE CONCORDE: TECHNOLOGICAL NATIONALISM

The Concorde supersonic aircraft illustrates what can go wrong with nationalized industries: They can build the wrong product for the wrong reason and cost taxpayers a fortune. The Concorde's development began in 1962 as a joint Anglo-French enterprise to give their lagging aircraft industries a technological jump on the Americans. They thought the graceful bird would be purchased by airlines all over the world.

Things didn't work out that way. Huge overruns boosted development costs to $4.28 billion and the price per plane to $92 million, close to ten times what had been estimated. The Concorde consumed three times the fuel per passenger mile of a Boeing 747. Only British and French airlines purchased Concordes and then only because the nationalized air carriers were required to by law. Because they seldom filled their one hundred seats, the airlines lost money on Concorde runs. Only fourteen Concordes were ever finished before production shut down in 1978.

Why did Britain and France do it? A na-

tionalized industry often has different priorities than a normal commercial venture. In this case "technological nationalism" was a factor; that is, they felt they had to boost their high-tech industries in the face of American competition. Employment was another factor; both Britain and France created thousands of jobs with the Concorde. Once the project was underway and the cost overruns mounting, neither country wanted to admit it had made a mistake. Because the Concorde's makers had access to their national treasuries, they did not have to undergo the discipline of raising capital in the marketplace.

This is not to say that nationalized industries always do things wrong. Aerospatiale of France, once it made the decision to drop Concorde and participate in a European consortium to produce the more conventional Airbus (purchased by some U.S. airlines), started doing much better, although it is still subsidized. Nationalized industries tend to inefficiency because they get government subsidies.

Many believe the key problem is European **labor-force rigidities**. These are related to West Europe's generous welfare and unemployment benefits, which discourage many unemployed Europeans from seeking new jobs. Wages and **social costs** are so high that European firms are reluctant to hire new workers. A French employer pays almost half as much in taxes as in wages, a German employer even more. And there are some two-dozen taxes that must be enumerated on pay stubs, drastically increasing paperwork. Laws in most of Europe prevent easy layoffs; if a firm lets a worker go it must give hefty severance pay.

The result is that French (and German) firms are reluctant to hire: It's too expensive, takes too much red tape, and you may not be able to let workers go in a downturn. The solution for business people: Either (1) don't hire anyone, or (2) hire on the **informal economy**, or (3) set up shop in another country. French businesses do all three. Europe's high off-the-books workforce indicates an economy choked with taxes and controls. In comparison, the United States has labor-force flexibility. Wages and social costs are low, and hiring and layoffs are easy. Result: The U.S. economy creates millions of new jobs a year, something West Europeans envy.

Key Terms

labor-force rigidities Unwillingness of workers to change jobs or location.

social costs Taxes for medical, unemployment, and retirement benefits paid by employers.

informal economy Under-the-table transactions to avoid taxes and regulations.

High French unemployment also puts a brake on further privatization. Some one-fourth of French workers are employed in the public sector, compared to one-seventh in the United States and Britain, and one-sixth in Germany. Those figures are not just "bureaucrats" but anyone who works for any form or level of government, including military personnel, schoolteachers, and workers in nationalized firms. French public-sector workers enjoy job security plus good pay, benefits, and retirement plans. Their unions stage strikes over any plans to trim these bounties, and Paris usually backs down. (Notice how Brazil, another statist system, has precisely the same problem.)

Key Term

austerity Drastically holding down government expenses.

Another contributor to high unemployment: In order to join Europe's single-currency club, Chirac had to bring France's budget deficit down to 3 percent of GDP and maintain a *franc fort* (strong franc). Britain said to hell with the euro and dropped out of the single-currency club, but Chirac was determined, partly for reasons of prestige, to stay in the club whatever the domestic economic costs. Many considered Chirac's **austerity** policy foolishly rigid and the chief cause of high unemployment and his loss in the snap parliamentary elections of 1997. Socialist Premier Jospin vowed to end the austerity policy, but the classic way to do this—as we shall see in Russia and Brazil—is to simply print more money. As the new euro currency took over, however, France surrendered its ability to print money to the European Central Bank (ECB) in Frankfurt, which limits the amount of euros to prevent inflation.

How to fix the unemployment problem? All French governments in recent decades have sworn to make it their top priority, but most were voted out in part because of it. The Jospin government's bright idea came from Germany: The French work week was cut to 35 hours (down from 39 hours) without cuts in pay. The theory here was that this would force firms to hire more workers. Most economists doubted that it would work in the long run. Initially, there were few new hires; firms bought more machinery and gave their workers more overtime

COMPARISON

EUROPEAN AND U.S. ATTITUDES ABOUT WELFARE

France, like most of Europe, approves of a far more extensive—and expensive—welfare state than Americans do. The French constitution, for example, promises a "decent means of existence." French welfare recipients get about 50 percent more than their U.S. counterparts. Most Americans are delighted to cut welfare benefits and drop recipients off welfare rolls.

There is clearly a major cultural difference here. Many European politicians, especially but not exclusively leftists, attack the "savage" unrestrained capitalism of America and point to its large underclass. "We will not become like the cruel U.S. economy," they say. Not many Americans see their economy as savage or cruel; most see it as flexible and competitive with opportunities for all. Making something of that opportunity is up to individuals. Sociologist Seymour Martin Lipset defined the American ethos as "competitive individualism." Europeans tend more to solidarity, to the view that society as a whole should look out for its weakest members. Like any element of culture, this view does not change easily.

KEY CONCEPTS

EUROPE AND U.S.-STYLE CONSERVATISM

One of the hardest points for American students of Europe to understand is that conservatism in Europe is not the same as in the United States. For Europeans, U.S.-style conservatism isn't conservatism at all; it's the classic liberalism of Adam Smith: minimum government and a free market. European conservatism hearkens back to a much older time, when monarchs and aristocrats ruled and a strong state supervised the economy for the sake of national power. In the twentieth century, European conservatives transferred their loyalties to strong leaders and saw nothing wrong with statism and the welfare state. Prime example: de Gaulle and the Gaullists.

Gradually, though, U.S.-style conservatism took hold in European conservative parties, spurred by intellectuals who saw that just defending old class privileges and uncompetitive, state-owned industries block competition and the creation of new jobs. They called the movement "neo-liberalism," a revival and updating of Adam Smith. Prime example: Margaret Thatcher and the Tory "dries." The movement showed itself in France with Premier Raymond Barre's efforts in the late 1970s to liberalize the French economy. It deepened when the Socialists realized in the early 1980s that state ownership of industry was no way to go. First Mitterrand and then Chirac privatized much French industry. France has cultural difficulty going all the way to a U.S.-style free market, precisely because it's American, and cling to the French model of a *dirigiste* state.

because that does not much increase the high social taxes for every employee. Managers also cleverly used a provision in the new law to make 35 hours the average week worked over a year, meaning they could give extra hours during peak times and fewer during slack times. One ironic side-effect of French job rules: France now has the world's highest labor productivity. That, however, works against adding new jobs.

Another 1997 Jospin promise was to create 350,000 jobs, mostly for young people, in health services, schools, welfare, transportation, and construction. Recipients were to get five-year contracts at minimum wage ($1,100 a month), most of it from government. Little came of the program. Hiring for public projects, a drain on the taxpayer, seldom yields long-term solutions.

For long-term solutions, France will have to rid itself of the structural impediments that keep private employers from hiring. The French, like many Europeans, have difficulty understanding that making it more expensive to hire people means fewer new hires. No one has come up with a legislative cure for unemployment.

France's Racial Problem

Even more than Britain and Germany (and the United States), France has a problem with immigrants. There are some 9 million foreigners living in France (if one counts naturalized citizens and the second generation), about 16 percent of the French population. France has long assimilated European immigrants. From 1880 to 1960 some seven million Italians, Spaniards, Portuguese, Poles, and Russians were integrated into French society.

But between 4 and 5 million **Muslims**, mostly from former French colonies in Equatorial and North Africa, have created major racial tensions. From unemployment and misery in Algeria, Morocco, Tunisia, Senegal, and Mali, immigrants come to France to take the hardest, dirtiest, lowest-paid work—tasks French workers won't do anymore. Some immigrants, often illegals, become street peddlers or petty criminals. They live in poor, shabby housing (although nothing nearly as bad as urban U.S. ghettos). When I lived in a suburb north of Paris in 1989, I reckoned that one-third of my fellow rail commuters were black or North Africans. One French homeowner in this area, in Aulnay-sous-Bois, ruefully wisecracked that it had become "Aulnay-sous-Cameroun." In a 1998 poll, four out of ten French admitted to being racist, a much higher percentage than other Europeans.

In public, few French will say or do anything hostile to the African immigrants. The French have a tradition of tolerance and personal freedom. In private, though, many indicate their fear and dislike of Muslims. Some would like immigrants sent home, a feeling that the National Front feeds on. All of France's main parties are against further immigration, so that now (legal) immigration is as tight as in Britain.

Meanwhile, what to do with the black and North Africans currently in France? Many wish to become French and work hard at improving their French language and job skills. But France has Europe's largest Islamic community, and Muslims resist assimilating to European cultural norms. Some become more Islamic, as if to underscore their pride in their religion and culture. One point of friction among many is Muslim girls coming to school defiantly wearing head scarves as a sign of their religion. Should they be suspended? Thundered one *imam* (Muslim cleric): "Allah's law takes precedence over French law." (The French deported him.) Now, as one official observed, "for the first time, we have people born in France who are not French."

The result has been the de facto creation of U.S.-type ghettos, where angry, uneducated youths slide into crime and drugs. The French police harass them, and some Muslim youths have died at police hands in recent years. From time to time, the youths riot. "We have American cities as a warning of what could happen here," said one official.

Most French politicians agree that the immigrants should be better integrated into French economic and cultural life, but they disagree on how to do this. Improving the immigrants'

Key Terms

Muslim   Follower of the Islamic faith.

value-added tax   Large, hidden national sales taxes used throughout Europe.

COMPARISON

WHAT IS VAT?

Throughout West Europe, governments raise close to 30 percent of their revenues through hefty (10 to 20 percent) **value-added taxes** (VAT). In contrast, U.S. sales taxes, mostly at the state level (America has only luxury sales taxes at the national level), account for some 15 percent of all U.S. taxes (federal, state, and local). But European VATs are invisible; they are calculated at every stage that value is added to a product (for example, after pieces of cloth are sewn together to make a shirt), not added to the purchase price at the cash register, as in America. Accordingly, European governments reason that it's not so painful as other kinds of taxes.

GEOGRAPHY

THE GEOGRAPHY OF MIGRATION

Everywhere the Third World is trying to sneak into the First. The reason: economic opportunities. Pakistanis in Britain, Algerians in France, Turks in Germany, and Mexicans in the United States are all expressions of the same problem: not enough jobs in the home country. Japan tries to block foreign job-seekers, but even there one finds Filipino, Thai, Sri Lankan, and other workers. There is one place on earth where you can walk from the Third World into the First: the Mexico-U.S. border. It's a kind of osmosis: migrants are drawn through a membrane (border) to escape unemployment and low living standards.

But is this a problem? From a purely economic standpoint, no. The immigrants take the hardest, dirtiest, and lowest-paying jobs, ones local people shun; they'd rather live on welfare. And, as we shall consider in Chapter 16, the rich countries have few babies and rapidly growing numbers of retirees. Without immigrants, there would be too few workers to pay for the oldsters' pensions.

The problem is in the cultural area, where immigrants form a distinct subculture that insists on preserving its ways in the new country. In France, discrimination and limited schooling mean immigrants and their children do not master French, gain no job skills, and become ghettoized into crime and drugs. This in turn fuels resentment against immigrants and has led to the British and French National Fronts and the German National Republicans. Notice how the same causes and same feelings are found in the United States.

Key Term

social mobility The movement of individuals from one class to another, usually upward.

housing, schooling, and jobs all costs money. The tax burden falls most heavily on the municipalities where there are the most immigrants. One mayor of a working-class suburb pointed out that Muslim immigrants have prodigious numbers of children "whose schooling our town has to pay for." This is one reason the National Front vote is the strongest where there are more Muslims. The parties on the left, Socialist and Communist, are more willing to spend additional funds. A National Front activist, on the other hand, said, "The solution for the immigrants is not integration; it's sending them back to their country."

Racial amity got a brief boost when the French soccer team won the 1998 World Cup: Eight of the twenty-two-man team were black or brown. France erupted with pride. The winning goal was made by Zinedine Zidane, born in Marseilles of Algerian parents. Sports may be more important than government programs in fostering racial integration. (Is that true in the United States?)

France's Education Problems

France has rapidly expanded educational opportunity in order to improve **social mobility** and integrate all, even immigrants, into French society. This effort is praiseworthy, reminiscent of U.S. efforts to solve social problems by increased school integration. But, as in the United States, it leads to new problems.

First, immigrant children tend to live in ghettos. Sending them to schools with each other, with few French children in the classroom, makes it difficult to teach them proper French language and culture. Many cannot speak any French when they first enter school. The threat of having their schools inundated by a wave of immigrant children prompted local French authorities in some cases to prohibit enrolling African and Arab children, a move that was shot down by national authorities. Leftists put up banners proclaiming "the right to school for all children." Rightists support the anti-immigrant stance.

The government decided that a much larger portion of French young people should achieve the "bac," discussed in Chapter 9. The Socialist government in 1985 announced an ambitious plan to send 80 percent of all young people to *lycées* by 2000, a goal largely achieved. The bac has been enlarged to include technical and vocational options to form a literate and qualified labor force needed by a modern economy. But even with a major upsurge in education spending, the public *lycée* system became severely overburdened, as evidenced by dilapidated buildings, crowded classrooms (some with over 40 students per teacher), and crime in the hallways and restrooms. Sound familiar? (Middle-class French parents, afraid of school decay, increasingly send their children to private *lycées*.) French student street protests from time to time shake the Paris government, for the protests remind them of the 1968 Events of May.

The Covering Up of Things Past

Every few years a new trial reminds France of its collaboration with Nazi Germany. It is a source of continuing shame that no postwar government has been able to handle. The official French line, started by de Gaulle, is that Vichy was an illegal and temporary regime run by Germans. The real France, led by de Gaulle, and the vast majority of French people were clean. Recent cases have underscored the degree of French collaboration.

THE NATIONAL FRONT: THE ANGRY PARTY

Somewhat like the Poujadists of the 1950s, the National Front (FN) sprang from out of nowhere to capture around 15 percent of the French vote in the 1990s. But the FN did not soon fade. The National Front's leader is Jean-Marie Le Pen, a former French paratrooper in Algeria and Poujadist deputy, who preaches a racist and nationalist line against France's Muslim immigrants and its longstanding Jewish community. Le Pen, a spellbinding orator, knows just how to push French anti-Muslim, anti-black, and anti-Jewish psychological buttons. He denies that he is a racist; he's just pro-French. In 1984 he authored *Les Français d'Abord* (The French First).

FN voting strength, although rarely a majority, is concentrated in localities where there are many black and North African immigrants. Some FN supporters were earlier Republican, Gaullist, and even Communist activists. The working class can be quite racist, especially in times of high unemployment. With the immigrant problem so large and visible, the FN will have a constituency for many years. Notice how Britain and Germany, facing the identical immigrant problem, produced, respectively, the anti-immigrant National Front and National Republican parties. (Is there a U.S. equivalent?)

COMPARISON

HOW U.S. AND FRENCH YOUTH HANDLE THE SCHOOL PROBLEM

American and French school problems sound quite similar, but U.S. and French young people part company in how they handle the problem. In America, young people, especially from disadvantaged groups, simply drop out of school. Dispirited, they act like they are beaten before they start. In France, angry but hopeful students take to the streets in protest. They strike for the right to study hard! Thousands of high-school students march to demand cleaner, newer schools, more teachers, smaller classes, and more security officers in schools.

Can you imagine U.S. high schoolers demanding the right to study hard? The difference is that American youth often dislike school, culture, and books and no longer see education as their ticket to the middle class. French students, including immigrant children, see schooling with some enthusiasm as their way up and out of the ghetto. They look at the one-quarter of French under the age of twenty-seven who are unemployed and conclude they need a good education to make them competitive on the job market. They also come from a tradition of mass protest to change government policy. In comparison, many American youth are passive and aimless. An earlier generation of Americans, especially immigrant children, embraced education as their path to upward social mobility. What has happened in America to change this attitude?

In 1983 Klaus Barbie, the Gestapo's wartime chief of Lyons, was extradited from Bolivia to France. Barbie had tortured and killed dozens of Resistance members and shipped hundreds of Jews, including small children, to death camps. His 1987 trial showed he could not have done these things without many French collaborators. Barbie was sentenced to life and died in prison.

In 1990, the high Vichy police official who rounded up Jews and put them on death trains was tried before the Special High Court of the Liberation, a court that had not existed for decades. Critics accused the government of stalling until the eighty-one-year-old René Bousquet died in order to avoid embarrassment. Mitterrand—who served both Vichy and the Resistance—had worked with Bousquet during the war and allegedly kept him from trial. A flamboyant eccentric solved the Bousquet problem by plugging him with a handgun.

In 1994, a high-ranking officer of the collaborationist French *Milice* (militia), Paul Touvier, then seventy-nine, received a life sentence for crimes against humanity. Touvier had hidden forty-four years in some fifty fundamentalist Catholic monasteries. His arrest in 1989 pointed up the connection between the Catholic right and the Vichy regime. Touvier had been tried in absentia after the war and sentenced to death, but his Church friends sheltered him and his family.

In 1998, a Bordeaux court found Maurice Papon, eighty-seven, who retired after serving in top positions in the Fifth Republic, guilty of complicity in Nazi crimes for turning over Jews for shipment to death camps. Papon argued that he was a minor Vichy official who had no choice and actually tried to shield Jews from deportation. Why did it take so long for Papon's case to come to light? Critics charge that his powerful friends in government shielded him. Official France does not like to talk about these matters.

The underlying problem is that France has never fully come to grips with its past, especially its Vichy past. To see how another land has tried to come to grips with its past, let us turn to Germany.

Key Terms

austerity (p. 153)

Common Agricultural Program (CAP) (p. 149)

conservatism (p. 151)

flash party (p. 149)

hypermarché (p. 149)

indicative planning (p. 148)

informal economy (p. 152)

labor-force rigidities (p. 152)

Muslim (p. 155)

petit bourgeois (p. 147)

protective tariff (p. 148)

social costs (p. 152)

social mobility (p. 156)

supranational organizations (p. 151)

value-added tax (p. 155)

Further Reference

Adams, William James. *Restructuring the French Economy: Government and the Rise of Market Competition since World War II*. Washington, D.C.: Brookings, 1989.

Chafer, Tony, and Brian Jenkins, eds. *France: From the Cold War to the New World Order*. New York: St. Martin's, 1996.

Estrin, Saul, and Peter Holmes. *French Planning in Theory and Practice*. Winchester, MA: Allen & Unwin, 1983.

Favell, Adrian. *Philosophies of Integration: Immigration and the Idea of Citizenship in France and Britain*. New York: St. Martin's, 1998.

Flynn, Gregory, ed. *Remaking the Hexagon: The New France in the New Europe*. Boulder, CO: Westview, 1995.

Fysh, Peter, and Jim Wolfreys. *The Politics of Racism in France*. New York: St. Martin's, 1998.

Gildea, Robert. *France since 1945*. New York: Oxford University Press, 1996.

Keeler, John T. S., and Martin A. Schain, eds. *Chirac's Challenge: Liberalization, Europeanization, and Malaise in France*. New York: St. Martin's, 1996.

Schmidt, Vivien A. *From State to Market? The Transformation of French Business and Government*. New York: Cambridge University Press, 1996.

Simmons, Harvey G. *The French National Front: The Extremist Challenge to Democracy*. Boulder, CO: Westview, 1996.

Smith, W. Rand. *The Left's Dirty Job: The Politics of Industrial Restructuring in France and Spain*. Pittsburgh, PA: University of Pittsburgh Press, 1998.

PART III

Key Websites

Basic Law for the Federal Republic of Germany   This site has the following topics: View of the Acts, Basic Rights, The Federation and the Laender, The Lower House of Parliament (Bundestag), The Upper House of Parliament (Bundesrat), The Joint Committee, The Federal President, The Federal Government. Legislative powers, joint tasks, and administrative duties provide detailed information about the government of the Federal Republic of Germany.
http://www.law.qub.ac.uk/consti/germany/gg0.htm

The Weimar Republic   This paper by Professor Gerhard Rempel at Western New England College details the economic and political problems of the Weimar Republic.
http://mars.wnec.edu/~grempel/courses/germany/lectures/20weimar1.html

Bundestag   Topics covered at this site include the following: Organization—the Bundestag's structures, procedures, powers, and rules; Members—an alphabetical list of all the Members of the German Bundestag; Legislation; and Database—a world directory of Parliamentary Libraries.
http://www.bundestag.de/btengver/e-index.htm

Political Parties of Germany   This site features the parties represented in the Bundestag in the Lower House of the German Parliament, including the following: the Christian Democratic Union; its sister party, the Christian Social Union; the Social Democratic Party; the Free Democratic Party; Alliance '90/The Greens; and the Party of Democratic Socialism.
http://www.policy.com/issuewk/98/0928/092898h.html

The American Institute for Contemporary German Studies at Johns Hopkins University   This site contains extensive studies, policy briefs and analyses, reports, seminar schedules, papers, discourses on current and historical events, and more. Topics include the following: Examining Critical Issues—The Berlin Republic; Germany's New Government; the European Union; Telecom and Data Protection; Responses to Globalization; and Foreign Policy.
http://www.aicgs.org/index2.html

Der Spiegel   This site features Germany's influential newsweekly—*Der Spiegel*.
http://www.spiegel.de

Germany:
The Impact of the Past

12

Questions to Consider

1. What are Germany's geographic problems?
2. How was Germany the opposite of French centralization?
3. What did *cuius regio* attempt to solve? How?
4. What did Prussia contribute to Germany?
5. How did nationalism combine with racism in Germany?
6. What were the First, Second, and Third Reichs?
7. How did Bismarck retard Germany's democratic development?
8. Why was the Weimar Republic doomed?
9. What were the main elements of Nazism?

Britain has natural borders. France claims to have natural borders, but one of its six sides (the northeast) has been disputed. Germany, however, has natural borders only on its north and south (the Baltic Sea and Alps), and this fact has contributed to its tumultuous history. Germany has expanded and contracted over the centuries, at times stretching from Alsace (now French) to East Prussia (now Polish and Russian). After World War II its eastern wing was chopped off, and the country was divided into eastern and western occupation zones, which in 1949 became East and West Germany. The Federal Republic of Germany that reunified in 1990 is considerably smaller than the mighty Second Reich at the turn of the century.

Germany's location in the center of Europe and the flat, defenseless North European Plain imposed two unhappy options on the nation. When Germany was divided and militarily weak—its condition throughout most of history—it was Europe's battleground. On the other hand, when Germany united and became militarily strong enough to deter any combination of potential attackers, it was also strong enough to beat all its neighbors one at a time. When Germany unified in the nineteenth century, it automatically became a threat to the rest of Europe; it was big, populous, and strategically located. Some Europeans still fear a united Germany. Geography, in making a united Germany a threat, has been unkind to Germany.

GEOGRAPHY

MOUNTAINS

Mountains can serve as defensive barriers, making a country hard to invade. The Alps help guard Germany's southern flank; the Pyrenees do the same for France. Russia, with no mountains until the Urals rise up to form Europe's border with Asia, lay nearly defenseless before the horsemen of the east (who passed south of the Urals), the Swedes of the north, and the Germans of the west.

Mountains can also slow political and economic development. Very mountainous countries, such as Spain and Colombia, may be harder to unify, as the nation's capital cannot easily penetrate regions shielded by mountains. As the West Virginia motto says, *Montani Semper Liberi* (Mountaineers are always free). Because much of Japan is too mountainous for farms or factories, most Japanese are forced to live in narrow and crowded coastal strips.

Who Are the Germans?

Contrary to Nazi race theory, the Germans are as much an ethnic mixture as any people in Europe, maybe more. The original Germans identified by the Romans were a collection of several barbarian tribes, some of which became Romanized. The invasion of the Huns in the fourth century set off gigantic migrations throughout Europe as everyone fled from their advance. Many Germans sought refuge in Roman territory, and soon Germanic tribes were roaming through and destroying the Roman Empire, eventually settling in various parts of it.

Since that time Germans have presented one face to the West and another to the East. To the West—to France and Italy—the heirs of Rome, they were awed and respectful of their superior culture, which they tried to copy. To the East, however, they saw barbarians—first Huns, than Slavs—whom they either Germanized, exterminated, or pushed back. Whole Slavic- or Baltic-speaking areas were Germanized, and many of today's Germans are of East European descent. The Nazis hated to admit it, but Germans are a combination of Celts, Romans, Jews, several Germanic tribes, Slavs, and Balts. When the Nazis introduced their model of the perfect Nordic specimen, some Germans quietly chuckled, for practically none of the Nazi leaders matched the tall, athletic, blond, blue-eyed image.

The Fragmented Nation

The Germanic tribes were so impressed by Rome—whose empire they were destroying—that they pretended to continue the empire. When in 800 the Frankish king Charlemagne (German: Karl der Grosse) was crowned in Rome, he called his gigantic realm the Holy Roman Empire (which, Voltaire later quipped, was "neither holy, nor Roman, nor an empire"). Although it soon fell apart, the German wing continued calling itself that until Napoleon ended the farce in 1806.

The Changing Shape of Germany

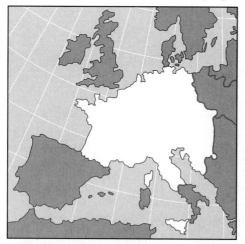

800: Charlemagne's Holy Roman Empire

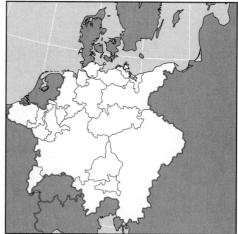

1648: After Westphalia

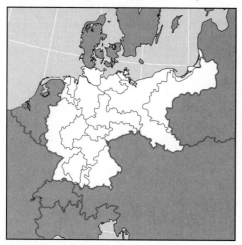

1815: The German Confederation

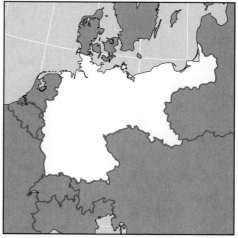

1871: The Second Reich

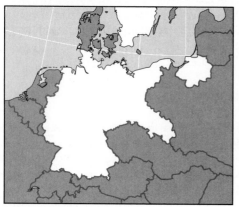

1919: The Weimar Republic

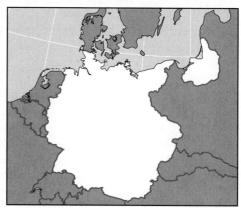

1939: Hitler's Third Reich

The Changing Shape of Germany (cont.)

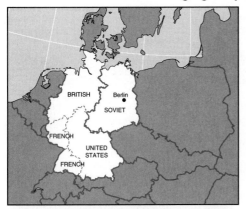

1945: Occupied Germany (Four Zones)

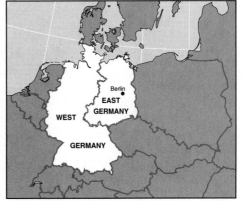

1949: Two Germanies

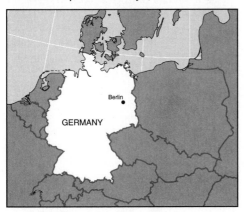

1990: Reunited Germany

In England, as we saw, power between king and nobles was kept in balance, resulting in a constitutional monarchy that moved in spurts toward civil liberty, limited government, and rule by Parliament. In France, absolutism upset the balance and the French kings amassed more and more power leading to a centralized, bureaucratic state. Germany went the other way: The nobles gained more and more power until, by the thirteenth century, the emperor was a mere figurehead while princes and leading churchmen ran ministates as they saw fit. Germany was not one country but a crazy quilt of hundreds of independent principalities and cities.

The split between Roman Catholics and Protestants accentuated Germany's fragmentation. Protestant reformer Martin Luther in the early sixteenth century reflected the feeling of much of northern Germany that the Roman church was corrupt and ungodly. The North German princes especially didn't like paying taxes to Rome and found Lutheranism a good excuse to stop. South Germany and the Rhineland stayed mostly Catholic, the north and east predominantly Protestant, a pattern that still characterizes modern Germany.

Two wars resulted from the religious question. In the first, the Schmalkaldic War (named after the town of Schmalkalden where Protestant princes formed a coalition) of 1545–55, the **Habsburg** Emperor Charles V nearly succeeded in crushing Lutheranism, when the

Key Term

Habsburg Leading Catholic dynasty that once held Austria-Hungary, Spain, Latin America, and the Netherlands.

GEOGRAPHY

BOUNDARIES: LINES ON A MAP

Exactly where one state leaves off and another begins is often unsettled. Looking at maps, you get the feeling that boundary lines are real, perhaps decreed by nature or at least hallowed by time to demarcate each people's allotted territory. Would that it were so. There are practically no natural boundaries in the world. Almost all boundaries are artificial, some more artificial than others.

Germany's boundaries, for example, consolidated, expanded, and contracted with great fluidity. Consider the maps of Germany over the centuries. Germany's boundaries were drawn widest under Bismarck in 1871 and under Hitler before and during World War II. The Second Reich included much of present-day Poland and a large sweep of Prussia to the east. With defeat in World War I, Germany lost part of Prussia and Pomerania to make a "Polish corridor" to the Baltic. Alsace returned to France. Hitler expanded the map of Germany by adding Austria, Bohemia (now the Czech Republic), Alsace, and parts of Poland. These lands were immediately stripped away with Germany's defeat in World War II. Germany was also broken into two countries from 1949 to 1990.

Which are the "correct" boundaries for Germany? It is impossible to apply historical, moral, or even demographic standards to determine with certainty Germany's boundaries. One might attempt, as Hitler did, to draw Germany's borders so as to include all Germans. But the peoples of Europe—as in most of the world—are not neatly arrayed in demographic ranks, with, say, Germans on one side of a river and Poles on the other. Instead, they are often "interdigitized," with some German villages in Polish territory and Poles living in some German cities. Whatever border you draw will leave some Germans in Poland and some Poles in Germany.

The boundaries of Poland are a perplexing example of border questions. As the empires that had partitioned Poland since the 1790s—the German, Austrian, and Russian—collapsed in World War I, Polish patriots under Pilsudski reestablished Poland, but it included many Lithuanians, Belorussians, and Ukrainians. During World War II Stalin pushed Soviet borders westward. In compensation, Poland got former German territories, so that now its western border is formed by the Oder and Neisse Rivers. Millions of Germans were expelled. In effect, Poland was picked up and moved over 100 miles westward! After much hesitation (because of German interest groups from the Oder-Neisse territories), Germany confirmed the new boundary.

Only boundaries that have been set up and observed over the centuries are without controversy. To be legal, a border must be agreed upon in a boundary treaty and demarcated with physical indicators, such as concrete pylons. Few borders in the world are like that.

Control of borders is a chief attribute of sovereignty, and nations will go to great lengths to show that they are in charge of who and what goes in and out across their borders. One of the first points of violence in Lithuania and Slovenia were their passport and customs houses. In forcibly taking over these border checkpoints, Soviet and Yugoslav federal forces respectively tried to show that they, rather than the breakaway republics, were in charge of the entire national territory.

Boundary questions abound, such as India's border with Pakistan (especially over Kashmir), China's borders with India and with Russia, Venezuela with Guyana, Argentina with Chile (over Tierra del Fuego) and with Britain (over the Falklands), Syria with Lebanon (over the Bekaa Valley), Morocco with Algeria (over the former Spanish Sahara), and Iraq with Iran (over the Shatt al-Arab waterway). Such questions cause wars.

GEOGRAPHY

BOUND GERMANY

Germany is bounded on the north by the Atlantic, Denmark, and the Baltic Sea on the east by Poland and the Czech Republic; on the south by Austria and Switzerland; and on the west by France, Luxembourg, Belgium, and the Netherlands.

To reinforce your knowledge, sketch out and label Germany and its neighbors. Note also the old border between East and West Germany that disappeared with unification in 1990.

Protestants allied with Catholic France to beat Charles. Trying to decide which parts of Germany should be Catholic and which Protestant, the Religious Peace of Augsburg in 1555 came up with the formula *cuius regio eius religio*—"whoever reigns, his religion." Thus the religion of the local prince decided an area's religion, a point that deepened the disunity of Germany and the power of local princes.

The peace proved shaky, though, and in 1618, as the Habsburgs again tried to consolidate their power, a much worse war broke out, the **Thirty Years War**. Again, at first the Catholic Habsburgs won. By 1631, help from other countries arrived. Cardinal Richelieu feared Habsburg power would encircle France, so he aided the Protestants. In international relations, power and national interests are more important than religious or ideological affinity. A strong Swedish army under Gustavus Adolphus battled in Germany for the Protestants. Germany suffered terribly, losing perhaps 30 percent of its population, most by starvation. Until World War I, the Thirty Years War was the worst in human history. The Treaty of **Westphalia** in 1648 confirmed *cuius regio* and left Germany atomized into 360 separate political entities.

Consider the political impact of religion on the three countries we have studied so far. England broke with Rome; the return of Catholic kings merely confirmed the power of Parliament. In France, the Catholic Church and *ancien régime* stayed loyal to one another while many French turned anticlerical, leading to a division of French society into conservative Catholics and anticlerical radicals. Germany didn't split into clerical and anticlerical but into Catholic and Protestant. The result was ghastly: a long and ruinous war, further breakup of an already fragmented country, and centuries of ill will between Germans of different faiths.

The Rise of Prussia

One German state eventually came to dominate the others. Brandenburg, later known as **Prussia**, expanded greatly during the eighteenth century, taking over the eastern German conquests of the Middle Ages along the Baltic and adding Silesia and parts of the Rhineland. In the eastern Baltic regions, a type of nobility had developed, descended from the old Teutonic knights, that had a major impact on German history. The **Junkers** held great estates worked by

Key Terms

Thirty Years War 1618–48 Habsburg attempt to conquer and Catholicize Europe.

Westphalia Treaty ending the Thirty Years War.

Prussia A powerful North German state; Berlin is its capital.

Junker From *junge Herren*, young gentlemen (pronounced YOON care); Prussian nobility.

GEOGRAPHY

BOUND POLAND

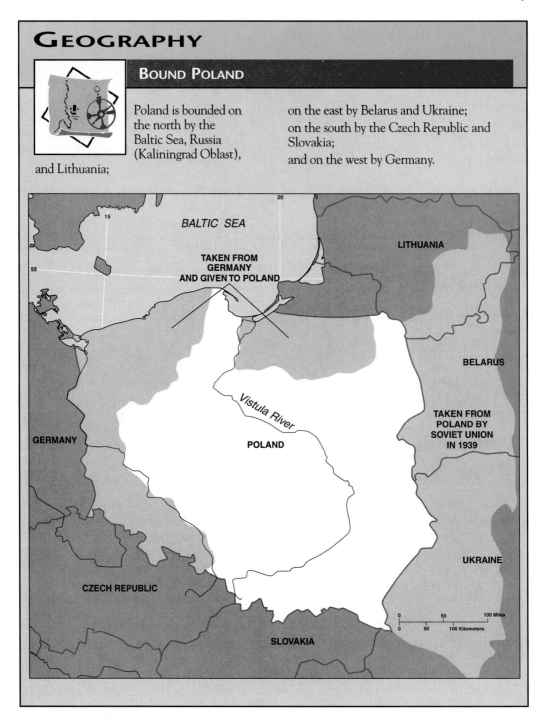

Poland is bounded on the north by the Baltic Sea, Russia (Kaliningrad Oblast), and Lithuania;

on the east by Belarus and Ukraine;

on the south by the Czech Republic and Slovakia;

and on the west by Germany.

BALTIC SEA

LITHUANIA

TAKEN FROM GERMANY AND GIVEN TO POLAND

BELARUS

TAKEN FROM POLAND BY SOVIET UNION IN 1939

GERMANY

Vistula River

POLAND

UKRAINE

CZECH REPUBLIC

SLOVAKIA

0   50   100 Miles
0   50   100 Kilometers

obedient serfs. Unlike the English lords, however, they did not retain their independence and act as a counterweight to the king but became a state nobility, dependent on the government and controlling all the higher civil-service and military positions. Famous for their discipline and attention to detail, the Junkers contributed to modern Germany a passion for excellence in both military and civil administration.

Key Terms

nationalism Belief in the greatness and unity of one's country and hatred of rule by foreigners.

Volksgeist German for "spirit of the people"; has racist connotations.

Lebensraum German for "living space" for an entire nation.

Prussian kings, with potential enemies on all sides, became obsessed with military power, leading to Voltaire's wisecrack that "Prussia is not a country with an army but an army with a country." In the early eighteenth century, King Frederick William acted as drillmaster to his entire people, demanding military obedience and Prussian efficiency, not only on the parade ground—where he personally marched his handpicked corps of oversize soldiers—but in civilian life as well. Especially in Prussia, obedience to authority became a German character trait.

His son, Frederick the Great, who ruled from 1740 to 1786, perfected what he inherited, as did France's Louis XIV. In Frederick's case this inheritance was the Prussian army, which he kept in such a high state of readiness that it frightened the monarchs of larger states. Administering his kingdom personally, Frederick became known as the "enlightened despot" who brought art and culture (Voltaire stayed at his court for a while), as well as military triumphs and territorial expansion, to Prussia. A brilliant commander and daring strategist, Frederick served as a model for expansion-minded German nationalists. Trying to identify himself with Frederick the Great, Adolf Hitler in 1933 announced the founding of the Third Reich from Frederick's tomb in Berlin.

German Nationalism

At the time of the French Revolution, there were still over three hundred German states. Prussia and Austria were the strongest of them, but they too were pushovers for Napoleon's conquering legions. German liberals, fed up with the backwardness and fragmentation of their country, at first welcomed the French as liberators and modernizers. Napoleon consolidated the many German ministates—but not Prussia or Austria—into about thirty, calling them the Confederation of the Rhine, and introduced new laws to free the economy and society from archaic laws.

The French brought with them more than liberalism, however; everywhere they went they infected conquered lands with the new idea of **nationalism**, the most contagious *-ism* of all; when one country catches it, the fever soon spreads to neighboring lands. In short order, Germans, Russians, and Spaniards were fired with anti-French nationalism. Napoleon, without realizing it, had let an imp out of the bottle; the push he gave to German nationalism indirectly led to three German invasions of France. Great historical events have highly unpredictable aftereffects.

As we saw in the case of France's borrowing English and American notions of freedom, ideas conceived in one country often become warped, exaggerated, or distorted when applied to another. This happened with German nationalism, which became romantic, angry, and racist and hearkened back to a mythical past. German nationalist intellectuals of the nineteenth century spoke of a **Volksgeist**, a combination of *Volk* (people) and *Geist* (spirit), that implied a Germanic tribal spirit that was superior to other peoples. German geographers coined the term **Lebensraum** and argued that Germany was entitled to more

Metternichian system
Contrived conservative
system that tried to restore
pre-Napoleon European
monarchy and stability.

Reich   German for empire.

Reichstag   Pre-Hitler
German parliament; its
building now houses
Bundestag.

Kaiser   German for Caesar;
emperor.

territory. (Japanese militarists argued precisely along these lines as well.) Long before Hitler, many Germans favored expansionist nationalism.

Germany looked to Prussia for leadership in throwing off the French yoke, and Prussian troops did contribute to Napoleon's downfall. Like France, Germany after Napoleon was not the same. Caught up in nationalism and liberalism—more of the former than the latter—German thinkers wanted a unified and modernized nation. The ultraconservative Austrian Prince Metternich, who hated both nationalism and liberalism, helped create a German Confederation of thirty-nine states, which he thought would contribute to European stability after Napoleon.

In 1848 revolution broke out all over Europe as discontented liberals and nationalists sought to overthrow the **Metternichian system**. In the midst of urban uprisings, German liberals met in Frankfurt to try to set up a unified, democratic Germany. They sent a delegation to Berlin to offer the king of Prussia leadership of a German constitutional monarchy, but he contemptuously refused it with the remark that he "would not accept a crown from the gutter." The army cleared out the National Assembly in Frankfurt, and German liberals either converted to pure nationalism or emigrated to the United States.

The Second Reich

In contrast to the attempts of liberal nationalists in 1848, German unification came not from the people but from above, from the growth of Prussia. Neither was it the work of liberals but rather of a staunch conservative, Otto von Bismarck, who had seen the liberals in action in 1848 and thought they were fools. Bismarck, who became Prussia's prime minister in 1862, wasn't really a German nationalist; he was first and foremost a loyal Prussian servant of his king who saw German unification under Prussian leadership as the only way to preserve and defend Prussia. As such, Bismarck's goals were quite limited; he had no intention of turning a united Germany into a military, expansionist state.

For Bismarck, armies and warfare were simply tools. In 1862, when the Prussian parliament was deadlocked over whether to increase the military budget, Bismarck ordered new taxes and spent the money without parliamentary approval. He declared: "Not by speeches and majority decisions will the great questions of the time be decided—that was the fault of 1848 and 1849—but by iron and blood."

Bismarck used his military tools to solve the great question of his day: Who was to lead a unified Germany, Prussia or Austria? In a series of three limited wars—in 1864 against Denmark, in 1866 against Austria, and in 1870 against France—Bismarck first consolidated the many German states behind Prussia, then got rid of Austria, then firmed up German unity. The new Second **Reich** (Charlemagne's was the first) was actually proclaimed in France, at Versailles Palace, in 1871.

The Second Reich, lasting from 1871 to 1918, was not a democracy. The legislature, the **Reichstag**, had only limited power, namely, to approve or reject the budget. The chancellor (prime minister) was not "responsible" to the parliament—that is, he couldn't be voted out—and handpicked his own ministers. The German **Kaiser** was not a figurehead but actually set policy. The individual states that had been enrolled into a united Germany retained their autonomy, a forerunner of the present federal system.

DEMOCRACY

BISMARCK'S DUBIOUS LEGACY

Otto von Bismarck, Germany's chancellor from 1871 to 1890, was a Prussian Junker to the bone, and the stamp he put on a unified Germany retarded its democratic development for decades. Bismarck and Disraeli liked each other, and many compared them as dynamic conservatives. But English and German conservatism are two different things. Disraeli's Tories widened the electorate and welcomed a fair fight in Parliament. Bismarck hated parties, parliaments, and anyone who opposed him. Bismarck left Germany an authoritarian and one-man style of governance that was overcome only by Allied occupation following World War II. Bismarck's **Kulturkampf** with the Catholic Church, which he wished to subordinate to the German state, sharpened Catholic resentment against the Protestant north, a feeling that lingers.

Bismarck's most dangerous legacy to Germany was in his foreign policy. He practiced both **Machtpolitik** and **Realpolitik** to manipulate first his own Prussia and then the rest of Europe to produce a unified Germany. War for Bismarck was just a tool. Cynical amorality was another pattern Bismarck bequeathed to Germany.

Germany's real problem was that Bismarck was a tough act to follow. Bismarck used power politics for a limited end—the unification of Germany. His successors picked up his amoral *Machtpolitik* but forgot about the limits, the *Realpolitik*. Bismarck, for example could have easily conquered all of Denmark, Austria, and France, but he didn't because he knew that would bring dangerous consequences. Bismarck used war in a controlled way, to unify Germany rather than to conquer Europe. Once he got his Second Reich, Bismarck concentrated on making sure potential enemies would not form coalitions against it.

Bismarck cautioned that an alliance with Austria, supporting Austrian ambitions in the Balkans, could eventually lead to war. "The entire Balkans," he said, were "not worth the bones of one Pomeranian grenadier." His fear came true, for that was precisely the way World War I came about. Bismarck's successors, men of far less ability and great ambition, let Austria pull them into war over the Balkans. The tragedy of Bismarck is that he constructed a delicate balance of European power that could not be maintained without himself as the master juggler.

Germany, which had been industrially backward, surged ahead, especially in iron and steel. The once-pastoral Ruhr region became a smoky workshop. With the growth of industry came a militant and well-organized German labor movement, starting in the 1860s. In 1863 Ferdinand Lassalle formed the General German Workers' Association, partly a union and partly a party. In 1875 the group became the Sozialdemokratische Partei Deutschlands (**SPD**), now the oldest and one of the most successful social-democratic parties in the world.

Bismarck hated the SPD and suppressed it in 1878. He tried to take the wind out of the Socialists' sails by promoting numerous welfare measures himself in the Reichstag. In the 1880s Germany

Key Terms

Kulturkampf Culture struggle, specifically Bismarck's with the Catholic Church.

Machtpolitik Power politics (cognate to "might").

Realpolitik Politics of realism.

SPD German Social Democratic party.

became the first country with medical and accident insurance, a pension plan, and state employment offices. Germany has been a welfare state ever since.

The Catastrophe: World War I

The Second Reich might have evolved into a democracy. Political parties became more important. After Bismarck was fired in 1890, the SPD came into the open to become, before World War I, Germany's largest party, with almost one-third of the Reichstag's seats. Gaining responsibility in elected offices, the German Socialists grew moderate, turning away from their Marxist roots and toward **revisionism**, the idea that socialism can grow gradually through democratic means rather than by radical revolution. So domesticated had the SPD become that in 1914, when the emergency war budget was placed before the Reichstag, SPD deputies forgot about the "international solidarity of all workers" and voted like good Germans—for it.

After Bismarck, Germany's foreign policy turned expansionist. Kaiser Wilhelm II saw Germany as a great imperial power, dominant in Europe and competing with Britain overseas. A program of naval armament, begun by Germany in 1889, touched off a race with Britain to build more battleships. Wilhelm supported the Boers against the British in South Africa and the Austrians who were coming into conflict with the Russians over the Balkans. By the time the shots were fired in Sarajevo in 1914, Germany had managed to surround itself with enemies, exactly what Bismarck had worked to prevent.

The Germans, with their quick victories of half a century earlier in mind, marched joyously off to war. In early August of 1914 the Kaiser told his troops: "You will be home before the leaves have fallen from the trees." All of Europe thought the war would be short, but it took four years and ten million lives until Germany surrendered.

Many Germans couldn't believe they had lost militarily. Right-wing Germans swallowed the **Dolchstoss** myth that Germany had been betrayed on the home front by democrats, socialists, Bolsheviks, and Jews. Fed nothing but war propaganda, Germans didn't understand that the army and the economy could give no more. The war ended before there was any fighting on German soil, so Germans didn't see their troops beaten. Worse was the **Versailles Treaty**, which blamed the war on Germany and demanded an impossible $33 billion in reparations. Germany was stripped of its few colonies (in Africa and the South Pacific) and lost Alsace and the Polish corridor. Many Germans wanted revenge. If a treaty is to be judged on what it produces, then Versailles was a catastrophe, for it led straight to Hitler and World War II.

Key Terms

revisionism   The rethinking of an ideology or reinterpretation of history.

Dolchstoss   German for "stab in the back."

Versailles Treaty   1919 treaty ending World War I.

Weimar Republic   1919–33 democratic German republic.

Republic without Democrats

We can see how the **Weimar Republic**—which got its name from the town of Weimar, where its federal constitution was drawn up—started with three strikes against it. First, Germans had no experience with a republic or a democracy, yet suddenly Germany became a democratic republic when the Kaiser fled to Holland at the war's end. Second, for many Germans the Weimar Republic lacked legitimacy; it had been forced upon Germany by the victorious allies and "back stabbers" who had betrayed the Reich. Third, the Versailles Treaty was so punitive and its demands for payment so high that Germany was humiliated and economically hobbled.

GEOGRAPHY

BOUND HUNGARY

Hungary is bounded on the north by Slovakia; on the east by Ukraine and Romania; on the south by Yugoslavia (Serbia) and Croatia; and on the west by Slovenia and Austria.

It has been estimated that only one German in four was a true democrat. Another quarter hated democracy. The rest went along with the new republic until the economy got rough and then shifted sympathies to authoritarian movements of the left or right. Weimar Germany, it has been said, was a republic without republicans and a democracy without democrats.

The German government, in a crisis with France over reparations, printed money without limit, bringing a **hyperinflation** so insane that by 1923 it took a wheelbarrowful of marks to buy a loaf of bread. Especially hard hit were middle-class families who saw their businesses and savings wiped out; many of them became eager recruits for the Nazis. The period left an indelible mark on Germans, and to this day the German government places great emphasis on preventing inflation.

By the mid-1920s the economy stabilized and things looked better. Cabinets changed frequently: twenty-six in fourteen years. The Social Democrat, Catholic Center, and Conservative parties were the largest; the Nazis were tiny and considered something of a joke. Hitler did resemble Charlie Chaplin. Then the world Depression started in 1929, and German democracy went down the drain. Moderate parties declined, and extremist parties—the Nazis and the Communists—grew (see box on page 174). Unemployment was the key: The more people out of work, the higher the Nazi vote.

One combination might have blocked the Nazis' rise to power. If the Social Democrats and Communists had formed a united front, the Weimar system might have been saved. But the German Communists, who split off from the SPD after World War I, reviled the Social Democrats as cowards and "social fascists." Under Stalin's orders, the German Communists rejected a joint program with the Socialists on the theory that Hitler would be a passing phenomenon and, when Germany collapsed, the Communists would take over. This was one of Stalin's greatest blunders, and Communists and Socialists alike paid for it with their lives.

By late 1932, the Nazis had won a third of the German vote, and the aged President Hindenburg, a conservative general, named Hitler as chancellor in January 1933. The Weimar Republic, Germany's first try at democracy, died after a short life of fourteen years.

The Third Reich

Nazi was the German nickname for the National Socialist German Workers party. Nazism, like other forms of fascism, had a pseudosocialist component that promised jobs and welfare. The Nazis did not

Key Term

hyperinflation Very rapid inflation, more than 50 percent a month.

KEY CONCEPTS

THE HORRORS OF POLARIZED PLURALISM

Italian political scientist Giovanni Sartori described what happens when a multiparty democracy such as Weimar's or Spain's in the 1930s gets terribly sick. The leading parties in the center face nasty opposition on both their right and left. In competing for votes in a highly ideological atmosphere, parties engage in a "politics of outbidding" by offering more radical solutions. Votes flee from the center to the extremes, to parties dedicated to overthrowing democracy. Sartori called this syndrome **polarized pluralism**, and the last years of Weimar are a good example of it. Compare the percentage of votes parties got in 1928 with what they got in 1933, and the "center-fleeing" tendency is clear.

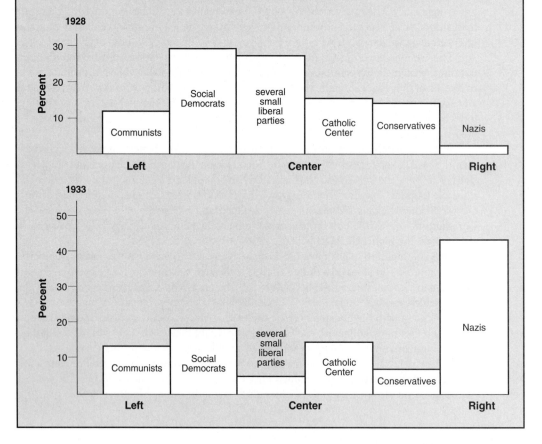

put industries under state ownership like the Communists in the Soviet Union; instead they practiced **Gleichschaltung** (coordination) of the economy under party supervision. Many Germans were delighted to get work on government projects, such as building the new **Autobahnen**. Although the Nazis never won a majority in a fair election, by the late 1930s it is certain that a majority of Germans supported Hitler, whom they saw as restoring prosperity.

Since most Germans had not been enthusiastic about democracy, not many protested the growth of tyranny. Some Communists and Socialists went underground, to prison, or into exile, and some old-style conservatives disliked Hitler, who they felt was nothing but an Austrian guttersnipe. But most Germans got along by going along. Centuries of being taught to obey authority led them to accept Nazi rule.

For some, membership in the Nazi party offered better jobs and sometimes snappy uniforms. Many ex-Nazis claimed they joined only to further their careers, and most were probably telling the truth. You don't need true believers to staff a tyranny; **opportunists** will do just as well. The frightening thing about Nazi Germany was how it could turn normal humans into coldblooded mass murderers.

Among the first and worst to suffer were the Jews, who formed less than half a percent of the German population. Exploiting widely held racist feelings, Hitler depicted the Jews as a poisonous, foreign element who aimed to enslave Germany in the service of international capitalism, international communism, or both. Logical consistency was never the Nazis' strong point. Jews were deprived, one step at a time, of their civil rights, their jobs, their property, their citizenship, and finally their lives.

Few Germans were aware of it, but Hitler ached for war. At first he seemed to be merely consolidating Germany's boundaries, absorbing the Saar in 1935, Austria and the Sudetenland in 1938, and Czech lands in 1939. And it was so easy! Germany's enemies from World War I, still war weary, did nothing to stop the growth of German power and territory. Hitler's generals, it is now known, were ready to overthrow him if the British had said no to his demands at Munich in 1938. It looked as though Hitler could amass victories without even fighting, and the German generals suppressed their doubts. Finally, when the Germans invaded Poland in September 1939, Britain and France declared war. France was overrun, Britain contained beyond the Channel, and by the summer of 1940 Germany or its allies ruled virtually all of Europe.

In 1941 Hitler ordered his **Final Solution** to begin. Death camps killed some six million Jews and a similar number of inconvenient Christians (Poles, gypsies, and others). A new word was added to mankind's vocabulary: **genocide**. The Nazis kept their death camps secret, and many Germans claimed they didn't know what was going on.

Key Terms

polarized pluralism   A sick multiparty system that produces two extremist blocs with little in the center.

Gleichschaltung   Nazi control of Germany's economy.

Autobahn   Express highway, like U.S. interstate.

opportunist   Unprincipled person out for self.

Final Solution   Nazi program to exterminate Jews.

genocide   Murder of an entire people.

DEMOCRACY

THE PLOT TO KILL HITLER

On July 20, 1944, a group of high-ranking German officers tried to kill Hitler. Had he not stepped away from the map table, the briefcase-bomb under it might have succeeded. More than two hundred anti-Nazi Germans were cruelly executed for their part in the plot. They came from all walks of life: generals, diplomats, Weimar politicians, trade unionists, scholars, theologians of both Christian confessions, and students. They were united in their opposition to totalitarianism, mass murder, and the war, which they would have ended as quickly as possible. Although they failed, they left a valuable legacy: the symbol that Germans fought Hitler, a moral statement for present-day German democracy.

The main extermination camp of the Nazi regime was at Auschwitz-Birkenau in southern Poland. Here millions of Jews and inconvenient Christians were gassed and incinerated. (Michael Roskin)

Hitler—just a week before he attacked Poland in 1939—had completed a **nonaggression pact** with Stalin. In the summer of 1941, however, Hitler assembled the biggest army in history and gave the order for "Barbarossa," the conquest and enslavement of the Soviet Union. Here, at last, Hitler's dream parted company with reality. The Russian winter and surprising resistance of the Red Army devoured whole German divisions. From late 1942 on it was all downhill for Germany.

The Occupation

This time there could be no Dolchstoss myth; Germans watched Russians, Americans, British, and French fight their way through Germany. German government ceased to exist, and the country was run by foreign occupiers. At Yalta in February 1945, the Allied leaders agreed to divide Germany into four zones for temporary occupation; Berlin, inside the Soviet zone, was similarly divided.

The Cold War grew in large part out of the way the Soviets handled Germany. The Soviets, having lost over twenty-five million people in the war, were intent on looting the conquered nation. They dismantled whole factories, shipped them home, and flooded the country with inflated military currency. The British and Americans, on the other hand, distressed at the brutal Soviet takeover of East Europe, decided to revive German economic and political life in their zones. The U.S. **Marshall Plan** and other aid programs pumped $3.5 billion into German recovery. In 1948 the British and Americans introduced a currency reform and a new **deutsche Mark (DM)**, which effectively cut out the Soviets from further looting the western zones. In retaliation, the Russians blockaded Berlin, which was supplied for nearly a year by an incredible British-American **Berlin airlift**. The Cold War was on, centered in Germany.

Key Terms

nonaggression pact
Treaty to not attack each other, specifically the 1939 treaty between Hitler and Stalin.

Marshall Plan   Massive U.S. financial aid for European recovery.

deutsche Mark (DM)
German currency since 1948.

Berlin airlift   U.S.-British supply of West Berlin by air in 1948–49.

ANOTHER TALE OF TWO FLAGS

As in France, Germany's divided loyalties have been symbolized by its flags' colors. The German nationalist movement flag was black, red, and gold, colors of a Prussian regiment that fought Napoleon. By 1848 it symbolized a democratic, united Germany. For the Second Reich's flag Bismarck chose Prussia's black and white, plus the white and red of the medieval Hansa commercial league.

The Reich's collapse in 1918 and the founding of the Weimar Republic brought back the democratic black, red, and gold German flag. Hitler, a fanatic for symbols, insisted on authoritarian black, red, and white colors. The Bonn republic designed the present German flag with the original democratic colors.

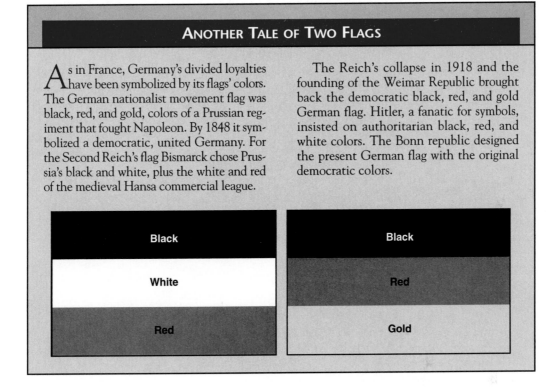

In 1949, the Western allies gave governing power back to West Germans in order to ensure their cooperation against Soviet power. A few months later, the Soviets set up East Germany. Accordingly, both German regimes were children of the Cold War with the Americans and the Soviets acting as respective foster parents. When the Cold War ended—according to some, by the fall of the Berlin Wall in 1989—prosperous and democratic West Germany swallowed weak and dependent East Germany. To examine how West Germany succeeded, let us turn to Germany's institutions.

Germany's Political Eras

Name	Years	Remembered for
Holy Roman Empire	800–1806	Charlemagne, fragmentation, religious wars.
Nineteenth century	1806–1871	Consolidation, modernization stir.
Second Reich	1871–1918	Bismarck unites Germany; industry and war.
Weimar Republic	1919–1933	Weak democracy; culture flourishes.
Nazis	1933–1945	Brutal dictatorship; war; mass murder.
Occupation	1945–1949	Allies divide and run Germany.
Federal Republic	1949–	Democracy; economic miracle; unification; from Bonn to Berlin.

Key Terms

Autobahn (p. 175)   Kulturkampf (p. 171)   Reich (p. 170)
Berlin airlift (p. 176)   Lebensraum (p. 169)   Reichstag (p. 170)
deutsche Mark (p. 176)   Marshall Plan (p. 176)   revisionism (p. 172)
Dolchstoss (p. 172)   Machtpolitik (p. 171)   SPD (p. 171)
Final Solution (p. 175)   Metternichian system (p. 170) Thirty Years War (p. 167)
genocide (p. 175)   nationalism (p. 169)   Versailles Treaty (p. 172)
Gleichschaltung (p. 175)   nonaggression pact (p. 176) Volksgeist (p. 169)
Habsburg (p. 165)   opportunist (p. 175)   Weimar Republic (p. 172)
hyperinflation (p. 173)   polarized pluralism (p. 175) Westphalia (p. 167)
Junker (p. 167)   Prussia (p. 167)
Kaiser (p. 170)   Realpolitik (p. 171)

Further Reference

Berghahn, Volker R. *Imperial Germany, 1871–1914: Economy, Society, Culture, and Politics.* Providence, RI: Berghahn Books, 1994.

Bracher, Karl Dietrich. *The German Dictatorship: The Origins, Structure, and Effects of National Socialism.* New York: Praeger, 1970.

Carr, William. *A History of Germany, 1815–1990,* 4th ed. New York: Routledge, 1992.

Craig, Gordon A. *Germany, 1866–1945.* New York: Oxford University Press, 1978.

Feldman, Gerald D. *The Great Disorder: Politics, Economics, and Society in the German Inflation, 1914–1924.* New York: Oxford University Press, 1993.

Fest, Joachim. *Plotting Hitler's Death: The Story of the German Resistance.* New York: Holt, 1996.

Maier, Charles S. *The Unmasterable Past: History, Holocaust, and German National Identity.* Cambridge, MA: Harvard University Press, 1989.

Marshall, Barbara. *The Origins of Post-War German Politics.* New York: Croom Helm, 1988.

Martell, Gordon. *Modern Germany Reconsidered, 1870–1945.* New York: Routledge, 1992.

Merkl, Peter H. *The Origin of the West German Republic.* New York: Oxford University Press, 1963.

Peukert, Detlev J. K. *The Weimar Republic: The Crisis of Classical Modernity.* New York: Hill & Wang, 1992.

Pulzer, Peter. *Germany, 1870–1945: Politics, State Formation, and War.* New York: Oxford University Press, 1997.

Sartori, Giovanni. *Parties and Party Systems: A Framework for Analysis.* New York: Cambridge University Press, 1976.

Stern, Fritz. *Dreams and Delusions: The Drama of German History.* New York: Alfred A. Knopf, 1987.

13

Germany: The Key Institutions

Questions to Consider

1. How does the debate over Berlin as Germany's capital represent a question of core areas?
2. Is federalism the best route for Germany? Why?
3. How do the French and German presidencies differ?
4. How do the British and German prime ministries differ?
5. Does Germany have a U.S.-type constitutional court? How does it differ?
6. What is the German lower house? How does it differ from the upper house?
7. What are Germany's main parties?
8. How does the German electoral system work?

I n 1949, the founders of the **Federal Republic of Germany** were hopeful that the east and west sections of their country would be reunified. Accordingly, in drafting their founding document—based in part on the 1848–49 Frankfurt and 1919 Weimar constitutions—they called it the **Grundgesetz** (Basic Law) rather than *Verfassung* (constitution), which was to come only when Germany reunified. They meant to indicate that the Federal Republic was temporary and operating under temporary rules. Half a century later, the question is a legal quibble; the Basic Law continues as unified Germany's constitution, and an excellent one at that.

After World War II, West Germany revived an old pattern in German history, **federalism**. Germany's **Länder** have at least as much power as American states, maybe more. Education, medical care, police, and many other functions are the province of the *Land* government. Part of the reason for this strong federalism was to repudiate the centralization of the Nazi period and to make sure that such power could never again become so concentrated.

Berlin was a strange situation. Located 110 miles (180 kilometers)

Key Terms

Federal Republic of Germany West Germany, now all of Germany.

Grundgesetz Basic Law; Germany's constitution.

federalism A system in which component areas have considerable autonomy.

Land plural *Länder*; Germany's first-order civil division, equivalent to a U.S. state.

Key Term

Mitteleuropa Central
Europe.

inside East Germany, Berlin was nominally governed by the four occupying powers. The Soviet sector, however, was turned into the capital of East Germany, and the American, British, and French sectors became to all intents and purposes a part of West Germany. Bonn counted West Berlin as its eleventh *Land*, but the wartime Allies did not recognize it as such. So, officially, West Berlin was not part of the Federal Republic, but in practice it was. West German currency, laws, and passports applied in West Berlin, but the city sent only nonvoting representatives to the Bonn parliament. The anomaly was solved in 1990 with the unification of the two Germanys. With the Berlin Wall down, Greater Berlin became a *Land* and in 1999 the official capital of united Germany, although six ministries (including defense) remained in Bonn.

GEOGRAPHY

FROM BONN TO BERLIN

The 1991 debate that led to the restoration of Berlin as the capital of united Germany was essentially a conflict over core areas. Bonn, a small town in the Catholic Rhine area well to the west, had served as West Germany's capital since 1949. It shifted Germans' attention westward in values, economics, and alliances. Berlin, a major city near the eastern border of Germany, had earlier been the capital of Protestant Prussia but served as Germany's capital from 1871 to 1945. Moving back to Berlin shifted Germans' attention to the problems of the poorer, former-Communist, eastern part of their country. Some critics feared that in the long run it would turn Germany from the West and toward the old concept of a German-dominated **Mitteleuropa**.

Berlin clearly aims to become a world-class city; it is the world's biggest construction site. Hugh cranes litter the horizon as ministries, parliamentary offices, embassies, hotels, and office buildings arise. Berlin is the world's most wide-open city for innovative architecture; curving and soaring metal and glass structures predominate. Even the old Reichstag building was redone with a new glass dome visitors can climb via spiral ramps. By virtue of location, vitality, and architecture, Berlin already is the de facto capital of Central Europe.

Reichstag Dome, the work of British architect Lord Norman Foster, has become Berlin's top tourist attraction. Inside the redone building below the dome, the Bundestag meets. (Michael Roskin)

GEOGRAPHY

FEDERATIONS

Diversity is the advantage of federalism, a system that yields major autonomy to the components, be they U.S. or Brazilian states, German *Länder*, or Russian republics. The components cannot be legally erased or split or have their boundaries easily changed; such matters are grave constitutional questions. Typically, certain powers are reserved for the federal government (defense, money supply, interstate commerce, etc.) while other powers are reserved for the components (education, police, highways, etc.). Large countries or those with particularistic languages or traditions lend themselves to federalism.

The advantages of a federal system are its flexibility and accommodation to particularism. Texans feel Texas is different and special; Bavarians feel Bavaria is different and special; Québécois feel Quebec is different and special; and so on.

If one state or province wishes to try a new formula for funding health care, it may do so without upsetting the state-federal balance. If the new way works, it may be gradually copied. If it fails, little harm is done before it is phased out. U.S. states in this regard have been called "laboratories of democracy": You can try something in one state without committing the entire nation to it. Governments at the *Land* or state level also serve as training grounds for politicians before they try the national level. Clinton and Schröder are two examples of this.

The disadvantage is the inconsistent and sometimes sloppy administration among components. Many federal systems cannot achieve nationwide standards in education, environment, welfare, or health care. One state wants something and can afford it; another state cannot. One state says a certain type of person is eligible for a program; another says he or she is not. Federal systems are generally less coherent than unitary systems. To correct such problems, many federal systems have granted more power to the **center** at the expense of the states. The United States is a prime example of this; compare the relative powers of the states and of Washington over the course of a century. One might say that in unitary systems there is a tugging in the direction of federalism, whereas in federal systems there is a tugging in the direction of unitary systems. This does not necessarily mean that the two will eventually meet in some middle ground; it merely means that neither unitary nor federal systems are finished products and are still evolving.

A federal system may also achieve a stable balance between local and national loyalties, leading gradually to a psychologically integrated country, as the United States, Germany, and Switzerland. This does not always work, though. Soviet, Yugoslav, and Czechoslovak federalism actually fostered resentments of the republics against the center. When Communist party strength weakened, local nationalists took over and declared independence.

East Germany, set up by the Communists in 1949, continued the Nazi pattern of centralized rule with fourteen administrative districts, each named after its leading city, without autonomy. Unification in 1990 brought back to life East Germany's five *Länder*, so now the Federal Republic has sixteen *Länder*, ten from West Germany, five from East Germany, plus Greater Berlin.

Key Term

center   In federal systems, the powers of the nation's capital.

The President

Germany's federal president (*Bundespräsident*) is the classic European president, a figurehead with few political but many symbolic duties. Like the monarchs of Britain and Scandinavia, the German president is an official greeter and ambassador of good will rather than working executive. The French president of the Third and Fourth Republics and today's Italian president are other examples of forgettable presidencies. De Gaulle, of course, greatly strengthened the French presidency.

The president is the "head of state" rather than "chief of government" (for the distinction, see Chapter 3), and as such receives new foreign ambassadors who present their credentials to him rather than to the people they will actually be working with, the chancellor and foreign minister. In addition, the president proclaims laws (after they've been passed by parliament), dissolves the **Bundestag** (upon the chancellor's request), and appoints and dismisses the chancellor (after the leading party has told him to). In short, the German president is, to use Bagehot's terms, a "dignified" rather than "efficient" part of government.

The president is elected by a special Federal Assembly composed of all Bundestag members plus an equal number from the state legislatures. The president serves five years and may be reelected once. The dead-end job is usually given as a reward to distinguished senior politicians. In 1999, the SPD's Johannes Rau was elected president with the support of Green deputies.

Key Terms

Bundestag   Lower house of the German parliament.

chancellor   German prime minister.

constructive no-confidence Requires parliament to vote in a new cabinet when it ousts the current one.

The Chancellor

Germany has a weak president but a strong **chancellor**. Unlike the changing chancellors of the Weimar Republic, the FRG chancellorship has been a stable and durable office. Part of the reason for this is that the Basic Law makes it impossible to oust the chancellor on a vote of no-confidence unless the Bundestag simultaneously votes in a new chancellor. This reform ended one of the worst problems of parliamentary (as opposed to presidential) governments, namely, their dependence on an often-fickle legislative majority.

The German reform is called **constructive no-confidence** because Bundestag has to offer something constructive—a new chancellor—rather than a mere negative majority to get rid of the old one. This has happened only once, in 1982, when the small Free Democratic party abandoned its coalition with the Social Democrats in midterm and voted in a new Christian Democratic chancellor. Constructive no-confidence makes ousting a chancellor a rarity.

Who Was When: Germany's Chancellors

Konrad Adenauer	CDU	1949–63
Ludwig Erhard	CDU	1963–66
Kurt Georg Kiesinger	CDU	1966–69
Willy Brandt	SPD	1969–74
Helmut Schmidt	SPD	1974–82
Helmut Kohl	CDU	1982–98
Gerhard Schröder	SPD	1998–

DEMOCRACY

PREFIX TO DEMOCRACY

In Germany today almost everything associated with the federal government bears the prefix *Bundes-*, meaning "federal." Thus:

- *Bundesrepublik Deutschland* is the Federal Republic of German, FRG.
- *Bundestag* is the lower house of the federal parliament.
- *Bundesrat* is the upper house.
- *Bundeskanzler* is the federal chancellor (prime minister).

- *Bundeswehr* is the army.
- *Bundesbank* is the national bank.
- *Bundesministerium* is a federal ministry.
- *Bundesregierung* is the federal government.

The prefix *Bundes-* is new, stemming only from the founding of West Germany in 1949, and has a modern, democratic ring to it. The old prefix to many of the same words, *Reichs-* (imperial), has a slightly sinister, discarded connotation. In Germany, "federal" has become synonymous with "democratic."

Another reason the chancellor is strong stems from the first occupant of that office: Konrad Adenauer, a tough, shrewd politician who helped found the Federal Republic and served as chancellor during its first fourteen years. First occupants, such as Washington in the American presidency, can put a stamp on the position, defining its powers and setting its style for generations. Adenauer—who was seventy-three when he first became chancellor—showed strong leadership and made numerous decisions without bothering parliament or his cabinet too much. A Catholic Rhinelander, he formed the CDU, set up a "two-plus" party system, pointed Germany decisively westward into NATO and the EU, and established a special relationship with France. Chancellors ever since Adenauer have been measured against him. His successor, for example, the amiable and intelligent Ludwig Erhard, was found wanting because he couldn't exercise firm leadership.

Partly thanks to the style Adenauer set, the German chancellor is approximately as powerful as the British prime minister, which is to say quite powerful. The chancellor picks his own cabinet—with political considerations in mind, like the British PM. He is responsible for the main lines of government policy and has to defend them before the Bundestag and the public. As such, he is implicitly held responsible for what his ministers say and do.

The Cabinet

The typical German cabinet is somewhat smaller than its French or British counterpart but still larger than the U.S. cabinet. In the late 1990s the German cabinet had fifteen ministers, including three Greens, one with no party affiliation, five women, and three Ph.D.s:

Minister of the Chancellery (chief of staff)
Foreign Minister

Interior Minister

Justice Minister

Finance Minister (that is, treasury)

Economics and Technology Minister

Minister for Nutrition, Agriculture, and Forestry

Minister for Labor and Social Affairs

Defense Minister

Minister for Health

Minister for Family, the Elderly, Women, and Youth

Transport, Construction and Housing Minister

Minister for Education and Research

Minister for Economic Cooperation and Development (foreign aid and trade)

Minister for Environment, Conservation, and Reactor Safety

As is usual in Europe, these ministries are added, deleted, combined, split, and reshuffled from one cabinet to another. For example, in the previous (Kohl) cabinet, there was a separate minister for posts and telecommunications, which was deleted in the Schröder cabinet. Schröder added two special-purpose advisors as "ministers of state in the chancellery" who were not heads of a ministry. Such redefinitions of who or what is in a cabinet are no big deal in Europe; what the leader of the largest party wants, he or she gets. Chief job of the Interior Ministry is protection of the constitution (*Verfassungsschutz*), which includes monitoring extremist parties and movements. The only police they have at their disposal, however, are the Border Police and Federal Criminal Office; all other police are at the *Land* or municipal level.

As in Britain (but not in France), practically all German cabinet ministers are also working politicians with seats in the Bundestag. Like their British counterparts, they are rarely specialists in their assigned portfolio. Most are trained as lawyers and have served in a variety of party and legislative positions. The job of parliamentary state secretary serves as a training ground for potential cabinet ministers. Below cabinet rank, a parliamentary state secretary is assigned to each minister to assist in relations with the Bundestag, in effect a bridge between executive and legislative branches, as in Britain.

The Bundestag

Konrad Adenauer, the authoritarian democrat, did not place great faith in the Bundestag. Germany never had a strong parliamentary tradition. Bismarck all but ignored the Reichstag (whose building the Bundestag now occupies). During the Weimar Republic, the Reichstag, unprepared for the governing responsibilities thrust upon it, could not exercise power. Then in 1949 came Adenauer who, like most Germans, had never seen an efficient, stable, responsible parliament, and so tended to disdain the new one. Since Adenauer's time, the Bundestag has been trying to establish itself as a pillar of democracy and as an important branch of government. Success has been gradual and incomplete. Many Germans still do not respect the Bundestag very much.

The Bundestag has at least 656 members, making it the largest democratically elected parliament in the world. Deputies are elected for four years and

Key Term

Jusos Short for Young Socialists, the radical youth wing of SPD.

GERHARD SCHRÖDER: A GERMAN BLAIR?

German Chancellor Gerhard Schröder was compared to British Prime Minister Tony Blair, who was popular all over Europe. Some things matched, but much did not. Both were young, moderate leftists who led their respective parties, Labour and the SPD, back into power after long spells in opposition. Both won in large part because voters were tired of the long conservative reign (Thatcher and Major from 1979 to 1997, Kohl from 1982 to 1998). Both were vague about where they stood—Blair for a "Third Way," Schröder for a *"Neue Mitte"* (New Center).

But there were differences. Blair had a vision and policies for change; Schröder did not. Blair had redone Labour into New Labour well before the 1997 elections; Schröder papered over splits in the SPD and pretended it was the New Center. Blair was from the comfortable middle class and well-schooled. Schröder came from grim circumstances. Born into a North German Protestant family in 1944, Schröder was three days old when his father was killed on the Russian front. His mother worked as a cleaning lady. Schröder dropped out of school at age 14 to help with family expenses but later won a scholarship to study law. (In contrast, Schröder's predecessor, Helmut Kohl, was a middle-class Rhineland Catholic.)

Schröder joined the **Jusos** at age 19 and led it in militantly leftist causes. Elected to the Bundestag in 1980, Schröder was the first deputy to address the house without wearing a necktie. (Greens later repeated the gesture.) Over time, however, Schröder became moderate and even friendly to business. In 1990 he led the SPD to an upset victory in the *Land* of Lower Saxony, where he governed with an SPD-Green coalition. After three divorces, he is married to wife number four. His spurned third wife calls him "a coward, an opportunist, and an egotist." (The French didn't care about Mitterrand's "parallel family," and the Germans don't care about Schröder's marriages. Why are Americans so different in these matters?)

After the SPD ran too-intellectual and too-leftist candidates against Kohl (Oskar Lafontaine in 1990 and Rudolf Scharping in 1994), Schröder offered his friendly, outgoing personality and vague centrist notions to reduce Germany's high unemployment to win for the SPD in 1998. Schröder, however, had no clear program or strong personal convictions. With the SPD and Greens still split among moderates and radicals, Schröder was pulled in different directions and delivered on little. The SPD declined in public-opinion polls but was given a boost by the revelations that the CDU had taken major and illegal "campaign funds" while Kohl was chancellor. An uptick in the German economy further boosted Schröder's standing.

Chancellor Gerhard Schröder. (German Information Center)

Key Term

grand coalition   A government composed of the largest parties, leaving only minor parties in opposition.

paid $89,000 a year. Under a parliamentary (as opposed to presidential) system, the legislature can never be a severe critic of the administration in the manner of the U.S. Congress. After all, the Bundestag's majority parties produce the government; they can't very well criticize it too harshly. Neither is the Bundestag the tumultuous assembly of the French Third and Fourth Republics; the FRG legislature can unmake a government only when it makes a new one. Nor is the Bundestag the docile rubber stamp that de Gaulle made of the French National Assembly. Still less is it the colorful debating chamber of the House of Commons, where brilliant orators try to sway the public for the next election. On balance, the Bundestag has less independent power than the U.S. Congress but more than the French National Assembly and possibly even the British House of Commons.

One interesting point about the Bundestag is its relatively high number of women members, about a quarter, typical of North European systems that use proportional representation, which allows parties to place women candidates on party lists. Over 40 percent of Sweden's parliamentarians are women. On the other hand, only 12 percent of U.S., 9 percent of British, and 6 percent of French national legislators are women, partly the result of single-member districts for elections.

The Bundestag's strong point is its committee work. Here, behind closed doors (most sessions are secret), Bundestag deputies, including opposition members, can make their voices heard. German legislative committees are more important and more specialized than their British counterparts. German party discipline is not as tight as the British so that deputies from the ruling party can criticize a government bill while opposition deputies sometimes agree with it. In the give and take of committee work, the opposition is often able to get changes made in legislation. Once back on the Bundestag floor—and all bills must be reported out; they can't be killed in committee—voting is on party lines with occasional defections on matters of conscience.

KEY CONCEPTS

THE GRAND COALITION

From 1966 to 1969 West Germany was ruled by a joint Christian Democrat-Social Democrat government, a so-called **grand coalition** because it included both the large parties and left only the small Free Democrats, who had but 6 percent of the Bundestag seats, to oppose and criticize. The advantage of a grand coalition is obvious: It has such an overwhelming majority in parliament that it can't be ousted and can pass any laws it likes.

The negative side became more obvious with time: People came to feel that nobody could criticize the government, that politics was a game rigged by the powerful, and that democracy was a sham. A leftist "extraparliamentary opposition" grew and criticized the government in radical terms. Some of West Germany's terrorists first became active in disgust at the wall-to-wall grand coalition, which is probably useful only for emergencies; if it stays in office too long it starts undermining faith in democracy. A good democracy requires a lively interaction between "ins" and "outs" rather than collusion between the two.

In 1999 the Bundestag met for the first time in its new Berlin home, the building that is still called the Reichstag and still bears the famous "For the German People." The Reichstag had met there from 1894 to 1933. (Michael Roskin)

The approximately twenty standing Bundestag committees are almost exactly the same as the cabinet ministries listed earlier in this chapter. The system is designed that way: Each cabinet minister can deal directly with a parallel, relevant Bundestag committee. The ministers, themselves Bundestag members, sometimes come over from their executive offices to explain to committee sessions a proposed piece of legislation.

In a parallel with French deputies, Bundestag membership is heavy with civil servants. German law permits bureaucrats to take leaves of absence to run for and serve in the Bundestag. Another important category is people from interest groups—business associations and labor unions. Together, these two groups usually form a majority of the Bundestag membership. While we can't be sure that this does any harm to German democracy, it does contribute to a public feeling that parliament is a place where the powerful meet to decide matters with little reference to popular wishes.

The Constitutional Court

In very few countries is the judiciary equal in power to the legislative or executive branches. The United States and Germany are two; both allow the highest court in the land to review the constitutionality of laws. The **Federal Constitutional Court** (*Bundesverfassungsgericht*, BVerfG), located in Karlsruhe, was set up in 1951 partly on American insistence. The American occupiers reasoned that something like the Supreme Court would help prevent another Hitler, and many Germans agreed with what was for Germany (and indeed all of Europe) a new concept.

The Karlsruhe court is composed of sixteen judges, eight elected

Key Term

Federal Constitutional Court Germany's top court, equivalent to U.S. Supreme Court.

Key Terms

extreme multipartism
Too many parties in parliament.

"two-plus" party system   Two big parties and several small ones.

monocolor   In parliamentary systems, cabinet composed of just one party.

by each house of parliament, who serve for nonrenewable, twelve-year terms. The BVerfG operates as two courts, or "senates," of eight judges each to speed up the work. Completely independent of other branches of German government, the court decides cases between *Länder*, protects civil liberties, outlaws dangerous political parties, and otherwise makes sure that statutes conform to the Basic Law.

The Constitutional Court's decisions have been important. It has declared illegal some right and left extremist parties on the grounds that they sought to overthrow the constitutional order. It found that abortion bills collided with the strong right-to-life provisions of the Basic Law and thus ruled them unconstitutional. (In 1993, however, it decided not to prosecute women who had first-trimester abortions.) In 1979 it ruled that "worker codetermination" in the running of factories was constitutional. In 1983 it found that Chancellor Helmut Kohl had acted within the constitution when he arranged to lose a Bundestag vote of confidence so he could hold elections early (which he won). In 1994 it ruled Germany can send troops overseas for peacekeeping operations. In 1995 it overrode a Bavarian law requiring a crucifix in every classroom. Judicial review has worked well in Germany, although the Constitutional Court, because it operates in the context of the more rigid code law, does not have the impact of the U.S. Supreme Court, whose decisions serve as precedents within the U.S. Common Law system.

Germany's "Two-Plus" Party System

Much of the reason the FRG government works rather well is the party system that has evolved since 1949. The Weimar Reichstag suffered from **extreme multipartism**; a dozen parties, some of them extremist, made forming stable coalitions difficult. Germany, more than Britain, now has a **"two-plus" party system**, because German governments almost always consist of one large party in coalition with one small party. Britain, with its majoritarian system, almost always gives one party a majority in parliament. Germany, with its proportional system, seldom produces **monocolor** governments. A two-plus party system is somewhere between a two-party system and a multiparty system.

For most of the FRG's history the largest party has been the Christian Democratic Union (*Christlich Demokratische Union*, CDU) with its Bavarian affiliate, the Christian Social Union (CSU). Sometimes the party is designated CDU/CSU. The original core of the CDU was the old Catholic-based Center party, one of the few parties that held its own against the growth of Nazism in the early 1930s. After World War II, Center politicians like Adenauer decided to go for a broader-based center-right party, one in which Protestants would also feel welcome. Like most European conservative parties, the CDU never embraced totally free-market capitalism, instead it went for a "social market" economy (see Chapter 16). The CDU/CSU has been the largest party in every election except 1972 and 1998, when the SPD edged it out. In 1998 it drew 35.2 percent of the national vote. Its current chairwoman is Angela Merkel, an East German physicist who was catapulted into leadership in 2000 by the CDU's fundraising scandal.

The Social Democratic party (*Sozialdemokratische Partei Deutschlands*, SPD) is the grand old party of European socialism and the only German party that antedates the founding of the Federal Republic. Originally Marxist, the SPD gradually became more and more "revisionist" until, in 1959, it dropped Marxism altogether. It was then that its electoral fortunes grew as it expanded beyond its traditional working-class base and into the middle class, especially intellectuals. Now a center-left party, the SPD's socialism amounts basically to support for welfare measures plus vague plans for reform. It won 40.9 percent of the national vote in 1998. An SPD problem: Its chancellor is centrist Schröder, but it still contains many firm leftists, who struggle with Schröder for control of the party.

The small Free Democratic party (*Freie Demokratische Partei*, FDP) is a classic liberal party, which in Europe is in the center of the political spectrum. It wants a free society, free market, more individual responsibility, and less government. (Note that liberalism in Europe means about the opposite of U.S. liberalism.) The FDP had trouble defining itself and often dropped to under 10 percent of the vote. In 1994 it won 6.9 percent. Like Britain's Liberals, the FDP is an alternative for voters mistrustful of the two big parties.

In 1983, a new ecology-pacifist party, the **Greens**, made it into the Bundestag. In 1998 it won 6.7 percent and became the coalition partner of the SPD. The leader of the Greens, Joseph Fischer, became foreign minister, the usual portfolio for the head of the second-largest party in a coalition. The Greens, once quite radical, became pragmatic and **regierungsfähig** during the 1990s. They want to phase out Germany's nineteen nuclear power plants and to put hefty "eco-taxes" on gasoline. Fischer, still known as "Joschka" (Little Joe), dropped out of high school, married three times, and engaged in street demonstrations. Now he wears a tie and understands the needs of business.

As soon as the Wall came down in 1998, West Germany's parties simply moved in and took over. The small, new East German parties that had spearheaded the ouster of the Communists were elbowed aside by the CDU and SPD, who had the money and organization. One regional East German party survives, the Party of Democratic Socialism (PDS), composed of ex-Communists and those who feel ignored by the new system. The PDS just made it over the 5 percent hurdle nationwide in the 1998 elections (but polled 21 percent in the former East Germany). Several small leftist and rightist parties, including Communists and neo-Nazis, win a few seats in local elections but have won no seats in the Bundestag.

Key Terms

Greens In Europe, environmentalist parties.

regierungsfähig Literally, "able to form a government," a party that has matured and become capable of ruling.

Bundesrat Literally, federal council; upper chamber of German parliament; represents states.

Landtag German state legislature.

The Bundesrat

Neither Britain nor France really needs an upper house because Britain and France are unitary systems. The German federal system has a useful upper house, the **Bundesrat**. Not as powerful as the U.S. Senate—an upper house that powerful is a world rarity—the Bundesrat represents the sixteen *Länder* and has equal power with the Bundestag on legislation that affects state affairs. On other issues the Bundesrat can veto a bill, but the Bundestag can override it.

The Bundesrat consists of sixty-eight members. Every German *Land*, no matter how small, gets at least three. More populous *Länder* get four; the most populous get six. Each *Land* has the right to appoint its delegates and in practice this has meant delegations of the leading state-level politicians, officials elected to the **Landtag**, who become cabinet members in the *Land* government. This often means that members of a state's delegation will all belong to one party. Each Bundesrat delegation must vote as a bloc, not as individuals. The theory here is that they represent states, not parties or themselves.

KEY CONCEPTS

GERMANY'S ELECTORAL SYSTEM: AN EXPORT PRODUCT

Germany's hybrid electoral system, which was technically called "mixed-member proportional" (MMP), was much talked about for decades. Then, in the early 1990s, several countries paid Germany the highest compliment by adopting similar systems, with national variations. The aim in all cases was to combine the simplicity of single-member districts with some of the theoretical fairness of PR. Some of the German-inspired hybrids:

- Russian elections since 1993 fill half of the 450-seat lower house by single-member districts and half by PR with a 5 percent threshold.
- In 1993, Italy voted to drop its traditional PR system to one in which 75 percent of the seats of both chambers are filled from single-member districts and 25 percent by PR.

- In 1994, Japan turned from its unique electoral system of multi-member districts with plurality victors to a system in which more than half the members of each house are elected from single-member districts, while the remainder are elected by PR in eleven regions (see pages 328–29).
- New Zealand in 1993 turned from straight Anglo-American single-member districts to a new system for its unicameral legislature of 60 such districts plus 60 elected by PR at the national level with a 5 percent threshold.
- The 1999 elections for Scottish and Welsh parliaments had single-member FPTP districts but "topped off" the parties' seats by PR so that they are roughly proportional to their vote share.

A Split Electoral System

Both Britain and the United States use single-member districts with plurality win (FPTP) in their parliamentary elections. The advantage with this system is that it anchors a deputy to a district, giving the representative an abiding interest in his or her constituents. The disadvantage is that the system does not accurately reflect votes for parties nationwide; seats are not proportional to votes. (It also gives U.S. Representatives too much interest in looking after the folks back home and too little interest in the good of the country as a whole.)

The alternative, proportional representation (PR), makes the party's percentage of seats nearly proportional to its votes. Weimar Germany had a PR system, which was part of its undoing. PR systems are theoretically the fairest but in practice often lead to difficulties. They permit many small parties in parliament, including antidemocratic extremist parties. They make coalitions hard to form and unstable because usually several parties must combine. Israel, with fifteen parties in parliament, suffers these consequences of pure proportional representation.

The German system combines both approaches, single-member districts and proportional representation. The voter has two votes, one for a single representative in one of 328 districts, the other for a party. The party vote is the crucial one, for it determines the total number

"You Have Two Votes": A German Ballot

of seats a party gets in a given *Land*. Some of these seats are occupied by the party's district winners; additional seats are taken from the party's *Landesliste* to reach the percentage won on the second ballot. This *Landesliste* (the right-hand column on the sample ballot above) is a list of persons whom the party proposes as deputies, starting with the names at the top of the list. The **party list** is the standard technique for a PR system. Leading party figures are assigned high positions on the list to ensure that they get elected; people at the bottom of the party list don't have a chance.

The German system works like proportional representation—

Key Term

party list   A party's ranking of its candidates in PR elections; voters pick one list as their ballot.

DEMOCRACY

THE STRUGGLE OF THE LIBERAL DEMOCRATS

With a **turnout** of 82 percent, the German elections in October 1998 ousted CDU Chancellor Kohl after four terms and made the Social Democrats the largest party in the Bundestag. An SPD coalition with the Greens gave them a twenty-one seat majority, enough to form a cabinet with Social Democrat Gerhard Schröder as chancellor.

The 1998 elections, the third for the newly unified nation, operated under the long-established FRG rules that are based on PR but add single-member districts. First, notice how close the percent of vote (on the right-hand, PR ballot) is to the percent of Bundestag seats (see table at end of box).

Notice also the discrepancies: These four parties got more seats than their percentage of the votes. This is partly because some small parties (e.g., the neo-Nazi Republicans) won less than 5 percent and got no seats. Further, ticket-splitting—voting, for example, for the CDU candidate on the left-hand half of the ballot but for the FDP on the right-hand side—won the two big parties more seats than did the percentage of their party votes. The FDP, in fact, wins seats only on the second ballot, the party list; almost nowhere are they big enough to win a single-member district.

Those who win in a single-member district (the left half of the ballot) keep the seat even if it exceeds the percentage their party is entitled to from the PR (right half of the ballot) vote. For this reason, the Bundestag often expands beyond its nominal size of 656 seats to accommodate these "bonus seats." The Bundestag now has 669 members to accommodate the thirteen bonus seats delivered by the 1998 elections.

Is the German electoral system now clear to you? Don't worry. Even many Germans don't fully understand it. Basically, all you have to remember is that it's a split system: roughly half single-member districts and half PR, but PR sets the overall number of seats.

	% of Vote	Seats
Social Democrats	40.9	298 (44.5%)
Christian Democrats	35.2	245 (36.6%)
Free Democrats	6.2	44 (6.6%)
Greens	6.7	47 (7%)
Party of Democratic Socialism	5.1	35 (5.2%)

percentage of votes equals percentage of Bundestag seats—but with the advantage of single-member districts. As in Britain and the United States, voters get a district representative. More than in straight PR systems, personality counts in German elections; a politician can't be just a good party worker but has to go out and talk with voters to earn their confidence on a personal basis. It is a matter of considerable pride among FRG politicians to be elected from a single-member district with a higher percentage of votes than their party won on the second ballot. It means that voters split their tickets because they liked the candidate better than his or her party.

For most of the postwar years, the partially single-member German system worked to slowly cut down the number of parties compared to Weimar days until it was a two-plus system (a big CDU and SPD, plus a small FDP). One reason: A party must win at least 5 percent nationwide or three single-member seats to gain admittance into the Bundestag. The **threshold clause** was designed to keep out splinter and extremist parties. More recently, however, some new

Key Terms

turnout   Percentage of those eligible who vote in a given election.

threshold clause   The minimum percent a party must win to gain any seats.

small parties have made it into parliament, the Greens and the Party of Democratic Socialism. Variations on the German hybrid electoral system were adopted by several countries (see box on page 190).

German parties get government help for campaign funds, but after the election. Every party that makes it into the Bundestag gets DM 1.30 ($0.70) for each citizen's vote up to five million votes, then DM 1 ($0.55) for each additional vote. Furthermore, parties' contributions and membership fees are matched 50 percent by federal funds. Typically, every German national election costs taxpayers $150 million or more.

Key Terms

Bundesrat (p. 189)

Bundestag (p. 182)

center (p. 181)

chancellor (p. 182)

constructive no-confidence (p. 182)

extreme multipartism (p. 188)

Federal Constitutional Court (p. 187)

Federal Republic of Germany (p. 179)

federalism (p. 179)

grand coalition (p. 186)

Greens (p. 189)

Grundgesetz (p. 179)

Jusos (p. 184)

Land (p. 179)

Landtag (p. 189)

Mitteleuropa (p. 180)

monocolor (p. 188)

party list (p. 191)

regierungsfähig (p. 189)

threshold clause (p. 192)

turnout (p. 192)

"two-plus" party system (p. 188)

Further Reference

Beyme, Klaus von. *The Legislator: German Parliament as a Centre of Political Decision-Making.* Brookfield, VT: Ashgate, 1998.

Conradt, David, Gerald R. Kleinfled, George K. Romoser, and Christain Soe. *Power Shift in Germany: The 1998 Election and the End of the Kohl Era.* Providence, RI: Berghan, 1999.

Johnson, Nevil. *State and Government in the Federal Republic of Germany: The Executive at Work,* 2nd ed. New York: Pergamon Press, 1983.

Klein, Hans, ed. *The German Chancellors.* Carol Stream, IL: Edition Q, 1996.

Moeller, Robert G., ed. *West Germany under Construction: Politics, Society, and Culture in the Adenauer Era.* Ann Arbor, MI: University of Michigan Press, 1997.

Nicholls, A. J. *The Bonn Republic: West German Democracy, 1945–1990.* New York: Longman, 1997.

Quint, Peter E. *The Imperfect Union: Constitutional Structures of German Unification.* Princeton, NJ: Princeton University Press, 1997.

Schweitzer, Carl-Christoph, et al., eds. *Politics and Government in the Federal Republic of Germany, 1944–1994—Basic Documents,* 2nd rev. ed. Providence, RI: Berghahn Books, 1996.

Thaysen, Uwe, Roger H. Davidson, and Robert Gerald Livingston, eds. *The U.S. Congress and the West German Bundestag: Comparisons of Democratic Processes.* Boulder, CO: Westview, 1990.

German Political Culture

14

Questions to Consider

1. What is meant by "liberal democracy"? Why was it difficult in Germany?
2. How have Germans handled the Nazi period and the Holocaust?
3. Have Americans attempted to blot out their past?
4. What is "postmaterialism"? Is it nearly everywhere?
5. What are Germany's "political generations"?
6. Why do Wessis and Ossis resent each other?
7. Is German democracy as solid as any? How can you tell?
8. How did Willy Brandt represent a turning point?

A German woman once recounted to me how the Americans, in the last days of World War II, had bombed her hometown, a charming North Bavarian place with a splendid church and no military value. The town was a mess: Bodies lay unburied, water and electricity were out, food supplies were unmoved. What did the people of the town do to meet this emergency? "Oh, nothing," she shrugged. "We waited for the Americans to come and tell us what to do."

Such were the beginnings of democracy in West Germany: A foreign implant grafted onto a people who were used to being told what to do. Can democracy be transplanted? Has it in fact taken root in Germany? This is the really bothersome question. The institutions are fine; in several ways the Federal Republic's Basic Law is a model constitution. But, as we saw with Weimar, good institutions aren't worth much if people don't support them. Are democratic values sufficiently strong and deep in Germany to withstand economic and political hard times?

Historically, there has long been a liberal tradition in Germany, an outgrowth of the Enlightenment, as exists in France. In Britain, democracy gradually triumphed. In France, democracy and reaction seesawed back and forth, finally reaching an uneasy balance. In Germany, on the other hand, democracy was overwhelmed by authoritarian forces. In 1849 the German liberals were driven out of the Frankfurt cathedral. In Bismarck's Second Reich they were treated with contempt. In the Weimar Republic they were in a distinct minority position, a pushover for authoritarians. Until the Bonn Republic, the democratic strand in German politics was a losing tradition.

East Germany tried to develop attitudes of "people's democracy" (communism) rather than **liberal democracy** in the Western sense. Although communism and fascism are supposedly opposites, some note that both aimed to make individuals obedient and powerless. This left many East Germans skeptical of the onrush of democracy from West Germany in 1990; they had known nothing but authoritarian rule since 1933. It will take years of intensive education for East German democratic attitudes to reach the levels of West Germany.

Key Terms

liberal democracy   A system that combines tolerance and freedoms (liberalism) with mass participation (democracy).

denazification   Purging Nazi officials from public life.

The Moral Vacuum

In addition to a lack of democratic tradition, Germany faced a more subtle problem after World War II. A liberal democracy requires certain moral foundations. If you are entrusting ultimate authority to the people through their representatives, you have to believe that they are generally moral, perhaps even a bit idealistic. When this belief vanishes, a democracy loses some of its legitimacy. People may go along with it but without deep faith. (Notice how this was one of the concerns during Clinton's impeachment.)

The Nazi period left a moral vacuum in Germany, and filling it has been a long, slow process, one still not complete. One problem that hindered the development of German democracy was the persistence of ex-Nazis in high places. Every time one was discovered, it undermined the moral authority of the regime. People, especially young people, thought, "Why should we respect democracy if there are still the same old Nazis running it?"

Immediately after the war, the Allied occupiers tried to "denazify" their zones. Party members, especially officials and the Gestapo (secret police), lost their jobs and sometimes went to prison. Henry Kissinger, then a U.S. Army sergeant, had a neat trick for rounding up Gestapo agents in the town he was running. He just put an ad in the newspaper for experienced policemen; when they showed up he slapped them in jail. Still, aside from the 177 war criminals tried at Nuremberg (twenty-five sentenced to death), **denazification** was spotty, and many Nazis got away, to Latin America or to new lives within Germany. Many Nazis made themselves useful to the occupation authorities and worked their way into business, politics, the civil service, and even the judicial system.

It is this last-mentioned group that kept Nazi mass murderers from coming to trial. There are laws on the books against such people, but Nazi criminals were rarely brought to trial until the 1960s. By then younger people had worked their way up the judicial ladder and were willing to prosecute cases their elders preferred to let pass. This helps explain why Nazi criminals were still being tried in the 1990s.

The Cold War also delayed a thorough look at the Nazi past. By 1948 if not before, the Western Allies decided they needed Germany to block the spread of Soviet power, so they stopped rubbing Germans' noses in the past. Tough questions about the wartime behavior of German civilian and military officials were not asked; now they were on our side. With the founding of the Federal Republic in 1949, such matters were placed in the hands of West German authorities, and many preferred not to "open old wounds."

Two presidents of the Federal Republic, Walter Scheel of the FDP and Karl Carstens of the CDU, and one chancellor, Kurt Kiesinger of the CDU, were once Nazi party members. All

POLITICAL CULTURE

HOW TO HANDLE THE HOLOCAUST

Keep it front and center, or retire it as an overworked issue from a bygone era? This was the dilemma Germany faced as it restored Berlin as the nation's capital in the 1990s. The problem was more subtle than nazism and anti-Semitism, of which there were little in the FRG. Some Germans felt that leftists had turned guilt for the Holocaust into an all-purpose tool to promote **multiculturalism** and political correctness. Some tired of hearing about the Holocaust, which only the oldest third of Germans had personally lived through.

Germany has paid some $60 billion in **reparations** for the Holocaust, and many Germans felt this was enough. Novelist Martin Walser created a storm in 1998 when he argued that Auschwitz should not be used as a "tool of intimidation" against Germans, who "have become a normal people now, an ordinary society." The head of Germany's Jewish community called Walser's comments "intellectual nationalism" and "understated anti-Semitism."

The specific question was whether and what kind of Holocaust memorial should be built in the heart of Berlin. CDU Chancellor Kohl had urged it; new SPD Chancellor Schröder and his party had some doubts. Some argued that there were already enough

such memorials. A new Jewish Museum opened in Berlin in early 1999 (designed and directed by Americans). Some argued that no memorial could possibly do justice to the magnitude of the horror. Some suggested that a death camp was the proper site. Some wanted a big memorial, others small. Some wanted a traditional memorial, others abstract. In 1999, the Bundestag finally authorized a large memorial by a U.S. architect in the heart of Berlin.

German businesses had a rough time with the Holocaust issue as well. Under the Nazis, they had benefited from the money and property seized from Jews and from Jewish (and other) slave labor. For decades, German businesses, banks, and insurance companies rejected survivors' demands for compensation with the claim that private firms, like everyone else, had to follow Nazi orders. They belatedly made efforts to settle when faced with class-action lawsuits in U.S. courts. In 1999, Chancellor Schröder, backed by twelve major German firms, set up a $5 billion compensation fund "to counter lawsuits, particularly class-action suits, and to remove the basis of the campaign being led against German industry and our country." Schröder's statement reawoke in some minds the old Nazi line that an international Jewish conspiracy was keeping Germany down.

asserted they were nominal rather than active members, "just opportunists" out to further their careers during a time when the Nazis controlled many paths to success. While none were charged with any crime, what kind of moral authority did "just an opportunist" lend to the highest offices of a country trying to become a democracy?

The Remembrance of Things Past

Can a society experience collective guilt? Was it realistic to expect Germans as a whole to feel remorse for what the Nazis did? The West German response was initially to flush the Nazi era down the memory hole, to say in effect, "Past, go away!" German fathers were reluctant to say much about what they had done. For some decades, German history textbooks stopped at 1933 and picked up again in 1945. The result was ignorance among young Germans in the 1950s and 1960s about the Nazis and the **Holocaust**. Then, in 1979, the American-made TV miniseries "Holocaust" riveted Germans' attention and triggered German books, movies, documentaries, and discussion. In the 1980s, curricula and textbooks changed to treat the Nazi period more fully. This belated Holocaust flood, however, made some Germans feel resentful and picked-upon.

Can a society simply forget its past, blot it out? West Germans tried. Climbing out of the ruins of World War II, Germans threw themselves with single-minded devotion into work, making money, and spending it conspicuously. The results were spectacular; the economy soared, and many Germans became affluent. The West German archetype became the *Wunderkind* (wonder child), the businessman who rose from rubble to riches in the postwar boom with a fat body, a fat cigar, and a fat Mercedes.

But material prosperity could not fill the moral and historical void. Many young Germans in the 1960s were greatly dissatisfied with the emphasis on materialism that seemed to be a cover-up for a lack of deeper values. Some of them turned to far-left and later "green" politics.

This factor probably contributed to the growth of radical and sometimes violent politics among young Germans in the 1970s and 1980s. Certainly it wasn't because they were poor; their society was prosperous, and often they were from wealthy families. Prosperity and materialism, in fact, rubbed them the wrong way. Said one rich girl: "I'm sick of all this caviar gobbling." Then she joined the terrorists and helped murder an old family friend, a banker. (She and other gang members were arrested in 1990 in East Germany, where they had been protected by the secret police, the Stasi.) The Baader-Meinhof gang committed murder and bank robbery in the name of revolution, and some young Germans sympathized with them. The terrorists, in their warped, sick way, put their finger on the German malaise: German society, avoiding its past, had developed a moral void with nothing to believe in but "caviar gobbling." The past, it seems, doesn't stay buried; it comes back to haunt the society trying to forget it. In the words of American writer William Faulkner: "The past is still with us; it isn't even past."

German Catholic writer Heinrich Böll in the 1950s coined the term **Vergangenheitsbewältigung** to direct Germans' attention to the moral vacuum. He meant that Germans must face the past and admit a degree of collective guilt. Many German intellectuals take this as the

Key Terms

Holocaust   Nazi genocide of Europe's Jews during World War II.

multiculturalism   Preservation of diverse languages and traditions within one country; in German, *Multikulti*.

reparations   Paying back for war damages.

Vergangenheitsbewältigung   Literally, "mastery of the past"; coming to grips with German's Nazi past.

GEOGRAPHY

SAILING THE BALTIC

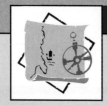

Back on your luxury yacht, you are sailing in a great, clockwise circle around the Baltic Sea, always staying with land a few kilometers to port (left). Upon entering the Skagerrak, which countries do you pass on your left?

Norway, Sweden, Finland, Russia, Estonia, Latvia, Lithuania, Russia again (Kaliningrad Oblast), Poland, Germany, and Denmark.

necessary foundation of German democracy. If Germans can't come to grips with their own past, if they try to cover it up, German democracy could again be taken over by mindless nationalists, cautioned former President Richard von Weizsäcker and leftist writer Günter Grass.

For most of the history of the Federal Republic there was a greater commitment to learning the lessons of the past on the left, among the SPD and Greens, than on the right. The Bavarian CSU shunned the notion that Germany's past needed examining. By the late 1990s, however, the shoe was on the other foot as leftists and liberals—including SPD Chancellor Gerhard Schröder—felt that the new generation of Germans had nothing to do with the Nazis and therefore should not be hectored by outsiders. They should look to the future, not the past. Many Germans agreed, but some worried that growing beneath the words was a self-pitying German nationalism that could turn angry.

Under Communist rule, the East Germans used a different approach to avoid coming to grips with the past: Deny it was their past. "We weren't Nazis," taught the Communist regime, "We fought the Nazis. So we have nothing to be ashamed of or to regret. The Nazis are over there in West Germany." East Germany avoided moral responsibility by trying to portray the Nazis as a foreign power, rather like Austria has done. In this area, as in many others, East German attitudes lagged behind West German attitudes.

The Generation Gap

As a guest in a German home long ago, I saw how the family reacted when one of the daughters found, in the back of a china closet, an old poem, *Die Hitlerblume* (the Hitler flower), comparing the *Führer* to a lovely blossom. The three college-age children howled with laughter and derision. "Daddy, how could you go along with this garbage?" they asked. The father, an

Memories of war are preserved in the Kaiser Wilhelm Church, which was deliberately left half-ruined in Berlin. (Michael Roskin)

KEY CONCEPTS

THE RISE OF "POSTMATERIALISM"

One of the trends among rich nations, especially pronounced in West Germany, is the feeling of some young people that modern society is too focused on material goods. Starting in the late 1960s, "countercultures" sprang up in every advanced country. Young people rejected the work-and-buy ethic of their parents and turned instead to beards, blue jeans, and "quality of life" questions. This caught on strongly in the Federal Republic as young Germans sought to repudiate the hypermaterialism of their parents.

Postmaterialism is found throughout the advanced industrialized world. Raised in conditions of **affluence** and never having suffered through depression or war, young Britons, French, Germans, Japanese, and Americans tend to ignore their parents' values and embrace few causes. The postmaterial generation is tolerant and fun-loving and not drawn to conventional political parties or religions or marriage and family.

Postmaterialism underlies the Federal Republic's Marxist, antinuclear, ecology, and pacifist movements, much of which came together in the Greens. Postmaterialism also plugged into German romanticism and nationalism. Will postmaterialism last or decline? If it has created a vacuum of values, what might eventually fill the vacuum?

old-fashioned authoritarian type, grew red in the face and stammered, "You don't know what it was like. They had everybody whipped up. The times were different." He was quite embarrassed.

The incident underscores the rapid generational changes in German political attitudes; simply put, the younger the generation, the more open, free-spirited, democratic, and European it is. Younger Germans tend to give unqualified allegiance to democracy and European unity. Only a handful of personality problems hanker for an authoritarian system. Feeling no personal responsibility for what the Nazis did, they are also less inclined to ponder Germany's past.

The younger generation has also freed up German society. No longer are German women confined to *Kinder, Küche, Kirche* (children, kitchen, and church); most now work outside the home and participate in politics. German youngsters are not as obedient as they once were, and German fathers no longer beat them as in the old days. If democracy starts in the home, Germany now has a much better foundation for democracy.

The typical German of today is far more democratic in attitudes than the typical German of 1949, when the Federal Republic was founded. Those who would support another Hitler, trade civil rights for "security," or think a one-party system is best have steadily dwindled, while those who think democracy and civil rights are worthwhile values in their own right have steadily increased. West German attitudes are now at least as democratic as any of their European neighbors, and the East Germans are likely to soon become so.

Is the change permanent? Political scientist Sidney Verba drew a distinction between **output affect** and **system affect** in his discussion of German political culture. The former means liking the system for what it produces (jobs, security, and material goods), the latter, liking the system because it is perceived as good. Verba thought

Key Terms

postmaterialism Theory that modern culture has moved beyond getting and spending.

affluence Having plenty of money.

output affect Attachment to a system based on its providing material abundance.

system affect Attachment to a system for its own sake.

DEMOCRACY

WILLY BRANDT AS TURNING POINT

One of the more optimistic signs that democracy had taken root in Germany was the 1969 election that made Willy Brandt chancellor. It would not have been possible even a few years earlier, for Brandt represented a repudiation of German history and society that few Germans could have then tolerated. First, Brandt was an illegitimate child, a black mark that Adenauer used in election campaigns. Second, Brandt was a Socialist, and in his youth in the North German seaport of Lübeck had been pretty far left (although never Communist). No Socialist had been in power in Germany for decades; the CDU kept smearing the SPD as a dangerous party, and many Germans believed it. Third, and most damaging, was that Brandt had fled to Norway in 1933, became a Norwegian citizen, and hadn't reclaimed his German nationality until 1947. Some even wrongly accused him of fighting Germans as a Norwegian soldier.

With a record like that, it seemed Brandt was starting into German politics with three strikes against him. But Brandt also had appeal for many Germans, especially younger ones. He was "Mr. Clean," a German who had battled the Nazis—literally, in Lübeck street fights—and who had never been "just an opportunist" who survived by going along. Brandt seemed to represent a newer, better Germany as opposed to the conservative, traditional values of Adenauer and the CDU.

As mayor of West Berlin from 1957 to 1966, Brandt showed how tough and anti-Communist he was by standing up to Soviet and East German efforts at encroachment. A leading figure in the SPD, Brandt supported the 1959 move away from Marxism.

In 1964 he became the SPD's chairman, and this boosted the party's electoral fortunes.

In 1966 the SPD joined the cabinet in a grand coalition with the CDU. As is usual in coalitions, the head of the second largest party is foreign minister. Here, Brandt showed himself to be a forceful and innovative statesman with his **Ostpolitik**. By 1969 the SPD had enough Bundestag seats to form a small coalition with the FDP, and Brandt became the FRG's first Socialist chancellor. The event was a symbolic breakthrough: Germany looked more democratic under an anti-Nazi than an ex-Nazi (Brandt's predecessor, Kiesinger).

The story, however, did not end happily. In 1974 it was discovered that a Brandt assistant was an East German spy. (West Germany was riddled with East German spies.) Brandt, regretting his security slip, resigned the chancellorship to become the grand old man of not only German but also West European social democracy. He lived to see the fruits of his Ostpolitik and died in 1992.

Willy Brandt, FRG Chancellor 1969–74. (Michael Roskin)

Germans showed more of the first than the second; that is, they liked the system while the going was good—they were "fair-weather democrats"—but had not yet become "rain-or-shine democrats" the way Britons or Americans are. Verba's point was made in the early 1960s. Since then, system affect among Germans has increased as the younger generation has come of age. Some East Germans, however, are still caught up in the output affect, judging democracy by the cars and jobs it provides them.

Key Terms

Ostpolitik   Literally "east policy"; Brandt's building relations with East Europe, including East Germany.

political generation   The theory that age groups are marked by the great events of their young adulthood.

A Normal Germany?

One of Chancellor Schröder's themes, echoed by many Germans, is that Germany has at last become a "normal" country. It should no longer bear any special guilt about the past. Most Germans were born after the Nazis. Its democracy is as solid as any. Its problems and hopes are the same as its European neighbors. As good Europeans, Germans should be willing to participate in preventing massacres in Bosnia and Kosovo, a majority of Germans felt, thus breaking the old taboo of using German forces outside of Germany. Is Germany now strictly a normal country, or could something go seriously wrong again?

The younger generation of Germans brings with them new concerns about jobs and the environment that the older generation didn't worry about. A distance developed between many young Germans and the mainstream political parties. In the German party system, newcomers must slowly work their way up party ranks, starting at the local and state levels, before they can have a say at the national level. By the time they can, they are no longer young. (One interesting exception: In 1998, a twenty-two-year-old SPD candidate from East Germany won a

KEY CONCEPTS

POLITICAL GENERATIONS IN GERMANY

German sociologist Karl Mannheim coined the term **political generations** to describe how great events put a lasting stamp on young people. We can see this in Germany. Today's young Germans were formed by the fall of the Berlin Wall in 1989. Sometimes called "89ers," they stand in marked contrast with previous German generations: the 45ers, who climbed out of the rubble and rebuilt a new Germany, and the 68ers, who rebelled against complacent materialism.

The 89ers are relatively few in number (because of the strong trend to one-child couples) and worry about unemployment, destruction of the environment, and having to pay off the staggering burden of German unification and the lavish pensions of older Germans. Generally liberal and tolerant, they are also fun-loving, individualistic, irreligious, and apolitical; they don't much care for hard work, marriage, families, or having children. Many don't vote, and few like the main political parties, but some are open to the Greens. Few join formal groups or associations. Their chief concern is music; many would just like to rave to a "techno" beat. Many young people around the world are like this.

DEMOCRACY

A BOUNCE-BACK EFFECT?

Germans, especially young Germans, are looser, freer, and more open than ever. Some observers think this is the way things are going all over the world, the generational shift to postmaterialism (see box on page 199). Historically, however, there have been **bounce-back effects** that have turned around values abruptly. American journalist William Shirer recalled that young Germans in the 1920s devoted themselves to being free and having fun. This did nothing to stop the Nazis, who quickly ended the party.

Many young Germans face long-term un-employment and resent foreigners who, they think, take their jobs. Germany has a number of **skinheads**; some of them rob and beat foreigners. Some young Germans say they have "had it up to here" with Holocaust guilt. They didn't do it, so why should it concern them? Contributing to this irritation are the years of politicians' dawdling on whether to build a major Jewish museum and a Holocaust memorial in Berlin. Young Germans will most likely continue to seek fun and freedom, which can sometimes turn destructive. What will come is highly unpredictable, but it will probably be to a rock beat.

seat in the Bundestag, the youngest German deputy ever.) In the meantime, they are expected to obey party dictates and not have much input. Some youth organizations of both the Social Democrats and Free Democrats became so rambunctious that they had to be disowned by their parent parties. For many young Germans, the Christian Democrats and Social Democrats, who alternated in power, looked a lot alike, staid and elderly, and neither was responsive to young people.

Belatedly, some German politicians recognized the problem. Former President Richard von Weizsäcker worried openly about "the failure of my generation to bring younger people into politics." Young Germans, he noted, "do not admire the moral substance of the older generation. Our economic achievement went along with a very materialistic and very selfish view of all problems."

Young Germans also developed resentment of the United States. In the 1950s and 1960s, young Germans nearly worshiped the United States; it was their model in politics, lifestyles, and values. Then events shook this. The assassination of President Kennedy—who had recently proclaimed "*Ich bin ein Berliner*" at the Berlin Wall—horrified Germans and made them wonder about the United States. The Vietnam War was worse; some young Germans compared it with Hitler's war of aggression. Finally, rising tensions between East and West and the warlike posture of President Reagan convinced many young Germans that the United States would be willing to incinerate Germany. A minority began to see Washington rather than Moscow as the source of tension. Some wanted the Americans out of Germany. It was ironic that the United States—which had tutored Germans to repudiate militarism—found itself the object of German antiwar feeling.

Key Terms

bounce-back effect Tendency of trends and values to reverse.

skinheads Racist youth, begun in England, with shaved heads and quasi-military attire.

The preceding attitudes fed the Green party. In elections, the Greens do better among young voters than among the total population. These attitudes also contributed to a new German nationalism that no longer followed in America's footsteps. Instead of automatically looking west, some young Germans look to a reunified Germany taking its rightful place as the natural leader of Central Europe. A few turned anti-United States and anti-NATO. The entirely new situation created by German unification, the end of the Cold War, and fighting in Bosnia and Kosovo is rapidly changing German attitudes, especially those of young people. We can no longer count on Germans to automatically look to the West or to the United States for guidance or solidarity.

The Disorienting Unification

There is still a big cultural gap between East and West Germans. When the Wall came down in late 1989, there was much celebration and good will. **Wessis** were generous to the **Ossis**, but soon the relationship soured. The Ossis kept demanding the bounties of the prosperous West as a right; after all, they were all Germans and the Wessis had so much. The Wessis didn't see things that way. "We've worked hard for more than forty years for this," they argued, "Now you Ossis must do the same." With newly acquired D-Marks, courtesy of West German taxpayers, Ossis snatched up modern products while their own economy collapsed. West Germans quickly developed negative stereotypes of East Germans living well at Wessi expense—like poor relatives who had come to sponge off them.

As the costs of bringing East Germany up to West German levels started to sink in, some Germans grew angry. The East German economy was found to be in far worse shape than foreseen and needed gigantic bailouts. Much industry simply had to be closed; unemployment shot up. West German business executives talk down to their East German counterparts. Wessis think Ossis have been trained into inefficiency by the Communists. Ossis feel talked down to and alienated from the West German system that was quickly imposed on them. This has led to an increase in East German consciousness, which is now greater than before unification. Nothing like togetherness separates people.

Politically, Ossi resentment benefits the Party of Democratic Socialism (PDS), which has been elected to the Bundestag since 1994, chiefly in the new eastern *Länder*. The PDS is supported by ex-Communists, retired people worried about their pensions, and Ossis who feel the other parties ignore them. The ideological collapse of East Germany's socialism left citizens disoriented and lacking something to believe in. "Freedom" is not clear enough; many are still ideologically socialist and crave order and a system that guarantees their livelihood. One of the lessons of Germany's unification: You have to pay as much attention to psychological and social transitions as to economic ones.

The economy too was a problem. For most of the 1990s German economic growth was slow or even negative, making many West Germans frightened about unemployment and the massive transfer of funds to the east. Some Germans wonder if unification had been worthwhile. Disoriented Germans ask which way for unified Germany in a vastly different Europe. Some left-wing intellectuals warn of the return of an aggressive, expansionist Germany. Some neo-Nazi and skinhead youths lent weight to the warnings by murdering resident Turks. Predicting a stable future for a united Germany is more difficult than was predicting it for West Germany alone.

Key Terms

Wessi Nickname for West German.

Ossi Nickname for East German.

The End of Shell Shock

Many Germans, especially the older generation who had gone along with the Nazis, felt so damaged by political involvement that they swore never to take an active part in politics again. To appreciate how an older German might feel shell-shocked and cautious about politics, imagine a German born at the turn of the century who was raised under a conservative monarchy and taught to obey authority. All of a sudden a republic comes that expects its citizens to be good democrats (they weren't). Then comes a dictatorship that demands the enthusiastic, unquestioning complicity of all Germans. After that come Allied occupiers telling the bewildered Germans that they have been very wicked and must now become democratic. No wonder that in the first decades of the Federal Republic many Germans said *ohne mich* (without me) to politics. Some East Germans still feel this way.

In their famous book, *The Civic Culture*, Almond and Verba described the German attitude of 1959 as one of detachment. Germans were often well informed about politics but didn't want to participate in much more than voting. They were pragmatic and sometimes cynical about politics. If the system worked it was okay, but there was no point in getting personally involved. Germans showed low levels of social trust or of willingness to discuss politics with others. In the decades since, however, this attitude receded, making West Germans among the most democratic and participatory in the world. Every decade there were fewer and fewer of the skeptical generation and more and more of the postwar generation. But now Germany, with unification, has entered the post-Cold War period, and it is becoming a time of testing.

The German Political Elite

German elite recruitment is quite mixed, more like that of the United States than Britain or France. There is no German equivalent of Oxbridge or the Great Schools. The three German political collapses of this century left a relatively clean slate for bright talent to achieve political office. Some (such as Brandt) were not even university graduates, although practically all politicians now are.

As in America, the typical German politician has studied law, although in Germany this is done at the undergraduate rather than the postgraduate level. German (and other European) legal systems produce different attitudes than the Anglo-American Common Law system. Continental law developed from Roman law—usually in the updated form of the Napoleonic Code—and it emphasizes fixed rules. The Common Law, on the other hand, is judge-made law that focuses on precedent and persuasion; it is flexible. The former system produces lawyers who tend to go by the book, the latter lawyers who negotiate and make deals. Consequently, German politicians with their legal background are heavily law-oriented rather than people-oriented.

Much of the work of the Bundestag, for example, is devoted to the precise wording of bills, making that house a rather dull, inward-looking chamber that has failed to win admiration from the German public. Likewise, cabinet ministers conceive of their role heavily in terms of carrying out laws. Several of Schröder's cabinet, including the chancellor himself, were lawyers.

Besides lawyers, a smaller group has had a disproportionate role in German politics: economists. In few other countries have professional economists achieved the stature they have in

the FRG. One German chancellor had a Ph.D. in economics: Ludwig Erhard. Under Adenauer, the rotund, jolly Economics Minister
Erhard charted Germany's rise to prosperity; later he became chancellor. Helmut Schmidt, an economics graduate, succeeded Brandt
as SPD chancellor and managed to keep both inflation and unemployment low in Germany while much of the world went through a
major recession. In Germany, economists are not just advisers but often become important
politicians themselves.

> ### Key Term
>
> **romanticism** Hearkening
> to an ideal world or mythical
> past.

The German Split Personality

The French, as we discussed, often seem split between demanding impersonal authority and
rebelling against it. The Germans have a sort of split personality, too, but it's between **romanticism** and realism.

Most of the time Germans are pragmatic realists: hard working, thrifty, clean, orderly, cooperative, family-oriented. But a persistent romantic streak runs through German history that
comes out every now and then: the nineteenth-century intellectuals (such as composer Richard
Wagner) who reveled in the *Volksgeist*, the Nazi youth who really believed they were building
a "thousand-year Reich," and in the 1970s far-left terrorists who thought they could build utopia
by assassination. The latest German romantics are the Greens, who long for an imaginary pas-
toral idyll free of atoms and industry. German romanticism also manifests itself in the striving
for perfection, which may lead Germans to undertake vast projects they may not have the resources for. Hitler's plan to conquer all of Europe, including Russia, is an infamous example.

Germans set high store by achievement. To work harder, produce more, and proudly let
others know about it seems to be an ingrained cultural trait. This helps explain Germany's rise
after the war to Europe's number-one economic power. Both East Germany's leader Walter
Ulbricht and West Germany's Helmut Schmidt toured their respective camps giving unso-
licited advice on how other countries should copy the German economic miracle. East Germany's, although not as spectacular as the Federal Republic's, nonetheless made it the
economic leader of the East bloc. I once told an anti-Communist West Berliner that East
Berlin also looked pretty prosperous. He didn't dispute me but nodded and said, "Of course.
They're Germans too."

Perhaps the archetypal German figure is Goethe's Faust, the driven person who can never
rest or be content with what is already his. This quality can produce both great good and evil.
Former Chancellor Helmut Schmidt, himself a stereotype of the German realist strain, once
said, "Germans have an enormous capacity for idealism and the perversion of it."

Key Terms

affluence (p. 199)

bounce-back effect (p. 202)

denazification (p. 195)

Holocaust (p. 197)

liberal democracy (p. 195)

multiculturalism (p. 197)

Ossi (p. 203)

Ostpolitik (p. 201)

output affect (p. 199)

political generation (p. 201)

postmaterialism (p. 199)

reparations (p. 197)

romanticism (p. 205)

skinheads (p. 202)

system affect (p. 199)

Wessi (p. 203)

vergangenheitsbewältigung (p. 197)

Further Reference

Ardagh, John. *Germany and the Germans: The United Germany in the Mid-1990s,* new ed. New York: Penguin, 1996.

Balfour, Michael. *Germany: The Tides of Power.* New York: Routledge, 1992.

Burns, Rob, ed. *German Cultural Studies: An Introduction.* New York: Oxford University Press, 1995.

Elias, Norbert. *The Germans.* New York: Columbia University Press, 1997.

Gedmin, Jeffrey, ed. *The Germans: Portrait of a Nation.* Washington, D.C.: American Enterprise Press, 1995.

Jarausch, Konrad H., ed. *After Unity: Reconfiguring German Identities.* Herndon, VA: Berghahn, 1997.

Kramer, Jane. *The Politics of Memory: Looking for Germany in the New Germany.* New York: Random House, 1996.

Kurthen, Hermann, Werner Bergmann, and Rainer Erb, eds. *Antisemitism and Xenophobia in Germany after Unification.* New York: Oxford University Press, 1997.

Markovits, Andrei S., and Philip S. Gorski. *The German Left: Red, Green and Beyond.* New York: Oxford University Press, 1993.

Mushaben, Joyce Marie. *From Post-War to Post-Wall Generations: Changing Attitudes Towards the National Question and NATO in the Federal Republic of Germany.* Boulder, CO: Westview, 1998.

Rohrschneider, Robert. *Learning Democracy: Democratic and Economic Values in Unified Germany.* New York: Oxford University Press, 1999.

Sa'adah, Anne. *Germany's Second Chance: Trust, Justice, and Democratization.* Cambridge, MA: Harvard University Press, 1998.

Yoder, Jennifer A. *From East Germans to Germans? The New Postcommunist Elites.* Durham, NC: Duke University Press, 1999.

Germany:
Patterns of Interaction

15

Questions to Consider

1. Why has coalition formation in Germany become more difficult?
2. Why is a unimodal distribution of opinion necessary for democracy?
3. How does the German distribution of opinion resemble the British and French?
4. What is the difference between *Weltanschauung* and catchall parties?
5. How do German elections resemble presidential ones?
6. Are fundraising scandals a part of democracy?
7. Describe the union-party linkup in North European countries.
8. In what ways does voting follow geography?

We saw how the Weimar Republic collapsed with the shrinking of the moderate parties and growth of extremist parties—"polarized pluralism." Could this happen in the Federal Republic? For most of the history of West Germany, the answer was "no." With only two-plus parties, they, for good political reasons, stuck close to the center of the political spectrum. Political competition in West Germany tended to be **center-seeking**. Voters had their choice of three moderate parties (there were several tiny parties on the ballot, but they were largely ignored), and these three parties could combine in only three different coalitions (CDU and FDP, CDU and SPD, SPD and FDP). This made West German politics stable compared to more tumultuous multiparty systems.

With unification—and even a little before—German politics became less stable and more complex. The party system is still "two-plus," but now the "plus" includes not just one small party but three. The two large parties lost some of their votes to smaller parties. This can make coalition formation more difficult, for now a German coalition may require three partners instead of the previous two. Now there are at least five possible coalition combinations (see box on page 208). This in turn makes German government less stable and predictable.

Key Term

center-seeking Parties trying to win the big vote in the center with moderate programs.

KEY CONCEPTS

GERMANY'S POSSIBLE COALITIONS

With five parties now in the Bundestag, coalition building is more complex, especially if either of the two large parties (CDU and SPD) gets less than 45 percent of the vote (and of Bundestag seats). Why 45 percent? One of the small parties, to get any seats at all, must have won 5 percent of the vote. Accordingly, two parties, one with 45 percent and the other with 5 percent, would be able to form a coalition with a (bare) majority of the Bundestag. By the same token, if one of the small parties won, say, 10 percent, it could form a winning coalition with a large party that won 40 percent. This situation gives rise to possibilities numbered 1 through 3, which were the standard coalitions for most of the FRG's history:

1. Christian-Liberal Coalition: The CDU/CSU wins about 40 percent and the FDP wins about 10 percent, allowing for the same coalition that had sustained Kohl and earlier cabinets in power.
2. Social-Liberal Coalition: The SPD edges out the CDU with about 40 percent and turns to the FDP with, say, 10 percent to rebuild the coalition that had supported Brandt and Schmidt in the 1970s.
3. Grand Coalition: Neither the CDU nor SPD do well in elections; say, each wins less than 40 percent. Rather than one of them attempting a coalition with two small parties, they make a coalition with each other, as occurred in the late 1960s with not-so-happy results (see page 186).
4. Red-Green Coalition (new): If the SPD (red, as it used to be called) gets 40-some percent and the Greens get 5 to 10 percent, they could put together a social-ecological coalition, which is what Schröder did in 1998.

Previously tried at the *Land* level, such governments had been unstable, as the idealistic Greens often dislike the daily grind of governing. Germany held its breath to see if it would work at the national level.

5. "Traffic Light" (*Ampel*) Coalition: Red, green, and yellow (for the FDP). If the SPD won under 40 percent, it might need two small coalition partners, each with 6 to 10 percent, to build a majority. Constructed once at the state level (Bremen), the Ampel is difficult to sustain, as the Greens and Liberals seriously dislike each other.
6. Red-Green Plus PDS Coalition: If the SPD won near 40 percent and the Greens and ex-Communist PDS won 5 or more percent each, they could form a left-wing coalition. A variation on this: the Swedish model in which the ex-Communists support the Social Democrats in parliament but get no cabinet positions. Why would the PDS accept such a deal? Because they would not like to see a conservative government.

One other theoretical possibility, a "government of national unity" of all parties, might be useful for an emergency situation such as war, but not for much else. According to the theory of coalitions, you stop adding partners once you have topped 50 percent; there is no point to adding more. And an all-party coalition would not stay together for long.

A Christian-Green or CDU-PDS coalition is unlikely; they are political opposites. If the neo-Nazi Republicans should cross the 5 percent barrier they would be fit coalition partners for no one. The recent fragmentation of the German party system makes one long for the old and relatively simple "two-plus" system in which the only alternatives were, with one brief exception, points 1 and 2.

Parties and the Electorate

Social scientists have found that political opinion in most modern democracies resembles a bell-shaped curve: A lot of people are in the center, with fewer and fewer as one moves to the left or right. If you want to sound more scientific you call this a **unimodal** distribution of

opinion. (**Bimodal** distributions indicate extreme division, even civil strife.) Routinely, citizens of the European Union are asked to place themselves on a one-to-nine ideological scale, one for the most left and nine for the most right. Germany comes out, like most West European countries, as a bell-shaped curve (see figure, below).

How does this affect political parties? When party leaders come to understand the shape of the electorate, either through modern polling techniques or by losing elections, they usually try to modify their party image so that it appeals to the middle of the opinion spectrum. If the Social Democrats position themselves too far left—say, at two on the nine-point scale—by advocating nationalizing private industry and dropping out of NATO, they may please some of the left-wing ideologues in the party but do poorly in elections. Fewer than 3 percent of Germans place themselves at the two position on the left. So the Social Democrats tone down their socialism and emphasize their commitment to democracy plus welfare measures, moving to the three or four position.

Now they do much better in elections, but the left wing of the party is unhappy with the dilution of socialist gospel. Finally, sniffing the possibility of becoming Germany's governing party, the SPD throws out socialism and tells the electorate that they will do a better job running the capitalist, market economy. At this point they are in roughly the four to five position. The party's left wingers are angry, accusing the SPD leadership of selling out to capitalism; some left-wing socialists even quit the party. But electorally, the SPD is doing well. By emphasizing democracy and minimizing socialism, they win the support of many citizens.

Key Terms

unimodal   A single-peaked distribution.

bimodal   A two-peaked distribution.

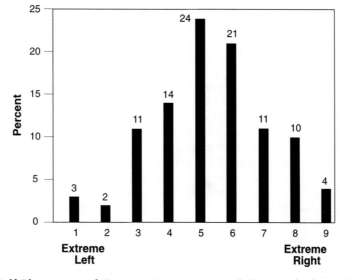

The Self-Placement of German Voters on a Left/Right Ideological Scale

POLITICAL CULTURE

UNHAPPY ON THE LEFT: THE JUSOS

When he was young, Gerhard Schröder was a typical Juso hothead; fortunately, he calmed as he aged. The youth branch of the SPD—the *Jungsozialisten*, or Jusos for short—has been a continual thorn in the left side of the party. Limited to people under thirty-five years of age, the Jusos attract some young zealots ablaze with Marxist notions of socialism. Impatient and idealistic, many Jusos find the mainstream SPD too moderate and gradualist. One favorite Juso target is now, ironically, Chancellor Schröder, their leader long ago.

Periodically, the SPD has to disown its offspring. If it doesn't, it costs the party votes. Some Jusos can't understand that Germans as a whole are moderate in their political views, and there is little support for pulling out of NATO, nationalization of industry, "cultural revolution," and massive taxes on the rich. When the Jusos helped move the SPD toward such positions in the early 1980s, the party lost four national elections in a row, just like the British Labour party. Some Jusos defected to the Greens or PDS. The SPD faces the question of whether to try to retain young radicals by moving leftward, or to win elections by staying centrist.

The preceding, in a nutshell, was the history of the SPD to their electoral high point of 45.8 percent in 1972. In the last century the Social Democrats started to shed their Marxism, in practice if not yet in theory. In the 1950s, seeing the CDU triumphantly win the center, they decided to break out of their left-wing stronghold. Meeting in Bad Godesberg (just outside Bonn) in 1959, they drew up a Basic Program so moderate one can hardly find any socialism in it. Marxism was *kaputt*; the SPD proclaimed itself "rooted in Christian ethics, humanism and classical philosophy."

Now, while the Social Democrats moved rightward, the Christian Democrats had already taken a broad swath of the ideological spectrum, claiming to stand for everything, a party of all Germans, just as the British Conservatives used to claim to represent all Britons. The CDU downplayed its conservatism, for it too understood that if the party image were too rightist it would lose the big prize in the center. The result, at least until recently, was two large parties that generally tried to be centrist but in so doing rubbed their respective left and right wings the wrong way (see boxes on pages 210 and 211).

The game is never finished, though. While they had transformed themselves into a center-left party, the SPD allowed the area on their left to be taken over by a newer, more radical party, the Greens. (In one study Green voters placed themselves at 3.4 on the scale.) Partly to try to win over these leftist voters, partly in response to Juso (see box above) influence within the SPD, and partly out of irritation at the hawkishness of the Reagan administration, the SPD moved leftwards in the late 1980s, much like the British Labour party had done earlier. The SPD came out against both U.S. nuclear missiles in Germany and nuclear power plants, two key Green demands. But the shift hurt the SPD electorally; they dropped from 42.9 percent of the vote in 1980 to 33.5 in 1990, their poorest showing since 1957.

The SPD is still pulled in two directions. Tugging leftward is the traditional socialist wing once headed by former party chairman and finance minister Oskar Lafontaine. This wing, based heavily on workers and older people, wants to help those in need and to preserve the welfare state. Tugging rightward is the Blairite wing of Chancellor Schröder, which wants reforms to cut taxes, pensions, subsidies, bureaucracy, unemployment, and regulations that slow economic growth. The two men had such serious differences that Lafontaine resigned from the cabinet and as party chair in 1999. His departure drew sighs of relief from the business community. The incoherence and indecisiveness of the SPD was not appreciated by the German voter. Tony Blair controlled a reformed Labour party; Schröder had trouble turning the SPD into a genuine New Middle.

Key Term

Weltanschauung party
Literally "world view"; a party that offers firm, narrow ideologies.

The Chancellor and the Electorate

Two factors especially hurt the SPD in the 1990s. The CDU's embrace of rapid unification made the SPD look narrow and carping in its warnings about the expense and economic impact of quick merger. Go slow and think it through, was the SPD message, not a popular one in 1990, although their "I told you so" won them some votes in 1994. SPD chancellor-candidate Oskar Lafontaine in 1990 was also part of the problem. He was too clever and radical for many German voters. The SPD's next candidate, the bearded young intellectual Rudolf Scharping came across in 1994 much the same way. In 1998, the SPD took a leaf from Tony Blair's 1997 success in Britain: Assume vague, centrist positions; emphasize that the conservatives have been in office too long; and offer a young, outgoing personality for prime minister. The SPD, in effect, learned the unimodal shape of the German electorate in the 1950s and 1960s, forgot it in the 1980s, and remembered it in the late 1990s.

In Germany, as in most advanced countries, personality has become more important than ideology in the mind of many voters. With the decline of **Weltanschauung parties** (see box on page 213) and the move of most large parties to the center of the political spectrum, the personality of candidates is often what persuades voters. This has long been the case in

POLITICAL CULTURE

THUNDER ON THE RIGHT: CSU

Bavaria is the Texas of Germany, a land with a raucous brand of politics all its own. On principle, the Christian Social Union (CSU) never let itself be absorbed into the CDU; instead it calls itself an allied party and sometimes threatens to burst out of Bavaria—where it sometimes wins a majority of the vote—and set itself up in nationwide competition with the CDU.

Current CSU chief and Bavarian state premier Edmund Stoiber makes no secret of wanting to become chancellor. The CSU is to the right of the CDU, demanding a tougher anti-immigrant stance, a firmer crackdown on radicals, and a rollback of welfare. The CSU's kingpin was the late Franz Josef Strauss, Germany's right-wing tough guy who minimized the Nazi past and used to say, "I do not care who is chancellor under me." Stoiber is more democratic but just as right-wing.

Key Terms

catchall party   A party that welcomes all and offers little ideology.

dealignment   Voters losing identification with any party.

the United States and is now becoming the European norm as well. Some call it the Americanization of European politics, but it is less a matter of copying than it is of reflecting the rise of **catchall parties**. Throughout Europe, election posters now feature the picture of the top party leader, the person who would become prime minister. Although voting may be by party list, citizens know that in choosing a party they are actually electing a prime minister.

German (and British) campaigns are conducted almost as if they were for the direct election of a president—as in the United States and France. Officially there is no "candidate for the chancellorship," but in practice the leading figures of the two big parties are clearly identified as such—in the media, on billboards, and in the public mind—so that much of the campaign revolves around the personalities of the two leading candidates.

A German candidate for chancellor must project strength and levelheadedness. In a country obsessed with fear of inflation, the candidate's economic background plays a bigger role than in most nations. Two of Germany's postwar chancellors have been economists. The candidate's adherence to democratic rules also plays a role, and Franz Josef Strauss's authoritarian streak contributed to his defeat in the 1980 race.

Personality contributed to the results of the 1990s elections, too. The CDU/CSU had the steady, optimistic image of Helmut Kohl. SPD candidates of the 1990s came across as radical intellectuals until Gerhard Schröder ran in 1998. By that point, many Germans were just plain tired of Kohl, who had been in office sixteen years and was showing his age. Much of postwar German politics can be described as parties groping for the right leader to bring them to power in the Bundestag and chancellor's office. When they find the right one—such as Adenauer and Kohl of the CDU—they stick with him for a long time.

German Dealignment?

For many years political scientists have worried that American voters were showing an increasing **dealignment** with the main parties. That is, some decades ago, U.S. parties used to present a fairly clear "party image" and most voters carried around in their heads a fairly clear "party ID." Where the two connected (for example, U.S. Democrats and blue-collar workers), you had reliable party-voter "alignments." These could change every few decades in what were called "realignments," new matches of voters to parties. But increasingly, U.S. voters are dealigning: Their preferences, often unfocused, connected with no party on a long-term basis. Their votes easily shift from one party to another in response to candidate personality and clever advertising.

Is electoral dealignment catching? Are West Europeans catching it? One sees evidence of it in Britain, France, and Germany. Increasingly, Germans dislike both major parties and doubt that either does any better in office than the other. German turnout in elections is falling, from a high of 91 percent in 1972 to a low of 79 percent in 1994 (but back up to 82 percent in 1998). More citizens now scatter their votes among a variety of small parties all over the political spectrum, from left to right. One center-right group that enjoyed brief notice called itself the *Statt* (instead of) party.

Where does dealignment come from? It is not a sinister plot (although it can have negative repercussions), but the normal and natural maturation process that many advanced democracies go through. One step in this process is the catchall party (see box on page 213). If two catchall parties face each other, as in the United States and Germany, their positions become so moderate and similar that they become boring. Neither offers much in the way of exciting new choices, programs, or personalities.

Meanwhile, the society is being hit by problems scarcely anyone could imagine a generation ago: immigration, environmental degradation, the movement of jobs to low-wage countries, and crushing tax and debt burdens. None of the catchall parties has any convincing solution; all waffle in some middle ground. Also, suddenly gone is the cement that helped hold the system together: the Soviet threat and the Cold War. It is a disorienting time, and none of the great catchall parties provides much in the way of guidance. (To what extent is this true of U.S. politics?) The public response is lower voter turnouts and small and less-stable shares of the vote for the catchall parties, in a word, dealignment.

Key Term

Rechtsstaat   Literally, state of laws; state based on written rules and rights.

The Bundestag and the Citizen

One reason German elections have turned into almost presidential elections for chancellor is the murky status of the Bundestag in the mind of many voters. They know what the chancellor does but aren't too clear on what the Bundestag does. Part of the blame for this is the concept Bundestag deputies have of their role. The **Rechtsstaat** tradition is focused on laws. The Bundestag, now housed in the old Reichstag building in Berlin, is staffed heavily by lawyers and civil servants and has become a law factory.

KEY CONCEPTS

THE "CATCHALL" PARTY

In prewar Europe, many political parties used to try to imbue their supporters with a "view of the world" (*Weltanschauung*) corresponding to the party's ideology and philosophy. This was especially true of parties on the left and came to a high point in Weimar Germany. After World War II most Weltanschauung parties disappeared as they broadened their appeal or merged into bigger parties.

Noting their demise, German political scientist Otto Kirchheimer coined the term "catchall party" to describe what was taking their place: big, loose, pluralist parties that have diluted their ideologies so they can accommodate many diverse groups of supporters. His model of a catchall party was the CDU, a political vacuum cleaner that draws in all manner of groups: farmers, businesspeople, labor, women, Catholics, Protestants, white-collar workers, blue collar, you name it.

For a while, under crusty Kurt Schumacher, the SPD tried to stay a Weltanschauung party, defining itself in rigid and ideological terms that turned away many middle-of-the-road voters. Since 1959, the SPD too has become a catchall party, appealing to Germans of all classes and backgrounds. Indeed, by now the catchall party is the norm in modern democracies. Almost axiomatically, any large party is bound to be a catchall party, for example, the French neo-Gaullists, Canadian Liberals, British Conservatives, Japanese Liberal Democrats, and, of course, both major U.S. parties.

DEMOCRACY

KOHL'S FUNDRAISING SCANDAL

At the start of the new millennium, former Chancellor Helmut Kohl and his CDU party were caught in a major fundraising scandal. Kohl admitted that when he was chancellor during the 1990s he personally accepted over $1 million in secret donations to the CDU. Ironically, Kohl himself had presided over the passage of Germany's strict **transparency law**, which requires that the source and amounts of all contributions over DM 20,000 ($10,500) be promptly declared.

The CDU as a whole took more than $70 million in kickbacks that were secretly funneled to state and local party organizations. This enhanced Kohl's personal power and helped him stay party chief for a quarter of a century. The CDU was fined $21 million for its misdeeds, and it declined in the polls. Even Kohl's successor, Wolfgang Schäuble, admitted he had accepted a bag of $52,000 in cash from a shady arms dealer. Both Kohl and Schäuble resigned in disgrace, and leadership of the CDU went to a 45-year-old woman physicist from East Germany, Angela Merkel.

Notice how all advanced democracies—the United States, Britain, France, Germany, and Japan—have party fundraising scandals. They seem to come with democracy. Elections cost big money, and it has to come from somewhere. The good news is that all over the world citizens are getting fed up with "money politics" and demanding reforms. For more on these scandals, see Chapter 25 on Japan, where they are especially pronounced.

But isn't a legislature supposed to legislate? Not entirely. By confining their activities to law books and committee meetings, Bundestag deputies have failed to grasp the less obvious functions of a legislature. Actually, the most important role of a legislature is probably in overseeing the activities of the national government, catching corruption and inefficiency, uncovering scandals, threatening budget cuts, and otherwise keeping bureaucrats on their toes.

The harsh glare of publicity is the best medicine for governmental wrongdoing. Too-cozy relationships between bureaucracy and business thrive in the dark. It is in this area that the Bundestag has been weak. Although there are commissions of inquiry and a question hour, the former are not pursued as thoroughly as on Washington's Capitol Hill—where televised committee hearings are a major preoccupation—and the latter is not carried out with as much polish as in the House of Commons. (Bundestag deputies can be quite insulting, but it comes across as crude rather than clever.) In functioning as little but lawmakers, German legislators have contributed to the boredom problem.

One function the Bundestag has failed to develop is that of education. The way a legislature operates, the arguments that are presented, the manner in which members of parliament conduct themselves, these are great teachers of democracy. Instead, Bundestag activity seems calculated to make a weak impression. The Bundestag doesn't generate good press because it's a dull story. U.S. Senators and Representatives get more attention because they do interesting and often unpredictable things, like disobeying their own party, something that rarely happens in Germany.

Another function of an effective parliament is to make people feel that someone who understands their point of view is speaking for them. In this the

Key Term

transparency law   A law requiring that political and economic information be made public.

Bundestag suffers from a problem common to all elected legislatures: It isn't representative of the voters. The average Bundestag deputy is close to fifty years old, male, trained as a lawyer, and employed as a civil servant, party leader, or interest-group official.

The strong German party system means that people must slowly work their way up in party ranks before they will be put on a ballot. Accordingly, candidates tend to be older, seasoned, party loyalists rather than bright, fresh, new faces. Unlike the American system, a German candidate cannot "come from out of nowhere" and win an election on his or her own. You're either a piece of the party machine, or you're nothing. The result is unrepresentative representatives. Said one German newspaper: "This gap between electorate and elected has become too wide." Many Germans do not feel represented; they feel that the Bundestag is the arena where the powerful interests of society work out deals with little reference to the common citizen, the little guy. Such feelings contributed to the Green vote.

The Union-Party Linkup

Unions in Germany are still strong but not what they used to be, another sign of the fraying of Germany's "consensus model" (discussed in the next chapter). One historical characteristic of North European political systems—and here we include Britain and Sweden along with Germany—has been the close relationship between labor union and political party, specifically the social-democratic parties. In these countries unions were large and cohesive; blue-collar workers were heavily organized, and their unions in turn formed a single, large labor federation. Such federations supported the social-democratic parties with money, manpower, and votes. Often union leaders actually ran for office on the party ticket.

Compare this pattern with the Latin European systems. Labor was weakly organized and fragmented into several federations—Communist, Socialist, Christian, and other. The fragmentation reduced the effectiveness of a working-class voice. American unions are also fragmented into several federations and historically did not tie themselves to one party. U.S. labor no longer has the same kind of political input as North European labor. In North Europe, labor unions founded the welfare state.

In Britain, TUC unions are actual constituent members of the Labour Party. In Sweden, the gigantic LO is so close to the Social Democrats that some of their top personnel are the same. The German Basic Law forbids a formal union-party tie, but here, too, everyone knows that labor support is an important pillar of SPD strength.

In the United States less than 15 percent of the labor force is unionized; in Germany 22 percent is (in Sweden, some 50 percent). Thirteen German unions—the largest being the metalworkers (*IG Metall*)—are federated into an umbrella organization, the *Deutscher Gewerkschaftsbund* (DGB) with 8.7 million members, a decline from 12 million in 1990. (Notice how U.S., British, French, and German unions have all declined. Is this permanent or reversible?) The DGB's voice is still heeded by the Social Democrats; its leaders are regularly consulted by SPD chiefs and get a good deal of what they want: an elaborate welfare system, a short work week, and even directors' seats on the boards of large companies (more on this in the next chapter). Many of the SPD's Bundestag deputies have union ties. The labor minister in Schröder's cabinet had been deputy chairman of IG Metall.

But the catchall nature of the SPD prevents its being dominated by any one group. The more the SPD seeks votes in the center of the political spectrum, the more it has to turn away from one-on-one cooperation with the DGB. (The British Labourites faced the same problem with the TUC; when they let the unions dominate, they lost.) Starting in the 1970s, the SPD

Variations on a Theme: Union-Party Links in Four Countries

Country	Union	Party Linkage
Britain	TUC	Labour
Sweden	LO	Social Democrat
Germany	DGB	SPD
United States	AFL-CIO	Democrat

and DGB found differences developing between them. Helmut Schmidt, representing the SPD right, was a better democrat and economist than he was a socialist. DGB relations with the SPD grew cool. Still, the DGB is locked into supporting the Social Democrats for the simple reason that no other party will treat them as well. The Schröder government pledged to work with unions and management in an "Alliance for Work" but still supported IG Metall in winning a 4 percent wage hike in 1999 at the very time unemployment was rising. Raising wages and benefits, many Germans saw, was no way to fight unemployment.

On the management side, there is a similar pattern. The powerful *Bundesverband der Deutschen Industrie* (Federation of German Industries, BDI) has warm connections with the CDU, but not as close as those of the DGB with the SPD. When the Social Democrats are in power, the BDI finds it can get along with them quite well, too. As in Britain and France, big business doesn't need to get closely involved with one party; it's to their advantage to be able to work with all parties. The major focus of business is the bureaucracy, not the parties. Providing information to the relevant ministry, explaining to civil servants why a given regulation should be modified, going along with government economic plans—in these and other ways business quietly cements ties with government.

The Länder and Berlin

Britain and France are unitary systems that have moved to devolution and decentralization. Germany is a federal system that some would like to make a little more centralized. The interesting thing here is that in both unitary and federal systems there are pressures to move toward a middle ground. Centralization in France was rigid, inefficient, and ignored local wishes and regional pride. Federalism in Germany is often uncoordinated, powerless, and deadlocked and encourages federal-state squabbles. In some ways the distinctions between unitary and federal systems are overdrawn; some see the emergence of a new "regional" pattern midway between the unitary and federal.

West Germany was founded as a federal republic for at least two reasons: (1) Germany has a history of particularism and regionalism, and (2) the occupying powers, fearful of a resurgence of German might in a centralized state, wanted it that way. The French in particular would have liked to see Germany broken up into several independent states that could never again threaten France. Postwar German politicians themselves, aware of the abuses of power of Hitler's centralized Reich and proud of their regional origins, were committed to a federal structure.

Germany is probably more federal than the United States: Its *Länder* run more of their own affairs and get a bigger portion of taxes than do U.S. states. For example, individual and corporate income taxes are split between Berlin and the *Länder* in approximately equal 40-percent shares; the cities get around 20 percent. The *Länder* also get some 40 percent of the

"Friendly to the environment" is the German phrase for using bikes and recycling glass (three, in the center) and paper. The ecology movement is big in Germany. (Michael Roskin)

value-added tax, the large but hidden sales tax used throughout Europe. Poorer *Länder*—the new eastern ones—get additional funds. German *Länder*, in addition to raising some of their own taxes, are directly plugged into the federal tax system, an idea Americans might consider.

Germany's federalism has some drawbacks. For example, there's really no nationwide police force (aside from the Border Police), so law enforcement is a *Land* affair. Terrorists who committed their crimes in one *Land* could flee to another, counting on communication and coordination foul-ups to delay police. The cleaning of the seriously polluted Rhine River still lacks a central authority because such matters are controlled by the states, and each state sees its environmental responsibilities differently. Only in 1986 did the Bundestag set up a federal environment ministry, but it could not override *Land* environment ministries. The decentralized nature of education has made it impossible for federal authorities to insist on the nationwide study of the Nazis and their crimes in schools.

Many Germans would like Berlin to have a little more control over things. But the German *Länder*, like American states, stoutly resist moves that would erode the powers of *Land* officials, and they have the perfect weapon to do so: the Bundesrat. Not directly elected, Bundesrat delegations are designated by *Land* governments, which usually means the state's political chiefs. The Bundesrat must concur on any move that would alter the balance of powers between federation and state. Under Kohl, the Bundesrat was dominated by Social Democrats (because they won the most *Land* governments), but after Schröder's election the SPD lost control of several states and with it control of the Bundesrat. The Bundesrat, like the U.S. Senate, acts as a check on both the cabinet and on the lower house.

As to the preferability of unitary versus federal systems, there is no simple answer. If you have one system, you usually want a little of the other. On balance, the German federation works pretty well. In founding a new democracy it was probably wise to give people a smaller unit to focus on, to serve as a building block for developing nationwide democratic loyalties.

German Voting Patterns

In Britain the vote is structured in part along lines of social class and region: Labour usually wins much of the working class, plus Scotland, Wales, and large industrial cities. French voting is similar, with the added factor of clerical or anticlerical attitudes. West German voting patterns also followed class, region, and religion, but the addition of East Germany in 1990 muddied some of these generalizations, and the general dealignment of the period muddied them further.

GEOGRAPHY

Virtually all elections when charted on maps show geographical voting patterns. There are almost always regional variations in party strength. Britain is a good example. The map of Britain showing where parties scored above average seldom needs to be changed; major parties tend to preserve their regional strength. Once rooted, regional voting patterns can persist for decades. Here are some of the patterns.

1. *Cities vote liberal.* Urban areas are usually to the left of rural areas. Many intellectuals live in cities, and they tend to criticize the existing state of affairs and to articulate a need to change and reform. Workers tend to live in cities, and they are often discontent over wages and the cost of living. The countryside tends to be calmer, more accepting of the status quo, and often still controlled by political bosses or old traditions. Rural and farming people often resent the "city slickers" for having more experimental notions than common sense. Accordingly, in most countries, big cities vote liberal or left while the countryside and small towns vote conservative or right.

England outside of the big cities votes Conservative; central London votes Labour. Catholic Bavaria votes Christian Social; swinging Munich votes Social Democrat. In Paris, the better-off people live in the city while the poor and working class live in the suburbs. This tends to give Paris a conservative core but a socialist belt around the city, now eroding as the old working-class suburbs gentrify. In recent Russian elections the big cities, led by Moscow and St. Petersburg, more strongly supported relatively liberal parties than the countryside, which was still partially under the thumb of Communist party bosses and feared economic disruption. Even in Iran, where open opposition is forbidden, cities tend to vote for more moderate or liberal candidates. The countryside tends to deliver the vote the mullahs want.

2. *Every country has regional voting.* Regions tend to vote their resentments, with the periphery voting against the core area. Part of the explanation is historical: Core areas usually acquire peripheral regions by conquest, and the conquered regions generally remember this. Scotland and Wales show their resentment of England by voting Labour; England stays Tory. France south of the Loire River and Spain south of the Tagus River tend to go more Socialist than the country as a whole, showing their resentment of, respectively, Paris and Madrid. The south of Italy has long been conservative; recently, the north of Italy, resentful of paying for the impoverished south, spawned a breakaway movement. As the Soviet Union's republics held free and fair elections, many nationalistic republic governments took office and proclaimed their independence. Lithuanians' and Georgians' hatred of Moscow led them to support nationalistic parties.

3. *Voting follows religion.* Religious attitudes tend to be regional. Indeed, the religion factor is one explanation for points 1 and 2 just discussed. Big cities tend to be less religious than small towns, and this inclines the former to vote liberal or left. Some regions have different religious affiliations than the core area. Scottish Presbyterians show their difference with Anglicans by not voting Tory. German Protestants are still a bit inclined to see the Christian Democratic Union as a Catholic party and to vote against it, a tendency muddied by other factors. In 1994 and 1998 largely Protestant East Germany swung away from the CDU and to leftist parties, the SPD, Greens, and PDS. Religion helped pull the Soviet Union apart, as Muslim republics installed pro-Muslim administrations that are implicitly anti-Christian. In the Caucasus and Central Asia, persons of Christian origin, even if non-practicing or atheists, feel threatened. Surrounded by hostile Islamic peoples, they elect implicitly anti-Muslim Christian governments, as in Armenia and Georgia.

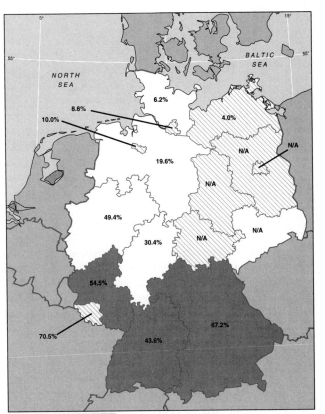

Percent of Catholics per Land (top) to Percent of CDU/CSU Vote per Land (bottom)

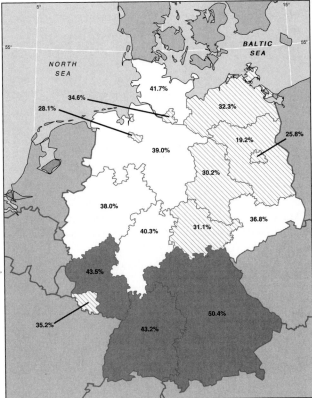

Close match: The percent of Catholics in each Land (see top map) predicts the percent of CDU/CSU vote in each Land (see bottom map). (Michael Baysore)

In Germany religion means Catholic or Protestant. German Catholics are likely to vote CDU, so heavily Catholic *Länder* such as Baden-Wurttemberg generally go CDU. The CSU has long had Catholic Bavaria sewn up. Further north, in the largely Protestant *Länder*, the SPD tends to do better, as they do in large cities. In Germany the rural and small-town vote tends to the CDU. German workers, especially labor union members, are generally more loyal to the SPD than British workers are to the Labour party. Thus, an **ideal-typical** SPD voter in Germany is a Protestant worker in a large northern city. His CDU counterpart is a middle-class Catholic in a small southern town. The Free Democrats appeal to some of the Protestant middle class, and the Greens attract the young, mostly at the expense of the SPD.

> ### Key Term
>
> **ideal-typical** Distilling social characteristics into one example.

East Germany, although mostly Protestant with a pre-1933 SPD voting tradition, went heavily Christian Democrat in 1990. As the costs of unification sank in, some East Germans in 1994 and 1998 moved to the SPD, a party more attractive to Protestants and to urban workers. But a good number of Ossis lent their votes to the Greens (who had merged with the East German Alternative/90 in early 1993) and to the ex-Communist Party of Democratic Socialism. German voting, like the German party system, has become more complex and less predictable.

Key Terms

bimodal (p. 209)	dealignment (p. 212)	transparency law (p. 214)
catchall party (p. 212)	ideal-typical (p. 220)	unimodal (p. 209)
center-seeking (p. 207)	Rechtsstaat (p. 213)	Weltanschauung party (p. 211)

Further Reference

Braunthal, Gerard. *Parties and Politics in Modern Germany*. Boulder, CO: Westview Press, 1996.

Dalton, Russell J., ed. *The New Germany Votes: Reunification and the Creation of a German Party System*. Providence, RI: Berg, 1993.

Downs, Anthony. *An Economic Theory of Democracy*. New York: Harper & Row, 1957.

Glees, Anthony. *Reinventing Germany: German Political Development since 1945*. Providence, RI: Berg, 1996.

Hancock, M. Donald, and Henry Krisch. *Germany*. Boulder, CO: Westview, 1998.

Huelshoff, Michael G., Andrei Markovits, and Simon Reich, eds. *From Bundesrepublik to Deutschland: German Politics after Unification*. Ann Arbor, MI: University of Michigan Press, 1993.

Jesse, Eckhard. *Elections: The Federal Republic of Germany in Comparison*. New York: St. Martin's, 1990.

Mayer, Margit, and John Ely, eds. *The German Greens: Paradox between Movement and Party*. Philadelphia, PA: Temple University Press, 1998.

Padgett, Stephen, ed. *Parties and Party Systems in the New Germany*. Brookfield, VT: Dartmouth, 1993.

Pulzer, Peter. *German Politics, 1945–1995*. New York: Oxford University Press, 1996.

What Germans Quarrel About

Questions to Consider

1. What made the German *Wirtschaftswunder*? Why can't it make a second one?
2. What did the German Model consist of?
3. Which country has the highest labor costs? What are its effects?
4. How were the major "left" governments of West Europe different? Who did the best job?
5. Could East and West Germany have merged gradually?
6. Why are immigrants necessary for a country like Germany?
7. How does the new Berlin Republic differ from the Bonn Republic?
8. What did the Helsinki Final Act do?

The great quarrel in Germany—indeed, in most of Europe—is how to trim an overly generous welfare state and cut its onerous taxes. If it doesn't, unemployment will likely stay high. But once a welfare benefit has been extended, it is terribly difficult to cut it, because people have come to expect it as a right. The debate over keeping or cutting the welfare state runs through all the major German parties. (Notice how U.S. politicians of both parties avoid even the appearance of slowing the growth of Social Security and Medicare.) German welfare benefits grew during the **Wirtschaftswunder** of the postwar years, when it seemed like the economy could afford almost anything. But now the miracle is over, and Germany's aging population requires ever-larger welfare subsidies.

Nothing produces economic miracles, it has been said, like losing a war. This is surely the case in West Germany and Japan following World War II. There was simply nothing to do but work. Some German factories were destroyed by Allied bombing. Many machine tools were ripped out and shipped back to the Soviet Union by the vengeful Red Army. The British and Americans patched up their old industries, but the Germans were forced to rebuild theirs with new and more efficient equipment.

The aftermath of war had some psychological benefits. Almost everybody was poor; food and fuel were barely sufficient for survival. This brought a kind of rough equality among Germans; income

Key Term

Wirtschaftswunder   German for "economic miracle."

Key Terms

Sozialmarkt "Social market"; Germany's postwar capitalism aimed at reconstruction and a welfare floor.

Modell Deutschland The German economic model.

consensus Agreement among all constituent groups.

Mitbestimmung "Co-determination"; unions participating in company decisions.

wage restraint Unions holding back on compensation demands.

distribution was more equitable in Germany (and Japan) than in the victorious countries. Consequently, the bitter class antagonisms found in Britain and France did not develop in Germany. Everyone started from a similar low level, and most West Germans felt that everyone got a share of economic growth. Furthermore, defeat in the war and empty stomachs following it left Germans with more modest expectations than Britons or Americans, who expected some kind of postwar paradise. For West Germans after Hitler, hard work to foster economic growth was about their only outlet for national pride.

Under the leadership of the CDU and Economics Minister (later Chancellor) Ludwig Erhard, Bonn pursued a largely laissez-faire policy. While Britain turned to Labour's welfare state and France to *planification* after World War II, West Germany relied mainly on market forces. During the 1950s, the West German economy recovered almost miraculously. It was built on the **Sozialmarkt** of Ludwig Erhard, which was basically a free market but aimed by bank loans to socially needed ends, such as rebuilding Germany's bombed-out cities. It continued and expanded the welfare state begun by Bismarck. Some called it "capitalism with a conscience."

During the 1970s the **Modell Deutschland** that stressed **consensus** among all social groups was successful and admired. In it, no one's views were ignored. Workers, for example, have **Mitbestimmung**, which gives unions a role in overall company policy. Each large firm must have a supervisory board with half its directors chosen by labor and half by top management and big shareholders. For example, in 1999, when BMW ousted its top management, the ten worker representatives on the board vetoed a proposed chief executive they didn't like and got one they did. Codetermination is one reason Germany has had very few strikes; workers feel they're part of the system.

The End of the Miracle

By the time of unification in 1990, however, the miracle had worn off, and not just from the heavy costs of unification. German wages and welfare benefits had climbed during the 1970s and 1980s, making Germany less of an economic dynamo. Basically, rapid economic growth comes from wages that lag behind productivity. That is, where you have skilled workers efficiently producing desired goods at prices that beat others, you will gain a large piece of the world market. Germany (and Japan, with a few years' lag time) fit this pattern. After the war, German workers' skills were still high, and much of Germany's infrastructure was intact. German labor unions practiced **wage restraint**; they did not demand every DM they could get but let capital grow until it provided jobs and good wages for all. This period—from the 1950s through the 1970s—was the time of Germany's rapid growth. In contrast, British and U.S. productivity lagged behind wage increases, meaning they sold less and less to the world.

By the 1980s, however, German wages surpassed U.S. wages, German social taxes were much higher, and German productivity was no longer growing quickly. In the meantime, America was getting more and more competitive; wages had been essentially stagnant (by the time you account for inflation) since the early 1970s, but productivity grew. The U.S. welfare floor, always much lower than the German, was less of a tax burden. By 1997, with U.S. labor averaging $18 an hour (including fringes and taxes) while German labor cost $28, and with U.S. productivity some 20 percent higher than in Germany, it cost two-thirds as much to make something in the United States as in the other major industrial countries (see box on page 225).

COMPARISON

EUROPE'S DIFFERENT "LEFTS"

In the late 1990s all of West Europe (except Spain and Ireland) voted in center-left governments, but notice—comparing Blair, Jospin, and Schröder—how they were quite different. Blair accepted the Thatcherite notion that business, not government, creates jobs. Instead of trying to undo her promarket reforms, he tackled important noneconomic issues (Northern Ireland, devolution, education) that the Tories had left untouched. In Blair's "Third Way," there was little left left.

Jospin, on the other hand, proclaimed "democratic socialism" and was a still-traditional *dirigiste* who never fully accepted the primacy of markets; he still saw a major role for the French state. For example, to cut unemployment he proposed publicly funded jobs and training. In France, the left was still left.

Schröder's "New Center" accepted the free market but turned almost reflexively to Germany's consensus model—his Alliance for Jobs—in an attempt to bring down the jobless rate. In a parallel to Jospin's plan, Schröder aimed to place 100,000 German youths in jobs or training programs. Yes, Europe did lurch to the left, but in each country left meant something different, something rooted in each land's political culture.

Furthermore, individual and corporate taxes are more steeply progressive in Germany than in America, and Germany has far more regulations. Under such economic pressures, German capital flees abroad. German investment in the United States, for example, has created some two-thirds of a million jobs for Americans while job growth in Germany stagnates.

By the 1990s, German workers enjoyed short work weeks (thirty-six hours), long vacations (a month or more), the world's highest pay, male retirement at sixty-three (women at sixty) with fat pensions, and almost no strikes. With the downturn of the 1990s, though, German workers got a jolt. Unemployment stayed above 10 percent overall (twice as high in the east as in the west), and union membership dropped. From 1986 to 1996, Germany's welfare spending more than doubled to some DM50 billion ($27 billion) a year—and this was under a conservative government. Can Germany's consensus model still work in a very different world from the 1950s when it was created?

In a 1996 "**austerity** package," the Bundestag cut Germans' health, unemployment, and welfare benefits and gradually raised the retirement age (to sixty-five for men and sixty-three for women). The Kohl government defended the cuts as moderate, necessary, and supported by most Germans, who were fed up with high taxes. Opponents of the cuts, including the SPD, called them "socially obscene" and the "destruction of the welfare state." The cuts helped the SPD win the 1998 elections, but in 1999 Schröder found he had to deliver another austerity budget; the economy allowed him no choice.

And here we see the trouble with the consensus model. With all major groups having a say, any one group can veto change. Try telling unions they'll have to accept lower pay and work longer hours. Not a chance. Try telling factories and farmers they must lose their subsidies. Not a chance. Try telling the jobless that their unemployment benefits must be cut. Not a chance. Try telling the sick that their

Key Term

austerity Cutting government expenditures, belt-tightening.

Key Term

blocked society   One in which interest groups prevent major, necessary change.

health-care benefits must be trimmed. Not a chance. Earlier, France had been called a **blocked society**; now the title may be passing to Germany. (Does the United States exhibit some of these same problems?)

Kohl passed Germany's economic problems on to Schröder, who promoted an "Alliance for Jobs"—labor, capital, and government together coming up with ideas to create jobs. Few jobs were created. It was an attempt to refurbish the old consensus model when there was no more consensus. Schröder then had to carry out—with much anger inside his own SPD—conservative-type reforms in taxation, welfare, and workforce flexibility.

How to Merge Two Economies

The sudden merging of two very different systems added to Germany's economic difficulties. Over forty-five years, the largely free-market West German economy had become a world giant, in some years exporting more (in dollar value) than the United States. The centrally controlled and planned East German economy, although it was the envy of the East bloc, had a per capita GDP half that of West Germany. Wessis were roughly twice as rich as Ossis. West German products were desired throughout the world; East German products were sold mostly to the Soviet bloc plus some Third World lands too poor to afford better. The two economies could exist side-by-side only with a wall between them to prevent direct competition.

In 1990, the physical and political barriers between the two Germanys suddenly disappeared. West German currency and products flooded into East Germany, and the East German economy collapsed with a speed and thoroughness no one had foreseen. It was thought to have been a working economy that just needed modernization. Many supposed that West German firms would bring their capital and know-how into East German enterprises and quickly lift them up to West German levels. This scenario was much too rosy. East Germans simply ceased

East Germany before and after the arrival of West German money: a Street in Stalsund (Stralsund) in 1990 (left) and in 1995 (right). (German Information Center)

COMPARISON

WHO WINS THE MANUFACTURING RACE?

Those with the lowest wages do not necessarily win the manufacturing race. To win in the global manufacturing race requires lower wages combined with higher productivity. Here's how the situation looked among our five industrialized democracies in the late 1990s:

	Total Hourly Labor Costs	Unit Labor Costs
Britain	$16	$106
Japan	19	103
France	18	100
Germany	28	100
United States	18	67

Source: Swedish Employers' Federation, OECD

Total hourly labor costs, here for 1997, include bonuses, fringe benefits, and social security and other taxes (such as health insurance), which in Germany add 80 percent to regular wages. These "social taxes" are low in the United States and Japan. **Unit labor costs**, a measure that combines total labor costs with productivity, in this table uses Germany as the standard "100" for comparative purposes. The clear winner: the United States. Productivity figures, though, change constantly. The German figures here are already an improvement; a few years earlier German labor costs were $32 and unit labor costs were 140.

buying East German products as soon as they could buy nicer West German goods. As gigantic state subsidies ended, East German factory and farm production plummeted. East German unemployment shot from essentially zero into the millions, and both East and West Germans turned angry. It was estimated that only one-fourth of East Germany's enterprises will ultimately survive the transition to a market economy.

Saving the East German economy required tons of money, far more than anticipated—over DM1 trillion ($530 billion)—from the federal government. Ultimately, of course, it comes from West Germans in higher taxes. Some 5 percent of Germany's GDP flows to its eastern region as subsidies. Thus, the first great quarrel of united Germany grew out of how to merge the two economies and who was going to pay for it. Chancellor Kohl said the bailout of the East German economy could be done without higher taxes. The opposition Social Democrats scoffed—their chief, Oskar Lafontaine, chided, "read my lips" (in English) in the 1990 election—and sure enough, the Kohl government next year put on a 7.5 percent "solidarity surcharge" on income taxes. Nobody liked the tax, which lasted for years, but Germany needed it to get its budget deficit below 3 percent, as required for the new European currency.

Can West Germany's earlier economic miracle apply to the East German economy? The desperate postwar feelings that made West Germans work so hard are not found in post-Wall East Germany. Under the Communists' centrally planned economic system, East Germans did not develop attitudes of hard work and **entrepreneurial** risk-taking. They got used to a vast welfare system that offered security for

Key Terms

unit labor costs What it costs to manufacture the same item in different countries.

entrepreneurial Starting your own business.

COULD UNIFICATION HAVE COME GRADUALLY?

Could unification have come gradually? No. The real problem behind the difficulties and costs of merging the two German economies is the speed with which it occurred. Some Social Democrats and economists urged merging only gradually, over several years. But that really couldn't happen, for once the ball started rolling, it could not be slowed. Events took on a fast-paced life of their own.

1. The hardline Honecker regime in East Berlin refuses all thought of reform for most of 1989. But East Germans, seeing reforms taking place elsewhere in the Soviet bloc, become more restless.

2. Hungary lets East Germans exit into Austria. The Communist regime in Budapest had pledged not to let East German tourists flee to the West, but in the summer of 1989 they stop enforcing this pledge. Why? My hunch is that debt-burdened Hungary, by then under reform-minded Communists, got some nice financing from Bonn. Economic carrots had long been part of West German policy in Eastern Europe. At an accelerating rate, thousands of East Germans "vacation" in Hungary but proceed to West Germany. East Berlin screams in protest, and Budapest shrugs. By September, more than 18,000 East Germans flee via Hungary, another 17,000 via Czechoslovakia. East Germany closes its border with Czechoslovakia to staunch the flow.

3. Massive demonstrations break out in East Germany in September, centered in Leipzig. In October Gorbachev visits to urge reform and warn Honecker, "Life punishes those who delay." Clearly, Gorbachev wishes to be rid of the problems and expenses of maintaining a Soviet empire in Eastern Europe. By now some 100,000 protesters are marching in Leipzig chanting "Gorby, Gorby!"

4. Honecker orders a "Chinese solution" (named after the massacre at Tienanmen Square that June) and tells his police to get ready to fire on the Leipzig demonstrators. Egon Krenz, in charge of security but sensing catastrophe, countermands the order. On October 18, Honecker is out and Krenz becomes party chief and president. By now a million East Germans, led by a intellectuals in the New Forum movement, are protesting for democracy.

5. On November 9, 1989, Krenz orders the Berlin Wall opened to gain some good will and time for reform. The Wall has kept East Germans locked in since 1961, and now tens of thousands pour into the West with no intention of returning. At this point, the days of a separate East Germany are numbered. Krenz resigns; much has happened because he countermanded the order to fire on protesters. Liberal and reform-minded Communists take over the party and government and pledge free elections.

6. Too many East Germans pour into the West because they are not sure that their own system is going to change. They want the good life of West Germany. Some half million come across in the four months after the Wall opens, overburdening West Germany's job and apartment market, financial resources, and patience. Stay home, Chancellor Kohl urges; we'll merge and rescue you soon enough.

7. Free East German elections in March 1990 put Christian Democrats in power. They see things Kohl's way and want speedy unification; this is why East Germans voted for them. Impatiently, East Germans want to get in on West German economic prosperity.

8. Bonn gives East Germans a favorable exchange rate. East German marks aren't worth much, but East Germans argue that they have worked for and saved Ostmarks for decades. They demand a one-to-one exchange. Bonn argues that Ostmarks are essentially funny

money and should be exchanged at a much lower rate. They compromise on one-to-one for each Ossi's first 2,000 marks (about $1,000) and one Westmark for two East above 2,000. It is a generous deal for East Germans, but if Bonn hadn't agreed to it, Ossis would have continued to pour into West Germany. In a sense, the one-to-one is a bribe to get them to stay put. On July 2, 1990, the Westmark becomes the official currency for both Germanys.

9. East Germans buy everything Western, nothing Eastern. With Westmarks in their pockets and Western products on store shelves, they turn their backs on their own products, now seen as junk. Suddenly, competing in a free market with the West, the East German economy collapses; it never had a chance to adjust.

Could anything have been done to prevent or slow the preceding sequence? We would have to go back to step one and get the Honecker regime committed to reforms that would gradually turn the East German economy into a market system that could compete with Western products. Then the two economies could merge without one of them collapsing. But Honecker was a devoted Communist. To marketize means abandoning communism, something he would not budge on. And once East Germans started pouring across, what could Bonn do? Rebuild the border fence between the two Germanys to make East Germans wait at home? The critics of too-rapid unification are right: It would have been better if it had been slower. But that was not in the cards.

Top: Brandenburg Gate in East Berlin behind the Wall. Bottom: Party time as the Wall comes down in November 1989. (German Information Service)

all but few incentives for individual exertion. Ossis say, "It's not our fault that the Communists saddled us with an inferior economic system. Besides, you Wessis got billions of dollars in U.S. Marshall Plan aid; we got ripped off by the Soviets. So it's only fair that you boost us up to your standard of living, and quickly."

Many West Germans are appalled at such attitudes, which seem like excuses to avoid work. Why set up factories in East Germany when you can get good productivity out of Poles and Czechs, whose wages are a fraction of the German level? Resentment flared in each half of Germany against the other half. From this resentment, especially in the East, grew some of the extremist groups that targeted foreign workers.

How Much Welfare?

As we considered with Britain, European countries are welfare states, and all are under pressure to cut welfare. One-third of Germany's GDP goes for social spending, a heavy tax burden on Germany's manufacturing competitiveness. Germany's welfare system is Europe's oldest, tracing back to Bismarck's innovations in the late nineteenth century. Since then, it has grown and become accepted by just about everyone, even conservatives. The CDU, for example, has a tradition of Catholic trade-unionism.

But now one of the great questions of European politics has become, "How much welfare can we afford?" Even previously committed social democrats worry that their generous welfare provisions are pricing them out of the market. In 1994, for example, with unemployment nearing 12 percent, the CDU/FDP government cut unemployment benefits from 58 percent to 55 percent of gross pay for married workers and ended the benefits after two to four years, depending on circumstances. This was still very generous unemployment compensation.

German pensions are also generous, but to pay for them German workers must contribute 20 percent of their wages, and this will soon rise to an impossible 30 percent if present trends continue. A complex of supplementary benefits essentially means that no Germans live in poverty, but this too is very expensive. The Kohl government argued it was time to move away from the "cradle to grave" concept of a welfare system that covers everyone for everything and to a "social safety net" limited to the truly needy. The fear is that if nothing is done to reform the German welfare system, the younger generation, which is having to bear the burdens (see box on page 230), will revolt.

The Flood of Foreigners

Like Britain and France, Germany too finds that foreigners from poor countries are attracted to its better jobs and higher pay. But in Germany the numbers—and the problems—are bigger. There are 7.4 million foreigners in Germany, mostly from Mediterranean nations (Turkey, ex-Yugoslavia, Greece, Italy, and Spain). Over 2 million are workers; the rest are spouses and children. All together, they comprise some 9 percent of the population of the Federal Republic.

The trend started in 1955 when the economic miracle had absorbed all working Germans and was still short of labor. Italians and later Spaniards were invited to West Germany and they came, eager for the plentiful jobs. Soon Germans began abandoning dirty, dangerous, and unskilled lines of work for better positions, leaving their old jobs to foreigners. At first the impact seemed temporary: The migrant workers were supposed to stay three years and rotate back

Turkish women in the Kreuzberg district of Berlin, a center for Turkish immigrants, of whom there are 2.1 million in Germany. (German Information Center)

home. But the "guest workers," faced with unemployment at home, often decided to remain and to send for their families. Large numbers began arriving from Turkey, where unemployment is especially high. There are now 2.1 million Turks in the Federal Republic; whole neighborhoods have turned into Turkish ghettos. The "guests" had come to stay.

By the 1980s, poor people worldwide had discovered Germany's very liberal asylum law. Simply upon arriving in Germany, a foreigner had only to claim that he or she was politically persecuted back home. Although more often the motivation was economic, legal tangles could let the asylum-seeker stay in Germany for years, all the while on welfare. As in Britain and France, antiforeign feeling grew among all social classes. Germans perceived foreigners as crime prone, lecherous, and disorderly. A new racism appeared in Germany, exaggerated by FRG law: A person of German descent arriving from Russia or Romania, whose ancestors had left Germany centuries ago, gets instant FRG citizenship; a Turk born and raised in Germany could not, until recently, become a German citizen.

With unification, all manner of people flocked to the Federal Republic from East Europe and even Asia, fleeing collapsing economies. Polish black marketeers and Romanian gypsies were not appreciated. Said a popular T-shirt: "I want my Wall back." The Federal Republic, along with Austria, strengthened border controls and expelled many undocumented visitors. Amid great political controversy (with the SPD fighting it), the asylum law was tightened to exclude most claimants.

The serious problem the **Gastarbeiter** presented was their families, especially the Turks. Originally, it was thought that only single workers would come, and no provision was made for educating children. But the Turkish families have about three times as many babies as do Germans. The result is a growing mass of underprivileged youth in Germany with inadequate schooling, few job skills, and few jobs. The situation has been called a social time bomb: hundreds of thousands of foreign children, many of them candidates for juvenile delinquency and drugs. Germany became Europe's number-one drug country; pure heroin from Turkey's poppy fields flowed in with Turkish Gastarbeiter.

Key Term

Gastarbeiter "Guest workers," temporary labor allowed into Germany.

GEOGRAPHY

THE GEOGRAPHY OF DEMOGRAPHY

Almost all industrialized countries produce few babies. In Germany, for example, despite hefty children's allowances (DM250 monthly each for the first two children, DM300 each for more than two), an average German woman bears only 1.26 children, one of the world's lowest **fertility rates** (which is not the same as the "birth rate," a different measure). In comparison, an average American woman bears 1.95 children, a French women 1.6, a British 1.7, a Japanese 1.45, and a Russian 1.1.

Replacement level is 2.1, the rate at which a population will hold steady, and it is found in few advanced industrialized countries. Large families are not prized, and women have increased educational and career options. These rates take no account of immigration

and are one reason why all of these countries need to have immigrants. Why? Because without immigrants, who is going to do the work that supports the increasing portion of the population that is retired?

By 2025, an estimated 24 percent of Germans and Japanese will be sixty-five or over; some 20 percent of Britons, French, and Americans will be in that age bracket. All of these countries face the problem of soon having too few people in the work force supporting too many people in retirement. Germany already has the heaviest burden, with three working persons supporting one retiree—one reason German taxes are so high. By 2040, the ratio could become an impossible 1:1 (and the same in France). The solution: either more babies, more immigrants, or (what is already happening) later retirements. **Demographics** leads to tough political choices.

Now, what to do with the immigrant workers and their families? Many German politicians, especially the more conservative ones, have tried to pretend it isn't Germany's problem: If the foreigners aren't happy in the Federal Republic, they should leave. Like the British and French National Front parties, a small anti-immigrant National Republican party sprang up in Germany that would like to expel the foreigners.

Leftist and green Germans, on the other hand, recognize that the immigrants aren't just temporary and that the problem will be helped only by integrating them into German society. This is happening, much like the U.S. melting pot a century ago. There are even SPD Bundestag members of Turkish origin. Under SPD sponsorship, a new law starting in 2000 allows German citizenship for those who have resided eight years (down from fifteen) in the FRG and makes it automatic for children born in the FRG, provided the parents lived there eight years. This is a major switch in Germany's definition of who is a German, and it provoked conservative opposition. From the traditional **jus sanguinis**, used throughout Europe, the SPD argued for a U.S.-style **jus soli**. *Land* elections went against the SPD over the citizenship issue. (Notice the parallel with U.S. Democrats and Republicans on rights for immigrants.)

Acting out of personal insecurities, limited job openings, and a hatred of foreigners, some young Germans became skinheads or neo-Nazis and attacked foreigners. Several Turks, members of families that had been working in Germany for many years, were murdered in firebomb attacks. In some cases, the

Key Terms

fertility rate   How many children an average woman bears.

demography   Study of population growth.

jus sanguinis   Latin for "right of blood"; citizenship based on descent.

jus soli   Latin for "right of soil"; citizenship given to those born in the country.

Although media attention focused on the crimes of a few against foreign workers in Germany, large crowds, such as this one at Cologne's Opera Square, turned out to protest antiforeigner sentiments as a type of racism. (German Information Center)

police and neighbors did nothing to stop the violence. Even members of the U.S. Olympic luge team were beaten by young toughs as they trained in Germany. On the other side, hundreds of thousands of young Germans attended rallies and protests against **xenophobia** and violence.

A Fourth Reich?

Does all the tension in present-day Germany have the makings of a major neo-Nazi movement? Unlikely. There are, to be sure, neo-Nazis in Germany (much of their literature is printed in the United States), and Germany will always bear watching in this regard. But extreme rightists and neo-Nazis are only a small percentage and divided into several parties—making it difficult to reach the 5 percent threshold. Many are simply confused and disoriented young people.

By most measures the Federal Republic of Germany is an unqualified success story. Its constitution, leading parties, and economy deserve to be studied by other countries. But some observers have wondered if, under the glittering surface, democracy has taken firm root. Could the present democracy go the way of Weimar's?

All survey data have said no. Decade by decade, Germans have grown more democratic in their values. By now they are at least as committed to a pluralist, free, democratic society as the British and French. They weathered terrorism and economic downturns as well as any of their democratic neighbors. Now, even East Germans are turning into free-market democrats, albeit with much pain and complaint.

Things have changed in both the domestic and international contexts of German democracy, however. Germany's consensus and welfare state has become rigid and costly. Like most of West Europe,

Key Term

xenophobia Fear and hatred of foreigners.

GEOGRAPHY

PERMANENT BORDERS FOR EUROPE

In Helsinki, 1975, thirty-five nations agreed to the Final Act of the Conference on Security and Cooperation in Europe (CSCE). Among its provisions to calm and stabilize Europe was Principle III of Basket I: "The participating States regard as inviolable all one another's frontiers as well as the frontiers of all States in Europe." Europe's boundaries can be changed only by peaceful means. Europe's boundary problems are over, especially the very touchy German-Polish border.

But other problems loom. First, the **Helsinki Final Act** is not a treaty, although it is treated virtually like one. It lacks the legally binding quality of treaties. Second, some of the CSCE's other provisions conflict with Principle III. For example, Principle VIII guarantees "self-determination of peoples," which was used to justify German unification and the dissolution of the Soviet Union, which left behind several potential boundary conflicts. Third, Serbia attempted to enlarge its boundaries by taking portions of Croatia and Bosnia, with great bloodshed and "ethnic cleansing" that tore a great hole in the CSCE agreement. Serbs were eventually pushed back but still hold part of Bosnia. Later, Albanians in Kosovo broke it away from Serbia. Which governs: permanent borders or self-determination?

Still, the CSCE Final Act was a praiseworthy attempt to settle Europe's boundaries, especially the German-Polish border. Conflicts may arise, as between Albania and Greece, Hungary and Romania, and Romania and Russia (over the Romanian-speaking republic of Moldova, annexed by Stalin in 1940). But the conflicts are likely to be peripheral and containable. Now called the OSCE (for Organization), the body shows a Europe trying to overcome centuries of warfare, much of it concerning boundaries.

Germany's wages, taxes, welfare benefits, and overregulation have led to high and seemingly incurable unemployment. Competition from low-wage countries is fierce, and many German firms have moved production to Poland and the Czech Republic. Berlin hotels send their laundry to Poland.

Both Germanys were children of the Cold War. At times, a third of a million U.S. soldiers were camped in West Germany, over half a million Soviet soldiers in East Germany. This situation was tense but stable. The FRG was firmly anchored to NATO and the European Union, the GDR to the **Warsaw Pact** and **Comecon**. Suddenly the international context changed. The Cold War is over. Germany is unified. The Soviet troops have left and only a few U.S. troops remain. The **Bonn Republic** was anchored to the West. Will the new **Berlin Republic** stay cemented to Western ideals and institutions, or could it someday go off on its own, with a nationalistic and expansionist foreign policy?

It is highly improbable that Germany could become a "Fourth Reich," as critics (including some Germans) fear. German democracy is solid. The new institutions of a uniting Europe are making Germans good Europeans, and all major FRG parties are committed to precisely that. The German army is small and has no ABC (atomic, biological, or chemical) weapons. Three of Germany's European neighbors have nuclear weapons, which by itself means that

Key Terms

Helsinki Final Act   1975 agreement to make Europe's borders permanent.

Warsaw Pact   Soviet-led alliance of Communist countries, now defunct.

Comecon   Trading organization of Communist countries, now defunct.

Bonn Republic   West Germany, with capital in Bonn.

Berlin Republic   Reunified Germany, with capital in Berlin.

Germany will never go on the warpath. Few Germans have any taste for militarism, for they have seen what it leads to. Germany has accomplished so much more by peaceful economic means than it could ever obtain by warlike means.

The Weimar analogy is misplaced on present-day Germany. For a gigantic country that may be on a Weimar-like brink of an abyss, let us now turn to Russia.

Key Terms

austerity (p. 223)
Berlin Republic (p. 232)
blocked society (p. 224)
Bonn Republic (p. 232)
Comecon (p. 232)
consensus (p. 222)
demography (p. 230)

entrepreneurial (p. 225)
fertility rate (p. 230)
Gastarbeiter (p. 229)
Helsinki Final Act (p. 232)
jus sanguinis (p. 230)
jus soli (p. 230)
Mitbestimmung (p. 222)

Modell Deutschland (p. 222)
Sozialmarkt (p. 222)
unit labor costs (p. 225)
wage restraint (p. 222)
Warsaw Pact (p. 223)
Wirtschaftswunder (p. 221)
xenophobia (p. 231)

Further Reference

Brubaker, Rogers. *Citizenship and Nationhood in France and Germany.* Cambridge, MA: Harvard University Press, 1992.

Edinger, Lewis, and Brigitte Nacos. *From Bonn to Berlin.* New York: Columbia University Press, 1998.

Garton Ash, Timothy. *In Europe's Name: Germany and the Divided Continent.* New York: Random House, 1993.

Hampton, Mary, and Christian Soe, eds. *Between Bonn and Berlin: German Politics Adrift.* Lanham, MD: Rowman & Littlefield, 1998.

Jarausch, Konrad H. *The Rush to German Unity.* New York: Oxford University Press, 1994.

Keithly, David M. *The Collapse of East German Communism: The Year the Wall Came Down, 1989.* Westport, CT: Praeger, 1992.

Markovits, Andrei S., and Simon Reich. *The German Predicament: Memory and Power in the New Europe.* Ithaca, NY: Cornell University Press, 1997.

Merkl, Peter H., ed. *The Federal Republic of Germany at Forty-Five: Union Without Unity.* New York: New York University Press, 1995.

Schmidt, Michael. *The New Reich: Violent Extremism in Unified Germany and Beyond.* New York: Pantheon, 1993.

Sinn, Gerlinde, and Hans-Werner Sinn. *Jumpstart: The Economic Unification of Germany.* Cambridge, MA: MIT Press, 1993.

Turner, Lowell. *Fighting for Partnership: Labor and Politics in Unified Germany.* Ithaca, NY: Cornell University Press, 1998.

Wolfgramm, Doris G. *The Kohl Government and German Reunification: Crisis and Foreign Policy.* Lewiston, NY: E. Mellen, 1997.

PART IV

Key Websites

The Russian Connection   This site contains insightful essays, links, and information on the political history of Russia.
http://home.freeuk.net/ethos/russia.htm

Russia on the Net   This is a site devoted to all aspects of Russian life, including art, culture, entertainment, recreation, and politics. The government and legislation section has many excellent links to all aspects of Russian political life.
http://www.ru/

Manifesto of the Communist Party   This site contains the classic *Manifesto of the Communist Party* by Karl Marx and Frederick Engels.
http://www.anu.edu.au/polsci/marx/classics/manifesto.html

Marxist Internet Archive   This takes a look at all aspects of Marxism.
http://www.marxists.org/

The Institute for the Economy in Transition   This is a comprehensive site created by Dr. E. Gaidar. It has monthly reports, hot news, and interviews on politics and economic issues concerning Russia.
http://www.online.ru/sp/iet/index.html

Stalinism: Its Origins and Future   This site offers an exhaustive series of articles, put together by Andy Blunden, covering the complete history of Joseph Stalin and his role in Russian history.
http://www.online.ru/sp/iet/index.html

Radio Free Europe/Radio Liberty   This site provides a first-rate analyses of current Russian (and regional) politics, including election coverage.
http://www.rferl.org

Russia:
The Impact of the Past

17

Questions to Consider

1. Does Russia's size make it inherently difficult to govern?
2. What geographic disadvantages has Russia faced over the years?
3. Why does Russia always seem to require modernization from above? Why can't it come from below?
4. How much practice has Russia had with democracy?
5. How does the clash of Westernizers and Slavophiles echo to this day?
6. Why did Marxism catch on in Russia, where it was not supposed to?
7. How did Lenin alter Marxism?
8. Could the Provisional Government have stayed in power? How?
9. Was Stalin an accident?

Russia is immense, stretching ten time zones across the northern half of Asia to the Pacific. Looking at a map of Russia, you notice only a small part of it is in Europe. (Look at a globe and you notice that Europe itself is only a small peninsula of Asia.) Although Russia has few natural boundaries, its very size and harsh winters make it difficult to conquer. Charles XII of Sweden, Napoleon, and Hitler discovered to their horror that Russia's size and fierce winters swallowed whole armies. These same winters give Russia a short growing season. Russian agriculture is a chancy business, with crops failing on an average of one year in three. Geography has not been as kind to Russia as it has been to the United States.

The vast territory that **Siberia** adds to Russia's size is problematic; its weather is hostile to settlement, and its mineral and forest wealth is hard to extract. Most of the Russian population continues to live in the "European" part, that is, west of the Ural Mountains. Most plans to settle in and develop Siberia, some of them going back to tsarist days, fall short of expectations. Industrial projects tend to be one-shot efforts by temporary labor. The promises of Siberia remain largely unfulfilled.

Another geographic problem has been the difficulty of reaching the open

Key Term

Siberia From the Russian for "north"; that part of Russia east of the Ural Mountains but not including Central Asia.

GEOGRAPHY

SIZE

Countries can be either too big or too small. If too small, the nation's resources and population may not be able to stave off foreign conquest or absorption. The map of Europe became simpler over the centuries as small principalities and dukedoms were drawn into larger units. Too big can also be a problem, especially when the country encompasses too many distinct ethnic groups.

The United States has generally integrated its many immigrants into an American culture. The Soviet Union, however, was not able to build a "new Soviet man" from its many nationalities. Perhaps a country as big and ethnically diverse as the Soviet Union was not meant to be. Just holding it together meant its rulers needed strong central control backed by force. Even now, the very size of Russia may incline it to tyranny.

sea. The first Russian states were landlocked; only under Peter the Great at the beginning of the eighteenth century did Russians overcome the Swedes to reach the Baltic and the Turks to reach the Black Sea. The North Russian ports ice over in winter, and the Black Sea is controlled by the Turkish Straits, still leaving European Russia without year-round, secure ports. Tsarists and Communists alike longed for warm-water ports under exclusive Russian control.

The Slavic People

Occupying most of East Europe, the Slavic peoples are the most numerous in Europe. Russians, Ukrainians, Poles, Czechs, Slovaks, Serbs, Croats, Bulgarians, and others speak languages closer to each other than are the Romance languages (Italian, Spanish, French) of West Europe. It is said a Slovak peasant can converse with any other Slavic peasant—so similar are their vocabularies and syntax.

The way the Slavic languages are written, though, has differentiated them. The Western Slavs (Poles, Czechs, and others) were Christianized from Rome; hence their alphabet is Latin. The Eastern Slavs (Russians, Ukrainians, Serbs, and others) were converted by Eastern Orthodox monks from Constantinople, and their languages are written in a variation of the Greek alphabet called **Cyrillic**, after St. Cyril, one of the monks who first converted Slavs.

Their Orthodox Christianity (as opposed to Roman Catholicism) and Cyrillic writing have contributed to the Russians' isolation from the rest of Europe. In addition to being at the geographical fringe of Europe, Russia was beyond its cultural fringe for centuries. The important ideas that helped modernize Catholic and Protestant Europe penetrated Russia only much later. Rome was a lively fountainhead of thought in West Europe, but the headquarters of the Orthodox faith, Constantinople, under the Turks ceased to provide intellectual guidance for its followers. At the same time West Europe was experiencing the invigoration of the Renaissance, which rippled outward from Catholic Italy, Russia stayed isolated and asleep. It missed the Enlightenment altogether.

Key Term

Cyrillic Greek-based alphabet of the Eastern Slavic languages.

GEOGRAPHY

NATURAL RESOURCES

Curiously, the quality of a country's soil and its mineral riches do not clearly determine its prosperity. Indeed, some of the richest countries in the world, such as Germany and Japan, are poorly endowed, whereas richly endowed countries like Russia and Indonesia may lag behind. The United States and France, to be sure, once had abundant mineral resources and still have fine farmland.

It is human resources—the skills, policies, and organization of societies—rather than natural resources that form the basis for growth. There is even the hint of an in- verse relationship between natural resources and politico-economic development: With little to fall back on, poorly endowed countries may develop their organization and techniques and turn themselves into rich countries. Lands naturally endowed may become dependent on their natural resources and fail to modernize. The big increases in oil prices in the 1970s, for example, enabled the Soviet Union—then the world's biggest producer and exporter of petroleum—to coast into the 1980s by importing food and technology. When world oil prices fell in the 1990s, so did the Soviet Union.

A more important factor in explaining Russia's isolation and backwardness was its conquest in the thirteenth century by the Mongols, later known as the **Tatars**. The Mongol khans crushed the first Russian state, centered at Kiev in present-day Ukraine, and enslaved much of the population. For two centuries, while West Europe moved ahead, Russian culture under the barbaric Mongols declined. Some historians believe even after the Tatar yoke was lifted, it still took five centuries for Russia to catch up with the West.

Russian Autocracy

Under the Tatars, the duchy of Moscow came to be the most powerful Russian state, first as a tax collector for the khans, then as their triumphant enemy. Moscovy's Ivan the Terrible (1530–84) had himself crowned **tsar**. Ivan was both murderous and successful; his brutal use of force set a standard for later Russian and Soviet rulers. To this day, many Russians think national greatness can be achieved only by the ruthless actions of a strong leader. Under Ivan, Russian territory expanded greatly, down the Volga to the Caspian Sea and into Siberia.

When the Russian nobles (*boyars*) came into conflict with Ivan, he used his secret police, the *Oprichnina*, to have them exiled or executed. Since that time, the Russian nobility never played an autonomous role in political life. It was as if the absolutism of France was applied early and completely to a culturally backward country. The result was **autocracy**, and the tsar was the autocrat. Unlike the countries of West Europe, Russia never experienced the mixed monarchy of nobles, church, commoners, and king, held in some kind of balance. Accordingly, Russians had no experience with limited government, checks and

Key Terms

Tatar Mongol-origin tribes who ruled Russia for centuries. (*Not* Tartar.)

tsar From "caesar"; Russia's emperor. Sometimes spelled old Polish style, czar.

autocracy Absolute rule of one person in a centralized state.

POLITICAL CULTURE

"MOSCOW IS THE THIRD ROME"

A fter **Constantinople** fell to the Turks in 1453, Russia felt itself to be the last and only center of true Christianity. Rome and Constantinople had both failed; now Moscow would safeguard the faith. Ivan the Terrible and other Russians intoned: "Moscow is the third Rome; a fourth is not to be." After the Bolshevik Revolution, Russia's new rulers felt the same way about world communism, namely, Moscow was its capital and there could be no other. Even today, some Russians still feel that Russia has a holy mission.

St. Basil's cathedral recalls Moscow's former role as a center of Christianity. Russia's tsars were not merely heads of state but also heads of the Russian Orthodox Church. (Michael Roskin)

balances, or pluralism. As Ivan grew older he became madder. Able to trust no one, he murdered those around him—even his own son—at the least suspicion. By the time he died he had carved out the modern Russian state, but his subjects suffered in fear.

Absolutism or Anarchy?

One of the reasons Russians put up with autocracy—and sometimes admired it—was because they felt that without a firm hand at the top the system would degenerate into anarchy. This happened in the early seventeenth century. Lacking a strong tsar, unrest, banditry, civil war, and a Polish invasion plagued the land; it was known as the Time of

Key Term

Constantinople   Capital of Byzantium, conquered by Turks in 1453. Now it's Istanbul.

GEOGRAPHY

BOUND RUSSIA

Russia is bounded on the north by the Arctic Ocean; on the east by the Bering Sea and Sea of Okhotsk; on the south by China, Mongolia, Kazakhstan, Azerbaijan, Georgia, and the Black Sea;

and on the west by Ukraine, Belarus, Lithuania, Latvia, Estonia, Finland, and Norway.

This does not include Kaliningrad Oblast (region), formerly Koenigsberg of old East Prussia, which is wedged between Poland and Lithuania.

Troubles. Russians accepted the idea that they had to serve a powerful state under a strong tsar. The Russian Orthodox church, which the tsar also headed, became a pillar of autocracy, teaching the faithful to worship the tsar as the "little father" who protected all Russians. The tsar integrated the offices of head of state and head of church, a pattern called **caesaropapism**. Russia has been called a "service state" in which all walks of life, from nobles to peasants to priests, served the autocrat. Western concepts such as liberty and individual rights did not take root in Russia.

During the fifteenth and sixteenth centuries, Russia actually moved backwards in one crucial area. Previously free peasants became serfs, tied to the land to labor for aristocrats as almost subhuman beasts. While West Europe ended serfdom centuries earlier, Russia found itself with the vast majority of its population poor and ignorant farm laborers.

From time to time these wretched people revolted. Some ran off and joined the Cossacks, bands of mounted freebooters in the border regions between the tsarist and Turkish empires. One Cossack leader, Stenka Razin, immortalized in ballad, led a peasant revolt that seized much of **Ukraine**. In time, the Cossacks turned into semimilitary federations, which the tsars enrolled as effective and ruthless cavalry.

Forced Modernization

Key Terms

caesaropapism Combining top civil ruler (caesar) with top spiritual ruler (pope), as in Russia's tsars.

Ukraine From the Slavic for "borderland"; region south of Russia, now independent.

By the time Peter I became tsar in 1682, Russia lagged behind the rest of Europe. Peter, an enormous man who stood six feet nine inches (206 cm.), was determined to modernize Russia and make it a major power. He didn't care about his people's wishes or their welfare; he would force them to become modern. Gifted with enormous energy, some of it dissipated on women and alcohol, Peter personally handled Russia's legislation, diplomacy, war, and technical innovation. He was the first tsar to travel in West Europe. Admiring its industries, he ordered them duplicated in Russia. Nearly continually at war, Peter pushed the Swedes back to give Russia an outlet on the Baltic. There he ordered built a magnificent new capital, St. Petersburg (later Leningrad), modeled after Amsterdam, to serve as Russia's window to the West.

Copying the tight Swedish administrative system, Peter divided Russia into provinces, counties, and districts, each supervised by bureaucrats drawn from the nobility. All male nobles had to serve the tsar from age fifteen until death, either as bureaucrats or military officers. Even the bureaucrats were organized on military lines, complete with ranks and uniforms. With Peter, the Russian government apparatus penetrated deep into society. A census determined the number of males available for military conscription, and each community had a quota. Draftees served for life. Taxation squeezed everybody as Peter ordered his officials to "collect money, as much as possible, for money is the artery of war."

Key Terms

Westernizers Nineteenth-century Russians who wished to copy the West.
Slavophiles Nineteenth-century Russians who wished to develop Russia along native, non-Western lines. Also known as "Russophiles."
zemtsvo Local parliaments in old Russia.

When Peter died in 1725, he left behind a more modern and Westernized Russia, but one still behind West Europe. Peter the Great contributed a pattern of forced modernization from the top, pushing a poor, gigantic country forward despite itself. Russia paid dearly. The mass of peasants, heavily taxed, were worse off than ever. The Westernized nobility—forced, for instance, to shave for the first time—was cut off from the hopes and feelings of the peasantry. The pattern was to continue for a long time.

Westernizers and Slavophiles

After Napoleon's invasion of Russia and capture of Moscow in 1812, Russian intellectuals became aware of the backwardness of their land, and many sought to bring in Western politics and institutions, including a constitutional monarchy that would limit the autocratic powers of the tsar. These were **Westernizers**. Others saw the West as spiritually shallow and materialistic. The answer to Russia's problems, they argued, was to dig into their own Slavic roots and develop institutions and styles different from and superior to the West's. "Russia will teach the world," was their view. These **Slavophiles** (literally, "lovers of the Slavs"), who stressed the spiritual depth and warm humanity of Russian peasants, were romantic nationalists who disdained West European culture. In our day this pattern continues, as countries like Iran claim they reject Western materialism in favor of traditional spiritual values. And in Russia today the old debate still echoes: Liberal reformers are still pro-West while conservatives are anti-West nationalists.

From Frustration to Revolution

Despite calls for far-reaching changes in Russia, reform during the nineteenth century made little progress. No tsar was prepared to give up any autocratic power in favor of a parliament. Even Alexander II, the "tsar-liberator," carried out only limited reforms. In 1861 he issued his famous Edict of Emancipation, freeing all serfs from legal bondage. Most of them remained in economic bondage, however. He set up district and provincial assemblies called **zemstvos**, but gave them only marginal local power.

The reforms were meant both to modernize Russia and to improve the living conditions of the masses. Under certain conditions, however, reforms may actually make revolution more likely rather than less. Alexander's reforms, which he saw as extensive and generous, were regarded by an increasingly critical *intelligentsia* (the educated class) as not going nearly far enough. Whatever he granted, they wanted more. The reforms merely whetted the critics' appetites. Many intellectuals became bitter and frustrated.

Some tried action at the grass-roots level. In the 1870s thousands of idealistic students put on peasant clothes and tried "going to the people" in the villages to incite radical action. These **Narodniki** made no progress; the suspicious peasants either ignored them or turned them over to the police. Others tried assassination, believing killing the right official constituted "propaganda of the deed," a way to arouse the inert masses. One group of committed terrorists, *Narodnaya Volya* (People's Will), made the tsar their special target and, after seven attempts, killed him with a bomb thrown into his carriage in 1881.

Actually, Russia did make considerable progress in the nineteenth century. Archaic usages were swept away, industry started (with an infusion of British, French, and German capital), railroads were built, and intellectual life flourished. But in the crucial area of political reform—parliaments, parties, elections, and the sharing of power—Russia essentially stood still. Political reforms do not make themselves, and in many ways they are more basic to the peaceful evolution of society than social, cultural, or economic reforms. A ruler who modernizes his economy but not his political system is asking for trouble.

Marxism Comes to Russia

According to Marx's theory, backward Russia was far from ready for proletarian revolution. There simply wasn't much of a **proletariat** in the still overwhelmingly agricultural land, where industrialization was just beginning in the late nineteenth century. Marx believed revolution would come first in the most industrially advanced countries, such as Britain and Germany. Curiously, though, Marxism caught on more strongly in Russia than anywhere else. Marx's works were eagerly seized upon by frustrated Russian intellectuals who badly wanted change but didn't have a theoretical framework for it. Here at last, they believed, they had found a reason and a means to carry out a revolution.

There were several schools of Marxism in Russia. The "Legal Marxists," noting Russia's economic underdevelopment, thought the country would first have to go through capitalism before it could start on socialism. Marx had a very deterministic view of history and saw it developing in clear stages based on the level of economic development. Loyal to Marx's historical analysis, the Legal Marxists believed they would have a long wait for revolution and must first work to promote capitalism.

Another school of Russian Marxism was called "Economism." Stressing better wages and working conditions through labor unions, the Economists thought the immediate economic improvement of the working class was the essence of Marxism. In this they resembled West European social democrats, whose Marxism mellowed into welfarism.

Opposing these two gradualist schools were impassioned intellectuals who wanted first and foremost to make a revolution. They argued they could "give history a shove" by starting a revolution with only a small proletariat, gaining power, and then using the state to move directly into socialism. Lenin made some theoretical changes in Marxism so it fit Russian conditions (see box on page 243). Since then, the doctrine of Russian **communism** was known as Marxism-Leninism.

In 1898, after several small groups had discussed Marxist approaches to Russia, the Russian Social Democratic Labor party was formed. It was penetrated by the *Okhrana*, the tsarist secret police, and many of its leaders went into exile in West Europe. Its newspaper, *Iskra* (the Spark), was published in Zurich and smuggled into Russia. One of its editors was Lenin.

Some claim that the dominant passion in Lenin's life was revenge against the tsarist system for hanging his older brother, Alexander, in 1887 for his part in a bomb plot against the tsar. It is clear Lenin was dominated by a cold, contained fury aimed at one goal: revolutionary socialism in Russia.

Born in 1870 as Vladimir Ilyich Ulyanov, son of a provincial education official, Lenin was from the intellectual middle class rather than the proletariat in whose name he struggled—a pattern typical of revolutionary socialist leaders. Expelled from university for alleged subversive activity after his first three months, Lenin was sent into rural exile. With the incredible self-discipline that became his hallmark, Lenin taught himself and breezed through law exams with the highest marks.

In the early 1890s Lenin discovered Marxism, read everything Marx wrote, and wrote Marxist analyses of the rapidly growing Russian economy. Recognized as a leading Marxist thinker, Lenin quickly rose to prominence in underground revolutionary circles.

In December 1895, while editing an illegal socialist newspaper, Lenin was arrested and sent to prison for a year followed by three years' exile on the Lena River in Siberia. There he took the name Lenin, the man from the Lena. The solitary hours gave him time to read, learn foreign languages, and write. Released in 1900, Lenin made his way to Zurich, Switzerland, where he spent most of the next seventeen years. Until taking power in Russia in 1917, Lenin never held a job.

At times during his exile Lenin feared there would never be a revolution in Russia. The working class was concentrating on higher wages rather than revolution. The Russian Social Democratic Labor party was small, with only a few thousand members in Russia and in exile.

Lenin was determined to transform this small party into an effective underground force. Size was not important; organization was everything. In his 1902 pamphlet *What Is to Be Done?* Lenin demanded a tightly disciplined party of professional revolutionaries, not a conventional social-democratic party open to everybody. Under Lenin the early Communists forged the "organizational weapon": the Party.

But how could a proletarian revolution happen in preindustrial Russia? This was the great theoretical problem Lenin faced. In solving it, he greatly changed Marxism. Marx theorized that revolution will come in the most advanced countries, where the proletariat was biggest. Lenin said not necessarily: Revolution could come where capitalism is weakest, where it is just starting. **Imperialism** had changed capitalism, Lenin argued, giving it a new lease on life. By exploiting weaker countries, the big imperialist powers were able to bribe their own working class with higher wages and thus keep them quiet. Where capitalism was beginning—as in Russia, with heavy foreign investment—was where it could be overthrown. The newly developing countries, such as Russia and Spain, were "capitalism's weakest link," said Lenin.

Lenin disagreed with Marx's insistence that the peasantry could never play a revolutionary role; Marx dismissed country life as "rural idiocy." Under certain conditions, Lenin believed, they could become highly revolutionary and, throwing their weight in with the small working class, provide a massive revolutionary army. (Three decades later, Mao Zedong elaborated on these two themes to argue that China, a victim of imperialism, could have a socialist revolution based entirely on the peasantry. Mao simply completed the train of thought Lenin started.)

Lenin showed himself to be not a great theoretician but a brilliant opportunist, switching doctrine to take advantage of situations. Lenin was less concerned with pure Marxism than with using it to overthrow the system he hated. Once in power, he practiced the same bloody ruthlessness that was later associated with Stalin's rule. It is not clear that had Lenin lived he would have been any better than Stalin.

Bolshevik "Majority" in Russian; early name for Soviet Communist party.

Duma Russia's national parliament.

In 1903 the small party split over a crucial question: organization. Some of its leaders wanted a normal party along the lines of the German SPD, with open but committed membership that tried to enroll the bulk of the Russian working class. Lenin scoffed at this kind of organization, arguing tsarist secret police would make mincemeat out of an open party. Instead, he urged a small, tightly knit underground party of professional revolutionaries, more a conspiracy than a conventional party.

Lenin got his way. At the 1903 party congress in Brussels, Belgium (it couldn't be held in Russia), he controlled thirty-three of the fifty-one votes. Although probably unrepresentative of total party membership, Lenin proclaimed his faction **Bolshevik** (majority), and the name stuck. The *menshevik* (minority) faction at the congress continued to exist, advocating a more moderate line.

Curtain Raiser: The 1905 Revolution

At the beginning of the twentieth century two expanding powers, Russia and Japan, collided. The Russians were pushing eastward, consolidating their position on the Pacific by building the Trans-Siberian Railway, the last leg of which ran through Manchuria. Japan was meanwhile pushing up from Korea to Manchuria, which was nominally a part of China. The tsar's cabinet, certain they could defeat any Asian army and hoping to deflect domestic unrest, thought war with Japan might be a good idea. Said the interior minister: "We need a little victorious war to stem the tide of revolution." Instead, the Japanese fleet launched a surprise attack against the Russians at Port Arthur, then beat the Russians on both land and sea.

The Russo-Japanese War revealed the tsarist regime as unprepared, inept, and stupid. Weak regimes shouldn't count on a "little victorious war" to paper over domestic unrest; wars make troubles worse. In Russia, rioting and then revolution broke out. Some naval units mutinied. (See Eisenstein's film classic *Battleship Potemkin*.) Workers briefly seized factories at St. Petersburg. It looked like revolution was breaking out.

Tsar Nicholas II, however, gave way and decreed potentially important reforms: freedom of speech, press, and assembly and the democratic election of a **Duma**. Briefly, his 1905 October Manifesto looked as if it would turn autocracy into constitutional monarchy. The tsar and his reactionary advisors backed down on their promises, however. Nicholas, none too bright, refused to yield any of his autocratic powers. Four Dumas were subsequently elected; each was dissolved when it grew too critical. Finally the Duma was turned into an undemocratic debating society without power. The Duma was Russia's last hope for a peaceful transition to democracy. People in modern times need to feel they participate at least in a small way in the affairs of government. Parties, elections, and parliaments may be imperfect means of participation, but they are better than violent revolution. Since the failed Decembrist revolt of 1825, Russian intellectuals had been trying to tell this to the tsar, but he refused to listen.

World War I and Collapse

Communists liked to speak of the Russian Revolution as inevitable, the playing out of historical forces that had to lead to the collapse of imperialism and capitalism. There was nothing inevitable about the October Revolution. Indeed, without World War I, there might have

KERENSKY: NICE GUYS LOSE

In the late 1950s at UCLA I had an eerie experience: seeing and hearing Alexander Kerensky speak. History lives. Still fit and articulate in his seventies, Kerensky recalled his brief stint (July to November 1917) as head of Russia's Provisional Government. One man in the audience, a Russian emigré, asked angrily why Kerensky didn't use his power to have Lenin killed. Kerensky reflected a moment and said, "Sometimes when you have power it's hard to use it."

That was Kerensky's problem. A decent man, he wouldn't have a political opponent murdered. The Western Allies begged him to keep Russia in the war, and he didn't have the heart to betray them. What Kerensky lacked in political ruthlessness he may have gained in longevity. Living in New York City, he spent his years justifying his brief rule and denouncing both the Bolsheviks and Russian rightists who tried to bring him down. He died in 1970 at age eighty-nine.

been no revolution in Russia at all, let alone a Bolshevik revolution. Lenin himself, in early 1917, doubted he'd live to see a revolution in Russia.

Things were not so terrible in Russia before the war. The Duma struggled to erode tsarist autocracy and in time might have succeeded. Industry grew rapidly. Peasants, freed from old restrictions on land ownership, were turning into prosperous and productive small farmers.

The war changed everything. Repeating their overconfidence of 1904, the tsarist military marched happily to war against Germany in 1914, and this doomed the system. It was a large army, but badly equipped and poorly led. Major offensives ground to a halt before the more effective German forces. The Russian economy fell apart. Troop morale disintegrated, and many deserted. Peasants seized their landlord's grounds. The government was paralyzed, but the tsar refused to change anything.

By 1917 the situation was desperate. In March of that year a group of democratic moderates seized power and deposed the tsar. Resembling Western liberals, the people of the Provisional Government hoped to modernize and democratize Russia. The Western powers, including the United States, welcomed them, thinking they would rally Russians to continue the war. The Provisional Government, which by July was headed by nominal socialist Alexander Kerensky, tried to stay in the war, and that was its undoing. If Kerensky had betrayed the Western Allies and made a separate peace with Germany, the moderates might have been able to retain power.

Meanwhile, the German General Staff, looking for a way to knock Russia out of the war, thought it would be clever to send the agitator Lenin into Russia to create havoc. In April 1917 Lenin and his colleagues traveled in a famous "sealed train"—so the Bolshevik bacillus wouldn't infect Germany, where revolutionary discontent was also growing—across Germany, Sweden, and Finland to Petrograd, the World War I name for St. Petersburg (which sounded too German). Without German help and funds, Lenin might never have made it back to Russia.

At Petrograd's Finland Station, Lenin issued his stirring slogan, "Bread, Land, Peace," speaking respectively to workers, peasants, and soldiers. Lenin immediately saw that a "dual authority" was trying to rule Russia. The Provisional Government controlled the army and

GEOGRAPHY

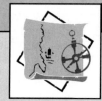

BOUND YUGOSLAVIA

Yugoslavia is bounded on the north by Hungary; on the east by Romania and Bulgaria; on the south by Macedonia and Albania; and on the west by the Adriatic, Bosnia, and Croatia.

There still is a Yugoslavia, but it is a **rump state**, a minifederation of Serbia and Montenegro. The old Yugoslavia of 1918–41 and 1945–91 included Slovenia, Croatia, Bosnia, and Macedonia, all of which are now independent. Why not just call it Serbia? Its government wished to preserve the boundary agreements that used the name Yugoslavia. If Montenegro (Black Mountain), which is restless, departs from the federation, Serbia will lose its outlet to the sea and will probably be called just Serbia, as it was before World War I. In 1999, Serbia lost Kosovo and its largely Albanian population.

Which European lands have not been named in our bounding exercises?

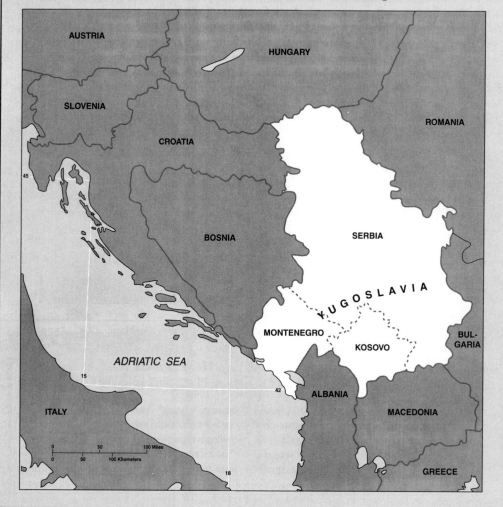

foreign policy. But in the most important city, Petrograd, a council (*soviet* in Russian) of workers, soldiers, sailors, and revolutionaries ran things. Soon these councils appeared in many Russian cities. The composition of these soviets was mixed, with the Bolsheviks a small minority. Lenin pursued a double strategy: Make the soviets the only effective governing power and make the Bolsheviks the dominant power in the soviets. Lenin's slogan for this: "All Power to the Soviets."

Key Term

rump state   Leftover portions of a country after dismemberment.

The Revolution and Civil War

The actual seizure of power in October (see box below) was amazingly easy. In a scene exaggerated by Soviet historians, soldiers and sailors loyal to the Petrograd soviet charged across a big square into the Winter Palace to oust the Provisional Government. But control of Petrograd and Moscow was one thing, control of all gigantic Russia was something else.

The tight organization and discipline of Lenin's Bolsheviks paid off. In a situation of almost total chaos, the best organized win. By a series of shrewd moves, the Bolsheviks were able to dominate the soviets and win many converts from deserting soldiers and sailors. Lenin headed the new government and immediately took Russia out of the war, accepting a punitive peace treaty from the Germans at Brest-Litovsk in March 1918. It was a dictated treaty (*Diktat* in German) that enabled the Germans to seize large areas of Russia and redeploy nearly a million troops to the western front.

Feeling betrayed and concerned that allied military supplies would fall into German hands, the Western Allies sent small expeditionary forces into Russia. American troops actually fought the Bolsheviks in North Russia and Siberia in 1918–19. This started the Soviet propaganda that the capitalist powers tried to strangle the infant Bolshevik regime in its cradle.

From 1918 to 1920 civil war raged. The White Army, led by reactionary Russian generals and admirals and supplied by the Western Allies, tried to crush the Communists' Red Army. Both sides displayed incredible ruthlessness in a life-or-death struggle. Millions

POLITICAL CULTURE

WHY THE OCTOBER REVOLUTION WAS IN NOVEMBER

Every November 7, Russia used to celebrate the anniversary of the Great October Revolution. If this sounds curious, it's because Russia, following its Orthodox church, in 1917 was still using the ancient Julian calendar, which (because it counted too many leap years) ran thirteen days behind the more-accurate Gregorian calendar, in use in Catholic countries since 1582. Protestant countries, fearing a popish plot, also delayed adopting the Gregorian calendar. The Bolsheviks finally switched Russia to the Gregorian calendar but then had to recalculate the October Revolution into November.

STALIN: "ONE DEATH IS A TRAGEDY; A MILLION IS A STATISTIC"

The Soviet system was not so much Lenin's as Stalin's. Lenin was fifty-four when he died in 1924, before giving definitive form to the system. Exactly who is to blame for the horrors that developed—Lenin or Stalin—is a matter of controversy both within and outside Russia. Some still argue that if Lenin had lived, his intelligence and sophistication would have set the country on the path to "true socialism." Others say the structure Lenin created—concentrating power first in the party, then in the Central Committee, and finally in his own person—made the misuse of power inevitable.

Stalin aptly illustrates Acton's dictum, "power corrupts." Stalin lived in order to amass political power, and he was very good at it. Born Yosif Vissarionovich Djugashvili in 1879, son of a poor shoemaker, Stalin lacked Lenin's intellectual family background and education. Some of Stalin's behavior can be traced to his homeland of Georgia, part of the Caucasus, a mountainous land with a warm climate and fiery people given to personal hatred and blood-feuds. In Georgia, "Soso" (his Georgian nickname) is still praised as a local boy who made good.

The young Djugashvili started to study for the Orthodox priesthood but soon turned to revolution. Expelled from the seminary, he joined the Georgian Marxist underground as an agitator and strike organizer. Repeatedly arrested, jailed, and exiled to Siberia, he always managed to escape. (There is some evidence that he was a double agent for the tsarist police.) Going underground, he took the name Stalin, Russian for "man of steel."

Never a great theoretician, Stalin attracted Lenin's attention as a non-Russian who could write the Bolsheviks' position on the nationalities question. Playing only a moderate role in the October Revolution, Stalin was named commissar for nationalities in 1918 and then, in what may have been

Lenin's worst mistake, chosen as the party's first general secretary in 1922. People thought the new office would be a routine job with little real power. Lenin and Stalin were never close—although Stalin's historians tried to make it look that way—and toward the end of his life Lenin had an inkling of what Stalin was like. In one of his last messages Lenin urged the party to reject Stalin as "too rude."

It was too late, however. Using his position as **gensek**, Stalin organized the **CPSU** to his advantage by promoting to key posts only those personally loyal to him. It was this organizational spadework that gave Stalin the edge over his rival, Leon Trotsky, organizer of the Red Army and a far more intelligent Marxist. Stalin beat him in party infighting and had him expelled from Russia in 1929 and murdered in Mexico City in 1940. Reviled as a deviationist traitor, Trotsky did try to organize an anti-Stalin opposition within the CPSU, a point that fed Stalin's natural paranoia and contributed to his ruthlessness in exterminating officials on the slightest suspicion of disloyalty.

Stalin, an uncanny manipulator, played one faction against another until, by the late 1920s, he was the Kremlin's undisputed master. Like Peter the Great, Stalin was determined to modernize regardless of human cost. In 1928 he instituted the first Five-Year Plan, beginning the forced industrialization of Russia. Farmers, very much against their will, were herded into collectives and forced to produce for the state, sometimes at gunpoint. Better-off farmers, the so-called *kulaks*, were "liquidated as a class," a euphemism for killed. Economic development was defined as heavy industry, and steel production became the chief goal of the man of steel.

In 1934, during the second Five-Year Plan, Stalin became obsessed with "Trotskyite" disloyalty in party ranks. Thus began Stalin's **purges:** up to one million party comrades killed, some after confessing to be British spies or Trotskyite "wreckers." People in positions of prominence trembled that they would be next—and many were. Stalin ordered all managers to train two replacements. Stalin even had all his generals shot, a blunder that hurt the Soviet Union in the 1941 German attack. Perhaps another ten million ordinary citizens, arrested on fake charges, also perished, many in Siberian forced-labor camps. In total, Stalin's orders led to the death of over fifteen million people during collectivization and the purges.

Was Stalin mad? There was some Trotskyite opposition to him, but he exaggerated it. It was Plato who first observed that any tyrant, even one who starts sane, must lose his mind in office because he can't trust anybody. More than a question of personality, Stalin shows what happens when one person assumes total power. The Communists didn't like to admit it, but it was their *system* that was at fault more than any particular individual.

During his lifetime Stalin was deified as history's greatest linguist, art critic, Marxist theoretician, engineer, agronomist, you name it. By the time he died in 1953—while preparing yet another purge—Stalin had turned the Soviet Union into *his* system, and, in basic outlines, it never did change much. When Mikhail Gorbachev attempted to seriously reform it, the system collapsed.

These three St. Petersburg graves of victims of Stalin's Great Purge convey some of the horror of Stalin's "cleansing" of people he supposed were unreliable. The family of the victim on the right, by erecting a life-size statue of a man in Bolshevik Young Guard uniform, meant to show that he was a faithful Communist all along. (Michael Roskin)

of citizens perished from starvation. Expecting their revolution to spread, the Red Army invaded Poland in 1920, hoping to trigger a Europe-wide socialist upheaval. Instead, the Poles threw back the Red Army and seized parts of Ukraine and Belarus. Lenin and his colleagues saw there would be no world revolution and settled for building the world's first socialist country.

War Communism and NEP

During the civil war, the Bolsheviks tried to plunge directly into their utopian system by running the ruined economy by executive fiat. This **war communism**, as it was euphemistically called, was due as much to the demands of a desperate civil war as to visionary schemes. To motivate workers, Lenin issued his slogan, "He who does not work, neither shall he eat" (first uttered by Jesus in 2 Thessalonians 3:10). War communism led immediately to starvation, and only the charity of American grain shipments (supervised by Herbert Hoover) held deaths to a few million.

Lenin saw Russia was far from ready for pure socialism, so he conducted a planned retreat of state control to the "commanding heights" of heavy industry and let most of the rest of the economy revert to private hands. This period of Lenin's **New Economic Policy (NEP)** brought relative prosperity; farmers worked their own land, "nepmen" behaved like small private entrepreneurs, and life in general relaxed. There was one catch: The NEP wasn't moving the Soviet Union, as it was now called, any closer to socialism, and industry grew only slowly. It is likely Lenin meant the NEP only as a temporary rest before moving on to socialist construction.

That changed when Stalin took full power in the late 1920s. In 1928 began the first of the government-enforced **Five-Year Plans** that accelerated collectivization and industrialization (see box on pages 248–49). Peasants resisted giving up their fields, farm production dropped, and millions (especially Ukrainians) were deliberately starved to death. In new factories, workers toiled with primitive tools to boost production of **capital goods**. Setting a pattern for all communist countries, **consumer goods** were deliberately neglected, and the standard of living declined. While many admit the forced industrialization of the 1930s was brutal, some argue it gave the Soviet Union the industrial base to arm against the German invasion in 1941.

As it was, the German invasion caused some twenty-seven million Soviet deaths. The Nazis cared nothing for Slavic lives; starvation was their standard treatment for Russian prisoners of war. Faced with extinction, the Soviet Union pulled together. Stalin, like Lenin, recognized the force of Russian nationalism beneath the Communist surface. Reviewing troops marching from Moscow to the front, Stalin mused: "They aren't fighting for communism or for Stalin; they're fighting for Mother Russia." In Russia today, World War II is known as the Great Patriotic War. By the time he died in 1953, Stalin had transformed a backward country into a gigantic empire and major industrial power. He had also founded a political system, the dismantling of which still preoccupies Russia.

Key Terms

gensek   Russian abbreviation for "general secretary," powerful CPSU head.

CPSU   Communist Party of the Soviet Union.

purge   Stalin's "cleansing" of suspicious elements by firing squad.

war communism   Temporary strict socialism in Russia 1918–21.

New Economic Policy (NEP)   Lenin's New Economic Policy that allowed considerable private activity, 1921–28.

Five-Year Plans   Stalin's forced industrialization of the Soviet Union, starting in 1928.

capital goods   Implements used to make other things.

consumer goods   Things people use, such as food, clothing, and housing.

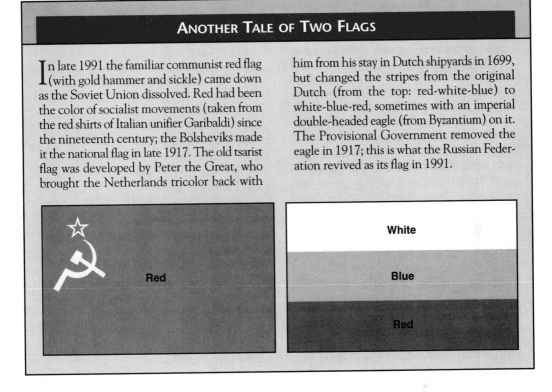

ANOTHER TALE OF TWO FLAGS

In late 1991 the familiar communist red flag (with gold hammer and sickle) came down as the Soviet Union dissolved. Red had been the color of socialist movements (taken from the red shirts of Italian unifier Garibaldi) since the nineteenth century; the Bolsheviks made it the national flag in late 1917. The old tsarist flag was developed by Peter the Great, who brought the Netherlands tricolor back with him from his stay in Dutch shipyards in 1699, but changed the stripes from the original Dutch (from the top: red-white-blue) to white-blue-red, sometimes with an imperial double-headed eagle (from Byzantium) on it. The Provisional Government removed the eagle in 1917; this is what the Russian Federation revived as its flag in 1991.

Red

White

Blue

Red

Key Terms

autocracy (p. 238)	Duma (p. 244)	Siberia (p. 236)
Bolshevik (p. 244)	Five-Year Plans (p. 250)	Slavophiles (p. 241)
caesaropapism (p. 240)	gensek (p. 250)	Tatar (p. 238)
capital goods (p. 250)	imperialism (p. 242)	tsar (p. 238)
communism (p. 242)	Narodniki (p. 242)	Ukraine (p. 240)
Constantinople (p. 239)	New Economic Policy (p. 250)	war communism (p. 250)
consumer goods (p. 250)	proletariat (p. 242)	Westernizers (p. 241)
CPSU (p. 250)	purge (p. 250)	zemstvo (p. 241)
Cyrillic (p. 237)	rump state (p. 247)	

Further Reference

Bater, James H. *The Russian Scene: A Geographical Perspective.* New York: Edward Arnold, 1989.

Conquest, Robert. *The Great Terror: A Reassessment.* New York: Oxford University Press, 1990.

Dukes, Paul. *A History of Russia: Medieval, Modern, Contemporary, c. 882–1996*, 3rd ed. Durham, NC: Duke University Press, 1998.

Figes, Orlando. *A People's Tragedy: A History of the Russian Revolution*. New York: Viking, 1997.

Fitzpatrick, Sheila. *Everyday Stalinism: Ordinary Life in Extraordinary Times*. New York: Oxford University Press, 1999.

Hosking, Geoffrey. *Russia: People and Empire*. Cambridge, MA: Harvard University Press, 1998.

Hughes, Lindsey. *Russia in the Age of Peter the Great*. New Haven, CT: Yale University Press, 1998.

Malia, Martin. *Russia Under Western Eyes: From the Bronze Horseman to the Lenin Mausoleum*. Cambridge, MA: Harvard University Press, 1999.

Mote, Victor L. *Siberia: Worlds Apart*. Boulder, CO: Westview, 1998.

Pipes, Richard, ed. *The Unknown Lenin: From the Secret Archives*. New Haven, CT: Yale University Press, 1996.

Radzinsky, Edvard. *Stalin: The First In-Depth Biography Based on Explosive New Documents from Russia's Secret Archives*. New York: Doubleday, 1996.

Thompson, John M. *Russia and the Soviet Union: An Historical Introduction*, 4th ed. Boulder, CO: Westview, 1998.

Ulam, Adam B. *The Bolsheviks: The Intellectual and Political History of the Triumph of Communism in Russia*. Cambridge, MA: Harvard University Press, 1998.

Volkogonov, Dmitri. *Lenin*. New York: Free Press, 1995.

Russia:
The Key Institutions

18

Questions to Consider

1. What were the main points of the Stalin system?
2. Why did all three Communist federal systems fail?
3. Would it be possible to have socialism without a large bureaucracy?
4. What is the CIS?
5. How is the Russian executive borrowed from France?
6. In what ways did Yeltsin resemble Gorbachev?
7. How is the Russian electoral system similar to but different from the German electoral system?
8. Describe the Russian party system. Does it resemble any of the ones we have studied previously?

Russian political institutions are still weak and evolving, and no one can say how or when they will stabilize. The best we can do in this chapter is describe two models of the Russian system, the old Soviet system formed under Stalin and a post-Communist system struggling to find stability. Some argue that the dramatic end of the Soviet Union in late 1991 and the birth of a new Russia was less than a **system change**. The new Russian government was not a new broom, and it did not sweep clean. Virtually all of the current leadership have roots deep in the old Soviet system; Russia's constitution overconcentrates power in the presidency; and the Communists and KGB are still important. Accordingly, we pay some attention to the old, Communist system, as its usages linger in today's Russia.

Key Term

system change The displacement of one set of political institutions by another.

The Stalin System

The Soviet system started by Lenin and perfected by Stalin lasted into Gorbachev's tenure. The system changed over time, but not much. Its main structural features were as follows:

The Communist Party in Command

Said Lenin: "The Communist party is not a party like other parties." Lenin meant that the Bolsheviks were not going to play the normal political games of democratic parties, contesting elections and leaving office when voted out. The CPSU was going to run Russia without opposition, and it did, for seven decades.

The CPSU was constitutionally defined as "the leading and guiding force of Soviet society." No other parties were permitted, and no factions were allowed inside the Party. The Party did not run things directly, however. It served as a nervous system and central brain that transmitted policy lines, kept tabs on the economy, reported discontent, and selected, promoted, and supervised the system's personnel. There was much overlap between Party and state system, so that at the top, most government ministers were also on the Party's **Central Committee**.

Party membership was tightly controlled. Less than seven percent of the Soviet population (at one point, about nineteen million out of 285 million) were Party members, selected on the basis of good records as workers, students, or youth leaders. The aim of the CPSU was to skim off the best of Soviet society. The Party was organized like a giant pyramid, with primary party organizations at the bottom; district, province, and republic party conferences in between; and an all-union party conference at the top. Presiding over each conference was a committee. Each level "elected" delegates to the next highest level (actually, they were handpicked from above) in what was called "democratic centralism." Party administrators, **apparatchiki**, were the cement that held the thing together.

The All-Union Party Congress of some five thousand delegates would meet for a few days every few years, ostensibly to elect the Central Committee of about 300 full and 150 candidate members. The Central Committee would meet twice a year, usually just before the meeting of its government counterpart, the Supreme Soviet, since the membership of the two bodies overlapped.

Above the Central Committee and really running things was the **Politburo**, a full-time decision-making body with about a dozen full members and six candidate members. Politburo decisions were automatically approved by the Central Committee, whose decisions were approved by the Party Congress, and so on down the line. Running the Politburo was a general secretary (*gensek*), usually called in the West the "party chief." This person in practice usually became supreme boss of both Party and state and could assume dictatorial powers. In most Communist systems, the party chief is the most powerful figure, for he controls the apparat and selects *apparatchiki* who are personally loyal to him.

A Less-Important State Structure

Outside observers agreed that the gigantic Supreme Soviet, with 1,500 members, could not serve as a real parliament. It met only a few days a year to rubber-stamp laws drafted by the top echelons of the Party. Nominally bicameral, the Supreme Soviet would "elect" a governing Presidium of twenty members that overlapped with the Politburo. The Presidium could decree whatever it liked, and its decrees had force of law. The Presidium also served as a collective presidency, and its chairman was often referred to as the "president" of the Soviet Union. Ever since Brezhnev, the Party general secretary also had himself named president, so as to make clear he headed both state and Party.

The Supreme Soviet also "elected" a sort of cabinet, the mammoth Council of Ministers, with some eighty-five highly specialized ministries, mostly concentrated on branches of the

POLITICAL CULTURE

THE KGB

Terror was called "the linchpin of the Soviet system," the key element that held it together. During Stalin's time there was a lot of truth to this, but after Stalin, terror—the fear of being arbitrarily arrested, imprisoned, sent to Siberia, or shot—receded as a means of political control. The political police, later called the Committee on State Security, or KGB, were active until the end (and still are), but their methods were more refined and subtle than the Cheka of Lenin's tenure or the NKVD of Stalin's. Putin was KGB.

Some three-quarters of a million KGB agents were everywhere: guarding the borders, in factories, hotels, and universities, keeping tabs on anyone who contacted foreign tourists, handled classified materials, or dissented against the Soviet system. Millions of Soviet citizens had KGB dossiers, and some found out, to their surprise, that the KGB was able to recite even trivial incidents from years earlier. Part-time informers, called *stukachi* (squealers), were everywhere.

While the political police lost the power to actually try most cases—which went to a regular court—they still had the power to frighten by selectively intimidating dissidents. Citizens could lose jobs, get sent to psychiatric hospitals, be denied university entrance, have their rooms bugged, lose the right to live in a city, and generally be made uncomfortable by a word from the KGB.

economy (for example, Ministry of Machine Building for Animal Husbandry and Fodder Production). The Council of Ministers rarely met for collective deliberation. Typically, only Politburo members could serve as prime minister, or minister of state security (KGB), interior (police), defense, and foreign affairs, the "power ministries."

A Centralized Federal System

The classic Soviet pattern was a federation—like the United States, Canada, and Germany—but one long dominated by the center. What the Politburo in Moscow laid down was implemented throughout the country by the Party. The Soviet Union had some two dozen major nationalities and many more minor ones—104 in all. The fifteen largest got their own Soviet Socialist **Republic** (for example, the Uzbek SSR), which together made the USSR (Union of Soviet Socialist Republics). The nationalities, however, are somewhat dispersed; there are ethnic Russians in every newly independent republic—one-third of the populations of Latvia and Kazakhstan are Russian—and this has sharpened a dangerous nationalities question.

The Russian Federative Republic was by far the biggest, and is still a federation of numerous autonomous regions for the variety of ethnic groups within it. The underlying intention of Soviet federalism was preservation of language rights. Stalin, who developed Soviet nationality policy, recognized that language and culture are potential political dynamite, and it was best to let each nationality feel culturally autonomous while in fact they were politically subordinate. Stalin's formula was: "National in form, socialist in content." This deception turned out to be unstable.

Key Term

republic The chief component of Communist federal systems, equivalent to U.S. states.

Who Was When: Soviet Party Chiefs

Party Chief	Ruled	Main Accomplishments
Vladimir I. Lenin	1917–24	Led Revolution; instituted War Communism, then NEP.
Josef Stalin	1927–53	Five-Year Plans of forced collectivization and industrialization; purges; self-deification.
Nikita Khrushchev	1955–64	Destalinized; experimented with economic and cultural reform; promised utopia soon; ousted.
Leonid Brezhnev	1964–82	Partially restalinized; refrained from shaking up system; let corruption grow and economy slow.
Yuri Andropov	1982–84	Cracked down on corruption and alcoholism; suggested major reforms but soon died.
Konstantin Chernenko	1984–85	*Nichevo.*
Mikhail Gorbachev	1985–91	Initiated sweeping change, unwittingly collapsed Soviet system.

A Gigantic Bureaucracy

Karl Marx argued that after socialism eliminated class differences, the state would "wither away." German sociologist Max Weber argued the opposite: that socialism required much more state power and a much larger bureaucracy. Marx was wrong; Weber was right. The Soviet bureaucracy became monstrous, with some eighteen million persons administering every facet of Soviet life. This bureaucracy spelled the ruination of the Soviet Union: slow, marginally competent, inflexible, indifferent to efficiency, corrupt, and immune to criticism except from high Party officials.

The Party, in fact, interpenetrated and guided the bureaucracy, what the Party called its *kontrol* function. The Party appointed and supervised all important officials, and this kept them on their toes. If they fouled up or were egregiously crooked, they could get demoted or transferred to a remote area. This tended to make officials extremely cautious and go strictly by the book. On the other hand, if officials were effective and successful, the Party could recommend them for higher positions.

The key tool in this was the **nomenklatura**, a list of some 600,000 important positions and another list of reliable people eligible to fill them, nearly all Party members. Once "nomenklatured," officials generally stayed on the list until retirement. The nomenklatura was unmentioned in Soviet law, but everyone understood it was the heart of the system.

Key Terms

nomenklatura Lists of sensitive positions and people eligible to fill them, the Soviet elite.

Gosplan Soviet central economic planning agency.

Central Economic Planning

The State Planning Committee, **Gosplan**, was the nerve center of the Soviet economic system, attempting to establish how much of what should be produced each year and setting longer-term targets for some 350,000 enterprises. Central planning produced both impressive growth and massive dislocations. Under Stalin, it enabled the Soviet Union to industrialize quickly, albeit at terrible human cost. But it also meant chronic shortages of items the Gosplan forgot about or deemed unimportant. One year no toothbrushes were produced in the entire Soviet Union, a Gosplan oversight.

GEOGRAPHY

WHY DID COMMUNIST FEDERATIONS FAIL?

All three of the world's Communist federal systems failed—messy in Russia, bloody in Yugoslavia, but peaceful in Czechoslovakia—and the huge Russian Federation could now fall apart just as the Soviet Union did. The tsarist system imposed a unitary pattern on the empire that was so hated that old Russia was called "the prison of nations." With the Bolshevik Revolution, Finland and the Baltic states of Lithuania, Latvia, and Estonia happily escaped to independence. (In 1940, Stalin swallowed the Baltics and treated their citizens cruelly.) Stalin thought he could retain the tsarist empire in a Soviet Union that, on paper, granted each republic great autonomy.

With Gorbachev's *glasnost* (openness) policy of relative freedom of speech and press, out came the nationalities question with a vengeance. Amid economic uncertainty, many republics prohibited shipment or sale of scarce commodities to other republics, thus nullifying the main point of a federation: economic integration of a large area. In 1991, all fifteen republics departed from the union and legally dissolved it. Many ex-Soviet nationalities fear, hate, or resent other nationalities. Attitudes border on racism. Particularly delicate is the question of the 25 million Russians who now live outside of Russia. The Russian army has made it clear that it will use force to protect them and has already done so in Moldova, where several hundred Romanian-speakers were gunned down. The newly independent republics are cautious about antagonizing Russia.

Why did Soviet federalism fail to integrate its peoples? There are many factors: First, there are so many national groups that not all could have their own territories. Second, the nationalities are dispersed; in Uzbekistan, for example, there are Tajiks, Russians, Jews, Tatars, Koreans, and many others in addition to Uzbeks. It would not be possible to draw a clean line separating nationalities. Third, the Soviet federal system was devised by Stalin, who drew the borders deliberately to make sure there would be ethnic tension. This enabled Stalin to arbitrate disputes and thus increase his power, the old "divide and rule" technique. Every republic would depend on Stalin. Fourth, the center held too much power, chiefly through the Communist party and KGB, so the federalism was less than genuine.

The Soviet Union paid the price for Stalin's fake federal system. Can a Russian federalism now be devised that will hold the Russian Federation with its eighty-nine component parts together by bonds of trade, laws, and mutual respect? Some feared the bloody fighting over Chechnya was a taste of things to come.

Soviet leaders claimed that a planned and centrally directed economy was more rational than a Western market economy. Actual results refuted that, but Soviet bureaucrats were reluctant to surrender central planning, an article of faith of "scientific socialism." In Gosplan, the hopes, aims, fears, and sometimes caprices of the Soviet system converged and struggled. Gosplan, itself quite sensitive to the wishes of the Politburo, determined who got what in the Soviet Union, whether steel grew at x percent this year and plastics at y percent next. Heavily computerized, Gosplan may be described as the steering wheel of the Soviet economy.

GOVERNMENT IN A FORTRESS

The Kremlin (from the Russian *kreml*, "fortress") is a walled city dating back centuries. (The present walls were built in 1492.) Triangular in shape and a mile and a half around, the ancient Kremlin houses both government buildings and cathedrals (now public museums). Right next to the Kremlin wall is Lenin's tomb, once used as a reviewing stand by the Politburo for parades in Red Square on May 1 (International Workers' Day) and November 7 (anniversary of the revolution). Also facing Red Square: the colorful onion-shaped domes of St. Basil's Cathedral.

The New System

In the months after the failed coup of August 1991, the old Soviet system collapsed, and from the rubble emerged a new system—one that may not last—with the following qualities:

No More Soviet Union

All of the fifteen Soviet republics took advantage of the turmoil of late 1991 to declare their independence. The Baltic republics especially—Lithuania, Latvia, and Estonia—led the way to full, immediate independence. They expelled Soviet police, issued their own passports and visas, and took control of their borders. The other republics soon followed and now all are independent. But some are more independent than others. Ukrainians voted overwhelmingly for independence. Although Ukraine had been part of tsarist Russia for centuries and was the breadbasket of the Soviet Union, many Ukrainians resented being ruled by Moscow, especially after they got a chance to hear and read about what Stalin's farm collectivization had done to them—deliberately starved to death six million people.

Belarus (formerly Belarussia, the area between Russia and Poland), which had never been an independent country or harbored much separatist feeling, voted for independence, too. But Belarus still uses the Russian ruble as currency and gets sweetheart trade deals with Russia. Its army is closely linked to the Russian army. Belarus in reality never cut its Russian ties.

Key Term

junta Pronounced Spanish-style, "khun-ta"; group that pulls military coup.

The scariest problem was the ethnic tension that came out in the republics. Minorities that had lived in peace for generations (because the KGB was watching) became the target of nationalist resentment. In the Caucasus, blood flowed. Many politicians at the republic level played the nationalist card, and this easily turned into chauvinism. Their messages were simple and effective: Georgia for the Georgians, Uzbekistan for the Uzbeks, Armenia for the Armenians, even Russia for the Russians.

A Commonwealth of Independent States

Is anything left of the old Soviet federal system? As it officially ceased to exist at the end of 1991, most of its component republics agreed to form a "Commonwealth of Independent States" (CIS), with headquarters in Minsk, Belarus. Conspicuously missing were the three Baltic republics and Georgia. Georgia was later forced, in the middle of a civil war abetted by the Russians, to sign the CIS treaty. No one quite knows what the powers of the CIS are. Some see it as a pretend organization, others as a trade bloc, but many suspect it is a Moscow plan to regain control over the other republics.

There are reasons for some republics retaining ties with giant Russia. First, eight of the twelve CIS member republics are landlocked and need Russia for access to the outside world. Industrially, all are tied to the Russian economy for manufactured goods and energy. Financially, over the decades many of these republics benefited from major Soviet aid.

1991: THE COUP THAT FAILED

In August 1991, as Gorbachev was on vacation in the Crimea, most of his cabinet tried to overthrow him. An eight-man **junta** (Russians used the Spanish loan word) of conservatives, calling themselves the "Emergency Committee," said Gorbachev had taken ill and declared his vice-president acting president.

Some Western experts had been predicting a coup for three years. Gorbachev's reforms, cautious as they might be, were threatening the Soviet system and the jobs and comforts of the Soviet ruling elite. Gorbachev had been warned repeatedly of their anger. In December 1990 Foreign Minister Eduard Shevardnadze resigned in public protest at what he said was a coming dictatorship.

Gorbachev zig-zagged between promising major reforms and reassuring Party conservatives that he would not change too much. In 1991 Gorbachev indicated he again favored reform and with the leaders of nine of the Soviet republics drafted a new union treaty that would give the republics great autonomy within a market economy. This was the last straw for the conservatives. The day before the treaty was to be signed they staged their coup.

For three days the world held its breath. Would the coup by not-very-bright Kremlin apparatchiks succeed? They seemed to hold the upper hand. Among them were the head of the military, the KGB, and the interior ministry. The following are some of the reasons the coup failed:

- Few supported the coup. Tens of thousands of citizens favoring democracy publicly opposed the coup. Gorbachev was not very popular, but the junta was much worse.
- Boris Yeltsin stood firm. About a mile and a half from the Kremlin is the parliament of the Russian Republic, then presided over by reformist Yeltsin. Yeltsin and his helpers holed up in the building and declared the junta's decrees illegal. A tank column sent to take the building instead sided with Yeltsin and defended it. Thousands of Muscovites came to stand guard and protest the coup. Yeltsin's toughness galvanized opposition.
- The Soviet armed forces started to split. Many commanders either stood on the sidelines or opposed the junta. The possibility of a bloody civil war loomed, and the junta lost its nerve.
- International pressure opposed the coup. All major foreign powers made it clear that the Soviet economy, desperate for foreign help, would get none if the coup succeeded. Foreign broadcasts (heard by Gorbachev himself) heartened the anti-junta forces.

A haggard Gorbachev returned to Moscow vowing further reform. The junta was arrested (one committed suicide). The coup attempt actually hastened the end of the Soviet Union. After it, Gorbachev was revealed as an indecisive failure. Yeltsin bumped him out of power and proclaimed an independent Russia.

GEOGRAPHY

THE FIFTEEN EX-SOVIET REPUBLICS

We should learn the names and approximate location of each of the fifteen former Soviet republics; they are now independent countries, some more independent than others. (See the map at the beginning of Chapter 17). To help you remember the republics, note that there are three groups of three, plus a large Central Asian group of five (the five "stans"), plus one oddball.

All of the Central Asian republics plus Azerbaijan have a Muslim majority. All speak a Turkic language except the Tajiks, who speak Persian (as in Iran). There has been Muslim-Christian violence between Azeris and Armenians and in Georgia. Inside the Russian Federation, Muslim Chechnya was bloodily crushed. All together, though, more were killed in ex-Yugoslavia. A big question is in which direction will the ex-Soviet Muslim republics go—toward the modern and secular example of Turkey, toward the Islamic fundamentalism of Iran, or back to an economically and militarily dominant Russia?

Slavic	Baltic	Caucasian	Central Asian
Russia	Lithuania	Georgia	Turkmenistan
Ukraine	Latvia	Armenia	Kazakhstan
Belarus	Estonia	Azerbaijan	Kirgizstan
			Uzbekistan
			Tajikistan

Romanian-Speaking
Moldova (formerly Moldavia)

A New Constitution

Along with voting for a new parliament, in late 1993 Russians also approved a new and completely different constitution, one with Western-type institutions, such as the following:

A Strong Presidency   Many observers worry that the presidency, borrowed from France, is too strong and is being misused. The Russian president—elected for a maximum of two four-year terms—sets basic policy, names the prime minister and other top officials, and can veto bills and dissolve parliament. In many areas the president can simply rule by decree. The president's power is somewhat offset by antireformist parties in the Duma. There is no vice-president; if the president dies or is incapacitated, the prime minister serves as acting president until elections are held within three months. This is what happened when Yeltsin suddenly resigned at the end of 1999.

A Prime Minister   Again on the French model, Russia has a prime minister as well as a president, and their relative powers are not completely clear or fixed. The president can name and fire prime ministers at will, but they must be confirmed by the Duma, and presidents sometimes have trouble doing this. When the Duma twice rejected Yeltsin's nominee in 1998, he backed down and named someone more to their liking. The Duma knows that if it rejects the president's nominee for prime minister three times, the president can dissolve the Duma and hold new parliamentary elections. In May 2000, President Putin named Mikhail Kasyanov, forty-two, as his prime minister with solid Duma approval. Kasyanov had been first deputy prime minister and finance minister.

A Federal System   The federal system is carried over from the old Soviet structure. The country's true name is the Russian Federation; it consists of eighty-nine regions—most of them "republics"—twenty-one of which are predominantly non-Russian. Each region is supposed to be bound by treaty to the Federation, but not all have signed, and many are virtually independent of Moscow's rule. Putin cracked down on their governors and recentralized power. One Caucasian Muslim republic, Chechnya, which had resisted Russian rule since its original tsarist conquest, won temporary **de facto** autonomy but was then shelled into submission.

DEMOCRACY

RUSSIA'S 2000 PRESIDENTIAL ELECTIONS

Russian presidential elections, modeled on the French two-round system, were held for the second time in 2000. The elections were three months early, because President Yeltsin resigned half a year before his second term was up. Under the 1993 Russian constitution, when that happens the prime minister becomes acting president but must hold elections in three months.

In the first round of Russian elections, almost any candidate can run; in March 2000, many did. Acting President Vladimir Putin won on the first round (but not by much). His chief competition, Gennady Zyuganov, head of the refurbished Communist party, had too few resources—money, media, and the powers that come with the presidency—to stand much of a chance. (See table for 2000 results.)

If no one had won a majority, a runoff would have been held two weeks later between the top two, as was done in 1996. Between the two rounds in 1996, French-style dealmaking took place that rounded up majority support for incumbent President Boris Yeltsin. In both 1996 and 2000, most of the Russian mass media, owned by newly rich "oligarchs," supported the incumbents, and voting irregularities were reported. They were not completely free and fair elections.

Were the elections democratic? Well, there was competition, which is probably the crux of democracy, but there was also a rigged quality about the campaign. Remember, historically the early stages of democracy in other lands were not completely democratic. Let us not expect too much from Russia at this stage.

Candidate	Party	Percent
Vladimir Putin	Unity	53.0
Gennady Zyuganov	Communist	29.0
Grigory Yavlinsky	Yabloko	5.8
Vladimir Zhirinovsky	Liberal Democrat	2.7

PUTIN: STEEL EYES, IRON HAND

In four months, Vladimir Putin (pronounced POOH-tin), a former KGB officer, rose from obscurity to powerful president of the Russian Federation, first as acting president and then elected on his own in 2000. It was an incredible story, the kind of thing that happens in chaotic situations where institutions are not yet firmly established. It also illustrates how much of the old Soviet system carried over into the new Russian system.

In August 1999, at age forty-six, Putin became President Yeltsin's fifth prime minister in seventeen months and his designated successor as president. As Yeltsin's health deteriorated, prime ministers took over more and more of the daily tasks of governing. Many expected Putin to be another temporary, but by year's end he had turned himself into Russia's most popular political figure. Yeltsin, extremely unpopular, resigned at the end of 1999, and Prime Minister Putin constitutionally became acting president. As popular incumbent, Putin easily won the presidential election of 2000. In Putin, Russians finally saw some of the firm leadership they had been craving, a cold-eyed, strong-hand type who combined tough crackdowns on corruption with willingness for economic reform.

Putin, although little known, knew a lot about politics. Born in 1952 in Leningrad (now St. Petersburg), Putin graduated law school in 1975 and went right into the KGB, where he became a lieutenant colonel in spy operations in East Germany, an important post. As the Soviet Union dissolved, Putin left the KGB to work in St. Petersburg's municipal government, where he became vice mayor in 1994. In 1996, Yeltsin brought him to the Kremlin to supervise relations among Russia's regions and in 1998 made him head of the FSB (see page 266). In March 1999 Putin was made secretary of the president's powerful Security Council.

Some believe that Putin's background in the KGB and FSB gives him leverage over Russia's most powerful people. He knows exactly who is corrupt and who is stashing money overseas. This includes most politicians and all oligarchs. Knowledge is power.

What made Putin popular among the masses, though, was the renewed war in Chechnya (see page 298). Bombs in several Russian cities—allegedly the work of Chechen terrorists, although none claimed credit—blew up apartment houses and killed nearly 300.

This time the Russian people and army wanted to settle some scores with Chechens. Putin's plan to crush all resistance in Chechnya won nearly complete support and made him top choice for president. Becoming acting president clinched his leading position.

Putin is no liberal and has a strong authoritarian streak, precisely why Russians like him. His political and economic views were vague, but he neither wants to return to communism nor copy the West. "Russia will not soon, if ever, become a copy of the U.S.A. or, say, Britain, where liberal values have deep historical roots," said Putin. Russian society, he claimed (accurately), "wants the restoration of a guiding and regulatory role of the state." The world held its breath to see if Putin would mark the stabilization of Russia's democracy and market economy or the rise of an authoritarian system.

A Bicameral Parliament   The bicameral parliament is like the United States but much weaker vis-à-vis the Russian presidency. The lower house, the **State Duma** (reviving the old tsarist name), consists of 450 deputies elected for up to four years (but not in synch with presidential elections). The Duma passes bills, approves the budget, and confirms the president's nominees for top jobs. It can vote no-confidence in a cabinet and, along with the upper house, can override a presidential veto with a two-thirds majority. The upper house, the Federation Council, consists of two members elected locally from each of the eighty-nine regions of the Russian Federation. Its duties are somewhat different from the Duma's. Only the Federation Council can change internal boundaries and ratify the use of armed forces abroad. It appoints the top judges and national prosecutor-general and can remove them. Some observers fear the Russian parliament's powers are only on paper and can be overridden by the president.

Key Term

State Duma   Lower house of Russia's parliament.

A Constitutional Court   The constitutional court is borrowed chiefly from the United States but with some French and German features. The Russian Constitutional Court has nineteen judges appointed by the president and confirmed by the upper house. These judges are supposed to be independent and cannot be fired. They may act both on citizens' complaints as well as on cases submitted by government agencies. The court is supposed to make sure all laws and decrees conform to the constitution. If this court operates as planned (that is, free of political control), it will be a great and essential step for the rule of law in Russia.

A Split Electoral System   This system is borrowed from Germany but is simpler. Half of the Duma's 450 seats are elected by proportional representation (with a 5-percent threshold), half by single-member districts with plurality win. Unlike Germany, in Russia the percentage from the PR side does not set the overall percentage.

A Party System under Construction

From one strong Party, Russia has gone to many weak parties. Russia's political parties spring up quickly but are weak, divided, constantly changing, and personalistic, like Brazil's parties. Russia's top parties are aimed chiefly at getting their leaders elected. In the 1999 Duma elections, five parties had present or former prime ministers as leaders. And not all Russian parties are democratic; some preach chauvinism or a return to communism. Fortunately, these parties lost ground in the 1999 elections.

GEOGRAPHY

RUSSIA'S COMPLEX FEDERALISM

Unlike U.S. states or German *Länder*, Russia's subdivisions are not the same or equal. Instead, there are a confusing four types, listed below:

- twenty-one republics, homelands of the major non-Russian nationalities. For example, Tatars have Tatarstan, and Buryats have Buryatia.

- fifty-two *oblasts* (regions), mostly populated by Russians.
- six *krais* (territories).
- ten autonomous *okrugs* (districts), ethnic portions of oblasts or krais which claim special status.

On paper, the republics have more autonomy. In practice, each place has as much autonomy as the local strongman is able to carve out for himself. Many do not obey Moscow.

The party system is perhaps the foundation of political stability in the modern world. Britain is basically a two-party system, France a multiparty system, and Germany a "two-plus" system. All have achieved stability. A system with too many parties, some of them extremist, poses a serious threat to democracy. Some thought Russia was headed that way, but the Duma elections of 1999 suggested a multiparty system that was starting to settle down. It may take some time, but we could someday see a Russian system much like West Europe's, where mostly two large parties, with only moderate differences between them, calms and stabilizes political life.

1993: THE SECOND COUP THAT FAILED

The 1991 coup attempt was carried out by members of Gorbachev's own executive branch and was stopped by members of the Russian (not Soviet) parliament in its White House some distance from the Kremlin. The October 1993 coup attempt was by conservative antidemocrats, only this time they occupied the White House and were crushed by armed forces under President Yeltsin, who was now in the Kremlin.

What triggered the 1993 attempt was Yeltsin's order to dissolve the Russian parliament and hold new elections. (The old Soviet Congress of Peoples Deputies disappeared with the USSR at the end of 1991.) The Russian parliament had been elected in 1989 under the old regime, when the CPSU still held sway; accordingly, a majority was cautious and conservative about reform. Yeltsin could no longer govern with this parliament, and, indeed, it was high time for free and fair parliamentary elections. But the old parliament didn't like being put out of business and called Yeltsin dictatorial, which turned out to be true. A majority of deputies declared the dissolution illegal and holed up in the White House, hoping that the country and especially the army would side with it. They did not; instead, tanks shelled the White House until it caught fire.

Yeltsin won but he lost. New elections were held in December 1993, but by then so many Russians were disillusioned with reforms that brought crime, inflation, and unemployment that they voted in a parliament, now called the State Duma, that was heavily antireformist and anti-Yeltsin. Yeltsin had to dump many reformist ministers.

Russian Parliament, the "White House" some distance from the Kremlin, was the scene of two dramatic showdowns. In 1991 Boris Yeltsin stood here and faced down the junta that attempted to oust Gorbachev, but in 1993 it was Yeltsin who ordered the building shelled to break a coup attempt by conservative parliamentarians. The White House was quickly restored and now houses Russia's State Duma. (Michael Roskin)

DEMOCRACY

RUSSIA'S 1999 ELECTIONS: DIRTY BUT DEMOCRATIC

Russia's 1999 Duma elections were dirty but democratic. In terms of mud-slinging and dirty tricks, they made U.S. elections look clean. In Russia, the big-money people who own the media delivered a sizeable bloc of seats to a new pro-Kremlin party, Unity. Dozens of newly rich *biznesmeny* ran for the Duma for the sole purpose of getting parliamentary immunity for themselves and their ill-gotten gains. Before we condemn Russia for dirty politics, we should remember that the early stages of democracy in other lands were quite similar. Democracy starts with competition and cleans itself up later. And in Russia in 1999, there was competition.

As with the 1993 and 1995 elections, the 1999 outcome shows Russia's party system still fragmented and inchoate. Of the twenty-six parties that ran for the State Duma in December 1996, six cleared the 5-percent threshold to win some of the 225 seats elected by PR and party lists. Other parties and independents won seats in 225 single-member districts. Several parties in the old Duma disappeared.

The still-biggest party, the revived (and somewhat changed) Communists, won a quarter of the PR vote and a quarter of the Duma's seats overall. President Putin got Communist support in the new Duma by offering them several choice positions. In second place, the surprise winner was Putin's newly formed Unity party. Putin was popular for his tough stand on the Chechen rebels. Unity, whose symbol and nickname was a bear (not a bad symbol for Russia), was a vague catchall with no clear program but had a superrich "oligarch" and his media empire behind it. Unity was basically aimed at setting up Putin to win the 2000 presidential elections.

Coming in third was ex-Prime Minister Yevgeny Primakov's and Moscow Mayor Yuri Luzhkov's new party, Fatherland–All Russia, considered a "centrist" party of moderate reformers. The Western-style Democrats of Yabloko (Apple) and economic reformers of the Union of Right-Wing Forces divided the liberal, promarket vote. The misnamed Liberal Democrats of Vladimir Zhirinovsky continued to decline, and the 1995 vehicle of former Prime Minister Viktor Chernomyrdin, Our Home Is Russia, nearly disappeared.

Ten seats were filled later, due to voting irregularities or the war in Chechnya. Party voting strength will change as the independents shift their support. Adding up Communist, Unity, and some small-party and independent seats, President Putin has a working majority in the Duma to support him.

Party	Orientation	% PR Vote	Seats from PR	Seats from Districts	Total Seats
Communists	Socialist	24	67	46	113
Unity	Catchall	23	64	8	72
Fatherland–All Russia	Centrist	13	36	30	66
Union of Right-Wing Forces	Reformist	9	24	5	29
Yabloko	Democratic	6	16	5	21
Liberal Democrats	Nationalist	6	17	0	17
eight small parties			0	16	16
independents			0	106	106

POLITICAL CULTURE

FROM KGB TO FSB

Although the Committee on State Security, or KGB, was formally dissolved with the Soviet Union, it reappeared divided into several new agencies. Chief among them is the Federal Security Service (FSB in Russian), which is staffed by old KGB hands and carries on with the same tasks: supporting the authorities and making sure they never lose power. Putin handpicked old KGB comrades for his most powerful aides. A special law gives the FSB strong powers to investigate and arrest. Although murder and corruption run rampant, the FSB arrests few. The implication: They're in on the crooked deals and are building files with which to blackmail leaders. Three of Yeltsin's prime ministers in a row were high up in the old KGB and then in the FSB. President Putin had been head of the FSB. The more it changes, the more it stays the same.

Key Terms

apparatchik (p. 254)

Central Committee (p. 254)

de facto (p. 261)

Gosplan (p. 256)

junta (p. 258)

nomenklatura (p. 256)

Politburo (p. 254)

republic (p. 255)

State Duma (p. 263)

system change (p. 253)

Further Reference

Gill, Graeme. *The Collapse of a Single-Party System: The Disintegration of the CPSU.* New York: Cambridge University Press, 1994.

Hahn, Jeffrey W., ed. *Democratization in Russia: The Development of Legislative Institutions.* Armonk, NY: M. E. Sharpe, 1996.

Huskey, Eugene. *Presidential Power in Russia.* Armonk, NY: M. E. Sharpe, 1999.

Knight, Amy. *Spies Without Cloaks: The KGB's Successors.* Princeton, NJ: Princeton University Press, 1996.

McFaul, Michael. *Russia's 1996 Presidential Elections: The End of Polarized Politics.* Stanford, CA: Hoover Institution Press, 1997.

Medish, Vadim. *The Rise and Fall of the Soviet Union,* 5th ed. Upper Saddle River, NJ: Prentice Hall, 1998.

Remington, Thomas. *Politics in Russia.* New York: Longman, 1999.

Sakwa, Richard. *Soviet Politics in Perspective,* 2nd ed. New York: Routledge, 1998.

Suny, Ronald G. *The Soviet Experiment: Russia, the USSR, and the Successor States.* New York: Oxford University Press, 1997.

Urban, Michael, Vyacheslav Igrunov, and Sergei Mitrokhin. *The Rebirth of Politics in Russia.* New York: Cambridge University Press, 1997.

Russian Political Culture

19

Questions to Consider

1. How can you grow democracy in a country where "democracy" has become a dirty word?
2. Why is establishing democracy in Russia more difficult than in the ex-Communist lands of Central Europe?
3. Was Solzhenitsyn right about American culture? Why then has it spread worldwide, especially among young people?
4. How can you tell if a system is based on ideology? Was the Soviet system? What empirical indicators could you look for?
5. What is "civil society" and how do you get it? Is it the same as "pluralism"?
6. Is the phrase "Weimar Russia" justified?
7. How would you explain to a Russian that America is not "out to get them"?
8. How were we mistaken in thinking Russia after the Communists would quickly become like us?

As the Soviet regime declined and collapsed in the late 1980s and early 1990s, the word "democracy" had a positive ring among Russians. It seemed to stand for a new beginning, for justice and prosperity, and for joining the Western world. The leading political party was *Demrossiya*, Democratic Russia. A decade later, with the economy in tatters and most Russians living more poorly than ever, "democracy" had become a swear word, a trick the Americans foisted on Russia to bring it down. For the average Russian, democracy has utterly failed. Most remember life under Brezhnev as better. Building a democracy from scratch is not so easy.

Ignoring the crucial factor of political culture, we naively assumed the collapse of the Communist regime would unleash stable democracy and free-market prosperity. Instead it has brought monumental lawlessness and poverty. A handful of **oligarchs** get very rich by plundering natural resources and state subsidies. Mafia gangs are into everything, including the government. Some call the current political system, half in jest, a

Key Term

oligarchy Rule by a few.

Key Terms

kleptocracy   Rule by thieves.

Gulag   The Soviet central prisons administration.

kleptocracy. The breakdown demonstrates what some scholars long suspected, that under the law-and-order surface of Soviet rule, Russian society was very weak—indeed, it had been made deliberately weak—and cannot sustain a free democracy, at least not for some time.

The Russian Difference

In Central Europe, Communist regimes were discarded in 1989, and within five years Poland, the Czech Republic, and Hungary were functioning democracies with growing, mostly private, market economies. During this same period, the Soviet Union, trying to make the same transition, collapsed both economically and politically and then its largest successor state, the Russian Federation, threatened to do the same. Why the difference between Central Europe and Russia?

GEOGRAPHY

HUNTINGTON'S "CIVILIZATIONAL" DIVIDE IN EUROPE

In an influential but controversial article in the Summer 1993 *Foreign Affairs*, Harvard political scientist Samuel P. Huntington argued that with the Cold War over, profound differences of culture were dividing the world into several "civilizations" that have trouble understanding each other. What Huntington called "civilizations" mostly follow religious lines: the West European (with a North American branch), the Slavic/Orthodox, Muslim, Hindu, Confucian, Japanese, and Latin American.

In Europe, said Huntington, the key geographic line is still where Eastern Orthodoxy meets the two branches of Western Christianity, Catholicism and Protestantism, a line running south from the Baltic republics (Lithuania is mostly Catholic, Latvia and Estonia Protestant) and along the eastern borders of Poland, Slovakia, Hungary, and Croatia. West European civilization, initially in Protestant countries, led the way to democracy and capitalism. The Catholic countries followed more recently. Poland, the Czech Republic, and Hungary turned quickly to market systems and democracy after ousting their Communist regimes in 1989.

But notice the difficulty experienced by Slavic/Orthodox countries such as Russia, Ukraine, Serbia, and Romania in making this transition. Basic assumptions about individual freedom and choice, private property, personal rights, and the rule of law that are widespread in West Europe have not developed in the same way in Slavic/Orthodox Europe. One key point: Orthodox culture is much less individualistic, and this helps account for economic behavior. Economic "shock therapy" (the sudden introduction of a free market) soon brought rapid growth to Poland. Applied in Russia, it simply collapsed the economy: "shock without therapy." Many observers suggest the differences between Poland and Russia are cultural, that Poland has always faced west and Russia not. Huntington's theory does not mean that other civilizations cannot become free-market democracies, just that it may take some time.

POLITICAL CULTURE

SOLZHENITSYN, A RUSSIAN MYSTIC

In 1963 a short, grim novel, *One Day in the Life of Ivan Denisovich*, burst on the Soviet literary scene like a bombshell. In detailing the horrors of Siberian forced labor, its author spoke from intimate experience: Alexander Solzhenitsyn had lived in such a camp from 1945 to 1953 and then in Siberian exile for another three years. His crime: As an artillery captain he criticized Stalin in a letter to a friend.

But the nightmare conditions did not break Solzhenitsyn; on the contrary, they made him stronger. Freed during Khrushchev's brief period of liberalization, Solzhenitsyn resolved to tell the whole story of Soviet repression through novels and nonfiction. But *One Day* was about as much of the truth as the regime was prepared to allow—and that was under the unusual circumstances of Khrushchev's destalinization drive—and Solzhenitsyn soon found himself expelled from the official writers' union and unable to publish.

Smuggled to the West, though, his works found a growing audience. Solzhenitsyn has a boundless love for Russia and long believed communism was a temporary mistake—imported from the West—that could be cured. In the classic mold of the nineteenth-century Slavophiles, Solzhenitsyn wrote a long letter to the Kremlin's rulers urging them to abandon communism, world empire, heavy industry, and domination over non-Slavic nationalities and to return to the Orthodox faith, a simple agricultural life, and the tremendous spiritual roots of old Russia.

In 1973 his monumental *Gulag Archipelago* was released in Paris. A massive compilation of the reports of 227 other camp survivors, **Gulag** showed that capricious ter-

ror was part and parcel of the Soviet system, that by the 1940s there were from 12 to 15 million people in the Gulag at any one time, and that most had committed no crime. That was the last straw for Soviet authorities, who bundled Solzhenitsyn onto a plane in 1974 and didn't let him back.

Solzhenitsyn is not merely anti-Communist. He also hates anything Western: rationality, technology, materialism, legalism, even personal freedom (which, he holds, has degenerated into license). He was not particularly impressed by the United States and lived as a recluse on a Vermont estate. At the 1978 Harvard commencement, he thundered:

> Should someone ask me whether I would indicate the West such as it is today as a model to my country, frankly I would have to answer negatively. Through intense suffering our country [Russia] has now achieved a spiritual development of such intensity that the Western system in its present state of spiritual exhaustion does not look attractive. After the suffering of decades of violence and oppression, the human soul longs for things higher, warmer, and purer than those offered by today's mass living habits, introduced by the revolting invasion of publicity, by TV stupor, and by intolerable music.

Although Solzhenitsyn became a U.S. citizen, he never became culturally American. Instead, he returned to Russia in 1994 with his mystical Russian nationalism. There his TV show flopped, and he was widely ignored. Things had changed since Solzhenitsyn lived in Russia; material longing had largely replaced spiritual longing. The materialist West had won.

First, there are some very basic cultural differences between the mostly Roman Catholic countries of Central Europe and Eastern Orthodox Russia (see box on page 268). Second, the Communists succeeded in capturing Russian nationalism, so that a Russian could take a certain pride in communism. For Central Europeans, communism was put and kept in place by Soviet bayonets and was profoundly at odds with local nationalism.

Perhaps more basically, communism had been implanted in Central Europe much later (after World War II) than in the Soviet Union; it didn't have as much time to take hold. Russians had nearly three-quarters of a century of Communist rule (1917–91), enough for three generations to know only one system. Furthermore, the previous tsarist system had not been democratic either and was just in the early stages of capitalist economic development.

The system Russians had gotten used to provided them with jobs (constitutionally guaranteed) and a low but generally predictable standard of living. An apartment, once you got one, was tacky by Western standards but cost only a few dollars a month. Few Russians worked hard; there was little point to it. Now, suddenly Russians are told their jobs are not guaranteed and that reward is linked to individual achievement.

The result has been psychological disorientation and fear. The economy declines, inflation grows, unemployment increases, and parents worry over how to feed their children. The old legitimacy of Party and leadership has collapsed, and nothing has taken its place. First Gorbachev and then Yeltsin lost their early credibility; they had indecisively zigged and zagged so long on the economy that few saw them as leaders.

In the vacuum of belief, cynicism and despair reign. While some Russians have rediscovered their Orthodox Church, many believe in nothing and say everything is going wrong. But people have to believe in something; cynicism cannot sustain a society. Western values of a free society, of morality rooted in religion, of civil rights, and of individual achievement in a market economy are talked about by some intellectuals but not widely held. Seven decades of Communist rule have stomped them out; they will have to be painfully relearned.

The Mask of Legitimacy

For decades, the CPSU tried to pound into Soviet skulls the feeling that the regime was legitimate—that is, it had the right to rule—and was leading the country through the difficulties of "building socialism" to the working utopia of communism. It is impossible to say how many really believed this. At various times, many did. Foreigners were treated to performances of marchers, youth delegations, and seemingly frank conversations with officials that were designed to show that Soviets believed in the system. In private, Western journalists were sometimes able to establish contacts who told them otherwise: dissident intellectuals, bitter workers, and even Party members who had come to doubt the worth of the system.

When Gorbachev permitted increased freedom of expression in the late 1980s, **glasnost**, torrents of criticism poured out. Freed from fear of the police, the media bitterly criticized the bureaucracy, the Party, and the corruption of both. The mask of Soviet legitimacy slipped away to reveal a system that satisfied few. The trouble was that there was no consensus on what should replace it. The broad masses (Russian: *narod*) generally wanted a cleaned-up socialism that guaranteed everyone a good standard of living. They showed little understanding of democracy or a market system. Many of the better-educated, on the other hand, understood that socialism was defective and should be scrapped in favor of free politics and free economics. Those whose jobs depended on the old system saw change as a threat. And many Russians simply didn't know what to think. They had never before been asked for their opinions.

Many Russians have turned to Russian nationalism, a powerful impulse long manipulated by the Communists, and to newly freed Russian Orthodox Christianity, which has enjoyed an upsurge. Russian nationalism and the Orthodox faith, however, cannot cement Russia together: Twenty-one ethnic republics are non-Russian, mostly Tatar and Muslim, and they react against Russian nationalism with separatism. No symbols unite Russians. Some like the new tricolor flag (based on a tsarist design); others want to bring back the red flag with hammer and sickle. National day is no longer November 11 to celebrate the revolution but June 12 to celebrate Russia's declaration of independence in 1990. Many Russians, however, deplore the breakup of the Soviet Union.

The Illusion of Ideology

Some textbooks on the Soviet Union used to pay considerable attention to Marxism-Leninism, the ideology of communism. Ideology counted for little in the Soviet Union for many years; with *glasnost* it disappeared from sight. Much of Soviet "ideology" was little more than Russian national pride masking feelings of inferiority. Marxism, by predicting the collapse of the capitalist West, tried to reassure Russians that they would eventually emerge superior. They were "building socialism," which at a certain point would surpass the United States and turn into a Communist utopia with no social or economic problems. In earlier decades some Soviets believed it, but many American academics went way overboard in supposing ideology was the basis of the Soviet system.

Actually, young people joined the Party out of self-interest: to get into universities, to win job promotions, to become military or civilian officials. Most were cynical and cared nothing for Marxism-Leninism. They were motivated by careers, not ideology.

Marxism is basically a method of analysis, one that stresses social classes and their conflicts. As such, it stayed far livelier in the West, where it faced constant argument and challenge. In the Soviet Union, it atrophied. Applying this tool of analysis to Soviet society was the last thing the *apparat* wanted, as it would have revealed a pampered Party elite lording it over a wretched proletariat. Soviet Marxists thus focused on the West and cranked out the standard clichés, such as the "sharpening of contradictions" and "increasing tempo and magnitude of crises." They were getting ready for the West to collapse any minute. After some decades, few took it seriously. Soviet students shuffled off to required classes on Marxism-Leninism with the enthusiasm of American students going to compulsory chapel.

The constant mouthing of a dead doctrine created a climate of cynicism, hypocrisy, and opportunism. With the collapse of the Soviet system, Marxism-Leninism collapsed like the house of cards it always was. Marxist ideology was always a defective foundation, but what kind of society can they build with no foundation?

The Rediscovery of Civil Society

Some analysts hold that the crux of the Soviet system was the stomping out of society by the state. Nothing was to be autonomous; everything in society was to be under strict state supervision. There were to be no independent enterprises, churches, associations, clubs, educational

POLITICAL CULTURE

HOW TO BUILD A CIVIL SOCIETY: THE PHILOSOPHICAL GAP

One of the key differences between us and the Russians is philosophical; namely, we are the children of John Locke and they are not. Although few Americans study the philosopher who is at the root of much of our thinking, most have assimilated what the seventeenth-century English thinker had to say: People are rational and reasonable; they have a natural right to life, liberty, and property; and government is good if it preserves these rights and bad if it infringes on them. If this sounds like the Declaration of Independence, it is; Jefferson was an ardent Lockean, as were most of the Founding Fathers. Ever since, Americans have taken to Locke like a duck takes to water; we love his common-sense emphasis on small government and individuals working for the good of themselves and their families. To Russians, this is not common sense.

Russian thought comes out almost the opposite of Locke and traces back to the geographical dilemma of living on a defenseless plain: Either build a strong state or perish. Plugging into the Russian tradition of a strong state is Jean-Jacques Rousseau (see page 94), the radical eighteenth-century French thinker whose theory of the "general will" rejected Lockean individualism in favor of using state power to "force men to be free." With Locke, people form society, and then society sets up a state, all with an eye to preserving property. With Rousseau, the flow goes the other way: The state, guided by the general will, molds society and then redoes individuals. Marxists added a class-struggle gloss to this; Lenin bought the package and then sold it to the Russian people.

Many Americans thought that once communism was overthrown the Russians would rapidly become like us: capitalist entrepreneurs and democrats. This neglected the centuries of philosophical underpinning that is utterly lacking in Russia. If there is to be a Peace Corps in Russia, the teaching of the philosophical basis of markets, pluralism, and limited government might be one of its first and most urgent tasks. Without a new philosophical outlook, one taken mostly from the West, the Russians will likely stay trapped in their statist frame of mind. (For more on statism, see the Brazil chapter.)

---

institutions, or morality. State power, in turn supervised by the Party, ran amok. The Communist system partly succeeded in crushing civil society, and its collapse has left a kind of vacuum where there should be society. Some thinkers argue that Russia must urgently reconstruct the **civil society** that the Soviet state annihilated.

The concept of civil society starts with the notion that state and society are two different things, although they clearly influence each other. Society over time evolves informal manners, usages, and customs that make living together possible. The "civil" (as in civilized) indicates a reasonable level of trust, politeness, public spirit, and willingness to compromise. A civil society through parents, churches, and schools **socializes** its members to right behavior and "rules of the game" that continue even when the state, through its police and bureaucrats, is not watching.

The state, the formal institutional structures that wield power, cannot substitute or replace civil society, although the Communists tried. Attempting

Key Terms

civil society Everything bigger than the family but smaller than the government: churches, businesses, associations, and the pluralistic values that come with them.

socialize To teach political culture, often informally.

such a substitution creates a system where people lack basic civility and see no need to play by informal rules of the game. Businessmen cheat, and mafia gangs muscle into all sectors of the economy. Politicians attack each other hysterically, immoderately, with no possibility of compromise; they have never learned restraint. Citizens feel little need to obey the law if they can get away with breaking it. Legitimacy is terribly weak.

POLITICAL CULTURE

HOW TO BUILD A CIVIL SOCIETY: THE MORAL GAP

America has its share of crooks and criminals, but what would America be like if one could go back over three generations and systematically strip out most moral teachings? What if parents, churches, and schools did not attempt to inculcate a sense of innate right and wrong in young people? What if no one could trust anyone else? The result, I suspect, would be rather like Russia today. This is another area we overlooked in thinking that once communism ended, Russians would quickly become like us.

Russians had ethical training, but it was relativistic, superficial, and based on Marxist theories of social class. That which helps the working class is good, went the litany. The Communist party helps the working class, so it must be good. The Soviet state is totally devoted to the working class, so it must be very good. The Party and the state must therefore be obeyed, respected, and defended. Anyone who goes against them is insane, a wrecker, or a spy. Crime is something that happens only in capitalist countries, where the poor are forced to steal. Private property is inherently wicked, because it has been stolen from the workers who produced it. Under communism, there were no moral absolutes.

Rhetoric aside, Russians soon learned to treat the system with cynicism. With the KGB and its informants everywhere, no one could trust anyone else, and they still don't. With no individual responsibility, stealing, especially from the state, was okay. After all, it really didn't belong to anyone. Under communism, monstrous rip-offs became standard: Everyone stole.

When the Party and the Soviet state collapsed, things got even worse. Knowing the Party and KGB were watching them restrained some Soviets to small rip-offs. Once these external controls vanished, a spirit of "anything goes" was unleashed. People who were smart, ruthless, or well-connected grabbed whole industries. Russia was robbed from within by its own bureaucrats. Since Soviets had always been taught that capitalists and *biznesmeny* (long a term of derision, now adopted as a loan word) were crooks and their gains were ill-gotten, many Russians went into business with that image as their norm. The crime rate shot into outer space. Russia's massive protection rackets, backed up by professional *keelers*, were alright because they were just stealing from capitalist thieves.

What escaped both Russians and Americans is that a modern capitalist culture has a considerable moral basis; people have to be able to trust each other. Such a system draws from religious and ethical teachings, legal enforcement, a spirit of trust, and the knowledge that cheating businesses don't get repeat customers. It may take a long time to build up this moral consensus. We made the mistake of thinking it would automatically arrive with the free market, which we take to be generally self-policing. For most Russians, a free market means legal cheating. For capitalism to work right in Russia, the moral gap must be filled.

The West has had centuries to build up its civil societies. Philosophers such as Hobbes and Locke explained rationally why civil society is necessary. Churches, often with threats of eternal damnation, inculcated right behavior. The market system generated usages aimed at keeping dealings fair and predictable. Laws and courts enforced this with a system of contracts, both written and unwritten. All of this has been missing in Russia since the 1917 Revolution. Americans failed to notice that civil society is the basis of their system; they thought the sudden imposition of democratic institutions and a market economy in Russia would quickly bring the customs of civil society. We now see that without the philosophical, moral, economic, and legal understandings of civil society, Russia will revert to authoritarianism. One key question for Russia, then, is how quickly can a civil society be built.

Natural Egalitarians?

Marxism-Leninism may have vanished in Russia, but many Russians display a sort of crude, inborn tendency toward extreme equality, a natural socialism. Russians resent differences of wealth or income and enviously try to bring the better-off down to their level. Some observers argue that the Russian peasantry, who for centuries tilled the soil in common and shared the harvest, developed highly egalitarian attitudes, which the Communists nourished. Perhaps so, but attitudes are not genetic; they are learned and can be unlearned, given the right conditions. Until new attitudes are learned, however, the old ones can trip up the best-laid plans of reformers.

Americans also favor equality, but it's "equality of opportunity": Everyone has a chance; the results are up to you. An American who gets ahead is usually applauded for his or her ability and hard work. Most Russians do not understand this kind of equality; they expect "equality of result," with each person collecting the same rewards. Those who get ahead are presumed to have cheated, exploited, or bribed. In a 1995 poll, two-thirds of Russian respondents said the free market and small state are wrong for Russia; only 22 percent thought them right. American attitudes of individual work and achievement lend themselves to capitalism; Russian attitudes generally do not.

Russian Racism

With glasnost, hate-filled attitudes latent among Soviet nationalities came into the open, attitudes so strong as to be racist. Under Soviet law, every citizen had his or her nationality stamped in their internal passports, and, contrary to U.S. usage, nationality throughout East Europe and the ex-Soviet Union does not equal citizenship. For example, one can be a Russian citizen of the Komi nationality. This approach is asking for trouble, because it encourages people to demand an independent state. Educated Russians admire the U.S. approach, which prohibits the official identification of citizens by race or national origin.

And Russians tend to pigeonhole everyone on the basis of their nationality. Some nationalities are acceptable, others despised. Russians, for example, respect the Baltic peoples as European, civilized, and "cultured." On the other hand, Russians speak scathingly of the Muslim-Turkic peoples of the Caucasus and Central Asia as lawless and corrupt mafiosi (the loan word *mafiya* is much used in the Soviet Union) who do nothing but make babies. The theme of the differential birthrate comes up often. Russian families nowadays rarely have more than two children; one is the norm. (This is also true in much of West Europe.) Muslim families have many children, sometimes eight or more. Some Russians fear that their stagnant numbers will be swamped by a rising tide of inferior peoples. When bombs blew up apartment houses in 1999, killing close to 300 people, the Russian government and the people eagerly blamed alleged Chechen terrorists and strongly supported a new war to crush Chechnya.

The non-Russian nationalities feel little affection or affinity for the Russians. In Central Asia, several republics have made their local language the only official language. Educated Uzbeks, for example, know Russian perfectly, but now they speak only Uzbek as a way of making local Russians feel unwelcome. Many Russians are getting the message and leaving Central Asia. Virtually none have fled from the Baltic republics, however, and some Russians there even support independence. They feel they would be treated fairly by the cultured Balts. They fear the Muslims of Central Asia.

Antisemitism, deliberately cultivated in tsarist Russia, is again on the rise. Russian nationalists point to the handful of Russians of Jewish or partly Jewish origin who have made big money recently and see a sinister international conspiracy called "Zionism." Even some Communist deputies voice this classic antisemitic line, and the Duma was unable to pass a resolution condemning such racism. (In a public-opinion poll, however, 83 percent of Russians considered the antisemitic statements "unacceptable.") A small nationalist party with black uniforms, Nazi salutes, and swastika-like logos, urges violence against Jews. Sensing a coming horror, tens of thousands of Russian Jews have moved to Israel.

Learning a Democratic Political Culture

Can a democratic political culture be learned? Sure. How else did Germans and Spaniards become democrats? How else did you acquire your democratic culture? (There is an element of **tautology** here: Culture by definition is any learned behavior.) The question for Russia is can it be learned before the system slides back into some sort of authoritarianism? All manner of undemocratic people want to take over and "restore order": ex-generals, factory managers, Party apparatchiki, fascists, and gangsters. A coalition-from-hell of all of the above is conceivable.

Some compare the present situation to the Time of Troubles in the early seventeenth century. Others use the phrase "Weimar Russia" to suggest a coming fascism. In a 1999 poll, 60 percent described the situation in Russia as "tense"; another 29 percent described it as "critical" or "explosive." Sixty-three percent saw the rise of anarchy; only 9 percent saw democracy building. A hefty 41 percent named Prime Minister (later President) Putin as the one who could bring order to Russia. Russians like a strong hand at the top.

We now realize that in the early 1990s, when Communist rule cracked and then collapsed, we were expecting too much. We paid insufficient attention to crucial factors of political culture and assumed that capitalism and democracy bring their own political culture with them. They do, but it takes a long time, and Russia doesn't have much time. Thrust onto an unprepared population in the midst of economic decline, democracy and capitalism have not yet taken root in Russia.

Russia: Paranoid or Normal?

"We could have been contenders," Russians seem to be saying. We once had a great empire that challenged the Americans; suddenly it is gone. Although support of client states around the globe was a net

Key Term

tautology   A statement that repeats the same thing in different words.

POLITICAL CULTURE

HOW TO BUILD A CIVIL SOCIETY: THE ECONOMIC GAP

In addition to the philosophical and moral foundations of a civil society, another basic point has been overlooked in the eager assumption that Russians would quickly become like us: People have to learn capitalism. A market economy may be something that occurs naturally (whenever buyers and sellers meet), but it is not understood naturally. You have to take courses in market economics and read books and articles about it. Soviet universities covered "bourgeois economics" as part of the history of economic thought but gave it short shrift as a doomed system riven with contradictions, unfairness, and depressions. When their system collapsed, only a minority of economists had a decent grasp of what makes market economies work.

Especially missing was any appreciation of how money plays an autonomous role in the economy. In Communist countries, there simply was no theory of money. For example, I have tried the following mental experiment on a seminar of U.S., Central European, and Russian colonels, all mature and well-educated. Imagine, I tell them, a miniature country with ten citizens, each of whom works in one hamburger shop. The ten workers make a total of ten hamburgers a day and each is paid $1 a day. Then each buys one hamburger a day with their $1. The government decides to raise the pay of each to $2 a day (by printing an extra ten $1-bills). The output of the workers is still ten hamburgers a day. Within a day or two, what is the price of a hamburger?

The Americans respond fast and almost instinctively: $2! The East Europeans and Russians don't get it. "You haven't given us enough data," they say. Well, how would you explain it to them? It's not so simple. Phrases like "supply and demand" by themselves don't explain much. What we accept as basic and self-evident, Russians do not. (By the way, once you can really explain the parable, you've got a rudimentary theory of money.)

---

drain on the Soviet economy, many Russians were proud of their empire. Some analysts have argued that the feeling of belonging to a mighty empire served to quiet discontent over shortages and poor living conditions. Every time a new client signed up—Cuba, Vietnam, Ethiopia, Angola—Russians could say, "See, we really are the wave of the future." The loss of empire was a real letdown for many Russians.

Russians used to feel they were the equals—maybe the superiors—of the Americans; now the arrogant Americans sneer at Russia. Indeed, it was they who craftily engineered the fall of the Soviet Empire and the collapse of the Soviet Union. Now they are moving in for the kill: the destruction of Russia. What else could the extension of NATO eastward—by adding Poland, the Czech Republic, and Hungary—mean? See what they are doing to our little Slavic brother Serbia. The Americans gave little money and a lot of bad economic advice, making sure our economy collapsed. Now that we are starving, they cut us off.

Remembering the definition of paranoia—unreasonable suspicion of others—observers were distressed at the signs of paranoia that grew as the Russian economy worsened. The images carried by many Russians are terribly untrue. The Soviet and later Russian systems collapsed from their own chiefly economic weaknesses; it was not a U.S. plot. Moscow tends to reject Western economic urgings and then gets angry when Western banks refrain from investing. Moscow aids Belgrade and then gets angry when Western aid dries up. Such a victim mentality contributes to the rise of a nationalist authoritarian regime, one that still has thousands of nuclear warheads.

At the same time, there are indications of political normalization in Russia. Voting patterns resemble those of stable democracies. City dwellers and young people tend to vote for continued reforms leading to a market economy. In other countries, we would call this a "liberal" or "left" vote, typical of urban areas. The Communists score best among old Russians, whose pensions have disappeared with inflation, and country dwellers, who have trouble adapting to the new market system. Russians, like Americans, may actually prefer the executive and legislative branches in the hands of opposing parties. All in all, not a bad record for a new democracy in a country with a devastated economy and with no previous democratic experience.

One of the leading studies of Nazi Germany blamed its rise on "the politics of cultural despair," a situation where everything seems to have failed, where the bonds of civil society have dissolved and nothing has taken their place. How far can despair go before something snaps?

POLITICAL CULTURE

HOW TO BUILD A CIVIL SOCIETY: THE LEGAL GAP

The rule of law is weak in Russia, in part because Soviet law paid minimal attention to property. Any big property (land, factories) automatically belonged to the state, and stealing state property could be punished as treason. The Lockean notion that property is a natural right and basis for human freedom was rejected out of hand. Russians, having been inculcated with the Marxist notion that "all property is theft," have trouble grasping the democratic and capitalist notion that "private property means personal freedom."

Weak or absent in the old Soviet socialist legal code, which Russia inherited, are such basics of the Common Law as ownership, contracts, torts, and bankruptcy. If you set up a business in the United States, Canada, or much of West Europe, you are reasonably confident your property and earnings will not be taken from you. In Russia, you have no such confidence. Not only are there few laws on the books in these areas, there is no legal culture built up over the years that regards these areas as sacred. One result is that foreigners and Russians alike are reluctant to invest in Russia. The climate is literally lawless, and they may lose everything. Russian law institutes are attempting to import Western legal concepts quickly, for they understand that the present uncertain situation stunts Russian economic growth. Said one Russian law expert ruefully, "The only lawyer around here is a Kalashnikov."

By way of contrast, Poland adopted its excellent Commercial Code in 1935, borrowed heavily from the Italian. The Polish Communist regime never repealed this code and after the Communists' ouster in 1989, Polish jurists simply dusted it off and put it into practice. Both Poles and foreigners who invest in Poland enjoy legal protections. Result: The Polish economy was the fastest growing in Europe. There is still no equivalent Russian commercial code.

Key Terms

civil society (p. 268)   oligarchy (p. 267)
Gulag (p. 268)   socialize (p. 272)
glasnost (p. 270)   tautology (p. 273)
kleptocracy (p. 272)

Further Reference

Brudny, Yitzhak M. *Reinventing Russia: Russian Nationalism and the Soviet State, 1953–1991*. Cambridge, MA: Harvard University Press, 1999.

Eckstein, Harry, Frederic J. Fleron Jr., Erik P. Hoffmann, and William M. Reisinger, eds. *Can Democracy Take Root in Post-Soviet Russia? Explorations in State-Society Relations*. Lanham, MD: Rowman & Littlefield, 1998.

Kramer, Mark. *Travels with a Hungry Bear: A Journey to the Russian Heartland*. Boston, MA: Houghton Mifflin, 1996.

Löwenhardt, John. *The Reincarnation of Russia: Struggling with the Legacy of Communism, 1990–94*. Durham, NC: Duke University Press, 1995.

McDaniel, Tim. *The Agony of the Russian Idea*. Princeton, NJ: Princeton University Press, 1996.

Petro, Nicolai N. *The Rebirth of Russian Democracy: An Interpretation of Political Culture*. Cambridge, MA: Harvard University Press, 1995.

Popov, Nikolai. *The Russian People Speak: Democracy at the Crossroads*. Syracuse, NY: Syracuse University Press, 1995.

Randolph, Eleanor. *Waking the Tempests: Ordinary Life in the New Russia*. New York: Simon & Schuster, 1996.

Remnick, David. *Resurrection: The Struggle for a New Russia*. New York: Random House, 1997.

Schmemann, Serge. *Echoes of a Native Land: Two Centuries in a Russian Village*. New York: Knopf, 1997.

Shalin, Dmitri N., ed. *Russian Culture at the Crossroads*. Boulder, CO: Westview, 1996.

Smith, Gordon B. *Reforming the Russian Legal System*. New York: Cambridge University Press, 1996.

Urban, Joan, and Valerii Solovei. *Russia's Communists at the Crossroads: Leninism, Fascism, or Social Democracy*. Boulder, CO: Westview, 1997.

Weigle, Marcia A. *Russia's Liberal Project: State-Society Relations in the Transition from Communism*. University Park, PA: Pennsylvania State University Press, 2000.

Russia:
Patterns of Interaction

20

Questions to Consider

1. In what way are we watching an old problem in Russia?
2. What did Khrushchev attempt to do and why? Why did he fail?
3. What is the difference between totalitarian and authoritarian?
4. What did Gorbachev attempt to do and why? Why did he fail?
5. Did Moscow end up borrowing cohabitation from Paris?
6. Who are Russia's "oligarchs" and how do they play politics?
7. Why did reforms work in Central Europe but not in Russia?
8. Is Putin building an authoritarian system?

Russian politics may be described as a tug-of-war between reformist and conservative forces. The two block each other, little gets done, problems worsen, and criminals operate freely. This suggests an authoritarian solution or something less than an open democracy. Post-Communist Russian politics reflects, and to some extent continues, Soviet and even earlier Russian patterns. What we are watching today is not completely new. It is, rather, a very old pattern—going back to tsarist times—of a system that cries out for reform but contains many conservative forces able and happy to block reform. A hundred years ago, educated Russians could recognize the problem: how to reform the unreformable system? Many have tried, and all have failed to both reform and keep the system intact.

Reformers versus Conservatives

The trouble with Russia is that there are few rules or institutions to regulate and moderate political clashes. Without experience in multiparty competition, a free press, voluntary associations, tolerance, and simple politeness, the new forces freed by the ending of Party control started to play a new game without knowing the rules. Their clashes were bound to be chaotic, and they were made worse by bureaucrats and others who quickly got in on the unregulated privatization by grabbing up state enterprises cheap.

279

Key Terms

shock therapy   Sudden replacement of a socialist economy with a free-market one.

red-brown   A possible combination of Communists and Fascists, the brown standing for Hitler's brownshirts.

Earlier editions of this book argued that under the uniform surface of political life in the old Soviet Union existed a permanent struggle between liberals and conservatives, the former for major change in a generally westward direction, the latter for standing pat with the essentially Stalinist system. It is here argued that this conflict continues in the post-Soviet era, but now it's more open.

Most of the reformers who rallied to Gorbachev and then to Yeltsin have resigned or been dismissed from high office. In many respects they hearken back to the Russian Westernizers of the nineteenth century who wanted to import Western ways nearly wholesale: a market economy, free democracy, and individualistic philosophy. This led them to attempt the economic **shock therapy** recommended by Harvard economist Jeffrey Sachs, which earlier worked in Bolivia and Poland. In Russia, such therapy was never fully and correctly applied, and the economy plunged downward. (See next chapter.)

What we are calling here "conservatives" covers a broad swath from moderates to extremists. What they have in common is their opposition to the thorough restructuring of the Russian economy. Russia may need reforms, some concede, but they must be *our* reforms tailored to *our* conditions. Some old-line Party types would go all or much of the way back to a centralized command economy. Like the old Russophiles of the nineteenth century, they reject Western models and would turn inward, to Russia's roots; accordingly, they are nationalistic, some rabidly so. With some oversimplification, we could compare their attitudes side-by-side.

These two general camps are halves of the Russian political spectrum that contains several graduations and combinations. The extreme end of the conservative side is sometimes called the **red-brown** coalition of old Party supporters plus extreme nationalists. Some feared that Zhirinovsky and his strange "Liberal Democratic" party could link up with someone like ex-General Alexander Lebed. More moderate conservatives cluster around Zyuganov's Communist party.

Under the label "centrist," another group seeks a middle ground of moderate reforms cushioned by continued state subsidies and ownership. The alignment Fatherland-All Russia is generally seen as centrist. Unfortunately, under Yeltsin this approach led to incredible

Liberals	Conservatives
reform	antireform
democratic	authoritarian
market	central controls
antiinflation	soft on inflation
soft on unemployment	antiunemployment
antisubsidies	prosubsidies
intellectuals	apparatchiks
younger	older
big cities	towns and rural
propresidency	proparliament
pro-Western	anti-Western
cosmopolitan	nationalistic

KEY CONCEPTS

TOTALITARIAN VERSUS AUTHORITARIAN

Since the 1930s, political science has debated the existence and nature of modern dictatorships. Some political scientists developed theories and models of **totalitarian** systems to explain Mussolini's Italy, Hitler's Germany, and Stalin's Soviet Union. Carl J. Friedrich and Zbigniew Brzezinski argued that totalitarian dictatorships have these six points in common:

1. An official ideology
2. A single, disciplined party
3. Terroristic police control
4. Party monopoly of the mass media
5. Party control of the armed forces
6. Central direction of the economy

Widely accepted for years, the totalitarian model gradually came under criticism as unrealistic and oversimplified. Far from total, the systems of Mussolini, Hitler, and Stalin were quite messy. Many citizens knew the regimes were frauds; plans were often just improvisations. The dictators like their systems to *look* total. Totalitarianism was an attempt at total control that always fell short.

Totalitarian fell into disuse, and **authoritarian** became the word used to describe modern dictatorships. It means a system with strong control at the top but one that does not try to achieve total control. In an authoritarian system, politics is in the hands of a dictator, such as Spain's Franco or Chile's Pinochet, but wide areas of the economy and cultural life are open. Most or all of the above six points are missing.

Political scientist Jeane J. Kirkpatrick in 1980 argued there are still useful distinctions between the two words. Authoritarian regimes, more loose and open, can change and reform themselves into democracies. This happened throughout Latin America in the 1980s. Totalitarian systems, especially Communist ones, she argued, cannot reform; they are too rigid. In a way, Kirkpatrick was right. The Communist regimes of East Europe and the Soviet Union never did reform; they collapsed.

corruption. Thoroughgoing reformers and democrats, such Yabloko, are a weak force in parliament. One interesting possibility emerged with the 1999 Duma elections. Prime Minister and later President Putin, whose Unity catchall spanned all political views, indicated he could work with the economic reformers of the Union of Right-Wing Forces. A stable, proreform coalition in the Duma could do wonders for Russia.

President versus Parliament

Executive and legislative are at serious odds in Russia, and their competing claims have led to anger and violence. The initial problem, as noted earlier, was the carryover from Soviet times of a Russian parliament elected under the old rules and under the Communists in 1989. Most members of this parliament stood firm with Yeltsin during the abortive coup of 1991.

Key Terms

totalitarian Political system that attempts total control of society, as under Stalin and Hitler.

authoritarian Dictatorial system that bypasses democratic procedures, as Spain under Franco and Chile under Pinochet.

FAILED REFORMER: NIKITA KHRUSHCHEV

Faced with a Soviet Union that had petrified under Stalin, Nikita Khrushchev attempted to revitalize the system and get it moving toward communism again. He was only partly and briefly successful, for much of the Soviet Party and bureaucracy resisted him. We now realize Khrushchev was far from the undisputed master of the Kremlin that Stalin was and that he in fact had to overcome many conflicting forces. Like Gorbachev, he failed.

Born in 1894 of an ethnic Russian family living in Ukraine, Khrushchev joined the Bolsheviks shortly after the revolution and worked his way up through party jobs. A protégé of Stalin, Khrushchev did some of the dictator's dirty work in the 1930s, which earned him a full Politburo membership in 1939. During the war he was made a political general and sent to the Ukrainian front. After the war he organized party work in Ukraine and then the Moscow region, and carefully packed the party leadership with his supporters, the key to success in Soviet politics.

Stalin's death in 1953 opened a period of jockeying for power. All the Politburo knew was that Stalin had been a monster; they longed for stability and personal security. Accordingly, one of their first steps was to have the head of the secret police, Lavrenti Beria (like Stalin, a Georgian), arrested and shot. This effectively put the KGB under Party control. The first post-Stalin premier was Georgi Malenkov, who advocated relaxing the Stalin system and producing more consumer goods. But Khrushchev was made party first secretary, a post that was always more powerful.

Khrushchev craftily built a coalition against Malenkov (and then later adopted his policies). Malenkov was depicted as weak, nothing more than a "clerk," and was deposed in 1955. But it was not a Stalin-Trotsky type of struggle; Khrushchev merely had Malenkov demoted to minister for power stations. The Soviet leadership seems to have agreed that violent death is no way to run a political system; after all, anybody might be the next loser.

To consolidate his power, Khrushchev resorted to perhaps the most dramatic incident in CPSU history: He denounced Stalin to a Party congress. Khrushchev did this not so much to set the record straight or to clear his conscience but to trounce his enemies within the Party. A Party that was still Stalinist was immobile, incapable of reform or innovation. The productive potential of the Soviet Union lay under a blanket of fear and routine. To storm through, Khrushchev chose the direct route: Get rid of the symbol of the whole system, Stalin.

At the Twentieth Party Congress in February 1956, Khrushchev delivered a stinging, hours-long tirade against the "crimes of Stalin" who, he said, had murdered thousands of Party comrades and top military officers. Khrushchev neglected to mention his own role in the purges or the millions of nonparty people killed. The problem, claimed Khrushchev, was that Stalin had built a **cult of personality**, something that must never be allowed again.

The supposedly "secret" speech did have dramatic impact but not precisely in the intended way. Communist parties the world over had based themselves on Stalin-worship, and when the speech leaked out, all hell broke loose. A Hungarian uprising was crushed by Soviet tanks; Poland nearly revolted. In the West, many longtime Communists resigned from the party. Most ominous of all, in China, Mao Zedong decided he couldn't trust someone who was undermining the Communist camp by denouncing its symbol.

Next, to revitalize the Soviet economy, Khrushchev proposed a sweeping decentralization. Outvoted in the Politburo, Khrushchev called a 1957 Central Committee meeting packed with his supporters and backed by the army, which forced his opponents to resign. They were designated the "antiparty group," but none were persecuted.

CPSU leaders, however, grew increasingly irritated at his "harebrained schemes" to boost production (especially of consumer goods), eliminate class differences (everyone would have to work before college, even the children of big shots), and outfox the Americans by placing missiles in Cuba. To the West, at that time, Khrushchev appeared as simply another dictator, the "butcher of Budapest," and the man who banged his shoe on the table at the UN. His opponents in the Kremlin, however, considered him a reckless experimenter and liberalizer. In retrospect, the Khrushchev era brought major changes in both domestic and foreign policy. An entire generation of young Party members—including Gorbachev—came of age wanting and planning economic reform. These people, "Khrushchev's children," later staffed the Gorbachev reform effort.

In October 1964 the hitherto unthinkable happened: The leader of the Soviet Union was *voted* out of office by a majority of the Politburo who disliked his economic and

Party "adventurism." He went into retirement and died in 1971.

Khrushchev was a flamboyant, can-do character, who promised much and delivered little. The first Soviet leader to visit the United States, he saw in the Midwest the wonders of corn production and ordered wide regions of the USSR to convert to corn, even areas not suited to it. In his Virgin Lands program in Kazakhstan, he ordered ploughing and planting. But rainfall is unreliable there, and after a few good harvests, much of the land turned into a dust bowl. By stressing consumer goods, he downplayed the traditional emphasis on heavy industry, and this infuriated both managers and the military. Culturally, he permitted the publication of anti-Stalin works (including Solzhenitsyn's *One Day*), then backed off when he felt things were getting out of hand.

We now see that Khrushchev was trying to reform in the face of the ingrained conservatism of Party *apparatchiki*, sometimes giving way to them and finally defeated by them. Gorbachev, whose reform efforts were inspired by Khrushchev but went farther, suffered a similar fate.

But then Yeltsin gathered more power into the office of the presidency. The Russian parliament reacted, claiming Yeltsin was becoming dictatorial. They also disliked seeing their own power and perquisites diminished. Some deputies who had earlier counted themselves as reformers began to discover the negative side of reforms and to slide into the conservative camp. To make clear who was in charge, in 1993 Yeltsin sponsored and won a referendum that endorsed both reform and the power of the presidency. Later that year, he pushed through a new constitution with Gaullist-type presidential powers. The last straw was Yeltsin's dissolution of parliament in order to hold new elections; that produced the parliamentary coup attempt of 1993.

Subsequent parliamentary elections were slaps at Yeltsin. Some of the biggest votes were for the Communists and other antireform parties. Yeltsin backed down, jettisoned his main reformers, and made cautious reformers, several of them very briefly, his prime ministers.

But isn't this just democracy in action? An executive starts showing dictatorial tendencies and implements policies that go farther and faster than citizens want, so the citizens, through their elected representatives in parliament, put on the brakes. That is the way the State Duma would like to see itself, but the problem in Russia is trickier. Without major economic reforms, democracy in Russia doesn't stand a chance. But such reforms are seldom initiated by purely democratic means; they can't

Key Term

cult of personality   A dictator who has himself worshiped.

"Life punishes those who delay," said the Soviet president in 1989 as he urged the East German Communist regime to reform before it was too late. The East Berlin regime ignored Gorbachev and collapsed. What Mikhail Sergeyevich Gorbachev didn't grasp was that he too was engaging in delayed and halfway reforms that collapsed the Soviet regime and led to his own ouster from power.

Amid great hopes Gorbachev assumed the top Soviet political position—Party general secretary—in 1985. The Soviet Union had been running down. Under Brezhnev's eighteen-year reign, growth rates slumped while cynicism, alcoholism, and corruption grew. Two elderly temporaries, Andropov and Chernenko, followed as the Soviet system began to atrophy. Gorbachev—age fifty-four, a mere kid in Politburo terms—announced wide-ranging reforms to shake up the Soviet system.

Born into a peasant family in the North Caucasus in 1931, Gorbachev graduated from Moscow University's law school in 1955 and returned to his home area for Party work. As Party chief of Stavropol province in 1970, he impressed Brezhnev, who summoned him to Moscow in 1978 to become a Party secretary with responsibility for overseeing agriculture. (Gorbachev had taken another degree, in agronomy, by correspondence.)

Gorbachev by now was under the wing of Andropov, head of the KGB, and Mikhail Suslov, a Politburo kingmaker from Stavropol. Gorbachev was elected to the Party's Central Committee in 1971, to candidate member of the Politburo in 1979, and to full member in 1980. When Andropov took over in 1982, Gorbachev assisted him closely and implemented his tough anticorruption policies.

In 1985, Gorbachev began his reforms as the hero who would turn the Soviet Union into a modern, possibly democratic, system. He announced "new thinking" in foreign policy that led to arms control agreements with the United States and to the freeing of Eastern Europe from the Communist regimes that had been imposed by Stalin after World War II. With these steps, the Cold War ended.

Gorbachev ordered *glasnost* in the Soviet media, which became more pluralist, honest, and critical. Corrupt big shots were fired. Gorbachev also urged *demokratizatzia*; competitive elections were introduced, and a partially elected parliament convened.

Gorbachev first tried to fix the creaky economic system with the old remedies: verbal exhortations, antialcohol campaigns, "acceleration," and the importation of more foreign technology. Then, after having hesitated too long, he ordered **perestroika** (economic restructuring) that slowly and gingerly began to decentralize and liberalize the Soviet economy. Farms and factories made more of their own decisions and kept more of their own profits. Private businesses called "cooperatives" were permitted and grew. But it was too little, too late. By 1989 economic disaster loomed. Economic dislocations lowered Soviet living and dietary standards and angered everyone.

With a freer press, the many nationalities (including Russians) demanded greater autonomy or even independence. Violence between ethnic groups flared. The *apparat* and *nomenklatura* sabotaged economic reforms by hoarding food and raw materials. Some generals and the KGB indicated they wouldn't stand for the growing chaos, which would have soon led to the dismemberment of the Soviet Union, so Gorbachev pulled back from reforms and tightened up in late 1990.

In early 1991, Gorbachev appeared to favor reform again. In opposition, conservative hardliners in his cabinet—every one hand picked by Gorbachev—attempted a coup against him in August 1991. The coup failed due to splits in the Soviet armed forces and the stubbornness of Russian President Boris Yeltsin, who took the initiative in pushing a weakened Gorbachev from office and in breaking up the Soviet Union into its component republics.

In part, Gorbachev had himself to blame for the Soviet collapse. He had dawdled too long and changed course too many times. He sought to preserve the Party and "socialism." He never did adopt an economic reform plan. Life indeed punished him who delayed.

be, as they inflict too much pain, at least temporarily. Major reforms need strong executive leadership; a fragmented parliament cannot do it. If the executive is blocked, the result will likely not be democracy but chaos, and out of chaos grows dictatorship.

Key Term

perestroika Russian for "restructuring"; Gorbachev's proposals to reform the Soviet economy.

The Oligarchs

Moscow privatized ("piratized" might be more accurate) the Russian economy in such a way as to make a few people incredibly wealthy. Clever wheeler-dealers, some of them members of the *nomenklatura*—who understood the value of state-owned firms, chiefly in the oil and natural-gas industries—bought them at giveaway prices. Most of what they did was legal because there are few laws in these areas. Russia privatized badly.

RUSSIA'S THROWAWAY PRIME MINISTERS

Yeltsin's first prime minister, Yegor Gaidar, privatized Russia's economy rapidly, angering many. He was out in half a year. To patch things up with conservative forces, Yeltsin kept Viktor Chernomyrdin as prime minister from 1992 to 1998. Chernomyrdin, a state-enterprise director, recemented relations with parliament, which was heavy with such people. He carried out several reforms but, as former Communist energy minister, tilted toward state-owned businesses and spoke of the need to reform slowly so as not to destroy Russian industry. He also amassed a personal fortune as head of Gazprom, Russia's giant natural-gas company. Results: halfway restructuring, corruption, and economic decline.

In a typical outburst in March 1998, Yeltsin fired his entire cabinet and named as prime minister a total unknown, thirty-five-year-old Sergei Kiriyenko, and a cabinet of similar young reformers. Five months later, he fired them and called back Chernomyrdin. This time, though, the Duma would not accept Chernomyrdin, so in September 1998 Yeltsin named Foreign Minister Yevgeny Primakov, then age sixty-eight, as prime minister, and the Duma went along with it, probably because Primakov came from deep in the heart of the old Communist regime, the KGB.

Primakov was moderately effective, and his support grew as Yeltsin's vanished, making Primakov a good bet in the 2000 presidential race. It was perhaps out of jealousy that Yeltsin fired Primakov after nine months and named the obscure intelligence official Sergei Stepashin prime minister. He lasted three months. Then in August 1999 he named another FSB chief (and former KGB spymaster in East Germany) Vladimir Putin, whom he also designated as his successor in the presidential elections of 2000.

What does this turmoil mean? In addition to Yeltsin's obvious instability—he was estimated to be lucid 10 percent of the time—the constant changes in prime minister suggest poor institutions, or at any rate institutions poorly suited to Russia at this stage of its development. As we discussed in France, quasi-presidential systems may be inherently unstable. In France, they part-way remedied the defects by the device of "cohabitation," where the president, faced with a parliament dominated by his opposition, names an opposition figure prime minister and takes a cut in presidential power. It worked in France, but Yeltsin would stand for no cut in his presidential power. He really did have dictatorial tendencies. His throwaway prime ministers can be seen as a crude attempt at cohabitation that made no one happy and hurt Russia's chances for democracy. One solution: Get rid of this crazy quasi-presidential system.

Key Term

mafia   A criminal
conspiracy.

These oligarchs, as they were soon called, either had or quickly developed ties to leading politicians. One of the best-known oligarchs was Boris Berezovsky, a former math professor turned used-car king and then media and oil magnate. Berezovsky's money, newspapers, and TV network helped first Yeltsin and then Putin win elections in 1996 and 2000. Berezovsky had extensive financial ties with Yeltsin and his daughter.

The trouble is, these oligarchs do not act like Western-style capitalists, who invest and then reinvest to make the economy and jobs grow. Russian oligarchs strip assets from their companies—for example, selling oil abroad—and do not reinvest the money but stash it in foreign (Swiss, Cayman Islands, Cyprus) banks. They do not like paying taxes or economic restructuring. In the meantime, Russian companies are broke and their workers are unpaid for months.

How to fix? Stop subsidizing industries and let the money-losers go bankrupt. Institute a Polish-type commercial code to regulate banks and businesses. Force the oligarchs to behave like real capitalists. But the oligarchs are well-connected and have many politicians on their payroll. They helped oust the reform-minded Kiriyenko cabinet in just five months. Kiriyenko vowed to collect taxes. In the name of keeping a vital industry alive and of not increasing unemployment, the subsidies, sweetheart contracts, and tax breaks continue. Another name for the process is corruption. Western executives call Russia one of the most corrupt countries in the world. Russians, with their penchant for equality, hate the oligarchs and could rally to a populist who promises to end their games.

The Mafia

The **mafia** (Russians used the loan word *mafiya*) is an important interest group in Russia, for it stands for much more than the criminal underworld. In Russia, the word covers a multitude of meanings, ranging from local strongarm rackets (virtually all businesses pay protection money) to the sophisticated takeover of natural resources by the Communist *nomenklatura* that used to run industry. Anyone in their way gets murdered (by *keelers*, another loan word). Bankers, journalists, old people (for their apartments), an American businessman, and even members of the Duma have been shot dead by mafiosi. Most "banks" are simply money-laundering operations. And no wrongdoers ever get caught because people in high office, including the former KGB, are in on the deals. Russia is not ruled by law.

Russian mafiosi flaunt their new wealth, flashy cars (any make you can name, often stolen), clothes, lady friends, and parties. The average Russian hates those who have rapidly enriched themselves as they have degraded Russia, and this hatred feeds support for politicians who vow to crack down on them. Thus, lawlessness could help promote an authoritarian takeover. Russians have long argued that without strict supervision and draconic controls they are the most lawless of peoples. Americans, they say, have internal controls that Russians have not. Historically, freedom in Russia meant chaos and bloody anarchy, and many Russians have welcomed rule by a strong hand, however harsh.

The Army

The new Russian armed forces are much smaller (nominally 1.2 million members) than the old Soviet armed forces (some 4 million) but still poorly fed and led. Many soldiers and officers work off-base to feed themselves. (In comparison, U.S. armed forces total 1.4 million and are superbly fed and led.) Russian armed forces are absurdly top heavy, with as many officers as enlisted soldiers (U.S. ratio: 1:6). Officers, fearful of losing their jobs and starved for decent housing, are angry. Soldiers go unpaid for months and have to grow much of their own food. Hundreds of conscripts, hazed and starved, commit suicide each year. Many young men ignore the twice-yearly draft calls. Former General Lebed warned of a possible military mutiny.

KEY CONCEPTS

THE TIMING OF REFORMS

In addition to the cultural factors already discussed, the timing of reforms can make a crucial difference to the successful founding of democracy. The differences in timing between what happened in Central Europe and what happened in Russia are instructive.

First, in Central Europe (Poland, Czechoslovakia, and Hungary) a broad anti-Communist movement formed while the Communists were still in power. By the time liberal Communists held free elections in 1989 or 1990, an aware electorate completely ousted the Communists from power, from the president's and prime minister's office to the main parties of parliament. It was a new broom sweeping clean. The initial winner was the broad catchall of anti-Communist forces, the leader of which became either the president (Walesa of Poland and Havel of Czechoslovakia) or the prime minister (Antall of Hungary). Later, these catchalls fell apart, but they had done their job: Communism was out, and democracy and market economics were established.

In Russia, there was no new broom and the old one did not sweep clean. There was no nationwide anti-Communist catchall movement like Solidarity or Civic Forum. The Communists never allowed that. Instead, the Communists held semifree elections but did not allow themselves to be neatly ousted from power. Gorbachev, who was never elected anything, stayed in office believing he was supervising major reforms.

But Gorbachev still faced major conservative (that is, Party) forces and continually changed course in the face of them. Sensing his weakness, Party conservatives attempted to overthrow him. After their defeat, the Party was finally ousted from office (late 1991) but still retains important influence in parliament, industry, and the countryside. Yeltsin, with no mass movement behind him, attempted serious reform but was still blocked by conservative forces, some of them remnants of the Party.

If Russia had done it like Central Europe, there would have been multiparty elections in late 1991 instead of late 1993. At the earlier date, there might have been sufficient enthusiasm to elect a proreform majority; by the latter date, the declining economy had produced despair and a backlash. But isn't that what happened in Central Europe? Quite so; in both Poland and Hungary economic hardship gave electoral wins to their Socialist parties (ex-Communists). But by then both democracy and the market economy were established and could not be rolled back. The Socialists had no intention of dismantling a working market system; instead, they made minor adjustments in the "social safety net" of Poland and Hungary.

The desirable sequence, as illustrated by Central Europe, seems to be as follows: First, form a broad mass movement; second, thoroughly oust the Communists in parliamentary elections; third, institute political and economic reforms. The Russians tried to do it backward.

REMEMBERING THE MARSHAL

New York Times editor Leslie Gelb recalled a private conversation he had in 1983 with the Chief of the Soviet General Staff, Marshal Nikolai Ogarkov, who worried semi-publicly that the Soviet military was falling behind technologically. He was later pushed out of high office for his outspokenness. "Modern military power is based upon technology," Gelb recalled him saying, "and technology is based upon computers," an area where the Americans were well ahead. Then, said Gelb, came his punch line:

We will never be able to catch up with you in modern arms until we have an economic revolution. And the question is whether we can have an economic revolution without a political revolution.

By the early 1980s, at least the high-tech sectors of the Soviet military, fearful of falling behind, favored major reform. The proof, if Ogarkov needed it, came with the quick U.S.-led victory over Soviet-equipped Iraq in 1991.

Several leading generals either supported the 1991 coup or did not oppose it. Many Soviet higher officers were fired. One, Marshal Sergei Akhromeyev, committed suicide. The Soviet armed forces had been consuming a quarter of the country's gross national product, a figure that was cut drastically. The army is still one of the few semistable institutions in Russia and may yet play a direct political role.

When a political system starts falling apart, whatever groups are best organized amid growing chaos are most likely to seize power. This usually means the army. (See the box entitled "Praetorianism" in Chapter 28, page 429.) In much of the Third World, military coup is the standard way to change governments. Some believe the Russian army could play such a role, although historically it never has. In 1991 and 1993 the military was divided and most of it hung back, afraid of being used by politicians and of starting a civil war among army units.

The army must surely be counted as an important pressure group within Kremlin politics. For decades, especially under Brezhnev, the military got a growing defense budget and a leading role in foreign policy. Everything else in the Soviet economy took second place to the defense needs defined by the generals. The Russian military now complains its budget is completely inadequate and demands more. Since Yeltsin was saved by the army twice, he supported an increase in defense spending, which the Duma rejected. This kept the army on Yeltsin's side.

The Soviet and now Russian army has gone through a series of humiliations. Gorbachev tried to limit the size of the Soviet military. In 1988, he admitted that the Soviet invasion of Afghanistan had been a mistake and withdrew Soviet forces. He gave up East Europe in 1989 as a waste of resources, even though the Soviet military defined East Europe as an indispensable defensive shield. The quick 1991 defeat of Iraq also hurt, because it was Soviet equipped and trained. Many high officers are angry at the obvious retreat of Russian power, at their shrinking defense budget and manpower, and at the growth of NATO. Their real humiliation came in 1994–96, when Chechen "bandits" beat them. In revenge, in 1999–2000 the army mercilessly demolished Chechnya.

FAILED REFORMER: BORIS YELTSIN

Gorbachev was the first *prezident* (they use the loan word) of the Soviet Union. Boris Yeltsin was the first prezident of the Russian Federation. As with Gorbachev, both Russians and the world initially hailed Boris Yeltsin as the great reformer who would make a prosperous and peaceful Russia. Both disappointed with halfway, half-hearted reforms that ruined the economy and their approval ratings. Neither were convinced democrats; by background and training both acted like Party big shots. In addition to his weak political position, Yeltsin had health and drinking problems.

Born in 1931 (as was Gorbachev) near Sverdlovsk (now Yekaterinburg) in the southern Urals of a poor peasant family, Yeltsin studied engineering and worked in the housing industry in his hometown. Joining the Party in 1961 at age thirty, Yeltsin was promoted to the Central Committee in 1976. Yeltsin drew attention as an energetic manager and reformer, and Gorbachev elevated him to head the Moscow Party organization in 1985 and made him a candidate member of the Politburo. A natural populist, Yeltsin, unlike other Soviet leaders, mingled with the people and denounced the privileges of the nomenklatura. The common people rallied to him.

Then came a bizarre series of events that, if the Soviet system had not been collapsing, would have led to Yeltsin's permanent banishment if not imprisonment. In a 1987 speech to the Central Committee celebrating the Bolshevik Revolution, Yeltsin attacked Party conservatives by name for dragging their feet on reform. For that, he was relieved of his Party posts and demoted to a midlevel government job.

But he bounced back. In the first partly competitive election in 1989, he ran on his populist credentials and easily won election to parliament. Increasingly, Yeltsin criticized Gorbachev for dawdling on reforms. Shifting his attention to the Russian (as opposed to the Soviet) government, Yeltsin won election to the Russian parliament in 1990. Yeltsin sensed that the Soviet Union was doomed, but Russia would survive. In July 1990 Yeltsin pulled another surprise by resigning from the Party. Now he was free to be as critical as he wished. As a non-Communist, he won fair elections to become president of the Russian Federation in 1991. This gave him another edge on Gorbachev, who, Yeltsin pointed out, had never been popularly elected to anything.

In the attempted coup of 1991, Yeltsin turned himself into a hero, standing firm on a tank in front of the Russian parliament. Mocking Gorbachev as an indecisive weakling, Yeltsin pulled the Russian Federation out of the Soviet Union in late 1991, thus collapsing the entire structure. Conservatives think it was a terrible mistake to break up the Soviet Union.

As president, Yeltsin went from bad to worse. Frequently drunk or ill, Yeltsin and his ministers bungled privatization, the economy tanked, corruption soared, and the Russian people turned bitterly against him. Consulting with no one, Yeltsin ordered the crushing of breakaway Chechnya (see page 298). Although reelected in 1996 as the lesser of two evils, during his last years in office Yeltsin's public approval rating was under 5 percent. The Duma tried to impeach him but was too divided to follow through. One of Yeltsin's favorite stunts was, every few months, to blame his prime minister for economic failures and replace him. One of the great questions of today's Russia is whether a personality at the top other than Yeltsin would have done things differently or better.

Veterans, like these in Moscow, wear war medals on their suits, a Soviet custom. Generally conservative, most veterans oppose reforms leading to capitalism. (Michael Roskin)

Key Terms

authoritarian (p. 281)   perestroika (p. 285)   shock therapy (p. 280)
cult of personality (p. 283)   red-brown (p. 280)   totalitarian (p. 281)
mafia (p. 286)

Further Reference

Brown, Archie. *The Gorbachev Factor*. New York: Oxford University Press, 1996.

Dobbs, Michael. *Down with Big Brother: The Fall of the Soviet Empire*. New York: Knopf, 1997.

Fish, M. Steven. *Democracy from Scratch: Opposition and Regime in the New Russian Revolution*. Princeton, NJ: Princeton University Press, 1996.

Handelman, Stephen. *Comrade Criminal: Russia's New Mafiya*. New Haven, CT: Yale University Press, 1995.

Lane, David, and Cameron Ross. *The Transition from Communism to Capitalism: Ruling Elites from Gorbachev to Yeltsin*. New York: St. Martin's, 1999.

Löwenhardt, John, ed. *Party Politics in Post-Communist Russia*. Portland, OR: F. Cass, 1998.

McAuley, Mary. *Russia's Politics of Uncertainty*. New York: Cambridge, 1997.

Murray, Donald. *A Democracy of Despots*. Boulder, CO: Westview, 1996.

Nogee, Joseph L., and R. Judson Mitchell. *Russian Politics: The Struggle for a New Order*. Needham Heights, MA: Allyn & Bacon, 1997.

Shevtsova, Lilia. *Yeltsin's Russia: Myths and Reality*. Washington, D.C.: Brookings, 1999.

Taranovski, Theodore, ed. *Reform in Modern Russian History: Progress or Cycle?* New York: Cambridge University Press, 1995.

White, Stephen, Richard Rose, and Ian McAllister. *How Russia Votes*. Chatham, NJ: Chatham House, 1997.

What Russians Quarrel About

21

Questions to Consider

1. What is to blame for Russia's current troubles?
2. How did political scientists fail to understand what was happening to the Soviet Union?
3. Is it fair to compare Poland's economic "shock therapy" with Russia's?
4. Does Russia now have capitalism? Why or why not?
5. What happened to Russia's economy in 1998? How does it compare to Brazil's economy?
6. What happened in Chechnya? Could similar things occur?
7. What is the "near abroad" and why do Russians want it?
8. What are the difficulties of "middle ways"?

We are interested in why the Soviet Union collapsed not out of purely historical curiosity but to serve as a warning about what can go wrong again. Whatever happened to the Soviet Union can happen to Russia; the problems and resistance Khrushchev, Gorbachev, and Yeltsin faced, Putin still faces. The question is also an important part of current Russian politics.

Why the Soviet Union Collapsed

Many Russians, especially strong nationalists, refuse to believe that the Soviet Union collapsed largely due to the inherent economic inefficiency of socialism. They prefer to blame sinister forces, especially the Americans. It is the functional equivalent of the "stab in the back" myth that so harmed Weimar Germany.

The real explanation is that socialist economies—meaning state-owned and centrally planned, "Communist," if you prefer—work poorly. They do not collapse overnight but over time slowly run down. Under certain circumstances, to be sure, centrally planned economies can grow very fast, as did the Soviet Union under Stalin's Five-Year Plans in the 1930s. A

Key Term

input-output table   A spreadsheet for the economy of an entire nation.

backward country borrowed capitalist technology and threw all its resources, including labor, into giant projects, chiefly into making steel and then making things from steel. From the 1930s through the 1960s, many observers assumed that the Soviet Union would catch up with and eventually overtake the United States in terms of economic production.

But as the Soviet Union tried to catch up, its economy became more complex and harder to control. **Input-output tables** required hundreds of mathematicians to make the thousands of calculations necessary to set the targets of the Soviet economy on a centralized basis. Products were often of poor quality, as only quantity was calculated and required. Designs, often copied from old Western products, were out of date. Efficiency counted for nothing; there was not even a Russian word for efficiency (the closest was effective). Many factories produced things nobody wanted.

The consumer sector, deliberately shortchanged, offered too few products to motivate Soviet workers, who had to wait years for an apartment or a car. Accordingly, workers refrained from exerting themselves. Chuckled workers: "They pretend to pay us, and we pretend to work." Many simply took afternoons off to shop for scarce goods; standing in lines took hours each week. All these factors and many others made Soviets angry with the system. By the early 1970s, the Soviet economy was slowing down, especially in comparison to the surging economies of West Europe and the Pacific Rim.

This by itself, however, was not enough to bring down the system, which could have lumbered on for a long time in shabby decay. The real killer was technological backwardness, especially as it impinged on the Soviet military. The computer age had arrived, and thinking machines were spreading fast into Western businesses, research labs, and military systems. The Soviets could not nearly keep up in computerization, and the Soviet military knew what that meant: getting beat. (See the box on Marshal Ogarkov in Chapter 20, page 288.) With U.S. President Ronald Reagan came an even worse technological menace: a "Star Wars" shield in space that would make America invulnerable. An important sector of the Soviet military thus turned to economic and technological reform out of the fear of falling behind.

Many thinking Soviet Party people, especially younger ones, knew by the 1980s that economic reforms were necessary and were itching for someone like Gorbachev to lead the way. But by themselves, they could not prevail against the conservative forces of managers and *apparatchiki*, many of whose jobs were at stake. It took, I believe, the high-tech sections of the armed forces to ally themselves with Gorbachev and give the green light to economic reforms in the expectation that these would lead to military technology to equal the Americans.

Oil played a roller-coaster role in first keeping afloat and then sinking the Soviet economy. The rapid increase in oil prices in the 1970s meant that Soviet petroleum exports—at that time the USSR was the world's biggest oil producer and exporter—could for a time pay for Soviet imports of food and technology. They became too dependent on oil exports. Then the sharp fall in world oil prices greatly harmed the Soviet and Russian economy. The 1999 upturn in world oil prices gave President Putin valuable breathing room.

How to Reform?

At no time did Mikhail Gorbachev adopt a thoroughgoing plan of economic reform. His advisors presented him with several, each bolder than the previous, but he never made them policy. He never wanted capitalism; instead, he sought a middle path or "third way" between

KEY CONCEPTS

LACKING FACTS, THEY THEORIZED

The most stupendous change of the late twentieth century took political scientists by surprise. Why did we fail to anticipate—notice that I'm not asking for prediction—the collapse of the Soviet Union? Only a handful of historians and economists sounded any warnings. Political scientists tended to see more of the same, with some reforms.

Why did political scientists do so badly? I can see at least six mental blocks that we built for ourselves, mostly by reading each others' books and articles.

1. *Lousy Empirical Data:* Many aspects of the Soviet system were closely held secrets; outsiders had to piece together flimsy indicators and infer how things worked. They filled the informational vacuum with theory, much of it misleading. In Yugoslavia, by way of contrast, researchers could get accurate data and candid interviews. As early as the 1960s some saw cracks in the Yugoslav federation. Little theory came out of studies of Yugoslavia, as researchers didn't need to theorize; they had facts. Lacking facts, Soviet specialists theorized. The moral: We are only as good as our data.

2. *Systems Theory:* Since at least the 1960s, political scientists had been trained to see all countries as "political systems" that have varying structures but perform the same functions. Whenever the system is thrown off balance, it always corrects itself, by new governments, parties, or reforms. Systems were thus presumed to be highly durable, possibly immortal. Systems theorists could simply not envision system collapse.

3. *Anti-Anticommunism:* The anticommunist hysteria of the early Cold War years, especially McCarthyism, was so primitive that it persuaded some thinkers to give Communist systems the benefit of the doubt. Specialists tended to accept Communist systems as givens (much like the systems theorists) and to conduct detailed studies of how the system worked. Anyone who suggested Communist systems were inherently flawed and doomed was read out of the profession as speculative, right wing, and unscholarly.

4. *Undervaluing Economics:* Many Soviet specialists paid little attention to economics; they assumed politics dominated economics. (Economists assume the opposite.) Few appreciated that a nation's economy can deteriorate only so far before it drags the entire country down with it. A few economists issued such warnings on the USSR years in advance, but political scientists largely ignored them.

5. *System Reformability:* Political scientists supposed Soviet problems could be fixed with a few reforms. (This too derives from systems theorists.) If the system has an economic or structural problem, it will correct it, was the bland assumption. Eventually, some thought, the Soviet system would reform itself into a sort of social-democratic welfare state. The brittleness of the Soviet system occurred to few.

6. *Fixation on Personalities:* Because reforms are necessary, they will be carried out; they just need the right personality to get things moving. Ah! Here comes Gorbachev, the man both we and Russian liberals have been waiting for. His reforms will produce a much nicer Soviet Union. In this way, we read into Gorbachev heroic and reformist qualities he never had. Clueless would be more like it.

Apartment houses in Russia are prefabricated and small. There is a terrible housing shortage, so flats like these in a Moscow suburb are eagerly sought. (Michael Roskin)

capitalism and socialism. Gorbachev hesitated and changed his mind more or less annually, one year for economic reform, the next year against. Later, he admitted several mistakes. First, he now says, he should have liberalized agriculture, as the Chinese did under Deng (see Chapter 27). Instead, Gorbachev tried a couple of timid steps he inherited from his mentor, the late Andropov: "intensification" and an antialcohol campaign. Both failed.

When it came to real reforms, Gorbachev choked, both out of fear for the consequences and in the face of massive resistance by conservative Soviet forces. Gorbachev finally freed most prices, but he did not privatize industry. The result was far too many rubles chasing too few goods: inflation. Everyone wanted dollars as the ruble dwindled in value. Worried citizens muttered that things could not go on like this. It was against this background that Gorbachev's own cabinet plotted a coup in 1991. Before the year ended, the Soviet Union was dissolved, Gorbachev was a private citizen, and Yeltsin was president of the Russian Federation. At last, reform started looking serious, but Yeltsin too faced opposition from conservative forces.

Can Russia Now Reform?

Gorbachev never restructured the Soviet economy. Yeltsin did not fully restructure the Russian economy. Are we asking for the impossible? You can rapidly reform a socialist economy. Poland initiated a "shock therapy" at the beginning of 1991 and within two years had gone through the worst of its inflation and industrial decline to emerge as the fastest growing economy of Europe.

Yeltsin's first prime minister (until late 1992) and later finance minister, the dynamic reformer Yegor Gaidar, tried to induce shock therapy as he privatized the large, obsolete industrial enterprises the Communists had built. Terribly inefficient and overstaffed and with no concern for consumer needs, many actually *subtracted* value from the raw materials they processed. But these industries were the wealth and power of the bureaucrats and *apparatchiks* who took them over and gave employment for those who listlessly worked in them. Accordingly, they were able to pressure Moscow to keep the subsidies flowing. In any rational system, they would have been declared bankrupt immediately. But you can't throw millions of people out of work all at once, protested many Russians.

Key Term

asset-stripping   Selling off a firm's property and the raw materials it controls for short-term profit.

Privatization in Russia (and some other ex-Communist lands) was carried out badly. A handful of clever operators bought up factories and raw materials cheap and turned themselves into a new class of capitalists. Many of these industries still get government subsidies (such as cheap energy), which allows the new owners to reap enormous profits as they export oil, natural gas, and minerals. Much of the profit does not return to Russia, though; it goes into foreign banks, a pattern typical of South America. Because this capital is not recycled back into the Russian economy, the rest of the economy declines, making poor people poorer. Capitalism in Russia has so far not worked like capitalism elsewhere; it has turned into **asset-stripping**, which is no basis for the country's long-term future.

For a while, though, the economy seemed to stabilize on new, sounder footing. Chernomyrdin, former head of the Soviet gas industry, as we discussed in the previous chapter, carried on with some reforms in order to meet IMF limits on budget deficits. Over two years, Gaidar, Chernomyrdin, and privatization minister Anatoly Chubais achieved a lot. Most of Russia's state-owned enterprises were privatized, and inflation was down. In 1997, the economy stopped declining and grew a little (0.8 percent). Many people and firms were making goods and money but concealing them to avoid taxes and payoffs to the mafia. State-owned industrial production was down, but consumption of goods, like refrigerators and television sets, was

KEY CONCEPTS

THE TERMINOLOGY OF ECONOMIC REFORM

- **liberalize** Cutting prices free to find their own level. Instead of using centrally designated prices, businesses may charge whatever they can get on the free market (thus sometimes called to "marketize").
- **privatize** Putting state-owned enterprises and land in private hands by selling them to local investors, foreign investors, workers, or the citizenry at large through vouchers. In Russia, only a few benefitted.
- **shock therapy** Liberalizing and privatizing simultaneously and rapidly. This proved successful in Central Europe but not in the ex-Soviet Union.
- **currency convertibility** The ending of

fake, imposed exchange rates by letting the local currency be exchanged for foreign currency at whatever rate the market sets. Convertibility makes it impossible to disguise inflation.
- **stabilization** Controlling the amount of currency in circulation, both by limiting the printing of money and by denying government loans to industry, so as to slow inflation and make currency worth fairly predictable.
- **tradeoff** The choice between inflation and unemployment, allowing one to rise in order to keep the other low. Most ex-Soviet type economies elect to let inflation roar in order to hold down unemployment.

Traveling Salesmen: These young Russians make a niche in the economy by buying Russian medicines (in the big bags) and selling them in outdoor markets in Sofia, Bulgaria. After a few days at the market, they return home for more, bribing their way across borders. They showed me how to catch a train from Romania to Bulgaria without a ticket: "Just bribe the conductor," they shrugged, "It's a Russian train." (Michael Roskin)

up. Many factories making military equipment or things nobody wanted closed. Meanwhile, private industry—now producing some three-fourths of Russia's GDP—is undercounted and wishes to remain so.

Then, in August 1998, the bottom fell out. Some observers saw trouble coming well in advance, in the area of **public finances**. Russia collects less than half the taxes it is supposed to. (New York City collects more in taxes than all of Russia.) Everyone cheat on taxes. As a result, the budget went dangerously into deficit, so the Yeltsin government simply printed more money. Banks—and anyone in Russia can open a bank—were unregulated and made unsecured loans to friends. Chief monetary instrument of Russian banks: U.S. $100 bills, some of them counterfeit. Knowing the perils of the Russian economy, Russian oligarchs have anywhere from $150 billion to $350 billion in **flight capital** offshore. Eventually, this Brazilian-type system (see Chapter 28) had to crash. When it did, the ruble lost some three-quarters of its value in relation to **hard currencies**. Many banks closed, leaving depositors with nothing. Russia's fledgling stock markets dived. Industries just getting on their feet collapsed. Russia **defaulted** on its loans (biggest losers: German banks, with over $30 billion loaned to Russia) and had to beg for new credit. Badly burned, foreign investors stayed out of Russia.

Russians felt angry and betrayed. We had told them that the free market is the path to prosperity, but it brought them only misery. A third now fell below the official (very low) poverty line. Actually, Russia had never fully implemented a functioning market system. Much Western advice was ignored. There were too many government subsidies and tax breaks and too few rules and regulations that keep a market economy steady. Money, always a weak point with Russians (see page 276), was not treated as an autonomous factor with important signaling functions. It was just something you printed. Even with "the most expensive economic education in history" (in the words of one Russian reformer), Russia's defective system has still not been reformed.

Before the 1998 collapse, some people got rich fast while ordinary workers

Key Terms

public finances What a government takes in, what it spends, and how it makes up the difference.

flight capital Money the owner sends out of the country for fear of losing it.

hard currency The noninflating, recognized currencies used in international dealings, such as dollars and deutsche Marks.

default Not being able to pay back a loan.

and their families went hungry. Having long been taught by the Communists that equality of material living standards is good and just, Russians witnessed the explosive growth of inequality. (Income inequality in Russia is now greater than in the United States.) Some *biznesmeny* and mafiosi (the two words are linked in the Russian mind) enjoyed new wealth while most Russians lived worse than ever. Mercifully, by 2000 there were signs of an economic turnaround, helped by the runup in world oil prices.

Recover the Lost Republics?

So far, we have been talking about the complex Russian Federation, a difficult situation itself. But what of the non-Russian republics that departed from the Soviet Union, what Russians call the **near abroad**? Most of them had been incorporated into the tsarist empire, and many Russians still think of them as belonging to Russia. They make no secret of their desire to restore the Russian empire. This feeling is especially prominent in the Russian army, which still has troops in most of the ex-Soviet republics. By hook or by crook, conservative nationalists intend to get back the old Soviet borders. Even the more liberal element envisions a Russian sphere of influence over the old republics.

This will be difficult. Local Communist elites at the republic level were never happy with subservience to Moscow. They felt that central control limited their power and possibilities of

GEOGRAPHY

WILL RUSSIA FALL APART?

Russia is an extreme example of center-periphery tensions, one that could lead to the breakup of the Russian Federation. As starvation loomed and Russia's eighty-nine republics and regions got no help from Moscow, many ignored the center and set up their own economic systems, with price controls, limits on "exports" to other parts of Russia, and even barter systems. Some talk about introducing their own currency. Many regions refuse to pay taxes to Moscow.

Many of the republics are authoritarian dictatorships where opposition candidates or media are not tolerated. Moscow is too weak to crack down on these minidespots. Local generals are often beholden to republic or regional governments for salaries and food for the troops. Several of these republics, especially in the Caucasus, are mostly Muslim and are undergoing an Islamic reawakening, which pushes them toward seeking independence, like Chechnya. The mixture of economic decline, local despotism, and Islam is explosive, and a series of Chechnyas is possible.

Just as the Soviet Union fell apart, so could the Russian Federation. Increasingly, as the economy declines, peoples in the outlying regions see less and less reason to stay part of the federation. Many distinct ethnic groups claim sovereign rights of republics; a few have even declared their independence. Since they are landlocked, however, Moscow can ultimately control them. If the Pacific Maritime region of Russia, on the other hand, should decide that its best deal is independence plus massive Japanese investment, Moscow could lose a huge, rich chunk of its territory. If that happens, we could see civil war.

THE TWO CHECHEN WARS

There were two bloody wars over the small Caucasian republic of Chechnya. The first, 1994–96, Chechen rebels won; the second, 1999–2000, the Russians won. The Caucasus, a crazy quilt of distinct nationalities, mostly Muslim, was subdued by tsarist forces only in the nineteenth century. The Muslim Chechens always hated being ruled by Russians and revolted from time to time. The Russians in turn despise Chechens as bandits. In 1944, Stalin accused the Chechens of being pro-German and brutally exiled them to Kazakhstan.

One Chechen, Jokar Dudayev, became a general in the Soviet air force. Assigned to an Estonian airbase in the 1980s, Dudayev came to sympathize with the Estonians, who, like Chechens, hated Russian rule. Dudayev blocked the landing of Soviet troops in early 1991, helping Estonia win independence. He then retired, won an election in Chechnya, and proclaimed his country's independence as the Soviet Union broke up in late 1991. But Chechnya, unlike Estonia, had never been a "union republic"; it was part of the Russian Federation, and Moscow feared its departure would set an example for dozens of other restive regions inside Russia. Chechnya also became the center for much crime, including drugs, mafia, and wholesale kidnappings.

Yeltsin in late 1994—with no discussion among military professionals, parliamentary debate, or publicity—gave the order to quickly crush Chechen independence. But the military campaign stalled; the Russian army was pathetic, and Chechens fought boldly and tenaciously. Some 80,000, mostly civilians, were brutally killed, and the capital, Grozny, was shelled into ruin.

Most Russians, even military officers, hated the war; partly because of it, Yeltsin's popularity plummeted. Ex-General Lebed worked out a peace with Chechen fighters in 1996, leaving them an undefined autonomy. The situation was inherently unstable.

In 1999, Chechen-led Muslim fundamentalists tried to take over neighboring Dagestan. Moscow retaliated sharply, pursuing the guerrillas back into Chechnya. In Russian cities, several apartment houses were blown up, killing nearly 300. Moscow immediately blamed Chechen terrorists and launched a major invasion of Chechnya. This time the Russian army was in much better shape, and the Russian people were behind them. Putin's tough stance boosted his popularity. Fighting was fierce, and the war took longer than Moscow foresaw. Grozny was again shelled, and tens of thousands of Chechens fled.

Although many foreign leaders condemned the horror, no one offered a plan to solve it and none dreamed of intervening. Cutting or delaying international loans was the only leverage the outside world had. Putin made clear that Chechnya was part of Russia and that Russia had every right to wipe out terrorism. Yeltsin bluntly reminded Washington that Russia still had a big nuclear arsenal. Chechnya marked the end of Western good will to Russia and the renewal of fears that Russia was abandoning democracy for authoritarianism.

graft and corruption. On purely ethnic grounds, most Soviet nationalities did not like the Russians, whom they saw as a colonial, or occupying, power. And the Russians returned the favor, with attitudes toward Muslim and other Asian peoples that can only be called racist.

In many ex-Soviet republics, the "new" leaders are old Party big shots, and rule by a Party elite continues uninterrupted and intact. In Central Asia, some of these leaders are descended from pre-Soviet elites. Not counting the Baltic republics, Russia had the most progressive and most reform-minded leadership. Other republics lagged behind. A particularly tragic example is Ukraine, potentially rich and European, whose ex-Communist leaders instituted no economic reform program. The result was a hyperinflation that made the Russian economy look good.

One crucial fact in Russian thinking are the 25 million ethnic Russians who live in the near abroad. (The term does not refer to the former satellites of East Europe, such as Poland or Hungary.) Some Russians in these republics are made to feel unwanted and even threatened. Any outright violence against these Russians, however, provokes the Russian army, which still has units stationed in other republics. In such situations, Russians feel their army has a right and duty to come to the rescue. This could someday be used as an excuse to seize all or part of neighboring republics.

Recovery of the lost republics could come about by more subtle means as well: economics. As the economies of many other republics kept plunging downward, some of them turned desperately to Moscow for help. Under the banner of the Commonwealth of Independent States, Moscow delivers some aid (for example, a good deal on oil and natural gas) but in return gets trade concessions and general obedience. Moscow successfully used this approach on Belarus—which now uses the Russian ruble as currency—and seems to be trying it on Ukraine.

GEOGRAPHY

YUGOSLAVIA: A MINIATURE SOVIET UNION?

The former multiethnic Balkan federal system of Yugoslavia bears some resemblance to the ex-Soviet Union. Both countries had a Slavic core nationality: Russians in the Soviet Union and Serbs in Yugoslavia. Serbs and Russians are both of the Eastern Orthodox Christian tradition and use the Cyrillic alphabet. Both define themselves as the founders and guarantors of their respective nations. They regard breakaway republics as traitors to the nation.

The other nationalities resent this overbearing attitude. In each country an advanced northwest (the Baltic republics in the Soviet Union and Slovenia in Yugoslavia) grew tired of being held back by the less-developed core nationality, which economically drained the advanced area. Interestingly, the Baltics and Slovenia declared their independence first.

The second largest nationality in each country is also Slavic but with a distinctive culture and resentments at being bossed by the center; thus, Ukraine and Croatia quickly broke away. In the south, feisty Muslim nationalities demand greater autonomy and fight neighboring Christian nationalities (the Azeris against the Armenians and the Bosnian Muslims and Kosovar Albanians against the Serbs). In most of the newly independent republics in both the ex-Soviet Union and ex-Yugoslavia, the "new" leaders had been local Communist bosses prior to independence.

A final touch: Russians and Serbs, respectively, formed the bulk of the officer corps of the old Soviet and Yugoslav armies and now of the Russian and Serbian armies. The top officers are conservative and dedicated to keeping their countries intact. They are not adverse to using force to do so. In 1991, both armies started intervening directly in politics. The key difference so far is that conservative Communists took over in Belgrade and, with the army's general staff in agreement, attempted to hold Yugoslavia together by force. When that quickly failed, they turned to building a "Greater Serbia" by military conquest, coupled with "ethnic cleansing." In the ex-Soviet Union, the death toll has not been as large, but it too experienced wars in the Caucasus region.

Key Term

middle way   Supposed
blend of capitalism and
socialism; also called "third
way."

A tricky approach appeared in Georgia, which itself is home to many non-Georgian nationalities. The Muslim Abkhazians of western Georgia broke away by force of arms, many of them supplied quietly by the Russian army. Georgia had originally refused to join the CIS in 1991 but, faced with military defeat, did so in 1994. Then the Russians changed sides and began supporting Georgia with arms and troops. They called it "peacekeeping," but it was more like a protection racket.

Should U.S. citizens criticize Russians for wishing to recover the near abroad? What did President Lincoln do when faced with the breakup of the Union? Americans should understand holding unions together. And hasn't West Europe turned into the EU with Germany as its economic powerhouse? If Moscow can build a CIS similar to the EU by economic means, it should not bother us, provided the trade deals are voluntary. But if Russia tries to regain the lost republics by military force, it will mean that a dangerous crowd has taken over in the Kremlin.

A Middle Way for Socialism?

Putin's ultimate problem (inherited from his predecessors) was that he thought there was a **middle way** between a centrally planned socialist economy and a free-market economy. Reforms, some argue, can blend a market economy with a socialist economy. They do it in Sweden, don't they? (No, they don't. See box below.) Some Russians think they can reserve the "commanding heights" of heavy industry for the state while permitting small enterprises to return to the free market. This is what Lenin did under the NEP in the early 1920s, and the NEP was frequently

COMPARISON

SCANDINAVIAN-TYPE SOCIALISM FOR RUSSIA?

Confusion surrounds the term "socialism." Many Russians and East Europeans now tell you they no longer know what the word means. Some call the welfare states of Scandinavia "socialist" because freely elected Social Democratic governments have gradually introduced elaborate medical, unemployment, educational, housing, and other programs to lift up the lower rungs of society: "cradle-to-grave welfare." These Social Democratic parties started out Marxist but all of them shed it. They are all based on large labor-union federations. The aim of these parties is to wipe out poverty without resorting to coercion or state control.

And here's where Scandinavian "welfarism" differs sharply from Communist-style socialism. The Scandinavian lands have little nationalized industry, and what was nationalized was done so for nonideological reasons (for example, to hold down unemployment). The bulk of the economy is private and capitalist. Swedish managers especially developed a ferocious reputation for efficient, money-making plant operation. Taxes, to be sure, are high, but the economy is otherwise free.

In sum, Scandinavia is not socialist; it's a variation on capitalism called "welfarism." If you wish to call it "socialism," of course, you may. But please note that it was developed after and on top of Scandinavia's capitalist industrial base. First came capitalism, then came welfare. It is doubtful if the order can be reversed or if they can be built simultaneously.

COMPARISON

THE HORROR OF RUSSIAN HEALTH

Russian health standards illustrate why economic growth is imperative. Officially, the Russian **infant mortality rate** was 25, but many thought it was closer to 33. Either figure is much worse than West Europe. Expectant mothers are poorly nourished and so are their babies, 60 percent of whom suffer protein deficiency. There have been isolated reports of children starving to death. Health care is supposed to be free, but no public money is available so medical personnel must be bribed to deliver services.

Under such circumstances, it is easy to understand why most Russian families have only one child. In 1989, Russian women bore 2.17 children, a little above the replacement rate; ten years later it was down to 1.1, well below replacement. Meanwhile, the Russian death rate climbs; life expectancy of adult men dropped to fifty-eight years, lower than in much of the Third World. Result: Russia's population shrinks by a million a year.

One of the causes of death is prodigious alcohol consumption (some of it poisonous homebrew) leading to industrial accidents. Heroin addiction and AIDS cases areexploding. Russian environmental poisoning, both chemical and nuclear, is among the world's worst, and environmentally caused diseases are common. (Russia's closest rivals: East Europe.) Even the air in industrial cities is dangerous. "To live longer," said one official, "we should breathe less." Many factories just dumped toxic and nuclear wastes into shallow landfills. Even once-pristine Lake Baikal, long revered as a symbol of Mother Russia, is getting polluted. The declining health situation feeds extreme nationalist politics.

mentioned as a model by Gorbachevites. But the NEP was inherently flawed and was running down in the late 1920s when Stalin dropped it in favor of forced industrialization.

No one has yet found a way to combine capitalism and socialism on a long-term, stable basis. For a while, such a combination sometimes seems to work. Then the private sector starts bumping into the restricted, slow-moving state sector. The private sector needs raw materials, labor, infrastructure, and transportation on a flexible, ever-changing basis. The state sector, still run by a central plan, can't possibly deliver and has no incentive to. If you allow state enterprises to enter the private-sector market, you are gradually desocializing the economy. It gets more efficient but less socialist. Eventually, you come to a point where you must either bury the socialist sector as a bad experiment or curb and recontrol the private sector. The mix won't hold steady; you must go one way or the other. China is caught up in this dilemma.

Many Russians, including Putin, still think they can find a middle way that is uniquely Russian. Experience suggests that if they try to build a middle way, it will lead to an unstable, declining system with high inflation.

Which Way Russia?

Observers of Russia split into two camps—optimists and pessimists. Pessimists see a botched job. Capitalism has not taken root; instead, a new class of oligarchs has simply looted the state enterprises and stashed

Key Term

infant mortality rate
Number of live newborns who die in their first year, per thousand; a standard measure of a nation's health.

the money abroad. Corruption and lawlessness have led to a series of linkups between authorities (including the police) and mafias. The average Russian lives worse than ever. The unity of the country is eroding as provincial ex-Party bosses set up their own criminal fiefdoms. Yeltsin was a catastrophe; he presided over a deepening mess with no program to reverse the decay. Eventually, either Russia will collapse or be taken over by an authoritarian.

The optimists point out that most of Russia's economy is private and, after the collapse of 1998, is showing signs of recovery. It has shifted from the looting of materials and importation of consumer goods to production, a healthy sign. Even if privatization was chaotic and crooked, the new class of owners has a stake in preserving a nonsocialist system. Reasonably free and fair elections have been held in which most Russians rejected both Communists and extreme nationalists. Yeltsin was not perfect but was better than any alternative available at the time. Democracy and a free market are now being built in Russia, although it may take a few years.

Which way will Russia go? Will a friendly, democratic Russia be our trading partner, or will we return to hostility? Many Russians blame America for their decline. True, U.S. economists gave advice that overlooked the lack of cultural and institutional bases for capitalism in Russia, assuming that Russia was a big Poland. But Russia never really swept out the old system.

Hostile as Russia may become, it is too poor and too weak to stand up to the West. Whatever regime rules in Moscow will have to bend to external pressures. To attract foreign investment, Russia must have rule of law. To get major loans it must adhere to austere IMF limits on budget deficits. With NATO expanded eastward and Russia's military terribly weak, Moscow

GEOGRAPHY

FEAR OF INVASION

Russians are unhappy about their former Central European satellites—Poland, the Czech Republic, Hungary—joining NATO in 1999. Starting under the tsars but reemphasized by Stalin during and after World War II, it became an article of Kremlin faith that Russia needed Eastern Europe as a defensive shield against attack from the west. There have indeed been many such invasions; the Nazi invasion of 1941 was the most recent. Until Gorbachev, all Soviet leaders accepted this argument, as did all Soviet generals. To prevent East Europe's departure from the Soviet orbit, Khrushchev crushed the 1956 Hungarian uprising and Brezhnev crushed the 1968 Prague Spring. Both came close to invading Poland.

But East Europe was a major economic and military drain on the Soviet Union, and it blocked improved relations with the West. By 1989, Gorbachev had decided to no longer support the Communist regimes of East Europe, and the regimes quickly fell. Central Europe quickly became democratic with free markets. Russia's strategic situation actually improved, for the end of the Cold War removed the military threat from the West. NATO, with declining defense budgets and small armies, poses no danger. Costs to Russia, in garrison troops and subsidized trade deals, have been drastically cut. Instead of selling Russian gas and oil at sweetheart prices to their satellites, Russia can get world-market prices for them, and in hard currency. Potentially, Russia is now open for trade with and investment from the West, the ticket to prosperity. Still, many Russian conservatives argue that Gorbachev gave away Russia's defensive shield; a few want it back. The very old fear of invasion from the West played into the hands of demagogic Russian politicians.

must be strategically very cautious; few fear them any more. No, the future will not duplicate the past. As Marx said: "History repeats itself, the first time as tragedy, the second time as farce."

Is Russia now a democracy? "Rough democracy" may be the best grade we can give it. There is competition, but elections are far from spotless. Institutions are unbalanced, the presidency too powerful and the legislature too weak. Corruption dominates everything. A democratic sprit of tolerance and fair play is absent. The whole thing could slide into authoritarianism.

Can Russians eventually govern themselves in a moderate, democratic fashion? They can, but it will take awhile. Russians aren't genetically authoritarian. Earlier in the twentieth century Germans and Spaniards were deemed unfit for self-government, but now they're practicing democracy as well as any Europeans. I believe Russia is going to make it, although there may be some reversals on the road to democracy and a market economy. What the Japanese have done the Russians can do. Let us now turn to this country of amazing adaptability and growth.

Key Terms

asset-stripping (p. 295)	input-output table (p. 292)
default (p. 296)	middle way (p. 300)
flight capital (p. 296)	near abroad (p. 297)
hard currency (p. 296)	public finances (p. 296)
infant mortality rate (p. 301)	

Further Reference

Allensworth, Wayne. *The Russian Question: Nationalism, Modernization, and Post-Communist Russia.* Lanham, MD: Rowman & Littlefield, 1998.

Åslund, Anders, and Martha Brill Olcott, eds. *Russia After Communism.* Washington, D.C.: Carnegie Endowment, 1999.

Cox, Michael, ed. *Rethinking the Soviet Collapse: Sovietology, the Death of Communism and the New Russia.* New York: Pinter, 1998.

Ellman, Michael, and Vladimir Kontorovich, eds. *The Destruction of the Soviet Economic System: An Insiders' History.* Armonk, NY: M. E. Sharpe, 1998.

Lieven, Anatol. *Chechnya: Tombstone of Russian Power.* New Haven, CT: Yale University Press, 1999.

Reddaway, Peter, and Dmitri Glinski. *The Tragedy of Russia's Reforms: Market Bolshevism against Democracy.* Herndon, VA: U.S. Institute of Peace, 2000.

Shlapentokh, Vladimir, Roman Levita, and Mikhail Loiberg. *From Submission to Rebellion: The Provinces Versus the Center in Russia.* Boulder, CO: Westview, 1997.

Solnick, Steven. *Stealing the State: Control and Collapse in Soviet Institutions.* Cambridge, MA: Harvard University Press, 1998.

Strayer, Robert. *Why Did the Soviet Union Collapse? Understanding Historical Change.* Armonk, NY: M. E. Sharpe, 1998.

Suraska, Wisla. *How the Soviet Union Disappeared: An Essay on the Causes of Dissolution.* Durham, NC: Duke University Press, 1998.

Woodruff, David M. *Money Unmade: Barter and the Fate of Russian Capitalism.* Ithaca, NY: Cornell University Press, 1999.

PART V

Key Websites

The Constitution of Japan   This site features the entire constitution of Japan: Preamble; Chapter I—The Emperor; Chapter II—Renunciation of War; Chapter III—Rights and Duties of the People; Chapter IV—The Diet; Chapter V—The Cabinet; Chapter VI—The Judiciary; Chapter VII—Finance; Chapter VIII—Local Self-Government; Chapter IX—Amendments; Chapter X—Supreme Law; and Chapter XI—Supplementary Provisions.
http://www2.gol.com/users/michaelo/Jcon.index.html

Japanese Customs   This site offers information on Japanese customs: traveling customs; business customs; workplace customs; dining customs; and customs in attire, manners, and non-verbal communication.
http://www.shinnova.com/part/99-japa/abj13-e.htm

The National Diet of Japan: House of Councillors   This site provides election information and information about the different political parties in Japan, with links to each party's website. Some of the parties included are the following: the Liberal Democratic Party, the Social Democratic Party, the New Party, Sakigake, the New Frontier Party, the Japanese Communist Party, and the Democratic Party of Japan (Minshuto).
http://kanzaki.com/jinfo/PoliticalParties.html

Prime Minister Keizo Obuchi   This is the official website of the prime minister. The site includes an overview of the prime minister's action plan, political strategies, statements, speeches, and economic strategies, as well as a transcript of the press conference held at the closing of the 142nd session of the Diet.
http://www.kantei.go.jp/foreign/index-e.html

Kochi City: Leaders of the Modern Period   During a time of intense ideological struggle and social upheaval, some remarkable men went about the business of molding a new nation through their industry, study, and service. The influential people featured in this website represent the age since the Meiji Restoration, and they are Kochi's outstanding contribution to modern Japan.
http://www.city.kochi.kochi.jp/ijin/kcd_modfig.htm

Asahi News   This frequently updated site features stories from Japan's top daily, the *Asahi Shimbun*, in English (or Japanese, if you prefer).
http://www.asahi.com/english/asahi/index.html

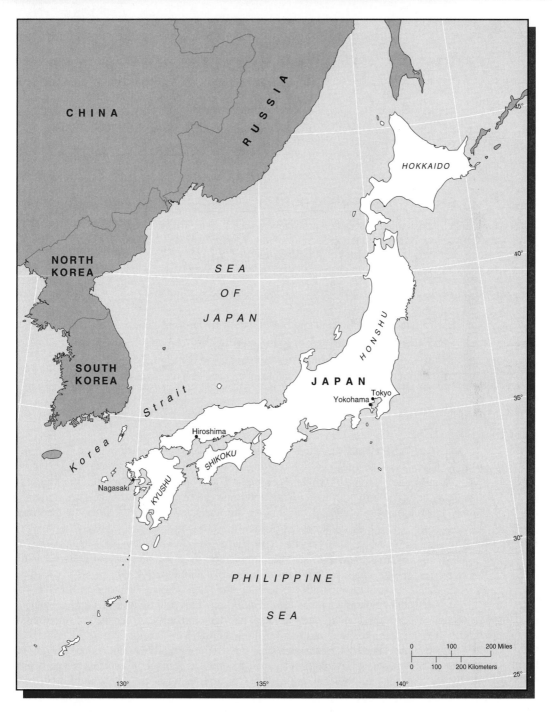

CHINA

RUSSIA

NORTH
KOREA

SOUTH
KOREA

Korea Strait

SEA

OF

JAPAN

HOKKAIDO

HONSHU

JAPAN

Tokyo
Yokohama

Hiroshima

SHIKOKU

KYUSHU

Nagasaki

PHILIPPINE

SEA

45°

40°

35°

30°

25°

130°   135°   140°

0   100   200 Miles

0   100   200 Kilometers

Japan:
The Impact of the Past

22

Questions to Consider

1. If geography is an important factor, why haven't the histories of Britain and Japan been more alike?
2. Was feudalism in Japan longer than in Europe?
3. Was the Tokugawa policy of keeping Japan isolated wise?
4. How were the Meiji reforms a logical outcome of Japan's opening by Perry?
5. What were the *zaibatsu* and how did they modernize Japan?
6. In conquering Asia, was Japan just copying the West?
7. Could Japanese-style modernization be copied elsewhere?
8. Was a U.S.-Japan war inevitable? What could have headed it off?

As with other countries, geography helps explain Japanese history, politics, and culture. Japan was close enough to China to be heavily influenced by Chinese culture but far enough away to resist Chinese conquest. The rough mountainous terrain of most of Japan and division into four main islands and hundreds of small islands made Japan hard to unify. Japan has little **arable** land, much of it historically devoted to rice, a crop so important it took on religious significance over the centuries.

The Japanese like to see themselves as a pure-blooded single tribe, but they are the descendants of immigrants from various parts of the Pacific Rim, especially from the Korean peninsula. The Japanese language has the same grammatical patterns as Korean, and some scholars even suggest that the imperial family may be of Korean origin. This finding is hotly controversial, as Japanese see Koreans as racial inferiors. In truth, both Japan and Korea drew much of their culture from classic China, a civilization so magnificent that it held most of Asia in awe. One can see the clear Chinese influence today in the pictographic writing of Japan and Korea, the architecture, ancient weapons, and the philosophical influence of **Confucianism** (see page 381) and **Buddhism**.

The early Japanese gradually pushed back the original inhabitants of the islands, whom they called *Ainu*, until only a handful now remain on the

Key Terms

arable Useable for agriculture.

Confucianism Chinese philosophy of social and political stability based on family, hierarchy, and perfection of manners.

Buddhism Asian religion that seeks enlightenment through meditation and cessation of desire.

northernmost island of Hokaido. In doing this, Japanese developed a warrior ethos that lasted for millennia. The Japanese were undisturbed on their islands for many centuries, and this allowed their culture and social structure to evolve away from the Chinese model. What came in from China was often accepted, but bent and trimmed to suit Japanese needs. Buddhism and Confucianism arrived in Japan in the sixth century from China along with Chinese writing, but all soon took on Japanese characteristics. This pattern of borrowing ideas and usages but changing them reappeared more recently in Japan's history.

Key Term

Shinto Japan's original religion; the worship of nature, of one's ancestors, and of Japan.

The name Japanese gave to their land, *Nihon* ("sun origin") reflects their mythology that all Japanese are descended from the Sun Goddess. An alternative and more elegant pronunciation of the characters "sun" and "origin" is *Nippon*, a name that was originally used in the West for Japan but has since died out. Marco Polo seems to have recorded the Mongol name *Zipangu*, which among Westerners turned into Japan.

In 1274 and 1281, Japan trembled when the Mongol emperor of China, Kublai Khan, who controlled much of Asia, sent invasion fleets against Japan. Japanese warriors fought the Mongols to a standstill and both times the invasion fleets were hit by typhoons and were wrecked or withdrew. The Japanese thus claim that a "divine wind" (*kamikaze*), plus the fighting ability of their samurai, saved Japan. The Japanese nobility treasured and celebrated an image of themselves as a superior warrior race until 1945.

Japanese Feudalism

One of the strongest patterns of Japanese history is its long domination by clans and their leaders. According to Japanese tradition (still practiced in the **Shinto** faith), Jimmu, a descendant of the sun goddess, founded the Land of the Rising Sun in 660 B.C. Myth aside, a kingly court appeared in Yamato in the third century A.D. and by the seventh century had largely unified central Japan on the Chinese imperial model, bolstered by the Confucianism and complete with a *tenno* (emperor). The forms of Chinese centralized rule took hold, but not the substance. Under the surface, the clans exercised their control. The emperors' powers were soon usurped by powerful clan chiefs, who could make or break figurehead emperors and hold them prisoner in the palace.

As we discussed in connection with Britain, feudalism is a pattern that tends to develop spontaneously as central authority breaks down. This breakdown occurred in Japan from the ninth to the twelfth centuries and led to seven centuries of feudalism, ending only in the nineteenth century. China overcame feudalism early to become a bureaucratic empire. England overcame feudalism slowly and in a way that set up limited, constitutional government. France overcame feudalism by means of absolutism. Japan, it has been argued, was feudal so long and so deeply that feudal characteristics are still powerful in Japanese politics

The essence of feudalism is power diffused and quarreled over among several aristocratic lords, each of whom has many warrior-helpers, who become the noble or knightly class. Typically, only these men are allowed to bear arms in normal times. They subscribe to a knightly code—in Japan, *bushido*, the way of the *bushi* (warriors)—that turns obedience and honor into religious virtues and places knights at a higher social level.

The sure sign of feudalism is castles, as each lord needs a secure base from which to rule his lands and resist infringements from other lords and from the king or emperor. Japan has many

COMPARISON

THE UNIQUENESS TRAP

The key question for Japan is whether it is a country like other countries or something unique. Many Japanese and some foreign observers would like outsiders to believe that the Japanese are a race and society like no other, sort of a tribe or large family. Indeed, during World War II, Japanese propagandists cultivated this image for domestic consumption. More recently, some have used this image to explain Japan's economic successes.

It is the view of this book—and indeed probably the basis of comparative politics—that descriptions of a country as totally unique are unwarranted. Granted, Japanese political culture is plenty different from the European political cultures we have discussed so far. When you compare, though, you discover any country's political patterns can be understood. Much of Japan can be explained by prolonged feudalism. You find that people everywhere are quite human. For example, Japanese politicians take money from interest groups just like politicians everywhere. Avoid the uniqueness trap and the related Mystique Mistake, the overly romantic fascination with another country.

lovely castles. To guard his autonomy, the lord had to be ready to fight at any time. War and feudalism tend to go together. Medieval Europe—with its trinity of king, lords, and knights—corresponds fairly closely with medieval Japan, where they respectively were the *tenno* (starting in 1600, eclipsed by the **shogun**), **daimyo**, and **samurai**. Japan was different from Europe, but not totally. Europe started growing out of feudalism in the fifteenth century or earlier, as modernizing monarchs crushed their aristocratic competitors to found the "strong state" of centralized power and sovereignty. Japan lagged far behind this pattern.

The European Jolt

Key Terms

shogun Feudal Japanese military chief who ruled in name of emperor.

daimyo Feudal Japanese regional lords.

samurai Literally, "those who serve"; Japanese knights.

Tokugawa Dynasty of *shoguns* who ruled Japan from 1600 to 1868.

shogunate Political system with a *shogun* at its head.

The first Europeans to reach Japan were Portuguese navigators in their caravels in 1543, followed by the Spanish in 1587 and the Dutch in 1609. The Japanese couldn't keep them out, and Portuguese traders and Catholic missionaries made great inroads. St. Francis Xavier turned the Jesuits to converting Asia by learned argumentation. Dedicated Jesuit priests learned Japanese and made as many as 150,000 converts (2 percent of Japan's population) by 1582. But Japan's rulers instinctively feared foreign takeover and banned Christianity in 1597. Gradually, over the next few decades, missionaries were excluded and Japanese Catholics slaughtered. In 1635, Japanese were forbidden to travel abroad.

During this period, the **Tokugawa** clan managed to defeat the others and establish a powerful **shogunate** in 1600. (The 1978 TV miniseries *Shogun*, a fictionalized portrayal of this period, may be available on video cassette.) The Tokugawa shogunate was a combination of military rule and police state. Spies were everywhere, especially watching the *daimyo* to make sure none got any ideas about rising up against the shogun. As in France under Louis XIV, lords

GEOGRAPHY

JAPAN AND BRITAIN

There are interesting geographical similarities between Japan and Britain. Both are offshore islands that derived much of their culture from the nearby continent. Why then are Japan and Britain so different? England very early became a great industrial seapower, exploring, trading with, and colonizing much of the world. Aside from a short-lived invasion of Korea in the 1590s, Japan stayed home and did not develop industry beyond the craft level. There was some Japanese piracy off the China coast, but no fleets or explorations. England evolved from feudalism to democracy. Japan stayed feudal.

One clue to this puzzle is the power each faced on their respective nearby continents. Europe was fragmented into many competing states and was rarely a threat to England. Indeed, England played power-balancer on the Continent by injecting its armies at the right time and place into Europe's wars.

Japan faced a unified China that was a nearly permanent threat. Only Korea was a possible takeover target. Early on, Japan decided isolation was its safest course. In the ninth century, Japan cut most of its contacts with and borrowings from China and turned inward. Unlike European monarchs, Asian monarchs did not engage in competitive expansion, so Japan had no incentive to discover new lands. (Imagine if Japan had crossed the Pacific about the same time England crossed the Atlantic.)

had to spend much time or leave their family at the palace. The long period of fifteen hereditary shoguns thus laid down early the tradition of the Japanese police state.

The Tokugawa era brought Japan two centuries of peace, prosperity, isolation, and stagnation. Aside from one small Dutch trading post allowed on an island in Nagasaki harbor, Japan effectively shut the door to foreign contact. (Unlike the Portuguese Catholics, the Dutch Protestants did no missionary work.) **Gaijin** were too threatening to Japanese stability.

The shoguns moved the capital from Kyoto (now an important Buddhist cultural treasure) to Edo (modern Tokyo). They kept discreet track of happenings in the outside world through Chinese couriers. The Japanese people were kept deliberately ignorant of the outside world, which was portrayed as barbaric and threatening. Actually, considering what the Europeans, led by Britain, were doing in and to China, the picture was not totally wrong. The Europeans penetrated China by trade, military power, missionaries, and education, slowly deranging and collapsing a great civilization. The Japanese, by keeping the foreigners at bay, preserved their civilization and territorial integrity until they were ready to accept the West on Japanese terms in the mid-nineteenth century.

The Forced Entry

By the middle of the nineteenth century Japan was an unusual country. It had a distinctive and highly developed civilization with essentially no Western influence. It had enjoyed internal peace for two

Key Term

gaijin Japanese for "foreigner." (The Japanese suffix "jin" means person, thus Nihonjin and America-jin.)

Key Terms

spheres of influence
Understandings among
imperial powers as to which
held sway in given areas.

caste Hereditary social
stratum or group.

Meiji Period starting in
1868 of Japan's rapid
modernization.

centuries. Although lacking industry and trade with the outside world, the Japanese were reasonably prosperous. A merchant middle class emerged, and with their wealth the arts flourished. If it were up to the Japanese, they might have preferred to have been left alone forever. But the West would not leave Japan alone.

The United States did a great deal of business on the China coast, which, by the 1840s, was carved up into **spheres of influence**. The Americans, proud of not being colonialists, had no such sphere but tagged along after the British, concentrated in Shanghai. Shipwrecks in the East China Sea sometimes washed Western sailors onto Japanese shores. (Even then, Japan controlled the Ryukyu Islands, chief of which is Okinawa, which rim this sea on the east.) These sailors could be gotten back only with difficulty, through the Dutch trading post. Furthermore, Japan looked like a tempting target for commercial expansion.

In 1846, two U.S. warships called at Yokohama Bay (Tokyo's port) to request relations; they were rebuffed. Then U.S. President Millard Fillmore ordered Commodore Matthew Perry to sail into the port and force the Japanese to have dealings with us. Perry arrived in 1853 with four ships that combined steam power with sails. The Japanese were frightened by these black, fire-belching sea monsters. Unprepared and confused, they begged Perry to return next year, when they would have an answer to his call for diplomatic relations.

How to best deal with the *gaijin* was a difficult and divisive issue for Edo. Ultimately, Japan's rulers decided they could keep out the world no longer, and when Perry returned in 1854, a large, splendidly attired Japanese imperial delegation met him and acceded to his demands for both diplomatic and trade relations. Soon Europeans followed in Perry's wake, and Japan quickly opened. But the Japanese managed to do it their way.

The 1868 Meiji Restoration

One of the results of a long period of internal peace in Japan was that it made the samurai **caste** unemployed and superfluous. With the challenge posed by the opening of Japan to the West, a group of these samurai found a new calling: to save Japan by modernizing it quickly and beating the West at its own game. Taking advantage of the accession of the new Emperor Mutsuhito, whose era took the name **Meiji**, these samurai had the emperor declare a restoration of his power and issue a series of "imperial rescripts" in 1868 that ordered the modernization

GEOGRAPHY

SAILING THE EAST CHINA SEA

Now your luxury yacht is entering the East China Sea from the south, the Taiwan Strait. Sailing clockwise in a great circle that in- cludes the Yellow Sea to the north, which countries do you pass on your left?

China, North Korea (steer well away), South Korea, Japan (including its Ryukyu Islands), and Taiwan.

GEOGRAPHY

CRUISING THE SEA OF JAPAN

Your luxury yacht is now entering the Sea of Japan from the south, through the Korea Strait. Cruising in a clockwise direc- tion, which countries do you pass to port (left)?

South Korea, North Korea, Russia, and Japan. (It looks like China has a tiny outlet to the sea here, but it doesn't.)

of everything from education and military organization to industry and commerce. Although called a "restoration" of the emperor's power (from the hands of the shoguns), the emperor re- mained a figurehead for rule by samurai clans.

The slogan of the Meiji modernizers: "Rich nation, strong army." Everything changed. Within a generation Japan went from the Middle Ages to the modern age. The Tokugawa were out. The *daimyo* lost their big hereditary estates (but got good deals in the new industries). Feudalism ended, and, on paper at least, all Japanese were legally equal. No more could a samu- rai legally kill someone who disrespected him. (Even today, those of samurai origin are proud of it, but it confers no special advantages.)

It was a controlled revolution from above, the only kind of rev- olution Japan has known.

Various daimyo and samurai clans were given monopolies on branches of industry and ordered to develop them. These formed the basis of the industrial groupings known as **zaibatsu**. Japanese emis- saries were sent out to study and bring back the best the West had to offer: British shipbuilding and naval warfare, French commercial law

Key Term

zaibatsu Industrial conglomerates headed by samurai clans; formed under Meiji period and lasting through World War II.

The traditional Japanese house features ex- treme simplicity. Shoes are removed to walk on rice mats. Diners sit or kneel on the floor in front of a low table. Futons are generally rolled aside every morning. (Michael Roskin)

and bureaucratic organization, and German medical care, steelmaking, and army organization. All was faithfully copied and put into operation. For taxes, the Meiji modernizers unmercifully squeezed the peasants.

The Meiji elite wanted Western technology but few wished Western values and philosophies on democracy, equality, and individual rights. On questions of governance and social structure, Japanese values were deemed superior. The Western ideas crept in anyway and, among many Japanese intellectuals, were highly influential. The Meiji modernizers copied the political system of newly unified Germany; they liked Bismarck's authoritarianism. The 1889 Japanese constitution included a monarch, an elected parliament, and political parties, but underneath, patterns of governance were thoroughly Japanese and largely brokered by traditional holders of power. It only looked democratic and modern.

Japan enjoyed rapid economic growth. In thirty-four years, from 1885 to 1919, Japan doubled its per capita GDP. Although puny by today's standards, this 2 percent annual growth rate was probably the world's fastest up to that point in time. Japanese products, starting with textiles and simple handicrafts, charged onto the world market using cheap labor to undercut Western producers. The purpose of Japanese economic growth, however, was less to make individual Japanese prosperous in the style of Adam Smith than to make Japan powerful as a nation. Some argue that this impulse never ceased to dominate the thinking of the Japanese government.

The Path to War

As soon as Japan was sufficiently armed in the Western style, it picked a fight with and beat China in 1895, seizing Taiwan as its prize. Then it proceeded to gradually take over Korea—which was even more of a hermit kingdom than Japan had been—finally making Korea a Japanese colony in 1910. If these moves sound wicked, we might pause and ask just what was it that the West had done in Asia over the previous couple of centuries. The West had taken Asia with the sword, so why should not Japan do the same?

In 1904, amid growing diplomatic tensions and military preparations, Japan attacked the Russian fleet at Port Arthur on the Manchurian coast. With a combination of disciplined and enthusiastic soldiers, bright and daring officers, and British naval and German army advisors, the Japanese devastated the incompetent Russians on both land and sea. U.S. public opinion favored the Japanese—Teddy Roosevelt called them "plucky little Nips"—partly because tsarist Russia had a terrible, repressive reputation in the United States. President Roosevelt personally mediated an end to the war in Portsmouth, New Hampshire, and won a Nobel Peace Prize for it.

Several *zaibatsu* grew into economic giants that bought control of political parties. Japanese politicians, like those of today, eagerly took money from private industry. In 1927, even before the Great Depression, the Japanese economy collapsed. The rich *zaibatsu* got richer as the middle class got poorer and peasants starved. The Japanese army officers, whose families and soldiers were often just off the farm, bitterly resented the economic concentration and crooked politicians who made it happen. The officer corps, long a hotbed of fanatic right-wing nationalism and emperor-worship, turned its hatred against the democracy and capitalism that began to bloom in the 1920s and moved gradually to bend and subvert them.

The Japanese military had zero civilian control but ran itself as it saw fit, without even informing civilian authorities or diplomats. In the cabinet, the war minister was a general and the navy minister was an admiral; they got whatever budget they wanted. The Japanese armed

COMPARISON

THE JAPANESE MODEL OF INDUSTRIALIZATION?

A couple of points should be noted about Japan's impressive, rapid modernization, which is sometimes offered as an example for the Third World to follow. It was not carried out on the basis of purely free-market capitalism; it had a great deal of government guidance and funding. Furthermore, it was not particularly nice or painless; some families, especially those of certain favored samurai, got rich, but many peasants were turned into a downtrodden proletariat.

Next, its centralization set up Japan for takeover by fascistic militarists and later, after World War II, by bureaucrats intent on making Japan a major industrial power no matter what the foreign or domestic costs. It bequeathed present-day Japan the problem of how to reform a government-led industrializing machine that lumbers on long after it has become a hindrance. We might wish to think twice before prescribing the Japanese style of modernization for other countries. Besides, could it work in a country with a completely different culture?

forces were also riven by rival cliques—feudalism again—who sometimes put each other down by gunfire. In a theme that we will explore more fully later, no one was in charge.

Established in Korea and southern Manchuria, the Japanese army built a state within a state aimed at further conquests. Any civilian politicians in Tokyo who protested the army's expansionist program were assassinated. By the early 1930s, the army was in control of the Tokyo government, although for public purposes most of the official leaders were still civilians. Ordinary Japanese soon learned to say nothing critical, as the dread **Kempeitai** kept tabs on everyone and were soon called the "thought police." Even Emperor Hirohito disliked the military takeover and urged it curbed, but he did not have the power to prevent it. He was still a figurehead.

The ideology of the militarists—who supposed that the "Japanese spirit" was invincible—was quite similar to that of the Nazis, a combination of racism, extreme nationalism, militarism, and a bit of socialism. Both defined their peoples as a biologically superior, warrior race, destined to conquer their parts of the world and exterminate or dominate inferior neighboring peoples. Both were convinced that they needed new lands for their growing populations. Both built societies structured on military lines into tight, obedient hierarchies. Both offered the working class and farmers minimum economic standards. The difference is the Nazis did it through a party, the Japanese through the army; parties in Japan were unimportant. It was no great surprise when Imperial Japan linked up with Nazi Germany in the 1936 Anti-Comintern Pact and in 1940 joined the Axis. The two had little contact during the war and, fortunately for both Russians and Americans, did not coordinate their military campaigns.

The Japanese propaganda line was "Asia for the Asians." The evil European colonialists were to be kicked out and the nations of the region were to be enrolled in the **Greater East Asia Coprosperity Sphere**, led, of course, by Japan, which would make all Asians

Key Terms

Kempeitai   Japan's army-run security police before and during World War II.

Greater East Asia Coprosperity Sphere   Asia run by Japan, Tokyo's World War II propaganda line.

prosperous. Some anticolonial Asians stepped forward to serve the Japanese (Ne Win of Burma, Sukarno of Indonesia, and Subhas Chandra Bose of India), although the Japanese were worse colonialists and racists than the Europeans had been. The Japanese governed with a bloody hand, mostly through the *Kempeitai*.

The Great Pacific War

In 1931, the Japanese army in **Manchuria** detonated a bomb on some railway tracks at Mukden and claimed the Chinese Nationalist army had done it. Using this as an excuse, the Japanese army quickly conquered all of Manchuria and set up a fake country named **Manchukuo**. The civilian prime minister in Tokyo protested and was assassinated. The Tokyo government was simply not in charge; the army was operating on its own. The world did not know what to do. The League of Nations condemned Japan, so Japan simply walked out of the League. Britain and France, with extensive Asian colonies, did not want to antagonize Japan, so they kept silent. The United States, as an avowed "big brother" to China, protested with words but not with military power, which simply made the Japanese militarists more contemptuous of the Americans, who obviously were bluffing.

In 1937, the Japanese army began its ambitious conquest of all of China. Sharply opposed but wishing to avoid war, the United States increasingly applied economic **embargoes** on Japan. Starting in 1940, no U.S. scrap steel was shipped to Japan. The Japanese, with no iron ore of their own, had been major buyers on the world scrap metals markets; this was also one of the reasons they needed Manchuria. Later that year, the United States, then a major oil exporter, barred shipments to Japan. This convinced the Japanese militarists that they had to conquer the Dutch East Indies (now Indonesia) for their petroleum. Washington thought its moves were important restraints and warnings to the Japanese; Tokyo thought they were steps in an undeclared war the Americans were waging. Washington never fully comprehended that these steps were leading to war. The mercenary Flying Tigers, for example, were all U.S. soldiers on leave from their military branches, as if this fooled anyone.

The last straw for Tokyo came in 1941 when Washington froze Japanese assets in American banks, a serious and hostile move. One clique of the Japanese military—few in the Tokyo government even knew about it—immediately began planning Pearl Harbor, which, as far as they were concerned, was retaliation for U.S. economic warfare that had been going on against them for some years. The militarists never dreamed of physically conquering and occupying the United States. They hoped that by knocking out the U.S. Pacific Fleet they would persuade Washington to leave the Western Pacific to them. This ignored, however, the crucial if irrational factor of American rage, something the militarists could not comprehend across the cultural gap. They thought the Americans were cowardly bluffs. The Japanese people were informed of and consulted on nothing.

The war itself, probably due to cultural and racial differences, was unusually cruel, even by twentieth-century standards. It was, as one U.S. author put it, "war without mercy." Both Japanese and Americans killed many war prisoners and inflicted tremendous civilian damage. The Japanese fought like fanatics, partly because surrender meant shame and partly because they thought they'd be killed if they were captured (many were). This fanatic quality persuaded President Truman—in order to avoid what all thought would be a costly invasion of Japan's main islands—to drop the newly developed atomic bomb on Hiroshima and Nagasaki. This finally brought Tokyo to surrender in August 1945.

Key Terms

Manchuria   Northeasternmost area of China.

Manchukuo   Japanese puppet state set up in Manchuria.

embargo   Not selling certain goods to a disfavored country.

THE UNITED STATES AND JAPAN: COLLISION IN THE PACIFIC

The United States and Japan turned imperialistic at precisely the same time, in the late nineteenth century. Both were relative latecomers to the imperial game, and, with both expanding in the Pacific, it was only a matter of time before they collided. The United States constructed a modern fleet in the 1890s and was eager to use it against Spain in 1898. The cause was supposed to be Cuba, but Washington used the war as an excuse to seize the Philippines from Spain. At the same time, the United States took Hawaii, Midway, Wake, Guam, and Western Samoa. One of the unstated reasons for the U.S. expansion in the Pacific was the fear that if we didn't take the islands the Japanese would.

Why couldn't America and Japan have lived side-by-side in the Asia/Pacific region? The problem was the U.S. policy of protecting China, a policy that began in 1900 with the **Open Door** notes. Originally designed to make sure that China trade was open to all, they soon turned into U.S. guarantees for the "territorial and administrative integrity" of China. As the Japanese military began conquering China, starting in Manchuria in 1931, they put themselves on a collision course with the United States.

Even then it was touch and go. Some of the militarists wanted to keep fighting to the last Japanese. They were even willing to disobey the emperor they professed to worship. Emperor Hirohito himself had never favored the military or their war. The atomic bombs gave him the chance to end the madness. If the war continued for another year, Japan would starve. The Japanese language is extremely subtle and usually tries to avoid blunt or harsh statements. Thus in August 1945, Hirohito went on radio to explain to his ruined country and army why Japan would have to "endure the unendurable" and surrender: "Developments in the war have not necessarily gone so well as Japan might have wished." It was a classic Japanese understatement, but it ended the war.

Up from the Ashes

Japanese cities were seas of grey rubble at the close of World War II. The old capital of Kyoto was spared upon the pleas of American scholars, who knew it was a world cultural (chiefly Buddhist) treasure and of little military value. U.S. bombs had burned much of Japan's crops in the field; starvation loomed. U.S. submarines had sunk a greater percentage of Japanese shipping than German U-boats had sunk of British shipping. In 1945, the Japanese were desperate, even more desperate than the Germans were.

Without the slightest resistance, General Douglas MacArthur and his staff moved into one of the few buildings in Tokyo still standing, that of the Dai-Ichi Bank (later one of the world's largest). Emperor Hirohito soon called on MacArthur to express his willingness to take the blame for everything Japan had done. MacArthur, speaking as one emperor to another, told him that would not be necessary and that he could keep his throne, but as an ordinary mortal, not as a "living god." Most Japanese already understood that

Key Term

Open Door U.S. policy of protecting China.

ANOTHER TALE OF TWO FLAGS

In keeping with the myth that they are descended from the sun goddess, some ancient Japanese clans used a sun in their flags at least six centuries ago. After Perry opened the country, Japanese ships needed a national flag to identify themselves. The present Japanese flag, *Hinomaru* (or rising sun), suggested by the head of the powerful Satsuma clan in southern Japan, was first used in 1860 (by the first diplomatic delegation to visit the United States).

The sinister Japanese flag shows the sun's rays radiating out; it became a symbol of militaristic expansion. The army version had thicker red rays, the navy version thinner red rays. The U.S. occupation government abolished the sun-ray flag, but the Naval Self-Defense Force resumed using it in 1954.

Neither the *Hinomaru* nor the national anthem (*Kimigayo*, "His Majesty's Reign"), however, were written into law or required at ceremonies. Some nationalistic politicians wanted to do that in the late 1990s, but they were opposed by the leftist teachers' union, who feared a recrudescence of nationalism. The Diet finally made both official and legal in 1999.

the emperor was no living god, but some still revered him. MacArthur's decision was probably wise, for the continuation of millennia-old throne helped calm and stabilize Japan.

In 1946 MacArthur's staff wrote a new constitution in five days, somewhat modeled on the British pattern. Why the hurry? The Americans wanted to block a Japanese attempt to just lightly revise their prewar constitution. Instead, U.S. Colonel Charles Kades, a lawyer in civilian life, produced a document to guarantee freedom, parliamentary democracy, and peace. Japanese elites did not like the **MacArthur Constitution**—among other points, it made the emperor merely the symbol of Japan—but grudgingly accepted it when the emperor endorsed it. Many educated Japanese were delighted to see Japan back on the path of democracy and equality and the old elite thrown out.

Although it has been Japan's constitution since 1947, it has not functioned precisely as written, as Japanese power does not flow in neat, Western-type channels. Industry was revived, much of it under the supervision of the old militarists who had run it as part of the Japanese war machine. The old *zaibatsu* conglomerates were broken up, but as the Cold War loomed MacArthur let banks reassemble them under the new name of **keiretsu**, giant

Key Terms

MacArthur Constitution Japan's U.S.-drafted postwar constitution.

keiretsu Japan's postwar industrial conglomerates.

POLITICAL CULTURE

JAPAN'S POLITICAL ERAS

Since the Tokugawa shogunate, Japan's political eras are named for the reigns of each emperor. Indeed, for domestic use only, years in Japan are those of the emperor's reign. Thus 2000 is given as year 12 of the reign of Akihito (add 1988 to this imperial year to get the Western year). Wherever they can, the Japanese do it their way.

Name	Years	Remembered for
Tokugawa	1600–1868	Conservative shogunate; military feudalism; isolated Japan.
Meiji	1868–1912	Rapid modernization under a "restored" emperor; military expansionism begins.
Taisho	1912–1926	Normal but corrupt democracy.
Showa	1926–1989	Militarists take over, lead country to war; postwar economic boom.
Heisei	1989–	Economic slowdown; efforts at reform.

industrial-financial combinations with the same names as the old *zaibatsu*. For the same Cold War reason, MacArthur let many of the old elites worm their way back into political power. In Japan, as in France, the more it changes, the more it stays the same.

The Japanese economy revived, and spectacularly, as we shall see in Chapter 26. The economy did not function on a strictly *laissez-faire* basis, however; much economic growth was supervised and encouraged by government bureaucracies. A democracy also revived, but it did not function on a strictly Western basis either, as we shall explore in the next chapter.

Key Terms

arable (p. 306)

Buddhism (p. 306)

caste (p. 310)

Confucianism (p. 306)

daimyo (p. 308)

embargo (p. 314)

gaijin (p. 309)

Greater East Asia Coprosperity Sphere (p. 306)

keiretsu (p. 316)

Kempeitai (p. 313)

MacArthur Constitution (p. 316)

Manchukuo (p. 314)

Meiji (p. 310)

Open Door (p. 315)

samurai (p. 308)

Shinto (p. 307)

shogun (p. 308)

shogunate (p. 308)

sphere of influence (p. 310)

Tokugawa (p. 308)

zaibatsu (p. 311)

Further Reference

Banno, Junji. *The Establishment of the Japanese Constitutional System*. New York: Routledge, 1992.

Beasley, W. G. *The Rise of Modern Japan*, 2nd ed. New York: St. Martin's, 1995.

Dower, John W. *War without Mercy: Race and Power in the Pacific War*. New York: Pantheon, 1986.

———. *Embracing Defeat: Japan in the Wake of World War II*. New York: Norton, 1999.

Hane, Mikiso. *Modern Japan: A Historical Survey*, 2nd ed. Boulder, CO: Westview, 1992.

Koseki, Sochi. *The Birth of Japan's Postwar Constitution*, ed. and tr. by Ray A. Moore. Boulder, CO: Westview, 1997.

McDougall, Walter A. *Let the Sea Make a Noise: A History of the North Pacific from Magellan to MacArthur*. New York: Basic Books, 1993.

Reischauer, Edwin O. *Japan: The Story of a Nation*, rev. ed. New York: Knopf, 1974.

Samuels, Richard J. *"Rich Nation, Strong Army": National Security and the Technological Transformation of Japan*. Ithaca, NY: Cornell University Press, 1994.

Sansom, G. B. *Japan: A Short Cultural History*, rev. ed. New York: Appleton-Century-Crofts, 1962.

Storry, Richard. *A History of Modern Japan*, rev. ed. Baltimore, MD: Penguin Books, 1968.

Tiedemann, Arthur E. *An Introduction to Japanese Civilization*. Lexington, MA: D.C. Heath, 1974.

Japan:
The Key Institutions

23

Questions to Consider

1. In what ways do Japanese institutions resemble British?
2. How does the Japanese diet contrast with the Japanese Diet?
3. Why does Japan's prime minister not function the way other prime ministers do?
4. With very dissimilar political cultures, how can Japan's LDP and Italy's DC closely resemble each other?
5. What's wrong with a coalition of many parties?
6. How can Japan be described as having a "dominant party system"?
7. How closely does the "generic prime minister" match the current one?
8. How does the new Japanese electoral system work?

If we were to go strictly by appearances and by what many Japanese want us to believe, we would portray Japanese political institutions as variations on the British pattern that was foisted on Japan by the Americans in 1946. As is often the case with appearances in Japan, this would be deceptive. Several British-type institutions are present in Japan, but none of them function as they do in Britain.

The Monarchy

The Japanese monarchy, which was constitutionally divine until 1945, still claims it can trace its direct lineage back to 660 B.C. But for most of history, the monarch was a figurehead, a court prisoner of the real power. For some Japanese, especially elders and conservatives, the monarch still is divine, symbolizing the entire nation in a way that has vanished in Europe. Right-wingers punish critics of the monarchy, sometimes by killing them. Most young Japanese pay the monarchy no special attention. The two royal marriages since the war were both to commoners, and this has helped demystify the Imperial Household.

319

COMPARISON

DEFERENCE TO MONARCHS

Both the British and Japanese monarchs are respected figureheads, but the Japanese much more so. Neither has anything but symbolic duties. Much of the British press see nothing divine in the younger generation of "royals." The media snoop on and photograph them and take particular delight in their marital troubles. The Japanese media would never snoop around the Imperial Household. The *Washington Post* first broke the story of the engagement of Crown Prince Naruhito in 1993, a story the Tokyo press wouldn't have touched until the official announcement. Once the *Post* dared to pierce the "chrysanthemum curtain" around the Imperial Household, however, the Japanese media began to comment on their royalty, especially on the mood swings of the empress.

Another interesting point of difference: The prince picked a commoner (but of very good family), Masako Owada, to be the future empress, the second time this has happened in modern Japan. The prince's own mother, Empress Michiko, was herself a commoner (but of a rich family). So far, British royal marriages of those directly in line for the throne have all been with aristocrats. In Britain in 1936, Edward VIII abdicated after less than a year on the throne "to marry the woman I love," an American divorcée. The British press printed nothing on the drama until the formal announcement; Britons in 1936 could read of it only in the American and Continental press.

Japan's imperial family: From left, Emperor Akihito, Crown Prince Naruhito, Crown Princess Masako, Empress Michiko. (Japan Information Center)

It is not clear if the emperor can influence Japanese politics. The constitution specifies he has no "powers related to government." A prisoner of ritual and ceremony, he goes along with what is expected of him. In 1945, Emperor Hirohito did play a policy role in deciding for peace; with the cabinet deadlocked but many generals willing to keep on fighting, Hirohito threw his weight behind the peace party, and it tipped the balance.

In public speeches nowadays, Emperor Akihito, son of Hirohito, who died in 1988, is generally vague and idealistic. Some observers believe, however, that the emperor gives a kind of tacit assent; that is, if things are not going horribly, he says nothing. This could continue for decades. If during a crisis an emperor should take a clear stand on an issue, however, he might have considerable impact. Japan is waiting to see if Crown Princess Masako will produce an heir to the throne, especially a male one. If she continues childless, the line of succession may go to the eldest daughter of the crown prince's younger brother, giving Japan its first female head of state in modern times.

Key Term

Diet Name of some parliaments, such as Japan's and Finland's.

The Diet

The Japanese diet is optimal, light on fat, cholesterol, and calories. The Japanese Diet is marginal, heavy on payoffs, pork, and political squabbling. The 1947 constitution, in the best Lockean style, specifies the **Diet** (legislature) as the "highest organ" of Japanese government. Not strictly true in Europe, it is even less true in Japan. While the bicameral Diet selects the prime minister and can oust him on a vote of no-confidence, much of Japan's real decision-making power lies elsewhere, in the powerful ministries.

Starting in 2000, Japan's lower house, the House of Representatives, has 480 members, 300 elected from single-member districts and 180 on the basis of proportional representation by party lists in eleven regions. The house's term is a maximum of four years. The new Japanese system, which began with the elections of 1996, resembles the German hybrid system but, like the Russian system, does not use PR to set the overall number of seats per party.

The Japanese Diet in Tokyo, a product of the 1920s, was completed in 1936. By then the military ran Japan. (Michael Roskin)

A WOMAN SPEAKER FOR JAPAN'S DIET

In 1993, Japan's House of Representatives elected its first woman speaker, Social Democrat chairwoman Takako Doi. Curiously, Britain's House of Commons had elected its first woman Speaker, Labourite Betty Boothroyd, the previous year. Doi at first didn't want the politically neutral administrative job but was persuaded to take it as a way to help hold together the new, non-LDP coali-

tion. With one of their own as speaker, Social Democrat deputies might be more loyal to the centrist-led cabinet. Symbolically, Doi's election was another small step to political equality for Japanese women. Unlike Britain's lifetime tenure for Speaker, Doi served only one term, until the 1996 elections, when the speakership passed to LDP chief Keizo Obuchi, who became prime minister in 1998.

As is standard in parliamentary systems, the House can be dissolved early for new elections, which happened after a vote of no-confidence in 1993 and when the premier thought his LDP would do best in 1996. The non-LDP coalition of 1993 rewrote some of the rules that were widely (if not necessarily accurately) blamed for Japan's endemic political corruption. (See the box on reforming Japan's electoral system, on page 353.)

As is usually the case with parliamentary systems, Japan's lower house has more power than the upper. If the upper chamber rejects a bill from the lower chamber, the latter may override the objection with a two-thirds majority vote. The upper chamber, the House of Councillors, has 252 members elected for six-year terms; half are elected every three years. Japan's forty-seven prefectures and districts elect 152 councillors. Since 1982, another one hundred councillors are elected nationwide according to party preference. The upper house cannot be dissolved early for new elections.

Key Terms

Liberal Democrats (LDP) Japan's dominant party, a catchall.

pork barrel Government projects that narrowly benefit legislators' constituencies.

With only one break from 1955 to the present, the lower house of the Diet (and usually the upper house as well) was firmly in the hands of the **Liberal Democrats (LDP)**. The Diet served as a sometimes raucous debating society in which the opposition parties, led by the doctrinaire Socialists, attacked the Liberal Democrats, and Liberal Democratic factions attacked each other, sometimes with fists as well as with words.

Beyond the parties, elections, and debates, the larger question of any parliament is whether it controls government policy. The career professionals who staff the Tokyo ministries feel that most members of the Diet pass around the **pork barrel** to get reelected but do not have much knowledge or interest in running the government. The Diet, like the British parliament, has a Question Time, but bureaucrats answer most of the questions, not ministers. The attitude of Japan's bureaucrats: Let the parliamentarians play their games, so long as they leave the running of Japan to us. This attitude of civil servants toward elected legislators is found in many governments; it is just stronger in Japan.

The Prime Minister

Contrary to most European systems, Japan's prime minister is not the real seat of power. Americans especially mistakenly equated a Japanese prime minister with his British or German counterpart. In trade talks, for example, the Japanese prime minister would make some concessions to the U.S. side, but then nothing would change. The prime minister doesn't have nearly the power, in the face of major interest groups and their friends in government ministries, to accomplish much.

A Japanese prime minister is not the analog of a European or Canadian prime minister; he is more of a figurehead. Few can name the Japanese equivalent of a Thatcher or Adenauer, tough leaders who really got things done; there have been none in Japan. Some observers suspect that Japanese do not want strong leadership. The big question now is whether Japan's reformers have really changed this pattern.

On average, Japanese prime ministers are in office for less than two and a half years, some for just a few months. By far the longest-serving prime minister was Eisaku Sato, who served from 1964 to 1972. (In Japanese, as in Chinese and Hungarian, family names are first, so we should say "Sato Eisaku.") Ordinary cabinet ministers average about a year in office. The limits to their tenures are not votes of confidence or the splintering of coalition cabinets, as was often the case in Europe. Until 1993, the Liberal Democrats had a comfortable majority in the House of Representatives and brushed off no-confidence motions.

Who Was When: Japan's Prime Ministers

	Dates Served	*Months in Office*	*Party*
Yoshida Shigeru	1946–47	12	Liberal
Katayama Tetsu	1948	10	Socialist
Ashida Hitoshi	1948	8	Democratic
Yoshida Shigeru	1948–54	74	Liberal
Hatoyama Ichiro	1954–56	24	Democratic
Ishibashi Tanzan	1956–57	3	Liberal Democratic
Kishi Nobusuke	1957–60	42	Liberal Democratic
Ikeda Hayato	1960–64	53	Liberal Democratic
Sato Eisaku	1964–72	92	Liberal Democratic
Tanaka Kakuei	1972–74	30	Liberal Democratic
Miki Takeo	1974–76	24	Liberal Democratic
Fukuda Takeo	1976–78	24	Liberal Democratic
Ohira Masayoshi	1978–80	18	Liberal Democratic
Ito Masayoshi	1980	1	Liberal Democratic
Suzuki Zenko	1980–82	29	Liberal Democratic
Nakasone Yasuhiro	1982–87	60	Liberal Democratic
Takeshita Noboru	1987–89	19	Liberal Democratic
Uno Sosuke	1989	2	Liberal Democratic
Toshiki Kaifu	1989–91	27	Liberal Democratic
Miyazawa Kiichi	1991–93	20	Liberal Democratic
Hosokawa Morihiro	1993–94	8	Japan New
Hata Tsutomo	1994	2	Japan Renewal
Murayama Tomiichi	1994–96	18	Social Democrat
Hashimoto Ryutaro	1996–98	30	Liberal Democratic
Obuchi Keizo	1998–		Liberal Democratic
Mori Yoshiro	2000–	20	Liberal Democratic

Prime Minister Mori of the Liberal Democratic party took office in 2000. (Japan Information Center)

Key Terms

faction   A party within a party.

shadow shogun   Unofficial term for top faction chief who names and controls Japan's prime minister.

dominant-party system A party system in which one party is much stronger than all the others and stays in office a very long time.

The problem, rather, is the fragmented nature of the Liberal Democratic party (LDP), in which the leaders of the several **factions** make and unmake prime ministers and ministers according to behind-the-scenes deals. The ministers are simply front-men for their factions. Many observers of Japanese politics allege the LDP faction leaders are considerably more powerful than prime ministers. There are instances when powerful LDP politicians passed up a chance to become prime minister because faction chief was a more important job. Typically, the leader of the dominant LDP faction, called only half in jest the **shadow shogun**, calls the shots and names the prime minister.

For eight months in 1993–94 Japan had an eight-party coalition, possibly a world record. Poland in 1991–93 had five- and seven-party coalitions. Such governments are recipes for instability. Short-term Prime Minister Hosokawa had his hands full as the many parties jockeyed for power within the coalition, just as the LDP factions had done. Indeed, many of the members of "new" parties had recently fled from the LDP as its electoral fortunes started to crumble. They brought with them the LDP traditions of infighting and power-brokering. Look for how long a Japanese prime minister stays in office and why he or she is replaced. The real weakness in the Japanese prime ministership is the parties, either fragmented, as in the case of the LDP, or splintered, as in the case of the newer coalitions.

The Parties

Japan, until recently, was (and maybe still is) an example of a **dominant-party system**, one with several parties but with one much stronger than any of the others. In such systems, the dominant party can theoretically be voted out but seldom is. Mexico and India have also been dominant-party systems. For most of the postwar period in Japan, one party, the LDP, was so strong that some jested that the Japanese system was a "one-and-a-half party system." (The much-weaker Socialists were the "half" party.) This system is changing, but perhaps less than anticipated.

FILL IN THE BLANKS: A GENERIC PRIME MINISTER

*B*ecause Japan's prime ministers change so quickly there is little point to printing the latest one in a textbook: By the time students read it, there will likely be a new prime minister. Instead, students may fill in the name of Japan's latest prime minister (in pencil, please; you may have to erase it) and the other details. The purpose of this exercise is to illustrate that the more things change in Japan, the more they stay the same.

Vowing to free up the Japanese economic system and break rule by bureaucrats, Prime Minister _____ took office in 200_. Although he billed himself as a reformer, _____'s roots go deep into the old system. After graduating from _____ University and working briefly as a _____, he worked his way up through the Liberal De-

mocratic party (pick one) (a.) and stayed loyal to it (or b.) but split from it.

Reform is difficult for the _____ government, though, as the cabinet is prone to disagreement and breakup. The bureaucrats whose power he intended to curb know how to fight back. And Japan's special interests were as influential as ever. Rumor says _____ received "campaign expenses" from a shady _____ company.

The real question: Is _____ a power in his own right or simply a front-man for _____, the shadow shogun who puts together cabinets behind the scenes? Japan's new "reformed" system works so much like the previous system it is doubtful Japan's politicians can or even want to seriously change it.

The Liberal Democrats were actually an amalgamation of several existing centrist and conservative parties that had been ruling Japan since 1947. With the growth of the **Cold War**, however, the United States grew concerned that radical Japanese parties, the Communists and Socialists, might either come to power or make Japan ungovernable. The Americans therefore encouraged the mergers that created the LDP. Only one thing mattered: Do not let Japan go Communist or turn neutral between East and West.

The Liberal Democrats, although they enjoyed unbroken electoral success and controlled the government until 1993, barely cohered as a party; only the winning of elections and gaining of spoils kept the LDP from breaking up. Some saw it less as a party and more an **electoral alignment** of factions grouped around powerful chiefs, much as samurai clans in olden times gathered around daimyo. Instead of swords, the faction chiefs used money. This feudal arrangement meant that no single faction or chief dominated for long, and no one was interested in or responsible for policy. There were no important ideological divisions within the party, only loyalties to chiefs, some of whom were unsavory holdovers from the World War II militarist government. Asked his political views, one local LDP activist proudly proclaimed, "I am a soldier in the Tanaka faction."

Japan's party system is messy and constantly changing. In the early 1990s, the LDP fell into disarray. Dozens of leading LDP politicians stalked out of the LDP to form three centrist-reformist parties: Japan Renewal, Japan New Party, and New Party Harbinger. The first two of these reshuffled some of their members, drew in some other smaller groups, and renamed themselves the New Frontier party for the 1996 election. The New Party Harbinger split, and the breakaway wing

Key Terms

Cold War Period of armed tension and competition between the United States and the Soviet Union, approximately 1947–89.

electoral alignment Temporary coalition of parties in order to win elections.

Party Systems

System	Example	Probable Causes
two-party	Britain	Single-member plurality election districts; not-so-complex history.
multiparty	France	Historical complexity; runoff elections.
two-plus	Germany	Hybrid single-member and PR elections.
fragmented	Russia	New, unconsolidated; personality struggles; partly PR system.
dominant-party	Japan	Postwar consolidation; weak opposition; obedient political culture.

named itself the Democratic Party of Japan (DPJ). As in Russia and Brazil, new parties in Japan—most simply personal vehicles to get their leaders elected—constantly emerge, split, and merge.

The "half party" of the old system, stuck in permanent minority status, was the Japan Socialist party (JSP), which had actually been born with the warm approval of MacArthur's occupation government because it seemed to repudiate the militarist regime. (Actually, some Japanese socialists had cooperated with the wartime regime.) The JSP hit an electoral high in 1958 with nearly one-third of the vote, but has declined ever since because it was extremely doctrinaire and rigid, caught up in the sort of Marxist slogans that Europe's postwar Socialist and Social-Democratic parties soon abandoned. The JSP, for example, proclaimed its neutralism, giving the Soviet Union and North Korea the benefit of the doubt while strongly criticizing the United States. Renamed the Social Democrat Party of Japan, it joined and ditched the shaky 1993–94 coalition, then bizarrely joined with its LDP archenemies in a 1994–96 coalition with Social Democratic leader Murayama as a weak figurehead prime minister. This sellout for the appearance of power alienated many Social Democratic voters, and the JSDP now has only one-quarter of the seats it had in 1990.

Some less-privileged Japanese, aware that the LDP was corrupt but who were unattracted to socialism, turned for many years to the strange Komei, or Clean Government, party. It too was stuck in minority status because it was a 1960s offshoot of the Soka Gakkai religious movement of evangelical-fundamentalist Buddhism, which many Japanese think is warped and fanatic. **Komeito's** program, aside from clean government, remained vaguely in favor of improved welfare benefits and quality of life. In 1996 Komeito split into three small parties, but the well-heeled Soka Gakkai tried to cement them back together for the 2000 elections. The main branch, called New Komei, joined the LDP-headed coalition in 1999.

Key Term

-to   Japanese suffix for party; the Komei party is Komeito.

A small Communist party, rooted in certain sectors of the working class and among radical intellectuals, consistently wins a few seats in the lower house and actually enjoyed an uptick in 1996. Torn between support for Beijing or for Moscow, the JCP was in a quandary when both headed for capitalism. Surveying Japan's messy and rapidly changing party system, it could be said that no party was strong, not even the LDP, but the opposition parties were too fragmented to unseat the LDP. Japan's dominant-party system may rumble on pretty much as before.

Japan's Electoral System

Until 1993, at least part of the blame for the weakness of Japan's parties and party system was placed on its electoral system, which was like no other. Under that system, elections for the more-important lower chamber, the House of Representatives, were by 130 districts, 128 of

COMPARISON

THE LDP AND ITALY'S DC

There is an uncanny resemblance between the Japanese Liberal Democratic party and the Italian Christian Democratic party. Both were founded after World War II, with U.S. blessings and CIA dollars, by combining preexisting political conservative-to-centrist groups to fight Communist or neutralist takeovers of Japan and Italy.

Both parties were successful and dominated their country's political life for most of the postwar decades. The LDP, with an outright majority of parliamentary seats, was mostly able to govern alone; the DC needed a multiparty coalition. Both parties oversaw major economic growth but neither were totally free-market, as both Japan and Italy had major state oversight of the economy (and, in the Italian case, major state-owned industries).

The negative side of the two parties was even more similar. Both were riven by at least half-a-dozen factions grouped around strong personalities who hated each other. Corruption was rampant in both parties and scandals were frequent. They stayed in power because not enough voters would switch to the radical parties, the Japanese Socialists or Italian Communists. The LDP and DC were the lesser of two evils in the minds of many voters.

With the Cold War over and the anti-Communist pressure removed, both parties declined in the early 1990s. The DC changed its name to the Popular party. Voters, who could no longer stomach the crooked ruling parties, scattered their votes among several new, smaller parties. In the same year, 1993, both countries reformed electoral laws by shifting heavily to single-member districts with an eye toward curbing corruption and party factions.

which sent from two to five deputies to the Diet, supposedly based on district population. (One small district sent one deputy, and one very large district sent six.)

But instead of European-style proportional representation, Japanese voters voted for one candidate rather than for one party, and the winners were simply those with the most votes. If there were seven candidates in a four-person district, the four highest vote-getters were elected. Candidates of the same party actually competed directly against each other in the same constituency, a system that begged for factionalism within the parties and helped explain why the LDP became so terribly faction-ridden and corrupt. The need to spread around campaign money became desperate and with that the opportunity for corrupt political payoffs by private industry.

The new coalition put into office by the 1993 election blamed the Japanese electoral system for many of the political system's ills and immediately reformed it. First, they divided Japan into three hundred single-member districts with roughly the same number of people. This was to solve one problem that cried out for reform: unfairness in number of voters per elected representative. The 1947 constitution was devised at a time when Japan was still two-thirds rural and used the electoral districts of 1925. Since then, Japan has become over three-quarters urban, but the size of electoral districts changed only a little, some by legislation and some by court order. In 1980, it took up to five times as many urban votes to elect someone to the Diet as rural votes. In the 1993 election, after some reforms, it still took up to three times more urban votes than rural votes to elect one deputy. The system greatly magnified the voice of Japan's farmers and gave the LDP an advantage in the countryside, since they promised to bar imported food and lavishly subsidized inefficient Japanese farmers. This gave Japanese consumers some of the highest food prices in the world and angered foreign food exporters, such as the United States.

Now, after the 1993 and 2000 reforms, three hundred districts elect only one member each, and by simple plurality (not necessarily a majority) of the votes. This was supposed to do at least two things: First, it was supposed to cut the number of parties in the Diet, since such systems penalize small parties. But this is not absolutely the case, as third and fourth parties that are territorially concentrated have good chances to win in at least a few districts. Next, by ending the old Japanese system of candidates from the same party competing against each other in multimember districts, the reform was supposed to overcome some of the dreadful factionalism within the LDP or any other large party.

The remaining 180 members of the lower house are now elected by proportional representation based on parties. This, too, was supposed to heal the factionalism that paralyzed the LDP. In such a system, candidates from the same party have to run as a team rather than as

DEMOCRACY

THE 1996 ELECTIONS: A HYBRID SYSTEM IN ACTION

Japan held its first elections under the new system in 1996. Change was less than breathtaking. The Liberal Democrats remained the largest party, just as they had been since 1955. The LDP, however, fell short of a majority and needed support from two small parties in order to govern. The election, which had the lowest turnout ever (59 percent), distributed seats as shown in the table below.

Some new parties that appeared in the 1993 elections, such as Japan Renewal and New Party Japan, merged and renamed themselves for 1996. All were composed of LDP politicians who walked out of the party when it seemed incapable of reforming itself or the system. Ideologically, though, there are no important differences between the LDP and its main opposition parties. All ran against the power of the bureaucrats and in favor of economic deregulation. The real loser was the JSP, running under its new name of Social Democratic party, which saw its seats cut in half from the 1990 to the 1993 elections, then in half again in 1996.

Did the new electoral system fail to accomplish its goal? The new lower house of the Diet looked as fragmented as before, with the LDP still the kingpin. The 1996 Diet had 500 members, trimmed in 2000 to 480 members. But did the overall makeup of the Diet change much in 2000?

	Outgoing Party Strength	*1996 Elections*
Liberal Democrat	239	211
Social Democrats	30	15
Democratic Party of Japan	52	52
New Frontier	160	156
Communists	15	26
New Party Harbinger	9	2
others	16	10

competitors. This was supposed to give Japan's parties greater ideological coherence. The reformers' end goal: a responsible two-party system with some alternation in power, like a real democracy.

Elections for the House of Councillors, in which half the members are up for reelection every three years, are different. Each prefecture has from two to eight councillors based on population, and here voters also have two ballots, German-style. One goes for an individual candidate, with the top vote-getters winning, as for the lower house. These account for 152 seats. Proportional representation at the national level fills another one hundred seats, a 1982 innovation. The electoral system for both Japan's upper and lower houses thus resembles the system for Germany's lower house. The LDP's 1998 electoral setback in the upper house—it won only 44 of the 126 seats being contested—served as a warning of voter discontent over the economic downturn and pushed Prime Minister Hashimoto to resign.

> ### Key Term
>
> **MITI** Japan's powerful Ministry of International Trade and Industry.

The Ministries

Who, then, does have the power in Japan? First, there is no strongly focused single center of power in Japan as in most other countries; power tends to be diffused among several centers. Many observers, however, point to the 19,000 career bureaucrats who staff the executive levels of the ministries, particularly the Finance Ministry and Ministry of International Trade and Industry—the famous **MITI**—as the real seat of power in Japan. The Ministry of Construction has clout, too, as it distributes public-works projects to benefit this or that locality or political chief.

The Japanese cabinet, like most European cabinets, can be easily changed from year to year, with ministries combined, renamed, or instituted. The cabinets of the late-1990s contained the following ministries:

Agriculture, Forestry, and Fisheries	Home Affairs
Construction	International Trade and Industry (MITI)
Education	Justice
Finance	Labor
Foreign Affairs	Posts and Telecommunications
Health and Welfare	Transport

In addition, the cabinet included several specialized agencies.

Economic Planning Agency	National Land Agency
Environment Agency	Okinawa Development Agency
Hokkaido Development Agency	Science and Technology Agency
Management and Coordination Agency	Self Defense Agency

There are a few interesting points about this cabinet. Notice that Self Defense is in the cabinet but does not rate the title of ministry. According to the constitution, Japan is not supposed to have armed forces. At least six ministries or agencies deal directly with economic

Key Terms

vice-minister   Top bureaucrat in a Japanese ministry.

prefecture   First-order Japanese civil division, like a French department.

development. The Minister of Foreign Affairs usually doubles as deputy prime minister. In addition to the above, a state minister serves as chief cabinet secretary under the prime minister.

At least half of the ministers must be members of the Diet, and most are. The ministers are not necessarily experts in their portfolios (ministerial assignments), which are based more on political criteria than on subject-matter competence. Bureaucrats run the ministries, not ministers. Occasionally, respected specialists or academics without party affiliation are named ministers.

As is the case in Europe, every party in a coalition has at least one top leader named to be a minister. The eight-party coalition of 1993, for example, had representatives of eight different parties in the cabinet. Even the small parties got a portfolio, but the coalition-member parties with the most seats got several. Such distributions of ministries are payoffs used to form and hold a cabinet together. After the 1996 elections, in which the LDP fell short of a majority of seats, LDP prime ministers governed in coalition with small parties, the Liberal, Conservative, and Komei parties. Most portfolios stayed in LDP hands.

Below the minister, a civil-service **vice-minister** generally runs a ministry. The Japanese vice-ministers, who correspond to the British "permanent secretaries," are more powerful than their nominal bosses, also the case in most of Europe. The top appointed officials—and they are appointed internally on the basis of merit, as defined by the individual ministry, not on the basis of political connections—have years of experience and knowledge; the minister may last only a few months in office. This gives the top bureaucrats a great deal of power and the feeling that they alone should run Japan.

Japanese Territorial Organization

Japan is a unitary system that looks a bit like a federal system. It has forty-seven administrative divisions, forty-three of them **prefectures**, after the French name for the head of a *département*. The other four are special situations: Tokyo, Osaka, and Kyoto are run as large metropolitan districts, and the thinly populated northernmost island of Hokkaido is one big district.

Each Japanese prefecture has an elected governor and unicameral assembly to decide local matters and raise local taxes. These taxes, though, cover only about 30 percent of prefectural needs, so the prefectural government is always beholden to Tokyo for additional revenues. Japanese call this "30 percent autonomy." The Ministry of Home Affairs in Tokyo still oversees prefectural matters and can override the local governor. The Japanese situation resembles the modern French territorial structure: unitary, but with certain local-democracy features. Many Japanese, who are proud of their local communities, wish they had greater autonomy from Tokyo.

Key Terms

Cold War (p. 325)

Diet (p. 321)

dominant-party system (p. 324)

electoral alignment (p. 325)

faction (p. 324)

Liberal Democrats (LDP) (p. 322)

MITI (p. 329)

pork barrel (p. 322)

prefecture (p. 330)

shadow shogun (p. 324)

-to (p. 326)

vice minister (p. 330)

Further Reference

Abe, Hitoshi, Muneyuki Shindo, and Sadafumi Kawato. *The Government and Politics of Japan.* Tokyo: University of Tokyo Press, 1994.

Dolan, Ronald E., and Robert L. Worden, eds. *Japan: A Country Study.* Washington, D.C.: U.S. Government Printing Office, 1992.

Hartcher, Peter. *The Ministry.* Boston, MA: Harvard Business School Press, 1998.

Hayes, Louis D. *Introduction to Japanese Politics.* New York: Paragon House, 1992.

Jain, Purnendra, and Takashi Inoguchi, eds. *Japanese Politics Today: Beyond Karaoke Democracy?* New York: St. Martin's, 1997.

Kataoka, Tetsuya. *The Price of a Constitution: The Origin of Japan's Postwar Politics.* Bristol, PA: Taylor & Francis, 1991.

Kim, Paul S. *Japan's Civil Service System: Its Structure, Personnel, and Politics.* Westport, CT: Greenwood, 1988.

Shibata, Tokue. *Japan's Public Sector: How the Government Is Financed.* Tokyo: University of Tokyo Press, 1992.

Stockwin, J. A. *Governing Japan: Divided Politics in a Major Economy,* 3d ed. Malden, MA: Blackwell, 1998.

Japanese Political Culture

24

Questions to Consider

1. How do postwar German and Japanese political cultures differ?
2. How can you tell if Japanese feel guilt or just shame?
3. How might you describe "Japaneseness"?
4. Why does Christianity have an uphill struggle in Japan?
5. Are the United States and Japan destined to misunderstand each other?
6. How does a *sarariman* differ from his U.S. counterpart?
7. What is *wa*? How does it relate to *nemawashi*?
8. Will the *shin jinrui* transform Japanese culture?

Japan is one of the few non-European countries that modernized while retaining its own culture. Japan took on some appearances of Western culture but kept its inner core of Japaneseness. For this reason, Harvard political scientist Samuel Huntington sees Japan as a unique civilization. Germany and Japan, although both suffered defeat and occupation, came out quite differently after World War II.

Missing from the U.S. occupation of Japan was the sort of denazification that was practiced, however imperfectly, in Germany. The Western Allies, by means of the Nuremberg War Crimes Tribunal and their control of the media and schools, were able to instruct many Germans on the horrors of the Nazis and on the merits of democracy. Little such instruction took place in Japan, partly because there was no Nazi-type party to blame or put on trial (just some generals) and partly because MacArthur did not dismantle the Japanese government but rather used it to run Japan. These Japanese bureaucrats and politicians quietly resolved not to change Japan too much.

One result of the U.S. occupation is that many Japanese to this day do not believe that Japan did much evil during the war. The way they see it, the victors vindictively punished the Japanese losers by hanging some seven hundred officers who had done their patriotic best. Bayonet practice on Chinese babies? Never. Germ warfare experiments on U.S. prisoners? No way. Korean "comfort ladies"? Not our doing. If you want to see war crimes, say some Japanese, look at Hiroshima and Nagasaki. The Japanese tend to see themselves as poor, downtrodden victims.

Only recently have some Japanese officials begun to admit war guilt (or is it shame?) for World War II. In 1991, Emperor Akihito apologized to Koreans for Japan's colonial occupation (1910–45). In Beijing in 1992, he told Chinese officials that he "deeply deplored" Japan's long (1931–45) war in China, which killed, by Beijing's estimate, 35 million Chinese. His father, Hirohito, had maintained a discreet silence about World War II. Prime Minister Hosokawa began his brief term in office by describing the Pacific War as Japanese aggression and apologizing for the "pain" Japan inflicted on other countries. In Germany, such admissions came decades earlier and were put into schoolbooks.

Many Japanese are still loath to admit the truth or to apologize. A 1995 Diet proposal for a resolution of apology was dropped in the face of an antiapology petition signed by five million Japanese and supported by most of the ruling party. One Japanese countered Hosokawa's atonement by claiming Japan had fought only "for self-defense and the independence of Asian countries," the old Greater East Asia Coprosperity Sphere line. In 1994, a minister resigned

Key Terms

guilt   Deeply internalized feeling of personal responsibility and moral failure.

shame   Feeling of incorrect behavior and violation of group norms.

POLITICAL CULTURE

GUILT VERSUS SHAME

Some foreign observers of Japan have argued that Japanese, unlike Westerners, are not driven by a sense of **guilt** but by the more superficial feeling of **shame**, of not upholding group standards. Guilt is woven into the Judeo-Christian ethos, starting with the Fall and continuing through the Crucifixion. The idea that God gives you moral choices and judges you is an important component of Western civilization and, according to some, the basis of Western individualism.

Japanese religion—and the Japanese are now probably the most irreligious people in the world—has no such reference points. Shintoism, a form of animism in which one's ancestors play a major role, now means basically worshiping Japan. There is no God or code of morality besides serving and obeying. State Shinto was refined into an organized religion by the Meiji modernizers to ensure loyalty during times of tremendous change, and as such lent itself to militarism. Buddhism, which exists side-by-side with Shintoism, is vague on the existence of God; Lord Buddha was merely enlightened, not divine. Either way, from Shinto or Buddha, few Japanese are on guilt trips.

Instead of guilt, according to this theory, Japanese are strongly motivated by shame. To let down the group is a terrible thing. In World War II, many Japanese preferred death to surrender, which meant shame. (Americans who surrendered were shameless cowards worthy only of harsh treatment.) One Japanese soldier who hid on Guam until 1972 said upon his heroic welcome back in Japan, "I have a gun from the emperor and I have brought it back." He also apologized: "I am ashamed that I have come home alive." There are few Japanese criminals, as trial and conviction brings devastating shame to the family. (The shame technique has been suggested for use on American criminals, but it doesn't work too well here.) The shame theory helps explain Japanese antiindividualism and the leitmotif of suicide that runs through the Japanese warrior code, politics, and even personal relationships.

Ritual dance at the Shinto shrine on Miyajima, home of the famous "floating torii" (gate, in background), teaches Japanese schoolchildren about their culture. (Michael Roskin)

after creating an uproar by claiming the 1937 Japanese "rape of Nanking" was a fiction. A book by a Chinese-American author with the same title could not find a Japanese publisher.

Prime ministers routinely pay homage to Japan's war dead at the controversial Yasukuni Shrine, the final resting place of many Japanese war criminals hanged by the Americans. LDP chiefs also cultivate the important Bereaved Families Association as well as political right-wingers and militarists who cluster in the Liberal Democratic party. Every year a couple of hundred members of parliament, right-wing LDP nationalists, visit the shrine.

Japan's Education Ministry carefully screens textbooks to promote unity and harmony. Truths that could provoke doubt and discord tend to get screened out. How history books handle World War II has long been a touchy subject, as in Germany. One older Japanese textbook said mildly, "We must not forget that Japan caused inconvenience to neighboring Asian countries in the past." China and Korea protested such a deceptive understatement, and the Education Ministry in 1992 ordered a tougher line substituted: "We must not forget that Japan caused unbearable suffering to neighboring nations in the past." The shift illustrates a couple of points: Japan at long last is starting to admit guilt, and Tokyo's ministries are still very powerful.

The view of themselves as the permanent disadvantaged underdogs colors many aspects of Japanese life. Japanese point out that all 126 million of them are confined to an **archipelago** about the size of California, most of it useless for crops, too mountainous to build on, and with zero mineral resources. We have to take special steps to ensure our survival, they argue; we cannot afford to be as free and open as big, rich countries. Furthermore, we have just been devastated in a terrible war.

In the immediate postwar years, there was clearly great validity in these attitudes. But after a quarter-century, by 1970, Japan was a sparkling, rich society with no need for special protection for any of its sectors. Psychologically, though, many Japanese, especially older people, act as if they are trapped in the worst years of wartime and postwar poverty and scarcity. Thus they "make do" with high tariffs, outrageous prices, cramped living quarters, and obedience and loyalty to company and bureaucratic authority.

Older Japanese especially display the psychological overshoot of insecure, worried people who have had to claw their way out of poverty. Such people work extremely hard and accomplish much, but they are often difficult to deal with, as it is impossible to calm their sense of deprivation. Mercifully, the younger

Key Term

archipelago Chain of islands.

generation, raised in postwar comfort, is repudiating the old attitudes, and we may expect policies to shift accordingly as more of this generation enters politics. This will take some time, however, as the generation currently ruling in Japan was born before World War II and still has vivid memories of the war and postwar period.

The Cult of the Group

Americans pride themselves on their individualism, Japanese on their groupness. We are trained from childhood to "be ourselves" and to attract attention: "Hey, look at me!" Japanese are trained to fit into the group and not attract attention: "It is the nail that sticks up that gets pounded down," goes a Japanese folk adage.

Almost like a big family, Japanese feel they can communicate with and understand only other Japanese. Foreigners, even if they live in Japan a long time and master the language, cannot do this, believe many Japanese, implying that Japanese have evolved to a higher human level. More plausibly, Japanese groupness is the result of centuries of isolation and feudal patterns, which taught that everyone has a place and must keep it.

Viewed in a less benign light, Japanese groupness is an expression of Japanese obedience. And Japanese are rather obedient. The crime rate is very low. There are fewer murders in all of Japan in one year than in Baltimore most weeks. (There are practically no private handguns in Japan.) Students hit the books with little complaint. Japanese bureaucrats instruct businesspersons on correct strategies, something no American businessman would tolerate for a moment.

The simplest explanation of where the emphasis on obedience comes from may be the

---

POLITICAL CULTURE

THE ROOTS OF JAPANESENESS

Japanese political culture is so distinctive, even from other East Asian cultures, that it has given rise to many theories of how it came to be. The truth is probably a combination of all.

- *Shintoism* taught that Japan and the Japanese are a perfect society that must not be changed or diluted.
- *Buddhism* still teaches the renunciation of desire, enduring pain and difficulties, and being careful and mindful of all persons and things.
- *Confucianism* taught that one is born into a strict hierarchy and must obey authority and treat superiors with great politeness.

- *Feudalism*, deep and prolonged in Japan, taught all to obey and honor superiors but diffused power among several centers.
- *Dependency* is inculcated into young Japanese by their parents and teachers. Unlike young Americans, Japanese are not trained for independence but to remain dutiful and submissive to authority of both the job and the government.
- *Crowded* into a small land, Japanese had to develop nice manners and cooperation to make daily life possible. (This would not explain New Yorkers.)

best: centuries of feudalism where even the hint of disobedience—such as not bowing low enough—to higher authority could be punished by beheading on the spot. Reinforcing this was the basic unit of the Japanese feudal system (borrowed from China through Confucianism), the *ie* (household), in which the patriarch had complete control over his wife and children. To this day, one can distinguish the social ranking of Japanese by noticing who bows lower. An underling bows very low and from the waist; his superior returns it with a curt, slight bow of the head. The Japanese do not have some special group or obedience gene; they were simply late in getting out of feudalism.

Unlike Western (especially American) individualists, Japanese generally try not to make waves. One should not attract attention to oneself or make a fuss, an attitude called **enryo** (more or less opposite of *chutzpah*, widely practiced by Americans). One should be polite and smile at all times, even in adversarial situations. One should not take legal actions, certainly not take someone to court, but should settle disputes quietly. (Japan has fewer lawyers than U.S. law schools produce each year.) One should not go to the doctor too much; small maladies will go away by themselves. (Japanese medical costs are half of America's, and Japanese have lower infant mortality and live longer.) Wow, maybe we should try a little *enryo*.

Key Term

enryo   Nonpresumptuousness; not asking for too much.

There is a negative side to this group-minded obedience: Japanese are severely shortchanged in the civil-rights and legal areas Americans take for granted. Some American lawyer-haters celebrate the fact that the Japanese rarely sue; they settle quietly, allegedly for the sake of social harmony. But this almost always leads to settlement in favor of the stronger party, no matter how rightful is the claim of the aggrieved party. In Japan, the rich and powerful company or bureaucracy is always right; the individual is always wrong.

Education for Grinds

The Japanese are strong on education, and this is possibly one of the keys to their success. The Japanese work force is considerably better educated than the American, especially in mathematics, the basis of all high-tech operations. On average, a Japanese high-school graduate

Traditional Japanese gardens feature the close control that is a prominent part of Japanese life. Note the small trees in enclosed settings—nature tamed. Indeed, the famous miniature bonsai trees are deliberately stunted rather than encouraged to grow. Some say Japanese children are also raised that way. (Michael Roskin)

knows more math than an American college graduate. Children do their homework—often supervised by "education mamas," mothers intent on their children's academic success—with a determination that puts even French grinds to shame. Of course, if Japanese students do poorly on exams, they may commit suicide out of shame.

Japanese youngsters run a demanding obstacle course to get into the right schools and universities. As an almost perfect **meritocracy**, all admissions are based on tests; athletic ability or family connections do not help. Cram courses may help, and many Japanese youngsters attend them after regular school hours. Getting into the right high school or university means "examination hell," a period of several days during which entrance exams are given.

Once into college, however, many Japanese students relax and do little work until their junior year, when they take exams that lead to jobs. Probably more important than what you learn in college is the fact that you got into a top college. If you've been admitted to the best, Tokyo University, you've got a head start over those who have been admitted to lesser institutions. Every prefecture has a public university—the U.S. occupation adopted the U.S. model of state universities—and they are generally good. In addition, Japan has hundreds of private colleges and universities of varying quality. Few Japanese students do graduate study, so few need a high grade-point average. Where you studied rather than grades matter for getting a job.

Key Term

meritocracy Advancement based only on intellectual ability.

THE UNITED STATES AND JAPAN: DESTINED TO MISUNDERSTAND?

Viscount Eiichi Shibuzawa (1840–1931), one of the founders of modern Japanese business and an advocate of strong U.S.-Japanese ties, grew exasperated with the difficulties he encountered. Wrote Shibuzawa: "No other countries exist which are as different from each other as the United States and Japan. These two countries seem to have been destined to misunderstand one another."

POLITICAL CULTURE

JAPAN'S CRITICAL CHRISTIANS

Religion everywhere has a major influence on political culture, and one clear difference between Japan and the West is the former's lack of Christianity. Christians of all denominations (mostly mainstream Protestant) form less than 1 percent of Japan's population and are not growing. (The Jesuits in the sixteenth century did better, gaining 2 percent.) Although Christian-related schools and colleges (many with U.S. ties) are numerous and popular, few students are drawn to Christianity. Western-style weddings, complete with marriage chapels and evening dress, are the rage but just for show.

Japan's Christians see themselves as an embattled, prophetic minority. They no longer face discrimination, just indifference. They deplore the lack of higher values among Japanese, whom they see caught up in "secular materialism"—the godless getting of money and things. They see Shinto and Buddhism as empty ritual, providing no moral grounding. The Japanese who drop in on a Buddhist service for a few minutes are simply doing a little relaxation therapy. Japanese Christians are among the few willing to face Japan's responsibility and guilt for World War II and to warn of the dangers of fanatic Buddhist-nationalist sects that spring up in Japan.

Christianity always had an uphill struggle in Japan, where it was regarded as a foreign subversion of Japaneseness. There is much truth to this, as Christianity brings with it individualism, guilt, and equality (especially between the sexes). Christianity would have greatly changed Japan, but this is unlikely to happen. The Japanese are content in their irreligiosity. In South Korea, by contrast, Christianity has reached majority status. Koreans, under the long Japanese oppression, saw churches (many U.S.-sponsored) as a comfort and support for their Koreanness.

Most Japanese students care and know nothing about politics. In some of the better universities, however, a few students under the influence of leftist professors learn to criticize the system that produced them. A few go into radical politics and protests, a handful into extremist terrorism. With graduation, though, almost all Japanese students get a haircut and new suit and dutifully become obedient **sararimen**. College in Japan is a brief respite of protest and freedom between the grind of grade school and the grind of work. Entrepreneurialism is rare; you either get a job with a big company or you're nothing. (Only recently have some young Japanese begun starting their own companies.)

The content of Japanese education is heavily slanted to rote learning and multiple-choice exams. Creativity and innovation are not highly prized; going along with the group is. Debate is normally taught only as part of English-language instruction, as if to imply that only with foreigners does one have disagreements. One interesting difference with U.S. classrooms: In Japan, the fast learners are assigned to help the slow. This is good for the education of both of them and builds groupness.

Americans and even some Japanese criticize the rote aspect of Japanese education, arguing that it hampers flexible, new thinking later in life. But problem-solving in mathematics does precisely that, and Japanese growth rates and labor productivity indicate that Japanese are plenty innovative. As U.S. classrooms have moved away from rote learning, they have left behind the

Key Term

sararimen Literally, "salary men"; mid-level employees.

self-discipline that comes with it. We might actually wish to reintro-
duce a bit of roteness. Besides, Japanese schooling is changing, producing a more spontaneous, questioning sort of student. Japanese
education is losing some of its rigidity.

Key Term

nemawashi   Literally,
"root-binding," as in
gardening; the formation of
group consensus.

Death of a Sarariman

The typical Japanese *sarariman*—who wears a suit no matter what the weather—would probably like to spend his entire working life with the same company. (We say "he" because, as yet,
most Japanese women are content to be "office ladies" for a few years before marriage, although
this is rapidly changing.) The company would like to reciprocate by offering "lifetime employment" to its people. Keep in mind, however, that at its peak only about 30 percent of the Japanese work force was covered by lifetime commitment from employers, chiefly large concerns,
and this has dwindled during Japan's long economic downturn. Smaller companies are forced
to hire and lay off as economic conditions dictate, although for most of the postwar period, economic growth has been so consistent that unemployment appeared only in the late 1990s.

Until recently, most Japanese employees felt duty-bound to stay with their firm. American-
style job-hopping was frowned upon as opportunistic and disloyal. Decades ago, I assured a
Japanese colleague from the Associated Press's Tokyo bureau it would be perfectly alright for him
to leave AP for a much better paying job. It just went against his grain to desert a company. He
was finally persuaded, he told me, when he saw me leave AP in New York for a better job, an
easy decision for an American. This has changed; along with corporate downsizing has come
job-hopping.

THE UNITED STATES AND JAPAN: MANAGING DIFFERENCES

Two business seminars are held in New
York City, one for twenty-five Japanese
executives in America, the other for twenty-
five American executives working for Japanese firms in the United States. The Japanese,
all males, arrive in dark suits and keep their
coats on even though the room is hot. They
take exactly the allotted ten minutes for a
coffee break. They ask no questions until
they get to know each other over lunch.
They politely defer to the speakers.

The American group includes eight
women. Many of the men immediately take
off their coats in the hot room. Chatting during the coffee break lasts more than twenty
minutes. The Americans ask many questions, and some dispute the speakers.

These are just a few of the cultural differences between Japanese and American managers. Americans view conflict within the
firm as normal; Japanese practice **nemawashi**, patient discussion leading to a
consensus which then all follow. American
managers want quick profits; Japanese want
bigger market share and greater efficiency,
building for the long run. American firms
hire people for specific skills, then downsize
them when they are no longer needed.
Japanese firms hire for what the person can
learn and contribute to improved efficiency
and try to not let the employee go. American
managers respond to questions quickly and
directly, for that indicates frankness. Japanese managers pause before answering and
give discreet replies, for that indicates
thoughtfulness. Sometimes one wonders if
we are indeed destined to misunderstand
each other.

HOW WOULD YOU DO ON A JAPANESE EXAM?

This solid-geometry problem is from a recent entrance examination to Japan's elite Tokyo University. It is aimed at young Japanese in their last year of high school.

A regular pyramid with a height of V and a square base of width *a* rests on a sphere. The base of the pyramid passes through the center of the sphere, and all eight edges of the pyramid touch the surface of the sphere, as is shown in the illustration.

How do you calculate (1) the height of V and (2) the volume that the pyramid and sphere share in common?

Well, you say, I'm not a math major and should not be expected to know such advanced stuff. But this question is from the exam for *humanities* applicants.

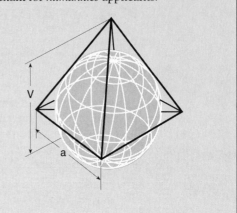

Japanese work very hard, probably too hard. An eight-hour day is rare for a *sarariman*; twelve hours is common. Some Japanese literally die of overwork, an illness they call **karoshi** (not to be confused with bar-singing *karaoke*, which is how many *sararimen* relax). Cases keep cropping up of *karoshi* victims working fifty or more days without a day off or working one hundred or more hours of overtime a month. Recently, though, some bereaved families have sued the companies that worked the husband into an early grave. (One benefit offered by some large firms: burial in the corporate cemetery, so you can be with your group for eternity.) The new generation of Japanese does not like to work so hard (or be buried in the company plot). They prefer leisure time to overtime and ask, "Why kill yourself for the company?"

One of the great puzzles of postwar Japan is why its people work so hard and produce so much but ask for so little. *Sararimen* are willing to live in rabbit-hutch apartments and commute for hours standing up in a crowded rail car to their urban jobs. The cost of living is among the highest in the world, especially for housing. Europeans and Americans would long since have gone out on strike in such conditions. Japanese unions are weak, many are organized by and for companies, and, if they must strike, do so over lunch hour so as not to disrupt work.

How can the Japanese put up with it? The explanation is that Japanese culture really is different—or at least has been different until now. Centuries of obedient, feudal relations have taught the Japanese not to ask for a great deal but to work hard for the lord (or company) and take pride in living modestly, even frugally. Japan never developed a social safety net or social-security system, so the Japanese learned to save for hard times and for their retirement. The Japanese are bigger savers than the Germans, and the capital this made available to banks and businesses helps explain much of Japan's magnificent postwar economic growth: plentiful supply of capital.

Key Term

karoshi Death by overwork.

POLITICAL CULTURE

WHY IS WA?

Some argue that the Japanese word **wa** is the key to Japanese culture. Japanese are trained to seek and cultivate harmonious relations with each other. *Wa* is what gives Japan its cooperative, group-mindedness where everyone looks out for everyone else. (Notice how the only way to play Pokémon is by cooperation.) Critics argue, however, that the concept of *wa* is deliberately hyped to provide a cover story for promoting conformity and obedience. Under the doctrine of harmony, anyone questioning or criticizing the way things are run is disturbing the domestic peace and tranquility and is therefore a troublemaker. *Wa* can be a device for social control.

Wa can also lead to terrible financial losses when corporations and government bureaucrats cover up financial problems rather than face them early and honestly. Several giant Japanese corporations have lost fortunes in financial mistakes—all kept quiet until too late. Sumitomo Corporation revealed in 1996 that a single copper trader had compounded one mistake into another and lost the company $1.8 billion. And the company had known about it all along but didn't want to disturb the harmony.

Political Suicide

Now a minor part of Japanese culture is the willingness to commit suicide under certain circumstances. Originally a component of *bushido*, the nobles' code of honor, *seppuku* (vulgarly known as *hara-kiri*) showed that a samurai was willing to die to avoid shame on himself and his family. Although only a small fraction of the Japanese population is of knightly descent, a greater number pretend to be and admire and affect its styles. As U.S. forces took Saipan in 1944, some four thousand Japanese women and girls committed suicide by jumping off cliffs. Prince Konoe, prime minister just before the war and grandfather of Prime Minister Hosokawa, when ordered to turn himself in for trial as a war criminal by the U.S. occupation, committed suicide in 1945.

In addition to atoning for personal shame, suicide has another use: It induces a sense of shame in others. If I sincerely believe in a cause but am not getting my way, by committing suicide before those I am trying to convince I make them ashamed and thus pressure them to follow my way. By dying, I win. This is still understood if no longer widely followed. In 1993, for example, a right-wing politician went to Japan's leading newspaper, the Asahi, to complain about its liberal slant. After rambling on before bored editors, he pulled out two guns and shot himself to death with both. In 1999 a Bridgestone manager disemboweled himself before the company president to protest downsizing.

Japan's most famous postwar suicide was that of Yukio Mishima in 1970. At age 45, Mishima was internationally acclaimed as Japan's greatest writer. He was also a fanatic right-wing militarist (and homosexual) who sponsored his own private army to inculcate young men with the old warrior spirit of Japan. Mishima specifically hated the clause of Japan's constitution that forbade it from having an army, even though it does have a

Key Term

wa Japanese for social harmony.

The United States and Japan: The Minamata Pietà

An environmental catastrophe on Japan's Minamata Bay illustrates the different moral and legal attitudes between the United States and Japan. A chemical company had long dumped mercury waste into the bay. The children of those who ate mercury-contaminated fish from the bay were born deformed. Famed U.S. photographer W. Eugene Smith, a man of great humanistic conscience, felt he had to tell the story. Few Japanese photographers or news media were interested. One of Smith's moving photos, of a Minamata mother bathing her deformed child, won the accolade "Minamata **pietà**," as it reminded viewers of Renaissance paintings and sculptures.

Many Japanese were not moved by the moral or legal challenge of toxic-waste dumping. Chisso Chemical, the cause of the horror, was a major employer, and government policy stressed the economy, not ecology. Chisso workers severely beat Smith for daring to impugn their company's honor. Smith had trouble getting his photos displayed until the manager of a big Tokyo department store decided to take the heat for the sake of artistic and ethical truth. He was criticized for disturbing the harmony of Japanese society. The victims finally sued Chisso, but the courts let the case drag on for one-third of a century before making Chisso pay a paltry $60,000 each to the 3,000 worst-harmed victims and $22,000 each to thousands of others.

In the United States, the media and photographers, many with a strong environmentalist slant, would cover the situation fully. American lawyers would be eager to take the victims' case. U.S. courts generally rule that companies face "strict liability" in such cases; if they caused the damage they must pay for it. Japanese courts make plaintiffs prove "negligence," that the company not only caused the damage but should have known it was doing so. In Japan, judges decide cases, not juries. Lawyers, courts, and lawsuits do have their uses; America may have too many, but Japan has too few. Indeed, Japanese universities are now expanding their law programs by adding U.S.-style three-year postgraduate law schools.

Key Terms

pietà   Italian for "piety"; artistic representations of Mary cradling the body of Jesus.

shin jinrui   Shin = new, jin = person, rui = class of; Japanese for new human race; the younger generation.

hefty "self-defense force." Mishima tried to change this by seizing the old Imperial Army Headquarters in Tokyo with a small group. When the takeover failed, Mishima, in a military-type uniform, committed *seppuku* on a balcony at the Headquarters before hundreds of horrified officers. Mishima ritually disemboweled himself with a special knife; then a friend beheaded him with a sword. His aim was to convince the officers to shake off the lethargy of peace and return to the way of the warrior. Suicide, because it is so traditional, tends to be used by conservatives who harken back to old ways. As such, it occurs less and less frequently.

The "New Human Race"

As you have noticed, the generation gap is wide in Japan, the widest of all the countries we study in this book. Older Japanese are amazed and not completely happy at how much the younger Japanese have changed and call the youngsters the **shin jinrui** because they are so different.

Physically, Japanese 20-year-old males are on average nearly 4 inches taller than those of three decades earlier, females 2.7 inches taller. Almost all of the Japanese gain has been in the

POLITICAL CULTURE

THE HONOR OF ON

Another remnant of feudalism in Japan is **on**. It is social and symbolic rather than legal and monetary and underlies the Japanese sense of obligation. If someone has done you a small favor, he or she has incurred your *on*, and you are expected to remember it and return the courtesy someday. *On* lubricates much Japanese social life. If you visit Japan, bring small, inexpensive gifts for your hosts.

For example, I repeatedly invited an American friend and his Japanese wife to visit me and my family for a weekend, but I was always politely turned down. My American friend explained why. My invitation had come without any basis in *on*, so his Japanese wife felt awkward in accepting. My friend had an idea to overcome the problem. He sent me two lovely books of photos as a gift, thereby incurring my *on*. At that point it was honorable for them to come and visit. The offering of gifts is also a normal and even required part of Japanese political life.

legs and is believed to be related to a more Western-type diet that is richer in protein than the traditional Japanese rice-based diet. Indeed, rice has been declining in popularity while McDonald's and Kentucky Fried Chicken have become, respectively, Japan's first and second most popular restaurants. With the growth spurt, however, the higher-fat diet has brought some obesity, never before known among Japanese youngsters. Another factor: Japanese no longer kneel in the home and office but sit in chairs; this has eliminated the constant pressure on the knees that stunted the growth of Japanese legs. (Earlier, the children and grandchildren of Japanese immigrants to America showed precisely the same startling increases in size.)

But more importantly, Japanese attitudes are rapidly changing among young people. Working long hours for the sake of the company is no longer seen as normal and desirable. Desire for leisure time for family, hobbies, and travel makes younger Japanese similar to their European and American counterparts. Holding down consumption for the sake of saving is no longer so attractive. Many younger Japanese have traveled or studied in the United States and have sampled the indulgent lifestyle of American youth. American fashions are the norm. (One recent craze: the expensive outdoors look of L.L. Bean, imported from Maine and sold exclusively in Bean stores in Japan.) They have learned to want the good life and to want it now.

To a considerable extent, it is the coming of age of the "new human race" that made the political changes of the 1990s possible. The older generation, schooled in discipline and deprivation, simply obeyed for most of the postwar period. What the company and government offered was good enough. Younger Japanese have lost some of these characteristics and are more likely to switch their jobs and their votes. Older Japanese could tolerate the corruption and factionalized leadership of the LDP; after all, the party had led Japan to prosperity. Younger Japanese are more likely to say the system needs a thorough housecleaning. Japanese political attitudes are not entirely different from the attitudes of other advanced industrial countries and with time are likely to increasingly resemble them.

Looked at over the span of a century and a half—since Perry—Japanese political culture appears as a continual rear-guard action designed to preserve the core of Japaneseness. Gradually and grudgingly

Key Term

on Duty or debt of honor.

COMPARISON

CHANGING POLITICAL CULTURES IN GERMANY AND JAPAN

West German political culture shared some characteristics with Japan. Both had a history of strong feudal hierarchies and stress on obedience. Both marched eagerly to war under dictators who knew how to manipulate traditional-looking symbols. Neither country took to democracy until it was imposed on them after World War II. After the devastation of the war and the lean postwar years, Germans too worked hard and did not ask for much. A reliable conservative party, the CDU, delivered growing prosperity, and Germans were not in the mood for experiments. Student radicals could fuss over the U.S. alliance and nuclear weapons, but solid citizens understood they were necessary. The difference is, Germany shed its postwar stability in about a generation; the Japanese took two generations.

Why was Japan slower? First, Japan's feudalism lasted longer and its obedience patterns were inculcated deeper than Germany's. Second, Japan was more isolated even after World War II and its people traveled less than West Germans. Third, Japan did not go through the reeducation that West Germany did after the war. Fourth, Japan was a poor country, poorer than most of West Europe, until it sprinted forward in the 1960s and 1970s. As Japan gets richer and more open to the world, its political culture may become less distinctive.

over time, Japan gives way to the *gaijin* ways, accepting some superficially and altering others. The Meiji modernizers in effect said: "Alright, we've got to modernize to prevent the West from taking us over. But we'll do it our way." After World War II, Japan in effect said: "Alright, we've got to become a capitalist democracy. But we'll do it our way."

After many such changes, Japanese political culture does shift, but never in a rapid or revolutionary way. It is the nature of a system that you cannot change just one thing, for when you do everything else changes. For example, equality of women, although in the MacArthur Constitution, is just now slowly being implemented. Women are going to college in large numbers. A few even seek the executive track in corporations. They drive cars, marry later, and work outside the home after marriage. This slowly changes male attitudes (many don't like it), childrearing patterns, household income, and eventually political attitudes. But they will always preserve that inner core of Japaneseness. Japan does change, but changes are usually incremental and nearly invisible, almost as if the elites of Japan meet quietly for a great *nemawashi* (see page 339) to construct a new consensus that will give in partway to the *gaijin*.

Key Terms

archipelago (p. 334)

enryo (p. 336)

guilt (p. 333)

karoshi (p. 340)

meritocracy (p. 337)

nemawashi (p. 339)

on (p. 343)

pietà (p. 342)

sarariman (p. 338)

shin jinrui (p. 342)

wa (p. 341)

Further Reference

Cutts, Robert L. *An Empire of Schools: Japan's Universities and the Molding of a National Power Elite*. Armonk, NY: M. E. Sharpe, 1997.

Fallows, James. *Looking at the Sun*. New York: Pantheon, 1994.

Feiler, Bruce. *Learning to Bow: Inside the Heart of Japan*. New York: Ticknor & Fields, 1992.

Garon, Sheldon. *Molding Japanese Minds: The State in Everyday Life*. Princeton, NJ: Princeton University Press, 1998.

Kumagai, Fumie, and Donna J. Keyser. *Unmasking Japan Today: The Impact of Traditional Values on Modern Japanese Society*. Westport, CT: Praeger, 1996.

Martin, Curtis H., and Bruce Stronach. *Politics East and West: A Comparison of Japanese and British Political Culture*. Armonk, NY: M. E. Sharpe, 1992.

Martineau, Lisa. *Caught in a Mirror*. New York: Macmillan, 1993.

McCargo, Duncan. *Contemporary Japan*. New York: St. Martin's, 2000.

McVeigh, Brian J. *The Nature of the Japanese State: Rationality and Rituality*. New York: Routledge, 1998.

Stronach, Bruce. *Beyond the Rising Sun: Nationalism in Contemporary Japan*. Westport, CT: Praeger, 1995.

Japan:
Patterns of Interaction

25

Questions to Consider

1. Aren't most countries run by "iron triangles"?
2. Is Japan a good example of a free-market economy?
3. Which are more important in Japan, interest groups or the bureaucracy?
4. Compare and contrast top French and Japanese bureaucrats.
5. Could something like MITI work in America?
6. Does corruption indicate political underdevelopment?
7. Can Japan's "money politics" be reformed?
8. Is the "no one in charge" theory valid?
9. What are "shadow shoguns" and do they still run things?
10. Did the 2000 elections change Japanese politics?

Japanese political interactions are sometimes described as an **iron triangle** consisting of the Liberal Democratic party, economic interest groups, and the ministries. Since the 1993 electoral upheaval, with its promise of major change, all new prime ministers have vowed to break the iron triangle. Such triangles, however, are not easily broken.

The classic Japanese pattern formed during the long reign of the LDP works as follows. Liberal Democratic politicians promise most of the country's economic interest groups—with agriculture and the construction industry prominent among them—to look out for their interests. In return, the interest groups deliver plentiful campaign funds, enabling the LDP to greatly outspend rival parties. (Some LDP politicians also put some of the funds in their own pockets.)

The LDP, however, rarely translates interest-group demands directly into law and policy; instead, they let the ministries and agencies adjudicate the demands by means of contracts, regulations, subsidies, and trade protection. The ministries have been there longer, know all the right people and how to deal with them, and can generally come up with workable compromises.

The ministries, the commanding corner of the triangle, have their own agenda, and it is not Adam Smith's vision of a free and open market in which competition delivers the best products and the lowest prices. Instead, the Tokyo

Key Term

iron triangle An interlocking of politicians, bureaucrats, and business people to promote the flow of funds among them.

ministries focus narrowly on their industries and sectors and seek to
protect them by controlled markets in which domestic competition
is limited lest it become cutthroat, and foreign competition is artful-
ly excluded wherever possible. This setup makes the Japanese economy—which superficially looks like a free-market economy—one of
the most regulated in the world. Until recent reforms, some eleven
thousand bureaucratic regulations governed every aspect and branch
of the Japanese economy. The Japanese economy has not been a good
example of a free-market system.

Key Terms

guided capitalism State
supervision but not ownership of the economy.

public corporation
Special-purpose economic
unit owned in whole or in
part by government (U.S.
example: TVA).

The ministries do not serve the interest groups, the way things
often work in the United States or Europe. Rather, the interest groups get some of what they
want from the ministries in return for overall obedience to the ministries' schemes to build regulated markets under the control of bureaucrats. The Japanese arrangement, reminiscent of the
controlled, mercantilist system of the French kings, suits practically all Japanese interest groups.
Japanese consumers, on the other hand, get robbed by outrageous prices.

Bureaucrats in Command

In emphasizing the political importance of top civil servants, we must understand where Japan's
ministries came from. They are not the product of a free-market democracy but of a militaristic system planning for and conducting World War II. Munitions, heavy industry, the development of Manchuria, transportation and communications, and many other sectors of Japan's
economy were under state control and supervision. Indeed, the very founding of the modern
Japanese economy during the Meiji Restoration was ordered and controlled by the state. Japan
has not really known a free-market economy.

After the war, precisely the same bureaucrats who ran Japan's war economy were given the
job of economic recovery. This they proceeded to do—and do very well—in the same spirit
they had displayed during the war: Economic development is too important to be left to capitalists. Japan is fighting for its economic life and does not have the luxury of slowly finding its
way by means of the inefficient system of supply and demand, went the postwar argument.
The attitude of Japan's top bureaucrats was that nothing but Japan's economic growth mattered,
and we are the only folks who know how to make it happen.

This would not properly be called a "socialist" system, for it kept ownership private and
did not attempt to redistribute wealth or income from the rich to the poor. It was not directly aimed at rapid improvement of individual living standards but at the growth of the Japanese economy as a whole. Some call such a system "statist," a system, as we have considered in
France and will examine again in Brazil, where the state is the number-one capitalist and owns
major industrial and financial institutions. This is not the case in Japan, which has little state-
owned industry. Perhaps the best name we can come up with for Japan is **guided capitalism**.

The Japanese government does not own much, but it has numerous **public corporations**
aimed at aiding various industries and economic development of several regions, especially
poorer ones, such as Hokkaido. The Japanese method of control is to leave most industry in
private hands but to prod—often over dinner and drinks—the industry to go this way or that
by rational persuasion and bank loans. The targets are the likely areas where Japanese advantages allow them to undercut foreign producers and then secure an overwhelming world-market share. (The strategy with the Japanese camera industry against the German was one such
success. See the box about this in the next chapter, on page 361.)

JAPAN'S MAJOR INTEREST GROUPS

Japanese interest groups tend to follow the French model; that is, they are usually subordinate to bureaucratic authority, but even more than the French groups, the Japanese interest groups until recently have seldom disputed or ignored the ministry that supervises them. Japanese pluralism is weaker than American pluralism, where interests tend to either capture the relevant agency or, failing that, fight it. That said, here are some top Japanese interest confederations:

- *Keidanren*, Federation of Economic Organizations, the most important business group, speaks for most large corporations and used to work closely with MITI to promote exports. Now it is working around ministerial control in favor of deregulation and competition.
- *Shin Rengo*, Japanese Trade Union Confederation, formed from the 1989 merger of smaller union federations, speaks for eight million members in a moderate and voice, even though it still has some ties to the Social Democrats.
- *Nissho*, Japan Chamber of Commerce and Industry, with good ties to the LDP, seeks to curb competition, large stores, discounting, and foreign imports.
- *Nokyo*, Central Union of Agricultural Cooperatives, argues for self-sufficiency in food and the exclusion of farm imports to its friend, the LDP.

- *Nikkyoso*, Japan Teachers Union, left-wing, pacifist, critical of government and powerful among grade-school teachers; tied to the Social Democrats.
- *Jichiro*, the Prefectural and Local Public Employees Union, is Japan's largest single union and is quite influential. It is also leftist and tied to the Social Democrats.

The leftist union of Japanese school-teachers protests against Japanese re-armament, NATO, and the United States, and for socialism, in a peaceful demonstration across the street from the Diet. (Michael Roskin)

Those industries certified as growth leaders get long-term, low-interest loans from banks that are connected with the important ministries. Those industries not moving down the desired paths did not get big loans. This is a far more subtle way of steering an economy than the outright state control of Soviet-type socialism. (It also meant, by the 1990s, that many loans were mistakes that ruined many Japanese banks. There's a down side to everything.) The Japanese approach is similar to the French "indicative planning" but stronger and more effective because it can make the cash flow and takes place in the cooperative Japanese setting where business generally obeys government.

For the most part, the top bureaucrats of Finance and MITI do a good job. Handpicked from the brightest graduates, they are promoted rapidly and given major responsibilities while young. Their salaries, however, are not high, and if they wish to move into lucrative positions in private industry in mid-career (what the Japanese call "descent from heaven" and the French call "putting on the slippers"), so much the better. That way the ministry broadens its ties with private industry (and, with it, the breeding grounds for corruption). Japan recovered quickly after World War II and went on to set economic growth records. As we shall explore in the next chapter, however, the bureaucratic guidance may have led to dangerous distortions in the Japanese economy that plunged it into difficulties later.

For some time, defenders of Japan claimed proponents of the overpowerful-bureaucracy theory were engaging in Japan-bashing. Then in 1993 the reformist Hosokawa government publicly agreed that the ministries were too powerful and needed to be curbed and coordinated. By the 1996 elections, virtually all parties agreed and made reforming the bureaucracies and regulations part of their campaign promises. (What they actually carried out is another matter.) Yesterday's Japan-bashing became today's conventional wisdom.

It will not be easy; the bureaucrats are used to their power. Fumed one high official of the powerful and conservative **Okurasho** about some changes proposed by a reformist cabinet: "We won't accommodate them, I assure you. They will accommodate us." In an unheard-of move,

Key Term

Okurasho Japan's finance ministry.

COMPARISON

BUREAUCRATIC ELITES IN FRANCE AND JAPAN

The concept of a strong bureaucracy operating on its own, with little guidance or input from elected officials, is nothing new. France had such a system for decades, and it is doubtful if de Gaulle's Fifth Republic or Mitterrand's reforms made French bureaucrats answerable to the electorate. The Japanese bureaucratic elite is a moderately close analog to the French *grand corps*. Both are very bright and highly educated and placed into the top executive positions with mandates to modernize and upgrade the economies of their respective countries. Both tend to think that they alone can save their countries and that elected politicians are a necessary evil that come and go and are not to be taken seriously.

The French are trained in a Great School, such as the National Administration School or Polytechnical, whereas the brainiest young Japanese gain admission to the prestigious Tokyo University ("Todai"), which is publicly funded. Upon graduation, both enter bureaucratic fast tracks for the executive level, and both may retire early into a better-paying job in private industry. The French bureaucratic elite disdains the views of interest groups as un-French and unobjective. The Japanese bureaucrats generally listen earnestly to the views of the interests it is assigned to supervise, but then it gently tries to persuade the interest group to change its views to match those of the ministry.

A big difference is that French bureaucratic elites tend to read from the same sheet of music and to cooperate across ministries. The Japanese are soon inculcated with their ministries' particular point of view and pay little attention to the views of other ministries. There is no grand plan in the Japanese model, and sometimes ministries work at cross-purposes.

THE UNITED STATES AND JAPAN: AN AMERICAN DITI?

If Japan's Ministry of International Trade and Industry helped speed Japan to the upper ranks of the industrialized countries after World War II, could not a U.S. equivalent—a Department of International Trade and Industry (DITI)—do the same for the United States? Here, we see how hard it can be to transfer institutions from one country to another.

MITI functioned well in a Japanese political culture of cooperation and obedience. MITI bureaucrats, to be sure, did not order businessmen to do things. They persuaded them, often by lengthy wining and dining. Soon enough, businessmen could get the point that what was good for them was also good for Japan.

A DITI would have to operate in a far more individualistic American context, one where businessmen are taught to disdain government and go their own way. Washington has no national "industrial policy" and is unlikely to develop one any time soon. U.S. antitrust laws might make collaboration between firms illegal, not a problem in Japan. The U.S. government's ability to provide bank loans would mean a whole redo of the U.S. banking system. Actually, the United States is trying government-led technological development. Sematech brought together five U.S. computer-chip manufacturers, exempt from antitrust laws, to share manufacturing technologies. The results of this small experiment have been positive.

in late 1993 the minister in charge of MITI fired a top career bureaucrat. The cabinet seemed to be telling the bureaucracy, "All right, you want a showdown?"

The economic downturn of the late 1990s showed the bureaucrats were unable to pull Japan out of its slump; the formulas of yesteryear no longer worked. Impatient, the top industrialists of Keidanren organized their own Competitiveness Committee and made some hard-hitting recommendations to the government, bypassing MITI altogether. Keidanren's message to the cabinet and the Diet: Fix this creaky economic machine or we move our factories overseas, which is what they were doing anyway. The bureaucracy lost prestige too. Law students at the elite Tokyo University, who used to compete to enter the civil service, now turn to private industry. Said one senior: "The bureaucrats have a bad image now—rigid, inflexible, annoying." If Japan cuts the power and status of its bureaucrats it will mark the evolution of Japan into a more normal country.

Key Terms

corruption Use of public office for private gain.

scandal A corrupt practice publicized by the news media.

walking-around money Relatively small payments by politicians to buy votes.

Corruption Scandals

Another leg of the "iron triangle," connecting the LDP to interest groups, is the fertile ground for **corruption**. There seems to be a new **scandal** every year. It used to be widely accepted, among both foreign and Japanese observers, that a little corruption was normal in Japan—an artifact of the electoral system—and that most Japanese did not especially mind it. **Walking-around money** is part of many political systems, and voters expect favors from politicians.

Few books on Japanese politics mentioned corruption except in passing; it did not seem to be an important point. Japanese, according to many area experts, like other Asians, understand and tolerate graft up to a certain level and object only when takers get conspicuously greedy. Maybe this was once the case, but by the early 1990s, with a well-educated postwar generation taking an interest in politics, attitudes changed. The corruption scandals got bigger, the previously rather docile Japanese media started going after corrupt politicians, and the Japanese public was less and less tolerant of political corruption.

In 1974 Lockheed was found to be delivering major bribes to Japanese politicians to get them to purchase Lockheed jet fighters for the Japanese air force. Lockheed said that it was just doing business like everyone else in Japan. Japanese politicians said they needed the money for party campaign expenses, but much of it stayed in private pockets. Energetic Prime Minister Kakuei Tanaka (1972–74) was brought down by the scandal and arrested and jailed briefly in 1976.

In 1988 and 1989 the Recruit Corporation privately sold untraded shares of stock to many LDP (including later Prime Minister Mori) and a few opposition politicians at bargain prices. Some made as much as $1 million overnight. The public was enraged, and Prime Minister Noboru Takeshita resigned in shame in 1989. A top aide committed suicide. Former Prime Minister Yasuhiro Nakasone, also implicated in the scandal, resigned from the LDP.

In 1992 Sagawa, a parcel express firm, was found to be paying off more than sixty politicians, with the top prize of $4.2 million going to LDP faction chief Shin Kanemaru of the old Tanaka faction. During the war, right-winger Kanemaru was an Imperial official in Manchukuo and later became the LDP's main fund-raiser. Kanemaru's sources included organized crime. His office safe held $50 million in cash and gold bars, but Kanemaru was fined less than $2,000. Public outrage mounted and carried over into the following year's elections.

The signs that corruption was a serious problem in Japan had been evident for some time. Everyone knew that public works, such as highways, bridges, and retaining walls (widely used in mountainous areas) rewarded both constituents and contractors, who were expected to kick back a percentage into party or personal coffers. Komeito was founded in the 1950s as the "clean government party," an obvious indication that corruption existed and that a certain fraction of the Japanese electorate wanted to do something about it.

COMPARISON

CORRUPTION INTERNATIONAL

Corruption is not just a Japanese problem; it's nearly everywhere. This is the finding of Transparency International, a Berlin-based organization that polls business people on their perceptions of having to pay off government officials and ranks countries on a ten-point index, ten being totally clean. Some of their 1999 findings:

Denmark	10.0
Canada	9.2
Singapore	9.1
Britain	8.6
Germany	8.0
United States	7.5
Chile	6.9
France	6.6
Japan	6.0
South Africa	5.0
Brazil	4.1
China	3.4
Mexico	3.4
India	2.9
Russia	2.4

Key Terms

money politics   Lavish use of funds to win elections.

¥   Symbol for yen, Japan's currency, worth about 100 to the dollar.

Many believe corruption is rooted in Japan's **money politics**, as the candidates (until the 1993 reforms) did not distinguish themselves by party platform or personality but by size of cash gifts. Under the old electoral system, LDP candidates often ran against other LDP candidates, a system that begged for factionalism and corruption. Prior to 1993, neither the government nor the party provided much funding for candidates or incumbents, who were left to raise funds for themselves.

And running for and holding office in Japan is not cheap. In addition to the usual local offices and constituent services, Japanese politicians by tradition must endear themselves to voters by attending weddings and funerals in their districts and giving nontrivial presents of cash to newlyweds and the bereaved. (It incurs their *on*.) A typical LDP incumbent spent an estimated ¥120 million (over $1 million) a year but got an allowance of only ¥20 million. The remaining ¥100 million (about $1 million) had to be raised somewhere, by the donations of friends, supporters, businesses, and even the gangster underworld.

Although supposedly controlled by law, money politics led to one scandal after another when the amounts were too big, the conflicts of interest too obvious, the methods of donation secretive, or the sources too dirty. The new electoral system was designed in part to break this pattern. To further break the money politics system, other new laws allowed corporate contributions only to parties, not to individuals, and offered public subsidies totaling ¥30.9 billion (about $300 million) to parties for campaign expenses.

By the early 1990s, the entire LDP was looking dirty, and some LDP politicians, generally younger and with an eye to the future, began bailing out of the party before it also tarnished them and began forming new parties. In 1993, voters, many now openly fed up with corruption, deserted not only the LDP but the perennial second party, the Social Democrats, who were also tarred with scandal. The immediate reason was both parties' failure to devise and lead the reforms necessary to curb corruption, make voting fair, and break out of the rigid patterns of a state-led export economy that was in difficulty.

The increasing clamor related to corruption shows the Japanese voting public is growing more mature and more democratic. What an older generation accepted as normal, a younger generation brands as dirty, dishonorable, and undemocratic. Notice how at this same

Japanese Communists politely try to interest passersby in Kyoto but get few takers. The JCP was always a small party. (Michael Roskin)

DEMOCRACY

CAN "MONEY POLITICS" BE BROKEN?

One of the questions of interest to political scientists in the Japanese electoral and campaign-funding reforms of 1993 is whether money politics is so deeply rooted into Japanese political culture that no amount of legal tinkering can end it. It is an example of a classic question: Which is more important in political systems, **structure** or psychology? In 1993, the Diet changed the structure. Did the psychology also change as a consequence?

Japan's money politics seemed to continue with subsequent elections, but we may have to give the new system more time.

Electoral reforms do not always work as planned. The United States has gone through several reforms of campaign financing only to find that both candidates and contributors come up with new ways to beat the system. (Now it's **soft money**.) The underlying prob-lem is the desperate need for prodigious campaign funds, in America for televised spots and in Japan for soundtrucks and gifts.

The Japanese reformers proposed that changing their electoral system would help eliminate some of this desperate need for campaign money. But will it? The United States, France, and Germany have very different electoral systems, but each have recurring scandals related to fund-raising. Why? Because in each system parties and candidates figure out ways to skirt the law. And in each system, some candidates use campaign contributions—both legal and illegal—for personal expenses, which often leads to additional scandals. Notice the underlying similarity: All politicians—American, Japanese, French, and German—are addicted to money. In the words of California political boss Jesse Unruh, "Money is the mother's milk of politics."

time Italian and Brazilian politicians were also brought down by the sort of corruption that had been going on for decades. These scandals were good signs, for they showed that people world-wide really do understand that they are ill-served by corrupt governments. A Japanese party that lets itself be drawn into the old patterns now understands that it will suffer electoral pun-ishment. Even the LDP vowed to reform itself and the system, although once the LDP was back in power influence-buying scandals continued to plague its top politicians.

No One in Charge?

One of the most damning accusations of the "Japan-bashers"—chief among them Karel van Wolferen, a Dutch journalist with many years of experience in Japan—is that behind an impressive façade of powerful and orderly government, there is no real center of decision-making power in Japan, no one in charge.

Prime ministers do not lead; they hang on to office for perhaps two years until the LDP faction chiefs dump them. The faction chiefs do not lead; they simply amass feudal power with which to bat-tle each other. Parliamentarians do little but collect money from

Key Terms

structure The institutions of government such as constitution, laws, and branches.

soft money In U.S. politics, funds given to parties and other groups rather than to candidates, in order to skirt restrictions.

private interests to ensure their reelection. And even the mighty bureaucracies, such as the *Okurasho* and MITI, lead only in their narrow subject areas. They promote their particular vision of the growth of Japanese industry and exports, nothing else. Japanese government, in this light, looks like a computerized, high-tech juggernaut: It rumbles on very efficiently, crushing anything in its path, but no one is steering; it doesn't even have movable wheels and thus proceeds in a straight line.

The "no one in charge" theory—still controversial—helps explain the uncoordinated drift of Japan into World War II: The government in Tokyo says peace; the army in China keeps on conquering. It helps explain the maddening difficulty in getting genuine trade commitments from Tokyo: The prime minister may promise very clearly to open up the Japanese market to American products, but Japanese bureaucrats quietly veto the idea by failing to implement any policy changes that come from outside their ministry.

Each Tokyo ministry is like a feudal fiefdom, answerable to no outside power. Neither do these government agencies have any common purpose or leadership. Each is dedicated to supervising its sector of the economy. The agencies and ministries do not so much respond to the calls of interest groups as direct the various interest groups to go along with bureaucratic plans, few of which are coordinated at the top.

If the "no one in charge" theory is approximately accurate, it means Japan suffers from serious institutional underdevelopment. A government that still operates under a basically feudal arrangement is not able to handle the economic problems of the twenty-first century, including a monumental and ever-growing trade imbalance that puts Japan on a collision course with many other countries.

No Losers

Related to the "no one in charge" theory of Japanese politics is the principal that no one gets injured by economic change. Although whale meat is now a trivial part of the Japanese diet, Tokyo still defends the right of Japanese whalers to keep on slaying the great beasts, who are fewer and fewer every year. Why? To give in to international pressures would put whalers out of business, and in this country no one gets hurt. A single farmer on three acres of eggplants blocks the badly needed expansion of Tokyo's overburdened Narita airport, which has only one runway. Why? To expand the airport would put him out of business, and in this country we don't do that.

The "no losers" impact on Japanese politics is to stifle change. In France (Chapter 11), we considered how economic modernization, such as hypermarkets, drives out small shops. In Japan, interest groups such as small retailers have been able to block and delay construction of big department stores and supermarkets. It took years to get permission for Toys "R" Us to open in Japan; small shopkeepers objected. (It is now Japan's biggest toy retailer.) Slowly and with a great lag time, Japan is modernizing its retail sector, and now most Japanese are happy to shop in large stores, such as the Daiei hypermarkets.

Japan has what is called a **unit veto** system, although this is nowhere stated. Any component of the system, no matter how small, can veto an innovation desired by most. Farmers especially have benefited from this. Even within the Tokyo area—at 35 million people the world's largest metropolitan area—there are small patches of farmland that the owners won't sell to make way for badly needed apartment houses, and they are supported by laws and lavish subsidies. Actually, it's not quite right to say there are no losers in this arrangement. Japanese consumers lose through the high prices and cramped life they must endure.

Key Term

unit veto   Ability of one component to block laws or changes.

POLITICAL CULTURE

SHADOW SHOGUNS IN CHARGE

Who really organized the reformist governments of 1993 and 1994? It was not the men who became prime minister, Morihiro Hosokawa of the Japan New Party or Tsutomu Hata of the much-larger Japan Renewal party, but Ichiro Ozawa, then the leader of Japan Renewal. Ozawa, himself a former LDP politician, put together out of public view the complex coalitions but took no portfolio for himself. Ozawa, in effect, continued the Japanese pattern of powerful faction chiefs who could make or break cabinets.

Who got Keizo Obuchi named prime minister in 1998? It was former Prime Minister Noboru Takeshita, who resigned during the Recruit scandal of 1989, but still controlled *Keiseikai*, the largest LDP faction. Obuchi had

been his protegé since entering the Diet in 1963. Obuchi had to form a coalition with his archenemy Ozawa, who was now the head of the Liberal party.

Japanese newspapers sometimes announce that the last shadow shogun has passed from the scene, opening the way for a new and more democratic type of politics. I wouldn't count on it. When something like this persists for many decades, it is probably a matter more of structure than of personality. With cases like these, we should not evaluate any Japanese prime minister as a "strong" or "new type" of prime minister but rather look behind the scenes to see who sets up deals. Hosokawa and Hata lasted precisely as long as Ozawa wanted them to last. Let's see how long Mori lasts and who engineers his replacement.

The Dangers of Multiparty Coalitions

Japan gives us the chance to examine something that is getting rarer in the West European systems that we studied earlier: multiparty systems leading to difficult coalition governments. France and Germany, to be sure, had two-party governments (UDF and RPR in France, SPD and Greens in Germany), but they do not capture the complexity and difficulty of coalitions composed of many parties. France under the Third and Fourth Republics and Weimar Germany often had such governments. Nowadays Italy, Sweden, and Israel are examples of multiparty cabinets. Japan in the 1990s plunged into this situation with no practice; as long as most people could remember, it was governed by a single party that had no need of coalition partners. Japan's recent multiparty coalitions tend to bear out the experience of other countries with such governments. The problem, obviously, is getting the several member parties to agree sufficiently that the coalition hangs together. This often means that bold new policies must be compromised or even abandoned if one or more coalition partner objects and threatens to walk out of the cabinet, thus opening the government to a vote of no-confidence in the Diet. In Japan, this dissenting partner has tended to be the Social Democrats, often the second-largest party in the coalition but also the one with the least in common with the other parties, which are middle-of-the-road in outlook. If the SDPJ withdraws its support, the coalition parties will no longer command a majority in parliament.

There are areas in which the Social Democrats have actually become a rather conservative party in the sense that they wish to preserve the status quo rather than reform it. The

SDPJ, for example, portraying itself as defender of farmers, became the most protectionist of all Japanese parties; it would lock out most foreign farm products. This made cooperation difficult between the Social Democrats and the centrist-reformist parties of the coalition that would open up Japan to more imports.

Short-lived reformist Prime Minister Hosokawa was very successful in getting the initial electoral reforms of 1993 passed in the Diet; his coalition held together because all member parties were committed to those reforms. Many LDP members even voted for the reforms. As cabinets attempted to move into economic reforms—namely, upsetting the "iron triangle" described earlier—one or more coalition partners balked and dropped out of the cabinet.

The more members in a coalition, the more likely this is to happen. Then holding the coalition together becomes a full-time job and major initiatives become impossible. This leads to immobilism—getting stuck over a major issue—which was the fate of Italy's long-ruling *pentapartito* (five-party) cabinets. Poland had a seven-party coalition in 1992–93 and suffered from immobilism on the crucial question of privatization. Japan under Hosokawa had an eight-party cabinet—probably a world record—and could not function for long. In the 1990s, the LDP had to ally itself with the JSDP, Komeito, and several small spinoff parties.

If any Japanese prime minister is to survive and thrive, one of his major concerns must be to decrease the number of parties he needs to form a coalition. This means a change in the party system toward fewer and bigger parties. Unfortunately, the 1996 elections did not produce this change, and the LDP still needed support from other parties.

The next major step must be to consolidate the three LDP-breakaway parties—New Frontier, Democratic, and New Party Harbinger—into one. There are no ideological differences among them, only personality struggles, just as within the old LDP. These struggles are not trivial, as powerful political personalities do not want to give up their leadership positions. What they need is a forceful leader to point out to these parties that under the new, partly single-member system one large party gets a bonus in seats compared to three small parties running separately. Merger talks have been held off and on. Precisely because they did not succeed, electoral power slid back into the hands of the LDP.

The Blocked Society

France and Germany have been described as blocked societies, systems that need change and modernization but are prevented from reform by entrenched interests. Typically, such systems continue unchanged for decades until pressures for change become so great that old structures suddenly give way to new ones. De Gaulle's 1958 arrival in power exemplified how a blocked society dramatically unblocks. Japan has a similar but perhaps worse problem, for there is no one in charge and no single center of power that can bring about major change.

Some observers see Japan as stuck in an institutional paralysis that is causing its economy to slow and its status as regional leader to lapse.

For years, Japanese prime ministers have pledged programs to deregulate the Japanese economy, but they get carried out only in bits. Instead of major, sweeping reforms that would in effect reinvent the Japanese way, prime ministers offer minor, almost cosmetic reforms that change little. Most

Key Term

alternation in power   The electoral overturn of one party by another.

DEMOCRACY

CAN JAPANESE POLITICS ALTERNATE?

One of the defining features of a democracy is **alternation in power**. If the same party stays in office seemingly forever, the system is probably not a democracy. The ruling party, of course, claims that it is the voters' choice, but its control over the media and ballot boxes makes sure it wins. Few observers count Mexico, whose Institutional Revolutionary party (PRI) has been in power for most of the twentieth century, as a true democracy. Occasional alternation in power, as when India's Congress party is voted out, indicates India is a democracy.

Does power alternate in Japan? Briefly, it did, but only in 1993–94. Then the LDP, with Social Democrat Murayama as figurehead prime minister, took over again. Will the LDP ever be really ousted and spend a few years in opposition? There are both structural and psychological reasons for the LDP's long tenure. The previous electoral system, with its rural overrepresentation and unwillingness of Japanese to throw out the party that had brought prosperity, explain much of the LDP's longevity. Money politics is another part. Have these factors now faded?

In 1998 elections to the (less-important) upper house of the Diet, voters delivered a stinging rebuke to the LDP, which declined sharply. In typical Japanese fashion, Prime Minister Hashimoto resigned and took the blame for "my lack of ability." But was this the beginning of a long-term, mass movement away from the LDP? Or was it just a temporary punishment for the bad economy?

The 2000 elections for the lower house could mark a turning point. If a young reformer can build up a party that offers a viable alternative, it could challenge the LDP at the polls. Every reformer, though, tends to get tainted with wrong-doing and see his glow fade. Prime Minister Hosokawa looked like the clean reformist who would engineer a breakthrough, but he admitted taking money on the side and resigned in shame in 1994. In the late 1990s, Naoto Kan organized the Democratic Party of Japan (DPJ) and briefly seemed to offer an alternative. Kan, a former health minister who blew the whistle on his own ministry for covering up AIDS-tainted blood (exactly the same scandal that rocked the French government), was favored by younger people and city dwellers, whom he called "the taxpayers," implying it was time to break the subsidies the LDP lavished on Japan's farmers, whom Kan called "tax-eaters." But Kan was tainted too, over an affair with a secretary that he tried to cover up. (Sound familiar?) Kan's star faded, and he was bumped out as DPJ leader.

So far, little marks the beginning of a more decisive break with Japan's dominant-party system than Hosokawa was able to bring about. Many Japanese were ready for a two-party system with alternation, the aim of Hosokawa's election-law reforms. On the other hand, Japan has always shown a strong persistence of pattern; nothing changes dramatically in Japan.

Japanese favor major reforms—Keidanren strongly backs them—hoping to kill as many as four birds with one stone. Namely, by deregulating the strongly regulated Japanese economy, including its barriers to foreign imports, reforms could fight recession, raise living standards, reduce trade surpluses, and curb the bureaucracy. Let us now consider some of the problems Japan faces.

Key Terms

alternation in power (p. 356)	public corporation (p. 347)
corruption (p. 350)	scandal (p. 350)
guided capitalism (p. 347)	soft money (p. 353)
iron triangle (p. 346)	structure (p. 353)
money politics (p. 352)	unit veto (p. 354)
Okurasho (p. 349)	walking-around money (p. 347)

Further Reference

Broadbent, Jeffrey. *Environmental Politics in Japan: Networks of Power and Protest*. New York: Cambridge University Press, 1998.

Junnosuke, Masumi. *Contemporary Politics in Japan*. Berkeley, CA: University of California Press, 1995.

Kohno, Masaru. *Japan's Postwar Party Politics*. Princeton, NJ: Princeton University Press, 1997.

Kyogoku, Jun-Ichi. *The Political Dynamics of Japan*. New York: Columbia University Press, 1993.

Mitchell, Richard H. *Political Bribery in Japan*. Honolulu, HI: University of Hawaii Press, 1996.

Murphy, R. Taggart. *The Weight of the Yen*. New York: W. W. Norton, 1996.

Nakano, Minoru. *The Policy-Making Process in Contemporary Japan*. New York: St. Martin's, 1997.

Richardson, Bradley. *Japanese Democracy: Power, Coordination, and Performance*. New Haven, CT: Yale University Press, 1997.

Rothacher, Albrecht. *The Japanese Power Elite*. New York: St. Martin's, 1994.

Schlesinger, Jacob M. *Shadow Shoguns: The Rise and Fall of Japan's Postwar Political Machine*. New York: Simon & Schuster, 1997.

Schwartz, Frank J. *Advice and Consent: The Politics of Consultation in Japan*. New York: Cambridge University Press, 1998.

Smith, Patrick. *Japan: A Reinterpretation*. New York: Pantheon, 1997.

Wolferen, Karel van. *The Enigma of Japanese Power: People and Politics in a Stateless Nation*. New York: Vintage Books, 1990.

Woodall, Brian. *Japan Under Construction: Corruption, Politics, and Public Works*. Berkeley, CA: University of California Press, 1996.

What Japanese Quarrel About

26

Questions to Consider

1. What explains Japan's economic success?
2. What went wrong with the state supervision of Japan's economy?
3. What does Japan suggest about income equality?
4. Has Japan overcome the downturn of the 1990s? How?
5. How does Japan resemble Germany demographically?
6. What is purchasing power parity?
7. What is *gaiatsu* and why does Japan resist it?
8. Does Japan practice a kind of mercantilism?
9. Is Japan's no-war clause now a dead letter?
10. Is Japan changing?

For some years after the war, "made in Japan" suggested a product was junk, probably tin cans recycled from the ashes of Japan's cities. In some cases, the term "junk" was justified. All countries that are just starting their economic climb seem to produce cheap products of dubious quality. Many, however, soon climb out of the junk stage, as Japan did in the 1950s.

The Japanese Economic Miracle

In 1960, Japan was the richest country in Asia but still had a per capita GDP of only $380 (around $2,000 in today's dollars), one-eighth the American. By 1990, Japan's per capita was nominally higher than America's. (This is tricky to measure. See the box on "Purchasing Power Parity" on page 366.) The catalyst was the Korean War that began in June 1950. U.S. forces in East Asia suddenly found themselves underequipped and gave contracts for clothing, footwear, and other items to low-bid Japanese producers. (South Korea's industrial takeoff followed precisely the same pattern in the late 1960s, only now the catalyst was the Vietnam War.) The quality of the Japanese goods was not bad. After the war, many U.S. manufacturers of civilian goods followed the U.S. military lead and gave the Japanese similar contracts. The quality got better all the time, and the costs were a fraction of U.S. producer costs. In the 1960s,

Key Term

geopolitics   The influence of geography on politics and the use of geography for strategic ends.

Japanese cars were looked down on as something of a joke, but by the 1970s they commanded world respect for economy and fine workmanship. A continual pattern has been to underestimate the Japanese product—until it puts you out of business.

As in postwar West Germany, workers in postwar Japan did not ask for too much; they were glad to have a job that put some food on the family's table. In politics they were also cautious and mostly gave their vote to the moderate conservative party with the misleading name Liberal Democrat. This party—more accurately, a collection of political factions—ruled Japan with only a brief pause from the time of its formation in 1955 until the present, and thus became an important institution and pillar of stability. The Liberal Democrats offered the Japanese growth and jobs. For most Japanese, this was enough. They lived to work and, accustomed to modest living standards and obedience, did not vote for change—at least not until recently.

By the 1990s, several things had changed. Japan's period of extraordinary economic growth finally ended with a major recession that brought unemployment for the first time in a generation. In 1999, Japanese unemployment, officially at 4.6 percent, was higher than the U.S. rate. And large Japanese firms are overstaffed ("in-house unemployment"); if they let excess employees go the Japanese rate would double. The Tokyo stock market and real-estate market bubbles burst, leaving many corporations and banks looking poorer and foolish. The long-ruling LDP started looking incompetent. A younger generation of Japanese were well-educated and well-traveled and saw how people in other industrialized countries do not live in rabbit hutches and pay exorbitant prices. Many no longer are willing to support the LDP.

The Secret of Japan's Success

Since the 1960s, when the West realized how fast the Japanese economy was growing, many observers have tried to explain the "Japanese model" as a new, different, and better system, combining elements such as confucianism, productivity, education, savings, and state supervision.

GEOGRAPHY

LIVING WITHOUT LEBENSRAUM

Geography influences international relations, both because of its real, physical impact and because decision makers *think* that certain geographic features are important, even if they aren't. As in many areas of human endeavor, the real feeds into the psychological, which in turn feeds back into the real.

German philosophers of the nineteenth century, for example, came up with overly deterministic theories of **geopolitics**. The Nazis and Japanese militarists eagerly accepted theories such as *Lebensraum* (living space) as justification for their imperial expansion. After their defeat, Germans and Japanese learned that they have never lived so well as when confined to their present crowded countries. If you've got the economy, you don't need much land. Prosperity depends not so much on territory as on smart and energetic people.

Confucianism

As comparativists, we make comparisons to solve puzzles like Japan's rapid economic growth. First, do other countries show similar patterns of rapid growth? Yes, in fact many East Asian countries do. In addition to China (see our later discussion of China's economic growth), the **Four Tigers** have, for the last couple of decades, also shown remarkable growth. Culturally, all share a Confucian background because all were under the cultural sway of China. Confucianism stresses hard work, stability, and obedience. It frowns on high personal consumption; people should save, not spend. Some have argued that a Confucian work ethic gave East Asia the functional equivalent of a Protestant work ethic, a religious or psychological motivation to work hard.

Key Term

Four Tigers South Korea, Taiwan, Hong Kong, and Singapore.

Productivity

Another factor for rapid growth is a level of productivity higher than the level of wages; that is, workers who produce a lot without getting paid a lot. (See the "Productivity" box on page 77.) In Britain, we saw how productivity increases were mediocre while wages and other costs

---

JAPAN DESTROYS THE GERMAN PHOTO INDUSTRY

One of the first indicators of what the Japanese could do in terms of quality came in the photo-optical industry. Photojournalists covering the Korean War tried Japanese-made lenses from Nikon and Canon on their German-made camera bodies and found, to their surprise, that they were excellent, sometimes better than expensive German lenses. Then they tried the Japanese-made bodies and found they were pretty good, too. The German photo industry should have started running scared, but, like most Westerners, tended to scoff at anything made in Japan.

In addition to lower wages, the Japanese photo industry had something going for it: a compulsion to constantly innovate. The Germans might bring out a new model every decade; the Japanese firms, desperately competing with one another, brought out new models every couple of years. In 1959, Nikon introduced the landmark Nikon F, a top quality single-lens reflex that allowed the photographer to see exactly what the film saw. Photographers turned from the pricey German Leica rangefinder cameras and embraced the Nikon F, the professional workhorse for more than a decade that was constantly modified and improved. Boasted Nikon ads: "Today, there's almost no other choice." During the 1960s, the Japanese photo industry captured essentially the entire world market as the German photo industry shrunk into irrelevance. Change or die.

In this process we see some of the factors that contributed to Japanese manufacturing success in other areas. With low wages (now no longer the case), a skilled and dedicated work force, constantly innovative designs, government encouragement, and far-sighted bank loans, Japan went on from cameras to consumer electronics, where it also became the world leader. Whether it can keep its lead is another question. With high labor costs, much of the Japanese photo and electronic industries have set up in other East Asian lands with cheap labor. My latest Nikon was made in Indonesia, my latest Minolta in China.

were high, gradually squeezing British products off the world market. In Germany, we saw how wage restraint coupled with increases in productivity gave German products a competitive edge and a major export market. More recently, however, German wages climbed out of line with productivity. The same happened in Japan. For some decades, Japanese productivity stayed ahead of wages, giving Japan an opening to produce much of the world's advanced consumer electronics. Japanese factories could simply put more high-quality labor into a product than other countries, but this is no longer the case.

Education

As we discussed in earlier chapters, productivity is partly the result of new, more efficient machines and partly of increasingly skilled workers and managers who know how to use them. Japan (and the Four Tigers) paid a lot of attention to education, especially at the primary and secondary levels (from elementary through high school). Such education is supervised at the national level and is compulsory. This gave Japan a highly skilled labor force, one that can read, follow instructions, and do math computations. (Much of the U.S. labor force can't.) Interestingly, Japan and its high-growth neighbors pay little attention to higher (college and university) education, finding that much of it contributes little to economic growth. Young Japanese are not encouraged to "find themselves" in college.

Savings

Japanese save a lot (nearly 13 percent of disposable household income), far more than Americans (4 percent). Japanese save for at least two reasons. First, thrift is an old tradition. Second, Japanese pension plans and social security are weak for an advanced country; to have a comfortable old age, Japanese know they must put aside their own money. Some economists think that savings alone is the biggest element in explaining Japanese economic growth. More recently, however, some say Japanese save too much; their reluctance to spend helps keep Japan in recession. The government even gave spending coupons to Japanese families to encourage purchases. It didn't work; they just used the coupons for daily necessities and saved their own income.

The propensity to save, for most of the postwar period, made Japanese banks the world's biggest and made available tremendous capital resources for investment in growth industries. Unfortunately, Japan's banks encouraged businesses to expand until they overexpanded and went broke, inflicting $1 trillion in bank losses.

State Supervision

This is where a discussion of Japanese economic growth gets controversial, although probably more Americans quarrel about it than Japanese. Is state supervision, going back to the Meiji modernizers and continuing with MITI and the Finance Ministry in our day, the key factor in Japan's rapid growth? Most of the other fast-growth East Asian economies have some degree of Japanese-style state supervision as well. (Hong Kong has none, and China's vigorous free-market sector, based heavily on foreign investment, is essentially unplanned; only China's money-losing state sector is supervised.)

What do we mean by "state supervised"? Does it mean simply getting the **macroeconomy**, sometimes called "the fundamentals," in order—little public

Key Term

macroeconomy The big picture of a nation's economy, including GDP and its growth, productivity, interest rates, and inflation.

debt, plentiful savings, low inflation, sufficient investment capital—and then standing back and letting the market do its stuff? Macroeconomic management probably describes the postwar German *Sozialmarkt*. Or does it mean government intervention in the **microeconomy** as well, with state technocrats choosing which industries to foster or phase out? This would be the Japanese model.

Some critical Western economists are skeptical about any "Japanese model" and say there is little evidence that state supervision boosted Japanese growth rates. Japan got its macroeconomy or "fundamentals" right, which was all that really mattered, and might have done just as well or even better without a MITI. Some Japanese firms prospered with no help from a ministry, and some with plenty of help did poorly. (Sony founder Akio Morita disdained the ministries.) Which is right, the "Japanese model" or its doubters? The only way you could demonstrate that Japanese economic intervention worked is to have two very similar countries operate under different policies, say, one with a MITI and the other without, and see which grows faster. Such controlled experiments are hard to come by in the real world.

COMPARISON

EQUALITY WORKS

Do big income differentials spur economic growth? Ronald Reagan and Margaret Thatcher thought so; under them, incomes in America and Britain grew more unequal. The reasoning: If rich people make a lot more money than poor people, there will be a greater incentive to work hard and get rich. Furthermore, rich people invest more. Accordingly, inequality and growth are twins. This theory, widely believed for years, came into doubt with a 1996 UN Human Development Report that showed more or less the opposite. The ratio of the top fifth of incomes to the bottom fifth in several countries was as follows:

Japan	4.0
Germany	6.0
France	7.5
United States	8.0
Britain	10.0
Russia	12.0
Brazil	32.0

Japan, with by far the fastest economic growth over the decades, has the most equal incomes. Brazil, with stop-and-go growth, has extremely unequal incomes. Good-sized differentials in the United States and Britain accompanied occasional economic growth. The theory that inequality produces growth is much too simple. People work hard and produce a lot for many reasons, not just to enjoy higher incomes. They may have an internalized work ethic, nationalistic pride, or good company morale. Japanese chief executives, who work like maniacs, make less than half what their American counterparts do, and the cost of living in Japan is high. Another point: Poor people have no money to save; middle-class people do. This may explain why the most equal countries on the list, Japan and Germany, are the biggest savers, and savings mean investment and hence growth.

From Bubble to Burst

Japan's economy grew at an amazing average rate of 10 percent a year from 1955 to 1973. The world had never seen anything like it. But from 1973 to 1991 it grew at an average of 4 percent a year, still good but hardly spectacular. And during the 1990s it grew at an average of only 1 percent a year and in some years actually declined. Some suspected the years of fast growth were over for good. No longer could Japan simply copy foreign products or quickly improve productivity. Japanese wages and other costs were high, and most Japanese investment flowed to countries with lower wages and fewer regulations.

To fight the slowdown of the 1990s, the Japanese government threw money into the economy—more than $1 trillion, mostly in public-works spending—until Japan's 1999 budget deficit was a dangerous 9 percent of GDP and its public-sector debt exceeded its GDP, both much worse than the corresponding U.S. or West European figures. The massive government spending produced little economic growth. Tokyo was doing what it had always done—bail out any sector of the economy that's in trouble. But no government can bail out everything forever.

Under MITI prodding and financing, Japanese electronics firms sunk and lost vast sums trying to develop the "fifth generation" of computers and high-definition television. Both projects bombed. MITI geniuses encouraged Japanese car makers to go for ever-larger world market shares—instead of the usual capitalist goal of profitability—so that during the recession of the early 1990s, Japan's eleven car companies had major excess capacity and most lost money. MITI had pushed the car makers to expand until they had overexpanded.

Government and banks had pushed the export sectors (cars, electronics) of Japanese industry into high levels of automation, productivity, and efficiency. Other sectors got left behind. Distribution was largely in the hands of neighborhood mom-and-pop stores that were convenient and friendly but did not compete on the basis of price. Until recently, U.S.-style discounting was hated, feared, and denounced in Japan as ruinous of family shops and family values. Gradually, though, as more Japanese traveled and found they could buy Panasonics and Minoltas cheaper in the United States, foreign retail chains started opening in Japan.

RUNNING OUT OF JAPANESE

In 1975, the number of births in Japan started to drop and kept declining for the rest of the century. Japan's barely growing population will soon start shrinking. Japan's colleges and universities worry that the number of eighteen-year-olds, which has declined from 2.2 million in 1974 to 1.2 million in 1999, will not be enough to fill classrooms. Industry worries about sufficient workers. The biggest worry, however, is how to support all the Japanese on retirement—and Japanese are the longest-lived folks in the world; seventy-seven years for men and eighty-three for women—when there are so few workers. By 2010, Japan's pension system will be in the red. Can two Japanese workers support one retiree? Notice that Germany has exactly the same problem, but Japan admits very few foreign workers.

THE UNITED STATES AND JAPAN: AMERICA-BASHING

Some Japanese leaders have turned nationalistic and anti-American. The underlying cause is the inner core of Japaneseness that doesn't easily give in to **gaiatsu**, but there were two specific causes. First, many Japanese grew tired of the United States hectoring them, especially about opening the Japanese market to U.S. products and ending bureaucratic supervision of Japan's economy. "Who are you to tell us how to run our economy?" they asked. "We do things the Japanese way, not to please you." The founder of Sony and a flamboyant politician coauthored a bestseller along these lines entitled *A Japan That Can Say No*. Actually, the downturn of the 1990s demonstrated that much of the American criticism was accurate. Still, hectoring wins no friends.

A second area of Japanese complaint concerned security arrangements: Should Japan follow the U.S. lead in regional defense, and should U.S. bases stay on Japanese soil? That flamboyant politician, Shintaro Ishihara, was elected governor of Tokyo in 1999, partly on an America-bashing platform. One of his demands (rejected) was return of a U.S. air base in suburban Tokyo. Such bases—the biggest is on Okinawa—have long been irritants; they occupy scarce land, their jets make too much noise, and their personnel commit occasional crimes. Some Japanese would like to be rid of all U.S. bases. Tension with China and North Vietnam curbed some of this sentiment, but it shows a Japanese nationalism not far under the surface.

Agriculture got left behind. The typical small Japanese farm of a few acres was hopelessly inefficient, but the Agricultural Ministry protected Japanese farmers from cheaper imports. This cost Japanese consumers dearly and angered Japan's trading partners. Many Japanese farmers turned to part-time farming anyway, a pattern typical of industrializing countries. Unprotected, many of these people would soon decide to sell their small holdings, either to larger and more-efficient farmers or to developers who could build badly needed apartments. There is protected and tax-exempt farmland in and near major cities that should be subject to market forces. Its sale would make some "farmers" rich while helping solve Japan's housing shortage.

Japanese were generally well satisfied with their economic growth since World War II. During the 1990s, however, they grew less satisfied. The shortcomings of their supervised market system became increasingly clear. Under bureaucratic guidance, the Japanese economy produced **excess liquidity**, which fueled stock-market and real-estate bubbles, which both burst in 1989. The Tokyo stock exchange lost half its value and was slow to recover. Real-estate prices plunged as well, and many Japanese banks and corporations were insolvent or nearly so.

Throwing money at the economy is one standard way of fighting recession, but Tokyo does it big time. In the 1990s, they pushed out so much money that Japan ran the biggest government deficits of all industrialized lands. They pushed out money in two ways: bailing out industries and massive public-works projects. But bailouts merely disguise firms' illnesses and block the market's signals that it's time for this company to change or fold. In 1998, for example, Prime Minister Obuchi promised to not allow any of Japan's nineteen large banks to collapse. Actually, all governments tend to react that way—they think of angry depositors and shareholders—but if they do it too much, they prop up industries that should be forced to change.

Key Terms

gaiatsu   Foreign pressure.
excess liquidity   Too much money floating around.

KEY CONCEPTS

PURCHASING POWER PARITY

Per-capita GDP figures can be deceptive because they do not include the cost of living in each country. The Japanese, on average, make more money a year than Americans but live more poorly. To correct this seeming discrepancy, economists now calculate **purchasing power parity (PPP)** in addition to the usual per-capita GDP that is translated into dollars at the "market exchange rate." See how the two differ in the figures from 1997 (see table below).

Which figure is the most valid? In terms of judging a nation's international economic power—what it can buy on the world market—the exchange rate is the one to use. In terms of who lives well, the PPP is more accurate. On average, Americans still live best even though several countries have larger per-capita GDPs, as measured by exchange rate.

What happens when the two measures are seriously out of line? It indicates that the country's currency is overvalued or undervalued, sometimes by market forces and sometimes by deliberate government policy. Using these figures, the four currencies from advanced countries are overvalued in relation to the dollar, but the four currencies from poorer countries are undervalued. For example, Chinese live a lot better—although still only one-eighth the American level—than the exchange-rate figure of $860 would indicate.

	GDP Per Capita at Exchange Rate	Purchasing Power Parity
Japan	$37,850	$23,400
Germany	28,260	21,300
United States	28,740	28,740
France	26,050	21,860
Britain	20,710	20,520
Russia	2,740	4,190
Brazil	4,720	6,240
South Africa	3,400	7,490
China	860	3,570

Source: World Bank

Key Term

purchasing power parity (PPP) Adjustment of GDP figures to take cost of living into account.

Increasingly, both Japanese and foreign analysts doubt that Japan's throwing money at problems will work in the new age, an age of lower-cost competitors and open markets. Already, other lands have seized the initiative in several areas that used to be Japanese: steelmaking, shipbuilding, and even consumer electronics. (My latest VCR was made in Mexico.) China is a growing economic giant. If China uses the same approach to economic growth that Japan used, who will be able to compete? Some Japanese are already worried; they fear their really good years of rapid growth are over. This is not necessarily a cause for despair; it just means Japan is becoming an ordinary country with a mature economy.

Should Japanese Live Better?

Key Terms

trade surplus   Exporting more than you import.

strategic   Important to the life of a nation.

national interest   What is good for the country as a whole in international relations.

If Japanese lived better it would be good for them and for us, because they would buy more U.S. products, such as foodstuffs and building materials. They have earned it. They lifted their country from the rubble of World War II to heights few Japanese dreamed of. Holding down domestic consumption while accumulating vast capital resources was a great prescription for rapid economic growth. But pursued too long, it overshot the mark and produced serious imbalances. The yen, held too low for too long, suddenly shot from 330 to the dollar to 80 to the dollar at one point in 1995 (more recently about 100 to the dollar). The too-strong yen hurt many Japanese firms that lost foreign sales, for now their products were too costly.

One of the problems with Japan's guided capitalism was the mammoth **trade surpluses** Japan accumulated, especially with the United States. They did no earthly good, but for decades MITI was obsessed by them, a sort of latter-day mercantilism. In effect, Japan produced goods that Americans eagerly bought, accepting dollars in payment. They accumulated a mountain of dollars but this forced the dollar to decline in relation to the yen. In effect, Japan sold its products too cheaply to Americans and got not enough in return. They only hurt themselves.

If the Japanese had consumed more, including more imported goods, at an earlier date, they might have avoided the excess liquidity that fueled the stock-market and real-estate bubbles. Too many yen chased investments to the sky; then the bubbles burst, harming Japan's growth and stability. Ironically, Japanese investors got burned in buying U.S. firms. They overpaid, found

GEOGRAPHY

U.S. STRATEGIC INTERESTS IN EAST ASIA

Should the United States, probably allied with Japan, play the role of strategic balancer in East Asia? It's an important question that Americans must face. Much depends on the precise nature of China: Is it transitioning to a market democracy or stuck under a Party dictatorship that aims at expansion? (We will consider this in the next chapter.)

We have to be careful, for once an area has been labeled **strategic** it becomes in the mind of many genuinely strategic, even if it is not. In the 1960s the United States defined South Vietnam as strategic. By the 1980s, hardly any Americans thought it had been strategic. In the heat of the moment, we may overuse the

term. You can end up calling every point on the globe strategic. And if you call something strategic, your adversary will likely do it too. Are the Senkaku Islands, just north of Taiwan and claimed by both China and Japan, really in anyone's **national interest**?

Accordingly, we have to make some clear-headed judgments on America's interests in East Asia and if they should be defended by force. As China and North Korea made threatening noises, the United States, Japan, South Korea, Taiwan, and other countries of the region were drawn together defensively. Remember, without fully understanding it, U.S. support for China in the 1930s drew us into a war with Japan. Could the reverse now happen?

KEY CONCEPTS

POOR MAN'S PPP: THE BIG MAC INDEX

Purchasing power parity, described in the box on page 366, is a more accurate measure of how well people live, but it is hard to calculate. Economists must find a market basket of goods and services that is the same in each country. A quick and cheeky way to approximate PPP was devised by the British newsweekly *The Economist*: Compare the price of a Big Mac sandwich at the local Mc-Donald's with its U.S. (big-city) price. Since a Big Mac requires the same ingredients, labor, and overhead wherever it is produced, it is actually a mini-market basket that reflects local costs fairly accurately. Some 2000 prices of Big Macs are listed in the table below.

Wherever a Big Mac is more expensive than the U.S. price of $2.51, it implies that the local currency is overvalued, the case in Britain and Japan, where the cost of living is high. Where the Big Mac is cheaper, it implies that the local currency is undervalued, as in Brazil, China, Russia, and South Africa. Notice how the Big Mac Index generally points the same way (overvalued or under-valued) as the more complex PPP calculation explained in the box on page 366. The Big Mac Index is only a rough approximation of PPP because it is too urban and tourist-oriented, and thus often overpriced. In 1998, the Russian ruble plunged in value, making a Big Mac a bargain for tourists (but not for Russians).

	Price in Local Currency	*in Dollars*
Brazil	Real 2.95	$1.65
Britain	£ 1.90	3.00
China	Yuan 9.9	1.20
France	F Fr 18.50	2.62
Germany	DM 4.99	2.37
Japan	¥ 294	2.78
Russia	Ruble 39.50	1.39
South Africa	Rand 9.00	1.34

the firms were not so profitable, and often had to sell at a loss. Americans for a while were afraid of Japanese investments. They shouldn't have been. The investments were all to our good. If rich people want to overpay for your property, don't discourage them.

But it was foolish for Japan. If more profits had been channeled into pay and dividends, the Japanese could have consumed more and lived better. But, curiously, some Japanese don't want to live better, at least not if that means harming the livelihood of other Japanese. For example, Japan, by keeping out foreign rice and subsidizing Japan's small, inefficient rice farms, was forced to pay about six times the world price for rice. Many didn't mind, for they understood they were keeping Japanese farmers employed. Thus, overpriced Japanese food-stuffs were a sort of indirect welfare transfer to help cousin Kenji on the farm. And it's not just food; the Japanese pay above world prices for just about everything, at an annual cost to them of many trillions of yen.

A Japanese shopper carefully selects steak, which costs several times the U.S. price. Modern hypermarkets, like this Daiei, have forced many small merchants to close. (Michael Roskin)

More and more young Japanese think this is ridiculous. They notice that cousin Kenji works only part-time on his rice patch anyway because he can't earn a living from it; most of the week Kenji works in town. Young Japanese are more likely to have traveled and been amazed at the cheap cost of living abroad. They find the taste of American rice acceptable—California growers now mostly plant short-grain oriental-style rice—and even bring back a bag as tourists. Many have developed a taste for beef and want it at $5 a pound, not $25. Younger Japanese are thus more likely to want a Japan open to two-way world trade than are their parents, who prefer the one-way model. Young Japanese also tend to dislike their cumbersome merchandising system—in which everything passes through costly layers of trading companies to small retail outlets—and carries few foreign goods. By law, it was very difficult for foreign firms to break into Japanese retail commerce.

It is this clash of generations that underlies much of recent Japanese politics. Younger voters are more likely to reject the LDP and turn to one of the new parties that seem to promise a Japan more open to foreign imports and the lower prices that come with them.

Should Japan Re-Arm?

Since World War II, Japan has preached and practiced peace. In the aftermath of a devastating war and at the behest of MacArthur's staff, a "no-war clause" (Article 9) was made part of Japan's postwar constitution. It states that the Japanese people "forever renounce war as a sovereign right of the nation and the threat or use of force as a means of settling international disputes" and adds that "land, sea, and air forces, as well as other war potential will never be maintained." In 1947 this seemed like a fine idea, but with North Korea's attack on South Korea in 1950, some Americans and Japanese began to have second thoughts. Would Article 9 mean that Japan would stay defenseless in a rough neighborhood or depend forever on U.S. protection? The question went back on the front burner in the late 1990s as China staked out territorial claims far into the the South and East China Seas and North Korea lobbed rockets over Japan as "tests." As a result, the United States and Japan dusted off their defensive alliance.

Key Terms

Article 9   The no-war clause in Japan's constitution.

de facto   In practice although not officially stated.

In the 1950s, Japan began building "Self-Defense Forces." Defense spending has been informally limited to 1 to 2 percent of GDP, and there is no draft. Nonetheless, given the size of Japan's GDP, its defense budget is now among the world's highest, even though its military manpower, at about 238,000, is low. Japan's Self-Defense Forces are small but well-funded and well-equipped.

Japanese leftists argue that their Self-Defense Forces are clearly at odds with both the letter and spirit of the constitution, and expanding them would compound the error. Most Japanese think their forces, which are not supposed to be used outside of Japan, are a prudent and necessary shield; some would be willing to drop Article 9. The United States also thinks Japan should be able to defend itself and take a leadership role in regional security—as Japan has done splendidly in Cambodian peacekeeping—and has encouraged Japan to do more. That is the great question: Should Japan expand its Self-Defense Forces to the point where they can defend Japan on their own and keep the peace regionally? For much of the postwar period, Japan's neighbors feared expansion of Japanese military power, but with the possibility that China could seize Taiwan and North Korea could again invade South Korea, many East Asian countries now see Japan as a strategic partner in a defensive situation. The question parallels the controversy Germany has gone through over military forces. Many Germans and their neighbors opposed them, but now most say it's time Germany became a normal country and participated in regional security, as in Kosovo.

Japan's **Article 9** will probably not be directly changed, but the way it is interpreted might be. Directly repealing Article 9 would be too controversial. One defense minister was forced to resign after he touched off a political furor by suggesting such a constitutional revision. Instead, look for new laws or interpretations permitting the Japanese Self Defense Forces to participate more fully in UN and other multilateral peacekeeping efforts. The move will be sold to the public as part of Japan's contribution to world and regional peace. Also look for Japan to reinforce its claim to the Senkaku Islands near Taiwan, which China also claims. Look for Japan to form **de facto** alliances with Taiwan and South Korea.

Hiroshima, Ground Zero: This municipal building partially withstood the first atomic bomb blast and now reminds Japanese of what war does. (Michael Roskin)

POLITICAL CULTURE

THE JAPANESE NON-WELFARE STATE

Japan is almost the opposite of the West European welfare state; it provides almost no welfare. Instead, families are obliged to provide (an echo of the old *ie* system of household responsibility). Only those without families and physically unable to work may qualify for a dole under strict standards. Never mind if they can't find a job. This harsh setup bothers few Japanese, who have almost no sense of American-style entitlement. Result: Only 0.7 percent of Japanese receive welfare benefits, compared to about 10 percent of the U.S. population. Another result seen during the downturn of the late 1990s: homeless Japanese men camping out in parks and public places.

This is not to say the Japanese have absolutely no welfare system. In a way, the whole Japanese economy has been rigged to make sure no one loses their jobs. Inefficient firms, farms, and stores are kept in business by regulations, subsidies, and the keeping out of imports, the costs of which are passed on to the Japanese consumer. One might call it welfare by indirect means.

The really explosive question is whether Japan should acquire nuclear weapons. Before North Korea began its ambitious and dangerous program to build nuclear weapons, the answer to that in Japan was a resounding "no." But with the North Korean program ready to produce bombs—and with North Korean missiles able to reach Japan—more Japanese have begun to think Japan should acquire a few nukes as a deterrence. The United States has not encouraged the idea and has pledged its armed might to protect Japan from, say, a North Korean bomb. Like de Gaulle decades earlier, some Japanese have begun to wonder if this U.S. promise is reliable. As the Cold War ended, more and more Japanese do not like to remain dependent on U.S. protection, and fewer Americans are willing to defend distant countries.

Even if the world could persuade or force North Korea to cease its nuclear program, Japan would still face two nuclear powers in Asia: China and Russia. If it faces them alone, it will increasingly debate the need for nuclear weapons. As history's only victims of nuclear war thus far, many Japanese adamantly oppose any nukes on Japanese soil. Even hinting at a nuclear program could set off massive protests. Accordingly, the issue is likely to linger out of public debate for a long time, but it will always be there.

Before Japan can play a major role in East Asian security, it will have to reflect deeply on its World War II atrocities and put them in school textbooks, as Germany has done. This is hard to do in Japan. Many Japanese politicians, especially in the LDP, cannot or will not say they are sorry for Japan's World War II aggressions. Instead, they honor Japanese war dead. Tojo's granddaughter still mourns him as a patriot. Some LDP politicians even let slip that Japanese occupation of Taiwan and Korea was a good thing. Amid howls of protest from Taipeh and Seoul, they usually resign.

In 1996, gangster-supported nationalistic Japanese groups reinforced Japan's claim to the small, uninhabitable Senkaku Islands near Taiwan. The Tokyo government gave quiet assent. China, Taiwan, and even Hong Kong joined in angry opposition, for China claims the islands as well. (The real reason: possible oil under the seabed around the islands.) Germany has more or less mastered its past, and now Germany's small army is a necessary and welcome participant in Europe's security. Japan could play the same role in East Asia, but first it must face its past.

A New Japan?

Japan is difficult to write about now because it is undergoing considerable change. The certainties of a few years ago—the Liberal Democrats would always lead Japan, corruption doesn't count, and the Japanese economy would keep up its rapid growth—have eroded and are not likely to be restored, at least not in their old shape. This is a new and exciting but unpredictable era in Japanese politics.

Will it come out where we want it to come out? Will we have a new, clean democratic partner across the Pacific ready to trade with us on a two-way basis? Or will we face an angry, protectionist Japan where some of the old nationalism links up with an enlarged military?

Neither the Japanese nor Americans fully understand the political implications of Japan's burst economic bubble. If, instead of being a growing economic giant with jobs for all, it undergoes years of slow or no growth, how will the Japanese people and political parties react? If Japan is at last becoming a "normal" country, one with approximately the same problems as other advanced, industrialized democracies, the changes are all to the good. If not, we may wish we had the old Japan of the LDP and cheap transistors back. How Japan fits into the modern world will determine a great deal for the peace of Asia. To see how another Asian giant is handling the onslaught of modernity, let us now turn to China.

Key Terms

Article 9 (p. 370)

de facto (p. 370)

Four Tigers (p. 361)

gaiatsu (p. 365)

geopolitics (p. 360)

macroeconomy (p. 362)

microeconomy (p. 363)

national interest (p. 367)

purchasing power parity (p. 366)

strategic (p. 367)

trade surplus (p. 367)

Further Reference

Anderson, Stephen J. *Welfare Policy and Politics in Japan: Beyond the Developmental State.* New York: Paragon House, 1993.

Berger, Thomas U. *Cultures of Antimilitarism: National Security in Germany and Japan.* Baltimore, MD: Johns Hopkins University Press, 1998.

Ito, Takatoshi. *The Japanese Economy.* Cambridge, MA: MIT Press, 1992.

Katz, Richard. *Japan: The System That Soured: The Rise and Fall of the Japanese Economic Miracle.* Armonk, NY: M. E. Sharpe, 1998.

McCormack, Gavan. *The Emptiness of Japanese Affluence.* Armonk, NY: M. E. Sharpe, 1996.

Okimoto, Daniel. *Between MITI and the Market: Japanese Industrial Policy for High Technology.* Stanford, CA: Stanford University Press, 1989.

Ozawa, Ichiro. *Blueprint for a New Japan: The Rethinking of a Nation.* New York: Kodansha International, 1994.

Sato, Kazuo. *The Japanese Economy*. Armonk, NY: M. E. Sharpe, 1996.

Smith, Dennis B. *Japan Since 1945: The Rise of an Economic Superpower*. New York: St. Martin's, 1995.

Tabb, William K. *The Postwar Japanese System: Cultural Economy and Economic Transformation*. New York: Oxford University Press, 1995.

Williams, David. *Japan and the Enemies of Open Political Science*. New York: Routledge, 1994.

Wood, Christopher. *The Bubble Economy: Japan's Extraordinary Speculative Boom of the 80s and the Dramatic Bust of the 90s*. New York: Atlantic Monthly Press, 1993.

PART VI

Key Websites

China—A Country Study   This site conducts an online study of the history, people, geography, and government of China, and includes a searchable database.
http://lcweb2.loc.gov/frd/cs/cntoc.html

U.S. Department of State China Homepage   This site includes statements about and background information on China.
http://www.state.gov/www/current/debate/china.html

Brazil   This site provides a wide variety of basic information about Brazil.
http://darkwing.uoregon.edu/~sergiok/brasil/brafacts.html

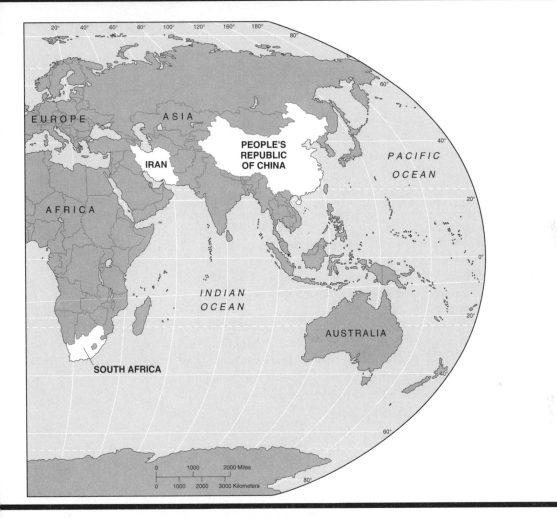

Brazil: A Country Study   This site features documents from the Library of Congress covering the economy, geography, history, society, and government of Brazil.
http://lcweb2.loc.gov/frd/cs/brtoc.html

The Parliament of South Africa   This site is the home page of the Parliament of South Africa.
http://www.parliament.gov.za/

Mohammad Khatami, President of the Islamic Republic of Iran   This site provides translations of recent speeches, essays, and articles, and also includes photos and e-mail addresses.
http://www.persia.org/khatami/index.html

China

27

Questions to Consider

1. What is the trouble with the term "Third World"?
2. Why was it easy for Europeans to penetrate and derange China?
3. How did Mao and the Communists beat the Nationalists?
4. Why does Beijing inflict periodic upheavals on China? What were the big ones?
5. What is a "technocrat" in the Chinese context?
6. What is "voluntarism" and how did Mao exemplify it?
7. What forms of nationalism could dominate in China?
8. What goes wrong when you mix capitalism and socialism?
9. Explain second- and third-order consequences.
10. What should U.S. policy regarding China be? Why?

The Impact of the Past

China's population is over 1.2 billion and slowly growing, even though the regime promotes one-child families. Less than one-third of China's territory is arable—rice in the well-watered south and wheat in the drier north. China's **man-land ratio**—now only one-quarter acre of farmland (and currently shrinking) for each Chinese—long imposed limits on politics, economics, and social thought.

With little new territory to expand into, Chinese society evolved **steady-state** structures to preserve stability and contentment among peasants rather than encourage them to pioneer and innovate. Labor-saving devices would render peasants jobless and were therefore not encouraged. China's achievements in science and technology—which put China far ahead of medieval Europe—remained curiosities instead of contributions to an industrial revolution.

Commercial expansion was also discouraged. Instead of a Western mentality of reinvestment, growth, and risk taking, Chinese merchants sought only a steady-state relationship with peasants and government officials; they depended heavily on government permits and monopolies.

Key Terms

man-land ratio How much arable land per person.

steady-state A system that preserves itself with little change.

GEOGRAPHY

WHAT IS THE THIRD WORLD?

Coined by French writers in the 1950s, *le Tiers Monde* (**Third World**) referred to the majority of humankind that was in neither the Western capitalist First World nor the Communist Second World. It is an awfully broad term that permits few firm generalizations. Now, with the collapse of communism in East Europe and the ex-Soviet Union, the Third World is simply everything that is not "the West," meaning Europe, the United States, Canada, Australia, and now Japan. Some say the only meaningful dividing line is now "the West and the rest."

The Third World is mostly poor, but some oil-producing countries are rich, and some of its lands have industrialized so fast that they are already affluent. It is mostly nonwhite. Almost all of it, at one time or another, was a colony of a European imperial power. Most of it is hot and closer to the equator than the rich countries, so some writers suggest we call it the Global South. The U.S. State Department and some international banks call it the LDCs (less-developed countries). The ones making fast economic progress are called NICs (newly industrializing countries). Business calls these countries the "emerging markets."

Call it what you will, one generalization stands up fairly well: It is politically unstable. The political institutions of almost all of its 120-plus countries are weak, and this is their chief difference with the West. Most Third World lands are wracked by political, social, and economic tensions that explode in revolution, coups, and upheavals and often end in dictatorship. Few have yet made it into the ranks of stable democracies, the characteristic now of all of the West. India is an amazing exception—although it went through a bout of authoritarian rule under Indira Gandhi. Pakistan is a more typical example: unstable elected governments alternating with military rule.

Scholars find a fairly clear connection between economics and democracy. Countries with per capita GDPs above $6,000 (middle-income countries and higher) are almost all stable democracies and do not revert to authoritarianism. Countries with per capita GDPs below $5,000 have trouble establishing and sustaining democracy; they often revert to authoritarianism. Notice how several of the countries discussed in this book are in this borderline area.

We should really come up with some better names than Third World to describe the complexity of the lands that are home to more than three-quarters of the human race, but until such a term has established itself, we use Third World.

Neither was there much interest in overseas expansion. Once they had their Middle Kingdom (because it was in the center of heaven) perfected, the Chinese saw no use for anything foreign. All outlying countries were inhabited by barbarians who were permitted to **kow-tow** and pay tribute to the emperor. China had all the technology for overseas expansion but simply didn't bother. Expeditions—one of which visited Africa—brought back the news that there wasn't anything worthwhile beyond the seas. Thus, for centuries, China remained a stay-at-home country.

Key Terms

Third World Most of Asia, Africa, and Latin America.

kow-tow Literally, head to the ground; to prostrate oneself.

The People's Republic of China

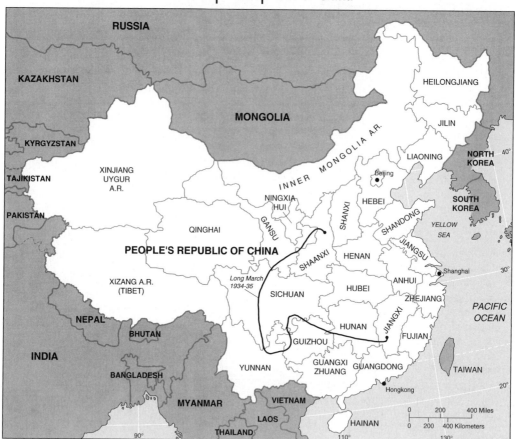

The solid black line shows the approximate route of the 1934–35 Long March.

A Traditional Political System

Politically too, China was steady-state. China unified very early. Feudalism was replaced by a bureaucratic empire, complete with impartial civil-service exams to select the best talent. The resulting Mandarin class—schooled in the Confucian classics, which stressed obedience, authority, and hierarchy—was interested in perpetuating the system, not changing it. A gentry class of better-off people served as the literate intermediaries between the Mandarins and the 90 percent of the population that were peasants. The words of one peasant song are as follows:

When the sun rises, I toil;
When the sun sets, I rest;
I dig wells for water;
I till the fields for food;
What has the Emperor's power to do with me?

Dynasties came and went every few hundred years in what is called the **dynastic cycle**. As the old dynasty became increasingly incompetent, water systems went unrepaired, famine broke out, wars and banditry appeared, and corruption grew. In the eyes of the people, it looked as if the emperor had lost the "Mandate of Heaven," that is, his legitimate right to rule. A conqueror, either Chinese or foreign (**Mongol** or **Manchu**), found it easy to take over a demoralized empire. By the very fact of his victory, the new ruler seemed to have gained the Mandate of Heaven. Under vigorous new emperors, things went well; the breakdowns were fixed. After some generations, though, the new dynasty fell prey to the same ills as the old, and people, especially the literate, began to think the emperor had lost his heavenly mandate. The cycle was ready to start over.

Two millennia of Chinese empire left an indelible mark on the China of today. Not a feudal system like Japan, China early became a unified and centralized system, with an emperor at the top setting the direction and tone, Mandarins carrying out Beijing's writ, gentry running local affairs, and peasants—the overwhelming majority of the population—toiling in the fields. New dynasties soon found themselves lulled into accepting the system and becoming part of it. Even the Communists were not able to totally eradicate the classic pattern of Chinese civilization.

Key Terms

dynastic cycle The rise, maturity, and fall of an imperial family.

Mongol Central Asian dynasty, founded by Genghis Khan, that ruled China in the thirteenth and fourteenth centuries.

Manchu Last imperial dynasty of China, also known as *Qing*; ruled from seventeenth century to 1911.

Middle Kingdom China's traditional name for itself, as if it were in the middle of the heavens.

The Long Collapse

For some 2,000 years the **Middle Kingdom** proved capable of absorbing the changes thrown at it in the form of invasions, famines, and new dynasties. The old pattern always reasserted itself. But as the modern epoch impinged on China, at least two new factors arose that the system could not handle: population growth and Western penetration.

In 1741, China's population was 143 million; just a century later, in 1851, it had become an amazing 432 million, the result of new crops (corn and sweet potatoes from the Americas), internal peace under the Manchu dynasty, some new farmland, and just plain harder work on

GEOGRAPHY

BOUND CHINA

China is bounded on the north by Russia, Mongolia, and Kazakhstan; on the east by Korea and the Yellow, East China, and South China Seas; on the south by Vietnam, Laos, Burma, India, Bhutan, and Nepal; and on the west by Tajikistan, Afghanistan, and Pakistan.

If you know China's boundaries you can label most of mainland Asia. Only Cambodia, Thailand, and Bangladesh do not border China.

GEOGRAPHY

RAINFALL

A focus on Europe may cause us to overlook one of the most basic physical determinants of a politico-economic system. Rainfall in Europe is generally sufficient and predictable, but in much of the world it is not. There is plenty of land in the world; water to grow crops is the limiting factor. An average Chinese has available only about 20 percent of the water of the global average. Irrigation can supplement rainfall, but this requires a high degree of human organization and governmental supervision. This may explain why high civilizations arose so early in China and Iran. Large desert or semi-desert areas of our four Third World examples—China, Brazil, South Africa, and Iran—will never be able to sustain much development.

the part of the peasants. Taxation and administration lagged behind the rapid population growth, which hit as the Manchus were going into the typical decline phase of their dynastic cycle in the nineteenth century.

At about the same time the West was penetrating and disorienting China. It was a clash of two cultures—Western dynamism and greed versus Chinese stability—and the Chinese side was no match at all. In roughly a century of collapse, old China went into convulsions and breakdowns, which ended with the triumph of the Communists.

The first Westerners to reach China were Portuguese seamen in 1514. Gradually, they and other Europeans got permission to set up trading stations on the coast. For three centuries the Imperial government disdained the foreigners and their products and tried to keep their number to a minimum. In 1793, for example, in response to a British mission to Beijing, the emperor commended King George III for his "respectful spirit of submission" but pointed out that there could be little trade because "our celestial empire possesses all things in prolific abundance."

But the West, especially the British, pushed on, smelling enormous profits in the China trade. Matters came to a head with the Opium Wars of 1839 to 1842. The British found a product that Chinese would buy, opium from the poppy fields of British-held India. Opium smoking was illegal and unknown in China. The British, however, flouted the law and popularized opium smoking. When at last a zealous Imperial official tried to stop the opium trade, Britain went to war to keep the lucrative commerce open. Britain easily won, but the Chinese still refused to admit that the foreigners were superior. Moaned one Cantonese: "Except for your ships being solid, your gunfire fierce, and your rockets powerful, what good qualities do you have?" For the Chinese, war technology was not as important as moral quality, a view later adopted by Mao Zedong.

The 1842 Treaty of Nanjing (Nanking in the now-obsolete Wade-Giles transcription) wrested five **treaty ports** from the Chinese. Britain got Hong Kong as an outright possession. In the treaty ports the foreigners held sway, dominating the commerce and governance of the area. The Westerners enjoyed **extraterritoriality**, meaning they were not subject to Chinese law but had their own courts, a point deeply resented by both Chinese and Japanese. In the 1860s, nine more Chinese treaty ports were added.

Key Terms

treaty ports   Areas of the China coast run by European powers.

extraterritoriality   Privilege of Europeans in colonial situations to have separate laws and courts.

Around the treaty ports grew **spheres of influence**, understandings among the foreign powers as to who ran things there. The British, French, Germans, Russians, and Japanese in effect carved up the China coast with their spheres of influence, in which they dominated trade. The Americans, claiming to be above this sort of business, tagged along after the British. China was reduced to semicolonial status.

Key Terms

sphere of influence Semicolonial area under control of major power.

Taiping Major religion-based rebellion in nineteenth-century China.

Boxer Major Chinese antiforeigner rebellion in 1900.

From Empire to Republic

Internally, too, the Empire weakened. Rebellions broke out. From 1851 to 1864, the **Taipings**—espousing a mixture of Christianity (picked up from missionaries), Confucianism, and primitive communism—baptized millions in South China and nearly overthrew the Manchu (Qing) dynasty. In 1900, with the backing of some reactionary officials and the empress dowager, the antiforeign **Boxer** movement, based on traditional temple boxing-type exercises, killed missionaries and besieged Beijing's Legation Quarter for fifty-five days. An international expedition of British, French, German, Russian, American, and Japanese troops broke through and lifted the siege. The foreigners then demanded indemnities and additional concessions from the tottering Imperial government.

Could the Qing (pronounced "Ching") dynasty have adapted itself to the new Western pressures? The Japanese had; with the 1868 Meiji Restoration they preserved the form of empire but shifted to modernization and industrialization with spectacular success. (See Chapter 22.) Many young Chinese demanded reforms to strengthen China, especially after their humiliating defeat by Japan in 1895. In 1898 the young Emperor Guangxu gathered around him reformers and in the famous Hundred Days issued more than forty edicts, modernizing everything from education to the military. Conservative officials and the old empress dowager would have none of it; they carried out a coup, rescinded the changes, and put the emperor under house arrest for the rest of his short life. (He was probably poisoned.)

KEY CONCEPTS

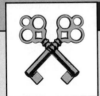

CONFUCIANISM: GOVERNMENT BY RIGHT THINKING

The scholar Confucius (551–479 B.C.) advised rulers that the key to good, stable government lay in instilling correct, moral behavior in ruled and rulers alike. Each person must understand his or her role and perform it obediently. Sons were subservient to fathers, wives to husbands, younger brothers to elder brothers, and subjects to rulers. The ruler sets a moral example by purifying his spirit and perfecting his manners. In this way, goodness perpetuates the ruler in power. Japan, as we discussed, picked up Confucianism from China.

The Confucian system emphasized that good government starts with thinking good thoughts in utter sincerity. If things go wrong, it indicates rulers have been insincere. Mao Zedong hated everything old China stood for, but he couldn't help picking up the Confucian stress on right thinking. Adding a Marxist twist, Mao taught that one was a proletarian not because of blue-collar origin but because one had revolutionary, pure thoughts. Confucius would have been pleased.

KEY CONCEPTS

CYCLICAL VERSUS SECULAR CHANGE

China offers good illustrations of the two kinds of change that social scientists often deal with. Cyclical change is repetitive; certain familiar historical phases follow one another like a pendulum swing. China's dynastic cycles are examples of cyclical change; there is change, but the overall pattern is preserved.

Secular change means a long-term shift that does not revert to the old pattern. China's population growth, for example, was a secular change that helped break the stability of traditional China. One of the problems faced by historians, economists, and political scientists is whether a change they are examining is secular—a long-term, basic shift—or cyclical—something that comes and goes repeatedly.

A system that cannot reform is increasingly ripe for revolution. Younger people, especially army officers, grew fed up with China's weakness and became militant nationalists. Many Chinese studied in the West and were eager to westernize China. Under an idealistic, Western-trained doctor, San Yatsen (Sun Yat-sen in Wade-Giles), disgruntled provincial officials and military commanders overthrew the Manchus in 1911. It was the end of the last dynasty but not the beginning of stability. In the absence of central authority, so-called **warlords** in effect brought China into feudalism from 1916 to 1927.

Gradually overcoming the chaos was the **Nationalist** party, or Guomindang (in Wade-Giles, Kuomintang, KMT). Formed shortly after the Manchu's overthrow, the Nationalists were guided by intellectuals (many of them educated in the United States), army officers, and the modern business element. Their greatest strength was in the South, in Guangzhou (Canton), especially in the coastal cities where there was the most contact with the West. It was no accident that they made Nanjing their capital; the word in fact means "southern capital." (North-South tensions exist to this day in China.)

Power gravitated into the hands of General (later Generalissimo) Jiang Jieshi (Chiang Kai-shek), who by 1927 had succeeded in unifying most of China under the Nationalists. While Jiang was hailed as the founder and savior of the new China—Henry Luce, the son of a China missionary, put Jiang ten times on the cover of *Time*—in reality, the Nationalist rule was weak. The Western-oriented city people who staffed the Nationalists did not reform or develop the rural areas where most Chinese still lived, usually under the thumb of rapacious landlords. Administration became terribly corrupt. And the Nationalists offered no plausible ideology to rally the Chinese people.

Key Terms

warlord   In 1920s China, a general who ran a province.
Nationalist   Chiang Kai-shek's party that unified China in late 1920s, abbreviated KMT.

Still, like Kerensky's provisional government in Russia, the Nationalists might have succeeded were it not for war. In 1931 the Japanese seized Manchuria and in 1937 began the conquest of the rest of China. By 1941 they had taken the entire coast, forcing the Nationalists to move their capital far up the Changjiang (Yangtze) River from Nanjing to Chongqing. The United States, in accordance with its long support of China, embargoed trade with Japan, a move that eventually led to Pearl Harbor. For the Americans in World War II, however, China was a sideshow. Jiang's forces preferred fighting Communists to Japanese, while waiting for a U.S. victory to return them to power.

The Communist Triumph

One branch of Chinese nationalism, influenced by Marx and by the Bolshevik Revolution, decided that communism was the only effective basis for implementing a nationalist revolution. The Chinese Communists have always been first and foremost nationalists, and from its founding in 1921 the Chinese Communist party (CCP) worked with the Nationalists until Jiang, in 1927, decided to exterminate them as a threat. The fight between the KMT and CCP was a struggle between two versions of Chinese nationalism.

While Stalin advised the Chinese Communists to base themselves on the small proletariat of the coastal cities, Mao Zedong rose to leadership of the Party by developing a rural strategy called the "mass line." Mao concluded that the real revolutionary potential in China, which had little industry and hence few proletarians, was among the long-suffering peasants. It was a major revision of Marx, one that Marx probably would not recognize as Marxism.

In 1934, with KMT forces surrounding them, some 120,000 Chinese Communists began their incredible Long March of more than 6,000 miles (10,000 km) to the relative safety of Yan'an in the north. It lasted over a year and led across mountain ranges and rivers amidst hostile forces. Fewer than twenty thousand survived. The Long March became the epic of Chinese Communist history. Self-reliant and isolated from the Soviets, the Chinese Communists had to develop their own strategy for survival, including working with peasants and practicing guerrilla warfare.

While the war against Japan drained and demoralized the Nationalists, it strengthened and encouraged the Communists. Besides stocks of captured Japanese weapons from the Russian takeover of Manchuria in 1945, the Chinese Communists got little help from the Soviets and felt they never owed them much in return. Mao and his Communists came to power on their own, by perfecting their peasant and guerrilla strategies. This fact may have contributed to the later Sino-Soviet split.

After World War II, the Nationalist forces were much larger than the Communists', and they had many U.S. arms. Nationalist strength, however, melted away as hyperinflation

Chairman Mao Zedong proclaims the founding of the People's Republic of China on October 1, 1949. (Xinhua)

KEY CONCEPTS

MAO AND GUERRILLA WAR

In what became a model for would-be-revolutionaries the world over, the Chinese Communists swept to power in 1949 after a decade and a half of successful guerrilla warfare. During these years, Mao Zedong, often in his Yan'an cave, developed and taught what he called the **mass line**. His lessons included the following:

1. Take the countryside and surround the cities. While the enemy is stuck in the cities, able to venture out only in strength, you are mobilizing the masses.

2. Work very closely with the peasants, listen to their complaints, help them solve problems (for example, getting rid of a landlord or bringing in the harvest), propagan-dize them, and recruit them into the army and Party.

3. Don't engage the enemy's main forces but rather probe for his weak spots, harassing him and wearing him out.

4. Don't expect much help from the outside; be self-reliant. For weapons, take the enemies'.

5. Don't worry about the apparent superior numbers and firepower of the enemy and his imperialist allies; their strength is illusory because it is not based on the masses. Will-power and unity with the masses are more important than weaponry.

6. At certain stages guerrilla units come together to form larger units until at last, as the enemy stumbles, your forces become a regular army that takes the entire country.

destroyed the economy, corrupt officers sold their troops' weapons (often to the Communists), and war weariness paralyzed the population. The Nationalists had always neglected the rice roots of political strength: the common peasant. The Communists, by cultivating the peasantry (Mao himself was of peasant origin), won a new Mandate of Heaven. In 1949, the disintegrating Nationalists retreated to the island of Taiwan while the Communists restored Beijing ("northern capital") as the country's capital and proceeded to implement what is probably the world's most sweeping revolution. On that occasion, Mao, reflecting his deeply nationalistic sentiments, said: "Our nation will never again be an insulted nation. We have stood up."

The Key Institutions

The Soviet Parallel

The institutions of China's government are essentially what the Soviet Union had—interlocking state and Party hierarchies—but China adds a Third-World twist: The army is also quite important, at times intervening directly into politics, as happens in other developing countries. China, no less than Brazil (see the next chapter), has experienced upheaval and chaos, which has led to army participation in politics. In this regard, the People's Republic of China (PRC) is still a Third-World country.

Key Term

mass line   Mao's theory of revolution for China.

As in the old Soviet model, each state and Party level ostensibly elects the one above it. In China, production and residential units elect local People's Congresses, which then elect county People's Congresses, which in turn choose provincial People's Congresses. China, organized on a unitary rather than federal pattern, has twenty-one provinces. The provincial People's Congresses then elect the National People's Congress (NPC) of nearly three thousand deputies for a five-year term.

As in the ex-Soviet Union, this parliament is too big to do much at its brief annual sessions. Recent NPC sessions, however, have featured some lively debate, contested committee elections, and negative votes—possibly indications that it may gradually turn into a real

TANDEM POWER: MAO AND ZHOU

For over a quarter of a century, until both died in 1976, power in Beijing was not concentrated in the hands of a single Stalin-like figure but divided between Party Chairman Mao Zedong and Premier Zhou Enlai. This Chinese pattern of tandem power may now be sufficiently deep to continue into the future.

Both men were of rural backgrounds, but Mao was born in 1893 into a better-off peasant family, while Zhou was born in 1898 into a gentry family. As young men, both were drawn to Chinese nationalism and then to its Marxist variation. Neither of them went much further than high school in formal education, although both studied, debated, and wrote in Chinese leftist circles. Zhou was in France from 1920 to 1924, ostensibly to study but actually to recruit Chinese students in Europe. Mao had no experience outside of China.

As instructed by the Soviets, the young Chinese Communist party worked closely with the Nationalists. Zhou, for example, was in charge of political education at the Nationalist military academy. In 1927, when Chiang Kai-shek turned on the Communists, both Mao and Zhou barely escaped with their lives. (Zhou was the model militant Chinese revolutionary for French writer André Malraux's novel *Man's Fate*, set in 1927 Shanghai.)

The next decade set their relationship. Mao concluded from his work with peasants that in them lay the path to China's revolution. Zhou, who briefly remained loyal to Moscow's proletarian line, by 1931 had changed his mind and joined Mao in his Jiangxi redoubt. From there, the two led the arduous Long March to the north. By the time they arrived in Yan'an, Mao was clearly the leader of the CCP, and his "mass line" of basing the revolution on the peasantry prevailed.

Mao dominated mainly by force of intellect. Other CCP leaders respected his ability to theorize in clear, blunt language. Mao became the Party chief and theoretician but did not concern himself with the day-to-day tasks of survival, warfare, and diplomacy. These became, in large part, Zhou's jobs. Zhou Enlai became the administrator of the revolution. Never bothering to theorize, Zhou was a master at shaping and controlling bureaucracies, smooth diplomacy, and political survival amidst changing lines.

Was there tension between the two? Probably, but Zhou never showed it. Publicly Zhou dedicated himself completely to fulfilling Mao's desires, although at times, in the shambles of the Great Leap Forward (1958–60) and the Cultural Revolution (1966–69), he seemed to be trying to hold things together and limit the damage.

Mao was the abstract thinker while Zhou was the pragmatic doer. This made Mao more radical and Zhou more conservative. Mao could spin out his utopian dreams, but Zhou had to make the bureaucracy, military, and economy function. Different roles require different personalities.

parliament with some checks on the executive. This, if it ever happens, would be a major step to democratization. A Standing Committee of about 155 is theoretically supreme, but it too does not have much power in overseeing the executive branch. The chairman of the Standing Committee is considered China's head of state or president, a largely honorific post currently held by Party Chairman Jiang Zemin.

THE INVISIBLE PUPPETEER: DENG XIAOPING

Deng Xiaoping was a strange leader. He had been purged from Chinese politics twice before becoming "senior vice-premier" in 1977, a deliberately deceptive title to cover the fact he was China's undisputed boss. And Deng sought no fame or glory; unlike Mao, he built no personality cult. Deng seldom appeared in public or in the media but governed in the ancient Confucian tradition: quietly, behind the scenes, chiefly by picking the right personnel. MIT political scientist Lucian Pye called him the "invisible puppeteer." This former protégé of Zhou Enlai—who, like Zhou, was a pragmatic administrator rather than a theorizer—set China on its present course and gave China its current problems.

Deng was born in 1904 into a rural landlord family. Sent to study in France, Deng was recruited by Zhou Enlai and soon joined the Chinese Communists. As a political commissar and organizer of the People's Liberation Army, Deng forged strong military connections. Rising through major posts after 1949, Deng was named to the top of the Party—the Politburo's Standing Committee—in 1956.

Deng was not as adroit as Zhou and kept getting into political trouble. An outspoken pragmatist, Deng said after the Great Leap: "Private farming is alright as long as it raises production, just as it doesn't matter whether a cat is black or white as long as it catches mice." During the Cultural Revolution this utterance was used against Deng to show he was a "Capitalist Roader." Although not expelled from the Party, Deng dropped out of sight and lost his official position. His son was crippled by a mob during the Cultural Revolution.

But the little man—Deng was well under five feet tall—bounced back in 1973 when moderates regained control. In 1975, he seemed to be ready to take over; he spoke with visiting U.S. President Ford as one head of state to another. But just a month later Deng was again in disgrace, denounced by the radicals of the **Gang of Four** as anti-Mao. Again, he was stripped of his posts, but an old army buddy gave him sanctuary in an elite military resort.

But the adaptable Deng bounced back yet again. With the arrest of the Gang of Four in 1976, moderates came back out of the woodwork, among them Deng. In July 1977, he was reappointed to all his old posts. Many Chinese state, Party, and army leaders, badly shaken by the Cultural Revolution, felt that old comrade Deng was a man they could trust. In 1978 Deng, then already seventy-four, started China on its present course by splitting economics from politics. He in effect offered Chinese a new deal: Work and get rich in a semifree market but leave politics in the hands of the Communist party. This set the stage for China's amazing economic growth. But won't the massive economic changes eventually influence politics? Apparently, Deng never gave much thought to this problem, which is now China's chief problem.

Deng was no "liberal." He encouraged economic reform but blocked any moves toward democracy. In 1989, Deng brutally crushed the prodemocracy movement in Beijing's Tiananmen Square. Although weak and reclusive in the 1990s, Deng was still quietly in control of Beijing's top personnel and main policy lines until he died in 1997 at age ninety-two.

The top of the executive branch is the State Council, a cabinet of approximately forty ministers (specialized in economic branches) and a dozen vice-premiers led by a premier, China's head of government, since 1998 Zhu Rongji.

The formal structure of the executive does not always correspond to the real distribution of its power. In 1976, after the death of both Party Chairman Mao Zedong and Premier Zhou Enlai, a relative unknown, Hua Guofeng, was installed in both their offices. On paper, Hua appeared to be the most powerful figure in the land.

But an elderly, twice-rehabilitated Party veteran, Deng Xiaoping, named to the modest post of senior vice-premier in 1977, was in fact more powerful than his nominal boss, Hua. When Deng toured the United States in 1979, he acted like a head of state. Deng's power grew out of his senior standing in the Party and the army. In 1980, he demoted Hua and assumed power himself, still without taking over the job titles, which he left to others. By 1982, Hua was out of the Politburo and out of sight.

The Party

Like the old Soviet Communist party, the Chinese Communist party (CCP) is constitutionally and in practice the leading political element of the country. No other parties are allowed. With 61 million members, the CCP is large, but relative to China's population it is proportionately smaller than the CPSU was. In recent years, as China's economy has decentralized and shifted to markets, the CCP has lost some of its authority. Communist officials now use their positions for personal gain; massive corruption has set in.

In organization, the CCP parallels the defunct CPSU. Hierarchies of Party congresses at the local, county, provincial, and national levels feed into corresponding Party committees. At the top is the National Party Congress; composed of some 1,900 delegates and supposed to meet at least once in five years, this congress nominally chooses a Central Committee of about 200 members. Since both bodies are too big to run things, however, power ends up in the hands of a Politburo of about twenty Party chiefs. But this too is not the last level. Within the Politburo is a Standing Committee of five to seven members who really decide things. Power is extremely concentrated in China.

The CCP's structure used to be a bit different from the classic Soviet model. Instead of a general secretary at its head, the CCP had a Party chairman, Mao's title, which he passed on to Hua Guofeng. By then, however, the office was robbed of meaning, and Hua was eclipsed by Senior Vice-Premier Deng Xiaoping, who, to be sure, also held important Party and army positions. In 1982, under Deng's guidance, the Party abolished the chairmanship—part of a repudiation of Mao's legacy—and upgraded the position of general secretary, so that now the CCP structure more closely matches that of the old CPSU. Deng arranged to have his protégé Hu Yaobang named general secretary. Hu, however, proved to be too liberal and a bit unpredictable. He also failed to win approval of the army (see next section) and was dropped in 1987. His place was taken by another Deng protégé, Zhao Ziyang, who in turn was ousted in 1989 for appearing to side with student demonstrators. Replacing him was the hard-line mayor of Shanghai, Jiang Zemin, who was also named head of state in 1993.

China's nervous system is its Party **cadres**. There are 30 million CCP cadres, and whoever controls them controls China. In 1979, Deng Xiaoping began the ticklish job of easing out both the incompetent old guard—whose only qualification, in many cases, was having been on the Long March—and the extreme leftists who wormed their way into the cadre structure during the tumultuous Cultural Revolution. Quietly, Deng brought in younger, better-educated cadres dedicated to his moderate, pragmatic line.

The Army

Until recently, the top figures in the Chinese elite held both high state and high Party offices, as in the old Soviet Union. In China, though, they also held high positions atop the military structure, through the important Military Affairs Commission, which interlocks with the CCP's Politburo. Mao, Hua, and Deng were all chairmen of the Military Affairs Commission. In addition, the CCP Standing Committee usually has at least one top general. Indeed, from the beginning, the People's Liberation Army (PLA), earlier known as the Chinese Red Army, has been so intertwined with the CCP that it's hard to separate them. Deng named an active-duty general to the elite Politburo Standing Committee, and nearly a quarter of the Central Committee is PLA. Fighting the Nationalists and the Japanese for at least a decade and a half, the CCP became a combination of Party and army. The pattern continues to this day. Political scientist Robert Tucker called the Chinese system "military communism."

Mao wrote "political power grows out of the barrel of a gun," but "the Party commands the gun, and the gun must never be allowed to command the Party." Where the two are nearly merged, however, it's hard to tell who's on top. As the Communists took over China in the 1940s, it was the PLA that first set up their power structures. Until recently, China's executive decision makers all had extensive military experience, often as political commissars in PLA units. Said Zhou Enlai: "We are all connected with the army." When the Cultural Revolution broke out in 1966, as we shall see, the army first facilitated, then dampened and finally crushed the Red Guards' rampages. By the time the Cultural Revolution sputtered out, the PLA was in de facto control of most provincial governments and most of the Politburo. In 1980, a third of the Politburo was still occupied by active military men. At various times during mobilization campaigns, the army is cited as a model for the rest of the country to follow, and heroic individual soldiers are celebrated in the media.

What does PLA influence mean for the governance of China? Armies, as guardians of their countries' security, define whatever is good for them as good for the country. Anyone who undermines their power earns their opposition. During the Cultural Revolution, for example, the army under Defense Minister Lin Biao supported Mao's program to shake up the Party and state bureaucracy. (The army was not touched.) As the chaos spread, however, military commanders worried that it was sapping China's strength and military preparedness. Lin became increasingly isolated within the military. In 1971 Peking released the amazing story that Lin had attempted a coup and fled to the Soviet Union in a plane that crashed. Outside observers suggest Lin died by other means. His supporters were purged from the military. The PLA thus helped tame Maoist radicalism.

China's leaders seem to have decided that the army is not a good way to control domestic unrest. (They are right.) The PLA did not like mowing down students in Tiananmen in 1989. To deal with such situations, Beijing built up the People's Armed Police (PAP), now over 1 million strong. This paramilitary police, resembling the French CRS, could also be used as a counterweight to the PLA in case there is political infighting.

Even before Deng died, China's leaders paid special attention to the PLA and increased

TANDEM POWER CONTINUES

In 1989, when Deng Xiaoping at age eighty-five gave up his last formal post—as chairman of the powerful Military Affairs Commission—he made sure two protégés took over: Party General Secretary Jiang Zemin and Premier Li Peng. They were, respectively, sixty-three and sixty-one years old, the younger generation in Chinese politics. Although neither of the two had military experience, Jiang also took Deng's place on the Military Commission.

Jiang was born in Jiangsu province; little is known of his early years. He joined the Communist party in 1946 while a student at the Shanghai Technical University. He graduated as an electrical engineer and after the Communist takeover worked in several factories, finally becoming a top engineer at an automobile plant in the northeast of China. In 1980 Jiang arrived in Beijing as an export-import official and in 1982 was named minister for the electronics industry. As mayor of Shanghai from 1985 to 1988, Jiang was not well-liked and considered by some incompetent. He cracked down on prodemocracy Shanghai intellectuals.

Li Peng, born in Sichuan, was only two years old when his revolutionary father was executed. When he was eleven, Zhou Enlai's wife sent him for schooling to the Communist headquarters in Yan'an. From 1948 to 1954, Li studied at the Moscow Power Institute and then worked on power projects in China. Deng brought him onto the Politburo in 1985 and got him named education minister. Always considered a conservative, Li cracked down on student demands for more freedom and democracy. After two five-year terms, Li stepped down as premier in 1998 to become chairman of the National People's Congress.

The new premier is Zhu Rongji. Born poor in a poor province (Hunan) in 1928, Zhu studied electrical engineering and became an industrial planner. He was caught in Mao's Hundred Flowers campaign and demoted. Later, during the Cultural Revolution (see page 397) he was forced to work for years on farms. But Deng remembered him and, after twenty years as an outcast, promoted him rapidly. In 1992, Deng gave Zhu a "triple jump" right into the Standing Committee. Zhu became China's chief economic manager and cracked down on inefficiency and corruption. He cared only about the economy, not about democracy.

All three of these leaders were dedicated to keeping firm central control of politics while moving toward a partially market economy. All had experience silencing troublesome intellectuals. All were graduate engineers, and this gave their rule a technocratic bent. None were popular, nor did they seek to please the masses. None returned to the philosophy of Mao or to rapid change. With Jiang in charge of Party affairs and Zhu of the government, the two seem to continue the pattern of tandem rule.

its budget, but the PLA, with 2.8 million soldiers, is still poor and underequipped. Trying to supplement its meager budget, the PLA went massively into private industry, running some 15,000 businesses. Worried about the PLA's corruption, smuggling, and loss of mission, President Jiang ordered the army to get out of business and get back to soldiering. They complied, indicating that the Party still commands the gun. In general, the PLA has been a conservative force in Chinese politics, for almost axiomatically, an army stands for order and sees disorder as a security problem. In China, as will also be seen in Brazil, when chaos threatens, the army moves.

Chinese Political Culture

Traditional Culture

Mao used to say that his countrymen were "firstly poor, secondly blank," meaning that the Communists could start with a clean slate and create the Chinese citizens they wished. Mao was wrong. Plenty of traditional Chinese attitudes have carried over into the People's Republic. Indeed, even Mao's vision of perfecting human nature by thinking right thoughts is a deeply Confucian notion.

When the Communists restored Beijing as the capital in 1949, they were restoring an old symbol; Beijing had been the capital for centuries until Jiang's Nationalists moved it to Nanjing. Some government offices and elite living quarters now directly adjoin the old Forbidden City of the emperors, just as the Soviets made the Kremlin their home. Tiananmen (Gate of Heavenly Peace) Square is still Beijing's parade and demonstration area, much like Red Square is in Moscow.

In some ways, the Communists' bureaucrats and cadres perform the same function as the old Mandarins and gentry. Reciting the latest Party line instead of Confucius, the new elites strive to place a gigantic population under central control and guidance. Their aim now, to be sure, is growth and modernization, but still under a central hand. Mao himself recognized the similarity of old and new when he denounced the bureaucrats as the "new Mandarins" during the Cultural Revolution. Deng Xiaoping governed in the old Confucian style, almost invisibly, as if he had reverted to the old pattern.

To become one of the new Mandarins, Chinese youths must undergo twelve and a half hours of grueling university entrance exams. Of the millions who take them, only about 10 percent of China's college-age youths pass and enter institutions of higher education (as opposed to some 40 percent in the United States). The three days of exams resemble nothing so much as the Imperial examination system of old China. The new exams, identical and kept secret, are given simultaneously throughout China. They include sections on Chinese literature, math, science, a foreign language, and politics.

Mao argued against the examinations and had them dropped during the Cultural Revolution; they were restored only in 1977. Mao thought the exams were elitist and unrevolutionary, that they created a class of new Mandarin bureaucrats. Mao was quite right, but without the brutally competitive exams, educational standards slid, and incompetents got into universities based on their political correctness. Inferior graduates retarded China's progress in industry and administration, so the post-Mao moderates restored the examinations. It was another example of a long-functional process reasserting itself.

In another carryover from Old China, age confers special qualities of wisdom and leadership in the People's Republic. Mao died at eighty-two and Zhou at seventy-eight, both in office. When he returned to power in 1977, Deng Xiaoping was seventy-three. In his early nineties he was still politically influential although weak and deaf. President Jiang and Prime Minister Zhu are both in their seventies.

Nationalism

Overlaying traditional Chinese values is a more recent one, the nationalism that has dominated China's intellectual life since the turn of the century. Chinese nationalism, like Third World nationalism generally, is the result of a proud and independent culture suffering penetration,

disorientation, and humiliation at the hands of the West. This can induce explosive fury and the feeling that the native culture, although
temporarily beaten by foreigners, is morally better and more enduring.
In our day, Chinese, Russians, and Iranians still act out their resentment of the West, especially of America.

Key Term

voluntarism   Belief that
human will can change the
world.

In Asia, Chinese and Japanese nationalists vowed to beat the
West at its own game, building industry and weaponry but placing them at the service of the
traditional culture. The Japanese were able to carry out their designs in the last century; the
Chinese are still caught up in this process, which from time to time leaps out as bitter anti-Amer-
icanism. All of the founding generation of Chinese Communist leaders, including Mao and
Zhou, began as young patriots urging their countrymen to revitalize China and stand up to the
West and to Japan.

As in the old Soviet Union, one prevailing Chinese attitude is the nationalist drive to catch
up with the West. During their good economic-growth years—the mid-1950s, and 1980s and
1990s—Chinese leaders were proud of their rapid progress. The Great Leap Forward and the
Cultural Revolution ruined the economy. A pragmatic moderate such as Zhou or Deng always
has a powerful argument against such disruptions: They harm growth and weaken the country. Basically, this is a nationalist argument, and one used by pragmatists today.

Chinese nationalism flared anew in the 1990s. Tension with the United States over Taiwan and American pressures against China over human rights and copyright violations sparked
a government-approved anti-U.S. campaign. A popular book (modeled on an earlier Japanese book), *China Can Say No*, portrayed a vast conspiracy led by America to keep China down
(the same line put out by extreme Russian nationalists). Well, America better watch out, the
book said, because China will defend itself. Matters got worse when U.S. jets mistakenly
bombed the Chinese embassy in Belgrade in 1999. There was genuine mass resentment, carefully orchestrated by Beijing, which did not permit publication of U.S. apologies. Observers suggest China's decaying regime is using nationalism to prolong its hold on power.

Maoism

Maoism, or Mao Zedong Thought, as Beijing calls it, is now fading into the background. It draws
from both traditional and nationalistic values, despite its claim to be totally new and revolutionary. From traditional China, it takes the Confucian emphasis on thinking right thoughts,
based on the idea that consciousness determines existence rather than the reverse: Willpower has primacy over weaponry in wars; willpower has primacy over technology in building
China. The unleashed forces of the masses, guided by Mao Zedong Thought, can conquer anything. This extreme form of **voluntarism** is consonant with China's past.

From nationalism, Mao took the emphasis on strengthening and rebuilding China so
that it could stand up to its old enemies and become a world power. The trouble is that these
two strands are partly at odds with each other. Traditional values call for China to ignore the
West and its technology, but nationalistic values call for China to learn and copy from the
West. The continuing, unresolved conflict of these two streams of thought spell permanent
trouble for China.

Maoism is an outgrowth of Mao thoughts on guerrilla warfare (see page 384). According to Maoist doctrine, what the PLA did to beat the Nationalists, China as a whole
must do to advance and become a world leader: Work with the masses, be self-reliant, and
put willpower on a higher plane than technology to overcome obstacles. Mao can be seen

as a theorist of guerrilla warfare who continued to apply his principles to governance—with catastrophic results.

In the Great Leap Forward from 1958 to 1960, Mao tried guerrilla warfare tactics on the economy, using raw manual labor plus enthusiasm to build earthen dams and backyard blast furnaces. Engineers, experts, and administrators were bypassed. The Soviets warned Mao it wouldn't work and urged him to follow the Soviet model of building the economy by more conventional means; Mao refused to follow their lead. In 1960, the Soviets withdrew their substantial numbers of foreign-aid technicians, and the Sino-Soviet split came into the open.

For the Soviet Communists, the revolution was over; the proletariat triumphed in 1917 and moved Russia into the most advanced stage of history. For Mao, the revolution never ends. Mao held that at any stage there are conservative tendencies that block the path to socialism: bureaucratism, elitism, and opportunism. Mao resolved to combat these tendencies by means of "permanent revolution," periodic upheavals to let the force of the masses surge past the conservative bureaucrats.

Socialism and bureaucratism are closely connected—as Max Weber argued long ago—but Mao thought he could break the connection. He saw China settling into the bureaucratic patterns he hated and was determined to break them by instituting a permanent revolution before he died. The result was the Great Proletarian Cultural Revolution from 1966 to 1976, during which young people were encouraged to criticize, harass, and oust almost all authority except the army. Chaos spread through China, the economy slumped, and the army took over. Shortly after Mao's death, power returned to the bureaucrats; they won and Mao failed.

Mao refused to recognize the unhappy truth that if you want socialism you must accept the bureaucratism that comes with it. By trying to leap directly into some kind of guerrilla socialism without bureaucrats, Mao nearly wrecked China. On balance, Mao Zedong Thought is inherently inapplicable, and in post-Mao China, Mao is quoted infrequently.

Concealed Anger

As in Russia, wide sectors of China's population accord their regime less and less legitimacy. The Party, once respected as clean and competent, is now seen as corrupt and irrelevant. Even the peasants, at one time thought to be apathetic or even pleased at their increased

---

SLOGANS FROM THE CULTURAL REVOLUTION

- "Put destruction first, and in the process you have construction.
- "Destroy the four olds—old thought, old culture, old customs, old habits."
- "Once all struggle is grasped, miracles are possible."
- "Bombard the command post." (Attack established leaders if they are unrevolutionary.)

- "So long as it is revolutionary, no action is a crime."
- "Sweep the great renegade of the working class onto the garbage heap!" (Dump the moderate chief of state, Liu Shaoqi.)
- "Cadres step to the side." (Bypass established authorities.)
- "To rebel is justified."

GEOGRAPHY

REGION AND LANGUAGE

China illustrates the close connection—and problems—between a country's languages and its regions. All but small countries have regions, often based on language. In some cases, as between Serbs and Albanian-speaking Kosovars, the country splits apart. China is populated mostly by Han Chinese (there are important non-Han minorities in Tibet, Xinjiang, and elsewhere) but even Han do not all speak the same language.

Chinese rulers have always proclaimed the unity of China, but China has eight main language groups—mutually unintelligible—and hundreds of dialects, making it the world's most linguistically diverse country. The biggest by far is Mandarin, dialects of which are spoken by 800 million in a broad swath from north to south, but not in the important southern coastal provinces, where 90 million speak some form of the Wu language (including Shanghai) and 70 million speak Cantonese.

The regime has always feared that separate languages could lead to breakup. Since 1913 under the KMT, Beijing has tried to make Mandarin standard and universal, and the CCP carried this on, now pushing a largely Beijing dialect, *Putonghua* (common language), as the language of government and education. Most urban Chinese can now sort of speak it, but not country folk. The new prosperity in China's southern coastal provinces has actually boosted the use of their local dialects. Beijing is not pleased.

incomes from the "responsibility system," turned angry as corrupt local officials gouged them with fake taxes. Urban workers, Marx's "proletariat" that was supposed to be the backbone of communism, are trapped between uncertainty and inflation. Many sided with prodemocracy students and tried to start independent labor unions.

As ever, China's cities are the hotbeds of criticism and reform. Although a small minority, the urban educated classes have often taken the lead in changing China. Student protests in Beijing, for example, go back a century and contributed much to the overthrow of the Empire and the rise of first the Nationalists and then the Communists. The Communists under Mao in the 1930s, to be sure, had a peasant base, but many of the cadres were urban intellectuals. Accordingly, we probably get a better idea of where China is heading by focusing on city attitudes. In most countries, urban intellectuals are the spark plugs of political change.

During the twentieth century, educated Chinese have generally had a cause to believe in. At first it was building a new republic that would not be carved up by foreigners. Then it was in repelling the Japanese invaders. With the Communist takeover, many Chinese idealistically believed that Mao offered them a blueprint for a prosperous, socialist China. After Mao, Deng Xiaoping offered the encouraging image of a prosperous, semicapitalist China possibly moving to democracy. After the June 1989 massacre of prodemocracy students in Tiananmen Square, many Chinese fell into despair. Marx, Mao, and Deng have all been discredited, even among Party officials, although few say so openly. With nothing to believe in, a spiritual vacuum has opened up. What will fill it?

One classic answer is religion; both old (including Christianity) and new ones are growing rapidly despite harsh regime scrutiny and numerous arrests. What really got the regime nervous was a gathering in 1999 in central Beijing of over 10,000 practitioners of a new religion, *Falun Gong* (Buddhist Law), which attracts all kinds of Chinese with its belief in faith healing, traditional exercises, and the coming destruction of humankind (for the eighty-second time). As we saw in Japan, Buddhism generates offshoots without limit. The cult's founder and leader now lives in New York City and claims tens of millions of adherents in China. The believers in China were calm and peaceful, but they remind some of the Taipings and Boxers in the nineteenth century. Beijing in 1999 denounced Falun Gong as superstition, outlawed it, and arrested thousands of its followers. This is the reaction of a nervous regime.

Over the decades, the Chinese have become politically numb. They had to mouth slogans and participate in mass campaigns—one year anti-Confucius, the next anticapitalist roaders, then anti-Gang of Four, then anti-"spiritual pollution," then anti-"bourgeois liberalization"—without end. Most Chinese are awfully fed up with this nonsense and mentally tune out.

The great hope for Chinese students is to go abroad. Many study English and dream of joining the forty thousand Chinese students already in the United States. Many, of course, do not return to China. The regime, aware of this brain drain, changed its relatively open policy on sending students abroad and sharply restricts their numbers. Chinese university graduates must first work five years before they can apply for graduate study overseas. The great prize: a graduate degree, often an MBA, from a prestigious U.S. university. Several high-ranking Chinese leaders had children in such programs.

The Chinese way of handling the latest government crackdown on freedom and democracy is called *biaotai*, "to express an attitude." Chinese know how to crank out the current line while concealing their true feelings. This leads to what Chinese call *nei jin, wai song*, "tranquility outside, repression within." Everything looks calm, but only because people know they are being carefully watched. Just below the surface, though, repressed anger waits to erupt. Some of this shows up in the constant flow of nasty rumors about repression, economic incompetence, and the corruption of high officials. This has been called a struggle between the Big Lie and Little Whisper: The government tries to fool people with big lies, but the people fight back with little whispers. Chinese at all levels, knowing that all foreigners are closely monitored, refuse to discuss anything political (or religious) with visitors.

Such a tightly controlled system is obviously unstable. A considerable fraction of China's population dislikes and distrusts the regime. This feeling is especially prevalent in the South, which has long resented rule by the North. They know that patience is a Chinese virtue, but they are also frustrated that China's progress is blocked by a Party elite that simply wants to cling to its power and good jobs. They know that in the coastal Special Economic Zones (mostly in the South), where capitalism and foreign investment are allowed, the economy is booming. Why then not just expand the Special Zones until they cover all of China? They also know that Taiwanese enjoy five times the per capita income and far more freedom than mainlanders. Some Chinese students speak with shame that they didn't have the guts to do what the Romanians did in 1989: stand up to the government's guns and overthrow the regime. In time, Chinese student frustration could boil over again.

In the right situation—for example, a split in Beijing leadership over the personnel and policies—China's peasants, workers, and students could quickly come together and overthrow the regime. Needless to say, the police work hard to prevent a Chinese equivalent of Poland's Solidarity. Political repression, of course, solves nothing; it merely postpones the day of reckoning. What happened in East Europe could happen in China.

Patterns of Interaction

Cycles of Upheaval

Since the Communists came to power in 1949 there have been three major upheavals plus several smaller ones. Among major upheavals are the "agrarian reforms" (that is, execution of landlords and redistribution of land) of the early 1950s, the Great Leap Forward from 1958 to 1960, and the Cultural Revolution from 1966 to 1976. Smaller upheavals include the brief Hundred Flowers liberalization of 1956, the antirightist campaigns of 1957 and the early 1970s, the crushing of the Gang of Four and their supporters in the late 1970s, and the repression of the alleged "counterrevolutionary rebellion" of prodemocracy students in 1989.

The big upheavals and most of the smaller ones can be traced to the same underlying problem: Beijing's leaders, having inherited a poor and backward land, want to make China rich, advanced, and socialist. Mao Zedong Thought taught that everything is possible: China can leap into the modern age and even beyond it. But the old, stubborn, traditional China was unyielding; it frustrated the bold plans and tugged the system back toward the previous patterns and problems.

As long as China is not what its leaders wish it to be—modern, powerful, and respected—there is the possibility of another upheaval instituted from the top. Indeed, such upheavals seem to be inherent in the effort to modernize. Similar episodes occurred in Russia as leaders tried to force their country along: Peter the Great's Westernization, Stalin's industrialization, Khrushchev's experiments, and Gorbachev's reform attempts. The difference with China is that it is far more backward and hence the remedies put forward have been more extreme.

For China's periodic upheavals to cease, it will require the abandonment of the Communists' central tenet, namely, that communism delivers rapid progress. To admit that China is now making major economic progress—but only by the capitalist path of foreign investment, markets, and world trade—took a major psychological shift at the top of the CCP. Nothing has been announced publicly, but insiders report that under Deng's leadership China's elite

Radicals and Moderates in Chinese Politics

Radicals	*Moderates*
celebrate Mao Thought	selectively quote Mao
mass-oriented	elite-oriented
antiauthoritarian	hierarchical
demand purification	demand modernization
permanent revolution	stability
breakthrough growth	steady economic growth
politics in command	economics in command
learn from the people	follow the experts
wage equality	wage differentials
worker enthusiasm	material incentives
common sense	science and education
economically self-reliant	import technology
ideological	empirical

decided to have a largely capitalist economy but to call it "socialism with Chinese character-istics." We have to keep a careful lookout for a new round of revolutionary enthusiasm. The potential for extremism is still present, and there are no institutional mechanisms—compet-ing parties, free elections, an independent judiciary—to block a new round of it. The limiting factors now are the weariness of the Chinese people after all the regime-sponsored disruptions and the success of the "capitalist road."

Radicals and Moderates

Outside observers used to label CCP figures as "radicals" or "moderates" according to their willingness to support the kind of upheavals previously described. This may oversimplify, for there were no distinct groups in China bearing these names. And many Party leaders demon-strated how they could play both sides of the field, depending on their career advantage.

China's moderates were and still are those high up in the Party, government, or army. Al-most axiomatically, anyone who's part of the establishment will not be a radical. Mao was right: Bureaucrats are by nature conservative. China's radicals were drawn largely from those peripheral to power but ambitious for it: students, junior cadres, some provincial leaders.

One of the prime motivations for radicals, especially during the Cultural Revolution, was the scarcity of job openings in Party, state, army, industrial, and other offices. For the most part, positions until recently were staffed by aging Party comrades who go back to the 1949 lib-eration or even the Long March. They never retire, and their longevity in office breeds impa-tience and resentment among younger people with ambitions of their own. A further element fueling youthful discontent is the previously mentioned difficulty of getting into a university.

THE GREAT LEAP FORWARD: "TWENTY YEARS IN A DAY"

In 1958 Mao Zedong launched one of the strangest efforts in the Third World's strug-gle to move ahead: the Great Leap Forward. Vowing to progress "twenty years in a day" and "catch up with Great Britain in fifteen years," all of China was urged to "walk on two legs" (use all possible means) to industrialize rapidly. Most peasants—and China is still mostly peasant—were herded into gigantic communes, some with as many as 100,000 people. Deprived of their private plots, they were ordered to eat in communal dining halls, leave their children in nurseries, and even sleep in large dormitories.

The communes were ordered to participate in engineering and industrial projects. Rely-ing on "labor-intensive" methods to compen-sate for lack of capital, millions were turned out to move earth with baskets and carry poles to build dams and irrigation works. Backyard blast furnaces were ordered built so that every commune could produce its own iron.

Within a year the failure was plain for all to see. Even Mao had to admit it; he resigned as president of the PRC but kept his chair-manship of the CCP. Peasants—as in the So-viet Union—failed to produce without private incentives. Labor was wasted in fool-ish projects. A serious food shortage devel-oped, and over 30 million Chinese died of malnutrition. To meet Party quotas, peasants melted down their good tools to produce im-plements of miserable quality. The communes were phased out, broken first into "produc-tion brigades" and then into "production teams," which were in fact the old villages. Private farming was again permitted. Mao lost; old China won.

THE GREAT PROLETARIAN CULTURAL REVOLUTION

If the Great Leap Forward was strange, the Great Proletarian Cultural Revolution was downright bizarre. In it, an elderly Mao Zedong tried to make his revolution permanent by destroying the very structures his new China had created. Of the many slogans from the Cultural Revolution, "bombard the command post" perhaps best summarizes its character. Mao encouraged young people, who hastily grouped themselves into ragtag outfits called Red Guards, to destroy most authority, even the CCP. They did, and Chinese progress was set back years.

The Cultural Revolution began with a 1965 flap over a Shanghai play some radicals claimed criticized Mao by allegory. Mao turned what could have been a small literary debate into a mass criticism that led to the ouster of several Party officials. Then university and high-school students were encouraged to air their grievances against teachers and school administrators. Behind their discontent was a shortage of the kind of jobs the students thought they deserved upon graduation.

By fall 1966, most schools closed as their students demonstrated, humiliated officials, wrote wall posters, and marched to and fro. China was in chaos. Hundreds of thousands of victims of the Red Guards committed suicide. A much larger number were "sent down" to the countryside to work with the peasants and "learn from the people." This included physical abuse and psychological humiliation. An unknown number were murdered outright. Worried officials set up their own Red Guard groups to protect themselves. Different Red Guard factions fought each other.

Even Mao became concerned, and in early 1967 he ordered the army to step in. By the end of 1967 the People's Liberation Army pretty much ran the country. To replace the broken governmental structures, the army set up "revolutionary committees" on which sat PLA officers, Red Guard leaders, and "repentant" officials. By 1969, the worst was over, although officially the Cultural Revolution did not end until 1976 when Mao died and the ultra-radical Gang of Four (headed by Mao's wife, Jiang Qing), was arrested.

The effects of the Cultural Revolution were all bad. Industry suffered. Education, when it resumed, was without standards, and students were chosen on the basis of political attitudes rather than ability. The more moderate and level-headed officials, whom the Red Guards sought to destroy, laid low and pretended to go along with the Cultural Revolution. When it was over, they reasserted themselves and made sure one of their own was in charge: Deng Xiaoping.

And what became of the Red Guards? Claiming their energy was needed on the farm, the army marched more than sixteen million young city people to rural communes for agricultural labor and forbade them to return to their cities. By hook or by crook, many of them managed to get back to their homes to try to continue their studies. Some, utterly disillusioned with the way they had been used, turned to petty crime or fled to the British colony of Hong Kong. Some eventually became capitalist millionaires in the burgeoning Special Economic Zones of the South.

These kinds of tensions underlay the radical outburst of the Cultural Revolution. Those who aspired to power enthusiastically attempted to carry out Mao's designs. Those who held power pretended to go along with it, often by mouthing the correct slogans and self-denunciations. In Mao's words, they "waved the red flag to oppose the red flag." When the campaign burned itself out, the bureaucrats and cadres took over again, and it appeared that the moderates had won.

Chinese Liberal and Conservative Politics

With the Maoist demon back in the bottle, a new conflict appeared in Chinese politics, a split between liberal and conservative forces, similar to what the Soviets went through before their system collapsed. The Chinese moderates who opposed the extremism of the Cultural Revolution essentially wanted to go back to the way things were before that upheaval. They earned the nickname the "seventeen-years-before people," because they thought the seventeen years (from 1949 to 1966) before the Cultural Revolution were pretty good. These tended to be older people, with secure positions in the Party, army, and bureaucracy, much like Soviet *apparatchiks.* They wanted socialism on the Soviet model, with centralized control over the economy, politics, and cultural life.

Facing them were liberalizers, usually younger people, who saw the unfairness and inefficiency of central control. They pointed to the amazing growth in output that came with the introduction of private and cooperative enterprises. In the Special Economic Zones, industrial growth set world records. "See, the market system works," they said in effect. They also wanted Western-style political democracy and cultural freedoms.

The Chinese conservatives, just like their old Soviet counterparts, feared that such a system would no longer be Communist and, even worse, that their jobs would be scrapped. Fumed one CCP member who supported reforms: "What do the conservatives want? They want to go back to the '50s. Who wants that? Nobody."

It was this split that caused Deng and his successors much grief. They were prepared to liberalize cautiously, hoping to confine it to the economic sector. But demands came bubbling up to go farther and faster. In the spring of 1989, tens of thousands of Chinese university students staged giant protests and hunger strikes in favor of democracy. Deng fired his handpicked and liberal-minded successor, Zhao Ziyang, and had the PLA mow down the students in Tiananmen

ANTI-WESTERN CAMPAIGNS

Every few years China is hit with a campaign aimed at making the Chinese pull away from the Western model of economic and political freedom. The work of conservatives within the CCP, these campaigns warned that decadent Western ideas such as free enterprise, open discussion, and a loosening of Party control would mean the end of socialism in China.

In late 1983, the catchword was "spiritual pollution," meaning that Western styles in clothes, music, and thought were ruining China. Deng, fearing the campaign was being used to block his economic liberalization, called it off after only four months.

In 1986, a somewhat longer lasting campaign against "bourgeois liberalization" appeared, ruling out any discussion of ending the CCP monopoly on power and replacing it with Western-style liberalism. After the 1989 Tiananmen Square massacre, conservatives charged that it was a "counterrevolutionary rebellion" inspired by Western influences, which had to be curbed.

In 1996, Beijing permitted publication of a book by a group of young, non-Party intellectuals denouncing U.S. high-handedness in telling China what to do in human rights and trade policy. In 1999, the regime whipped up anti-U.S. anger over the bombing of the Chinese embassy in Belgrade (but quickly forgot it). The regime tries to harness Chinese nationalism for its own ends. We have likely not seen the last anti-Western campaign.

THE TIANANMEN MASSACRE

During the early morning of June 4, 1989, more than 100,000 Chinese troops opened fire on young demonstrators camped out in Beijing's Tiananmen (Gate of Heavenly Peace) Square, killing hundreds and injuring thousands. (The regime never released figures.) Much of the killing, including tanks crushing protesters and bicyclists shot at random, took place outside the Square, but the horror went down in history as "Tiananmen."

Tiananmen marked the point at which China's Communist chiefs choked over letting China's 1980s experiment with a partially free market economy spill over into political democracy. The economic results had been good, but they encouraged people to want democracy, never the intention of Beijing's rulers. The massacre illustrates the danger of halfway reform: It encourages people to want more.

Trouble began with the death of the liberal ex-Party chief Hu Yaobang in April 1989. Students began mourning him and protesting the current CCP leadership. On April 18, thousands began to occupy the Square. While the regime pondered how to handle the demonstration, the students organized, gave speeches, and built a Goddess of Democracy statue that resembled New York's Statue of Liberty. Around the country, many sympa-thized with the demonstrators, and criticism of the regime mounted.

If prodemocracy demonstrations had kept going, the regime would have been in trouble. The regime knew that and struck back. Zhao Ziyang, who succeeded Hu in 1987, went out to talk with the students. He was conciliatory and appeared to side with them. This gave Politburo hardliners the chance they had been looking for to oust Zhao. Deng Xiaoping, still the real power at age 84, wanted the army to crush the demonstrators. "We do not fear spilling blood," he said.

Troops and tanks poured into Beijing. The soldiers, mostly simple country boys, felt little in common with the urban students. In one memorable videotaped confrontation, a lone protester blocked a tank column; when the tanks tried to go around him, he quickly stepped in front of them again. It seemed to symbolize the individualism of democracy standing up to the coercion of dictatorship. After the bloodbath, thousands were arrested. The top protest figures received sentences of up to thirteen years, less for those who "repented." Hundreds were held for years without trial. China's elite decided to keep going with economic change but to keep the lid on political change. Some observers say the ingredients for a similar upheaval are again present.

Square. Several hundred died, and some ten thousand were imprisoned. A chill settled over Chinese life. Conservatives also launched anti-Western campaigns (see box on page 398). The conservatives had one serious drawback: Many were elderly. Time seemed to be on the side of the liberalizers, but not without rear-guard conservative actions.

The Underlying Problem

The earlier radical-moderate and current liberal-conservative struggles have some interesting points in common. First, the old "moderates" are basically today's "conservatives": older cadres who like bureaucratized socialism. They like it because they owe their jobs to it. Further, curious as it sounds, some of yesterday's "radicals"—the Red Guard punks who caused so much destruction in Mao's name—are now ardent "liberalizers," happy to discard Maoism.

Key Terms

yuan   China's currency, worth about 12 U.S. cents.

deflation   Overall decrease in prices; opposite of inflation.

devaluation   Decreasing the worth of your currency in relation to others.

Both radicals and liberalizers shared the same impulse in trying to break up the bureaucratized socialist system, the former attacking from the left, the latter from the right.

How could they switch from left to right? Some of the switch can be attributed to young people realizing that they had been cynically used during the Cultural Revolution. Badly burned by the experience, they are now turned off by Mao Thought and open to Western-style reforms and liberalization.

But a more basic factor is that the young people—especially university students and recent graduates—who faced bleak job prospects then, face them still. They have been trained and expect higher-level jobs in the government and economy, but few are available. Why? Because those old conservatives never retire; both Chinese tradition and CCP practice grants lifetime tenure. They stay in office until they die. Making the job situation even worse is the fact that socialism does not spontaneously grow new firms to hire graduates. (Capitalism does.) The result, now as before, is frustration and resentment among young and better-educated Chinese.

Mao tapped this resentment for his Cultural Revolution. The unstated message of the Red Guards who shouted "Destroy the four olds!" was "Get rid of the old guys and give us their jobs!" Now, in a partially market economy, these same people (or their younger brothers and sisters) see their path to success in greater economic decentralization that will let the number of firms multiply and open up new job possibilities. Some of the young Chinese protesting in favor of democracy had little idea what it meant; they just wanted to make sure the old conservatives didn't reimpose their stranglehold. And the old conservatives, fearing for their jobs and status, fought back.

One of the great underlying problems of China is what to do with the younger generation. One solution would be to impose a mandatory retirement age, but this goes against Chinese tradition. Deng Xiaoping ordered many old comrades to retire but hardly set a good example himself. Youthful energy that is badly misdirected, as in the Cultural Revolution, can wreck China. Given productive outlets in a free economy, it could make China the growth wonder of the world.

Ideology is often a mask for self-interest. The people who have the cushy jobs warn that democracy and liberalization mean "abandoning socialism." In analyzing Communist (and many other) systems, take ideology with a grain of salt; follow the jobs. (Think the jobs explanation is an exaggeration? What motivates you?)

What Chinese Quarrel About

A Market Economy for China?

Starting in 1978, some amazing changes took place in the Chinese economy. China, like all Communist countries, faced the question of how centralized the economy should be and decided on decentralization while retaining centralized political control. This, as in other countries that tried it, is proving to be an unstable combination.

The earliest changes came in the countryside, where most of China's population still live. Collectivized agriculture was reduced and families were permitted to go on the "responsibility system," a euphemism for private enterprise. Peasants lease land from the state for up to fifteen years—still no private owners—and must deliver a certain quota to the state at set prices.

Beyond that, they can sell their produce on the free market for the best price they can get. They can choose their own crops and decide how to use fertilizer and farm machinery, which they buy at their own expense. Farm production soared, Chinese ate better, and farmers' incomes went up; some even got rich.

KEY CONCEPTS

THE TROUBLE WITH MARKETS

The trouble with a market economy when introduced piecemeal into Communist countries, such as Yugoslavia, Hungary, or China, is that it tends to run out of control. The country experiences improved economic performance but also develops problems that wreck the socialist system.

Unemployment appears: In Communist systems unemployment was disguised by gross labor inefficiency, but once firms have to compete in a market and make profits, they prune unnecessary workers. Chinese workers under Mao had an "iron rice bowl"—jobs for life. Deng broke the bowl and made millions unemployed. China had to permit small-scale private enterprise to soak up some of these unemployed. More than 100 million Chinese, most without permission, left rural inland areas to seek jobs in the cities and coastal Special Economic Zones. More are on their way. Under arbitrary "custody and repatriation" rules, several million internal Chinese migrants are placed in detention camps each year.

Income inequalities develop: With a market system, some Chinese farmers, entrepreneurs, and whole provinces get richer than others. The ones who don't do so well—the inland provinces with poorer soil and fewer natural resources—become jealous and complain to Beijing to redistribute some of the wealth. The richer provinces in the South and along the coast (home of the Special Economic Zones) object, arguing they work harder and produce more. Tensions between regions, especially between North and South, are growing and producing regional tensions.

Economic instability grows, usually in the form of inflation: Most of China's food, clothing, and consumer goods are now produced and sold on a free market, and at times too many **yuan** chased too few goods, producing inflation that reached 25 percent a year in the early 1990s. In the late 1990s, however, caught with too much production during a time of East Asian recession, **deflation** actually lowered Chinese prices. Many thought China would **devalue** its currency in order to fight recession, and that this would trigger potentially dangerous regional economic instability.

Corruption increases: Corruption grows at the interface of private and governmental sectors. Economic liberalization multiplies such interfaces as more and more entrepreneurs need raw materials and permits from government officials. Some Party officials have become outrageously corrupt, helping themselves to "taxes," kickbacks, and whole enterprises.

Crime rates soar: Putting together all the above and adding weakened social controls, crime becomes a serious problem. With this come repeated campaigns to crack down on crime, including many thousands executed by firing squad each year.

The problem of an economy that mixes socialism and capitalism is its instability. It cannot find a middle ground but tends to slide more and more toward full capitalism until blocked by central control. The result is a zigzag every few years as the government alternately tightens and relaxes supervision of the economy, never finding a stable balance. China is caught in this situation.

By the 1990s, things weren't going so well in the countryside, where 70 percent of Chinese still live. The government held down farm prices and paid peasants IOUs for their grain. Farm incomes declined as inflation soared. In many rural areas, peasants rioted and attacked local authorities, who extort illegal "taxes" from them. In a pattern very typical of the Third World, more than 100 million rural Chinese moved to the jobs and riches of the coastal cities where market economies were flourishing, a destabilizing tide the regime cannot control.

The partly free market spread to the cities. Faced with substantial unemployment, the regime let individuals open small stores, restaurants, repair shops, and even manufacturing facilities. It was even permissible to hire workers, something any Marxist would call capitalist exploitation. But it worked. The Chinese applied individual hustle to produce and sell more and better products than the indifferent state factories and stores ever could. Hole-in-the-wall "department stores" had customers waiting in line to buy the fashionable clothing and footwear Mao used to scorn. People swarmed to outdoor markets to buy home-produced chairs and sofas.

Starting with the area around Hong Kong, large regions of coastal China were declared "Special Economic Zones," open to private and foreign investors. Capital poured in (much of it from Taiwan and Hong Kong) to take advantage of low Chinese wages, and production soared. These firms compete in a world market to make profits. Because of these firms—which cover only part of the Chinese economy—China's GDP grew at am amazing 10 percent a year during the 1980s and into the 1990s to become the world's second largest overall economy (but not per capita). Imagine if all the Chinese economy shifted to capitalism. By comparison, one-third of the more than 100,000 state-run enterprises lose money and have to be propped up by subsidies. Of these, half are reckoned to be hopeless. Whether to close the losers (and create unemployment) is one of the great questions facing Beijing.

While most Chinese liked their taste of the free market, many cadres did not. If you really go to a market system, what do you do with the cadres who make a good living by supervising a controlled economy? They dig in their heels and try to block major change. Deng purged or retired the old guard and replaced them with young technocrats who pursue capitalist-style economic growth and call it "socialism with Chinese characteristics."

But market economies produce problems of their own (see box on page 401) and awaken resentments and jealousies. Some suggest the Chinese economy is careening out of control at a time when political authority is weakening. Political reform has been deliberately blocked, for China is still very much a one-Party dictatorship. What will happen when the free-market economy gets totally out of kilter with the dictatorial political system?

A Middle Way for the Middle Kingdom?

The basic supposition of Deng Xiaoping and his successors was that there is a middle way between capitalism and communism, between a controlled and a free-market economy, between the Soviet and American models. (Russian President Putin entertained similar notions.) By bringing in elements of a market economy while retaining a large state sector, they sought a middle way. Is there one? Not really, and many observers now think the Chinese elite has quietly admitted it, at least among themselves.

When a Communist country introduces a bit of market economics—supply and demand, competing producers, profits, family farming, prices finding their own level—the first few years are usually good. Farm output especially grows, and everyone eats well. Consumer goods become far more available, and people live and dress better. New industries produce clothing and consumer electronics for the world market. Statistically, growth rates shoot up. It looks like they've found the happy balance: a market economy at the "micro" level to provide for consumer needs under the benevolent guidance of a state-run economy at the "macro" level. The farmers, shoemakers, and tailors are mostly private; many big industries, as well as banking and planning systems, are state-owned and under Party control.

But after a few years things start to go wrong. Shortages, distortions, and bottlenecks stall economic growth. Indeed, China's growth slowed in the late 1990s. The private sector keeps bumping into the state sector. Every time it does, there is a "crisis" that can only be resolved by expanding the private sector and shrinking the state sector. After some years of this, there is little socialism left, and this Beijing's rulers do not like.

KEY CONCEPTS

SECOND- AND THIRD-ORDER EFFECTS

China's fierce program to limit population growth shows what can go wrong with coercing society into what the government has decided is desirable. It also illustrates the problem of second- and third-order consequences, that is, how hard it is to predict the longer-term effects of a policy.

In the early 1980s China carried out a ferocious program to curb births. Urban women were ordered to have only one child and were fined and lost benefits if they had more. Many women were forced to have abortions. The first-order consequence, as might be expected, was to bring down China's rate of population increase to 1.3 percent a year, low for the Third World, much of which grows at 3 percent; only Europe shows less than 1 percent increase.

A second-order effect, however, was a large excess of boy over girl babies, both by abortion and female infanticide. About 5 percent of the girls expected to be born from 1979 to 1995 are missing, 10 percent in the 1990s. Like many Third World cultures, Chinese value boys above girls, both to work on the farm and to support the parents in old age. So, if they are allowed only one child, many Chinese strongly prefer a son. Bodies of newborn girls are frequently found floating in rural canals, a pattern that goes back centuries in crowded China.

Third-order effects flow from the second. The surplus of males over females mean that millions of Chinese men will never find brides. Further, the drastic restriction in fertility rates—to below the replacement rate of 2.1 births per average woman—means that China's retired generation—now much bigger and living much longer thanks to improved nutrition and health care—will not have enough working Chinese to support it. China, still a poor country, will thus face exactly the same problem as the rich countries. China's State Family Planning Commission, which now emphasizes education and contraception, never considered the second- and third-order consequences.

How then to handle the serious Third World problem of too-rapid population growth? Economic growth solves the problem without coercion. As the economy grows, more people become urban and middle class and decide for themselves to limit their number of children, as Japanese have done. As more women are educated they postpone marriage in favor of work and have fewer children. No rich country has a problem of too many babies (in fact, it's just the opposite), and newly industrializing lands show a dramatic falloff in births. China's demographic debacle is one example of Mao's (and, earlier, Stalin's) thinking that society can be forced into any shape the Party decrees.

The Chinese—like the Yugoslavs and Hungarians—found that a little bit of capitalism is like being a little bit pregnant. The choice Communist countries faced was difficult. If they went part of the way with a market economy, they experienced a few years of growth followed by dangerous distortions. If they called off the liberal experiment, they returned to the centralized, Stalinist system that was slowly running down, leaving them further and further behind the capitalist world. If they went all the way to a market system, they admitted they had been wrong all these decades.

Another problem cropped up with the financial problems that hit other East Asian lands in 1997: China's banks had also loaned recklessly and sometimes crookedly and faced insolvency. Some of their loans were under government orders, to prop up money-losing state industries. The central government itself was deeply in debt from subsidizing too much and collecting too little in taxes. With a faulty and foolish financial system, China's growth slowed.

Some observers argue that China's reforms were far more clever than the Soviet Union's and have a much better chance to succeed. First, China permitted private farming. The Soviet Union was still debating private farming when it collapsed. Then China permitted small businesses. China designated Special Economic Zones for foreign investment. Missing in China was the political liberalization that blew up in Gorbachev's face. None of Beijing's rulers wanted to be China's Gorbachev, hence they tolerated no democracy, competing parties, or free press, precisely the reforms that Gorbachev did first. Did the Chinese do it right, sequencing their reforms so as to build an economic basis for democracy before reforming their political system?

Other observers fear that China could collapse, that its partial economic reforms without political reforms could blow up.

With an increase in corruption, inflation, and inequality (see box on page 401) there is increasing mass unrest. So far, the only successful transitions from communism to free-market capitalism have come in Central Europe—Poland, the Czech Republic, and Hungary—where anticommunists completely threw out the communist regimes. No controlled, middle-way transition has worked.

Do Markets Lead to Democracy?

Economic liberalization tends to encourage political participation. You can't reform the economy alone, for economic reform generates demands for political reform, namely, democracy. Amidst economic improvement, the Chinese find they have plenty to complain about: rampant corruption, terrible medical care, rising prices, and continued economic controls and restrictions. Immediate and specific grievances turn into general criticism of the entire regime. Student complaints about wretched college conditions—no heat or toilets, incompetent teachers, food fit for hogs, no job prospects—underlay the 1989 student demonstrations, which turned into calls for full-blown democracy.

Many observers agree with political scientist Peter Burger: "When market economies are successful over a period of time, pressure for democratization inevitably ensues." A market economy generates a large, educated middle class and interest groups. People start resenting a corrupt government treating them like small children. They want democracy. If the regime is intelligent and flexible, it gradually opens up, usually by permitting a critical press, then opposition parties, and finally free and fair elections.

Taiwan is the textbook example of this transition from authoritarianism to democracy. Some thinkers argue that China will follow a similar path, but there are differences. Taiwan's elite, many of them educated in the United States, led the way to democracy in the late 1970s.

One of their motives: Show the Americans they are a democracy in order to win U.S. support against Beijing's demands to take over Taiwan. We must be careful in supposing the Taiwan model fits mainland China.

China's elite is still firmly Communist, has no desire for democracy, and is not trying to please the Americans. They have deliberately tried to prevent the formation of an autonomous middle class. Calls for democracy are ruthlessly crushed. Do not count on China moving to democracy automatically or peacefully.

Rather than achieve stable democracy, China could explode. Consider China's problems: a huge country hard to govern in good times, with up-and-down economic growth, corruption out of control, restive minorities, major splits within the Party, central authority weakening, and many Chinese unhappy with the regime. China could break up into the "warlord" pattern of the 1920s, some observers feared. Others feared Beijing would try to deflect unrest onto other lands by promoting expansionist nationalism, a common practice of nervous regimes.

Which Is the Real China?

As the millennium changes, we face two very different images of China. The first one, supported by many journalists and academics, is that China is having a difficult transition but will eventually turn into a free-market democracy. Beijing itself argues that amid all these changes China needs "stability," and this justifies keeping politics out of mass hands. Modernization theory predicts that economic growth leads to democracy. If China occasionally snarls at us, we must forebear. Just give them time.

The other image is not as optimistic. Some observers argue that Beijing craves economic growth, not to make its people prosperous but for national power and respect. It has no intention of letting itself be turned into a democracy. Dissidents who publicly argue for democracy serve many years in prison; some of the more troublesome dissidents are shipped off to the United States. Under tight surveillance, few Chinese discuss politics with foreigners. These policies betray the regime's extreme nervousness and fear of being ousted.

Beijing also aims to become the number-one military power of East Asia, eclipsing Japan. Said Party chief Jiang: "There will only be two superpowers by around 2020—China and the United States." Unlikely, no matter how many nuclear secrets they steal. One of China's priorities is its navy, with which it has claimed and fortified islets far from its shores in the East and South China Seas. This angers other countries in the region—Japan, the Philippines, Malaysia, Indonesia, and Vietnam. And Beijing proclaims the right to seize Taiwan, which it regards as a renegade province, any time. By a 1979 law, the United States is committed to a peaceful, voluntary reunification. But if Beijing applies force or intimidation, how should we react?

These optimistic and pessimistic images reflect the power struggle between reformist and conservative wings of the CCP. Beijing is clearly trying to keep a lid on political challenges, but will it be able to in the long run? Beijing is happy to join the World Trade Organization (WTO), but how can it control the flow of goods, money, and ideas that come with world trade? How will China control the Internet—widely used among educated Chinese—with its ability to communicate and inform instantly? Can any country now run without it? China clearly wishes to develop its military power, but its army is still poorly equipped and has little mobility. Underlying everything is a deep craving for dignity and respect for what was once the world's greatest civilization but one that was brought low by Western and Japanese imperialists. How China achieves this recognition will be one of the great chapters of twenty-first century history.

GEOGRAPHY

THE HONG KONG EXAMPLE

In mid-1997 the British colony of Hong Kong reverted back to China. Most of Hong Kong actually consisted of leased territory on the mainland—the source of the colony's water supplies—and the lease was up in 1997. The British decided to give the whole package back to Beijing. Many prosperous and hardworking Hong Kongese didn't want to be part of China, although Beijing guaranteed, under the formula "one nation, two systems," that Hong Kong can keep its autonomy for fifty years.

In 1999, China took over the even-smaller Portuguese colony of Macao near Hong Kong and also gave it autonomy. Beijing's intention, many believed, is to demonstrate to Taiwan that it could rejoin the mainland and still keep its political and economic system. Few Taiwanese are buying.

Beijing did not openly break its word, but slowly Hong Kong lost its autonomy and capitalistic vitality. Beijing court decisions eroded Hong Kong's special status. Critical Hong Kong editors lost their jobs. Corruption appeared, as certain cooperative Hong Kongese got special deals. Beijing seemed to favor Shanghai as China's financial hub, as it once was before World War II. Prime Minister Zhu—like President Jiang, a former mayor of Shanghai—said in 1999, "Shanghai will be China's New York." Hong Kong will be its "Toronto." Hong Kong, one of the world's great financial centers, did more and more business with mainland China and less and less with other Pacific Rim countries. As Hong Kong lost its glitter, Singapore tried to move into its place as the great trading post of the Pacific Rim.

Key Terms

Boxer (p. 381)	Manchu (p. 379)	Taiping (p. 381)
cadre (p. 387)	man-land ratio (p. 376)	Third World (p. 377)
deflation (p. 400)	mass line (p. 384)	treaty ports (p. 380)
devaluation (p. 400)	Middle Kingdom (p. 379)	voluntarism (p. 391)
dynastic cycle (p. 379)	Mongol (p. 379)	warlord (p. 382)
extraterritoriality (p. 380)	Nationalist (p. 382)	yuan (p. 400)
Gang of Four (p. 387)	sphere of influence (p. 381)	
kow-tow (p. 377)	steady-state (p. 376)	

Further Reference

Chinoy, Mike. *China Live: Two Decades in the Heart of the Dragon*, updated ed. Lanham, MD: Rowman & Littlefield, 1999.

Dreyer, June Teufel. *China's Political System: Modernization and Tradition*, 2nd ed. Needham, MA: Allyn & Bacon, 1996.

Evans, Richard. *Deng Xiaoping and the Making of Modern China*. New York: Viking, 1994.

Fairbank, John King. *China: A New History*. Cambridge, MA: Harvard University Press, 1994.

Gilley, Bruce. *Tiger on the Brink: Jiang Zemin and China's New Elite*. Berkeley, CA: University of California Press, 1999.

Gore, Lance L. P. *Market Communism: The Institutional Foundation of China's Post-Mao Hyper-Growth*. New York: Oxford University Press, 1999.

Hunter, Alan, and John Sexton. *Contemporary China*. New York: St. Martin's, 1999.

Kwong, Julia. *The Political Economy of Corruption in China*. Armonk, NY: M. E. Sharpe, 1997.

Lam, Willy. *The Era of Jaing Zemin*. Upper Saddle River, NJ: Prentice Hall, 1999.

Li, Cheng. *Rediscovering China: Dynamics and Dilemmas of Reform*. Lanham, MD: Rowman & Littlefield, 1997.

MacFarquhar, Roderick, ed. *The Politics of China: The Eras of Mao and Deng*. New York: Cambridge University Press, 1997.

Nathan, Andrew J. *China's Transition*. New York: Columbia University Press, 1998.

Walder, Andrew G., ed. *The Waning of the Communist State: Economic Origins of Political Decline in China and Hungary*. Berkeley, CA: University of California Press, 1995.

Wei Jingsheng. *The Courage to Stand Alone: Letters from Prison and Other Writings*. New York: Viking, 1997.

Winckler, Edwin A., ed. *Transition from Communism in China: Institutional and Comparative Analyses*. Boulder, CO: L. Rienner, 1999.

Yang, Benjamin. *Deng: A Political Biography*. Armonk, NY: M. E. Sharpe, 1998.

Zhu, Fang. *Gun Barrel Politics: Party-Army Relations in Mao's China*. Boulder, CO: Westview, 1998.

Brazil

28

Questions to Consider

1. How did Spanish and Portuguese colonialism differ?
2. How did the Old Republic typify "whig democracy"?
3. What did Vargas attempt to do with his "New State"?
4. Why did Brazil's generals take over in 1964? Why did they leave?
5. What are Brazil's institutional weaknesses?
6. Explain the role of inflation in Brazilian politics.
7. Compare Brazilian and South African racism.
8. What factors made Brazil democratic? Will it last?
9. How does Brazil illustrate "praetorianism"?
10. What are Brazil's economic problems?

The Impact of the Past

Portugal had a claim to Brazil even before its explorers arrived there. In 1494 the Treaty of Tordesillas gave Portugal lands in the yet-unexplored New World. The treaty drew a line 370 leagues (some 1,100 miles) west of the Cape Verde Islands; land to the east of the line went to Portugal, and land to the west to Spain. This arrangement sliced off the easternmost bulge of present-day Brazil; subsequent Portuguese settlements pushed their control further westward to give Brazil its present borders. The first Portuguese arrived in 1500, when Pedro Alvares Cabral, claiming he was blown off course, took formal possession of the land for the king of Portugal.

The Portuguese Influence

Portugal did not administer its new colony the way Spain did. The Spanish charged quickly into Latin America for "gold, God, and glory." The Portuguese did nothing for thirty years, partly because they were busy with the rich trade route around Africa to India and partly because Brazil seemed to offer little gold. About the only Portuguese interest in the new land was in its red wood that could be used to make dye. From the brazed color of brazilwood came the name Brazil (*Brasil* in Portuguese).

It was when the French started to settle there in 1530 that the Portuguese crown began to take an interest. Ordering the French expelled, Dom João (King John) III parceled out the coastline into fifteen *capitanías* or royal grants which he gave to wealthy Portuguese willing to finance settlement. The original *capitanías*, like the thirteen English colonies in North America, gave initial shape to Brazil's present-day states and laid the foundation for its federalism. Growth in the *capitanías*, however, was slow and spotty. Portugal's population at that time was only around one million, and there were not many people eager to become colonists. Compared to the Spanish colonies, there were no quick and easy mineral riches to be found in Brazil.

Economic life centered on sugar, for which Europe had recently acquired a taste. Sugar farming requires lots of labor, however. The Indians of Brazil were relatively few in number and made poor slaves; used to a life of casual hunting, many refused to work. With many trading posts down the African coast, though, the Portuguese found their answer in black slaves. From the 1530s to the 1850s, at least three million Africans (perhaps six times the number that were brought to the United States) were brought to Brazil and sold, chiefly to work in the sugar-cane fields. Interbreeding among the three population groups—Indians, blacks, and Portuguese— was rife, producing Brazil's complex racial mixture. The Portuguese always prided themselves on being nonracist, and this attitude, in public anyway, carries over into present-day Brazil.

Other Portuguese attitudes distinguish Brazil from the former Spanish colonies of Latin America. Portuguese have been less inclined to violence than Spaniards. As many Portuguese point out: "In a Portuguese bullfight, we don't kill the bull." Flexibility and compromise are more valued in Brazilian politics than in the politics of its Spanish-speaking neighbors.

A Painless Independence

Brazil's independence from Portugal is also in marked contrast to the long struggles waged by the Spanish colonies. Slowly, Brazil grew in population and importance. When the Netherlands made Pernambuco (now Recife) a Dutch colony in the mid-seventeenth century,

Black, white, and Indian blood flow together freely in Brazil, producing a complex racial mixture. (Michael Roskin)

GEOGRAPHY

BOUND BRAZIL

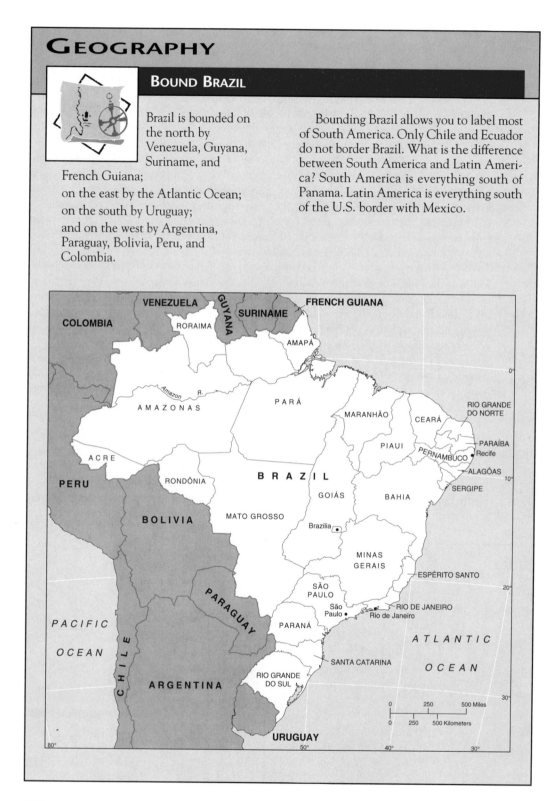

Brazil is bounded on the north by Venezuela, Guyana, Suriname, and French Guiana; on the east by the Atlantic Ocean; on the south by Uruguay; and on the west by Argentina, Paraguay, Bolivia, Peru, and Colombia.

Bounding Brazil allows you to label most of South America. Only Chile and Ecuador do not border Brazil. What is the difference between South America and Latin America? South America is everything south of Panama. Latin America is everything south of the U.S. border with Mexico.

Portuguese, blacks, and Indians together struggled to expel them and, in the process, began to think of themselves as Brazilians. In the 1690s, gold was discovered in what became the state of Minas Gerais (General Mines). A gold rush and later a diamond rush boosted Brazil's population. Economic activity shifted from the sugar-growing region of the Northeast to the South and stayed there. To this day, the growth area has been in the more temperate climes of the South, while the Northeast, impoverished and drought-stricken, has become a problem area.

By the late eighteenth century, Brazil had become more important economically than Portugal, and thoughts of independence began to flicker in the growing Brazilian consciousness, inspired, as throughout Latin America, by the U.S. and French revolutionary examples. Brazilian independence, curiously, came about partly because of Napoleon.

In trying to seal off the European continent from Britain, Napoleon sent an army to take Portugal in 1807. The royal court in Lisbon—some fifteen thousand people in all—at British prodding, boarded ships and sailed for Brazil. Dom João VI was at first wildly welcomed in Brazil, but the royal court was horrified at conditions in Rio and irritated leading residents by requisitioning their houses. Dom João ordered Rio cleaned, beautified, and turned into a true capital. In 1815, Brazil was raised in rank from colony to kingdom within the Portuguese empire.

In 1821, the British advised Dom João to return to Lisbon to make sure Portuguese liberals didn't get out of hand. He left his son, Dom Pedro, then age twenty-three, as regent in Brazil and gave him some parting advice: If Brazilian independence became inevitable, he should make sure he led it. It was a pragmatic, level-headed idea, an example of Portuguese flexibility in contrast to Spanish obduracy. In this way the Portuguese royal house served as a bridge between colonial and independent status. In 1822 Dom Pedro proclaimed Brazil independent, and Portugal did not resist.

From Empire to Republic

Monarchy is rare in the Western Hemisphere; it appeared only briefly in Haiti and Mexico (Maximilian). Brazil, however, was a true monarchy from 1822 to 1889, another point of contrast with the rest of Latin America. Dom Pedro I proved an inept ruler, and when the army turned against him he abdicated in 1831 while his Brazilian-born son was still a child. Under a regency—a council that runs affairs until a king comes of age—power was dispersed among the various states; an 1834 act set up states' rights and introduced de facto federalism. Politics became a series of quarrels among the states and the rich landowning families that ran them. The instability was so serious that it led finally to widespread agreement in 1840 to declare Dom Pedro II—only fourteen years old—of age to rule.

Dom Pedro II was beloved for his calm, tolerant manner and his concern for his nation. But he did not do much of anything. Basing his rule on big plantation owners (*fazendeiros*), Pedro let things drift while he exercised the "moderating power" of the liberal 1824 constitution in appointing and dismissing ministers. But the Brazilian economy changed. The large landowners mattered less while vigorous businessmen and bankers gained in importance. The growing modern element came to resent the conservative monarchy and to favor a republic. One big question Dom Pedro II couldn't handle was slavery. Under British pressure, the importation of new slaves ended during the 1850s, but slavery continued, deemed humane and necessary by Pedro's landowning supporters. Various formulas for phasing out slavery were considered, but Pedro let the question drift until his daughter, Princess Isabel, acting as regent while he was in Europe, signed an abolition bill in 1888. Brazil was the last Western country to emancipate its slaves.

KEY CONCEPTS

"ORDER AND PROGRESS"

French philosopher Auguste Comte (1798–1857) developed a doctrine known as **Positivism**. With its slogan of "Order and Progress," this optimistic philosophy held that mankind can and will progress by turning away from theology and abstract speculation and toward the scientific study of nature and of society. By applying the natural-science methods of empirical observation and data gathering, society can be analyzed, predicted, and then improved, not in a revolutionary way, but gradually and under the supervision of humanitarian specialists. Said Comte: "Progress is the development of order."

Comte's Positivism launched modern social science (and still holds sway in psychology) and took root especially in Brazil. By the 1880s many Brazilian army officers had been instructed in Positivism by the mathematics professor Benjamin Constant Magalhães, who taught in the national military academy. With the 1889 republic, Positivists put their motto into the Brazilian flag, where it remains to this day: *Ordem e Progresso.*

By now, wide sectors of the Brazilian population were disgusted with monarchy. Intellectuals, businesspeople, and army officers, imbued with Positivist philosophy (see box, above), wanted modernization. Deprived of their slaves, even the plantation owners turned against Dom Pedro. In 1889, a military coup ended the monarchy and introduced a republic without firing a shot.

The Old Republic

The relative stability conferred by Brazil's Portuguese heritage (bloodless independence and nineteenth-century monarchy) wore off during the **Old Republic**, and Brazil came to resemble its Hispanic neighbors. Revolts, rigged elections, and military intervention marked this period. The 1891 constitution was modeled after that of the United States, but power gravitated into the hands of **coronéis** and the military. For most of the Old Republic, the presidency alternated between the political bosses of two of the most important states, São Paulo and Minas Gerais.

Grumbling increased during the life of the Old Republic. New sectors of the population became aware that their interests were unheeded by the conservative political bosses. Idealistic army officers revolted in 1922 and 1924, believing they could save the republic. The Brazilian army at this time was by no means conservative. Many officers were imbued with Positivism and hated conservative politicians, who seemed to block progress. To this day, the Brazilian military sees itself as a progressive rather than as a conservative force.

What finally destroyed the Old Republic was the worldwide depression and the collapse of the price of coffee, a crop that Brazil depended upon heavily for export earnings. Further, in 1930 a split developed in the old Paulista-Mineiro combination, and a crafty politician from Rio Grande do Sul—the home of many maverick politicians—took advantage of it to run for the presidency. Getúlio Vargas claimed the election results had been rigged

Key Terms

Positivism   Philosophy of applying scientific method to social problems and gradually improving society.

Old Republic   Brazil's first republic, 1889–1930; a rigged democracy.

coronéis   "Colonels"; Brazilian state-level political bosses.

against him (entirely plausible) and, with help from the military and amid great popular acclaim, took over the presidency in Rio in October 1930.

Vargas's "New State"

Latin American populist strongmen (*caudillos* in Spanish, *caudilhos* in Portuguese) are hard to label, for they appear to be both leftist and rightist. They expand the economy by statist means (see box on page 414). They claim to be for the people and are proud of the many welfare measures they institute. Often they create a labor movement and give it a privileged status that is long remembered among the working class. But they are no more democratic than the old political bosses they overthrew and often support the interests of existing elites, such as keeping coffee prices high. And they are very much for "order."

Some called such figures as Vargas of Brazil and Perón of Argentina fascists, but they probably were not. Rather than building a party along ideological lines, these populist dictators **mobilized** the masses with their personal appeal. During the 1930s and 1940s, however, when fascism in Europe was having its day, they threw in some fascistic rhetoric.

Vargas, like Perón, looked after the working class. Under Vargas, Brazil instituted an eight-hour work day, minimum wages, paid vacations, and collective bargaining. Labor did not fight and win its rights; Vargas handed them over long before there was an organized labor movement to make demands. The result, as in much of Latin America, is a weak labor movement that constantly seeks the protection of a paternalistic state.

Vargas's 1934 constitution brought in a **corporatist** element—one-fifth of the legislature directly represented professional and trade groups—on the pattern of Italy and Portugal. The constitution also limited the president to a single four-year term. By 1937, however, Vargas decided he wanted to stay president and carried out a coup against his own regime, what is called in Latin America an **autogolpe**. Vargas proclaimed himself president, but this time there was no legislature to limit his powers. Vargas called his regime the **Estado Nôvo**. His critics called it "fascism with sugar." There was material progress—industry, highways, public health, social welfare—but there was also a loss of freedom. The United States got along well with Vargas, for he did not curb U.S. investments. In 1942, Brazil declared war on the Axis powers (but sent few troops).

Vargas discovered the power of the urban working class and mobilized them to his cause by setting up labor unions and the *Partido Trabalhista Brasileiro* (Brazilian Labor party, PTB for short). The military, however, became alarmed at his populistic dictatorship and forced him to resign in 1945. By then Vargas had become a hero to many Brazilians, who continued to support his PTB. In both Brazil and Argentina, the working masses longed for the return of their respective dictators and reelected them to office, Vargas in 1950 and Perón in 1946 and 1973. Once mobilized by a populistic dictator, the masses may prefer such rulers and their statism to democracy and free markets.

The Rise and Fall of Jango Goulart

The reelected Vargas was a poor president; corruption and inflation soared. Many Brazilians, including top military officers, demanded he resign in 1954. Instead, he committed suicide, blaming reactionary international (that is, U.S.) and domestic forces for blocking his good

KEY CONCEPTS

THE ADDICTION OF STATISM

The Old Regime in France started the tradition of "statism," the idea that the government should supervise the economy and own much industry, and it spread throughout much of the world. Regimes intent on rapid change—the Bolsheviks in Russia, Ataturk in Turkey, Perón in Argentina, and Vargas in Brazil—embraced statism as a seemingly logical solution to their problems of backwardness. Statism caught on like an addiction in Latin America: Once you had a little state supervision, you soon wanted more. Have a social or economic problem? A new government program, industry, or regulation can solve it.

Statism's basic premises have long been examined and found wanting. Adam Smith, for example, concluded that state intervention gets in the way of economic growth. State-owned industries often become monopolistic, uncompetitive, graft-ridden, and inefficient. Many have to be propped up with state subsidies, money that comes from citizens' pockets. But once established, statist structures defy reform. Politicians, fearful of unemployment and of appearing pro-American or pro-capitalist, hesitate to privatize inefficient and crooked state enterprises. Once addicted, an economy tends to stay statist. Only in our day have wide areas of Latin America begun to kick the habit and turn to the free market. Privatizing Brazil's state-owned industry has been one of its great steps forward.

works. One of Vargas's appointments had particularly angered the military. Vargas named a neighbor from Rio Grande do Sul, the radical João (Jango) Goulart, as labor minister, but the military forced him to resign in 1954.

Goulart, however, continued to head the PTB and in 1955 helped moderate Juscelino Kubitschek win the presidency with Goulart as vice-president. Kubitschek mobilized into his Social Democratic party (PSD) the old political class of state and local elites who had dominated Brazil before Vargas. Kubitschek tried to focus Brazilians' energies on developing the interior; he pushed construction of Brasília, which became the capital in 1960. Heedless of economic problems, Kubitschek promoted industrialization and allowed inflation to skyrocket.

Brazil's working masses were still responsive to populist appeals. In 1960 a Paulista populist, Jânio Quadros, won the presidency in a landslide with reformist promises; Goulart was vice-president. An unstable alcoholic, Quadros resigned after just seven months, leaving a quixotic note reminiscent of Vargas's. Now Goulart, the very man the military forced out in 1954, was in line for the presidency.

The Brazilian army started talking about a coup, but a compromise was worked out: Goulart could be president but with the powers of that office greatly curtailed. Goulart accepted but played a waiting game. As the economy got worse—inflation climbed to 100 percent a year by 1964—he knew the Brazilian masses, by now mobilized and seething with demands for radical change, would support him in a leftward course. Goulart's strategy worked: In a January 1963 plebiscite Brazilians voted five-to-one to restore full powers to the president so he could deal with the economic chaos.

Goulart now veered further left and called for "Basic Reforms": land redistribution, nationalizing the oil industry, enfranchising illiterates, legalizing the Communist party, and turning the legislature, which had blocked his schemes, into a "congress composed of peasants, workers, sergeants, and nationalist officers."

GEOGRAPHY

CENTRAL AMERICA

From northwest to southeast, the countries of Central America are: Belize, Guatemala, Honduras, El Salvador, Nicaragua, Costa Rica, and Panama. Mexico is considered part of North America.

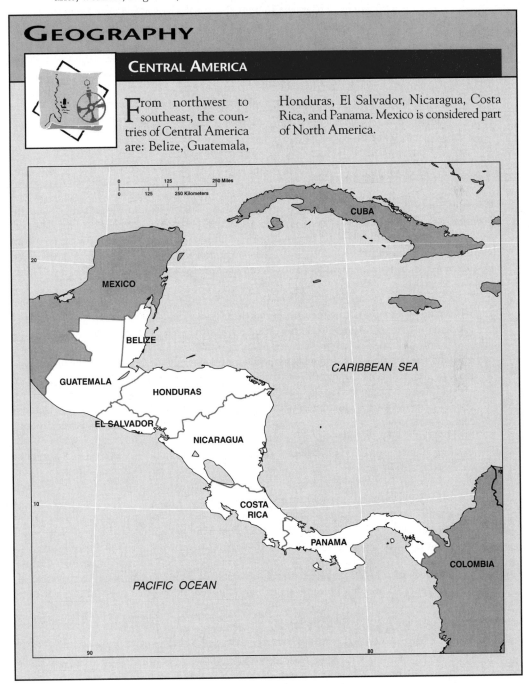

statute   An ordinary law, usually for a specific problem.

fiscal   Related to taxes and public spending.

Brazilian society—like France and Germany in earlier decades—split into leftist and conservative wings with little middle ground. Conservatives, including most middle-class Brazilians, were horrified at Goulart and his appointment of Marxists to high positions. The United States saw Goulart as another Castro, cut off financial aid, and stepped up covert activity to destabilize the Goulart government. Brazil seemed to be on the edge of a revolution.

What finally brought Goulart down was his challenge to the armed forces. Goulart publicly supported some mutinous sailors, which Brazil's generals saw as undermining their military discipline and command structure. On March 31, 1964, with scarcely a shot, the armed forces put an end to Brazil's tumultuous democracy.

The Key Institutions

Flawed Structure

Brazil illustrates what can go wrong if a country's basic institutions are defective: The best intentions and good will are stymied, and the country gets stuck in patterns of the past. The past is alive and well in Brazil's 1988 constitution. The Old Republic echoes today in the freespending powers of Brazil's states and their governors. Vargas's New State echoes in the state-owned industries and employee protections. Overcoming these roadblocks is much on the mind of reformist Brazilians, including President Fernando Henrique Cardoso.

Criticism focuses on Brazil's 1988 constitution, the country's seventh since independence. Its aims and general structure are fine, but its details seem designed to trip up needed reforms. Like most modern constitutions, Brazil's includes numerous social and economic rights—a forty-hour work week, medical and retirement plans, minimum wages, a 12-percent interest ceiling on loans, the right to strike, Indian rights, and environmental protection. Such details have no place in a constitution. But the writers of new constitutions, especially in the Third World, are often idealistic and think they can right all wrongs by mandating fixes in the constitution.

The problem with guaranteeing such rights is that they create expectations and demands that cannot possibly be met by a struggling economy, and this deepens popular discontent. Such details also fail to distinguish between a constitution and **statutes**. Even worse, it built in referendums—called "popular vetoes" and "popular initiatives"—to voice these discontents. California, with its myriad initiatives on each ballot, can get away with such hyperdemocratic nonsense; in Brazil it fosters instability. Another potentially disruptive feature of Brazil's constitution: Voting age now starts at sixteen.

Brazilian states and municipalities are more independent and less responsible than their U.S. counterparts. They raise some of their own taxes but are entitled to big chunks of federal revenue and run up big debts. (U.S. states have to stand nearly on their own **fiscally** and cannot run deficit budgets.) Brazilian states and cities are overstaffed with patronage civil servants who retire young on good pensions, one of the problems of Brazilian public-sector overspending. Trimming bureaucrats' pensions is a major reform effort, one that the bureaucrats resist.

Congress and the Presidency

The 1988 Brazilian constitution is basically presidential—a powerful president is directly elected. But the Congress is fragmented into many weak parties, often making it difficult to pass badly needed reforms. Until changed in 1997, Brazilian presidents could be elected for just one

COMPARISON

SPAIN TURNS DEMOCRATIC

In 1975, when Franco died, Spain was an authoritarian system with a hand-picked parliament, curbs on the press, and no legal political parties. Just two years later, Spain was a full-fledged democracy with a freely elected parliament, a lively and critical press, and a complete party system. The Franco system had become history. Spain has had free and fair elections ever since.

Dictators kid themselves that they have built lastingly. Their immediate successors like to think they can give a few tokens of democracy but preserve the authoritarian system. They can't. A little bit of democracy just whets people's appetites for more, and the system tends to slide all the way into full democracy. There are several points of comparison between Spain's rapid shift to democracy and Brazil's, with one important difference. Spain has a mostly middle-class population, and this tends to make for centrist politics. Brazil has a large class of extremely poor people, and this can still make for unstable politics.

five-year term; now they can be elected to two four-year terms. In 1993, a plebiscite decided to keep the presidential system—Brazil's tradition since 1889 and the pattern throughout Latin America—rather than go to a parliamentary system with a prime minister as chief executive.

Brazil's parliament, the National Congress, is bicameral. It is also utterly fragmented, undisciplined, and uncooperative, almost designed to block reforms (like Russia's Duma). The upper house, the Senate, consists of eighty-one members who are elected for eight-year terms. Each of Brazil's twenty-six states gets three senators. The lower house, the Chamber of Deputies, has 513 members, each elected for four-year terms based on a type of proportional representation that begs for trouble. Brazil's twenty-six states (plus the Federal District of Brasilia) have from eight to seventy deputies, depending on population. This overrepresents the rural, less-populous states and is unfair to the populous, economic-powerhouse states such as São Paulo.

Each state is a multimember PR district. Voters can pick either a party or write in the names of their preferred candidates. This system, known technically as "open-list proportional representation," means that candidates of the same party compete against each other, one of the flaws of the old Japanese electoral system. It also means that party matters little; candidates run on personality, contributing to the weakness of Brazil's parties.

The military presidents of Brazil were extremely powerful, their civilian successors much less so. Their power to initiate needed reforms is restricted by Congress on one side and state governors on the other. Members of Brazil's Congress, essentially the representatives of their states and its powerful interest groups, generally want to spend more, especially on their clients. They pay little attention to the budget deficits this creates, which in turn lead quickly to inflation. All their incentives push them to spend.

Brazil's presidents, especially Cardoso, understand what causes inflation and try to curb government spending. A series of reforms to do this, however, have rough going in the fragmented Congress. Few think of the good of the whole, only of their favored interest group. Some state governors have simply ignored Brasilia's decrees to balance their budgets, trim the bureaucracy, and stop borrowing. Brazilian politicians—like those of the French Fourth Republic—are good at blocking but not at building.

DEMOCRACY

THE INFLATION CONNECTION

Brazil's presidential elections of 1994 and 1998 were quite similar. The two top candidates were the same. Both times, Brazilians voted against inflation by electing Fernando Henrique Cardoso of the centrist Social Democratic party and against fiery Workers party leader "Lula." Just before the 1994 election, as finance minister, Cardoso had authored the "Real Plan" that introduced a new currency, the **real**, and drastically reduced Brazil's runaway inflation. (One real was worth 2.75 x 10^{15} of the *cruzeiros* of 30 years earlier.) Lula had been leading in the polls, but Cardoso beat him 54 to 27 percent in the first round. In 1998, Carodoso again beat Lula 53 to 32 percent in the first round. Lula was seen as a destabilizing radical, Cardoso as a realistic reformer.

Cardoso had himself been a radical, a sociology professor and promoter of **dependency theory**, a Marxist-type theory popular throughout Latin America, that the United States keeps Latin America poor (see box on page 426). Under the generals, Cardoso was arrested, barred from teaching, and forced into exile. Over the years, like many Latin American radicals, Cardoso abandoned dependency theory in favor of the free market and international trade as the way out of poverty. By the time he ran for president in 1994, Cardoso was pledging to rid Brazil of its state-owned and protected industries (the same promise Collor de Mello had made).

The taming of inflation is what won both times for Cardoso. Cardoso's Real Plan dropped inflation from a monthly rate of 45 percent in June to 1.5 percent in just three months. Economic stabilization gave Brazilians hope. Lula, on the other hand, spoke of socialist programs for the poor. Such programs are inflationary, something that even poor Brazilians don't want any more. Said one Rio *favelado*, "I'm voting for Fernando Henrique. He invented the Real Plan."

Cardoso's popularity went down after the 1998 election because he had to devalue the real, and this induced a **recession**. He did this to head off inflation. As the financial world held its breath, it worked. Carodoso's popularity **varied inversely** with the fear of inflation: when it went up, his popularity went down. Cardoso was able to form a four-party coalition and continue, with difficulty and setbacks, his reform agenda. With Brazil's recent economic growth, Brazil seems to have entered the ranks of stable democracies whose citizens do not fall for populist **demagoguery**.

Brazilian President Fernando Henrique Cardoso. (Embassy of Brazil)

An Inchoate Party System

Under the military, Brazil had essentially fake parties, one a total creature of the regime, the Renovating Alliance (*Aliança Renovadora Nacional*, ARENA), the other a tame opposition, the Brazilian Democratic Movement (*Movimento Democrático Brasileiro*, MDB). With the opening up (*abertura*) of the 1980s, the MDB turned itself into the Party of the MDB (PMDB), a moderate center party.

Several socialist or workers' parties sprang up. The main party of the left, the Workers party (*Partido dos Trabalhadores*, PT), is led by a charismatic union organizer, Luis Inácio da Silva, nicknamed "Lula," the PT's habitual candidate for president. Leonel Brizola, a radical intellectual and Goulart's brother-in-law, set up a center-left Democratic Labor party (*Partido Democrático Trabalhista*, PDT) and ran as Lula's vice presidential candidate in 1998.

At center-left (but more to the center), Cardoso's Brazilian Social Democratic party (*Partido da Social Democracia Brasileira*, PSDB) was formed in 1988 from a variety of centrist and reformist deputies. Cardoso won the presidential elections in 1994 and 1998. The Liberal Front party (*Partido da Frente Liberal*, PFL), a conservative party led by former President José Sarney, worked with the PSDB in congress. The populist former São Paulo mayor Paulo Maluf used his (conservative) Brazilian Progressive party to position him for presidential runs.

Brazil's parties and their members change like quicksilver. Like Russia's, they are founded, merge, and split so fast it's hard to keep up with them. Brazilians do not trust their parties; they see them as corrupt and irresponsible. In the 1990s, Brazil's Congress had nineteen parties. In the 1994–98 Congress, 230 representatives in the lower house (out of 513) switched parties, some more than once. These are the marks of an **inchoate** party system in which the poorly institutionalized parties are simply personalistic vehicles to get politicians elected.

Few parties articulate a clear program or implement coherent policies. Rather, once elected, leaders use government resources (jobs, contracts, loans, kickbacks) to keep themselves in power and get rich. Fernando Alfonso Collor de Mello, for example, created his own National Reconstruction party to win the presidency in 1989, but his party soon faded. He did not care, for he was then able to enrich himself and his friends. (Under impeachment for corruption, he resigned in 1992 and lives well in Miami.) Settling down into a stable, meaningful party system is one of the best things Brazilian democracy could do for itself. But such an evolution will take reforms, several elections, and patient organizational work, something Brazilians have not been good at.

Key Terms

real   plural *reís*; Brazil's currency, worth about $0.50.

dependency theory   Radical theory that rich countries keep poor countries poor by siphoning off their wealth.

recession   An economy going downward.

vary inversely   As one thing goes up, another goes down.

demagoguery   Crowd-pleasing promises that cannot be fulfilled.

inchoate   Not yet organized; incoherent.

The Military as Political Institution

As in much of the Third World, Brazil's political institutions are weak. Unlike Europe, with its well-established parliaments, parties, and bureaucracies, Brazil's political institutions are barely capable of handling the demands of mass politics in an orderly way. When the political system gets stuck or chaotic, the army is often the only institution capable of governing. Direct military participation ended in 1985, but if things get tumultuous again, another military takeover is possible.

The Brazilian military has intervened in politics many times: at the birth and through the life of the Old Republic, at first in support of Vargas and then against him, at the establishment of reasonably democratic regimes at the end of the two Vargas periods, and in 1964. Prior to 1964, however, the Brazilian military never tried to stay in power. They saw themselves in much the same way as Dom Pedro II had seen his role, that of a "moderating power" to restrain politicians from excesses. Step in when need be, set things right, then step out, was the Brazilian military pattern.

By 1964, both the Brazilian military attitude and the nation's situation had changed. Brazilian officers, partly thanks to U.S. guidance, had redefined their mission from defending Brazil against external enemies to guarding it against internal threats, especially communism. In the Superior War College, the ESG (see box, below), top officers studied politics, economics, psychology, and counterinsurgency.

Thus the Brazilian military, technically highly trained and newly motivated toward a more active role in their country's politics, was ready to upset a long-held view (especially by Americans) that truly professional military officers do not engage in coups. Looking around, the Brazilian officers found—almost like a case study—a Brazil that was sliding rapidly to the left. The Brazilian army chose to intervene, and it did so precisely because it was professionally trained to prevent revolution. This time the officers were determined to stay in power, block the return of divisive politics, and modernize their potentially rich country in an organized, rational manner.

COMPARISON

BRAZIL'S POWERFUL MILITARY SCHOOL

A school facing a luxurious Rio beach does not seem a likely spot for a powerful political institution, but in Brazil virtually an entire ruling class emerged from the Superior War College (*Escola Superior da Guerra*, ESG). Founded in 1949 on the model of the U.S. National War College (which trains midcareer officers for higher command), by the 1960s the ESG had shifted its emphasis from external to internal security. Still influenced by the old Positivism—which, in fact, had been spread in the last century through Brazil's military academy—ESG students came to the conclusion that only Brazil's rapid economic development would save it from chaos and communism.

The ESG trained not only the best colonels, but top civilians as well. Government administrators, private industrialists, and leading professional people tended to outnumber ESG's military students. The ESG drew its ninety students a year from key areas of the political and economic power structure: banking, mass communications,

education, and industry. ESG's graduates returned to their branches imbued with the authoritarian developmentalist doctrines they learned at the school. In civilian-ruled Brazil, ESG graduates are not so influential, although many are still in high positions. They still form a cadre of technocrats the military could rely on again should they return to power.

The ESG actually resembles a French *grande école*, such as the Polytechnique or ENA, except that ESG students are generally older and already established in careers. In both cases, however, the schools put their stamp on bright, carefully selected people, training them to think and act the same way and to maintain close ties with each other. This is what gave French and Brazilian policy making its cohesion and continuity. "We don't actually make government policy," said a senior Brazilian officer on the ESG staff. "The great contribution of the school has been to establish an elite of people who can think in the same language and who have learned the team approach to planning here." The French couldn't have said it better.

For two decades, Brazil was governed by a succession of generals, each chosen by a small group of generals. The Brazilian military did not rule the country directly, as if it were an army camp. Rather, they structured the political system so that only a military officer or a civilian who worked closely and cooperatively with the military could attain executive office. Once named president, a Brazilian general usually retired from active service and seldom wore his uniform.

Brazil's military regime was not just military, and that may be why it lasted so long. The Brazilian military had close ties to civilian bankers, educators, industrialists, and governmental administrators, many of whom trained together in the Superior War College in Rio. The weakness of most military regimes is their isolation and lack of contact with civilian elites. Unable to run the complexities of economy, society, and diplomacy without skilled civilians, military regimes frequently blunder so badly that they decide to give up power and responsibility.

Brazil's generals avoided this kind of isolation by partially integrating themselves with conservative civilian elites who held views and values close to the military's. Brazil's "military" regime was actually a civilian-military network of authoritarian developmentalists who controlled most of Brazil's economic, political, and military structures. In public, the government looked civilian. Most executive positions were occupied by civilian technocrats.

Can an army be a political institution? Historically, the evidence is against the military holding power permanently. Armies are clumsy tools to govern with. After some years, military regimes tend to return power to civilians, or turn into civilian regimes themselves, or get overthrown in a new military coup. The first is what happened in Brazil in the early 1980s.

A Lack of Institutions

The underlying reason that Brazil got its military governments was the lack of sturdy institutions that could handle the influx of newly mobilized sectors of the population and their demands. In the absence of firm, well-established parties and parliaments, demagogic populists aroused both the masses and the military. The military won, and, as we shall see, the masses lost. The trouble was that the Brazilian military did not really found durable institutions either.

One of the principal functions of political institutions is winning and channeling mass loyalty to the system. The chief mechanism for doing this is political parties. Without loyalty, mere technical arrangements, even if they work well in promoting economic growth, become more and more isolated from the population they rule. Franco's Spain supervised an economic boom, but there was little positive feeling among Spaniards for the Franco institutions. After his death in 1975, those institutions were dismantled with scarcely a protest.

By stunting the growth of political institutions, the Brazilian military did great harm to the country. We are now watching to see if Brazil can escape from its cycle of weak civilian institutions overthrown by clumsy military regimes, which in turn give way to weak civilian administrations again. Could there be another coup? From time to time, one hears muttering from top officers, but Brazil's economic growth has now moved it into the ranks of the middle-income countries (over $6,000 per capita GDP), and they tend to be stable democracies. Unless there is a terrible crisis, we are not likely to see military rule again in Brazil.

Brazilian Political Culture

The Easygoing Image

Both Brazilians and resident foreigners tend to describe Brazilians as easygoing people, seldom angry or violent, largely indifferent to politics, and unlikely to rise in revolt. There's a lot of truth to this image. In most of Brazil for most of the year it's too hot to make a revolution. People would rather go to the beach.

Brazilians have better things to do with their energies than take them out in politics. Brazilians are emotional; they laugh, joke, and embrace in public. They love children—possibly, some suggest, because the infant mortality rate is so high—and tend to spoil their offspring, especially the boys. This creates a male-centered society in which the men are expected to indulge themselves but not the women.

Many of the Portuguese who settled Brazil either were minor noblemen or pretended they were. They brought with them antiwork attitudes and looked down on tawdry moneymaking. Until fairly recently this attitude was still present in the Brazilian middle and upper classes, limiting their entrepreneurial energy. Many of the more vigorous business and government people have been of non-Portuguese origin (German, Italian, Japanese, and East European). Avoidance of work is common throughout the middle and upper classes in Latin America; people would rather attach themselves to the state bureaucracy than develop private industry. The elements of hustle and vigor are missing from much of Latin American capitalism, a point sometimes offered as an explanation of both backwardness and penetration by U.S. capital.

The image of Brazilians as lazy and laid-back amidst tropical languor, however, may have been overdone. An economy can't expand at several percentage points a year without people working hard. The "tropical languor" theory may have been deliberately cultivated in Brazil, for it serves as a rationalization for keeping the broad mass of Brazilians apolitical while leaving elites free to run the country as they wish. Brazilian elites tell themselves that the poor are content in their ignorance and are apathetic by nature. They, the elites, must shoulder the arduous tasks of running government and the business sector, both of which mostly benefit the elites.

Furthermore, there wasn't anything easygoing about Brazilian attitudes as the country has approached the brink of social collapse. Desperate people, some of them reduced from middle-class jobs to street peddling, turned angry. About 30 percent of Brazilians live in **absolute poverty**, and Brazil has practically no unemployment compensation, welfare benefits, or food stamps. When Brazilians have no more money for food, they are forced to starve or steal. Traditionally, Brazilians shrugged off their impoverished class as a normal thing that could not be helped. With the prospect of social breakdown and violence, however, some have begun to take notice and try to do something about it.

Key Term

absolute poverty
Extremely low income; defined by World Bank as living on under $1 a day.

Brazilian Racism

One area where the easygoing Brazilian attitude has helped to keep society calm and stable is their proclaimed indifference to race. At least one-third of Brazilians have African ancestors, giving Brazil the largest African-descended population outside of Africa. Precise classification is impossible, however, because of both racial mixing and the Latin American tendency to let culture decide race. Throughout the continent, a person with the right education, manners, and money is considered "European" with little regard to skin color. Brazilians have dozens of words to distinguish among the combinations that make up the country's racial spectrum: *branco*, *alvo*, and *claro* for the lighter skinned, *moreno* and *mulato* for the middle shades, and *negro*, *preto*, *cabo verde*, and *escuro* for the darker. In theory and in most public places, there is no discrimination in Brazil. Walking down the street, one Brazilian feels as good as another.

Brazil's dirty little secret, however, is that in fact it is a racist society, one that adheres to the old American song: "If you're white you're all right, and if you're brown stick around, but if you're black get back." Career chances are strongly related to skin color in Brazil. If you're white, your chances of going to a university, entering a profession, making lots of money, and living in a nice house are much, much higher. If you're black, you run a high risk of infant death, malnutrition, rural poverty, and the lowest jobs or unemployment.

The Brazilian economic and political elite is white, whether the government is civilian or military. A small number of blacks have moved upward, but their way is often blocked by job requirements specifying "good appearance" (that is, white or near-white). Individual blacks can succeed in entertainment and sports, but they are a handful. The world's greatest (and highest-paid) soccer star, Pelé, is black. Even he encountered discrimination early in his career. When he served as Cardoso's minister of sports, he was the only black in an all-white cabinet. Intermarriage is perfectly legal but seldom takes place. Problems of race are rarely discussed in Brazil's mass media. Increasingly, Brazil's blacks resent this.

Brazil's Poor: Passive or Explosive?

Do poor people turn naturally to social revolution, or are they too busy trying to stay alive to bother with political questions? In Brazil, we have a laboratory to test some of the longstanding debates about why people revolt. The answers depend not just on people being poor—

POLITICAL CULTURE

PERSONALISMO AND MACHISMO

Latin American politicians often rely on **personalismo** in politics rather than on clear thinking, party programs, or organizing. Many Latin Americans like to be perceived as strong, the men especially as macho, leading to **machismo**. Latin American leaders, civilian or military, traditionally combine personalismo and machismo in varying degrees. They figure it's the only way to gain mass respect.

The Brazilian generals, given the way in which they were selected for power, tended to downplay these qualities. With the return of civilian politics, however, personalismo and machismo reappeared in Brazilian politics. Both Collor de Mello in 1989 and Lula in 1994 exuded personalismo. A sign of Brazilians' maturity was the election and reelection of Cardoso, Brazil's first nonclownish civilian president.

Key Term

favela   Brazilian shanty-town, found around most cities.

most Brazilians through history have been poor—but on the context in which poor people find themselves.

In the dry, overpopulated Northeast, some people starve. Many rural poor, hoping to improve their condition, flood to the **favelas** surrounding the cities, where some do find work while others eke out a precarious living from peddling or crime. Rich Brazilians, on the other hand, live sumptuously. For most of the military era, there was little open class resentment. First and most important, the Brazilian underclass was deprived of its leadership and organizational alternatives. The radical parties and leaders of the Goulart period were, respectively, outlawed and exiled or had their political rights annulled, *cassado* in Portuguese. Anyone caught trying to form a radical opposition got into bad trouble—"disappeared" to torture or death.

The strong economic growth of the 1970s gave people hope and thus dampened protests, but with the economic downturns of the 1980s and 1990s hope dimmed. "I tell you frankly I'm desperate," said one sidewalk peddler whose pregnant wife stood nearby. "They keep telling us that things will get better, but who can afford to wait? Hunger doesn't wait. Yesterday I sold nothing. Our food is ending. When it ends, what do I do?" The answer for some Brazilians was

COMPARISON

APARTHEID, BRAZILIAN STYLE

Until *apartheid* ended in the early 1990s, South Africa classified population groups and then used elaborate laws to discriminate against nonwhites. From the Brazilian perspective this was not only unjust but expensive and stupid as well. The Brazilian system, while claiming that all are equal, assigns people to social roles on the basis of race as the South African system did, but without the obvious unfairness, the many laws, or the social tension that the apartheid system brought. By pretending to be color-blind, Brazilian society dampens the black resentment that could lead to rage and revolt.

Curiously, tacitly racist breakaway movements in Brazil's southernmost provinces, where the population is 85 percent European, parallel South Africa's apartheid. People in the clean, prosperous states of Rio Grande do Sul, Santa Catarina, and Parana, upset by the influx of impoverished darker Brazilians from further north, talk about setting up a new country, the Republic of the Pampas. It would

be the size of France and have 22 million mostly white citizens. German and Italian would be coequal languages with Portuguese.

One spokesman for this republic is businessman Irton Marx, the blond son of German immigrants, who argues Brazil is too big, too statist, and too corrupt. "Our culture and economy are different here in the south. We are part of the First World. We are subsidizing the whole country and getting nothing back." Denying he or his movement is racist, Marx contends his tidy region is threatened by the mass migration of poor northeastern Brazilians, who do not have the local "Teutonic" attitude toward work.

Some municipalities in the south of Brazil already make it difficult for poor nonwhites to settle. They deny them permits or even put them on buses back to where they came from. Chances are the breakaway movement will get nowhere, but it does illustrate (1) there is racism in Brazil, (2) Brazil is in a shaky condition, and (3) the crux of apartheid, whether in South Africa, Brazil, or U.S. suburbia, is influx control.

MARGINALS IN BRAZIL'S FAVELAS

Brazil's poor are sometimes called **marginals**. Many of them huddle in favelas. Some favelados hold regular jobs, others sell pop on the beach, and some steal. Brazil's crime rates are astronomical. There is no place for the marginals to go, and no one cares about them.

Politically they are on the margin, too. Unorganized and too busy just trying to get food, they riot only when faced with starvation. Brazilian sociologists point out that however wretched life seems in the favelas, it's worse in the countryside. Moving to a favela for many is a step up, for there they have access to some education and health services and may even find a job.

"Keep Your Distance," says this Rio road sign, but it could also serve as a warning about the favelas that nestle between Rio's peaks. (Michael Roskin)

to raid food stores. Everything from corner grocery shops to supermarkets were smashed open by hungry crowds and quickly looted. Brazil's food riots sent chilling warning signs throughout the Third World.

Especially ominous is that this arousal of Brazil's poor, from passive to active, comes at the time Brazil has democratized and formed parties, some of them with radical leadership. Even more explosive is the fact that many middle-class Brazilians find themselves getting pushed down into the lower classes, and middle-class people are far more likely to rise in revolt than those who have always been downtrodden. Sectors of the middle class, desperate to hold on to their tenuous positions, could serve as the sparkplug for major unrest.

In sum, the poor are not automatically passive or active but can become either, depending on the situation. If Brazilian radicals attempt once again to mobilize mass discontent, the military might decide to intervene again.

Uneven Democratic Attitudes

Most Brazilians respect democracy in the abstract, but a 2000 poll found that only 18 percent were satisfied with the way Brazil's democracy works in practice. Twenty-five percent said authoritarianism might be better; 28 percent didn't care. Some Brazilians, especially

Key Term

marginal Poor person on the edge of society and the economy.

among elites, are convinced democrats. Others, especially poorer and working-class people, are interested in little besides jobs and are willing to support whatever will put some food on the table, democratic or not. This is typical of the Third World—and even much of the First. Commitment to democratic values is stronger among those higher up on the socioeconomic ladder, people who don't have to worry about eating.

Researchers in Brazil and other Third World lands often find that poorer and less-educated people are more interested in law-and-order and bread-and-butter issues than in civil rights and democracy. Many actually prefer an authoritarian populist in command. One survey had found 63 percent of Brazilian illiterates named the dictatorial Vargas as the best president. Those with high school or college education favored Médici, the toughest of Brazil's military presidents. Their reasons? Poor people liked the way Vargas raised wages and looked after the poor; middle-class people pointed to industrialization under Médici.

The strong vote for Cardoso in 1994 and 1998 was not necessarily a vote for democracy; it was a vote for bread on the table. Only among better-educated and better-off Brazilians do we find an interest in democracy for its own sake, and even here it is not overwhelming. And these Brazilian findings are not unique. In many countries—including the United States—commitment to democratic values falls off as one moves down the socioeconomic ladder. The irony here is that democracy—a system that's supposed to be based on the broad masses of people—receives its strongest support from elites.

KEY CONCEPTS

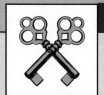

LATIN AMERICA'S CHANGING LEFTISTS

During much of the Cold War, Latin American intellectuals subscribed to fashionable leftist views that their region's poverty was the result of exploitation by wicked capitalists, especially by *Norteamericanos*. Some worked this into a Marxist type of theory called "dependency" that was accepted as an article of faith throughout much of the Western Hemisphere. Only by getting out from under U.S. corporations—who dictated what Latin American lands would produce (bananas and coffee) and what they would consume (Chevrolets and Coca Cola)—would Latins find prosperity. Accordingly, revolutionary regimes such as Cuba and Nicaragua were not bad, because they broke the Yankee connection.

In recent decades the Latin left has had to rethink its Marxist and dependency theories. The demise of Communist regimes in the Soviet Union and East Europe made many wonder if "socialism" really worked. The economic success of Chile, where a military dictator enforced capitalism, made many appreciate the vigor of market systems, especially those connected to the world economy. Argentina's restructuring in the early 1990s had a similar impact. And intellectually, many were persuaded by the arguments of Peruvian economist Hernando de Soto that the only effective and dynamic sector of Latin economies is the black market. Why? Every other sector is choked into stagnation by government controls.

The result of all this was that many Latin intellectuals, including Cardoso, abandoned statism and socialism. Free markets, international trade, and foreign investment no longer looked bad; maybe they were even good. The new attitude spread unevenly in Latin America, though. It was most pronounced in Mexico, Chile, and Argentina but weaker in Brazil and Uruguay.

This doesn't mean that democracy is impossible in Brazil, but it's an uphill struggle. Part of the impulse for Brazil's democratization comes from the educated upper-middle class, a group that's relatively small but strategically positioned to make its voice heard. Brazil makes us aware that democracy—or indeed any kind of political system—is usually the work of the few mobilizing the many.

Key Term

whig democracy Democracy with limited participation, typical of democracy's initial phases.

Patterns of Interaction

An Elite Game

Politics in Brazil has been largely a game for elites: big landowners, bankers and industrialists, and top bureaucrats and military people. Many do not welcome mass participation in politics. The stakes of the game are political power, the patronage jobs, and the control of funds that come with it. The rules of the game are that none of the players gets seriously hurt or threatened and that nobody mobilizes the Brazilian masses in an angry way, for that would destroy the game's fragile balance and hurt them all.

Accordingly, Vargas, himself a wealthy rancher, was an acceptable player when he supported coffee prices for the growers, but when he started to mobilize poor Brazilians he had to be ousted. Kubitschek was a good player who looked after his elite friends and deflected potential discontent with his grandiose plans to open Brazil's interior. Goulart, also a wealthy rancher, was a very bad player: He threatened all the elites and mobilized the masses at a furious rate. The PT's Lula, an antielite labor-union radical, mobilized Brazil's working class in a way that frightened most of Brazil's elites. If he had won, the military might have been inclined to move again.

Until recently, Brazil's political history has been the same elite game: Dom Pedro with his fazendeiro friends, the Old Republic with its Paulista-Mineiro alternation, and the military technocracy with its industrial and bureaucratic clientele. Since Vargas, however, the political mobilization of the masses has been a recurring threat to the game. Periodically, a politician who doesn't like the elite's fixed rules is tempted to reach out to Brazil's masses, both to secure his own power and to help the downtrodden. Seeing the threat, Brazil's elites, through the military, remove it and try to demobilize the masses. Mobilization and demobilization can be seen as a cycle.

The Mobilization-Demobilization Cycle

Scholars of the Third World in general and Brazil in particular often focus on "political mobilization." Mobilization means the masses waking up, becoming aware, and often becoming angry. Prior to the beginning of mass political mobilization in a country, few participate in politics, and decisions are made by traditional elites, such as Brazil's big landowners and political bosses. Some call this **whig democracy**, and it is standard in the opening decades of democratic development. Democracies typically start with participation limited to the better off (even in the United States). Some social stimulus, such as economic growth, brings new sectors of the population (in Brazil, the urban working class) to political awareness; they are "mobilized" and start participating in politics with new demands.

The problem with Brazil—and many other Third World countries—is that the existing institutions haven't been able to handle this influx of new participants and their demands. Well-organized, strong political parties can channel, moderate, and calm mass demands in a constructive way. But Brazilian parties are weak, little more than personalistic vehicles to get their chiefs into power. The chiefs, such as Vargas and Goulart, use their parties in a demagogic way, to whip up support among the newly mobilized and politically unsophisticated masses by promising them instant economic improvement. The more conservative elements in society—the wealthy, who often have close ties to the military—view this process with horror. The military sees it as "leftist chaos" and may end it by a military coup, the story of many Latin American countries. Thus mobilization, which could be the start of democratization, often leads to authoritarian takeovers.

The 1964 military takeover in Brazil ended one phase of what might be termed a mobilization-demobilization cycle. The generals had grown to hate civilian politics, especially political parties and their demagogic leaders. We can to a degree understand their hatred. As guardians of Brazil's unity and security, they witnessed their beloved republic falling into the hands of irresponsible crowd-pleasers.

Typically, the military tries the only solution they know: demobilization. Believing that the solution lies in an end to disruptive political activity, they ban most parties, hand pick

DEMOCRACY

POLITICAL MOBILIZATION, BRAZILIAN STYLE

The turnouts in Brazilian elections provide a graphic indicator of political mobilization. Even in 1962, the figure was rather small compared to the total Brazilian population, then about 76 million. But a literacy requirement held down the size of the electorate and eliminated the poorest from voting. Conservative, better-off Brazilians and the military were horrified at the prospect of Goulart's dropping the literacy test and letting lower-class Brazilians into the election booth with their potentially radical demands. Now there is no literacy requirement, the voting age is sixteen, and voting is compulsory (but not enforced). The 1998 election indicates the growth of apathy, as Brazilians discover that politics can't solve everything.

1930 and earlier	never more than .25 million
1933	1.25 million
1945	6.2 million
1950	7.9 million
1955	8.6 million
1960	11.6 million
1962	14.7 million
1989	63.0 million
1994	93.0 million
1998	84 million

KEY CONCEPTS

THE PRAETORIAN TENDENCY

As the Roman Empire ossified and crumbled, the emperor's bodyguard, the Praetorian Guard, came to play a powerful role, making and unmaking emperors. Political scientists now use **praetorianism** to indicate a situation where the military feels driven to take over the government.

Praetorianism is not just a problem of a power-hungry army but reflects deep conflict in the whole society. In praetorian societies, it's not only the army that wants to take power, but many other groups as well: students, labor unions, revolutionaries, and politicians would like to seize the state machinery. Institutional constraints and balances have broken down; nobody plays by the rules. In such situations of chaos and breakdown, it is the army among the many power contenders that is best equipped to seize power, so praetorianism usually means military takeover.

political leaders, and permit only rigged elections. Initially, things do calm down. Some people are thankful the army has stepped in to put an end to extremist politics and empty promises. Mass rallies, loud demands, and radical leaders disappear—the latter sometimes physically.

But the problems aren't solved. The demands—although no longer whipped up by politicians—are still there and growing. Indeed, as the economy grows, more people come to live in cities, and the pent-up demands for change increase. To repress such demands, the regime turns to the police-state brutality of arbitrary arrests and torture. Once people are awakened or mobilized they can never be fully demobilized, even by massive doses of coercion.

The Inflation Connection

Inflation is a political problem the world over, especially in Latin America, where regimes may fall over the rate of inflation. Inflation may also be seen as part of the mobilization-demobilization cycle. In Brazil, inflation in currency corresponds to the inflation in promises made by politicians seeking mass support.

Controlling inflation is an unhappy task. By restricting credit and cutting the amount of money being printed, an austerity policy can lower the inflation rate, but at a cost of unemployment and slow economic growth. Latin American inflation cutters are often conservative authoritarians, usually military men, who can pursue disinflationary measures without regard to mass desires. As in much of Latin America, the Brazilian military in effect says to its citizenry: "We don't care how much it hurts, the sooner inflation ends the better we'll all be. Take the bitter medicine now before inflation wrecks the entire economy." When Cardoso made Brazilians swallow this bitter medicine just after his reelection in late 1998, his popularity fell.

Encouraging inflation, on the other hand, is easy; regimes can almost do it in a fit of absent-mindedness. Politicians, wanting to make everybody happy, let the national mint's printing presses run to finance government projects. This is the way Kubitschek built Brasilia. Inflation tends to feed on itself and get out of hand, and soon people can't

Key Term

praetorianism Tendency for military takeovers.

make ends meet. Conservative industrialists and bankers become convinced that the politicians have gone insane. The military, whose fixed salaries are eroded by the galloping inflation, seethes in jealous rage and starts planning a coup to save both the republic and their incomes.

When the military does take power, their disinflationary measures correspond to the political demobilization they also try to enforce. Under the military, this consisted of controls on wages but not on prices, with the result that lower-class Brazilians have to work like dogs to keep up with food prices while some speculators enjoy an economic boom. Civilian regimes may try to do the opposite, with equally bad results (see box below).

Although the Brazilian generals had excellent economic planners, they did not end inflation, which by 1984 reached 223 percent, double what it was in 1964 when the military seized power. This extremely embarrassing fact undermined regime support among the businessmen and bankers who had welcomed the 1964 takeover. One reason Brazil turned democratic was that the military proved as inept as civilians in controlling inflation.

The Corruption Connection

One of the standard characteristics of the Third World is its massive corruption. Throughout Latin America, officials expect *la mordida* (the bite) to issue contracts and licenses. Some argue that corruption is simply a part of Latin American political culture. Perhaps, but corruption tends to flourish under certain institutional arrangements; namely, it grows at the interface of the public and private sectors. Latin America, with its large state sectors and regulated economies, is thus especially fertile ground for corruption. The solution? Cut the state sector back. Where this was done, in Chile, corruption also diminished.

BRAZIL'S STRUGGLE AGAINST INFLATION

Until recently, Brazil suffered seemingly incurable inflation, sometimes at more than 50 percent a month. At times the government froze wages and prices and took other drastic steps. "Prices, starting tomorrow, are halted," said the economy minister in 1991.

But the prices disobeyed. The 1991 effort was the fifth plan to control wages and prices in five years. Five years earlier, Brazilians saw how President Sarney's plan to do the same thing ended in disaster, with prices going up after a short pause and many producers driven out of business. Sarney's popularity plunged lower than ever, unions struck, crowds took to the streets, and the military glowered angrily, as if awaiting their turn to take over.

The real problem, one about which both Collor de Mello and Cardoso campaigned, is Brazil's overlarge state sector that has to be propped up with big subsidies, which are provided by simply printing more money. In the early 1990s, Brazil's Central Bank increased the nation's money supply severalfold each year, producing hyperinflation, which hit 1,149 percent in 1992, 2,489 percent in 1993, and 5,154 percent in early 1994. To turn off the printing presses, though, would mean shutting down a large part of the Brazilian economy, resulting in even more unemployment. Unions warned they wouldn't stand for it. Wage-and-price freezes, experience from many countries shows, simply do not work for more than a few months. They are instituted in desperation when the real cures would hurt too many politically influential groups.

THE BRAZILIAN POLITICAL CYCLE

With some oversimplification, Brazilian politics over the decades can be seen as a cycle or progression of phases that repeat themselves. If we were to sketch out our discussion of the last few pages, it would look like the diagram below:

The cycle could start all over with the mobilized masses falling under the sway of demagogic politicians. That's the way Brazilian politics worked earlier—for example, during the two "Vargas cycles."

Mobilization → Demagoguery → Military Takeover → Demobilization → Liberalization → Democratization
             (inflation)   (disinflation)

The interesting thing about Brazil (and some other Latin American countries) is that the public is increasingly fed up with corruption, especially in high places. The presidents of Brazil and Venezuela were hounded from office when the media uncovered the extent of their corruption. Dozens of Brazilian Congresspersons (most in the PMDB) enriched themselves through fake projects (such as pretend help for the poor). The chairman of the budget committee got $51 million over five years. (He said he was very lucky in the lottery.) As in Russia, parliamentary immunity shields such crooks.

This new public concern is a very good sign, an indication of growing political maturity. Stealing from the starving is no longer acceptable. Brazilian politicians have looted their country long enough; let them now face angry citizens. The danger here is that when Brazilians start to think that democracy equals corruption, the way is open for a coup. Brazil's top general warned Congress to clean up its act: "Beware the anger of the legions," the exact words once used by Rome's Praetorian Guard.

Resurgent Interest Groups

For most of the life of the military regime, the Brazilian government continued the corporatist model that Vargas had borrowed from Italy and Portugal. Under corporatism, interest groups are controlled or coordinated by the government. With the *abertura* of the 1980s, Brazil's interest groups emerged with a life of their own once again.

After the 1964 takeover, the military abolished the big union that had been fostered by Goulart and placed all labor unions under direct government control. Particularly drastic was the control of rural unions, whose impoverished and militant farm workers threatened the property of the conservative landowning allies of the military government. Union leaders were henceforth hand picked to make sure they would cooperate with the new order and not lead workers in excessive wage demands or strikes.

While this arrangement held down wages, prices rose until workers could stand it no more. New unions and leaders outside government control emerged as a major force. The largest and most radical Brazilian union, the United Confederation of Workers (CUT), is tied to Lula's Workers party. CUT is especially strong in São Paulo and has struck against many big industries there. The military does not like CUT. The tamer General Confederation of Workers (CGT) is tied to the large but corrupt PMBD.

Many businessmen had welcomed the 1964 coup only to find that the military technocrats would sometimes ride roughshod over their interests in the name of economic rationality. The theory of **constructive bankruptcy** let weak Brazilian firms go under rather than subsidize them with tariff protection against foreign competition. Now businesses generally want sound money and an end to government economic controls and restrictions. Other groups, such as students and farmers, also voice their discontent. Opposition to the rule of the generals developed across a broad front of conservative and radical Brazilians. The most interesting group, however, was the Catholic church, a force to be reckoned with in the world's largest Catholic country.

The Church as Opposition

The Roman Catholic church was the only large Brazilian group that maintained its autonomy and was in a position to criticize the military regime. Typically in Catholic countries the Church has been conservative and has favored conservative regimes. We saw in France how the long fight between clericalism and anticlericalism split society into two camps. The same thing happened in Spain and Italy.

Brazil never had this kind of split. With the 1891 republican constitution, modeled after the U.S. constitution, the Brazilian church consented to disestablishment, that is, to losing its special privileges as church and state were separated. Brazil settled this important and divisive issue quickly and early, leaving the church as an independent force.

Still, in social and economic outlook the Brazilian Catholic church was pretty conservative, urging the faithful to save their souls rather than to reform and improve society. With the **Second Vatican Council** of 1962–65, this conservative attitude changed, and many churchmen, especially younger ones, adopted the "theology of liberation" that put the church on the side of the poor and oppressed. In some Latin American countries, young priests actually became guerrilla fighters trying to overthrow what they regarded as wicked and reactionary regimes.

In the late 1960s, Brazilian church leaders denounced the regime for "fascist doctrines" and for arresting and torturing priests and nuns accused of harboring political fugitives. During the 1970s, the Brazilian church developed a strong stand for human rights and against Brazil's terrible poverty. When strikes flared in the 1980s, strikers often held meetings and sought refuge from police clubs in churches. As a whole, the Brazilian Catholic church was the most activist in Latin America, usually to the chagrin of the Vatican, which ordered priests out of direct political actions.

In 1980, John Paul II visited Brazil. He was visibly moved by what he saw in the favelas. In one, he removed the ring given him by Pope Paul VI when he became a cardinal and gave it to a local priest as a donation. John Paul seemed to be turning into an activist himself. In a Rio slum he called to Brazil's rich: "Look around a bit. Does it not wound your heart? Do you not feel remorse of conscience because of your riches and abundance?" But he stopped short of endorsing active church involvement in politics. Church people should guide spiritually but not politically. In Brazil, this middle road is hard to tread because concern for the poor tends to radicalize people.

Under the democratic regime, the Brazilian church continued its critical attitudes in support of the poor. Some Brazilian churchmen pretended not to hear the Vatican's order to steer clear of radical politics. Their argument is that in order to reach people to save their souls, the church must also help feed them. In poverty-stricken northeast Brazil, therefore, priests keep

Key Terms

constructive bankruptcy
Economic theory that weak firms should fold to make way for new enterprises.

Second Vatican Council
Series of meetings that modernized the Roman Catholic Church and turned it to problems of poverty; also called Vatican II.

CHICO MENDES: ANOTHER DEATH IN THE AMAZON

To Americans the murder of Chico Mendes in 1988 seemed to be part of an environmental outrage concerning the destruction of Brazil's Amazonian rain forest. Less noticed is the murder every year of dozens of leaders of the rural poor in land conflicts with farmers and ranchers intent on keeping their large holdings.

Mendes, who lived in Brazil's westernmost state of Acre, was national leader of rubber tappers who made common cause with environmentalists and Indians in trying to halt the destruction by ranchers and farmers of the lush jungle. The rubber tappers simply use existing trees and have no interest in burning down the forest. The ranchers and farmers, encouraged for decades by Brazil's government to develop the interior, cut and burn tens of millions of acres a year, contributing to global warming and to a shrinking of the earth's capacity to produce oxygen.

Mendes led major protests and legal actions to stop the developers. They in turn detested and frequently threatened him. In 1990, a rancher's son stunned an Acre court by admitting, "I killed Chico Mendes." He probably confessed to protect his father, who was charged with the murder of other peasant leaders. Guns for hire are cheap in the Amazon region, where some two thousand union leaders, small farmers, lawyers, priests, and nuns have been slain. (The Brazilian Catholic Church has taken a leading role in speaking for the rural poor.)

For most Brazilians, poverty is a bigger issue than the environment; people are more important than trees. The question is how and for whom the Amazon will be developed: for the masses of rural poor or for big ranchers who claim thousands of acres as their cattle pasture?

reminding the government of its land-reform program while they support the militant *Movimento Sem Terra* (Movement of Those Without Land). Conservative landlords charge that priests and nuns encourage the poor to illegally occupy private farms. Many are threatened with death.

Especially troublesome were radical French, Dutch, and other West European priests working in land reform. When the Brasilia government tried to keep them out, Brazil's bishops protested. The federal police chief said, "It's necessary to talk to them and pray, to pray above all that priests return to praying."

What Brazilians Quarrel About

How to Make a Second Brazilian Miracle

After the 1964 military takeover, the Brazilian economy improved. From 1968 to 1974 the annual growth rate averaged 10 percent, equal to Japanese rates at the time. A series of very bright economic technocrats used state-owned banks and industries to make a Brazilian miracle. The miracle had problems, however. It was based on foreign rather than Brazilian capital investment and on cheap imported oil. Brazilian capitalists, instead of reinvesting their money in industrial growth, preferred to spend it, speculate with it, or stash it abroad.

Key Term

capital flight Tendency of businesspersons in countries with shaky economies to send their money out of the country.

Capital flight is common in Latin America and more recently in Russia. For new capital investment they got government or foreign loans. This was one of the reasons Brazil accumulated one of the Third World's largest foreign debts, over $200 billion.

In the 1980s the cheap foreign loans and oil dried up, turning the boom into a declining GDP a decade later. From 1980 to 1993 Brazil's GDP grew at an annual average of only 1.5 percent. Per capita GDP (which takes into account population growth) declined an average of half a percent a year. Brazilians grew poorer. Some say this shows the limits of technocratic, state-led economic development, which can produce quick, one-time growth, but not for long.

How to turn this around? At this same time (as discussed in boxes on pages 418 and 426), Latin American intellectuals were starting to think that state-owned industries and government supervision of the economy might be mistaken paths. Cardoso made such a shift and privatized (by auction) state-owned telecommunication, electricity, mines, railroads, banking, and other industries. (Collor had begun the job by selling off steel and petroleum industries.) Cardoso also cut Brazil's nationalistic restrictions on foreign ownership, drastically trimmed the number of Brazil's bureaucrats and their pensions, and reined in state-level banks, who loan recklessly to friends of governors. Cardoso faced strong opposition every step of the way, for every one of these measures meant rich, powerful interests giving up their cushy deals. Brazil's congress represents these interests—some in Cardoso's own party—and often fought him.

The freeing up of Brazil's red-tape economy is analogous to the economic reforms undertaken in Russia and Japan. Many people see what needs to be done for the long-term good of the country, but those who will be hurt by the reforms do everything they can to block them. Cardoso, to his credit, made progress in freeing Brazil's economy and selling state-owned companies, but much work remains. By 1996, Brazil started registering growth rates of 2 percent a year, not great but a lot better than negative growth. With the currency collapse of late 1998 (triggered by the Russian collapse), growth again slumped.

THEY GOT AN AWFUL LOT OF EVERYTHING IN BRAZIL

Brazil has economic problems, but these should not overshadow its amazing achievements. In recent decades Brazil has developed rapidly to become the

- eighth largest economy of the world,
- fifth biggest food exporter in the world,
- third biggest shoe producer in the world,
- seventh biggest steel producer of the world,
- ninth largest producer of cars in the world,
- second largest producer of iron ore,
- eighth largest producer of aluminum,
- fifth biggest arms exporter, and
- of course, world's biggest coffee producer.

With a burgeoning economy that still has great growth potential, one can see why foreign banks put an awful lot of money into Brazil. If Brazil ever achieves economic stability, it could be a growth wonder. One Brazilian wisecrack: "Brazil is the country of the future and always will be."

GEOGRAPHY

MERCOSUR: A REGIONAL TRADE BLOC

One stimulus to Brazil's growth was **Mercosur** (*Mercosul* in Portuguese), a free-trade area formed in 1991 by Argentina, Brazil, Paraguay, and Uruguay. (Chile and Bolivia are associate members.) Just as West Europe's Common Market pushed its economy into greater competition, efficiency, and prosperity, Mercosur seems to be doing the same. Trade among members shot up. In time, Mercosur could expand to include all of South America and eventually even merge with our North American Free Trade Area (NAFTA) to form a common market for the whole Western Hemisphere.

Brazil's State Capitalism

While leftists point to foreign dependency as the root of Brazil's problems, many businessmen and economists point to Brazil's large state sector and red-tape controls on the economy. Brazil, they emphasize, has not really been a free-market country relying on private initiative. Until recent privatization, some 60 percent of Brazil's industry was in government hands—including mines, petroleum production, and electric companies. In addition, the majority of loans came from government banks, giving the state the power to determine what got built and where. Collor de Mello started to dismantle this statist empire, and Cardoso continued the task.

Statism—where the government is the number-one capitalist—can both accomplish big projects and make big mistakes. Some projects that Brazil poured money into were prestigious but money losers. For example, the government invested heavily in nuclear power in a country where hydroelectricity had scarcely been tapped. The nuclear program was a foolish waste—although it made Brazil look like an advanced country—and by 1980 it was greatly curtailed.

Government loans were sometimes extended foolishly, too. The interest on these loans was so low, and Brazil's inflation so high, that the credits amounted to free money, which the borrower could immediately loan out at high interest. Why work for a living when you can just shift some paper around? The subsidized loans from the government, however, ultimately came from working Brazilians in the form of inflation. Brazil's cheap government loans were another reason the rich got richer and the poor got poorer.

State control produces other distortions in the economy. There are so many laws and regulations that businesses have to employ red-tape specialists called *despachantes* (expediters) to jog the bureaucracy into giving a license or allowing a price change. Many despachantes are related to the bureaucrats they deal with; some are former bureaucrats themselves. The Brazilian word for getting around a regulation is *jeito*, literally "knack," meaning having someone who can fix it for you. The whole system feeds corruption.

Another problem area is minimum wages, a holdover from Vargas's populist paternalism. As in other countries, minimum wages dissuade employers from hiring unskilled workers. Many poor people then cannot find entry-level jobs. Minimum wages, aimed at helping the working poor, simply mean more unemployed marginals in the favelas.

Key Term

Mercosur "Southern market"; free-trade area covering southern part of South America.

HEADED FOR EXTINCTION: BRAZIL'S INDIANS

With Brazil's expansion into the vast Amazon frontier has come the pushing back of its Indians until they may be facing extinction. Brazil's constitution guarantees Indians rights to traditional rain-forest lands, but in practice the need of ranchers and miners for ever more territory has made enforcement spotty at best. Of the 270 tribes of Brazilian Indians found at the beginning of the twentieth century, ninety have disappeared altogether and others are slipping fast. Particularly vicious have been gold miners, who readily invade Indian reserves and kill them by guns and dynamite or by poisoning the water with the mercury they use to isolate gold particles. More intent on development and jobs, few Brazilians worry much about the plight of the Indians.

Even worse, many of Brazil's grandiose projects have been capital-intensive (using lots of machinery) rather than labor-intensive (using lots of workers). Brazil is short of capital but has lots of labor. More labor-intensive projects would kill two birds with one stone, alleviating both the capital shortage and tremendous unemployment. But such projects were not to the taste of Brazil's technocrats, probably because they were less prestigious than mammoth capital investments.

Who's right—the leftists, who point to dependency, or the businesspeople, who point to state strangulation? Actually, the two views complement each other. State control does stunt domestic capital formation, and this makes Brazil chronically dependent on foreign capital. Instead of a vigorous private sector of local businesses, the Brazilian economy is divided between the foreign multinationals and the state. Brazilians tend to attach themselves to one of the two. The cure for statism is privatization, which Brazil undertook during the 1990s. Most of the purchasers were foreign (especially U.S.) multinationals. Leftists objected, claiming that Brazil was giving foreign capitalists its wealth. Promarketeers cheered, arguing that the sales bring new investment, competition, and economic growth. Finally, with much hesitation, Brazil is moving away from statism.

Growth for Whom?

Another weakness of the Brazilian economy is that Brazil has one of the most unequal income distributions in the world (see box on page 363). The richest 20 percent of Brazilians rake in 65 percent of all income, while the poorest 20 percent get 2 percent. The rich get richer and the poor poorer. Half of Brazilians are reckoned as poor, and many are destitute. Per capita income in the Northeast is lower than in Bangladesh. The "Brazilian miracle" overlooked these people.

Critics on the left argue that the miracle, because it was controlled by U.S. multinationals and Brazilian technocrats, produced semiluxury goods and grandiose projects that benefited the better off. It made cars and swanky apartments rather than public transportation and basic housing. The leftists would redistribute income to the poor.

Those defending the system point out that Brazil contains two economies, a First World economy that is modern and productive and a Third World one that is traditional and unproductive. Actually, most Third World countries have First World sectors within them. In

For poor urban dwellers, streetcorner or beach hawking may be the only way to eke out a living. Here, a Rio woman and her children sell candles to light in the church behind them. (Michael Roskin)

Brazil the contrast is stark. But, argue the defenders, the gap cannot be bridged overnight. Brazil must first build up its modern sector until it gradually takes over the whole country. To simply redistribute income to marginals, who produce little or nothing, would be economic folly. The trick is to keep the economy growing so as to absorb the marginals and turn them into producers and consumers. This is known as the developmentalist solution to Brazilian poverty.

The critic on the left rejoins that Brazilian development, because it is capital-intensive, can't begin to create the 1.3 million new jobs needed every year.

The Population Problem

Brazil, like most of the Third World, has seen a hefty population increase. The Catholic church, of course, forbids any artificial method of birth control, and the military regime thought a high birth rate contributed to economic growth. Accordingly, in Brazil, until the 1970s, there was no emphasis on slowing population growth, and Brazil's population is now 168 million. The good news is that Brazil's fertility rate, like much of the Third World, has plummeted since 1970, when a Brazilian woman had an average of 5.8 children, to 2.1 in 1997, not much above First World levels. This showed the impact of birth control, television, and economic downturn. Brazil's popular TV soaps show small, affluent families with only one or two children, and this has become a national norm.

It is poor people, especially peasants, who have the most children. The poverty-stricken Northeast, where people have especially large families, is an inexhaustible reservoir of marginal Brazilians. However many millions of them pour into the cities of the South, there are millions more still coming. The result is **hyperurbanization**, common throughout the Third World, where cities are usually surrounded by huge slum belts created by peasants who can no longer live off the land. Two-thirds of Brazilians live in cities, an absurd situation for a big, empty country. São Paulo with 18 million inhabitants is the third largest city in the world (after Tokyo and Mexico City).

The rural immigrants to the cities settle in favelas. With no education—a majority of Brazilians haven't finished primary school—or job skills, many do not find regular work. Those that do usually

Key Term

hyperurbanization Over-concentration of populations in cities.

must travel hours to and from their jobs. With prices rising, most discover themselves getting poorer. If they cannot feed their numerous children, they are forced to abandon them. Millions of "nobody's children" live on the streets, usually by stealing.

Some of Brazil's urban poor, caught at the bottom of a worsening economic situation, turn to crime. With widespread gun ownership, Brazilian murder rates are among the world's highest. Brazilian citizens and police, fed up with crime, turn to extralegal remedies. Unofficial "death squads" of off-duty policemen execute thousands of criminal suspects a year in the favelas or streets. Sometimes shopkeepers pay them to clean up the sidewalks. Young purse and wallet snatchers are sometimes beaten to death on the street. Police shoot street kids as they sleep on the assumption they are petty criminals. And the police may be worse than the criminals. Some police set up roadblocks to shake down and even shoot motorists. Some gun down landless peasants. Policemen are rarely convicted of anything.

Is Democracy Here to Stay?

In the 1970s, almost all of Latin America was some form of dictatorship, but since then almost all of Latin America has returned to democratic, civilian rule (except Cuba). Democracy may be contagious. But will Brazil's democracy, or any of the others, last? The problems of all of Latin America's nations are incredible: severe economic difficulties, bloated state sectors, growing populations, military establishments accustomed to intervening in politics, and a lack of seasoned political institutions such as parties and parliaments. The good news is the bad news is wrong, or at least exaggerated. Democracy has been reasonably sturdy in Latin America, despite some economic hard times, and these hard times, widely trumpeted in the media, always pass.

What has changed? The region as a whole is richer and has a bigger middle class, the bearers of democracy. Better educated and informed, they no longer swallow demagogic promises. Many are now aware of the dangers of statism and inflation. Markets work, and trade between countries benefits all. Even Cuba may soon give way to the democratic tide. For another country with great potential also struggling toward stable democracy, let us now turn to South Africa.

Key Terms

absolute poverty (p. 422)

autogolpe (p. 413)

capital flight (p. 434)

constructive bankruptcy (p. 432)

coroneís (p. 412)

corporatism (p. 413)

demagoguery (p. 419)

dependency theory (p. 419)

Estado Nôvo (p. 413)

favela (p. 424)

fiscal (p. 416)

hyperurbanization (p. 437)

inchoate (p. 419)

machismo (p. 423)

marginal (p. 425)

Mercosur (p. 435)

mobilize (p. 413)

Old Republic (p. 412)

personalismo (p. 423)

positivism (p. 412)

praetorianism (p. 412)   statute (p. 416)
real (p. 419)   vary inversely (p. 419)
recession (p. 419)   whig democracy (p. 427)
Second Vatican Council (p. 432)

Further Reference

Abers, Rebecca Neaera. *Inventing Local Democracy: Grassroots Politics in Brazil.* Boulder, CO: L. Rienner, 2000.

Baaklini, Abdo I. *The Brazilian Legislature and Political System.* Westport, CT: Greenwood, 1992.

Bresser Pereira, Luiz Carlos. *Economic Crisis and State Reform in Brazil: Toward a New Interpretation of Latin America.* Boulder, CO: Lynne Rienner, 1996.

Diamond, Larry, Jonathan Hartlyn, Juan J. Linz, and Seymour Martin Lipset, eds. *Democracy in Developing Countries: Latin America*, 2nd ed. Boulder, CO: Lynne Rienner, 1999.

Eakin, Marshall C. *Brazil: The Once and Future Country.* New York: St. Martin's Press, 1997.

Goertzel, Ted G. *Fernando Henrique Cardoso: Reinventing Democracy in Brazil.* Boulder, CO: Lynne Rienner, 1999.

Hagopian, Frances. *Traditional Politics and Regime Change in Brazil.* New York: Cambridge University Press, 1996.

Hall, Anthony. *Sustaining Amazonia: Grassroots Action for Productive Conservation.* New York: St. Martin's, 1998.

Hunter, Wendy. *Eroding Military Influence in Brazil: Politicians Against Soldiers.* Chapel Hill, NC: University of North Carolina Press, 1997.

Kingstone, Peter R., and Timothy J. Powers, eds. *Democratic Brazil: Actors, Institutions, and Processes.* Pittsburgh, PA: University of Pittsburgh Press, 2000.

Levine, Robert M. *Brazilian Legacies.* Armonk, NY: M. E. Sharpe, 1997.

Mainwaring, Scott. *Rethinking Party Systems in the Third Wave of Democratization: The Case of Brazil.* Stanford, CA: Stanford University Press, 1999.

Purcell, Susan Kaufman, and Riordan Roett, eds. *Brazil Under Cardoso.* Boulder, CO: Lynne Rienner, 1997.

Roberts, Paul Craig, and Karen LaFollete Araujo. *The Capitalist Revolution in Latin America.* New York: Oxford University Press, 1997.

Rosenn, Keith S., and Richard Downes, eds. *Corruption and Political Reform in Brazil: The Impact of Collor's Impeachment.* Boulder, CO: L. Rienner, 1999.

Schneider, Ronald M. *Brazil: Culture and Politics in a New Industrial Power.* Boulder, CO: Westview, 1996.

Skidmore, Thomas F. *The Politics of Military Rule in Brazil, 1964–1985.* New York: Oxford University Press, 1988.

Weyland, Kurt. *Democracy without Equity: Failures of Reform in Brazil.* Pittsburgh, PA: University of Pittsburgh Press, 1996.

29

South Africa

Questions to Consider

1. Explain South Africa's population groups.
2. What did the Boer War do to South Africa's politics?
3. What and when was *apartheid*?
4. Why was Nelson Mandela important to South Africa's transformation?
5. How did South Africa escape revolution?
6. What are South Africa's parties and what do they stand for?
7. What is "consociation" and how did South Africa attempt it?
8. How does Inkatha illustrate the tribal nature of African politics?
9. What could go wrong in South Africa?

The Impact of the Past

South Africa began as a colony and continued until recently to have a **colonialist** structure and mentality, the elimination of which is not complete. It began when the Dutch East India Company sent Jan van Riebeeck with two hundred men to start a "refreshment station" at the Cape of Good Hope in 1652. They encountered the native Khoi Khoi, whom they enslaved, impregnated, and eventually killed off with smallpox. Needing more slaves, they imported them chiefly from the Indies and Madagascar. The resulting mixture—Khoi Khoi, Dutch, Malay, and other—produced the so-called Cape Coloureds. This process is reminiscent of the early settlement of Brazil, which also produced a racial mixture. The difference in South Africa was that the whites developed exclusivist attitudes about race and classified the Coloureds as an inferior group. As in the United States, racism started early and lasted.

As the Cape colony expanded, mostly Dutch farmers (*boers*) pushed outward, taking the land they wanted. When the soil was exhausted, they moved on. Their constant movement earned them the name *trekboers*, or farmers on the move. Farther inland, they met the primitive San people, whom they shot as "pests." Very early, Afrikaners had the attitude that the land was exclusively theirs and that the natives were to be either enslaved or exterminated.

Key Term

colonialism The gaining and exploitation of overseas territories, chiefly by Europeans.

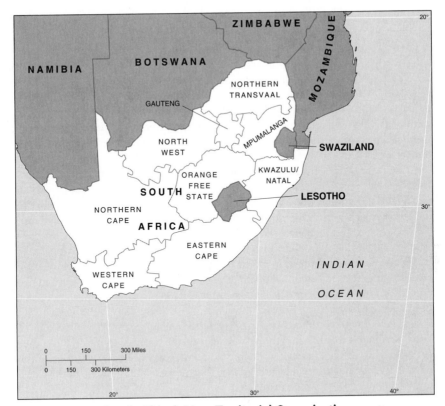

South Africa's New Territorial Organization

The Dutch didn't pay much attention to the Cape colony, but it grew, aided by the arrival of French Huguenots and Germans, who brought the French and German names found today among Afrikaners as well as wine-making skills. As the trekboers pushed along the Indian Ocean coast in the late eighteenth century, they met African Negroes, bigger, stronger, much better organized, and more warlike than Khoi Khoi or San. These Africans were moving south, away from population pressure, tribal wars, and slave raids. In a series of battles over a century, the so-called Kaffir Wars, the Boers subdued the Africans and again took the land they wanted.

Napoleon indirectly triggered the rise of both modern Brazil and South Africa. When a French revolutionary army occupied the Netherlands in 1795, the Dutch let the British take over the Cape to keep Table Bay—around which Cape Town is built—out of French hands. The British stayed as welcome guests until 1803 but returned in 1806, this time for good. In 1814, the Netherlands officially turned over the Cape to Britain, and the English moved to remake it into a British colony.

The Great Trek

Many Boers bristled at British rule. Not only did the British want everybody to speak English, they wanted everybody to be equal before the law. Even Coloured servants could bear witness against their masters. In 1834, to the outrage of many Boers, slavery was abolished.

Key Term

Zulu   Largest South African population group, living chiefly in KwaZulu/Natal.

The Boers became convinced that the English were destroying their language, institutions, way of life, and freedom.

Between 1836 and 1838, an estimated twelve thousand Boer men, women, and children—about one-quarter of the Cape's Dutch population—loaded up ox carts and, like American pioneers, moved into the interior seeking land and freedom. The epic is known as the Great Trek and is celebrated by Afrikaners today as a symbol of their toughness, courage, and go-it-alone attitude. At times the *voortrekkers* (pioneers) had to disassemble their wagons to get them over roadless escarpments. Some columns fought battles with Africans, drawing their wagons into a circle called a *laager*. One column disappeared without a trace, another was slaughtered by **Zulus**.

The voortrekkers' dealings with Africans paralleled the Americans' with Indians. Sometimes by force and sometimes by persuasion, the voortrekkers made treaties with chiefs to obtain land. The Africans, who had no concept of owning land, thought they were letting the Boers use the land for a while. Disputes were settled by the pioneers crushing the natives.

The rich soil and adequate rainfall of Natal, fronting the Indian Ocean, was the initial goal of most voortrekkers. But the British also took an interest in this lush province and annexed it in 1843. The British claimed it was to prevent further bloodshed between voortrekkers and Africans; the Boers retorted that it was to rob them of their land once again. In disgust, many voortrekkers repacked their ox wagons and moved back inland where, they thought, they would be forever free of the hated British.

The voortrekkers consolidated their inland settlements into two small republics, the Transvaal (meaning on the far side of the Vaal River) and the Orange Free State. Here, the Boers were at home. The language, religion (Dutch Reformed), governmental institutions, and way of life were all theirs. The Boer republics lived in uneasy peace with the British in the Cape and Natal until diamonds and gold were discovered.

The Boer War

With the discovery of diamonds in 1870 and gold in 1886, Europeans and even some Americans poured into the Cape and Transvaal. There, on the Witwatersrand (literally, "white-water ridge"), gold was mined in such quantities that a new city, Johannesburg, was built atop the waste rock. It soon became South Africa's largest city—and it was mostly English-speaking.

For the Boers, it looked as if the English were pursuing them and destroying their way of life. By 1895, the English-speaking *uitlanders* ("outlanders" or foreigners) outnumbered the Boers more than two to one. The Transvaal government under Paul Kruger, worried that it would be swamped by uitlanders, made life difficult for them, denied them the vote, and ignored their petitions. Disenfranchising other groups became an Afrikaner tactic to preserve dominance.

Meanwhile, to the south in the Cape, the British were plotting to add the Transvaal and Orange Free State to the British Empire. Sir Cecil Rhodes, the Cape millionaire who set up the Rhodes scholarships to Oxford, wanted the mineral wealth of the Boer republics. He had already sent a column around the Boers to the north to found Rhodesia. Said Rhodes: "Expansion is everything." With him was the British high commissioner in the Cape, Alfred (later Lord) Milner, who wanted a British-ruled swath of Africa from Cairo to the Cape. Using the issue of uitlander rights in the Transvaal, Rhodes and Milner provoked Kruger into declaring war in 1899.

The Boers fought tenaciously. Good riders and marksmen—and equipped with modern arms from a sympathetic Germany—the Boers at first set the British reeling back and laid siege to British-held cities. Wrote Kipling: "We have had a jolly good lesson, and it serves us jolly well

GEOGRAPHY

BOUNDARIES IN AFRICA

The boundaries of Africa are especially artificial. Many of them were settled at a conference in Berlin in 1885, the great "carve-up" of Africa to suit the imperialists. Many African boundaries cut through tribes and force together unworkable combinations of tribes. A river in Africa is a poor border because typically people of the same tribe live on both sides of it.

In 1963, with most of Africa independent, the new Organization of African Unity decided, however, not to change the Berlin borders and even put them in its charter. The new leaders were both afraid of unleashing chaos and of losing their governing jobs. Best to leave these artificial borders alone, they figured. Notice how several of Africa's borders are straight lines, the sure sign that a border is artificial. In Africa, the imperialists' land grabs became permanent boundaries.

right." Ultimately, Britain needed 450,000 soldiers to subdue 88,000 Boer fighters, who were reduced to guerrilla bands. To isolate the Boer "commandos" from food and supplies, the British resorted to rounding up Boer families and placing them in "concentration camps." Typhoid broke out and some 26,000 died in the camps. Even today, every **Afrikaner** family has the memory of losing at least one relative in a camp; they never forgave the English and depict themselves as the century's first concentration-camp victims.

Finally, in 1902, the Boers capitulated and signed a treaty ending the war, but the British, guilty over the misery they had inflicted, failed to follow up on their victory. Instead of suppressing the defeated foe, they gave them full political rights, and, over time, the Afrikaners used their legal powers ultimately to take over all South Africa. After half a century, the Boers won.

From Defeat to Victory

The defeated Boer republics were made British crown colonies but were soon given internal self-government. In 1908, a National Convention met in Durban to draw up plans for making the four colonies one country, and, in 1910, the Union of South Africa was proclaimed. Politically, the English and the Afrikaners, as they now called themselves, managed to cooperate and even form parties that included members of both language groups. Some of South Africa's leading statesmen, such as the famed General Jan Christiaan Smuts, had earlier fought the British. A spirit of good feeling and forgiveness seemed to reign.

But many Afrikaners opposed the alliance: First, it tied them to British foreign policy because South Africa was now a British dominion, and most Afrikaners didn't wish to fight for Britain. When South Africa entered World War I, many Afrikaners rebelled rather than help take over the neighboring German colony of South-West Africa. In 1939 when parliament voted to enter World War II, an Afrikaner fascist movement, the *Ossewa-Brandwag* (ox wagon torch guard), sprang up to oppose South African help for a traditional enemy against a traditional friend.

Key Term

Afrikaners White South Africans of mostly Dutch descent, who speak *Afrikaans*.

SOUTH AFRICA'S POPULATION (IN MILLIONS)

South Africa's white population increases at a modest 1.7 percent a year (high compared to Europe). The nonwhite population, however, increases at Third World rates, 2.5 percent for Africans, 2.2 percent for Coloureds (mixed descent), and 2.1 percent for Asians (chiefly Indians). Every year, whites become a smaller minority. Take these figures with caution; they may have undercounted the Africans.

	1960	1998
Africans	12.0 (70%)	32.0 (78%)
Whites	3.1 (18%)	5.0 (11%)
Coloureds	1.5 (9%)	3.5 (8%)
Asians	.5 (3%)	1.0 (3%)

This sign on a bus for blacks in Soweto shows what is on white minds: a rapidly growing black population. (Michael Roskin)

Second, and of equal importance, the Afrikaners were economic underdogs to the English, who nearly monopolized industry and commerce. The Afrikaners were largely farmers, and when farm prices collapsed worldwide between the two wars, many Afrikaners were reduced to poverty. Afrikaners streamed to the cities looking for work. Jobs for poor whites became their rallying cry.

Their path to salvation was "ethnic mobilization," organizing themselves to promote Afrikaners in business and politics. They built cultural associations, insurance companies, schools and universities, and, above all, the National party. The National party was founded in 1914 for Afrikaners, but its moderate leaders believed in cooperation with the English. When the party split in 1934, the militant Daniel F. Malan remade the Nationalists into the party of Afrikaner power. Malan stood not only for white supremacy but for making sure every Afrikaner had a job, a pseudo-socialist component that survived for decades.

Key Term

apartheid Literally, "apartness"; a system of strict racial segregation in South Africa from 1948 to early 1990s.

Slowly, the Nationalists built their strength. A well-organized party, the Nationalists indoctrinated Afrikaners with the idea that anyone not supporting the party had broken the laager and betrayed his brothers. By 1948, they had sufficiently mobilized Afrikaners, who were and still are a majority of the country's whites, to win the general election. Now at last the country was restored to them. No longer would the British push them around. They proceeded to build precisely the system they wished, **apartheid**, which ended only in the early 1990s.

The Key Institutions

Key Term

African National Congress
South Africa's largest and
oldest party, formerly a
vehicle for black liberation.

System in Flux

Until recently, South African institutions were designed to keep blacks
powerless. Beginning with the release of Nelson Mandela from prison
in early 1990, however, breathtaking changes occurred that culminated in Mandela's election
as president in 1994. In 1993 and 1994, an advisory committee representing all the population
groups hammered out an interim constitution that went into effect with the first multiracial elections of 1994.

The new parliament completed a permanent constitution in 1996 that was basically the
same as the 1994 constitution. One interesting point: A two-thirds majority of the new South
African parliament is needed to modify the constitution, and the largest party, the **African National Congress (ANC)**, is just short of that. Accordingly, the ANC must debate and bargain
for constitutional changes with other parties, and that's good, for it helps build consensus and
a gradual approach to change.

From 1910 to 1984, South Africa had been structured along British lines—"the Westminster model"—with a prime minister chosen by an all-white parliament. When South Africa
broke away from the British Commonwealth in 1961 (it returned in 1994), it instituted a figurehead president as honorific head of state of the new Republic of South Africa (RSA).

A Quasi-Presidential System

No more. In 1990 South Africa switched from a parliamentary to a quasi-presidential system.
We say "quasi" (almost) because South Africa's president is elected not by the population directly but by the National Assembly, now for a maximum of two five-year terms. The president
may also be ousted by a parliamentary vote of no-confidence. This makes South Africa's "president" more like a prime minister. The president, however, still has a lot of power, and this gave
reform-minded Presidents P. W. Botha and F. W. de Klerk the ability to institute reforms without being blocked at every turn by a conservative majority in the whites-only House of Assembly. As de Gaulle concluded in France, a presidential system is more effective in instituting
changes. South Africa has three deputy presidents, black, white, and brown.

GEOGRAPHY

BOUND SOUTH AFRICA

South Africa is
bounded on the
north by Botswana
and Zimbabwe;
on the east by Mozambique and
Swaziland;
on the south by the Indian Ocean;

and on the west by the Atlantic
Ocean and Namibia.

Lesotho, a residue of British colonialism,
is totally surrounded by South Africa, a rare
situation.

DEMOCRACY

WHY DID APARTHEID END?

With supreme self-confidence, the National party built its apartheid system. But starting in the mid-1970s the Afrikaner regime started to lose its nerve, which gave democracy a chance. Some of the key dates:

- 1975—Portugal, after years of fighting, pulls out of its colonies of Angola and Mozambique, where black Communists sympathetic to the ANC take power. A South African military incursion into Angola is mauled by Cubans and pulls out.
- 1976—Young Africans riot in Soweto and cannot be quickly controlled. Some sneak out to join ANC guerrilla forces.
- 1978—P. W. Botha is elected prime minister and soon promises a "new dispensation." He does little but heighten expectations.
- 1980—White-ruled Rhodesia turns into black-ruled Zimbabwe, and South Africa loses the last buffer zone on its north.
- 1985—Major international banks start doubting South Africa's creditworthiness and refuse new loans, jolting the South African business community.

- late 1980s—Pretoria government concludes black homelands are economically inviable and require too many subsidies.
- 1989—Soviet power collapses, and the Cold War ends. The ANC loses its Soviet support, and the Pretoria regime loses its U.S. support. Both sides realize they no longer have outside backers.
- 1990—F. W. de Klerk is elected, frees Nelson Mandela, rolls back the apartheid system, and negotiates an end to white rule.

This transition to democracy was not forced on the white regime, which suffered no military defeats or serious threats and could have stayed in power years longer. It was chiefly the product of sufficient Nationalist leaders coming to realize that the longer they delayed, the worse would be the revolution. They could clearly see the trend: no more protective belt of white-ruled colonies to their north, no more U.S. interest in stopping communism in Africa, and a black population that grew bigger and angrier every year. The Afrikaners split into liberal and conservative wings, and the liberals won. What we have witnessed is a "negotiated revolution" based on the power of human reason.

South Africa's capital moves twice a year. The parliament buildings are in Cape Town rather than in Pretoria, the administrative capital. When the president comes to Cape Town to officially open a parliamentary session, the capital comes with him. This means that every year hundreds of ministers, bureaucrats, journalists, and diplomats decamp to Cape Town and then trek back to Pretoria when parliament is over.

In response to demands from many groups (Zulus, some whites), South Africa shifted from a unitary to a federal system. The old colonies (the Cape, Natal, the Transvaal, and the Orange Free State) had been the country's four provinces. In 1994 the country was divided into nine provinces, and the "black homelands" were abolished, ending the fiction of independent black republics. Each province now has its own legislature concerned with local affairs such as police, education, health services, highways, and fish and game; it also elects a premier for the province. The provinces, which depend mostly on Pretoria for their revenues, became money pits of mismanagement and corruption that require repeated federal bailouts.

A Bicameral Parliament

In 1984 the all-white South African regime instituted a curious parliament consisting of three houses: a big one for whites and two smaller ones for Coloureds and Indians. White supremacy was effectively preserved. Blacks, three-quarters of the population, got no representation on the theory that they were represented in their tribal homelands.

GEOGRAPHY

BOUND THE DEMOCRATIC REPUBLIC OF CONGO

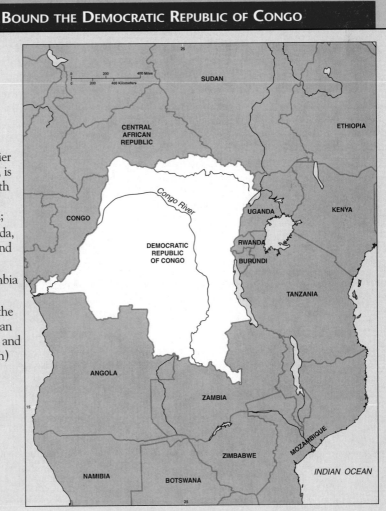

The Democratic Republic of Congo (formerly Zaire, earlier the Belgian Congo), is bounded on the north by Central African Republic and Sudan;

on the east by Uganda, Rwanda, Burundi, and Tanzania;

on the south by Zambia and Angola;

and on the west by the Atlantic, the Angolan exclave of Cabinda, and (the formerly French) Congo-Brazzaville.

For a man who spent twenty-seven years in prison for opposing apartheid, Nelson Mandela was extremely calm, showing no sign of hatred. He wanted to get on with building a prosperous and just South Africa where no one is penalized because of skin color, origin, or gender. He eschewed theories and focused on pragmatism and consensus-building.

Born into a chiefly clan of the Xhosa tribe in a village in the Eastern Cape in 1918, Mandela went to missionary boarding school and then to Fort Hare University, where he studied law (but got suspended for leading a student protest). His chiefly lineage showed in his calm self-confidence and ability to lead.

Mandela rejected an arranged marriage in his village in favor of the excitement of Johannesburg, where he opened his law practice and joined the African National Congress. Mandela learned to ignore ethnic differences and multiculturalism. "I no longer attach any value to any kind of ethnicity," he said.

With the Afrikaners building apartheid, Mandela and other young ANC members saw that mere petitions would get them nowhere. They organized a militant ANC Youth League and used it to take over the ANC leadership.

The 1960 Sharpeville massacre, where police gunned down sixty-nine peaceful protesters, persuaded the ANC leadership to turn to armed struggle. Mandela became founder and commander of a guerrilla group, *Umkhonto we Sizwe* (Spear of the Nation). The whites-only government banned the ANC and arrested ANC leaders. For plotting revolution, Mandela, then forty-four, was sentenced to life on Robben Island off Cape Town.

Prison did not break Mandela, and every year he grew more legendary, especially among young black South Africans. In 1982, Mandela was moved to comfortable quarters on the mainland and treated like a VIP. By 1986, the white regime knew it had to talk with Mandela, and secret meetings began.

Not long after F. W. de Klerk won election, in February 1990, he ordered Mandela released from prison. Here at last was a sign that major change was underway. In four laborious years of talks among all population groups, South Africa's first free and fair elections were held. Mandela, at age seventy-five, became president unopposed and by unanimous consent of the National Assembly. Even white conservatives knew there was no other possible choice. Mandela served only one term but set a standard of good sense and moderation.

In 1999 Mandela, then age eighty, was succeeded by his first deputy president, brainy Thabo Mbeki, then fifty-six, and like Mandela a Xhosa. Mbeki, a British-educated, multilingual economist, lived thirty years in exile. His father, a Communist, served decades in jail with Mandela. Mbeki's only son and a younger brother vanished, presumably killed by security forces. For a time, Mbeki was a socialist but more recently discovered markets. Mbeki did much of the daily work of governance while Mandela served as a calming and unifying symbolic figure.

What kind of a president will Mbeki make? A reserved person, he has none of Mandela's charisma but is a good backroom deal-maker. A no-nonsense administrator, he fired several incompetent officials. Mbeki demanded the opening of executive and managerial positions to blacks, a stronger version of U.S. affirmative action. Mbeki doesn't like rivals or criticism. Some see ruthlessness in Mbeki and the potential for a corrupt ANC dictatorship.

South Africa's President Thabo Mbeki (South African Embassy)

In general, parliaments with more than two chambers (Yugoslavia had a five-chambered legislature from 1963 to 1974) have been short-lived experiments. In the South African case, the tricameral parliament showed how desperate the Nats were getting.

The current parliament is fairly conventional: two houses, one representing population, the other provinces. As in Britain, elections must come every five years but can sometimes come sooner. The lower house, the National Assembly, consists of four hundred members elected by proportional representation but on two levels, one national, the other provincial. Two hundred are chosen from nationwide party lists, the other two hundred from the nine provinces with seats proportional to population. The large but arid and sparsely inhabited Northern Cape gets only four seats; the small but industrial and thickly settled Rand (now called Gauteng province) gets forty-four seats. Thus South Africa's new lower house represents the country as a whole as well as regional perspectives.

The upper house, the Council of Provinces, consists of ninety members, ten from each province, elected by provincial legislatures. The Council has less power than the lower chamber, the norm for all upper houses except the U.S. Senate. In 1994, voters also cast ballots for their provincial legislatures. Members of parliament are entitled to speak in any of South Africa's eleven official languages, but, mercifully, most use English, the country's **lingua franca**.

No population groups are directly represented. Zulus do not automatically get a certain number of seats; they are represented by being able to vote for whom they wish. In KwaZulu/Natal province, Zulus divide their votes between the Zulu-based Inkatha Freedom party and the African National Congress, both of whom run Zulu candidates locally. Tswanas, who live mostly in the Northwest province, generally vote for the ANC, whose local candidates tend to be Tswanas. The effort is to keep any one population group from identifying too closely with just one party, for that is the path of tribalism and civil conflict that has bedeviled much of Africa.

In 1999 the African National Congress again took most of these seats, 266 out of 400, but still short of the two-thirds needed to change the constitution. The ANC must earn the cooperation of other parties for such changes. This tends to inhibit the dictatorial and corrupting tendencies that arise when one party gains complete power. Early drafts of South Africa's electoral law contemplated a German-style 5-percent threshold, but numerous small groups protested, so the threshold was abolished. Theoretically, a party that wins as little as 0.25 percent could get a seat in parliament.

The Cabinet

The new South African cabinet has about twenty-seven ministers. Under the interim constitution, each party that won 5 percent of the popular vote was entitled to a share of cabinet ministers roughly proportional to its vote. Thus, in the national-unity government of 1994–96, the ANC, with 63 percent of the vote, got twelve ministries; the Nats, with 20 percent, got six; and Inkatha, with 10 percent, got three. This "consociational" (see box on page 461) provision was designed to make sure no major population group felt left out. This provision was dropped in the 1996 constitution.

The Parties

Theoretically, there are no longer "black" parties and "white" parties in South Africa. All citizens over eighteen years of age receive common ballots and may, in the secrecy of the voting booth, mark an X by whichever party they wish. Each party is identified on the ballot by name, symbol, and photo of its leader to help illiterates vote. Further, it is highly desirable in a democracy that some voters cross the color line and vote for parties not closely related to their own group. Most South African blacks, however, vote for black parties, and most nonblacks vote for traditionally white parties.

DEMOCRACY

HOW TO REFORM AN UNJUST SYSTEM

Since 1985 the South African government has repealed or liberalized almost all of the more than 350 apartheid laws. Some of these laws went back to 1913, but the Nationalists, starting in 1949, introduced far more specific, detailed legislation to keep blacks assigned to separate and inferior lands, housing, jobs, education, buses, beaches, rest rooms, and, ultimately, countries. The culmination of apartheid, in the Bantu Homelands Citizenship Act of 1970, was to make all Africans citizens of their tribal homelands and deprive them of South African citizenship. In all this, black South Africans had not one word of input, and protest was illegal.

The crux of apartheid was "influx control," keeping blacks from flocking to the cities. As we considered in Brazil, flight from the poor countryside to better opportunities in the cities is universal in the Third World. The white regime in South Africa tried to fight this by an elaborate system of passbooks that had to be carried by all blacks; these had to be officially "endorsed" to live in an urban area. Only long-term black residents and people with guaranteed jobs were entitled to remain; others could be "endorsed out" to some impoverished homeland with the thump of a police stamp. The single things blacks hated most were the passbooks, accompanied by the policeman's gruff demand, "Where's your pass, boy?"

P. W. Botha came to power in 1978 and spoke of a "new dispensation" that would give blacks a better deal. Just two years before, Soweto had erupted. "Apartheid is dead,"

proclaimed his government. A positive, almost joyous feeling began to emerge that major reforms would make South Africa a just and happy land. But the reforms came too little and too late. Fearful of backlash from white voters, Botha hesitated for years.

In 1985, the Immorality and Mixed Marriages Acts, prohibiting contact across the color line, were repealed. In 1986, the pass laws, influx controls, and citizenship laws were reformed to make it easier for blacks to live in cities and obtain citizenship in their own country. Some of the reforms were word games that left the system intact. Influx control became "orderly urbanization"; passbooks became "identity documents"; apartheid became "separate development." Blacks, now sensing they had the regime on the defensive, became angrier than ever. Halfway reforms can be worse than no reforms.

President de Klerk picked up in 1990 where Botha had chickened out. De Klerk's reforms went much further and faster than Botha's. For example, in 1990 and 1991 de Klerk had parliament repeal the segregationist Separate Amenities Act, Group Areas Act, Land Acts, and Population Registration Act, virtually ending the legal basis of apartheid.

Notice how the zig-zag of South Africa's reforms resemble those of Gorbachev in the Soviet Union. In both cases, leaders knew the system had to change but were terrified of losing power and unleashing chaos, so they alternated between promises and stalling. When an unjust, inefficient system is over-ripe for reform, hesitation can push the structure toward collapse.

A CONSTITUTIONAL COURT FOR SOUTH AFRICA

A first for South Africa (and rare worldwide), the constitution set up a Constitutional Court whose eleven members are appointed for seven-year terms by the president after consultation with political parties, current members of the court, and a judicial review commission. Theoretically above the political fray, like the U.S. and German high courts, South Africa's Constitutional Court interprets the constitution and settles disputes between levels of government. Included in the new constitution are U.S.-style guarantees of freedom of speech and assembly, equality of race and gender, and rights to hold property, join a union and strike, and receive a fair trial. The death penalty, amply applied by the old regime, is effectively banned.

Although it proceeds on the basis of cases brought before it, South Africa has moved away from the Common Law, which is what gives enormous power to the U.S. Supreme Court. Instead of the power of precedent, which is the heart of the Common Law, South Africa uses old Dutch-Roman law, based more on codes and statutes and less on precedent. Accordingly, the powers of South Africa's Constitutional Court may be less sweeping than those of the U.S. Supreme Court.

In 1990 black political parties were legalized in South Africa. They had existed over the decades, either labeled as cultural associations or underground and in exile. The oldest and most important black party is the African National Congress, not to be confused with the Afrikaners' National party ("the Nats"). The ANC was founded in 1912 by Africans educated in missionary schools. The ANC still likes to call itself "the world's oldest liberation movement." For half a century the ANC practiced nonviolent protest; its leader during the 1950s, the great and gentle Chief Albert Luthuli, won the 1961 Nobel Peace Prize. He was, nonetheless, banished to a remote village. The ANC was banned in 1960 and, as the regime brutally implemented its apartheid structure, came to the conclusion that violence was necessary to communicate its message. In 1964, the ANC's leaders were convicted of plotting revolution and sentenced to life imprisonment.

But the ANC did not die. Operating in exile, it gave young blacks weapons training (with Soviet-bloc help) and had them infiltrate the Republic for sabotage and attacks on police stations. Its leader, Nelson Mandela, grew more legendary with every year he spent in prison. When he was released, along with many other black leaders in 1990, mass rejoicing broke out. "He is the symbol of our struggle," said a black high-school student. "To me, he is like Jesus Christ." As expected, the ANC won the 1994 and 1999 national elections.

The ANC's leadership is heavily Xhosa, but it defines itself as a multiracial party, and some of its leaders were white (e.g., the late Joe Slovo, a Communist). Decades ago, the tiny South African Communist party (SACP) joined the ANC and came to be well represented in its leadership. In 1994 and 1999, the SACP did not run a separate slate but stayed under the wing of the ANC. Slovo (now deceased) became minister of housing and welfare. In 1992, five parliamentarians from the liberal white Democratic party moved to the ANC. Whites in the ANC, although few in number, do two things: They help educate ANC members away from revolution and toward liberalism, and they help calm white fears that the ANC is extremist and out for revenge against whites. A few percent of South Africa's whites vote for the ANC.

To the left of the ANC, the smaller Pan-Africanist Congress (PAC) originally was radical and violent. PAC broke away from the ANC in 1958 over the question of building a black society as opposed to a multiracial one. PAC's chilling slogan until 1994: "One settler, one bullet." It was PAC militants who slashed to death American Fulbright student Amy Biehl in 1993, not knowing or caring that she was proliferation. PAC did poorly in 1994 and 1999. Since then, PAC has moderated under the leadership of a Methodist bishop but still seeks return of lands taken by settlers generations ago. The even smaller Azanian People's Organization (AZAPO), wins almost no seats.

Meanwhile, to the right of the ANC, the Zulu-based Inkatha turned from a "cultural movement" founded in 1975 to the Inkatha Freedom party in 1990. The IFP, anti-Communist,

1999: A Proportional Representation System in Action

In 1999, South Africa stayed with its proportional representation system, which had been introduced in its first nonracial elections in 1994. Each South African voter casts two ballots, one for a national party list, the other for a provincial party list. Of the four hundred seats of the lower house—the National Assembly—two hundred are proportional to votes from the national list, and two hundred are proportional to votes from the provincial lists, which are also used to elect provincial legislators (who in turn choose senators).

As expected, the ANC again won nationwide to totally dominate parliament, but it fell one seat short of the two-thirds necessary to amend the constitution. Some breathed a sigh of relief. The big losers were the Nats, now renamed the New National party, who slumped from second place with eighty-two seats to twenty-eight. The new official opposition is the Democratic party, which tries to be multiracial but is heavily white. With only thirty-eight seats, it can do little to block the ANC.

South Africa's PR system, like all PR systems, fragmented the parliament into several parties, and that is just what South Africa needs. A single-member system exaggerates the rewards to the largest party, and in South Africa's case would have given parliament to the ANC with the ability to amend the constitution. From there it is but a few easy steps to rebellion by minority groups who feel they've been disenfranchised and then to dictatorship by the leading party. PR, especially with South Africa's extremely low minimum of 0.25 percent, makes sure all important groups win seats, and this can have a calming effect. The white separatists of the Freedom Front, who shrank from nine seats in 1994 to three in 1999, and the Zulu chauvinists of Inkatha, who dropped from forty-three seats to thirty-four, dislike the ANC majority, but they must ask themselves if they get a better deal by being in parliament or by leaving. (Correct answer: Stay in.) In this way, the fragmenting tendencies of PR paradoxically help South Africa hang together.

	Percent of Vote	Lower House Seats
ANC	65.7	266
Democrats	10.2	38
Inkatha	8.0	34
New Nationalists	7.5	28
United Democratic Movement	3.4	14
Freedom Front	0.8	3
others	17.0	

HOME FOR FOUR MILLION PEOPLE?

KwaZulu (meaning the "place of the Zulus") was supposed to be home to nearly half of the 8 million Zulus. Broken into twenty-nine fragments and overpopulated, there is no way it could have survived unless many of its people worked outside the homeland, and white industry set up facilities to take advantage of the plentiful, cheap labor. It is now part of KwaZulu/Natal province.

KwaZulu. (Michael Roskin)

pro-self-determination, and procapitalist, is well-organized and has a territorial base in KwaZulu, where IFP and ANC adherents murdered an estimated 12,000 of each other in virtual civil war. In voting, IFP controls the countryside of KwaZulu/Natal while the ANC controls its urban areas. Inkatha leader Mangosuthu Buthelezi, a Zulu chief, jealously guards his provincial power base. Inkatha attracts few non-Zulu Africans, and radical blacks despise Buthelezi as a sellout and Zulu fascist. Some Natal whites support and even belong to the IFP as protection against the danger of the ANC turning South Africa into a one-party state.

The National party dominated South Africa from 1948 to 1994. Originally a purely Afrikaner party, it crafted most of the institutions of apartheid. In the 1990s, F. W. de Klerk totally transformed the Nats by turning to a program of serious reform and welcoming all voters into National ranks. In short order, many English-speakers, Coloureds, and Indians concluded the Nats were their best ticket to survival. The Nats in 1994 became the leading nonblack party. Renaming itself the New National party, it shrunk greatly from 1994 to 1999.

Much of the white vote in 1999 went to the Democratic party, which was formed in 1989 from the old Progressive Federal party. A classic liberal party—free society, free economy—its votes are in English-speaking cities such as Johannesburg, Cape Town, and Durban. Much earlier than the Nats, the Democrats worked to dismantle apartheid and share power with blacks, Coloureds, and Indians. The Democrats now keep the ANC government on its toes by calling attention to corruption.

In protest at rolling back the apartheid system, in 1982 the right wing of the National party walked out to form a new Conservative party that ran well in the farming districts where the Nats used to hold sway. In the elections of 1994 and 1999 much of this electorate joined the Freedom Front, which sometimes talked about withdrawing to form a separate whites-only state. Further right, the small Afrikaner Resistance Movement (AWB), which used to wave Nazilike flags and vowed violence to preserve white power, did not run in 1994 or 1999 and has all but disappeared.

Is there no party that seriously brings together black and white? In 1997 the United Democratic Movement was formed to do that, but it enjoyed little success in the 1999 election.
The symbolism was good: Its leaders were former ANC and Nat officials, Bantu Holomisa and
Roelf Meyer, respectively. And its issues were good: Fight crime and unemployment, all within a framework of "national moral regeneration." But the UDM lacked a significant tribal base,
the foundation of most of Africa's parties. The ANC, however, smelling competition, lashed out
angrily at the UDM, several of whose officials were gunned down.

Farewell to the Homelands

One aim of apartheid, or separate development, was to make Africans citizens only of their
homelands and not of South Africa. This policy permitted South Africa to treat blacks as temporary workers in the Republic without voting or residency rights. Some of the homelands were
native reserves left after the Kaffir Wars of the last century. (Americans would call them Indian reservations.) Policy was gradually to turn the territorially fragmented black areas into homelands and then into "independent republics," one for each tribe.

These ten homelands, supposedly home to all of South Africa's black population, accounted
for only 13 percent of RSA territory. Half of Africans did not live in the homelands but in the
cities and on white farms. Many had never seen their homeland and didn't want to. The law
let authorities forcibly send Africans to their homelands if they were not needed in an urban
area or formed a "black spot" in a farming area designated for whites. Some 3.5 million were thus
"resettled" on hopeless, overcrowded, marginal lands. Even with large RSA subsidies, the homelands stayed terribly poor.

Four homelands, under pliant, hand-picked leadership, opted for nominal independence:
Transkei in 1976, Bophuthatswana in 1977, Venda in 1979, and Ciskei in 1981. Aside from
South Africa, no country granted them diplomatic recognition. Other homeland leaders, following the lead of KwaZulu chief minister Buthelezi, rejected independence as a sham designed
to deprive Africans of their national birthrights. In 1994, in time for elections, all the homelands were legally merged back into the RSA; in reality, they had never left.

South African Political Culture

The Africans

There is some truth to the view that the Africans are still tribal in outlook. Voting is heavily on
tribal lines: Xhosas go ANC, Zulus IFP. Chiefs are still strong; they settle disputes and can deliver much of the rural vote. When asked their nationality in a 1994 survey, 63 percent of South
African blacks named their tribe; only 16 percent said South African. But for the many millions—about one-third of all Africans—who reside in urban areas to work in mines, factories,
homes, or offices, this is changing. Here, under modern economic conditions, Africans from many
tribes integrated with Africans from other tribes and see themselves as Africans suffering a common fate in addition to their continuing identity as Xhosas, Tswanas, or others. The Zulus—
the largest group of Africans—see themselves as a superior, warrior race and tend to go their own
way. Murderous fighting, helped along by the white police of the old regime, has broken out between Zulus and members of other tribes.

GEOGRAPHY

BOUND KENYA

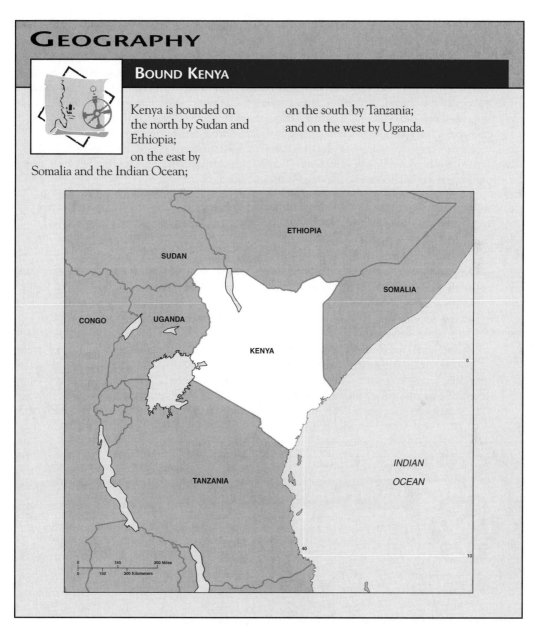

Kenya is bounded on the north by Sudan and Ethiopia; on the east by Somalia and the Indian Ocean; on the south by Tanzania; and on the west by Uganda.

It is white industry that helped break down tribalism and integrate Africans into a whole. During World War II, South African industry mushroomed, and the ensuing labor shortage led to a major black influx into the cities and factories. (Their squatter towns alarmed whites into voting for the Nats in 1948). Rapid black urbanization produced greater African education, sophistication, and integration. In the mines, for example, work teams composed of only one tribe were prone to fight teams of other tribes. When the work crews were integrated, the fighting stopped. The mining companies even invented a synthetic work language so men from different tribes could communicate. Many urban blacks (including Thabo Mbeki) are fluent in several African languages and generally get along with people from other tribes. Most also speak English, although they were long reluctant to learn Afrikaans, "the language of the oppressor."

Are all Africans revolutionaries? Far from it. African political opinion spans the range from mild, even conservative, to violent and radical. Older Africans especially tend to think in terms of specific problems: the long commute from the black township, decent housing, making ends meet, and so on. Some black South African religions teach submission to authority. A number of young black South Africans, especially in urban areas, are, however, radicalized. They want and expect speedy change. It was, in fact, high-school students who led the massive 1976 Soweto riots—triggered by a government order to teach Afrikaans in school—that left some seven hundred dead. Thousands of young blacks then sneaked out of the country to join the ANC. Decades of school boycotts subsequently left a generation of black youths uneducated.

The Afrikaners

Over the nineteenth century, the Boers began to think of themselves as Afrikaners rather than Dutch, German, or French. Their language, Afrikaans, had evolved from the original Dutch. No longer citizens of the Netherlands, they felt Holland had turned its back on them. They had become Africa's white tribe, *die volk* (the people), as they called themselves.

And Afrikaner attitudes are indeed tribal. Until recently, they frowned on marriage to English-speakers. Like tribes throughout Africa, they did not like to share power with other tribes. A dour people, Afrikaners take pride in their steadfastness, religiosity, strength, and determination. Until recently, most were convinced they were right and were rarely willing to compromise or admit they might be wrong. They are not, however, arrogant or elitist; among themselves they are quite democratic. Toward foreigners they are friendly if somewhat reserved.

POLITICAL CULTURE

FROM EUPHORIA TO DYSPHORIA

Great was the outpouring of joy and emotion at the election of South Africa's first African (or, more precisely, nonracial) government in 1994. Africans stood in line hours and even days to cast their first ballot, mostly for the ANC. All things seemed possible. Soon, many believed, Africans would enjoy improved living standards, education, and employment. They were euphoric.

But little improved; much of the change was superficial. Crime and corruption grew. Wealth seemed to stay mostly in white hands.

Elected leaders tried to explain there were no funds to fix everything immediately. It would take time and patient building up of the economy. Many Africans felt let down and lapsed into dysphoria, the opposite of euphoria.

In actuality, South Africans were passing through the standard psychological stages that accompany most revolutions. The ouster of a bad or repressive regime almost always brings euphoria. Soon, however, reality settles in. Life, amid scarcities and economic disruption, often gets worse. Now comes dysphoria, the letdown after the euphoric high. We will see parallel attitudes in Iran.

POLITICAL CULTURE

A LOST GENERATION OF AFRICAN YOUTH

From the Soweto riots of 1976 until the ANC electoral victory of 1994, a large portion of urban African youth dropped out of school and sought no employment. Instead, they busied themselves with revolutionary protests. Many wore ANC or PAC insignia and T-shirts, gave clenched-fist salutes, and called each other "comrade." They enforced rent-boycott programs and gave suspected police spies (and there were many) a grisly death: a "necklace" of a burning car tire around their head. And many just hung out and did little.

What to do with them now? Observers see them as a lost generation that is increasingly bitter that life has passed them by. Many have neither education nor skills. Upon release from prison, Nelson Mandela urged African youths to return to school. Unless integrated into the new South Africa, these urban Africans, many of them no longer "youths," are a potential disruptive and destabilizing force that could wreck the new democracy.

Afrikaners treat blacks firmly but (they think) fairly; on a personal level they may esteem individual blacks but are convinced blacks need white supervision. Although they no longer say so publicly, they see blacks as behind whites in civilization, work habits, and level of organization. Because blacks are still largely tribal, Afrikaners supposed until recently that they must not be accorded political equality with whites. Blacks are still, the Afrikaner believed, happiest with their own people; that's why the homelands struck Afrikaners as a plausible solution.

Afrikaner views of English-speaking whites have softened since the end of apartheid. They used to consider English liberals hypocrites and cowards who saw blacks exactly the way Afrikaners did but lacked the guts to say so. One important factor eluded outside critics of South Africa: The Afrikaners never saw themselves as oppressors but rather as the aggrieved party, the hurt victims of historical injustice at the hands of the British. Afrikaners expected ethnic solidarity from their fellow Afrikaners. An Afrikaner who criticized apartheid broke the laager, the voortrekkers' ring of ox wagons, and thus betrayed die volk. Actually, Afrikaners were never monolithic in their views. Some, such as novelist André Brink, Reverend Beyers Naude, and Afrikaner members of the Democrats were among the regime's severest critics. With de Klerk's takeover of the National party and the country's presidency in 1989, the Nats and many Afrikaners shifted to a reformist position that in five years led to the Mandela presidency. Hardline Afrikaners joined more conservative parties.

The English-Speakers

English-speaking people constitute about 40 percent of South Africa's whites. In terms of ethnic origin, English-speakers can be Greek, Irish, Italian, Jewish, Portuguese, German, or even Dutch. As in Canada, most new immigrants elect to learn English. Sometimes referred to as "the English" for short, they are a diverse group who clustered around the original British colonials.

The English, after winning the Boer War, walked away from politics, preferring business instead. As a result, they lost most political power but they continue to dominate commerce and

POLITICAL CULTURE

DO AFRIKANERS CHANGE?

Not long ago the conventional wisdom was that Afrikaner attitudes were set in concrete, that they had always been white supremacists and always would be. The common supposition that racial superiority was part of the Dutch Reformed faith of Afrikaners erred by looking at too narrow a time period. Afrikaner historian Hermann Giliomee examined the historical record and found that, over the centuries, Afrikaner thought on race changed quite a lot to accommodate new situations. Whatever seemed the way for Boers and later Afrikaners to survive soon turned into their religious and social teachings.

Accordingly, Giliomee suggested in the 1970s, Afrikaners were capable of adapting to the new situation of black political participation and were already beginning to change. Giliomee was right. Even at the time, one of the foundations of the Afrikaner community, the Dutch Reformed Church ("the National party at prayer," as it was called), was rethinking the church's position on race and finding racial inequality inherently unchristian. This shift in attitude enabled many Afrikaners to accept and even support the new political system. For example, in 1994 Wilhelm Verwoerd, grandson of Hendrik Verwoerd, chief architect of apartheid, campaigned for the ANC, and his wife, Melanie, was elected as an ANC member of parliament! These people do know how to survive.

industry. The rural Afrikaners discovered capitalism relatively recently; the urban English were capitalists from the start. This gave them a more liberal outlook: Let economics and market forces take care of social problems, rather than imposing numerous controls and regulations as the Nationalists have done. The English never formed an exclusively "English party" but were happy to join with Afrikaners in fusion parties, such as the old South Africa and United parties, which were usually Afrikaner-led.

The Afrikaners' scorn for English liberals was at least partly justified. Few protested as the Nationalists built the apartheid system, and many English-speaking business persons benefited from the cheap, controlled labor supply it produced. English liberals questioned the form but not the substance of apartheid. With the Nats' move to reform, many English switched to them. The English are more likely than the Afrikaners to voice their fears openly. Some wonder if South Africa is a safe place for their children; some ask visitors about jobs in other countries. Every year, several thousand quietly emigrate. (Favorite destination: Australia.) Some secretly retain British passports for a possible speedy escape.

Indians and Coloureds

Perhaps the saddest, most worried South Africans are neither the whites nor the blacks but the Indians and Coloureds. They are neither in the economically privileged position of whites nor in the numerical superiority with blacks. They are the middlemen, squeezed between forces they can't control. Held to an inferior status by whites, they are not particularly liked by blacks.

There is little feeling of solidarity between the Coloureds, most of whom live in the Cape, and the Indians, most of whom live in Natal. The Coloureds, who once had the vote in the Cape, became more politically restless and resentful. Sometimes counted as a subgroup among the Coloureds are the Cape's "Malays," descended largely from Indonesians the Dutch brought over who still practice Islam (some fiercely). The Indians—some Hindu, some Muslim—inched their way up from indentured sugar-cane workers to prosperous merchants. They are more inclined to leave national politics alone and settle for self-governance within the Indian community. The Indians brought with them a strong sense of identity and culture from their native country. The Coloureds have identity and culture problems: Most speak Afrikaans and wanted to be the little brown *baas* (Afrikaans for boss) but were rejected by the apartheid system.

What then happened is both amazing and logical. Many Coloureds and Indians went to the Nats, the party that had made them victims along with the black majority. As the 1994 election neared, Indians and Coloureds grew worried that black radicals would seize their property; some received threats. Quickly, they perceived their interests were with the party that might give them some protection, the Nats, who welcomed their votes. In 1999, many of them stayed with the New Nats. The two top leaders of the Western Cape, which includes Cape Town, are Coloured and New Nats.

Patterns of Interaction

Politics within the ANC

The African National Congress is a broad "catchall" party (see page 213), including everything from black-power extremists, militant trade-unionists, moderate Africans, black entrepreneurs, conciliatory persons, and Communists of every hue. So far, the ANC has hung together amazingly well. With Nelson Mandela as its head, it had one of the most attractive and charismatic figures of all Africa.

The ANC, to a considerable extent, is required to be two-faced. To its black voters it must promise jobs, housing, and education rapidly, no matter what the cost to whites. Moderate as it tries to be, the demands of Africans are so urgent that if the ANC delays, it risks losing its black supporters either to more radical movements—such as Winnie Mandela (divorced second wife of Nelson) and her militant wing of the ANC or the PAC—or to apathy and nonvoting.

The other face of the ANC, required under the circumstances, is to calm and reassure whites, especially white capitalists, who are their only hope for making the economy grow rapidly. Many ANC leaders understand the weaknesses of socialism and strengths of capitalism. They meet with white capitalists and favor a vigorous private sector in South Africa. But if they go for the economic rationality of free markets and private enterprise, they make white capitalists a little richer and move the ANC away from the urgent needs of black masses. What's good economics is sometimes bad politics.

One classic way to retain the loyalty of party activists is to hire them: **patronage**. The Nats over the decades of *apartheid* created bureaucratic monstrosities and gave Afrikaners a lock on civil-service jobs. Now the ANC is keeping the bureaucracies but bumping out the Afrikaners in favor of ANC loyalists. The South African government estimates that it has 54,000 unneeded civil servants on the public payroll. This sort of cronyism hurts in three ways: It leads to corruption; it builds an undemocratic party-state; and it builds a large class of civil servants with a strong incentive to block change.

Key Term

patronage   Using political office to hire supporters.

KEY CONCEPTS

CROSS-CUTTING CLEAVAGES

One of the puzzles of highly pluralistic or multiethnic societies is why they hold together. Why don't they all break down into civil strife? One explanation, offered by the German sociologist Georg Simmel early in the twentieth century, is that successful pluralistic societies develop **cross-cutting cleavages**. They are divided, of course, but they are divided along several axes, not just one. When these divisions, or cleavages, cut across one another, they actually stabilize political life.

In Switzerland, for example, the cleavages of French-speaking or German-speaking, Catholic or Protestant, and working class or middle class give rise to eight possible combinations (for example, German-speaking, Protestant, middle class). But any one of these eight combinations will have at least one attribute in common with the other seven (for example, French-speaking,

Protestant, working class). Therefore, the theory goes, Swiss always have some kindred feelings with other groups.

Where cleavages do not cross-cut but instead are **cumulative**, dangerous divisions grow. A horrible case is ex-Yugoslavia, where all Croats are Catholic and all Serbs are Eastern Orthodox. The one cross-cutting cleavage that might have helped hold the country together—working class versus middle class—had been outlawed by the Communists. The several nationalities of Yugoslavia had little in common.

Many of Africa's troubles stem from an absence of cross-cutting cleavages. Tribe counts for everything, and religious or social class differences do not cut across tribal lines. It will take both skill and luck for South Africa to build cleavages that cut across the color line. A few appear in voting, such as the Coloureds who went for the previously white parties and the white intellectuals who voted ANC.

The ANC and the Whites

The ANC leadership now has plenty of contact with the great economic engines of South Africa, such as the Anglo-American Corporation (which recently moved its headquarters to London). The dialogue goes both ways. The capitalists explain investment and growth to the former ANC radicals, and the ANC explains to the capitalists that if they wish to retain wealth and position in the new South Africa they will have to quickly deliver new jobs and mass economic improvement and promote blacks to the executive level. Otherwise, black discontent will give rise to radical politicians who preach nationalization of private industry and redistribution of wealth. This, of course, would lead to massive white flight and the impoverishment of South Africa. The ANC tries to persuade white capitalists to invest for rapid economic growth, putting jobs for blacks ahead of immediate profit. This will not be easy, as capitalists are by nature careful investors who aim precisely for profit.

Key Terms

cross-cutting cleavages Multiple splits in society that make group loyalties overlap.
cumulative Reinforcing one another.

Paradoxically, it is the richer, English-speaking white liberals of the Democratic party that are more likely to understand and accept this argument. As professionals and executives, they have little worry about their economic and social status. Much of the white working class, however, has to pay the price of rapid improvement for Africans. Working-class whites are being leveled downward. The "color bar" that kept blacks out of their jobs is over, their taxes rise, and government jobs (including schoolteachers) now go to Africans. The white resentment these shifts engender comes automatically with a regime dedicated to making blacks equal.

Initially, the Nats tried to cooperate with the ANC in the 1994–96 coalition, but it was strained from the outset. Mandela and de Klerk angrily blamed each other for South Africa's difficulties. In mid-1996 de Klerk (who was also second deputy president) and his Nats pulled out of the government. White confidence in the government declined.

The ANC versus Inkatha

The bloodiest interaction in South Africa was not black against white but black against black, namely the turf war between the ANC and the Inkatha Freedom party in its stronghold of KwaZulu/Natal. Inkatha staked out a claim to represent gradual, moderate change but engaged in a great deal of violence, mostly against ANC members. Outside of KwaZulu/Natal, the struggle was between Zulus and non-Zulu Africans. In the Rand townships, where Zulus live mostly in single-men's hostels, white authorities had long encouraged them to crush protest movements and break strikes. The authorities played to the Zulus' sense of warrior superiority over other tribes and pointed out that disturbances meant lost wages. Accordingly, in the

---

KEY CONCEPTS

CONSOCIATIONAL DEMOCRACY

Another explanation of why pluralistic democracies hold together focuses less on the social level (see box on "Cross-Cutting Cleavages" on page 460) and more on the political level. University of California at San Diego political scientist Arend Lijphart finds certain deeply divided countries can work if the elites of the several groups share executive power. This is quite different from conventional "majoritarian" democracy, where the majority rules. If there is too big a gap between the majority and minorities, civil strife may result. The majority thinks it can get its way, and minorities feel no need to obey.

Clever political leaders may calm such situations by making sure all important groups have a share not only of seats in parliament but of executive power as well. In a consociational democracy, the elites of each major group have struck a bargain to share power and restrain their followers from violence. Every group gets something; no one group gets everything.

Lijphart's chief example of **consociation** is his native Netherlands; he thinks it suitable for South Africa, where a straight majoritarian system would invite minority rebellion. Notice the consociational element in the 1994–96 interim constitution: Parties got one ministry in the cabinet for every 5 percent of the vote they won. Thus the Nats (representing whites, Coloureds, and Indians) got four portfolios, and Inkatha (representing Zulus, the largest tribe) got two. The 1996 constitution abandoned this consociational concept for a majoritarian one. But de facto consociation continued with Inkatha leader Buthelezi serving as home affairs minister in Mandela's and Mbeki's cabinets along with two deputy ministers from Inkatha. The appointments helped hold down ANC-Inkatha violence, exactly what consociation is supposed to do.

Key Term

divide and rule   Roman
and British imperial ruling
method of setting subjects
against each other.

townships the Zulus became extralegal enforcers of the status quo. Furthermore, the police, practicing the ancient tactic of **divide and rule**, quietly armed, funded, and sided with Inkatha.

In Natal, the Zulu home area, things are even worse. As noted, Buthelezi built up a power base in the Inkatha movement, which was never outlawed. Membership was to some degree coerced, and rival movements were not tolerated. Not all Africans in Natal are Zulus, however, and not all Zulus wish to join a Zulu nationalist movement. In the 1980s, many joined the ANC. Sensing ANC encroachment on its turf, Inkatha reacted violently, slaughtering any blacks suspected of ANC sympathy. ANC supporters defended themselves, leading to virtual civil war in Natal. Thousands were slain for political reasons, mostly in Natal, many by clubs and spears. At a somewhat lower level, the killing continues.

The real horror here is that violence got worse as the white regime eased its controls. The big increase in violence came after Nelson Mandela was released from prison and the ANC was unbanned in 1990. When all black politics were suppressed, there was relative calm, at least on the surface. With the legalization of black political parties in 1990, an immoderate struggle for turf and predominance broke out. Major reforms by themselves do not prevent bloodshed. Chief Buthelezi had no intention of giving up his power to Mandela (who is also of chiefly lineage, as a Xhosa, a tribe which has long fought the Zulus). Is this a political struggle or a tribal struggle? It is both, for in Africa, all politics is tribal.

A parallel with the ANC-Inkatha violence is that visited upon the small, new interracial party, the United Democratic Movement. The ANC views the UDM officials as scoundrels who were thrown out of the ANC and now serve reactionary white interests by dividing the black community. Although no one has taken responsibility, clearly the gunmen who assassinate UDM figures work for the ANC. The ANC, like most African parties, lashes out when it sees encroachments on its turf.

DEMOCRACY

SOUTH AFRICA'S BLOODSHED

Black-on-black violence causes some South African whites to smirk: "You see, we told you liberal foreigners that apartheid was the only workable system. Thought it was so easy, did you? Just abolish the old system and everything will be fine, eh? This bloodshed is your fault." This charge should make some critics of old South Africa think things over. To what extent did well-intentioned liberals naively underestimate the difficulty of achieving freedom and democracy?

The ultimate finding of fault has to carefully consider the steps—or nonsteps—the white government took in preparing black South Africans for political participation. Democracy needs an educated population. Why was black education so inferior? Democracy needs a substantial middle class. Why did apartheid all but prohibit black entrepreneurship? Democracy requires "cross-cutting cleavages," whereby members of different groups have some things in common. Why did apartheid prohibit contacts across the color line? Yes, there is black-on-black violence, but much of it could have been avoided if the white regime had, starting decades ago, begun preparing its black majority for full citizenship.

GEOGRAPHY

BOUND NIGER

Niger (a former French colony not to be confused with Nigeria) is bounded on the north by Algeria and Libya; on the east by Chad; on the south by Nigeria (a former British colony) and Benin; and on the west by Burkina Faso (formerly Upper Volta) and Mali.

A Dominant-Party System?

South Africa's party system looks like bad news for several reasons. First, the ANC with its big majority does not alternate in power. It seems likely to win elections well into the future, maybe forever. Even if all the other parties merged (an impossibility) they would still form a minority.

Second, in South Africa, we need not only a left-to-right axis but a black and nonblack one as well. In a rough schematic, the South African party system looks like this figure:

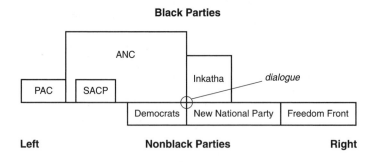

The areas where black and nonblack parties touch—where the ANC and Inkatha and the Democrats and New Nats intersect—enables them to dialogue although not necessarily agree. This area is crucial to South Africa's political stability. If the two predominantly black parties and the two predominantly white parties can continue their dialogue, we may yet see a free and democratic South Africa. If not, we may see bloodshed, white flight, and a black dictatorship.

Third, no party links Africans and nonblacks in a serious way. Fourth, the black political spectrum is further left than the nonblack spectrum, making policy consensus difficult. Fifth, the ruling ANC faces **bilateral opposition**, with forces tugging it left and right. The ANC has Inkatha on its right and PAC on its left. The small Communist party, not the most-left element working within the ANC, is actually rather moderate in its views. Faced with either being pulled apart or into immobilism, African party leaders tend to opt for strengthening and centralizing their power, eventually becoming dictatorial. Thabo Mbeki could go this route, and South Africa could become a dominant-party system, where the ANC holds perpetual sway.

Key Term

bilateral opposition
Centrist parties or governments being undermined from both sides.

NEW PLAYER: COSATU

In 1985, black South African unionists merged thirty-four black labor unions into an umbrella organization called the Congress of South African Trade Unions, COSATU. With some 1.8 million members, COSATU works for higher wages, better conditions, and an end to all vestiges of South Africa's segregated system. Long a front for the ANC, COSATU runs on a joint ANC-SACP-COSATU alignment. COSATU leaders serve in ANC and cabinet positions.

COSATU's biggest component is the National Union of Mineworkers, which claims a membership of a quarter of a million and has greatly boosted miners' pay. The trouble is, with the world price of gold now low, many mines are losing money and laying off workers.

COSATU General Secretary Sam Shilowa likes to quote Lenin and dislikes privatization of state-owned enterprises. COSATU is in a Latin American situation of a pampered government-related union speaking for a comparatively well-off black working class, blocking change rather than demanding it. With COSATU keeping wages too high, there are no new jobs for the millions of black unemployed, and foreign investment looks elsewhere.

President Nelson Mandela attempted to preserve good relations with former President de Klerk, then a deputy president. (South African Consulate General)

Harvest of Hatred

For over four decades, there was no constructive dialogue between South Africa's blacks and whites. The regime simply governed by coercion and repression. Avenues of legal protest were systematically closed off; black protests were automatically illegal and brutally stopped by the police. It was a virtual prescription for violence: plenty of injustice but no way to protest it legally. Riot police used dogs, whips, tear gas, clubs, shotguns, and automatic rifles to disperse crowds of Africans. Secret police and army "hit squads" assassinated dozens of regime opponents.

South Africa made its own contribution to the art of coercion with the **ban**, an order from the justice minister prohibiting a suspected troublemaker from normal contacts. A typical banning order might specify that for five years the subject would not be allowed to work in a large group (such as in a factory); might not have more than one visitor at a time; could not be quoted by others or by the press; and must be home by 6 P.M. Banning also could include exile to remote villages or round-the-clock surveillance by the security police. Since no court was involved, no banning order could be appealed.

Key Term

ban Apartheid punishment of isolating alleged troublemakers.

South Africa jailed prodigious numbers each year; those jailed for simple passbook violations could be released after a short time. Political detainees, on the other hand, could be held indefinitely without charges, beaten to death in jail, or shipped off to Robben Island for life. Under apartheid, life imprisonment meant life.

When some of the worst police-state restrictions eased in 1990 and black movements became legal, there were still few constructive interactions between blacks and whites. Instead of building bridges between the two groups, the Nationalists had deliberately, over the decades, destroyed them. Few whites had contact with Africans outside of a master-servant or boss-employee relationship. For decades there had been no church, club, university, sports association, or political party to serve as a meeting ground. Today, most whites wish a constructive dialogue with blacks. This is difficult. After decades of abuse, many blacks are angry. Their leaders have difficulty keeping them in check. In its dreadful way, the apartheid program worked: Now black and white South Africans really are apart.

What South Africans Quarrel About

How to Manage a Revolution

As political philosopher Hannah Arendt observed, rage is the indispensable ingredient for revolution, but it is absolutely worthless in building anything after the revolution. Such is President Mbeki's difficult task: to carry out a virtual revolution without spilling blood, and retain his government's legitimacy among all population groups. Blacks and whites are still deeply split. Africans call for "transformation," meaning shifting power in essentially all institutions from whites to blacks; change so far has been minor. Whites think they've already ceded a lot.

The government is pulled in different directions: Many black militants want "socialism," although they have a poor understanding of what that means, whereas whites generally want capitalism. Without paying much attention to theory, the impoverished black masses demand a rapid improvement in their living standard, and they recall the ANC promising precisely that.

Income inequality in South Africa is high, about at the level of Brazil. Black wages are about a fifth of white wages. Over a third of black South Africans are unemployed and below the poverty line, and there is only the beginnings of welfare or a social safety net. The white minority owns almost all the land and wealth. Nearly all young whites (along with most Indians and Coloureds) graduate high school; only one-third of blacks do. Black infant mortality is high, white low.

Campaigning in 1994 was easy for Mandela and the ANC. They simply promised African crowds free medical care and education, jobs for all, inexpensive houses, pensions for the old, loans for African entrepreneurs, and land for African farmers. This was subsequently called the Reconstruction and Development Program (RDP). "Each and every person will be entitled to decent housing, like the whites have now," Mandela told crowds. He admitted it couldn't happen overnight; "It is going to take a year, two years, even as much as five years" to lift up Africans to decent levels. It is taking much longer, even though more than half a million new homes were built under Mandela and millions more got water, electricity, and phones.

During the 1999 election Mbeki tried to deflect attention away from 1994 promises by stressing redistribution of executive-level jobs in favor of Africans. This is already happening; indeed, there is a shortage of educated Africans for managerial positions. Business sought African executives, especially the relatives of ANC leaders. This helps only a handful of Africans and leads to corruption. For most Africans, the grinding inequality still makes them wonder why abundance has not been redistributed. If all the wealth and land of South Africa now in white hands could suddenly be redistributed, it would make blacks only a little better off, and that would be temporary, for the white-run economic machine would shut down and poverty would increase.

Capitalism for South Africa?

For many decades the ANC and its SACP junior partner denounced capitalism and vowed a socialist future for South Africa. For a black South African, the capitalism practiced by whites looked an awful lot like brutal exploitation. Actually, South Africa never had a free-market economy; much of it was controlled and state-owned. When they took power in 1948, the Nats thought the law of supply and demand was strange and dubious. They fixed farm prices, severely restricted black labor mobility and entrepreneurship, and developed huge state industries. By the time Mandela took over, an incredible 50 percent of South Africa's fixed assets were state-owned. South Africa's white capitalists were the big liberals and progressives. When, in the late

1980s, white business leaders visited the ANC in Zambia to seek assurances against nationalization, they could get none. It looked like the ANC was committed to socialism.

But the release of Mandela and legalization of the ANC in 1990 came at an interesting time.
Communist governments had just collapsed in Eastern Europe, and the Soviet economy was revealed as a failure. Socialism (meaning here state ownership of industry) simply had no success

GEOGRAPHY

BOUND GUINEA

Guinea, a former French
colony in West Africa
(not to be confused with
Guyana in South
America), is bounded on the north by
Guinea-Bissau, Senegal, and Mali;

on the east by the Ivory Coast;
on the south by Liberia and Sierra Leone;
and on the west by the Atlantic Ocean.

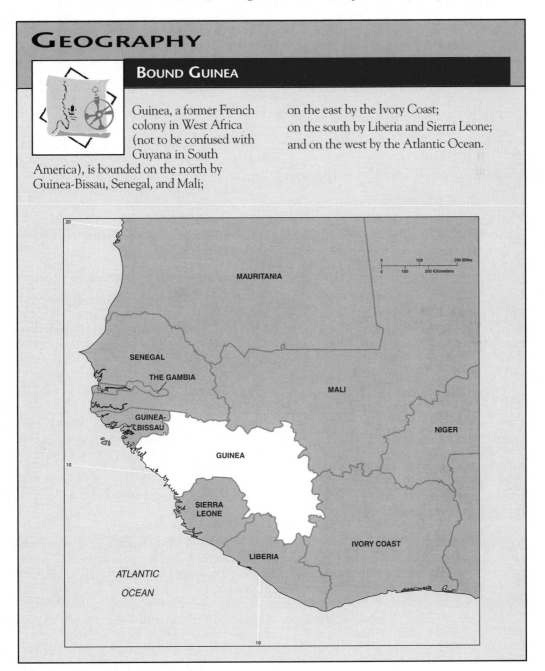

DEMOCRACY

HOW MUCH TRUTH CAN SOUTH AFRICA TAKE?

For years South African police and army units secretly bombed, tortured, beat to death, assassinated, and provoked black-on-black violence. How did postapartheid South Africa handle these horrors? In 1996 a Truth and Reconciliation Commission began work aimed at healing the wounds. It sought to get all the facts and publish them. Those who came forward with facts—including naming who their bosses were—could apply for amnesty.

The truths that came out were shocking. Witnesses from the police and army said orders came from the very top—including the defense minister and Presidents Botha and de

Klerk—to coldly "eliminate" antiapartheid "targets." Torture and beating to death was routine. The commission also found that the ANC had practiced "extrajudicial killing" in its struggle with the apartheid regime.

The commission concluded its work in 1998 with little reconciliation. South Africans on both sides faulted it. The doers, uncertain if they would get amnesty, were reluctant to testify. The Nats said it was just opening old wounds. And many black victims and their families wanted criminal prosecutions and civil lawsuits brought against former officials; amnesty was too good for these people. Argentina and Chile had earlier tried such commissions after brutal dictatorships with similar unsatisfying results.

stories. Gradually, the lesson began to penetrate the ANC. Maybe free markets and private initiative should be given a chance, especially if blacks could get in on the capitalist deal. By 1996, Mandela had come out in favor of privatizing South Africa's extensive state-owned sector. Some ANC members, however, still think state-owned industries are the way to go.

A government committed to socialism or statism could inflict economic catastrophe on South Africa. White people, with their skills and capital, are already quietly moving abroad. In 1998, for example, the giant Anglo-American Corporation moved its headquarters from Johannesburg to London. Black unemployment is around 40 percent (white: 4 percent). Highly productive white farms are folding before trained black farmers can run them. White farmers are murdered to drive them off the land. Starvation could break out. Responsible black leaders are increasingly aware of these dangers. As black politics came home from exile and out of the underground, it engaged in less ideological debate and in more pragmatic debate.

Tyrants-in-Waiting?

Actually, the Brazilianization of South Africa—crime and inflation—is not the worst thing that could happen. A greater possibility—and one feared by many South Africans—is to become like Zimbabwe, the formerly white-ruled Rhodesia to the north of South Africa. After a long and bitter guerrilla war plus an international embargo (which leaked through Mozambique and South Africa), in 1980 the white regime turned over power to Robert Mugabe, who revived the ancient name of Zimbabwe. Mugabe, intelligent and well-educated, keeps winning six-year terms as president, because his party is based on the country's largest tribe, the Shona.

After strife and looming violence between the Shona party and the parties of smaller tribes,

COMPARISON

THE BRAZILIANIZATION OF SOUTH AFRICA?

One point of resemblance between Brazil and South Africa is the shantytowns that spring up at an increasing rate around South Africa's cities. Much like Brazilians from the impoverished Northeast, poor Africans stream in from the countryside looking for work in the cities. With South Africa's terrible passbook, influx, and residential controls now scrapped, shantytowns grow.

Many critics of apartheid never understood that the original purpose of "influx control" was to prevent the black shantytowns that started with the rapid industrialization of World War II. The Nats bulldozed these shantytowns and offered "townships" instead: neat, planned rows of spartan cottages (without plumbing or electricity, so the "temporary workers" wouldn't get too comfortable) set up several miles from the main cities to be easily controlled by police and army. With the townships, the largest of which is Soweto (South West Townships) near Johannesburg, South Africa's white cities could have black labor by day but have them out of town by night.

"Why, without influx control," the Nats used to say with horror, "we'll become like Brazil." Now they have. Their influx controls just stored up people in the impoverished hinterlands; now they rush to the cities in a flood.

They delayed the shantytowns so characteristic of the Third World; they did not prevent them. South Africa vies with Brazil for the dubious honor of having the world's biggest gap between rich and poor. With the rapid printing of excess currency to pay its bills and fulfill some of its promises, the South African rand, once worth more than a U.S. dollar, is now seven to the dollar. With massive patronage hiring, corruption multiplies.

South Africa's crime rate, always high, is skyrocketing. Some twenty thousand people are murdered annually. On average, a South African is eight times more likely to be murdered than an American. Especially common and horrifying: car-jacking. (A recent South African invention: mini-flame throwers built into the sides of cars.) The old, white-dominated police have been thoroughly discredited for brutal illegality and covertly aiding Inkatha against the ANC. Now hundreds of police officers a year are accused of everything from corruption and robbery to murder, just like in Brazil. With uncontrolled influx and plentiful firearms, unemployed young men form criminal gangs. Whites hunker behind razor wire and security systems; crime pushes many to emigrate. Township dwellers form vigilante groups, and the security business booms. Every year, South Africa becomes more like Brazil.

Mugabe strongarmed them into joining his Zimbabwe African National Union (ZANU). Zimbabwe, which started as a multiparty democracy, has thus been a one-party state since 1987 under what seems to be a president-for-life. White farms are seized (with government approval) by poor blacks, opposition is silenced, and the media is muzzled. The problem is not simply individuals with dictatorial leanings. The underlying problem is a country with many poor people, a no-grow economy, and tribe-based politics. Under such circumstances, democracy is likely to fail and power go to the strongest, the story of much of Africa.

Could South Africa go this way? The ANC doesn't like checks and balances or the sharing of power. Its wars with Inkatha and the UDM demonstrate that. If an ANC government ever controls two-thirds of parliament, it could change the constitution and build a dictatorship.

GEOGRAPHY

A SEPARATE KWAZULU?

Inkatha chief Buthelezi was always at odds with the ANC and half-hearted about joining the national unity government of Mandela. What matters for Buthelezi is control of KwaZulu/Natal. His cooperation with the Mandela and Mbeki governments—in which he served as home affairs minister—was purchased at the price of ceding him control of this province. He hates ANC inroads into this area and goes to any lengths to stop them. Most of the bloodshed has been over this.

But if Buthelezi feels control slipping from him, he is likely to bolt from the Pretoria cabinet. In a bizarre move, Buthelzi once pulled his IFP deputies out of parliament but stayed in the cabinet. Conceivably, he could demand an independent KwaZulu/Natal. If it comes to that, what should South Africa do? Let the entire province go? Or fight a war to keep it? Neither is a very pretty choice. Either way there would be a great deal of bloodshed, as Zulus in other provinces come under pressure to flee homeward and as non-Inkatha people in KwaZulu/Natal are eradicated. South Africa has the potential of becoming a sort of Yugoslavia.

Thabo Mbeki is bright and well-educated, but the situation inclines South Africa toward dictatorship, if not under Mbeki then under someone else. As Archbishop Desmond Tutu, who fought apartheid for decades, put it, "Within the ANC are numerous tyrants-in-waiting."

Whatever the regime, South Africa's great challenge is how to shift from a revolutionary mode to a constructive postrevolutionary mode. One of the biggest challenges is education. Many of South Africa's black young people are enraged, uneducated, and unskilled. Education is also needed to stem the tide of AIDS that is engulfing Africa.

Black unemployment was earlier disguised by forcing many of them to live in the homelands. South Africa desperately needs rapid economic growth to create two million new jobs a year. In the mid-1990s, the economy did grow, but not the number of jobs. Hemmed in by labor restrictions, tough unions, high wages, and low productivity, businesses hired few new workers. Foreign investment is the key.

For this, South Africa must make up its mind on privatizing its gigantic state sector. State industries tend to generate little job growth, but in order not to arouse ANC and unionists still inclined to socialism, the government avoids the "p-word" but speaks of "restructuring of state assets." Although the ANC government needs foreign investment, it has gone slowly in selling off industries such as its airlines, railroads, buses, arms industries, energy industries (electricity, oil, gas), television stations, and the telephone company. Some economists say the sooner these are privatized the better; they will bring in new money, new technology, and new jobs.

As part of this, the regime must encourage white capitalists, who already know their futures are on the line, to invest and reinvest, especially in ways that employ more labor. For this, they must be firmly assured that they will keep their property. The unions and their friends in the ANC must understand that the high costs of South African labor and its low productivity relative to other economies doom it to slow growth and fewer jobs. The previously protected, high-cost South African economy now faces bruising international competition. Investment flows to where wages are low and productivity is high; South Africa has the opposite.

South Africa has intriguing economic possibilities. It has the only substantial industrial plant south of the Sahara. It has a treasure of minerals, some rare and important. It now has trade access to a potentially large market in all of Africa. It has a good infrastructure of highways, railroads, electric power, and communications. Will South Africa more resemble the economic tigers that rim Asia or the stagnant economies typical of much of the Third World?

Key Terms

African National Congress (p. 445)	colonialism (p. 440)	lingua franca (p. 449)
Afrikaners (p. 443)	consociation (p. 461)	patronage (p. 459)
apartheid (p. 444)	cross-cutting cleavages (p. 460)	Zulu (p. 442)
ban (p. 465)	cumulative (p. 460)	
bilateral opposition (p. 464)	divide and rule (p. 462)	

Further Reference

Abel, Richard L. *Politics by Other Means: Law in the Struggle Against Apartheid, 1980–1994.* New York: Routledge, 1995.

Adam, Heribert, Frederik van Zyl Slabbert, and Kogila Moodley. *Comrades in Business: Post-Liberation Politics in South Africa.* Concord, MA: International Books, 1998.

Alden, Christopher. *Apartheid's Last Stand: The Rise and Fall of the South African Security State.* New York: St. Martin's, 1996.

Holland, Heidi. *The Struggle: A History of the African National Congress.* New York: George Braziller, 1990.

Johnson, R. W., and Lawrence Schlemmer, eds. *Launching Democracy in South Africa: The First Open Election, April 1994.* New Haven, CT: Yale University Press, 1996.

Karis, Thomas G., and Gail M. Gerhart. *From Protest to Challenge: A Documentary History of African Politics in South Africa, 1882–1990.* Vol. 5: *Nadir and Resurgence, 1964–1979.* Bloomington, IN: Indiana University Press, 1997.

Lowenberg, Anton D., and William H. Kaempfer. *The Origins and Demise of South African Apartheid: A Public Choice Analysis.* Ann Arbor, MI: University of Michigan Press, 1998.

Marx, Anthony W. *Making Race and Nation: A Comparison of South Africa, the United States, and Brazil.* New York: Cambridge University Press, 1998.

May, Julian, ed. *Poverty and Inequality in South Africa: Meeting the Challenge.* New York: Zed Books, 1999.

O'Meara, Dan. *Forty Lost Years: The Apartheid State and the Politics of the National Party.* Athens, OH: Ohio University Press, 1996.

Sampson, Anthony. *Mandela: The Authorised Biography.* New York: Knopf, 1999.

Sparks, Allister. *Tomorrow Is Another Country.* New York: Hill & Wang, 1995.

Taylor, Stephen. *Shaka's Children: A History of the Zulu People.* New York: HarperCollins World, 1996.

Thompson, Leonard. *A History of South Africa.* New Haven, CT: Yale University Press, 1990.

Waldmeir, Patti. *Anatomy of a Miracle: The End of Apartheid and the Birth of the New South Africa.* New York: Norton, 1997.

Iran

30

Questions to Consider

1. What has geography contributed to Iran's development?
2. How does Iran differ from Arab countries?
3. What is a "modernizing tyrant"? Why do they fail?
4. What factors brought Iran's Islamic Revolution?
5. Explain Iran's dual executive. Who is more powerful?
6. Does secularization always come with modernization?
7. What kind of Iranians wish to liberalize their system?
8. Explain the power struggle in Iran.
9. How is attire a political debate in Iran?
10. How have America and Iran misunderstood each other?
11. Why is the Persian Gulf region strategic?

The Impact of the Past

Much of Iran is an arid plateau around 4,000 feet above sea level. Some areas are rainless desert; some get sufficient rain only for sparse sheep pasture. In this part of the world, irrigation made civilization possible, and whatever disrupted waterworks had devastating consequences. Persia's location, though, made it an important trade route between East and West, one of the links between the Middle East and Asia. Persia thus became a crossroads of civilizations and one of the earliest of the great civilizations.

A crossroads country becomes a natural target for conquest. Indo-European-speaking invaders took over Persia about the fifteenth century B.C. and laid the basis for subsequent Persian culture. Their most famous kings: Cyrus and Darius in the sixth century B.C. The invasions never ceased, though: the Greeks under Alexander in the third and fourth centuries B.C., the Arab-Islamic conquest in the seventh century A.D., Turkish tribes in the eleventh century, Mongols in the thirteenth century, and many others. The repeated pattern was one of conquest, the founding of a new dynasty, and its falling apart as quarrelsome heirs broke it into petty kingdoms. This fragmentation set up the country for easy conquest again.

GEOGRAPHY

BOUND IRAN

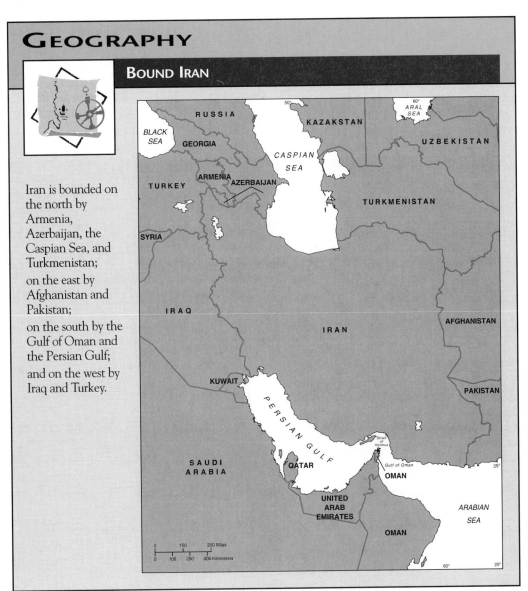

Iran is bounded on the north by Armenia, Azerbaijan, the Caspian Sea, and Turkmenistan;

on the east by Afghanistan and Pakistan;

on the south by the Gulf of Oman and the Persian Gulf;

and on the west by Iraq and Turkey.

Iran, known for most of history as Persia (it was renamed only in 1925), resembles China in that it is heir to an ancient and magnificent civilization that, partly at the hands of outsiders, fell into "the sleep of nations." When it awoke, it was far behind the West, which, like China, Iran views as an adversary. If and how Iran will move into modernity is a major question.

Although it doesn't look or sound like it, Persian (*Farsi*) is a member of the broad Indo-European family of languages; the neighboring Arabic and Turkic tongues are not. Today, Farsi is the mother tongue of about half of Iranians. Another fifth speak Persian-related languages (such as Kurdish). A quarter speak a Turkic language, and some areas speak Arabic and other tongues. The non-Farsi speakers occupy the periphery of the Farsi-speaking heartland and have at times been discontent with rule by Persians. In Iranian politics today, to be descended from one of the non-Persian minorities is held against politicians.

The Arab Conquest

Allah's prophet Mohammed died in Arabia in 632, but his religion spread like wildfire. **Islam** means "submission" (to God's will), and this was to be hastened by **jihad**. Islam arrived soon in Iran by the sword. The remnant of the Sassanid empire, already exhausted by centuries of warfare with Byzantium, was easily beaten by the Arabs at Qadisiya in 637 and within two centuries Persia was mostly **Muslim**. Adherents of the old religion, Zoroastrianism, fled to India where today they are a small, prosperous minority known as Parsis.

The Arab conquest was a major break with the past. In contrast to the sharp social stratification of Persian tradition, Islam taught that all Muslims were, at least in a spiritual sense, equal. The Arabic script was adopted, and many Arab words enriched the Persian language. Persian culture flowed the other way, too, as the Arabs copied Persian architecture and civil administration. For six centuries, Persia was swallowed up by the Arab empires, but in 1055 the Seljuk Turks invaded from Central Asia and conquered most of the Middle East. As usual, their rule soon fell apart into many small states, easy prey for Genghis Khan, the Mongol "World Conqueror" whose horde thundered in from the east in 1219. One of his descendants who ruled Persia embraced Islam at the end of that century. This is part of a pattern Iranians are proud of: "We may be conquered," they say, "but the conqueror ends up adopting our superior culture and becomes one of us."

A major step toward establishing a distinctly Iranian identity was the coming of the Safavid dynasty in 1501. The Safavids practiced a minority version of Islam called **Shia** (see box on page 488) and decreed it Persia's state religion. Most of their subjects switched from **Sunni** Islam and are *Shi'ites* to this day. Neighboring Sunni powers immediately attacked Safavid Persia, but this enabled the new regime to consolidate its control and develop an Islam with Persian characteristics.

Western Penetration

It's too simple to say Western cultural, economic, and colonial penetration brought down the great Persian empire. Safavid Persia was attacked from several directions, mostly by neighboring Muslim powers: the Ottoman Turks from the west, Uzbeks from the north, and Afghans from the northeast. It was in the hope of saving themselves from the Ottomans that Safavid rulers sought to make common cause with the early Portuguese, Dutch, and English sea traders in the late sixteenth and early seventeenth centuries. As previously in the region's history, the outsiders were able to penetrate because the local kingdoms had seriously weakened themselves in ruinous warfare, a pattern that continues in our day.

In 1722, Afghan invaders put an end to the Safavid dynasty, but no one was able to found a new dynasty or effectively govern the whole country. After much chaos, in 1795 the Kajar dynasty emerged victorious. Owing to Persian weakness, Britain and Russia became dominant in Persia, the Russians pushing in from the north, the British from India. Although never a colony, Persia, like China, slid into semicolonial status, with much of its political and

Key Terms

Islam   The religion founded by Mohammed.

jihad   Muslim holy war.

Muslim   A follower of Islam; also adjective of *Islam*.

Shia   Minority branch of Islam.

Sunni   Mainstream branch of Islam.

economic life dependent on what foreigners wanted, something Persians strongly resented. A particularly vexatious example was an 1890 treaty turning over to British traders a monopoly on tobacco sales in Persia. Mass hatred of the British tobacco concession was led by Muslim clerics, and the treaty was repealed.

At this same time, liberal, Western ideals of government seeped into Persia, some brought, as in China, by Christian missionaries (who made very few Persian converts). The Constitutional Revolution of 1906–07 (in which an American supporter of the popular struggle was killed) brought Persia's first constitution and first elected parliament, the **Majlis**. The struggles over the tobacco concession and constitution were led by a combination of two forces: liberals who hated the monarchy and wanted Western-type institutions and Muslim clerics who also disliked the monarchy but wanted a stronger role for Islam. This was the same combination that brought down the **Shah** in 1979; now these two strands have turned against each other over the future of Iran.

Notice how at almost exactly the same time—1905 in Russia, 1906 in Persia—corrupt and weak monarchies promised somewhat democratic constitutions in the face of popular uprisings. Both monarchies, dedicated to autocratic power and hating democracy, only pretended to deliver, a virtual prescription for increasing mass discontent. A new shah inherited the throne in 1907 and had his Russian-trained Cossack bodyguard unit shut down the Majlis. Mass protest forced the last Kajar shah to flee to Russia in 1909; he tried to return in 1911 but was forced back as Russian troops occupied Tehran. The 1907 Anglo-Russian treaty had already cut Persia in two, with a Russian sphere of influence in the north and a British one in the south. During World War I, Persia was nominally neutral, but with neighboring Turkey allied with Germany, Russia and Britain allied with each other, and German agents trying to tilt Persia their way, Persia turned into a zone of contention and chaos.

The First Pahlavi

As is often the case in such situations, military officers come to see themselves as the saviors of their nation. (See the box on page 429 on "praetorianism.") In 1921 an illiterate cavalry officer, Reza Khan, the commander of the Russian-trained Cossack brigade, seized power and in 1925 had himself crowned shah, the founder of the short-lived (1925–79) Pahlavi dynasty. The nationalistic Reza took the pre-Islamic surname Pahlavi and told the world to start calling the country by its true name, Iran, from the word *aryan*, indicating the country's Indo-European roots. (Nazi ideologists also loved the word aryan, which they claimed indicated genetic superiority. Indeed, the ancient Persian Zoroastrians preached racial purity.)

Like Ataturk, Reza Shah was determined to modernize his country (see box). His achievements were impressive. He molded an effective Iranian army and used it to suppress tribal revolts and unify Iran. He invented a modern, European-type civil service and a national bank. He replaced traditional and Islamic courts with civil courts operating under Western codes of justice. In 1935 he founded Iran's first Western-style university. Under state supervision and fueled by oil revenues, Iran's economy grew. Also like Ataturk, Reza Shah ordered his countrymen to adopt Western dress and women to stop wearing the veil. But Reza also kept the press and Majlis closely obedient. Troublemakers and dissidents often died in jail. Reza Shah was a classic **modernizing tyrant**.

World War II put Iran in the same situation as World War I had. It was just too strategic to leave alone. As an oil source and important conduit for U.S. supplies to the desperate Soviet Union, it could not possibly stay neutral. As before, the Russians took over in the north and the British (later the Americans) in the south. Both agreed to clear out six months after the war ended. Reza Shah, who tilted toward Germany, in September 1941 was exiled by the British to South Africa, where he died in 1944. Before he left, he abdicated in favor of his son, Mohammed Reza Pahlavi.

The Americans and British cleared out of Iran in 1945; the Soviets did not, and some argue this incident marked the start of the Cold War. Stalin claimed that Azerbaijan, a Soviet "republic" in the Caucasus, was entitled by ethnic right to merge with the Azeris of northern Iran and refused to withdraw Soviet forces. Stalin set up puppet Communist Azeri and Kurdish governments there. In 1946 U.S. President Truman delivered some harsh words, Iran's prime minister promised Stalin an oil deal, and Stalin pulled out. (Then the Majlis canceled the oil deal.)

The Last Pahlavi

Oil has determined much of Iran's twentieth-century history. Oil has been the great prize for the British, Hitler, Stalin, and the United States. Who should own and profit from Iran's oil—foreigners, the Iranian government, or Iranians as a whole? Major oil deposits were first discovered in Iran in 1908 and developed under a British concession, the Anglo-Persian (later Anglo-Iranian) Oil Company. Persia got little from the oil deal, and Persians began to hate this rich foreign company in their midst, one that wrote its own rules. Reza Shah ended the lopsided concession in 1932 and forced the AIOC to pay higher royalties.

COMPARISON

ATATURK AND REZA SHAH

During the 1920s, two strong personalities in adjacent Middle Eastern lands attempted to modernize their countries from above: Kemal Ataturk in Turkey and Reza Shah in Iran. Both were nationalistic military officers and Muslims but **secular** in outlook and both wished to separate **mosque** and state.

In economics, both were *étatiste* (French for "statist"; see page 414) and made the government the number-one investor and owner of major industries. Both pushed education, the improved status of women, and Western clothing. As such, both aroused traditionalist opposition led by Muslim clerics. Both

were authoritarian. Both thundered "You will be modern!" But religious forces opposed their reforms, and do to this day.

Their big difference: Ataturk ended the **Ottoman** monarchy and firmly supported a republican form of government in Turkey. He pushed his reforms piecemeal through parliament, which often opposed him. Reza Shah rejected republicanism and parliaments as too messy; he insisted on an authoritarian monarchy as the best way to modernize an unruly country, as did his son. Although Turkey has had plenty of troubles since Ataturk, it has not been ripped apart by revolution. Ataturk built some political institutions; the Pahlavi shahs built none.

THE UNITED STATES AND IRAN: THE BIG U.S. MISTAKE

We were much too close to the Shah. We supported him unstintingly and unquestioningly. The Shah was anti-Communist and was rapidly modernizing Iran; he was our kind of guy. Iranian unrest and opposition went unnoticed by the U.S. Embassy. Elaborate Iranian public relations portrayed Iran in a rosy light in the U.S. media. Under Nixon, U.S. arms makers sold Iran "anything that goes bang." We failed to see that Iran and the Shah were two different things, and that our unqualified backing of the Shah was alienating many Iranians. We didn't notice the Shah governed by means of a dreaded secret police, the SAVAK. We failed to call a tyrant a tyrant. Only when the Islamic Revolution broke out did we learn what Iranians really thought about the Shah. We were so obsessed by communism penetrating from the north that we could not imagine anything like a bitter, hostile Islamic revolution coming from within Iran.

The AIOC still rankled Iranians, who rallied to the radical nationalist Prime Minister Mohammed Mossadegh in the early 1950s. With support from Iranian nationalists, liberals, and leftists, Mossadegh nationalized AIOC holdings. Amidst growing turmoil and what some feared was a tilt to the Soviet Union, Shah Mohammed Reza Pahlavi fled the country in 1953. The British urged Washington to do something, and President Eisenhower, as part of U.S. **containment**, had the CIA destabilize the Tehran government. It was easy: The CIA's Kermit Roosevelt arrived with $1 million in a suitcase and rented a suitable mob. Mossadegh was out, the Shah was restored, and the United States won a battle in the Cold War. We thought we were very clever.

Like his father, the Shah was a modernizing tyrant, promoting what he called his "White Revolution" from above (as opposed to a red revolution from below). Under the Shah, Iran had excellent relations with the United States. President Nixon touted the Shah as our pillar of stability in the Persian Gulf. We were his source of money, technology, and military hardware. Some one hundred thousand Iranian students came to U.S. universities, and forty-five thousand American businessmen and consultants surged into Tehran for lucrative contracts. This point shows that person-to-person contacts do not always lead to good relations between countries.

What finally did in the Shah? Too much money went to his head. With the 1973 Arab-Israeli war, oil producers worldwide got the chance to do what they had long wished: boost the price of oil and take over oil extraction from foreign companies. The Shah, one of the prime movers of the Organization of Petroleum Exporting Countries (**OPEC**), gleefully did both. What Mossadegh tried, the Shah accomplished. Oil prices on the world market quadrupled. With more cash than ever, the Shah went mad with vast, expensive schemes. The oil revenues were administered by the state for the greater glory of Iran and its army, not for the Iranian people. This resentment was one of the prominent factors in the Islamic Revolution. Oil led to turmoil.

The sudden influx of new wealth caused great disruption. The Shah promoted education, but the more education people got, the more they could see the Shah was a tyrant. Some people got rich fast while most stayed poor. Corruption grew worse than ever. Millions flocked from the countryside to the cities where, rootless and confused, they turned to the only institution they understood, the mosque, for guidance. In their rush to modernize, the Pahlavis alienated the

Key Terms

containment   U.S. policy throughout Cold War of blocking expansion of communism.

OPEC   Cartel of oil-rich countries designed to boost petroleum prices.

GEOGRAPHY

CRUISING THE PERSIAN GULF

The countries bordering the Persian Gulf contain some two-thirds of the world's proven petroleum reserves. Some of you may do military service in the Gulf, so start learning the geography now. Imagine you are on an aircraft carrier making a clockwise circle around the Gulf. Upon entering the Strait of Hormuz, which countries do you pass to port? Oman, United Arab Emirates, Qatar, Saudi Arabia, Bahrain (an island), Kuwait, Iraq, and Iran.

Muslim clergy. Not only did the Shah undermine the traditional cultural values of Islam, he seized land owned by religious foundations and distributed it to peasants as part of his White Revolution. The **mullahs** also hated the influx of American culture, with its easy toleration of alcohol and sex. Many Iranians saw the Shah's huge military expenditures—at the end, an incredible 17 percent of Iran's GDP—as a waste of money. As de Tocqueville observed, economic growth paves the way to revolution.

Key Terms

mullah Muslim cleric.
ayatollah "Sign of God"; top Shia religious leader.

One of Iran's religious authorities, **Ayatollah** Khomeini, criticized the Shah and incurred his wrath. He had Khomeini exiled to Iraq in 1964 and then forced him to leave Iraq in 1978. Khomeini took up residence in a Paris suburb, from which his recorded messages were telephoned to cassette recorders in Iran to be duplicated and distributed through mosques nationwide. Cheap cassettes bypassed the Shah's control of Iran's media and helped bring him down.

In the late 1970s, matters came to a head. The Shah's overambitious plans had made Iran a debtor nation. Secular intellectuals and Islamic clerics alike were discontent. And U.S. President Jimmy Carter made human rights a foreign-policy goal. As part of this, the Shah's dictatorship was subject to U.S. criticism. Shaken, the Shah began to relax his grip, and that is when all hell broke loose. As de Tocqueville observed, the worst time in the life of a bad government is when it begins to mend its ways. Compounding his error, Carter showed his support for the Shah by exchanging visits, proof to Iranians that we were supporting a hated tyrant. In 1977, Carter and the Shah had to retreat into the White House from the lawn to escape the tear gas that drifted over from the anti-Shah protest (mostly by Iranian students) in Lafayette Park.

By late 1978, the Shah, facing huge demonstrations and (unknown to Washington) dying of cancer, was finished. Shooting into the crowds of protesters just made them angrier. The ancient Persian game of chess ends with a checkmate, a corruption of the Farsi *shah mat* ("the king is trapped"). On January 16, 1979, the last Pahlavi left Iran. *Shah mat.*

The Key Institutions

A Theocracy

Two and a half millennia of monarchy ended in Iran with a 1979 referendum, carefully supervised by the Khomeini forces, that introduced the Islamic Republic of Iran and a new constitution. As in most countries, the offices of head of state and head of government are split. But instead of a figurehead monarch (as in Britain) or weak president (as in Germany), Iran now has two heads of state, one its leading religious figure, the other a more standard president. Ultimately, the religious chief is the real power. That makes Iran a **theocracy**.

Theocracy is rare and tends not to last. Even in ancient times, priests, shamans, and holy men filled supporting rather than executive roles. Russia's tsar, head of both church and state, emphasized the state side; he wore military, not priestly, garb. Iran (plus Afghanistan and Sudan) tried a theocratic system. The principle of political power in the system devised by Khomeini is the **velayat-e faqih**. This leading Islamic jurist, the *faqih*, serves for life. *Jurist* means a legal scholar steeped in Islamic, specifically Shia, religious law. (The closest Western equivalent is **canon law**. In medieval Europe, canon lawyers were leading intellectuals and politicians.) Allegedly the *faqih*, also known as the "Spiritual Guide," can use the Koran and related Islamic commentaries to decide all issues, even those not connected to religion. (An **Islamist**, of course, would say everything is connected to religion.)

Key Terms

theocracy   Rule by priests.

velayat-e faqih   "Guardianship of the religious jurist"; theocratic system devised by Khomeini.

canon law   The internal laws of the Roman Catholic Church.

Islamist   Someone who uses Islam in a political way.

IRAN'S 1997 PRESIDENTIAL ELECTION

In a surprising landslide, a relative moderate came from obscurity to win Iran's presidential election in May 1997. Mohammed Khatami, age fifty-four, took nearly 70 percent of the vote to less than 25 percent for conservative Ali Akbar Nateq-Noori, the Speaker of the Majlis, who had been favored. Khatami's election, which had an amazing 90 percent turnout, showed that a big majority of Iranians were fed up with economic decline and clerical supervision of private life. Educated, urban Iranians, women, and young people ignored the urgings of the top mullahs to vote for Nateq-Noori and went strongly for Khatami. The Council of Guardians (see box on page 481) let only four candidates run out of more than two hundred hopefuls.

Khatami ran on a platform of greater personal freedoms, legalization of political parties, more jobs, and less male dominance, issues aimed at women and young people. Nateq-Noori ran on improving the economy and following strict Islamic law. All Iranians (male and female) age sixteen or older were eligible to vote. Both candidates, it should be noted, were Islamic clerics and in no sense opposed the Islamic Revolution. They just held different versions of that revolution, Nateq-Noori a harsh version and Khatami a tolerant one aiming at "civil society."

Indeed, Khatami is the son of a famous Islamic teacher and wears a black turban, permitted only to clerics who can prove they are direct descendants of the Prophet Mohammed. Khatami criticized the Shah's regime in the 1970s and in 1978 headed the Islamic Center in Hamburg, Germany. He speaks some German and English. With the triumph of the revolution in 1979, Khatami returned to Iran and served as Minister of Islamic Guidance from 1982 to 1992 but was forced out for allowing too much media and artistic freedom. Largely out of sight as head of Iran's national library, he advocated rights for workers, women, and young people. His views became known only during the last few weeks before the election but spread rapidly.

Within the limits set by the Council of Guardians, it was a fair and democratic election. Although party labels were not allowed, people knew where the candidates stood and voted accordingly. Not a liberal in our sense of the word, Khatami probably qualifies as a moderate, a cautious reformer (see page 481).

Khomeini, the first and founding *faqih*, died in 1989. He was nearly all-powerful. His successor—now referred to in the constitution as the "Leader"—is chosen by an elected Assembly of Experts. These eighty-six Muslim clerics, elected every eight years, choose from among the purest and most learned Islamic jurists. The man they elect (Islam permits no female religious leaders) will likely already be an ayatollah, one of a handful of the wisest Shi'ite jurists, or he will be named an ayatollah.

Iran's current *faqih* is Ayatollah Ali Hoseini-Khamenei. He names the heads of virtually all major state and religious organizations and may declare war. He therefore controls, at least indirectly, the judiciary, armed forces, security police, intelligence agencies, radio, and television. He is more powerful than Iran's president. Khamenei has neither the spiritual depth nor forceful personality of Khomeini, but he and his followers can still block any liberalizing moves.

Iran's Executive

Iran's working chief is a U.S.-type executive president, elected by popular vote for up to two four-year terms. The constitution specifies that this president is "the holder of the highest official power next to the office of the *faqih*," indicating he is inferior in power to the Leader. Khatami continually had to defer to the conservative policies of Khamenei. There was no open disagreement between the two, but it meant that Iran got stuck between Khomeini's original revolutionary design and attempts to reform and stabilize the country.

Both Khatami and his predecessor are Muslim clerics. Ali Akbar Hashemi-Rafsanjani, who earlier was the powerful Speaker of the parliament, served two terms as president (from 1989 to 1997), and was himself a *hojatolislam*, an Islamic jurist ranked just below *ayatollah*. An extremely shrewd and pragmatic individual, however, Rafsanjani served to quietly calm and secularize the Islamic revolution, never, of course, going directly against the top clerics. The cabinet conducts the real day-to-day work of governance. Practically all new laws and the budget are devised by the cabinet and submitted to parliament for approval, modification, or rejection.

Iran's Legislature

Iran has a unicameral (one-house) legislature, the Islamic Consultative Assembly (Majlis), consisting of 290 deputies elected for four-year terms. Iran uses single-member districts, like Britain and the U.S. Congress. Iran is divided into 265 constituencies, and each Iranian seventeen (raised from sixteen in 2000) and older has one vote for a representative. An additional five seats are reserved for non-Muslim deputies (one each for Assyrian Christians, Jews, and Zoroastrians; two for Armenian Christians; none for Baha'is).

Majlis elections are semifree. The actual balloting is free and fair, but all candidates must be approved by the Council of Guardians, which disqualifies candidates they suspect might not support the Islamic Revolution. Out-and-out liberals are thus discouraged from even putting forward candidates. The 2000 elections, however, produced a clear reformist majority.

The Speaker of parliament has emerged as a major position, first filled by Rafsanjani and now by the leader of the conservative Islamist forces that predominate in the Majlis, Ali Akbar Nateq-Noori, who lost the 1997 presidential election to the moderate Khatami. Nateq-Noori blocked President Rafsanjani's and Khatami's proposals for moderate liberalization.

IRAN'S STRANGE "COUNCIL OF GUARDIANS"

Iran's Council of Guardians is strange among political institutions, combining features of an upper house, a supreme court, an electoral commission, and a religious inquisition. It has twelve members; they serve six years each with half of them changed every three years. The *faqih* chooses six Islamic clerics; Iran's supreme court (the High Council of Justice) names another six, all Islamic lawyers, who must be approved by the Majlis.

The Council examines each Majlis bill to make sure it does not violate Islamic principles. If a majority decides it does, the bill is returned to the Majlis to be corrected. Without Council approval, a bill is in effect vetoed. Several important pieces of legislation have been blocked in this way. To settle conflicts between the Majlis and the Council, an "Expediency Council" appointed by the Leader has become like another legislature.

Perhaps more important, the Council of Guardians examines all candidates for the Majlis and has the power to disqualify them without explanation. Their criteria are unclear for rejecting candidates; anyone deemed not "politically correct" in their support of Islamic rule may be rejected. In the 1996 and 2000 Majlis elections, the Council scratched a large fraction of the candidates. While not as strict as Communist control over Soviet elections, the Council makes sure there is no serious opposition in the Majlis.

Emerging Parties?

Parties are legal under Iran's constitution, but the government does not allow them; only individual candidates run. This also makes Iranian elections less than totally free, for without party image the electorate cannot clearly discern who stands for what. It was not even possible, in the 1996 and 2000 parliamentary elections, to count which "tendencies" exactly won how many seats. In practice, however, candidates are linked through alignments, "lists," and "fronts." Over time, these may turn into legal parties. Observers see four main political groupings, all of which contain many factions and individual viewpoints.

Radicals, the most extreme supporters of the Islamic Revolution, want to adhere to what they perceive as Khomeini's design for an Islamic republic. Socialist in economics, they also favor state control over the economy. They wish to keep out all Western influences and continue Islamic supervision of society, such as squads who dictate women's attire.

Conservatives, more moderate than the radicals, want a nonfanatic Islamic Republic with special consideration for the economic needs of small merchants. They still oppose any U.S. contacts.

Moderates are reformers in Iranian terms, but are cautious and work within the system. They tend to be the educated middle class and favor privatization of state enterprises, fewer Islamic controls on society, elections open to most candidates (not just those approved by the Council of Guardians), and an end to confrontations with the West.

Liberals would go farther. Popular among Iranian students, they emphasize democracy and civil rights and want totally free elections. They would like to eliminate the social controls imposed by the Islamists. In economics, however, they are a mixed bag, ranging from free-marketeers to socialists. In the 2000 legislative elections, moderate and liberal reformists won a majority of Majlis seats.

A Partly Free System

Iran could be described as a partially free political system or one trying to become free. The 2000 elections were heartening. The spirited debates of the Majlis (mostly about the direction of the economy, statist or free-market), televised nationwide, show a parliament and society that wants to guide its future in a democratic way. Elections are lively and, within the limits imposed by the Council of Guardians, contested. The press is constitutionally free but a law also requires it "to enjoin the good and forbid the evil," as defined by the mullahs. Newspapers and magazines criticize some government policies and charge some high officials, mullahs, and their relatives with corruption. Critical papers are frequently closed, their editors tried, and dissidents mysteriously killed. As in much of the Third World, Iran's political institutions are vague and chaotic. It's hard to tell who has the power to do what. Much depends on personalities. Furthermore, researchers are not permitted to investigate Iran's government first-hand. We probably know more about the government workings in Russia and China—and we don't know much about them—than we do about how power flows in Iran.

Iranian Political Culture

As is often the case in the Third World, many Iranians do not wish to see their traditional culture erased by Western culture. "We want to be modern," say many citizens of the Third World, "but not like you. We'll do it our way, based on our values and our religion." Whether you can be a modern, high-tech society while preserving your old culture is a key question for much of the globe today. Will efforts to combine old and new cultures work or lead to chaos? In some cases, like Japan, it has worked. For Islamic nations, so far it has not. The key factor may be the flexibility and adaptability of the Third World culture, which is very high in the case of Japan. Japan learned to be modern but still distinctly Japanese. Can Muslim countries do the same?

Beneath all the comings and goings of conquerors and kingdoms, Persian society changed little over the centuries. As in China, the dynastic changes little disturbed the broad majority of the population, poor farmers and shepherds, many of them still tribal in organization. As in much of the Third World, traditional society was actually quite stable and conservative. Islam, the mosque, the mullah, and the **Koran** gave solace and meaning to the lives of most Persians. People were poor but passive.

Then came modernization, mostly under foreign pressure, starting late in the nineteenth century, expanding with the development of petroleum, and accelerating under both the Pahlavi shahs. Iran neatly raises the question of whether you can modernize and still keep your old culture. According to what political scientists call "modernization theory," a number of things happen more or less simultaneously. First, the economy changes, from simple farming to natural-resource extraction to manufacturing and services. Along with this comes urbanization, the movement of people from country to city. At the same time, education levels increase greatly; most people become at least literate and some go to college. People consume more mass media—at first newspapers, then radio, and finally television—until many people are aware of what is going on in their country and in the world. A large middle class emerges along with a variety of interest groups. People now want to participate in politics; they do not like being treated like children.

It was long supposed that secularization comes with modernization, and both Ataturk and the Pahlavis had tough showdowns with the mullahs. But

Key Terms

Koran Muslim holy book.
sharia Muslim religious law.

POLITICAL CULTURE

IS ISLAM ANTI-MODERN?

Most Middle-East experts deny there is anything inherent in Islamic doctrine that keeps Muslim societies from modernizing. Yet one finds no Islamic countries that have fully modernized. Under Ataturk, Turkey made great strides between the two wars, but Islamic militants constantly try to undo his reforms. In Huntington's terms (see page 268), Turkey is a "torn" country, pulled between Western and Islamic cultures. Recently Malaysia, half of whose people are Muslim, has scored rapid economic progress. Generally, though, Islam coincides with backwardness, as we define it. Some Muslim countries are rich but only because oil has brought them outside revenues.

Does Islam cause backwardness? By itself, no. The Koran does prohibit loaning money at interest, but there are ways to get around that. Historically, Islamic civilization was for centuries more advanced than Christian Europe in most areas (e.g., science, philosophy, medicine, sanitation, architecture, steelmaking). Europe got reacquainted with classic Greco-Roman thought, especially Aristotle, through translations from the Arabic, which helped trigger the Renaissance and Europe's modernization. Go back a millennium and you would find Muslims wondering if it wasn't Christianity that kept Europe backward.

But something happened; Islamic civilization faltered and European civilization modernized. By the sixteenth century, when European merchant ships arrived in the Persian Gulf, the West was ahead of Islam. Why? There are some historical causes. The Mongol invaders of the thirteenth century massacred the inhabitants of Baghdad and destroyed the region's irrigation systems, something the Arab empire never recovered from. (The Mongols' impact on Russia was also devastating.) Possibly because of the Mongol devastation, Islam turned to mysticism. Instead of being flexible, tolerant, and fascinated by learning and science, Islam turned sullen and rigid. When the Portuguese first rounded the southern tip of Africa in 1488, they opened up direct trade routes between Europe and Asia, bypassing the Islamic middlemen. Trade through the Middle East declined sharply and with it the region's economy.

Islam also has a structural problem in its combining of religion and government. The two are not supposed to be separate in Islam, and it is very difficult to split mosque and state in a Muslim country; those who try (such as Ataturk) are strongly resisted. Even today, many Muslims want **sharia** to be the law of the land. This sets up the kind of hostility Iran saw between secular modernizers and religious traditionalists, who compete for political power, with the latter constantly trying to reverse the efforts of the former. Until Muslim countries learn to separate mosque and state, this destructive tug-of-war will block progress.

Perhaps most important, the domination of European (chiefly British) imperialists starting in the nineteenth century created the resentment of a proud civilization brought low by upstart foreigners: "You push in here with your guns, your railroads, and your commerce and act superior to us. Well, culturally and morally we are superior to you, and eventually we'll kick you out." This attitude—which has some historical validity—spurs hatred of anything Western and therefore opposition to modernity, because embracing modernity would be admitting the West is superior. Islam teaches it is superior to other civilizations and will eventually triumph worldwide. Devout Muslims do not like evidence to the contrary.

If Muslim countries do not discard their antipathy toward the West and modernity in general, their progress will be slow and often reversed. Look for reforms in Islam that will make this possible; such movements are already afoot. Eventually, we could see societies that are both modern and Muslim. One of the best ways to promote this: Educate women.

Islamism   Islam turned into a political ideology.

Iran's Islamic Revolution and other religious revivals now make us question the inevitability of secularization. Under certain conditions—when things change too fast, when the economy declines and unemployment grows, and modernization repudiates traditional values—people may return to religion with renewed vigor. If their world seems to be falling apart, church or mosque give stability and meaning to life. This is as true of the present-day United States as it is of Algeria. In the Muslim world, many intellectuals first passionately embraced modernizing creeds of socialism and nationalism only to despair and return to Islam. (Few intellectuals, however, embraced free-market capitalism, which was too much associated with the West.)

The time of modernization is a risky one in the life of a nation. If the old elite understands the changes that are bubbling through their society, they will gradually give way toward democracy in a fashion that does not destabilize the system. A corrupt and foolish elite, on the other hand, that is convinced the masses are not ready for democracy (and never will be), hold back political reforms until there is a tremendous head of steam. Then, no longer able to withstand the pressure, they suddenly give way, chaos breaks out and ends in tyranny. If the old elite had reformed sooner and gradually, they might have lowered the pressure and eased the transition to democracy. South Korea and Taiwan are examples of a favorable transition from dictatorship to democracy. Iran under the Shah is a negative example.

The Shah was arrogant: He alone would uplift Iran. He foresaw no democratic future for Iran and cultivated no important sectors of the population to support him. When the end came, few Iranians did support him. Indeed, the Shah scorned democracy in general, viewing it as a chaotic system that got in its own way, a view as old as the ancient Persian attack on Greece. The mighty Persian empire, under one ruler, could surely beat a quarrelsome collection of Greek city-states. (Wrong!) The Shah, repeating the millennia-old mistake, supposed that Iran, under his enlightened despotism, would soon surpass the decadent West. When a Western journalist asked the Shah why he did not relinquish some of his personal power and become a symbolic monarch, like the king of Sweden, the Shah replied: "I will become like the king of Sweden when Iranians become like Swedes." By this he indicated that unruly, tumultuous Iranians need a strong hand at the top.

The answer to this overly simple view is that, yes, when your people are poor and ignorant, absolute rule is one of your few alternatives. Such a country is far from ready for democracy. But after considerable modernization—which the Shah himself had implemented—you've got a different country, one characterized by the changes discussed earlier. The educated middle class especially resents one-man rule; the bigger this class, the more the resentment builds. By modernizing, the Shah was sawing off the tree limb on which he was sitting. He modernized Iran until it no longer wanted him.

Islam as a Political Ideology

Ayatollah Khomeini developed an interesting ideology that resonated with many Iranians. Called by some **Islamism**, it was not only religious but also social, economic, and nationalistic. The Shah and his regime, held Khomeini, not only abandoned Islam but also turned away from economic and social justice. They allowed the rich and corrupt to live in Westernized luxury while the broad masses struggled in poverty. They sold out Iran to the Americans, exchanging the people's oil for U.S. weapons. They permitted large numbers of Americans to live in Iran with their "unclean" morals, corrupting Iran's youth with their alcohol, sex, and rock music. By returning to the Koran, as interpreted by the mullahs, Iranians would not only

KEY CONCEPTS

IS "ISLAMIC FUNDAMENTALISM" THE RIGHT NAME?

Some object to the term "Islamic fundamentalism." First used to describe U.S. Bible-belt Protestants in the nineteenth century, "fundamentalism" stands for inerrancy of Scripture: The Bible means what it says and is not open to interpretation. But that's the way virtually all Muslims view the Koran, so Muslims are automatically "fundamentalists." Some thinkers propose we call it "Islamic integralism" instead, indicating a move to integrate the Koran and sharia with government. "Integralism" too is borrowed,

from a Catholic movement early in the twentieth century whose adherents sought to live a Christ-like existence.

Political scientists, of course, like to stress the political angle. Some use the term "political Islam," indicating it is the political and nationalistic use of religion to gain power. Along this line, it has been called "sacral nationalism," indicating that its underlying impulse is a nationalistic resentment of the West. And the term "Islamism," a religion turned into a political ideology, has been gaining favor for the simple reason that it's shorter.

cleanse themselves spiritually but also build a just society of equals. The mighty would be brought low and the poor raised up by extensive welfare benefits administered by mosques and Islamic associations. Like communism, Islamism preaches leveling of class differences, but through the mosque and mullahs rather than through the Party and *apparatchiks*.

Islamism is thus a catchall ideology, offering an answer to most things that made Iranians discontent. It's a potent brew, but can it work? Probably not. Over time, its many strands fall apart and start quarreling among themselves. Islamism's chief problem is economics (as we shall consider in greater detail later). As Islamism recedes as a viable ideology, look for the reemergence of other ideologies in Iran.

Democracy and Authority

If rule by the mullahs is someday overturned, can Iranians establish a stable democracy, or was the Shah right—do Iranians need a strong hand to govern them? There were two impulses behind the 1979 revolution: the demands of secularist intellectuals to become a democracy and the demands of Islamists to become a theocracy. The secular democrats, always a small minority, threw in with the more-numerous Islamists, figuring they would be an effective tool to oust the Shah and that the two would form a sort of equal partnership. But the Islamists, better organized and knowing exactly what they wanted, used the secular democrats and then dumped them (in some cases, shot them). Many fled to other countries. Learning too late what was happening to them, some democratic supporters of the Revolution put out the slogan: "In the dawn of freedom, there is no freedom."

But these secular democrats did not disappear; they simply laid low and went along outwardly with the Islamic Revolution. To have opposed it openly could have earned them the firing squad. Among them are the smartest and best-educated people in Iran, the very people needed to make the economy function. With Iran's drastic economic decline, many either lost their

POLITICAL CULTURE

ARE IRANIANS RELIGIOUS FANATICS?

Only some Iranians are religious fanatics. Not even the supposed Islamic fundamentalists are necessarily religious fanatics. Many Iranians are perfectly aware that religion is a political tool (more on this in the next section) and are fed up with it. Neither are Iranians anti-American on a personal basis. Despite massive regime propaganda depicting the United States as the "great satan," most Iranians are very friendly to the few Americans who visit. Some have been in the United States or have relatives there; many remember that when

Iran was allied with America, Iraq didn't dare invade. Do not confuse regime propaganda with the attitudes of ordinary citizens.

Ironically, Iranians labeled the Taliban government of neighboring Afghanistan as Muslim extremists. Far stricter than Iranian Islamists, the Taliban confine women to the home and require all men to have beards. Why the conflict with Iran? Like most of Afghanistan, the Taliban are Sunni and attacked the Shia minority, some 1.5 million of whom fled to Iran. When Iranian diplomats tried to aid Afghan Shiites, the Taliban killed them. Dangerous stuff, religious extremism.

jobs or decided it was more prudent to develop private practices as consultants and specialists, working out of their apartments. Many of them—once they are sure you are not a provocateur for the regime—speak scathingly in private of the oppression and economic foolishness of the rule of the mullahs. "I believe in Islam, but not in the regime of the mullahs," said one Iranian.

People like these—who voted for Khatami in 1997—believe Iranians are capable of democracy. They argue that the anti-Shah revolution was hijacked by the Islamists but that its original impulse was for democracy, not theocracy, and this impulse still remains. Especially now that people have tasted the economic decline, corruption, and general ineptitude of the mullahs, they are ready for democracy. Look for the secular democrats to increasingly make their arguments public and to demand open elections with no parties declared ineligible.

Persian Nationalism

Islam is not the only political force at work in Iran. Remember, Islam was imposed on Persia by the sword, and Iranians to this day harbor folk memories of seventh-century massacres by crude, barbaric invaders. Iranians do not like Arabs and look down on them as culturally inferior and lacking staying power. By adopting Shia, Iranians were and are able to distinguish themselves from their mostly Sunni neighbors. "Yes, of course we are Muslims," is the Iranian message, "but we are not like these other Muslim countries." Accordingly, not far under the surface of Iranian thought is a kind of Persian nationalism, affirming the greatness of their ancient civilization, which antedates Islam by a millennium.

Key Term

The Shah especially stressed Persian nationalism in his drive to modernize Iran. The Shah was a nominal Muslim and had himself photographed in religious devotion, as on his **hajj**, required of all Muslims who can possibly afford it

hajj   Muslim pilgrimage to Mecca.

once in their lifetime. But the Shah's true spirit was secular and nationalistic: to rebuild the glory of ancient Persia in a modern Iran. If Islam got in the way, it was to be pushed aside. The Shah was relatively tolerant of non-Muslim faiths; Baha'is (a universalistic and liberal offshoot of Islam), Jews, and Christians were gen-

erally unharmed. Since the Islamic Revolution, non-Muslims have been treated harshly, especially the 300,000 Baha'is, Iran's largest minority religion, who are regarded as dangerous **heretics**. For centuries, Iran's sense of its unique Persianness coexisted uneasily with its Islam. The Shah's modernization program brought the two strands into open conflict.

But if you look closely, even the Islamic Revolution of 1979 did not totally repudiate the Persian nationalist strand of Iranian thought. Rather, it put the stress on the religious side of Persianness. The long and horrible war with Iraq, 1980–88, especially brought out the Persian nationalist side of the Islamist regime. They were fighting not only for their faith but for their country and against a savage, upstart Arab country, Iraq, that didn't even exist until the British invented it in the 1920s. Iran celebrates two types of holidays, Persian and Muslim. The Persian holidays are all happy, such as New Year (*Now Ruz*). The Islamic holidays are mostly mournful, such as the day of remembrance of the martyrdom of Hussein at Kerbala, during which young Shi'ite men beat themselves until they bleed. In analyzing Iranian political attitudes, remember that Persianness is about as strong as Islam, and Iranian regimes typically base themselves on both, although often giving more weight to one. As the Islamic Revolution tires, be on the lookout for an Iranian switch back to greater emphasis on Persianness.

DEMOCRACY

IRAN'S ANGRY STUDENTS

In the late 1970s, Iranian students, most of them leftists, battled to overturn the old regime. Twenty years later, Iran's students—who number over one million—are again willing to turn to street demonstrations for civil rights. Many students are outspoken liberals and want to push President Khatami to pluralism, a free press, and free elections. As before, they also protest the serious lack of jobs.

In 1999, when a hard-line court closed a relatively liberal daily, *Salaam* (Peace), and convicted its editor, Tehran students erupted in a week of street protests that spread to several cities. Some were killed. The editor was himself a Muslim cleric, helper of Khomeini, and ally of Khatami. To say one is Muslim in Iran doesn't say much; there are Muslim liberals and Muslim conservatives. Newspapers are closed all the time for showing too much "tolerance and leniency," that is, support for pluralism.

Both Ayatollah Khamenei and President Khatami, who must maintain good relations with the Leader and the conservative Majlis, denounced the student riots. To repeat: Khatami operates within the the system, not against it. Could students one day pave the way to democracy? By themselves, probably not. They are too few and not organized. But in combination with other groups, they could push moderates like Khatami to take stronger reformist stances.

KEY CONCEPTS

SUNNI AND SHIA

Over 80 percent of all Muslims practice the mainstream branch of Islam, called Sunni. Scattered unevenly throughout the Muslim world, however, is a minority branch (of 100 million) called Shia. The two split early over who was the true successor (*caliph*) of Mohammed. Shi'ites claim the Prophet's cousin and son-in-law Ali has the title, but he was assassinated in 661. Shia means followers or partisans, hence Shi'ites are the followers of Ali. When Ali's son, Hussein, attempted to claim the title, his forces were beaten at Karbala in present-day Iraq (now a Shia shrine) in 680, and Hussein was betrayed and tortured to death. This gave Shia a fixation on martyrdom; some of their holidays feature self-flagellation.

Shia also developed a messianic concept lacking in Sunni. Shi'ites in Iran hold that the line of succession passed through a series of twelve *imams* (religious leaders) of whom Ali was the first. The twelfth imam disappeared but is to return one day to complete the Prophet's mission on earth. He is referred to as the Hidden Imam and the Expected One. Such believers are thus sometimes called "Twelver" Muslims. Shi'ites are no more "fundamentalist" than other Muslims, who also interpret the Koran strictly.

Although the origin and basic tenets of the two branches is identical, Sunnis regard Shi'ites as extremist, mystical, and crazy. Only in Iran is Shia the majority faith and state religion. With their underdog status elsewhere, Shi'ites sometimes become rebellious (with Iranian money and guidance), as in southern Lebanon, southern Iraq, and scattered through Arabia. Shia imparts a peculiar twist to Iranians, giving them the feeling of being isolated but right, beset by enemies on all sides, and willing to martyr themselves for their cause.

Patterns of Interaction

Religion as a Political Tool

Manipulate, use, dump. This is how Khomeini's forces treated those who helped them win the Revolution. Like turbaned Bolsheviks, the Islamists in the late 1970s hijacked the Iranian revolution as it unfolded. First, they captured the growing discontent with the Shah and his regime. By offering themselves as a plausible and effective front organization, they enlisted all manner of anti-Shah groups under their banner—the democratically inclined parties of the National Front, the Iran Freedom Movement, the Marxist (and Soviet-connected) Tudeh party, and Islamic guerrilla movements. They had some of these groups do their dirty work for them, and then got rid of them, sometimes by firing squad. The flowering of democratic, Islamic, secular, and socialist parties that accompanied the Shah's overthrow was crushed within three years. As an example of revolutionary technique, Lenin would have admired their skill and ruthlessness.

In doing all this, the Islamists used their religion much as the Bolsheviks used Marxism, as a tool, a recruiting and mobilizing device, a means of gaining authority and obedience, and a way to seize and consolidate power. This is not to say they were not serious about their religion, but rather that in a revolutionary situation the instrumental uses of their faith predominated over the devotional. If you want to seize state power, you can't be otherworldly; you've got to be very shrewd and practical. There's nothing "crazy" about the Islamists who run Iran; they are perfectly capable of calm and rational decisions calculated to benefit themselves. They only look crazy.

After some time immersed in the world of politics, the power side takes over and the original religious (or ideological) side takes a back seat. As with the Bolsheviks, this soon leads to opportunism and cynicism among the politically involved and ultimately to regime decay. The ruling group turns into a self-serving new class. This is why regimes that base themselves on ideology or religion (Islamism combines both) have finite lifespans. After a while, the power and greed of the ruling class is noticed by all, and mass disillusion sets in; the regime loses its legitimacy. This is happening in Iran. Eventually Iran's Islamic revolution will burn out.

Radicals and Moderates in Iran

After the 1986 Iran-contra fiasco, in which White House aides attempted to secretly sell U.S. missiles to alleged Iranian "moderates," the term "Iranian moderate" disappeared from Washington's vocabulary. The Americans, led by Marine Lt. Col. Oliver North, fell for a sucker play by Iranian revolutionary leaders, who set up the deal and then leaked word that the United States was trading with Iran, illegal under U.S. law. These people never miss a chance to embarrass the United States. There are Iranian moderates; it's just that they've learned to keep their mouths shut and do nothing stupid, like having contact with Americans. Instead, the Iranians who fit under the labels "moderates" and "liberals" discussed earlier play a cautious game, not directly opposing the Islamic revolution while trying to tone it down. They are in a permanent power struggle with conservative forces.

Those who fit under the labels "radicals" and "conservatives" want an Islamic republic, one based on religious law and presided over by the *faqih*. Anything else means giving in to

POLITICAL CULTURE

DOES ISLAM DISCRIMINATE AGAINST WOMEN?

Iran is actually one of the better Muslim countries when it comes to the treatment of women. Unlike the Arab kingdoms on the southern shore of the Gulf, Iranian women drive cars, go to school, work outside the home, and participate in politics. But even in Iran there are tough restrictions on dress, contact with males, and travel.

Devout Muslims swear women are deeply honored in their societies; it's just that their place is in the home and nowhere else. Women are indeed kept at a subservient status in most Islamic countries; often they get little education, cannot drive a car, and their testimony is worth half of men's in courts of law. But such discrimination does not always come from the Koran. In some Muslim countries (not Iran), such customs as the seclusion of women, the veil, and female genital mutilation are pre-Islamic and were absorbed by Islam (much as Europeans adopted for Christmas the pagan worship of trees). These non-Koranic imports can therefore be discarded with no harm to the faith, maintain Muslim feminists. Yes, there are such people, and increasingly they are speaking out and organizing. If they succeed, they will greatly modernize their societies. The widespread education of Iranian women suggests social and legal change will arrive there before long.

Iran's enemies—the West in general, the United States in particular—with eventual loss of Iran's independence, culture, and religion. They do anything they can to block liberalizing reforms, from closing newspapers to voting out ministers to putting allies of Khatami on trial.

In a parallel with what we did earlier for Russia and China, we can construct a list of Iranian moderate and Islamist views (see table on page 492). On at least a couple of points there is no clear divergence between moderates and Islamists. First, both groups are Muslim and want to preserve a generally Islamic emphasis in public life, including the judicial system. Second, both groups want economic growth, both for the sake of Iran's national power and to improve the lot of its people. It's how to do this that is the bone of contention: free market or state controlled? In elections no one runs on an opposition platform; all seem to be supporting at least a version of the Islamic revolution. In Iran, direct opposition could be hazardous to your health. It is in the nuances among groupings that differences begin to appear.

There are some Iranians, both inside and outside the country, who would like to get rid of the whole Islamic revolution. A few monarchists, mostly people who got rich under the Shah, would like to restore the son of the last Pahlavi, a young man now living in the West, to the

THE UNITED STATES AND IRAN: THE U.S. EMBASSY TAKEOVER

The seizure of the U.S. embassy in Tehran by student militants in November 1979 brought American cries of outrage and a complete break in relations. The embassy takeover and holding of fifty-two American officials for 444 days indeed broke every rule in the diplomatic book and seemed to prove Iran was governed by mad fanatics.

Looked at more closely, the incident was a domestic Iranian power play, cynically manipulated by the Khomeini forces. The ayatollah had no further use for the prime minister he had appointed early in 1979, Mehdi Bazargan, a relative moderate. How to get rid of him and other moderates? The occasion was the admission of the ailing Shah to the United States for cancer treatment. Khomeini's cadres whipped up mass rage in Iran, claiming that this U.S. humanitarian gesture proved the United State still supported the Shah's ousted regime. Then they had a group of student militants invade and take over the U.S. embassy, which had already been reduced to a skeleton staff. No shots were fired; the U.S. Marine guards were ordered not to shoot. They took sixty-six Americans prisoner—but killed none and released fourteen—and published classified embassy documents (pieced together from the shredder) purporting to show how dastardly the Americans were.

The Islamic activists, using anti-American hysteria ("Death to USA!"), consolidated their hold on the country. Humiliated and powerless, Bazargan resigned. Anyone opposed to the embassy takeover was fired or worse. One foreign-ministry official (who had dropped out of Georgetown University to promote revolution) helped some Americans escape via the Canadian embassy. He was tried and shot. Khomeini's followers seemed to enjoy watching President Carter squirm, especially after the aborted U.S. rescue mission in April 1980. Carter's apparent weakness on Iran hurt him in the 1980 election, which he lost to Reagan.

At that point, the holding of U.S. diplomats had exhausted its utility for Khomeini. Knowing Reagan was not averse to military measures, Tehran released the diplomats just as he was inaugurated. The militants who had seized and held the Americans had also served their purpose. Considered unreliable, some were arrested and executed. Others were sent to the front in the war with Iraq, where they died in the fighting. The revolution devours its children.

COMPARISON

IS SAUDI ARABIA NEXT?

The bombings of U.S. servicemen in Saudi Arabia remind us that not all is well in the Kingdom, as Saudis call their country. Not far under the surface are the same kind of antiregime forces that overthrew the Shah in Iran. The Saudi regime, which established itself in the 1920s based on the Wahhabi brand of strict Islam, is vulnerable for the same reasons we reviewed earlier in Iran. The legitimacy of the royal family has come into question, because many of them play around, Western-style, in a non-Islamic fashion. The House of Saud has some four thousand princes, with more than five hundred of them eligible to become king, an invitation for a succession struggle.

Oil created some very rich people, including the princes, but left many poor Saudis behind. Earlier, oil revenues allowed the regime to buy off discontent with subsidies for everyone from wheat farmers (who use expensive desalinated seawater) to students (who got scholarships to study overseas). But oil prices dropped, and the Kingdom paid much of the cost of the 1991 Gulf War. Saudi Arabia now has a debt and budget deficit; it is no longer nearly so rich. Cushy jobs no longer await young Saudis, who must now work for a living.

Making matters worse, in the oil-producing Eastern Province are Shi'ites, who (with Iranian backing) carry out acts of terrorism. In 1979 Sunni fanatics (also with Iranian help) seized the holiest Islamic shrine in Mecca until dislodged by French special forces. News from the Kingdom is rigorously censored—nothing negative is allowed—and Washington never utters a word critical of or worried about our good friends, the House of Saud. It was the same way we treated the Shah.

What can be done? It may be too late to do anything, as attempting reforms can easily trigger revolution. Still, drawing lessons from the Iranian revolution, we might suggest that the Saudi government do the following:

Allow some opposition parties: Make sure they are moderate, and let them criticize the regime in a constructive way. Make sure there are many parties (some conservative, some liberal, none radical) to divide public discontent.

Permit a semifree press: Make it along the same lines as parties—limited criticism only.

Crush and suppress revolutionaries: Don't ease up on them. They are out to destroy you, and if they take over they will not be moderate or democratic. Be especially ruthless with any group getting Iranian or Iraqi support.

Hold legislative elections: But make them elections with a list of parties limited to the authorized ones (i.e., ranging from conservative to moderate). Gradually, over many years, you can expand the list.

Have the new legislature redistribute wealth in the form of heavy taxes on the rich: Impose taxes especially on members of the royal family, who must be seen taking a financial hit. This is to defuse mass anger over the great and unfair wealth of the royals. The princes don't like paying taxes? Point out to them they could lose everything—including their heads—if they aren't careful.

Limit the American presence; it is a cultural irritant: Women soldiers, American media, and foreigners on holy Islamic soil offer natural fodder for Islamic extremists. The handful of Americans left should be nearly invisible.

Crack down on corruption, especially among the highest officials and princes: Show that you mean business here, and that the crackdown will be permanent.

Have we learned anything from Iran? Would any of this work to head off a revolution? Maybe, but it would require the willingness of the House of Saud to cut its own wealth and power, and that is something ruling classes rarely do. But if Saudi Arabia cannot make the transition to some kind of democracy, revolution and then U.S. military involvement is likely. The Persian Gulf and its oil is one place we do not walk away from.

The spirit of Iran's Islamic Revolution lives on in this Tehran cemetery memorial to the fallen of the Iran-Iraq war of 1980–88. Losses were horrifying—some three-quarters of a million killed, many of them boys. Note the women in chadors in the foreground. (Mehrdad Madresehee)

throne. Only in conditions of extreme domestic chaos is this even dimly feasible. Even Iranians who think the Shah's rule was not so bad do not consider this option. The times are against monarchy; every decade there are fewer and fewer ruling (as opposed to figurehead) monarchs.

On the other side, some Marxist-type revolutionaries, the *Mujahedin-e Khalq* (Fighters for the People), who earlier worked with the Islamists to overthrow the Shah now try to overthrow the Islamists. Among them were some of the young militants who seized the U.S. embassy. Subsequently, it is estimated that over 10,000 Mujahedin were executed by the Khomeini forces. Their survivors have a headquarters in Paris and are sheltered in and sponsored by Iraq, which invaded and massacred Iranians (sometimes with poison gas), during the 1980s, so these Mujahedin have little resonance among Iranians.

Change is coming from the struggle between Iranian militants and moderates, not the influence of monarchists, leftists, or outside forces. For example, one of the key alliances of the 1979 Iranian revolution was between the mullahs, the Muslim clerics, and the *bazaaris*, the small merchants whose shops are often in a bazaar (a Persian word). Suffering under the Shah's top-heavy modernization—bakers were put out of business by bread factories, clothiers by department stores, cobblers by shoe factories, and so on—the *bazaaris*' shift to the Islamic revolution

Moderates	*Islamists*
shift power to Majlis	preserve power of *faqih*
permit all parties	outlaw non-Islamic parties
free press	controlled press
permit Western women's attire	Islamic attire only (veil)
improve relations with West	keep distant from West
stop hating America	keep hating America
don't spread Islamic revolution	keep spreading it
liberalize economy	keep economy statist

guaranteed its success. But now many *bazaaris* are also fed up with the mullahs, whose corruption and amassing of wealth has betrayed the revolution. Accordingly, some *bazaaris* back moderates in the Majlis, especially those who understand the needs of small businesspeople. Even in revolutionary Iran, interest groups are alive and well.

The Revolution Burns Out

Review Crane Brinton's classic theory of revolution on page 96. Notice how the Iranian revolution fits it well. To recapitulate: The old regime loses its legitimacy. Antiregime groups form, rioting breaks out, and the old regime folds. Initially moderates seize power, but they are soon dumped by more ruthless radicals, who drive the revolution to a frenzied high point. But people can't take that forever; eventually a "Thermidor," or calming down, arrives. Iran passed through each of these stages almost as if Iranians had read Brinton. Every stage, that is, except the last, and even that seems to be have happened without a clear-cut Thermidor. Instead, there may be a low-key, rolling Thermidor that led to Khatami's election in 1997.

No revolution lasts forever. In Iran we see an effort to become stable and normal, disputed, to be sure, by Islamic revolutionary militancy. Time is probably on the side of the normalizers. In the first place, many mullahs have corrupted themselves. Mullahs were placed in control of *bunyads*, foundations originally set up to redistribute the wealth of the Shah and his supporters. These *bunyads* now control billions of dollars and much of Iran's industry. They are supposed to be run for the good of all, a sort of Islamic socialism, but in practice they have made their mullahs rich, powerful, and corrupt while their industries are run poorly. As Lord Acton observed (see page 29), power corrupts.

Aware of this, many Iranians want the mullahs to return to the mosque and get out of government and the economy. Even some mullahs wish to return to the mosque. Here we have a parallel with the Brazilian generals, who bowed out when they came to realize that running a country was ruining their reputation and their mission in life. Chanted Iranian students in 1999: "The mullahs have become God, and the people have become poor." Another factor is that now half of Iranians were born after the Shah and have no personal commitment to the Islamic revolution. They want jobs and more freedom and they can vote at age seventeen. (In raising the voting age from sixteen to seventeen in 2000, the mullahs kept out some 1.5 million young voters, most of them favoring reforms.)

Will there be a point at which we can say the Iranian revolution has burnt itself out? The reestablishment of diplomatic ties between the United States and Iran would indicate that point had passed. Khatami has mentioned "dialogue" with Americans (but not with Washington) but pulled back when conservative forces objected. Other indications would be the mullahs giving up control of the *bunyads* and the *faqih* becoming a figurehead or "dignified" office.

What Iranians Quarrel About

Which Way for Iran's Economy?

Iran has changed rapidly, partly under the Shah and partly under the Islamic Revolution. The countryside has received schools, electricity, health care, and tractors. Infant mortality, a key measure of health care, fell from 169 per 1,000 births in 1960 to 33 in 1996. Average life expectancy

HOW MANY IRANIANS?

Islam frowns upon family planning: The more babies the better. After the revolution, Iran's mullahs urged women to produce a generation of Muslim militants; subsidized food helped feed them. Iran's rate of population growth for several years averaged 3.7 percent a year, one of the world's highest. Despite the murderous war with Iraq, in less than two decades after the Revolution Iran's population doubled from 34 million to 68 million.

By the early 1990s, though, the government, realizing it could not subsidize or employ the vast numbers of young Iranians, reversed the high-births policy. Amid economic decline, families now can afford fewer children. Clinics now offer all manner of contraception free of charge (but not abortions). Women agents go door-to-door to promote family planning. Food and other family aid is decreased after a family has three children. One Muslim cleric even issued a *fatwa* in favor of smaller families. From an average 7 births per woman during her life in 1986, the fertility rate dropped to half, to 3.6 births per woman over her life in 1993, actually much lower than before the revolution. By 1995, the rate of population growth was down to a more reasonable 2.3 percent (which, if held, would still double the population in thirty years.) The turnaround on births is an indication the revolution is over.

jumped thirteen years, from 50 to 69. Literacy has climbed from less than half to two-thirds. More Iranian women than ever are in schools (segregated from males, of course) and universities.

The Iranian economy—ruined by revolution, war, isolation, and mismanagement—declined steeply in the 1980s until now per capita income is about a third of what it was under the Shah. There is some growth, but inflation, although somewhat tamed, is still hefty. Many Iranian workers are unemployed. Pay is low so people hold two and three jobs to make ends meet. Many jobs and business dealings, as in Russia, are off the books. Even the oil industry, once the pride and basis of the Iranian economy, has suffered from lack of replacement parts and up-to-date technology. U.S. pressure has kept most oil companies from cooperating with Iran. The mullahs who run the *bunyads* run them badly and corruptly, and increasingly Iranians notice this.

By giving all Iranians a welfare floor—including subsidized food and gasoline—while simultaneously damaging Iran's great source of revenue, its petroleum connection with the West—Tehran has run out of money. Iran runs large annual budget deficits, which translate into persistent inflation. The Shah left a foreign debt of $8.4 billion, which the Khomeini regime, amid great hardship, repaid, swearing Iran would never fall into imperialist clutches again. But by 1996, Iran's foreign debt was a dangerous $33 billion. Under worsening material conditions, many of the early adherents of Islamism have dropped out or even come to oppose it. The true believers, the **hezbollahis**, still try to supervise much of Iranian society, but they are an increasingly resented minority, the functional equivalent of the old Soviet Communist party. And you recall what happened to them.

The Islamic Revolution did not dismantle the Shah's statist economy. State-owned business (the biggest: oil) still produce 86 percent of Iran's GDP. And much of the rest is in the hands of the *bunyads*. Theoretically, foreigners can invest in Iran, but the limits and regulations are so many and so tangled that

Key Term

hezbollahi "Partisan of God"; fanatic supporter of Islamism.

most investors are scared off. To get anything done requires numerous bribes. Iran's is not a free-market economy. The big question: Should it become one?

Opposing arguments show up in Majlis debates over economic policy, which have become thinly disguised battles over the future of strict Islamic rule. As we have considered, Islamism is a surrogate socialism; that is, it blends Islamic correctness with collectivist economics. In the minds of many Islamists, socialism is the logical extension of Islam, for Islam preaches equality and leveling of class differences. Thus, they claim, Islam is the true and best path to a just society of equal citizens, where no one is either rich or poor. What the Marxists, Socialists, and Communists talked about, they say, we can deliver.

Most moderates respond that socialism and/or statism is not the way to go, that they just keep Iran poor and backward. The collapse of the Soviet system demonstrates socialism doesn't work, and the decline of Iran's economy demonstrates statism doesn't work. Besides, they note, there is no Koranic basis for government control of the economy. It is perfectly feasible to combine free-market capitalism with the alms-giving required of faithful Muslims to achieve social justice. If we keep declining economically, moderates also worry, we'll never be able to build a first-class army and so will be vulnerable to hostile outside forces. And if our towering unemployment problem is not solved soon, the whole Islamic revolution could be doomed. The best and quickest way to solve these problems is the free market. State ownership of major industries, especially petroleum, is what the Shah tried, and we certainly don't want to follow in his footsteps. Such are the arguments of Iranian moderates. Notice that outright rejection of the Islamic revolution is not one of their points.

THE UNITED STATES AND IRAN: AMERICA, DON'T MESS WITH IRAN

We don't understand the Iranian revolution and have not been clever in dealing with it. Part religious, part nationalistic, part cultural, and part antityrannical, the Iranian revolution defied our predictions and efforts to tame it. When we tried to deal with alleged "Iranian moderates" in 1986, we were humiliated. When we tilted toward Iraq in its war against Iran, we supported a fiendish dictator (Saddam Hussein) whom we soon had to fight ourselves. In 1988 a U.S. destroyer mistook an Iranian jetliner for an attacking fighter, shot it down with a missile, and killed all 290 aboard. (Some specialists believe the downing of Pan Am 103 over Scotland later that year was a retaliation.) Iran, and indeed the whole Persian Gulf, is a tar baby: Once you punch it, you get stuck worse and worse.

But if we leave Iran alone, things may break our way. As pointed out in these pages, Iran's Islamic revolution is waning and relative moderates have a chance to take over. In the long term, Iran needs us. We can provide the petroleum technology and other means to modernize the country. If an aggressive Russia starts rebuilding its Caucasian empire, Iran would find U.S. support awfully handy. Historically, Russia always had territorial designs on Persia; the United States never did. We need not be enemies forever.

Anthropologists have pointed out that when two Iranian *bazaaris* quarrel, by long tradition they simply shun and ignore each other for some years. Gradually, the quarrel fades and they cautiously reestablish relations with each other. After a while, the quarrel is forgotten. Actually, it's a rather civilized way to handle a quarrel. We might take a leaf from a Persian folkway in dealing with Iran and avoid another Cold War.

THE UNITED STATES AND IRAN: IRAN, DON'T MESS WITH AMERICA

You Iranians don't understand American culture very well. Americans are in many ways the opposite of Iranians; we are direct, unsubtle, and prone to violence: cowboys. When we see something stamped "enemy," we destroy it. We like black and white, not shades of grey. Our presidents are especially afraid of appearing weak; it hurts their chances for re-election. Americans like tough, decisive action, especially if accompanied by good TV film clips.

Accordingly, Iranians, do not let yourselves be seen as hostile or dangerous to America. Do not chant *Marg bar Amrika!* ("Death to America!"), as we take it literally. The U.S. commitment to making sure the oil of the Persian Gulf flows in a friendly fashion is one point Americans agree on in foreign policy. No amount of bombings can persuade us to abandon this policy. And we can "make your economy scream." Those were Kissinger's

words describing what we did to Chile when it came under Marxist rule. (We're probably doing it to you now.)

So end all sponsorship and encouragement of terrorist activity, especially that aimed at Americans. Do not develop a nuclear device; remember, we have thousands of them. Turn to your tradition and simply shun America, doing nothing against us. And when you're ready to resume contact and economic growth, let us know in a public way. We understand that you are going through a terrible power struggle between conservatives and reformers and that you can't move prematurely. Eventually, there will be a thaw. We were friends once and can be again. One area of possible cooperation: an oil pipeline from Central Asia to the Persian Gulf. Another area: our mutual enmity toward Iraq. The Middle East, after all, is the origin of the famous diplomatic dictum: "The enemy of my enemy is my friend."

The Veiled Debate on Islam

Iran will always be a Muslim country, but what kind of Islam will it have? A relatively moderate kind that largely keeps out of direct political involvement or a militant kind that seeks to guide society by political means? Judging by the victories of reformists in elections, most would opt for the first kind.

Because outright liberal candidates are barred by the Council of Guardians, public debate on the religion question is muted. No one wants to risk being branded "anti-Islamic." Still, one can infer that such a debate is taking place. One of the stand-ins for a discussion of Islam in public life is the debate on what kind of clothing is admissible, especially for women. Even for men, though, blue jeans were frowned upon, partly because they represent American culture. Liberals say, no, they don't; jeans are simply a comfortable and international garment with no political connotations.

Before the Islamic revolution, urban and educated Iranian women dressed as fashionably as European women. Then suddenly they could wear no makeup and had to wear the veil and *chador*, the single-piece head-to-toe garment designed to cover feminine attractiveness. Devout Muslims, including many women, say this attire is better than Western clothing as it eliminates lust, vanity, and distinctions of wealth. (Notice how some U.S. schools are coming to similar conclusions about school uniforms.) Western clothes and makeup are the first steps toward debauchery and prostitution, they argue, and anyone who thinks otherwise is deemed anti-Islamic. But in subtle ways urban Iranian women dress in a manner that pushes to the limit of the permissible in public (and in private dress as they wish). The veil and *chador* are no longer mandatory on the street, so long as a woman is dressed modestly without makeup and with hair and forehead covered by a kerchief. Push beyond this and women run the risk of Islamic *komitehs* (morals police) stopping them on the street and sending them home or to jail. These volunteer squads have become one of the most obnoxious features of the Islamic revolution and have pushed urban and educated Iranians away from the revolution. The lifting of Islamically correct clothing requirements will mark an overall retreat in the political power of the mullahs.

What Kind of Foreign Policy?

The guiding lights of the Islamic revolution had aspirations beyond Iran. Some still have. They saw themselves as the revitalizers of the entire Islamic world and tried to spread their revolution, especially among Shi'ites but also among Muslims in general. One of their earliest areas of concern were the Shi'ites of southern Iraq, long a large, suppressed minority. Actually, by the time you subtract the Shi'ites of the south and Kurds of the north of Iraq, the Sunni Arabs of the middle of Iraq are a minority, but political power has always been in their hands, and they don't share it. Many of the main shrines of Shia are in southern Iraq, the area Khomeini was exiled to in 1964. Upon taking power in Tehran, the Khomeini people propagandized Iraqi

GEOGRAPHY

STRATEGIC WATERWAYS

These are mostly narrow choke points connecting two bodies of water. Hostile control of them causes one or more countries discomfort or fear. Here are the main ones:

Turkish Straits (Dardanelles and Bosporus), connecting the Black and Mediterranean Seas.

Strait of Gibraltar, connecting the Atlantic and the Mediterranean.

Suez Canal, connecting the Mediterranean and Red Seas.

Bab al Mandab, connecting the Red Sea and Indian Ocean.

Strait of Hormuz, connecting the Persian Gulf and Indian Ocean.

English Channel, connecting the Atlantic Ocean and North Sea.

Skagerrak, connecting the Baltic and North Seas.

North Cape, dividing the Atlantic from the Barents Sea.

Cape of Good Hope, where the Atlantic and Indian Oceans meet off the southern tip of Africa.

Strait of Malacca, connecting the Indian Ocean and South China Sea, the oil lifeline of East Asia.

Korea (Tsushima) Strait, connecting the East China Sea and Sea of Japan.

Panama Canal, connecting the Atlantic and Pacific Oceans.

You are the captain of a small tanker that has just loaded oil in Kuwait for delivery in Umea, Sweden. Which bodies of water—including seas, oceans, straits, and canals—do you pass through? (Note: Supertankers are too big for Suez; they have to go around Africa. But small tankers still pass through Suez.)

Shi'ites and urged them to join the Islamic revolution. This was one of the irritants—but hardly a sufficient excuse—for Iraqi dictator Saddam Hussein to invade Iran in 1980.

Wherever there are Shi'ites, Iranian influence turns up: southern Lebanon, Kuwait, Bahrain, and Saudi Arabia. Funds, instructions, and explosive devices flow through this connection. Iran, along with Iraq, Syria, and Libya, were placed on the U.S. State Department's list of countries sponsoring terrorism. Iran feels it must take a leading role in

GEOGRAPHY

BOUND ISRAEL

Israel is bounded on the north by Lebanon and Syria; on the east by Jordan; on the south by Egypt; and on the west by the Mediterranean Sea.

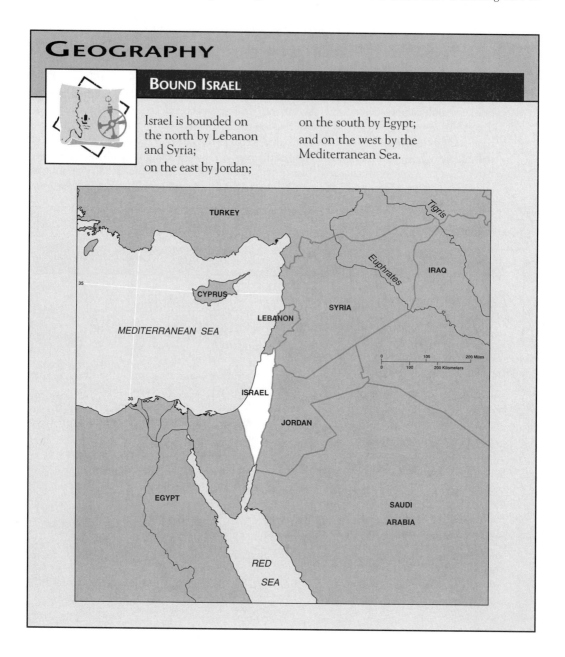

POLITICAL CULTURE

A FATWA ON RUSHDIE

One of the more horrifying examples of the Iranian revolution was the turning of a **fatwa** into an international death warrant. In 1989 Khomeini issued a *fatwa* ordering the execution of British author Salman Rushdie, a lapsed Muslim of Indian origin. Rushdie had just published his *Satanic Verses*, a fantasy on the life of Mohammed that was extremely offensive to devout Muslims. A semi-official Tehran foundation offered a reward of $1 million (later raised to $2.8 million) for killing Rushdie, who went into hiding for years. Even now, he appears rarely and cautiously; he knows they mean it.

The Western world was aghast at this order to kill someone in a faraway country for writing a book. The entire concept of the *fatwa* underscores the vast cultural differences between Islamic and Western civilizations. (In 1993, the top Saudi cleric issued a *fatwa* that the earth is flat and anyone claiming it round should be punished as an atheist.) Iran's relations with most of Europe deteriorated. Even many Iranians are embarrassed and apologetic over the *fatwa* and wish it rescinded. Khomeini's successors claim that he's the only one who can rescind it, and he died a few months after issuing it. Even though the Tehran government says it has dissociated itself from the *fatwa* on Rushdie, it continues as a block to improved Iranian relations with other countries.

destroying Israel, which it depicts as a polluter of Islamic holy ground (Jerusalem is also sacred to Muslims) and outpost of Western imperialism. Under the Shah, Tehran had good (but informal) relations with Israel and quietly sold it most of its oil. Suddenly that totally changed, and Iran supports Lebanon's *Hezbollah* (Party of God), which harasses Israel's northern border. (One of the best information sources for critical Iranians is Israeli radio, which broadcasts to Iran in Farsi.)

How many enemies can a country handle at once? On all sides but one—the northeast, namely the ex-Soviet Muslim republics of Central Asia—Iran now faces enemies. To a considerable extent, by trying to spread its revolution, it has made these enemies. And it has no allies that can do it any good. This has put Iran into a tight squeeze, limiting its economic growth and requiring it to maintain armed forces it cannot afford. Many thinking Iranians want to call off any attempt to spread the Islamic revolution. It brings nothing but trouble and no rewards. A few militant mullahs want to keep going, no matter what it costs the country. The ending of Iranian support for militant Shi'ites elsewhere will be another sign that Iran's moderates have prevailed.

Another nasty pattern revolutionary Iran has fallen into is terrorism, both as victim and practitioner. Antiregime forces, particularly the Mujahedin-e Khalk, assassinated several Iranian leaders, including one prime minister. In return, Iranian hit squads in Europe took out several regime opponents, including a former prime minister and the leaders of a breakaway Kurdish movement. This kind of "war in the shadows" simply deepens Iran's isolation from the world community.

Key Term

fatwa A ruling issued by an Islamic jurist.

Do Revolutions End Badly?

Burke (see box on page 31) was right: Revolution brings in its wake tyranny far worse than that of the regime it toppled. Iran is a good example: The Shah was a dictator, but rule of the mullahs is worse. Only in America did revolution lead to the establishment of a just, stable, democracy—and the American revolution was a very special, limited one, aimed more at independence than at revolution. The twentieth century is littered with failed revolutions: fascist, communist, and now Islamist. The few remaining Communist countries that still celebrate and base their legitimacy on an alleged revolution, Cuba and North Korea, are hungry and isolated. Communist China and Vietnam, by partly integrating their economies with world trade, have so far been spared this fate.

Why do revolutions end badly? Several writers have attempted to answer this question. Burke argued that the destruction of all institutional and political structures leaves people confused and ripe for dictatorial rule. François Furet (see box on page 121), wrote along similar lines that the French Revolution unleashed such chaotic forces that it had to "skid out of control." Crane Brinton wrote that revolutions fall into the hands of their most ruthless element, who then proceed to wreck everything until they are replaced in a "Thermidor." Hannah Arendt wrote that revolution goes astray when revolutionists try to solve the "Social Question" (how to bring down the rich and help the poor); to do this they must institute a tyranny. It is interesting to note all these writers were, to some extent, conservatives. Radicals and leftists often refuse to admit revolutions end badly; if something goes wrong they tend to blame individuals for "betraying" the revolution.

The unhappy revolution is something Iranians ponder. Although few want a return of the Pahlavis, many Iranians—in private conversation with people they can trust—indicate the Islamic revolution has turned out wrong. At least under the Shah there was economic growth, however unfairly distributed, and modernization. Now there is economic decline and unemployment. Most Iranians live more poorly now than before. Certain mullahs and their friends, those in charge of the *bunyads*, are doing well. Given a chance, many Iranians would be delighted to throw these rascals out. The mullahs, their security forces, and their *komitehs* try to make sure this won't happen. They have some bases of support—more than the Shah had—among the religious and certain groups of the poor who have benefited from Islamic handouts. President Khatami must fight a two-front war, against the conservatives and militants on his right and against the liberals and students on his left.

And what should we do? Only wait. Direct interference just gives the Islamists more nationalistic propaganda points: "You see, the U.S. imperialists are trying to destroy poor little Iran." Time and economic difficulties are breaking the Iranian revolution, just as it broke the Communist revolution in the Soviet Union.

Key Terms

ayatollah (p. 478)

canon law (p. 479)

containment (p. 477)

fatwa (p. 499)

hajj (p. 486)

heretic (p. 487)

hezbollahi (p. 494)

Islam (p. 474)

Further Reference

Arjomand, Said Amir. *The Turban for the Crown: The Islamic Revolution in Iran.* New York: Oxford University Press, 1988.

Bahrampour, Tara. *To See and See Again: A Life in Iran and America.* New York: Farrar, Straus & Giroux, 1999.

Baktiari, Bahman. *Parliamentary Politics in Revolutionary Iran: The Institutionalization of Factional Politics.* Gainesville, FL: University Press of Florida, 1996.

Esposito, John L., ed. *Political Islam: Revolution, Radicalism, or Reform?* Boulder, CO: Lynee Rienner, 1997.

Halliday, Fred. *Islam and the Myth of Confrontation: Religion and Politics in the Middle East.* London: I. B. Tauris, 1996.

Keddie, Nikki R. *Iran and the Muslim World: Resistance and Revolution.* New York: New York University Press, 1995.

Mackey, Sandra. *The Iranians: Persia, Islam, and the Soul of a Nation.* New York: Dutton, 1996.

Miller, Judith. *God has Ninety-Nine Names: Reporting from a Militant Middle East.* New York: Simon & Schuster, 1996.

Moin, Baqer. *Khomeini: Life of the Ayatollah.* London: I. B. Tauris, 1999.

Rahnema, Saeed, and Sohrab Behdad, eds. *Iran After the Revolution: Crisis of an Islamic State.* New York: St. Martin's, 1994.

Ramazani, R. K. *Revolutionary Iran: Challenge and Response in the Middle East.* Baltimore, MD: Johns Hopkins University Press, 1994.

Schirazi, Asghar. *The Constitution of Iran: Politics and the State in the Islamic Republic.* London: I. B. Tauris, 1998.

Watt, William Montgomery. *Islamic Political Thought.* New York: Columbia University Press, 1998.

Lessons of Nine Countries

31

1. States   States often precede and create nations. Countries are rather artificial things, the product of governments instilling a common psychology over many generations. A working, effective government is the crux of nationhood.

2. The Modern State   The modern state has existed only about half a millennium and is not necessarily the last word in political organization. The emergence of the European Union suggests possibilities beyond the nation-state.

3. Boundaries   Most boundaries are artificial. Where one country ends and another begins is a political decision, often contested. The expansion and contraction of Germany is an example of how fluid some boundaries can be.

4. Core Areas   Most countries have core areas, often where the state began, that are still home to the country's capital. Outside of these core areas, in the periphery, regionalism and resentment at being governed by a distant capital often grow. Thus peripheral areas often vote differently than core areas.

5. The Past   The past is alive and well and living in current politics. The past forms a country's political institutions, attitudes, and quarrels. The past is especially lively in the resentments of aggrieved people, for example among regions and social groups that feel they've been shortchanged.

6. Wars   Wars are dangerous to political systems and all living things. War, said Marx, is the midwife of revolution. Many of our nine countries have undergone total system change as a result of war. Moral: Think twice about going to war; it may mean the end of your system.

7. Economic Growth   Economic growth is destabilizing, especially rapid growth. Economic growth and change bring new people into politics, some of them bitterly discontent. Don't think economic growth solves political problems; it often makes them worse. Political change must accompany economic change in order to head off revolution.

8. Change   A system that cannot change to meet new challenges may be doomed. The wisest rulers are those who make gradual and incremental changes in order to avoid sudden and radical changes. Rulers who wait to reform until revolution is nigh may actually fan its flames by offering concessions. All regimes tend to petrify; the good ones stay flexible.

9. Institutions   Solid, time-tested institutions that people believe in are a bulwark of political stability. No political leader, however clever, has pulled functioning institutions out of a hat. They require time, intelligence, and continual modification.

10. Constitutions   Constitutions rarely work the way they're supposed to on paper. Many factors modify the working of constitutions: popular attitudes, usages that change over time, powerful parties and interest groups, and behind-the-scenes deals.

11. Parliaments   Everywhere, parliaments are in decline. Some have become little more than window dressing; some are under such tight executive and/or party control that they have lost their autonomy, and only a few are fighting to regain it. As governance becomes more complex and technical, power flows to bureaucrats and experts.

12. Bureaucracies   Everywhere, bureaucracies are in the ascendancy. In some systems, such as Japan, the permanent civil service is already the most powerful institution. Bureaucrats tend to see themselves as indispensable, the saviors of their countries. No country has yet devised a way to control its bureaucracies.

13. Multiparty Systems   Multiparty systems tend to be more unstable than two-party systems. Much depends on other factors, such as the rules for forming a cabinet or choosing the executive. Reforms can stabilize multiparty systems so that their behavior is not much different from two-party systems.

14. Electoral Systems   Electoral systems help determine party systems. Single-member districts with a simple plurality required to win tend to produce two-party systems because third parties have difficulty surviving in such systems. Proportional representation tends to produce many parties.

15. Federal and Unitary Systems   There are no longer purely federal or purely unitary systems. Instead, the trend is for federations to grant more and more power to the center, while unitary systems set up regional governments and devolve some powers to them.

16. Cabinets   Most cabinets consist of about twenty ministers. By American standards, other cabinets are large and their portfolios rather specialized. In the United States, there is a reluctance to add new departments. In Europe, ministries are added, deleted, or combined as the prime minister sees fit; the legislature automatically goes along.

17. Prime Ministers   In some ways, prime ministers in parliamentary systems are more powerful than presidents in presidential systems. Prime ministers, if they have an assured and disciplined majority in parliament, can get just about whatever they deem necessary. There is no deadlock between executive and legislative. Prime ministers who have to rely on coalitions, of course, are weaker.

18. Mass Participation   Most people, most of the time, aren't much interested in politics. As you go down the socioeconomic ladder, you usually find less and less interest in political participation. Radicals deny this when they call for "power to the people," but they are usually middle-class intellectuals, sometimes intent on power for themselves. Mass participation in politics tends to be simple and episodic, such as voting every few years.

19. Democracy   Democracy arouses little enthusiasm in most countries. Only countries with a history of democratic rule have democratically inclined masses. More typically, masses admire regimes that give them law and order, a feeling of national greatness, and a sense of material progress. More-educated people have stronger commitments to democratic values.

20. Political Culture   Political culture is at least as much a reflection of government performance as it is a determinant of the workings of government. Political culture can be taught—intentionally or inadvertently—by a regime. Countries with a cynical, untrusting political culture have usually earned it with decades of misrule. By the same token, when a democratic regime does a good job over many years, as Germany has, it firms up democratic attitudes.

21. Social Class   Social class is only one factor in establishing political orientations. Often other factors, such as religion and region, are more important. Usually these three—class, religion, and region—in varying combinations explain a great deal of party identification and voting behavior.

22. Religion   Religion is important in politics. In Iran, the two merge. More typical are political parties based on religion or religiosity (degree of religious feeling). Germany's Christian Democrats were originally based on and still draw Catholic voters. In Catholic countries such as France, the more religious vote for the more conservative parties.

23. Ideology   Political systems are rarely totally ideological, but neither are they totally pragmatic. Parties and regimes usually have at least some ideological underpinning—to justify themselves to the masses, if for no other reason—but at the top, rulers tend to be rather pragmatic in making decisions. Leaders may talk a certain ideology but find that in actual governance it is not wholly relevant. Using ideology as window dressing is a common political device.

24. Elites   Every country has its elites, the few with much influence. Depending on the system, party elites, labor elites, business elites, military elites, even religious elites may assume great importance. Elites pay attention to politics, usually battling to preserve and enhance the status of the groups they lead. Elites rather than masses are the true political animals.

25. Intellectual Elites   Elites, especially intellectual elites, create and articulate political ideas (ideologies, reform movements, media commentary), something the masses rarely do. Further, elite attitudes tend to be more democratic than mass attitudes.

26. Education   Education is the usual gateway to elite status. Except in revolutionary regimes, most elites now have university educations. Some elites are selected by virtue of the special colleges they attend. Educational opportunity is never totally equal or fair; the middle class usually benefits most from it.

27. Competition   Much of politics consists of competition and bargaining among elites. Occasionally elites, in order to gain leverage on competing elites, refer matters to the masses in elections or referendums and call it democracy. Of all the political interactions discussed in this book, notice how relatively few of them involve mass participation.

28. Mass Politics   Mass politics is easier to study than elite politics. With mass politics—elections, voter alignments, popular attitudes—political scientists can get accurate, quantified data. But since much of elite politics is out of the public eye, we have to resort to fragmentary anecdotal and journalistic data. This means that some of the most crucial political interactions are hard to discern and even harder to document.

29. Democracy   Democracy grows when elites open their decisions and deals to public scrutiny and approval. Typically, bargains are struck among elites and then presented to parliament and the public. Much legislative and electoral behavior is in ratifying decisions made earlier among elites.

30. Opportunism   Politicians are endlessly opportunistic. Most will do whatever it takes to get, keep, or enhance their power. To this end, they will change their views and policies. This is not necessarily deplorable, however; it lets democracy work because it makes politicians bend to the popular will.

31. Money   Politicians are addicted to money. They need it for election campaigns and sometimes to make themselves rich. Countries with very different institutions and political cultures thus often have similar fund-raising scandals.

32. Parties   Parties are balancing acts. Parties are invariably composed of different groups, factions, and wings. Some parties split apart over personal and ideological differences. To hold the party together, politicians dispense favors, jobs, and promises to faction leaders. This holds for both democratic and authoritarian parties.

33. Armies   Once an army has taken over a government, chances are it will do so again. Once a country catches praetorianism, it seems never to fully recover from the disease. Democracy and reformism are often short-lived phenomena between periods of military rule. Praetorianism can be seen as an incurable, self-reinfecting illness endemic in much of the Third World. Its cure is economic growth.

34. The Third World   Most of humanity lives in the Third World, defined somewhat simplistically as Asia, Africa, and Latin America. Some are making good progress to prosperity and democracy; others, encumbered by institutional, ideological and cultural rigidity, are not.

35. Foreign Workers   The Third World is trying to get into the First. One of the big problems of West Europe is the new class of foreign workers—Pakistanis in Britain, Algerians in France, Turks in Germany—that have come seeking jobs and often intend to stay. Likewise, the United States has become a magnet for Latin Americans. Given the differential rates of birth and economic growth, the trend is increasing and has become a major political issue worldwide.

36. Cities   Within Third-World countries, people are flocking to the cities. Overpopulation and few jobs in the countryside push people to the cities, where they often live in shantytowns. The Third World already has the globe's biggest cities, and they're growing fast. Some countries, such as China and South Africa, attempted "influx control," but most countries just let the slums grow.

37. Racism   Racism can be found nearly everywhere. Most nations deny it, but discrimination based on skin color, religion, or ethnic group is widespread. When asking if there is racism, look to see what a country does, not what it says. Underdog racial and ethnic groups are locked out of economic and political power.

38. Welfare   Cutting welfare benefits is extremely difficult; recipients protest too much. Conservatives often come to power with promises to end the welfare state, but they seldom touch the problem. Once a benefit has been extended, it's almost impossible to withdraw it. The most conservatives can do is restrain expansion of the welfare system.

39. State Sectors   Likewise, cutting state sectors of an economy is difficult. Most countries have state ownership, control, or guidance over the economy (the United States relatively little). In countries as diverse as Russia, Japan, Brazil, South Africa, and Iran, getting the government out of the economy meets great opposition from those who have something to lose. Thus many governments talk about privatization but delay doing it.

40. Economics   Much of what people and politicians quarrel about is economic. Some economists go so far as to claim that economics is the content of politics. That's going a little too far, since there are important political conflicts that are not directly economic, such as questions of region, religion, and personality. Still, on any given day, people are most likely to be arguing who should get what. Study economics.

41. Markets   At almost the same time, countries rediscovered the market economy. Most have found that statist control retards growth. Markets are now the intellectual trend.

42. Development   Democracy depends a great deal on economic development. Poor countries can rarely sustain democracy. Middle-income and richer countries mostly have stable democracies. The likely reason: Economic growth generates a large, educated, and moderate middle class that starts insisting on political participation.

43. Inflation   Inflation is easy to ignite, but it hurts growth, sours attitudes, and can even bring down governments. At least three of our countries endured revolutions after periods of galloping inflation that destroyed people's means of making a living and their confidence in government.

44. Unemployment   Unemployment is a problem nearly everywhere and one few governments solve. Worldwide, there is a struggle for jobs, ranging from difficult in West Europe to desperate in the Third World. The Soviet Union was able to provide jobs but only because its industry and agriculture were grossly inefficient.

45. Cures   Many political issues are insoluble. They are the surfacing of long-growing economic and social problems that can't be "fixed" by government policy. Often only time and underlying economic and social change gradually dissolve the problem. Politics has been overrated as a way to cure problems. Often the best politics can do is keep things stable until time can do its work.

46. Political Quarrels   Things are getting more political, not less. As government gets bigger and takes on more tasks, what were previously private social interactions become political interactions with all the fighting that entails. Modernization brings increased politicization. As more areas become political footballs, we can look for more political quarrels.

47. Controversies   No country has ever run out of problems or political controversies. As soon as one problem is solved—and they're rarely solved by politics alone—new ones appear, usually relating to the administration of the problem-solving mechanism. No country is so advanced that it has no more problems. Indeed, the more advanced a country, the more political problems it seems to have because everything becomes political.

48. Results   Political movements, parties, ideologies, and regimes are hard to judge by *a priori* criteria. We seldom know how something is going to work until we see it in practice for a while. We learn what's good and bad by studying results.

49. Complexity   Whenever you look closely at political phenomena, you find they are more complex than you first thought. You discover exceptions, nuances, and differentiations that you didn't notice at first. You can modify and sometimes refute generalizations—including the ones offered here—by digging into them more deeply.

50. Studying Ourselves   Ultimately, in studying other countries we are studying ourselves. One of the lessons that should have emerged from this book is that neither our country nor we as citizens are a great deal different from other countries and peoples. When you compare politics, be sure to include your own system in the comparison.

Glossary

Here are some frequently used words or technical terms from the field of comparative politics. Each is defined here in its political sense. The country where the term originated or is most commonly used is indicated where appropriate, but often the word is now used worldwide.

absolute decline   Growing weaker economically compared to one's own past.

absolute poverty   Extremely low income, defined by World Bank as living on under $1 a day.

absolutism   A royal dictatorship in which the king amasses all power.

affluence   Having plenty of money.

African National Congress   South Africa's largest and oldest party, formerly a vehicle for black liberation.

Afrikaners   White South Africans of mostly Dutch descent, speak *Afrikaans*.

alienated   Psychologically distant and hostile.

Allies   World War II anti-German military coalition.

alternation in power   The overturn of one party by another in elections.

anachronism   Something from the past that doesn't fit present times.

ancien régime   French for old regime, the monarchy that preceded the Revolution.

Anglican   Church of England, Episcopalian in America.

anglophile   Someone who loves England and the English.

anticlerical   Favoring getting the Roman Catholic Church out of politics.

antithetical   Ideas opposed to one another.

apartheid   Literally, "apartness"; system of strict racial segregation in South Africa from 1948 to early 1990s.

apparatchik   "Man of the apparatus"; full-time CPSU functionary.

arable   Useable for agriculture.

archipelago   Chain of islands.

aristocrat   Person of inherited noble rank.

Article 9   The no-war clause in Japan's constitution.

asset-stripping   Selling off a firm's property and the raw materials it controls for short-term profit.

austerity   Cutting government expenditures; belt-tightening.

authoritarian   Nondemocratic or dictatorial politics.

authority   The power of a political figure to be obeyed.

Autobahn   German express highway, like U.S. interstate.

autocracy   Absolute rule of one person in a centralized state.

autogolpe   Spanish for "self-coup"; top executive seizes more power.

autonomy   Partial independence.

ayatollah   In Iran: "Sign of God"; top Shia religious leader.

baccalauréat   Exam by which French finish high school.

ban   Apartheid punishment of isolating alleged troublemakers.

Bastille   Old and nearly unused Paris jail, the storming of which signaled the start of the French Revolution in 1789.

belle époque   The "beautiful epoch"; France around 1900.

Berlin airlift   U.S.-British supply of West Berlin by air in 1948–49.

Berlin Republic   Reunified Germany, with capital in Berlin.

bilateral opposition   Centrist parties or governments being undermined from both sides.

bimodal   A two-peaked distribution.

bloc   A grouping or alliance.

blocked society   One in which interest groups prevent major, necessary change.

Bolshevik   "Majority" in Russian; early name for Soviet Communist party.

Bonn Republic   West Germany, with capital in Bonn.

bounce-back effect   Tendency of trends and values to reverse.

bound   Pertaining to bordering countries.

Bourbon   French dynasty before the Revolution.

bourgeois   Middle-class.

Boxer   Chinese antiforeigner rebellion in 1900.

Buddhism   Asian religion that seeks enlightenment through meditation and cessation of desire.

Bundesrat   Literally, federal council; upper chamber of German parliament, represents states.

Bundestag   Lower house of the German parliament.

bureaucratized   Heavily controlled by civil servants.

burghers   Originally, town dwellers; by extension, the middle class; French *bourgeoisie*.

by-election   A midterm election for a vacant seat in Parliament.

cadre   French "framework"; used by Asian Communists for local Party leader.

caesaropapism   Combining top civil ruler (caesar) with top spiritual ruler (pope), as in Russia's tsars.

canon law   The internal laws of the Roman Catholic Church.

capital flight   Tendency of businesspersons in countries with shaky economies to send their money out of the country.

capital goods   Implements used to make other things.

carpetbagger   In U.S. usage, an outsider attempting to run in a different constituency.

Cartesian   After French philosopher René Descartes, philosophical analysis based on pure reason without empirical reference.

caste   Hereditary social stratum or group.

catchall party   A party that welcomes all and offers little ideology.

causality   Proving that one thing causes another.

Celts   Pre-Roman inhabitants of Europe.

censure   Condemnation of executive by legislative vote.

center   Politically moderate or middle-of-the-road, neither left nor right. In federal systems, the powers of the nation's capital.

center-peaked   Distribution with most people in the middle; a bell-shaped curve.

center-periphery tension   Resentment of outlying areas at rule by the nation's capital.

center-seeking   Parties trying to win the big vote in the center with moderate programs.

Central Committee   The large, next-to-top governing body of most Communist parties.

central office   London headquarters of British political party.

chancellor   German prime minister.

charisma   Pronounced "kar-isma"; Greek for gift; political drawing power.

chauvinism   After a Napoleonic soldier named Chauvin; fervent, prideful nationalism.

civility   Using reasonably good manners in politics.

civil society   Civilized humans. Modern usage: associations between family and government.

class voting   Tendency of a given class to vote for a party that claims to represent its interests.

coalition   Multiparty alliance to form a government.

cohabitation   French president forced to name premier of opposing party.

Cold War   Period of armed tension and competition between the United States and the Soviet Union, approximately 1947–89.

colonialism   The gaining and exploitation of overseas territories, chiefly by Europeans.

Comecon   Trading organization of Communist countries, now defunct.

Common Agricultural Program   EU program to subsidize farmers; biggest single part of EU budget.

Common Law   System of judge-made law developed in England.

commonwealth   A *republic*.

communism   The economic theories of Marx combined with the organization of Lenin.

compartmentalization   Mentally separating and isolating problems.

comprehensive school   A publicly funded British secondary school, equivalent to a U.S. high school.

Confederation of British Industry   Leading British business association.

Confucianism   Chinese philosophy of social and political stability based on family, hierarchy, and perfection of manners.

consensus   Agreement among all constituent groups.

Constantinople   Capital of Byzantium, conquered by Turks in 1453.

conservatism Ideology aimed at preserving existing institutions and usages.

consociation General agreement and power sharing among the leaders of all major groups.

constituency The district or population that elects a legislator.

constitution The written organization of a country's institutions.

constitutional monarchy Monarchy whose powers are limited.

constructive bankruptcy Economic theory that weak firms should fold to make way for new enterprises.

constructive no-confidence Requires parliament to vote in a new cabinet when it ousts the current one.

consumer goods Things people use, such as food, clothing, and housing.

consumption Buying things.

containment U.S. policy throughout Cold War of blocking expansion of communism.

Continent, the British term for the continent of Europe, implying they are not part of it.

coronéis "Colonels"; Brazilian state-level political bosses.

corporatism Representation by branch of industry, a device of Mussolini.

Cortes Spain's parliament.

corruption Use of public office for private gain.

counterculture Rejection of conventional values, as in the 1960s.

coup d'état Extralegal seizure of power, usually by military officers.

courtier Person who hangs around a royal court.

CPSU Communist Party of the Soviet Union.

cross-cutting cleavages Multiple splits in society that make group loyalties overlap.

Crown The powers of the British government.

CRS Republican Security Companies, French riot police.

culmination Logical outcome or end.

cult of personality A dictator having himself worshiped.

cumulative Reinforcing one another.

cynical Untrusting; belief that the political system is wrong and corrupt.

Cyrillic Greek-based alphabet of the Eastern Slavic languages.

daimyo Feudal Japanese regional lords.

deadlock Tendency of U.S. executive and legislature, especially when of opposing parties, to block each other.

dealignment Voters losing identification with any party.

decolonization The granting of independence to colonies.

de facto In practice, although not officially stated.

default Not being able to pay back a loan.

deferential Accepting the leadership of social superiors.

deflation Overall decrease in prices; opposite of inflation.

deindustrialization Decline of heavy industry.

demagoguery Crowd-pleasing promises that cannot be fulfilled.

democracy Political system of mass participation, competitive elections, and human and civil rights.

demography Study of population growth.

denazification Purging Nazi officials from public life.

département Department; French first-order civil division, equivalent to British county.

dependency theory Radical theory that rich countries keep poor countries poor by siphoning off their wealth.

deputy Member of French and many other parliaments.

deregulation Cutting government industrial rules.

deutsche Mark German currency since 1948.

devaluation Decreasing the worth of your currency in relation to others.

devolution A central government turning some powers over to regions.

Diet Name of some parliaments, such as Japan's and Finland's.

dignified In Bagehot's terms, the symbolic or decorative offices.

diplomatic recognition One state announces it is ready to do business with another.

dirigiste Bureaucrats directing industry; closely connected to French *statism*.

divide and rule Roman and British imperial ruling method of setting subjects against each other.

division A vote in the House of Commons.

Dolchstoss German for "stab in the back."

dominant-party system A system in which one party is much stronger than all the others and stays in office a very long time.

dries In Thatcher's usage, Tories who shared her *neoliberal* vision.

Duma   Russia's national parliament.

dynastic cycle   In China: The rise, maturity, and fall of an imperial family.

eclectic   Drawn from a variety of sources.

efficient   In Bagehot's terms, the working political offices.

Eire   The Republic of Ireland.

electoral alignment   Temporary coalition of parties in order to win elections.

electoral franchise   The right to vote.

elites   The top or most influential people.

Élysée   Presidential palace in Paris, equivalent to U.S. White House.

embargo   Not selling certain goods to a disfavored country.

Enlightenment   Eighteenth-century philosophical movement advocating reason and tolerance.

enryo   In Japan: Nonpresumptuousness; not asking for too much.

entitlement   Spending programs citizens are automatically entitled to, such as Social Security.

entrepreneurial   Starting your own business.

Establishment   Half in jest, the supposed monopoly of a clubby social elite in British politics.

Estado Nôvo   In Brazil: "New State"; Vargas's corporatistic welfare state.

Estates-General   Old, unused French parliament.

ethnicity   Cultural characteristics differentiating one group from another.

euro   Symbol €; currency introduced in 1999 for most of West Europe; approximate value $1.

Eurocommunism   Move in 1970s by Italian Communists away from Stalinism and toward democracy.

European Union (EU)   Federation of most West European states; began in 1957 as *Common Market*.

Europhile   Likes the EU and wishes to strengthen it.

Eurosceptic   Does not wish to strengthen the EU at the expense of national sovereignty.

Events of May   Euphemism for the riots and upheaval of May 1968.

Exchequer   Britain's treasury ministry.

extraterritoriality   Privilege of Europeans in colonial situations to have separate laws and courts.

extreme multipartism   Too many parties in parliament.

faction   A party within a party.

fatwa   A ruling issued by an Islamic jurist.

favela   Brazilian shantytown, found around cities.

Federal Constitutional Court   Germany's top court, equivalent to U.S. Supreme Court.

federalism   System in which component areas have considerable autonomy.

Federal Republic of Germany   Originally West Germany, now all of Germany.

fertility rate   How many children an average woman bears.

feudalism   Political system of power dispersed and balanced between king and nobles.

fiefdom   Land granted by a king to a noble in exchange for support.

Fifth Republic   French regime devised by de Gaulle, 1958 to present.

Final Solution   Nazi program to exterminate Jews.

first-order civil division   The main units countries are divided into, such as departments in France.

fiscal   Related to taxes and public spending.

Five-Year Plans   Stalin's forced industrialization of the Soviet Union starting in 1928.

flash party   One that quickly rises and falls.

flight capital   Money the owner sends out of the country in fear of losing it.

Fourth Republic   1946–58 French regime.

Four Tigers   South Korea, Taiwan, Hong Kong, and Singapore.

FPTP   "First past the post"; a short way of saying "single-member districts with plurality win."

francophobe   Someone who dislikes France and the French.

Free French   De Gaulle's World War II government in exile.

French Revolution   1789 popular ouster of the monarch.

fusion of powers   The combination of executive and legislative as in parliamentary systems; opposite of the U.S. separation of powers.

gaiatsu   Japanese for foreign pressure.

gaijin   Japanese for foreigner.

Gang of Four   Mao's ultraradical helpers, arrested in 1976.

Gastarbeiter   "Guest workers"; temporary labor allowed into Germany.

GDP   Gross Domestic Product; sum total of goods and services produced in a country in one year.

generalization   The finding of repeated examples and patterns.

general will   Rousseau's theory of what the whole community wants.

genocide Murder of an entire people.

gensek Russian abbreviation for "general secretary"; powerful CPSU head.

geopolitics The influence of geography on politics and the use of geography for strategic ends.

glasnost Gorbachev's policy of media openness.

Gleichschaltung Nazi control of Germany's economy.

Good Friday agreement 1998 pact to share power in Northern Ireland.

Gosplan Soviet central economic planning agency.

government A particular cabinet, what Americans call "the administration."

grammar school A private British nonboarding school, equivalent to a U.S. day school.

grand coalition Coalition of two or more large parties who previously opposed each other.

grande école French for "great school"; an elite, specialized institution of higher education.

Grands Corps Top bureaucrats of France.

Greater East Asia Coprosperity Sphere Asia run by Japan, Tokyo's World War II propaganda line.

Greens In Europe, environmentalist parties.

Grundgesetz Basic Law, Germany's constitution.

guided capitalism State supervision but not ownership of the economy, as in Japan.

guilt Deeply internalized feeling of personal responsibility and moral failure.

Gulag The Soviet central prisons administration.

Habsburg Leading Catholic dynasty that once held Austria-Hungary, Spain, Latin America, and the Netherlands.

hajj Muslim pilgrimage to Mecca.

Han Original and main people of China.

hard currency The noninflating, recognized currencies used in international dealings, such as dollars and deutsche Marks.

heckling Interrupting a speaker.

hegemony Being the top or commanding power.

Helsinki Final Act 1975 agreement to make Europe's borders permanent.

heretic Someone who breaks away from a religion.

hezbollahi "Partisan of God"; fanatic supporter of Islamism.

Holocaust Nazi genocide of Europe's Jews during World War II.

home rule A region governing itself.

hooliganism Violent and destructive behaviour.

Huguenots French Protestants.

human capital The education, skills, and enthusiasm of a nation's work force.

hyperinflation Very rapid inflation, more than 50 percent a month.

hypermarché French for "hypermarket"; a store that sells everything.

hyperurbanization Overconcentration of populations in cities.

ideal-typical Distilling social characteristics into one example.

ideology Belief system that society can be improved.

immobilisme Inability of a government to solve big problems.

imperialism Powerful, rich countries spreading their influence around the globe.

inchoate Not yet organized, incoherent.

indicative planning In France: Governmental economic research and suggestions for business expansion.

Indochina War The first Vietnam war, 1946–54, between French and Communist Viet Minh.

infant mortality rate Number of live newborns who die in their first year, per thousand; a standard measure of a nation's health.

inflation The systematic rise of almost all prices.

informal economy Under-the-table transactions to avoid taxes and regulations.

input-output table A spreadsheet for the economy of an entire nation.

Inspection Short for General Finance Inspection; very top of French bureaucracy, with powers to investigate all branches.

institution Established rules and relationships of power.

intendants French provincial administrators, answerable only to Paris; early version of *prefects*.

interested member MP known to represent an interest group.

interest group Association aimed at getting favorable policies.

interior ministry In Europe, department in charge of local administration and national police.

investiture crisis Fight between popes and monarchs over who had the right to crown the latter.

Irish Republican Army Anti-British terrorists who seek unification of all Ireland.

iron triangle An interlocking of politicians, bureaucrats, and business people to promote the flow of funds among them.

Islam   The religion founded by Mohammed.

Islamism   Islam turned into a political ideology.

Islamist   Someone who uses Islam in a political way.

jihad   Muslim holy war.

junior minister   An MP with executive responsibilities below that of cabinet rank.

Junker   Pronounced "yoon care"; Prussian nobility.

junta   Pronounced Spanish-style, "khun-ta"; group that pulls military coup.

Jusos   Short for Young Socialists, radical youth wing of SPD.

jus sanguinis   Latin for "right of blood"; citizenship based on descent.

jus soli   Latin for "right of soil"; citizenship given to those born in the country.

Kaiser   German for Caesar; emperor.

karoshi   In Japan: Death by overwork.

keiretsu   In Japan: Industrial conglomerates; new name for prewar *zaibatsu*.

Kempeitai   Japan's army-run security police before and during World War II.

knighthood   The lowest rank of nobility; in Britain carries title of "Sir."

kleptocracy   Rule by thieves.

Koran   Muslim holy book.

kow-tow   In China: Literally head to the ground; to prostrate oneself.

Kulturkampf   Culture struggle, specifically Bismarck's with the Catholic Church.

labor-force rigidities   Unwillingness of workers to change jobs or location.

"La Marseillaise"   French national anthem.

Land   Plural *Länder*; Germany's first-order civil division, equivalent to U.S. state.

landlocked   A country with no seacoast.

Landtag   German state legislature.

Law Lords   Britain's top judges, members of Lords.

Lebensraum   German for "living space" for an entire nation.

legitimacy   Mass perception that a regime's rule is rightful.

Levellers   Radicals during English Civil War who argued for equality and "one man, one vote."

liberal democracy   A system that combines tolerance and freedoms (liberalism) with mass participation (democracy).

Liberal Democrats   LDP; Japan's dominant party, a catchall.

life peers   Distinguished Britons named to the House of Lords for their lifetimes only, does not pass on to children.

lingua franca   In a multilingual situation, the one language used overall.

lycée   French academic high school.

MacArthur Constitution   Japan's U.S.-drafted postwar constitution.

machismo   Strutting, exaggerated masculinity.

Machtpolitik   Power politics.

macroeconomy   The big picture of a nation's economy, including GDP and its growth, productivity, interest rates, and inflation.

mafia   A criminal conspiracy.

Maginot Line   Supposedly unbreachable French defenses facing Germany before World War II.

Magna Carta   1215 agreement to preserve rights of English nobles.

Majlis   Arabic for assembly; Iran's parliament.

Malthusian   View that population growth outstrips food.

Manchu   Last imperial dynasty of China, also known as *Qing*; ruled from seventeenth century to 1911.

Manchukuo   Japanese puppet state set up in Manchuria.

man-land ratio   How much *arable* land per person.

marginal   Poor person on the edge of society and the economy.

Marshall Plan   Massive U.S. financial aid for European recovery.

Marxist   Follower of the socialist theories of Karl Marx.

mass   Most of the citizenry; all who are not *elite*.

mass line   Mao's theory of revolution for China.

Medef   French business association.

Meiji   Starting in 1868, period of Japan's rapid modernization.

mercantilism   Theory that nation's wealth is its gold and silver, to be amassed by government controls on the economy.

Mercosur   "Southern market"; free-trade area covering southern part of South America.

meritocracy   Advancement based only on intellectual ability.

Metternichian   Contrived conservative system to restore pre-Napoleon European monarchy and stability.

microeconomy   The closeup picture of individual markets, including product design and pricing, efficiency, and costs.

middle class   Class of professionals or those paid salaries; typically educated beyond secondary school.

Middle Kingdom   China's traditional name for itself.

middle way   Supposed blend of capitalism and socialism; also called "third way."

Midi   French for "noon"; the South of France.

minister   Head of a major department (ministry) of government.

Mitbestimmung   German for "codetermination"; unions participating in company decisions.

MITI   Japan's powerful Ministry of International Trade and Industry.

Mitteleuropa   German for Central Europe.

mixed monarchy   King balanced by nobles.

mobilize   To bring new sectors of the population into political participation.

Modell Deutschland   The German economic model.

modernizing tyrant   Dictator who pushes country ahead.

monetarism   Friedman's theory that rate of growth of money supply governs much economic development.

money politics   Lavish use of funds to win elections.

Mongol   Central Asian dynasty, founded by Genghis Khan, that ruled China in the thirteenth and fourteenth centuries.

monocolor   In parliamentary systems, cabinet composed of just one party.

mosque   Muslim house of worship.

MP   Member of Parliament.

mullah   Muslim cleric.

multiculturalism   Preservation of diverse languages and traditions within one country.

multinational   A country composed of several peoples with distinct national feelings.

Muslim   A follower of Islam; also adjective of *Islam*.

Narodniki   From Russian "people," *narod*; radical populist agitators of the late nineteenth-century.

nation   The cultural element of a country; people psychologically bound to one another.

National Assembly   France's parliament.

nationalism   Belief in the greatness and unity of one's country and hatred of rule by foreigners.

National Front   French anti-immigrant party.

national interest   What is good for the country as a whole in international relations.

Nationalist   Chiang Kai-shek's party that unified China in the late 1920s; abbreviated KMT.

near abroad   The non-Russian republics of the old Soviet Union.

nemawashi   Japanese for "root-binding," as in gardening; the formation of group consensus.

neo-Gaullist   Chirac's revival of Gaullist party, the Rally for the Republic (RPR).

neoliberalism   The revival of free-market economics.

New Economic Policy   NEP; Lenin's New Economic Policy that allowed private activity, 1921–28.

New Labour   Tony Blair's name for his very moderate Labour party.

nomenklatura   Lists of sensitive positions and people eligible to fill them, the Soviet elite.

nonaggression pact   Treaty to not attack each other, specifically the 1939 treaty between Hitler and Stalin.

Normans   Vikings who settled in and gave their name to Normandy, France.

objective   Judged by observable criteria.

October Revolution   1917 Bolshevik seizure of power in Russia.

Okurasho   Japan's finance ministry.

old boy   Someone you knew at boarding school.

Old Republic   Brazil's first republic, 1889–1930; a rigged democracy.

oligarchy   Rule by a few.

omnipotent   All-powerful.

on   Japanese for duty or debt of honor.

OPEC   Cartel of oil-rich countries designed to boost petroleum prices.

Open Door   U.S. policy of protecting China.

opportunist   Unprincipled person out for self.

opposition   In parliamentary systems, the parties in parliament that are not in the cabinet.

Orangemen   After King William of Orange (symbol of the Netherlands royal house), Northern Irish Protestants.

Ossi   Nickname for East German.

Ostpolitik   Literally "east policy"; Brandt's building relations with East Europe, including East Germany.

Ottoman   Turkish imperial dynasty, fourteenth to twentieth centuries.

output affect   Attachment to a system based on its providing material abundance.

Oxbridge   Slang for Oxford and Cambridge universities.

Palais Bourbon   Paris building of the French National Assembly.

parliament   A national assembly that considers and passes laws. When capitalized, Britain's legislature, specifically its lower chamber, *Commons*.

Parliamentarians   Supporters of Parliament in English Civil War.

Paris Commune   Takeover of Paris government by citizens during German siege of 1870–71.

particularism   A region's sense of its difference.

party identification   Psychological attachment of a voter to a particular political party.

party image   The way the electorate perceives a party.

party list   A party's ranking of its candidates in PR elections; voters pick one list as their ballot.

passé   Outmoded; receded into the past.

patrie   French for fatherland.

patronage   Using political office to hire supporters.

peerage   A British Lord or Lady; higher than *knighthood*.

per capita   GDP divided by population, giving an approximate level of well-being.

periphery   The nation's outlying regions.

perestroika   Russian for "restructuring"; Gorbachev's proposals to reform the Soviet economy.

permanent secretary   The highest British civil servant who runs a ministry, nominally under a minister.

personalismo   Politics by strong personalities.

petit bourgeois   Small shopkeeper.

pietà   Italian for "piety"; artistic representation of Mary cradling the body of Jesus.

plebiscite   *Referendum*, a mass vote for an issue rather than for a candidate.

pluralism   The autonomous interaction of social groups with each other and on government.

pluralistic stagnation   Thesis of Beer that interest groups out of control produce policy log jam.

plurality   The largest quantity, even if less than a majority.

polarized pluralism   A sick multiparty system that produces two extremist blocs with little in the center.

Politburo   "Political bureau"; the small, top governing body of most Communist parties.

political culture   The values and attitudes of citizens in regard to politics and society.

political generation   Theory that age groups are marked by the great events of their young adulthood.

political geography   The way territory and politics influence each other.

Popular Front   Coalition government of all leftist and liberal parties in France and Spain in the 1930s.

pork barrel   Government projects that narrowly benefit legislators' constituencies.

portfolio   Minister's assigned ministry.

Positivism   Philosophy of applying scientific method to social problems and gradually improving society.

postmaterialism   Theory that modern culture has moved beyond getting and spending.

praetorianism   Tendency for military takeovers.

pragmatic   Without ideological considerations, based on practicality.

precedent   Legal reasoning based on previous cases.

prefect   French *préfet*; administrator of a department.

prefecture   First-order Japanese civil division, like a French department.

premier   French for prime minister.

president   An elected head of state, not necessarily powerful.

prime minister   The chief of government in parliamentary systems.

privatistic   Tending to purely private and family concerns.

privatization   Selling a state-owned industry to private interests.

production   Making things.

productivity   The efficiency with which things are produced.

proletariat   Marx's term for the class of industrial workers.

proportional representation   Electoral system that assigns parliamentary seats in proportion to party vote.

protective tariff   Tax on imported goods to prevent them from undercutting domestic products.

protest vote   Ballot cast against the existing regime.

Prussia   Powerful North German state; Berlin was its capital.

public finances   What a government takes in, what it spends, and how it makes up the difference.

public corporation   Special-purpose economic unit owned in whole or in part by government.

public school   In Britain, a private boarding school, equivalent to a U.S. prep school.

purchasing power parity   Way of comparing cross-nationally how well people live based on how much they can buy rather than on how much currency they earn.

purge   Stalin's "cleansing" of suspicious elements by firing squad.

quarrels   As used here, important, long-term political issues.

quasi-federal   Halfway federal.

Question Hour   Time reserved in British Commons for MPs to question members of cabinet.

reactionary   Seeking to go back to old ways; extremely conservative.

real   Plural: *reís*; Brazil's currency, worth about $0.50.

Realpolitik   Politics of realism.

recession   An economy going downward.

Rechtsstaat   Literally, state of laws; state based on written rules and rights.

redbrick   British universities other than *Oxbridge*.

red-brown   A combination of Communists and Fascists, the brown standing for Hitler's brownshirts.

redistribution   Taxing the better off to help the worse off.

referendum   A mass vote on an issue rather than on candidates; same as *plebiscite*.

Reform Acts   Series of laws expanding the British electoral franchise.

regierungsfähig   German for "able to form a government"; a party that has matured and shown itself capable of ruling.

Reich   German for empire.

Reichstag   Pre-Hitler German parliament; its building now houses *Bundestag*.

reification   Taking a theory as reality.

Reign of Terror   Robespierre's 1793–94 rule by guillotine.

relative decline   Failing to keep up economically with other nations.

reparations   Paying back for war damages.

republic   A country not headed by a monarch. Also civil division of Communist federal systems and now of Russia.

republican   In its original sense, favoring getting rid of monarchy.

Résistance   Underground French anti-German movement of World War II.

revisionism   The rethinking of an ideology or reinterpretation of history.

revolution   The sudden and complete overthrow of a regime.

Rhodes scholarship   Founded by South African millionaire, enables top English-speaking students to attend Oxford.

romanticism   Hearkening to an ideal world or mythical past.

Royalists   Supporters of the king in the English Civil War.

rule of anticipated reactions   Friedrich's theory that politicians plan moves in anticipation of public reaction.

rump state   Leftover portions of a country after dismemberment.

Russification   Making non-Russian nationalities learn Russian.

safe seat   Constituency where voting has long favored a given party.

samurai   Literally, "those who serve"; Japanese knights.

sararimen   Japanese for "salary men"; mid-level employees.

scandal   A corrupt practice publicized by the media.

seat   Membership in a legislature.

Second Vatican Council   1962–65 meetings that modernized the Roman Catholic Church and turned it to problems of poverty; also called Vatican II.

secular   Long-term, irreversible trends; also nonreligious.

secularization   Cutting back the role of religion in government and daily life.

select committee   A specialized committee of the Commons focusing on a ministry.

semipresidential system   System with features of both presidential and parliamentary systems.

shadow shogun   Unofficial term for top faction chief who names and controls Japan's prime minister.

shah   Persian for king.

sharia   Muslim religious law.

Shia   Minority branch of Islam.

shin jinrui   In Japan: new human race, the younger generation.

Shinto   Japan's original religion; the worship of nature, of one's ancestors, and of Japan.

shock therapy   Sudden replacement of a socialist economy with a free-market one.

shogun   Feudal Japanese military chief who ruled in name of emperor.

shogunate   Political system with a *shogun* at its head.

Siberia   From the Russian for "north"; that part of Russia east of the Ural Mountains but not including Central Asia.

single-member district   Sends one representative to parliament.

skinheads   Racist youth, begun in England, with shaved heads and quasi-military attire.

Slavophiles   Nineteenth-century Russians who wished to develop Russia along native, non-Western lines.

sleaze factor   Public perception of politicians on the take.

snap election   An election called on short notice, ahead of schedule.

social class   A layer or section of a population of similar income and status.

social costs   Taxes for medical, unemployment, and retirement benefits paid by employers.

socialize   To teach political culture, often informally.

social mobility   The movement of individuals from one class to another, usually upward.

soft money   In U.S. politics, funds given to parties and other groups rather than to candidates in order to skirt restrictions.

solidarity   Feeling of cohesion within a social class.

sovereignty   The last word on law in a given territory; boss on your own turf.

Sozialmarkt   "Social market"; Germany's postwar capitalism aimed at reconstruction and a welfare floor.

SPD   German Social Democratic party.

sphere of influence   Semicolonial area under control of major power.

Stalinist   Brutal central control over a Communist party.

state   The institutional or governmental element of a country.

State Duma   Lower house of Russia's parliament.

state of nature   Humans before civilization.

statism   Idea that a strong government should run things, especially major industries.

statute   An ordinary law, usually for a specific problem.

steady-state   A system that preserves itself with little change.

strategic   Important to the life of a nation.

structure   The institutions of government such as constitution, laws, and branches.

structured access   Permanent openness of bureaucracy to interest-group demands.

subject   Originally, a subject of the Crown; now another term for British citizen.

subjective   Judged by feeling or intuition.

subsidy   Government financial help to private individual or business.

Sunni   Mainstream branch of Islam.

supranational organizations   Organizations that group together several countries; literally "above national."

swing voters   Those voters who change party from one election to the next.

symbol   Political artifact used to stir mass emotions.

system affect   Attachment to a system for its own sake.

system change   The displacement of one set of political institutions by another.

Taiping   Major religion-based rebellion in nineteenth-century China.

Tatar   Mongol-origin tribes who ruled Russia for centuries.

tautology   A statement that repeats the same thing in different words.

technocrat   Official, usually unelected, who governs by virtue of economic and financial skills.

temporal   Of this world, opposite of spiritual.

Thatcherite   The free-market, anti-welfarist ideology of former British Prime Minister Margaret Thatcher.

theocracy   Rule by priests.

theory   Firm generalizations supported by evidence.

Thermidor   Month when Robespierre fell, a calming down after a revolutionary high.

Third Estate   Largest chamber of the *Estates-General*, representing commoners.

Third Republic   France's democratic regime from 1871 to 1940.

Third World   Most of Asia, Africa, and Latin America.

Thirty Years War   1618–48 Habsburg attempt to conquer and Catholicize Europe.

threshold clause   Minimum percent a party must win to gain any seats.

-to   Japanese suffix for party.

Tokugawa   Dynasty of *shoguns* who ruled Japan from 1600 to 1868.

Tories   Faction of British Parliament that became Conservative party; now their nickname.

totalitarian   Political system that attempts total control of society, as under Stalin and Hitler.

Trades Union Congress   TUC; British labor federation equivalent to the U.S. AFL-CIO.

trade surplus   Exporting more than you import.

traditional Tory   Moderate or centrist Conservative, not a follower of Thatcher.

transparency law   A law requiring that political and economic information be made public.

Treasury   British ministry that supervises economic policy and funding of other ministries.

treaty ports Areas of the China coast run by European powers.

Trotskyist Follower of the Marxist but anti-Stalin theories of Leon Trotsky.

tsar From "caesar"; Russia's emperor. Sometimes spelled old Polish style, czar.

turnout Percentage of those eligible who vote in a given election.

tutelle French for tutelage; bureaucratic guidance.

"two-plus" party system Two big parties and several small ones.

tyrannical Coercive rule, usually by one person.

Ukraine From the Slavic for "borderland"; region south of Russia, now independent.

underclass Permanently disadvantaged people.

unilinear Progressing evenly and always upward.

unimodal A single-peaked distribution.

unitary system System in which power is centralized in capital and component areas have little or no autonomy.

unit labor costs What it costs to manufacture the same item in different countries.

unit veto Ability of one component to block laws or changes.

value-added tax Large, hidden national sales taxes used throughout Europe.

vary inversely As one thing goes up, another goes down.

Vatican Headquarters of the Roman Catholic church.

velayat-e faqih In Iran: "Guardianship of the religious jurist"; theocratic system devised by Khomeini.

Vergangenheitsbewältigung Literally, "mastery of the past"; coming to grips with Germany's Nazi past.

Versailles Palace and estate on outskirts of Paris built by Louis XIV.

Versailles Treaty 1919 treaty ending World War I.

vice-minister Top bureaucrat in a Japanese ministry.

Vichy Nazi puppet regime that ran France during World War II.

volatile Rises and falls quickly.

Volksgeist German for "spirit of the people"; has racist connotations.

voluntarism Belief that human will can change the world.

vote of no confidence Parliamentary vote to oust a cabinet.

wa Japanese for social harmony.

wage restraint Unions holding back on compensation demands.

walking-around money Relatively small payments by politicians to buy votes.

war communism Temporary strict socialism in Russia, 1918–21.

warlord In 1920s China, general who ran province.

Warsaw Pact Soviet-led alliance of Communist countries, now defunct.

Weimar Republic 1919–33 democratic German republic.

welfare state Political system that redistributes wealth from rich to poor, standard in West Europe.

Weltanschauung party German for "world view"; parties offering firm, narrow ideologies.

Wessi Nickname for West German.

Westernizers Nineteenth-century Russians who wished to copy the West.

Westphalia Treaty ending Thirty Years War.

wets In Thatcher's usage, Tories too timid to apply her militant neoliberalism.

Westminster The British Parliament building.

whig democracy Democracy with limited participation, typical of democracy's initial phases.

Whigs Faction of British Parliament that became Liberal party.

whip A parliamentary party leader who makes sure members obey the party in voting.

Whitehall The main British government offices.

Wirtschaftswunder German for "economic miracle."

working class Class of those paid an hourly wage, typically less affluent and educated.

xenophobia Fear and hatred of foreigners.

yuan China's currency, worth about 12 U.S. cents.

zaibatsu Prewar Japanese industrial conglomerates headed by samurai clans.

zemtsvo Local parliaments in old Russia.

Zionism Jewish nationalist movement, founded Israel.

Zulu Largest South African population group, live chiefly in KwaZulu/Natal.

Index